THE
SOCIAL AND ECONOMIC
HISTORY OF THE
HELLENISTIC
WORLD

THE
SOCIAL & ECONOMIC
HISTORY OF THE
HELLENISTIC
WORLD

By

M. ROSTOVTZEFF

Hon. D.Litt., Hon. Litt.D. (Cambridge)
Hon. Litt.D. (Harvard), Hon. Litt.D. (Wisconsin)
Professor of Ancient History in Yale University

VOLUME III

OXFORD
AT THE CLARENDON PRESS
M CM XLI

OXFORD UNIVERSITY PRESS
AMEN HOUSE, E.C. 4
LONDON EDINBURGH GLASGOW NEW YORK
TORONTO MELBOURNE CAPETOWN BOMBAY
CALCUTTA MADRAS
HUMPHREY MILFORD
PUBLISHER TO THE UNIVERSITY

PRINTED IN GREAT BRITAIN

3538 (cf. 1343)

CONTENTS

NOTES

CHAPTER I

[1] Droysen's brilliant presentation, and Niese's and Beloch's careful sifting, dating, and co-ordinating of the relative facts still remain the foundation of our knowledge of the political development of the Hellenistic world. To this foundation much new material and numberless suggestions regarding the interpretation, arrangement, and combination of the data have been contributed by a number of eminent scholars who, following Droysen and in some cases with the help of Niese and Beloch, have since dealt with the political history of the period and have greatly improved and enlarged our knowledge. This process has been much assisted by the enormous increase in our documentary evidence, especially in the form of inscriptions, papyri, and coins, many of them brought to light by scientifically organized excavations of ancient cities and temples, for instance at Athens, Olympia, Delphi, Delos, Rhodes, Cos, Samos, Thasos, Samothrace, Miletus, Priene, Pergamon, Ephesus, Halicarnassus, Magnesia, the various cities of Crete, Cyrene, several cities in Palestine, Antioch on the Orontes, Seleuceia in Pieria, Dura–Europus, Babylon, Uruk, Seleuceia on the Tigris, Susa, and many cities in Egypt, especially Alexandria, Ptolemais and various towns in the Fayûm and in Middle and South Egypt. The widening of our horizon as regards the political history of the Hellenistic period is principally due to these new documents and to their masterly interpretation by various scholars.

I cannot here give an exhaustive list of works bearing on the political history of the period. It will be sufficient to refer to the excellent bibliographies to the various chapters of *C.A.H.*, vols. vi, vii, viii, and ix. These chapters themselves, written chiefly by W. W. Tarn and M. Holleaux, give a short but full and excellent presentation of the facts. For a more condensed presentation I may refer to U. Wilcken, *Griechische Geschichte im Rahmen der Altertumsgeschichte*, 4th ed., 1939; M. Cary, *A History of the Greek World from 323 to 146 B.C.*, 1932; H. Berve, *Griechische Geschichte*, ii, 1933, pp. 204 ff.; and R. Cohen, *La Grèce et l'hellénisation du monde antique*², 1939. To these may be added the two most recent histories of Ptolemaic Egypt—E. R. Bevan, *A History of Egypt*, 1927 (French translation, 1934), and especially P. Jouguet, 'L'Égypte ptolémaïque', in G. Hanotaux, *Histoire de la nation égyptienne*, iii, 1933. At the last moment has appeared the first part of the fourth volume ('Alexandre et l'hellénisation du monde antique') of the *Histoire grecque* of the late G. Glotz. It deals with 'Alexandre et le démembrement de son Empire', and was written by G. Glotz, R. Cohen, and P. Roussel. I regret that this excellent contribution came too late to be fully used. In the section on the Successors, written by Roussel, the reader will find useful supplements to my notes to this chapter. This first part will be followed by a second, 'Les États gréco-macédoniens' by A. Aymard, E. Bikerman, and P. Collart.

These notes give references to some recently published documents and to the most important modern contributions which have appeared since the publication of the corresponding volumes of *C.A.H.*, and which I have utilized in writing this chapter. I have not aimed at completeness.

2 Modern scholars have shown much interest in the period between Alexander's death and the battle of Corupedion. Witness the large number of articles which have appeared since 1927 and are therefore not listed in *C.A.H.* vi, p. 606 and vii, pp. 880 ff. I give in this and the following notes references to some of these, of which I have made use in compiling this chapter. For the events immediately succeeding the death of Alexander, see W. Ensslin, *Rh. Mus.* lxxiv (1925), pp. 293 ff.; W. Schwahn, *Klio*, xxiii (1929), pp. 211 ff.; xxiv (1931), pp. 306 ff.; G. De Sanctis, *St. It. Fil.* ix (1931), pp. 5 ff.; P. Treves, *Riv. Fil.* lx (10) (1932), pp. 372 ff.; A. Neppi Modona, *Athenaeum*, x (1932), pp. 22 ff.; F. Miltner, *Klio*, xxvi (1932), pp. 39 ff.; W. Schur, *Rh. Mus.* lxxxiii (1934), pp. 129 ff.; F. Geyer, *P.W.K.* xix. 604 ff., esp. 608 (art. 'Perdikkas') (1937); H. Bengtson, 'Die Strategie in der hell. Zeit', pt. i, *Münch. Beitr. Pap.* xxvi (1937), pp. 63 ff.; cf. F. Heichelheim, Bursian's *Jahresb.* ccl (suppl.), p. 243 f.

3 I cannot here discuss the recent book of F. Hampl, *Der König der Makedonen*, 1934 (cf. the reviews by F. Geyer, *Ph. W.* lvi (1936), pp. 118 ff. and by A. Momigliano, *Athenaeum*, xiii (1935), pp. 3 ff.,), in which the author gives a new interpretation of the relations that existed between the king of the Macedonians and the various parts of his army, his vassals on the one hand and the Macedonian people under arms on the other. The events after Alexander's death show that the Macedonian phalanx was not a group of mercenaries in the service of Alexander which helped him to conquer the East, but that it regarded itself as the Macedonian people led by Alexander to a war which was not exclusively a private military enterprise of his. Nor is it certain that the ἑταῖροι of Alexander were exclusively his vassals who received δωρεαί from him in the territories conquered by Philip and Alexander in their own private wars. Some of Alexander's companions were feudal lords in the cradle-land that was the kernel of Alexander's kingdom, Macedonia proper. On Macedonia and its constitutional structure, cf. P. Zancan, *Il Monarcato ellenistico nei suoi elementi federativi*, 1934, pp. 110 ff., and esp. pp. 119 ff., and W. S. Ferguson's review of F. Granier, *Die makedonische Heeresversammlung*, 1931, in *Gnomon*, xi. (1935), pp. 518 ff.

4 The most important document bearing on the treaty of 311 B.C. is the letter of Antigonus to the Greek cities. Of this we still have a large part in the copy addressed to Scepsis in the Troad and discovered in that city (each Greek city probably received its own copy of the letter). The text of the letter with comments is to be found in *O.G.I.* 5 and in C. Bradford Welles, *Royal Correspondence in the Hellenistic Period*, 1934, no. I (the last with a full up-to-date bibliography and a useful survey of the political situation in 311 B.C.). Cf. A. Neppi Modona, *Athenaeum*, xi (1933), pp. 3 ff.; A. Heuss, *Hermes*, lxxiii (1938), pp. 156 ff.

5 V. G. Furlani e A. Momigliano, 'La cronaca babilonese sui diadochi', *Riv. Fil.* lx (10) (1932), pp. 462 ff., A. Neppi Modona, loc. cit.

6 For the League of 302 B.C., see U. Wilcken, 'Zu der epidaurischen Bundesstele vom J. 302 v. Chr.', *Berl. S.B.*, 1927, pp. 277 ff., cf. his 'Philipp II von Makedonien und die panhellenische Idee', ibid., 1929, pp. 291 ff., and *S.E.G.* i. 75; W. Schwahn, 'Zu I.G. II, 160 (Philipps Landfrieden)', *Rh. Mus.* lxxviii (1929), pp. 188 ff., and 'Heeresmatrikel und Landfriede Philipps von Makedonien', *Klio*, Beiheft xxi (1930), pp. 36 ff.; F. Taeger, 'Der Friede von 362/61', *Tübing. Beitr.* xi (1930), pp. 60 ff.; F. Schehl, 'Zum Korinthischen Bund vom J. 338/37 v. Chr.', *Öst. Jahresh.* xxvii (1931–2), pp. 115 ff.; J. A. O. Larsen, *Cl. Phil.* xx (1925), pp. 313 ff.; xxi (1926), pp. 52 ff.; xxvii (1932), pp. 395 ff.; F. Heichelheim, 'Griechische Staatskunde', Bursian's *Jahresb.* ccl (suppl.), p. 241 f.; A. Momigliano, *Filippo il Macedone*, 1934, pp. 161 ff.; G. Glotz, *Hist. gr.* iii, 1936, pp. 370 ff., and iv, 1, 1938, pp. 338 ff.; A. Heuss, *Hermes*, lxxiii (1938), pp. 160 ff., esp. pp. 189 ff.; P. Roussel, in G. Glotz, *Hist. gr.* iv. 1, pp. 306 n. and 339; H. Bengtson, 'Die Strategie in der hell. Zeit', *Münch. Beitr. Pap.* xxvi (1937), pp. 157 ff.

7 An interesting decree of the city of Aspendus conferring certain privileges on mercenary soldiers of Ptolemy Soter first published by Paribeni and Romanelli, *Mon. Ant.* xxiii, pp. 116 ff. (cf. A. Wilhelm, *Wien. S.B.* clxxix (1915), 6, p. 60), and later republished and commented upon by M. Segre, *Aeg.* xiv (1934), pp. 252 ff., is interpreted by M. Segre as referring to a war between Demetrius and Soter (otherwise unknown) which Demetrius conducted on behalf of his ally Seleucus some time between 301 and 298 B.C. in order to deprive Ptolemy of the parts of Asia Minor which he probably had occupied at the same time as Syria (the fact is not attested by other evidence). It is difficult to accept M. Segre's reconstruction of events, for it seems very probable that Demetrius at about this time was in diplomatic relations with Soter, G. N. Cross, *Epirus*, 1932, pp. 50 ff.

8 On Demetrius and his policy, see P. Treves, 'Dopo Ipso', *Riv. Fil.* lix (9) (1931), pp. 73 ff. and pp. 355 ff.; id., *Riv. Fil.* lx (10) (1932), pp. 194 ff., and *Athenaeum*, x (1932), pp. 187 ff. On the cult of Demetrius, O. K. Weinreich, *N.J. f. Wiss. und Jugend*, ii (1926), pp. 646 ff.; K. Scott, *A.J. Ph.* xlix (1928), pp. 149 ff. and pp. 228 ff.; V. Ehrenberg, *Die Antike*, vii (1931), pp. 279 ff.; P. Treves, *Riv. Fil.* lviii (8) (1930), pp. 278 ff. On Pyrrhus, G. N. Cross, *Epirus*, 1932, pp. 50 ff.

Two recently discovered inscriptions may bear on some events in the life of Demetrius. One found at Thasos (G. Daux, *B.C.H.* lii (1928), p. 46 f., cf. M. Cary, *J.H.S.* l (1930), pp. 253 ff.) is a decree of Lampsacus in honour of a Thasian Nossicas, who is praised for having saved some Lampsacene prisoners of war taken in a naval battle and for having helped them to return home. The battle in question is probably one of the battles in the war of Demetrius and Lysimachus, when Demetrius in 302 forced the Dardanelles and the Hellespont. The Lampsacenes evidently supplied some ships or crews to Lysimachus or Demetrius. The second inscription is the epitaph of a certain Chairippos, who fell probably in 287/6 fighting for the liberation of Munychia (N. Kyparissis and W. Peek, *Ath. Mitt.* lvii (1932), pp. 142 ff.). Cf. the inscription from Aspendus mentioned in the preceding note.

⁹ Cf. the recently discovered treaty between Aetolia and Boeotia, which is variously dated in 301–299 B.C., in 295 or 294 B.C., in 292 or 291 B.C., and in 281/0 B.C. *S.I.G.*³, 366, cf. G. De Sanctis, *Atti Acc. Tor.* xlix (1913–14), p. 684; Th. Walek, *Rev. Phil.* xxxvii (1913), pp. 262 ff.; K. J. Beloch, *Gr. Gesch.*, 2nd ed., IV. i, p. 213; R. Flacelière, *B.C.H.* liv (1930), pp. 75 ff.; M. Guarducci, *Riv. Fil.* lviii (8) (1930), pp. 329 ff.; G. Klaffenbach, *I.G.*² IX. 1. i. no. 170, and Suppl., p. 85, cf. p. xv, *sub anno* 291 B.C.; R. Flacelière, *Les Aitoliens à Delphes*, 1937, pp. 57 ff.; P. Roussel, in G. Glotz, *Hist. gr.* iv. 1, p. 348.

¹⁰ New evidence on Lachares is supplied by a fragment of a chronicle, *P. Ox.* 2082; F. Jacoby, *F.G.H.* II B, Fr. 1. 2. no. 257 a (p. 1194), cf. II B D, pp. 848 ff., discussed by G. De Sanctis, *Riv. Fil.* lvi (6) (1928), pp. 53 ff. W. S. Ferguson, 'Lachares and Demetrius Poliorcetes', *C.P.* xxiv (1929), pp. 1 ff.; P. Treves, *Riv. Fil.* lix (9) (1931), pp. 73 ff. and pp. 355 ff. A fragment of a violent speech found at Oxyrhynchus (now at Florence) and published by A. Porosa, *St. Ital. Fil.* xii (1935), pp. 2 ff., is interpreted by G. De Sanctis, 'Atene dopo Ipso', *Riv. Fil.* lxiv (14) (1936), pp. 134 ff. and pp. 253 ff., as bearing on the same civil war; cf., however, P. Roussel, *Mél. Desrousseaux*, 1937, pp. 429 ff.

¹¹ Two of the most important documents bearing on the situation in Asia Minor before and after Demetrius crossed to that country are reprinted and commented upon by C. B. Welles, *Royal Correspondence*, no. 5 (letter of Seleucus to the Milesians of 288 B.C.—*O.G.I.S.* 214; cf. Hiller, *P.W.K.* xv, 1604) and no. 6 (letter of Lysimachus to Priene of about 285—*O.G.I.S.* 12, concerning probably the military operations of Lysimachus before the decisive action of Agathocles).

¹² The best modern narrative of the events of the period under review will be found in the three chapters of vol. vii of *C.A.H.* by W. W. Tarn (chs. vi, xxii, and xxiii). An excellent bibliography appended to these chapters (pp. 874 ff.) relieves me of the necessity of giving a bibliography here: cf. note 1. I may add references to some books and articles of later date than 1927 (the date of *C.A.H.* vii) and not listed in the bibliography to chs. v–vii of vol. viii of *C.A.H.* (1930).

Most of the new contributions bear on the history of the Balkan peninsula and especially of Greece and Macedonia in the period under review.

MACEDONIA. On ANTIGONUS GONATAS, W. Fellmann, *Antigonos Gonatas König von Makedonien und die griechischen Staaten*, Diss. Würzburg, 1930; on the CHREMONIDEAN WAR, W. W. Tarn, 'The new dating of the Chremonidean war', *J.H.S.* liv (1934), pp. 26 ff., cf. W. Peremans, *Rev. Belge*, xii (1933), pp. 49 ff., and on the Acarnano-Aetolian treaty probably connected with the outcome of this war (*I.G.* IX ², no. 3 A—*S.I.G.*³ 421), G. Klaffenbach, *Klio*, xxiv (1931), pp. 223 ff.; cf. E. Pozzi, *Atti Acc. Tor.* xlvii (1911–12), pp. 222 ff., and P. Treves, *Riv. Fil.*, lx (10) (1932), pp. 276 ff. Note, however, that R. Flacelière, *Les Aitoliens à Delphes*, 1937, p. 192 f., is inclined to date the treaty a little earlier (270 B.C.).

On the BATTLES OF COS AND ANDROS and their dates, see E. Bikerman, *R.E.A.* xl. (1938), pp. 369 ff.; he makes the battle of Cos an event of the Chremonidean war and denies that it had any influence on the general political situation in the Aegean Sea; I cannot share his point of view and still believe in the rapid growth of Macedonian authority in the Aegean, which is reflected in the Delian inscriptions.

On DEMETRIUS II, P. Treves, 'La tradizione politica degli Antigonidi e l'opera di Demetrio II', *Rend. Linc.* viii (1932), pp. 168 ff. New evidence on the situation of Attica in the time of Demetrius II and of the attacks of Aratus on Athens is yielded by a recently found inscription published and interpreted by *Σ. Κουγέας* in *Ἑλληνικά*, iii (1930), pp. 281 ff., and by P. Roussel, 'Un nouveau document relatif à la guerre Démétriaque', *B.C.H.* liv (1930), pp. 268 ff.; cf. *Rev. É.G.* xliv (1931), p. 214 f.

On the relations between Athens and ANTIGONUS DOSON, see the inscription found in the Athenian agora which refers to an embassy sent by Athens to the king in 226/5 B.C.; the ambassador was the well-known peripatetic philosopher Prytanis of Carystus, see B. D. Meritt, *Hesp.* iv (1935), pp. 525 ff., no. 39; cf. L. Robert, *B.C.H.* lix (1935), p. 436 f., and P. Roussel, ibid., p. 520 f. On the relations between the Antigonids and Athens in general, A. Heuss, 'Stadt und Herrscher des Hellenismus', *Klio*, Beiheft, xxxix (1937), pp. 62 ff.

On the ACHAEAN LEAGUE in the third century and ARATUS, M. Levi, 'Arato e la "liberazione" di Sicione', *Athenaeum*, viii (1930), pp. 508 ff.; F. W. Walbank, *Aratos of Sicyon*, 1933 (with good bibliography).

On the AETOLIANS and especially their relations with Delphi and their history in the third century B.C., R. Flacelière, *Les Aitoliens à Delphes*, 1937. The most important chronological problem affecting not only the history of the Aetolians and of Delphi, but also the chronology of the third century in general, is that of the date of the Aetolian foundation or refoundation of the Soteria at Delphi, which is closely connected with the date of the Athenian archon Polyeuctus. The view generally accepted is that first suggested by P. Roussel, that the Soteria originally established by the Amphictions in 279 were remodelled and refounded by the Aetolians at a much later time (255/4 or 243/2). The only scholar who after Roussel still supports the old view that the Aetolians founded the Soteria in 279 and that this is the date of Polyeuctus' archonship is W. Kolbe, *Hermes*, lxviii (1933), pp. 440 ff., and ibid. lxix (1934), pp. 217 ff. On the position of the controversy and on the data which support the view of Roussel, see the most recent discussions of the problem by L. Robert, *R.E.A.* xxxviii (1936), pp. 5 ff.; S. Dow, *A.J.A.* xl (1936), pp. 57 ff., and R. Flacelière, *Les Aitoliens à Delphes*, 1937, pp. 138 ff. Cf. M. N. Tod, *J.H.S.* lvii (1937), p. 182 f., and U. Kahrstedt, 'Zu den delphischen Soterienurkunden', *Hermes*, lxxii (1937), pp. 369 ff. The date proposed by Roussel seems to be confirmed by a fragmentary inscription published by B. D. Meritt, *Hesp.* vii (1938), pp. 121 ff., no. 24. On the role of Aetolia in Greece and the Aegean, see the remarks of G. Klaffenbach, 'Asylievertrag zwischen Ätolien und Milet', *Sitzb. berl. Akad., phil.-hist. Kl.*, 1937, p. 159.

On EPIRUS, G. N. Cross, *Epirus*, 1932, pp. 88 ff. On AGIS and CLEOMENES, see the bibliography quoted below, Ch. IV.

EGYPT and SYRIA. The crucial problem of the chronology of the Syrian wars, depending as it does on the interpretation of the afore-mentioned Babylonian Chronicle and a Milesian and several other inscriptions, has been discussed recently in a group of papers which I will quote in full later in this book (cf. Ch. III, note 11). It may be mentioned here that the desire of Philadelphus after the Second Syrian war to restore his sea-power is reflected in some Delian inscriptions (K. J. Beloch, *Gr. Gesch.* IV. i, 2nd ed., p. 611 f.; cf. W. W. Tarn, *C.A.H.* vii, p. 715) and in an unpublished papyrus at Oxford which Mr. C. H. Roberts was kind enough to show me and which I mention here with his permission. It is a dossier of 251/50 B.C. concerning an order of Philadelphus to his famous *dioecetes* Apollonius to cut a large amount of local wood for the outfit of the νῆες μακραί, i.e. war-ships. It is evident that Philadelphus, after his heavy losses, was anxious to build up as strong a navy as possible in order to check the Macedonian and Seleucid influence in the Aegean.

On the ARABIAN policy of Philadelphus, W. W. Tarn, 'Ptolemy II and Arabia', *J.E.A.* xv (1929), pp. 9 ff. On ANTIOCHUS I, M. Segre, 'Per la storia di Antioco I Sotere', *Athenaeum*, viii (1930), pp. 488 ff. On the relations of the early Seleucids and the satrapies of the farther East, especially India and Bactria, W. W. Tarn, *The Greeks in Bactria and India*, 1938. On the history of PARTHIA, J. Wolski, *Arsaces I, Założytiel panstwa partyjskiego*, Diss. Krakow 1937, and N. C. Debevoise, *A Political History of Parthia*, 1938.

[13] References in R. Flacelière, *Les Aitoliens à Delphes*, 1937, pp. 268 ff.

[14] Modern study of the third period in the history of the Hellenistic world has been influenced by the relative importance of the events and by the character of our sources. The result is that whereas for the first part of the period—that of the Macedonian and the Syrian wars, including the history of Greece to the destruction of Corinth—there is a very large number of treatises and monographs analysing and interpreting the sources, the period after Antiochus III in Syria and in Egypt, and the history of Asia Minor after the end of the Pergamene kingdom and of Greece after the destruction of Corinth have been rather neglected by scholars.

An excellent presentation of the facts relating to the early part of the former period (down to Magnesia and the treaty of Apamea) will be found in various papers and works by the late M. Holleaux; these are summarized in his masterly chapters in *C.A.H.*, vol. viii (1930)—ch. 5, 'Rome and Macedon: Philip against the Romans'; ch. 6, 'Rome and Macedon: the Romans against Philip'; ch. 7, 'Rome and Antiochus'. To these chapters is appended an

excellent bibliography. In the same chapters Holleaux summarized, shortly
before his death, his views on the relations between Rome and the East, views
which in the main I have accepted in my summary (with some not unim-
portant modifications). The problem, however, of the reasons which led
Rome to begin an active policy in the East, her reasons, that is, for engaging
in war with Philip and with Antiochus, will always remain debatable. Cf.
F. Münzer, *Die politische Vernichtung des Griechentums*, 1925 (Das Erbe der
Alten, ix). It is therefore not surprising that it should have been again discussed recently by several scholars. I give a list of articles dealing with the
question which have been published since Holleaux wrote his chapters (1930):
First Macedonian war: J. van Antwerp Fine, 'Macedon, Illyria and Rome
220–219 B.C.', *J.R.S.* xxvi (1936), pp. 24 ff. Second Macedonian war and the
war with Antiochus: A. Passerini, 'Studi di storia ellenistico-romana. I. Le
relazioni di Roma con l'Oriente negli anni 201–200', *Athen.* ix (1931), pp.
260 ff.; II. 'I moventi di Roma nella seconda guerra Macedonica', ibid., pp.
542 ff.; III. 'La pace con Filippo e le relazioni con Antioco', ibid. x (1932),
pp. 105 ff.; IV. 'Lo scoppio della guerra Siriaca', ibid., pp. 325 ff.; V. 'L'ultimo
piano di Annibale', ibid. xi (1933), pp. 10 ff.; VI. 'I moti politico-sociali della
Grecia e i Romani', ibid., pp. 309 ff.; E. Bickermann, 'Bellum Antiochicum',
Hermes, lxvii (1932), pp. 47 ff.; id., 'Rom und Lampsacos', *Phil.* lxxxvii
(1931), pp. 277 ff.; id., 'Les préliminaires de la seconde guerre de Macédoine',
Rev. Phil. ix (61) (1935), pp. 59 ff. and pp. 161 ff.; and G. T. Griffith, 'An
early motive of Roman imperialism', *Cambridge Historical Journal*, v (1935),
pp. 1 ff; J. A. O. Larsen, 'The treaty of peace at the conclusion of the Second
Mac. War', *Class. Phil.* xxxi (1936), pp. 342 ff., and 'The Peace of Phoinice',
etc., ibid. xxxii (1937), pp. 15 ff.; A. H. McDonald and F. W. Walbank, 'The
Origins of the Second Macedonian War', *J.R.S.* xxvii (1937), pp. 180 ff.;
J. A. O. Larsen, 'Roman Greece' in T. Frank, *Econ.Surv.* iv, 1938, pp. 261–313.

On the attitude of Athens towards Philip and on the situation of the city
during his rule see the Athenian decree in honour of the well-known Cephisodorus, the head of the anti-Macedonian party (Paus. i. 36. 5), recently published by B. D. Meritt, *Hesp.* v (1936), pp. 419 ff., cf. F. Heichelheim, *Aeg.* xvii
(1937), pp. 61 ff. New light has been thrown on the organization of Philip's
army by several recently found inscriptions (quoted below, Ch. V). I may
mention here an inscription from Thessalonice: a letter of Philip to Archippus
and a *diagramma* of Philip relating to the Serapeum of the city, see Σ. Πελε-
κίδης, 'Ἀπὸ τὴν πολιτεία καὶ τὴν κοινωνία τῆς ἀρχαίας Θεσσαλονίκης, Παράρτημα
τοῦ Β' τόμου τῆς 'Επιστημονικῆς 'Επετηρίδος τῆς Φιλοσοφικῆς Σχολῆς (Πανεπιστήμιον Θεσσαλονίκης), 1933, pp. 7 ff. Cf. C. B. Welles, 'New texts from the
chancery of Philip V', *A.J.A.* xlii (1938), pp. 245 ff., and E. Bikerman,
Διάγραμμα, *Rev. d. Phil.* xii (64), 1938, pp. 295 ff.

Important contributions to our knowledge of Roman international law and
Roman foreign policy will be found in H. Horn, *Foederati, Untersuchungen
zur Geschichte ihrer Rechtsstellung im Zeitalter der römischen Republik und des
frühen Prinzipats*, 1930, and A. Heuss, 'Die völkerrechtlichen Grundlagen der
römischen Aussenpolitik in republikanischer Zeit,' 1933 (*Klio*, Beiheft 31,

N.F. 18). For the treaty of Apamea cf. M. Holleaux, *R.E.G.* xiv (1932), pp. 7 ff.

The history of Macedonia and Greece and the relations between Rome and the Hellenistic States from Magnesia to the destruction of Corinth are discussed by P. V. M. Benecke in *C.A.H.* viii, chs. 8 and 9, cf. J. A. O. Larsen, 'Was Greece free between 196 and 146 B.C. ?', *Cl. Phil.* xxx (1935), pp. 193 ff., and id., 'Roman Greece', loc. cit.; G. Daux, *Delphes au IIme et au Ier siècle*, 1936, pp. 303 ff.; F. Geyer, *P.W.K.* xix. 996 ff., art. 'Perseus' (1937), and a most interesting inscription from Athens—an honorary decree of 169/8 for a certain Calliphanes who had fought at Pydna on the side of the Romans and Eumenes and brought to Athens the news of the Roman victory—B. D. Meritt, *Hesp.* v (1936), p. 429, cf. ibid. iii (1934), no. 18. The history of Delphi after the end of the Aetolian domination is illuminated by some important Delphian inscriptions hitherto insufficiently known and wrongly interpreted: M. Holleaux, *B.C.H.* liv (1930), pp. 1 ff.; ibid. lv (1931), pp. 1 ff.; P. Roussel, ibid. lvi (1932), pp. 1 ff.; G. Daux, *Delphes au IIme et au Ier siècle*, 1936.

On the history of the Near East during the period under review, see the relative chapters of *C.A.H.*, namely vol. viii, ch. 16 ('Syria and the Jews', by E. R. Bevan), and ix, chs. 5 ('Pontus and its neighbours', by M. Rostovtzeff and H. Ormerod) and 14 ('Parthia', by W. W. Tarn). These chapters contain up-to-date bibliographies (cf. also the bibliographies to *C.A.H.* vii, chs. 4 and 5, and viii, chs. 18, 19, 20, by M. Rostovtzeff). To these bibliographies I may add some recent important contributions.

Some noteworthy new facts regarding SYRIA in the time of Seleucus IV have been revealed by an inscription from Seleuceia in Pieria interpreted in a posthumous paper by M. Holleaux, *B.C.H.* lvii (1933), pp. 6 ff. On the section of the trilingual decree of Tell-el-Maskutah bearing on the BATTLE OF RAPHIA, A. Momigliano, *Aeg.*, x (1930), pp. 180 ff. The relations between Rome and EGYPT are dealt with in a Breslau dissertation by H. Winkler, *Rom und Aegypten im II. Jahrh. v. Chr.*, 1933, and in a set of papers written on the subject of the now famous 'last will and testament' of Ptolemy Neoteros (Euergetes II) first published by G. Oliverio, 'La stele di Tolomeo Neoteros re di Cirene' (*Documenti antichi dell'Africa Italiana*, I. *Cirenaica*, i), 1932, and later discussed by many scholars, the most important contributions being: U. Wilcken, *Sitzb. Berl. Ak.*, 1932, pp. 317 ff.; G. De Sanctis, *Riv. Fil.* lx (10) (1932), pp. 59 ff.; L. Wenger, *Studi Riccobono*, i (1932), pp. 529 ff.; P. Roussel, *R.E.G.* xlv (1932), pp. 286 ff.; E. Bickermann, *Gnomon*, viii (1932), pp. 424 ff.; W. Schubart, *Phil. Woch.*, 1932, pp. 133 ff.; A. Gitti, *Aeg.*, xii (1932), pp. 145 ff.; M. Segre, *Il Mondo Classico*, ii (1932), pp. 424 ff.; U. Ratti, *Riv. Fil.* lx (10) (1932), pp. 375 ff.; A. Piganiol, *Rev. hist. du Dr. fr. et étr.* xii (1933), pp. 409 ff., 597 f.; A. Steinwenter, *Z. d. Sav.-St.* liii (1933), pp. 497 ff. Cf. the excellent bibliography and discussion by V. Arangio-Ruiz, *Studia et Documenta Historiae et Juris*, ii (1936), pp. 483 ff. On the SIXTH SYRIAN WAR, PTOLEMY PHILOMETOR and PTOLEMY EUERGETES II: W. Otto, 'Zur Geschichte der Zeit des 6. Ptolemäers', *Abh. Bayer. Akad.*, N.F., xi (1934), with copious bibliography; P. Jouguet, 'Les débuts du règne de Ptolémée Philométor et la sixième guerre Syrienne', *Rev. Phil.* xi (63) (1937), pp. 193 ff. and 'Eulaeos et Lénaeos', *Bull. Inst. d' Égypte*, xix (1937), pp. 157 ff. On ANTIOCHUS IV EPIPHANES, besides the papers quoted above, see W. W. Tarn, *The Greeks in Bactria and India*, 1938, Index, s.v. 'Antiochus IV Epiphanes'. On his domestic policy, below, Ch. V.

CHAPTER II

[1] See the excellent new edition of the treatise with very useful comments: B. A. van Groningen, *Aristote, le second livre de l'économique*, &c., 1933. Unfortunately the author has ignored some important modern contributions to the problem presented by the treatise, which are listed in A. M. Andreades, *A History of Greek Public Finance*, 1933, pp. 83 ff.

[2] On the milieu in which the Πόροι was written and on the treatise itself see K. von der Lieck, *Die xenophontische Schrift von den Einkünften*, Diss. Köln, 1933; cf. W. Jaeger, *Demosthenes*, 1938, p. 219, n. 17.

[3] The author certainly used literary sources for his work. These sources did not go beyond Alexander. The author himself may therefore have lived a little later.

[4] There are many surveys of the financial administration of the Persian kings, of their economic policy and of their sources of income, the most recent being that of Andreades, loc. cit., pp. 89 ff. I have not found, however, in modern books any attempt to analyse in detail the economic life of Persia and of her various satrapies, though as regards some parts of her dominions, such as Babylonia, Egypt, and Phoenicia, there is no lack of information, e.g. the clay tablets of Babylonia of the Persian period, the inscription recording the building of the palace of Susa, certain Egyptian texts, &c. The only exception in this respect is the recent book by F. Heichelheim, *Wirtschaftsgeschichte des Altertums*, 1938. Though he devotes no special chapter to Persia, in dealing in his sixth chapter (pp. 294 ff.) with the 'Classical time of the Polis-economy from Peisistratos to Alexander (ca. 560–ca. 330 B.C.)' he makes from time to time in his systematic subsections valuable remarks on the economic life of some of the constituent parts of the Persian Empire. Unfortunately the work came into my hands too late to be duly considered in this and the following chapters of my book.

On the Persian Empire in general (with a good survey of original sources and an up-to-date bibliography) A. Christensen, *Die Iranier*, Müller–Otto, *Handb. d. Altertumsw.* III. i. 3, cf. U. Wilcken, *D. Literaturz.* lvii (1936), pp. 1867 ff. New archaeological evidence on the Persian Empire and considerations on the political and religious history of Iran: E. Herzfeld, *Archaeological History of Iran*, 1935, pp. 1–44.

[5] On the political history of the Iranian plateau see G. G. Cameron, *History of Early Iran*, 1936, which lays special emphasis on the political history of

Elam and of the other pre-Iranian inhabitants of the plateau and pays due attention to the history of the Medes and early Persians. The book contains an excellent up-to-date bibliography. A similar book on the cultural, economic, and social history of early Iran, including the Iranian Nomads, remains for the time being a *pium desiderium*. Cf. E. Herzfeld's book quoted in the preceding note. On the early social structure of Eastern Iran as revealed by the Gāthās and the Yašts of the Avesta, H. S. Nyberg, *Die Religionen des Alten Iran* (transl. by H. H. Schaeder), 1938, esp. chs. 3 and 4.

⁶ On the political status of Syria and Mesopotamia during Persian rule and under Alexander, and particularly its division into satrapies, see the recent book by O. Leuze, *Die Satrapieneinteilung in Syrien und im Zweistromlande von 520–320*, 1935 (published after his death in *Schr. d. Königsberger Gelehrten-Gesellschaft*, xi. 4); cf. on the oriental satrapies, A. Foucher, 'Les Satrapies orientales de l'Empire Achéménide', *C.R. Ac. Inscr.*, 1938, pp. 336 ff. On the clay tablets of the Persian and Hellenistic periods found in Babylonia see the remarks of M. San Nicolò, *Beitr. z. Rechtsgeschichte im Bereiche der keilschr. Rechtsquellen*, 1931, p. 132, cf. A. Aymard, *Rev. É. A.* xl (1938), p. 6; innovations of Persian times in the field of civil law, A. Aymard, ibid., pp. 11 ff.; economic conditions and prices, ibid., pp. 23 ff.

⁷ On the successors of Babylonia, A. Götze, *Hethiter, Churriter und Assyrer*, &c., 1936. The connexion between Babylonia and the surrounding countries in the sphere of law, and the legal development on independent lines of each of her neighbours, have recently been set forth in the admirable general survey of P. Koschaker, 'Keilschriftrecht', in *Zeitschr. d. D. Morgenl. Ges.*, N.F., xiv (1935), pp. 1 ff. The same or similar relations between Babylonia and the surrounding countries may be noticed in the field of art (cf. A. Moortgat, *Bildwerk und Volkstum Vorderasiens zur Hethiterzeit*, 1934), and probably in that of economics and material civilization. Almost all recent careful excavations of Syrian and north Mesopotamian 'tells' have revealed a Persian period in the life of the settlements. I may quote *exempli causa* the excellent report of F. Thureau-Dangin and M. Dunand, *Til Barsib*, 1936, cf. M. E. L. Mallowan, *Antiquity*, xi (1937), pp. 328 ff.

⁸ M. Rostovtzeff, *Caravan Cities: Petra, Jerash, Palmyra, Dura*, 1932 (Italian edition 1934).

⁹ On Ras Shamra see the annual reports of C. F. A. Schaeffer in *Syria*, and the short summary of R. Dussaud, 'Ras Shamra', in *Liverpool Ann. of Arch. and Anthr.* xxi (1934), pp. 93 ff.; cf. C. F. A. Schaeffer, 'Die Stellung Ras-Shamra-Ugarit zur Kretischen und Mykenischen Kultur', *J.D.A.I.*, lii (1937), pp. 139 ff., and on the beginnings of Phoenician commerce, R. Dussaud, 'Le commerce des anciens Phéniciens à la lumière du poème des dieux gracieux et beaux', *Syria*, xvii (1936), pp. 59 ff. On the excavations at Byblus, which are now completed, P. Montet, *Byblos et l'Égypte*, 1928, and M. Dunand, *Fouilles de Byblos*, i, 1926–32, Atlas, 1937 (the volume containing the text has not yet appeared, see meanwhile his reports in *Syria*). On the relations between Syria

and Egypt in the time of the New Empire cf. P. Montet, *Les Reliques de l'art syrien dans l'Égypte du Nouvel Empire*, 1937. On Sidon, Honigmann's article in *P.W.K.* iv A, 221 ff. There is no good monograph on Tyre. On the coins, E. T. Newell, *Tyrus Rediviva*, 1923. On Carthage, S. Gsell, *Histoire ancienne de l'Afrique du Nord*, iv: *La Civilisation carthaginoise*, 1920. On the Phoenician cities and their trade in pre-Persian times, F. Heichelheim, *Wirtschaftsg.*, p. 226 f. Al Mina, below n. 19. On the excavations (still in progress) at Tal Atchana, ancient Alalkha, between Antioch and Aleppo, which testify to the relations between the early 'Phoenician' harbours and the cities of Northern Syria, Sir Leonard Woolley, *J.H.S.* lvi (1937), pp. 125 ff., *Antiquaries Journ.* xviii (1938), pp. 1 ff., and xix (1939), pp. 1 ff., and *Br. Mus. Quart.* xii (1938), p. 113 f., cf. Sir Arthur Evans, *J.H.S.* lvi (1937), pp. 133 ff. (on the local imitation of Minoan pottery); C. F. A. Schaeffer, *Syria*, xix (1938), pp. 30 ff., and S. Smith, *Antiquaries Journ.* xix (1939), pp. 38 ff. (on the cuneiform tablets found in the ruins and on the history of Alalkha).

[10] Phoenician trade with Greece: see the books and papers on the economic development of Greece quoted below, note 25. Phoenician trade with the West: E. Meyer, *Gesch. d. Altert.* ii. 2, 2nd ed. (1931), pp. 77 ff., and the bibliography by Heichelheim, *Festg. f. Sombart*, p. 177, n. 51; cf. below, notes 16 ff.

[11] I cannot here give a bibliography of books and articles dealing with the social and economic life of Palestine in the various periods of her prehistoric and historical life. On the period of Persian domination, S. A. Cook, *C.A.H.* vi (1927), pp. 167 ff., and bibliography p. 578, and especially C. Watzinger, *Denkmäler Palästinas*, ii, 1935, pp. 1 ff.

[12] On Anatolia see A. Götze in Müller–Otto, *Handb. d. Altertumsw.* iii. 1, 3; cf. U. Wilcken, *D. Literaturz.* lvii (1936), pp. 1862 ff., and A. Götze, 'The present state of Anatolian and Hittite Studies', *Haverford Symposion of Archaeology and the Bible*, 1937, pp. 136 ff, cf. the reports on the excavations of Tal Atchana quoted above. The more we know of 'Hittite' Asia Minor and North Syria, the more we realize how extensively the Hittite organization of Anatolia survived in the Persian and Hellenistic periods.

[13] On Egypt in Persian times, G. Posener, 'La première domination perse en Égypte', *Bibl. de l'Inst. fr. d'arch. or.* xi (1936), a collection of all the hieroglyphic inscriptions relating to the first Persian domination in Egypt with valuable comments on them. Cf. C. Préaux, *Chr. d'Ég.* xiii (1938), pp. 166 ff., and the following note.

[14] W. Schur, 'Zur Vorgeschichte des Ptolemäerreiches', *Klio*, xx (11) (1926), pp. 270 ff., cf. my remarks in *C.A.H.* vii, p. 110, and the bibliography, ibid., p. 892, cf. below, ch. IV. On the grave of Petosiris and its Iranian or Greek connexions, Ch. Picard, 'Mél. Victor Loret', *Bull. Inst. Fr. Arch. Or.* xxx (1930), pp. 201 ff. See pl. XII, 1.

[15] A. Andreades, 'Le montant du budget d'Alexandre le Grand', *XXIIᵉ session de l'Institut International de Statistique*, sect. 2, Comm., 1934, pp. 3 ff.

[16] There are no reliable statistical data relating to the Greek, especially Athenian, coins discovered in the eastern and Syro-Phoenician satrapies of the Persian Empire and in the non-coastal regions of Asia Minor. They are, however, well known to all numismatists. On this point and on the imitation of Athenian coins see K. Regling, art. 'Münzwesen' in *P.W.K.* xv. p 467. The many rich coin hoards of the fourth century found in this region are listed by S. P. Noe, 'A bibliography of Greek coin-hoards'², *Num. Notes and Monographs*, lxxviii (1937), for instance Antioch (no. 55, Greek coins exclusively), Beithir (no. 134), Cilicia (no. 252; cf. E. T. Newell, *Num. Chr.* xiv (1914), pp. 1 ff.), Qasr Naba (Syria, no. 846), and the river Tigris (no. 1109). An historical interpretation of the coin-hoards as listed by Noe has been recently suggested by F. Heichelheim in his paper 'Wirtschaftshistorische Beiträge zur klassisch-griechischen und hellenistischen Münzortstatistik', *Trans. of the Intern. Numismatic Congress*, 1936, pp. 68 ff. Cf. A. Blanchet, *Rev. Num.* xxxix (1936), pp. 1 ff.

Two recent finds illustrate the conditions in the fourth century B.C.: one made at Susa (Elam), the other in Palestine. At Susa a wooden box was discovered, apparently hidden by one of the soldiers of Alexander or one of his immediate successors. In it was a Phoenician necklace consisting of various beads and many small silver coins mostly of the fourth century. The coins give a good idea of the currency that was in use in the Persian Empire in that century. There was only one 'royal' coin (Xerxes I), the rest were local coins of the various satrapies, with those of Phoenicia and Asia Minor prevailing: Bagous, the satrap of Egypt, Aradus, Sidon, Tyre, Gaza, Pisidia, Cilicia, Hecatomnus of Caria, and perhaps Apollonia. In addition there were coins of Alexander the Great and of one of his immediate successors. Some coins have not been identified. See J.-M. Unvala, *Mém. de la Mission Arch. de Perse*, Min. Éd. Nat., xxv (1934), pp. 78 ff., and pl. II, cf. Allotte de Fuÿe, ibid., p. 89 (not listed by Noe).

Very similar in many respects is the recent find in Palestine near Gezer (probably a large hoard), see C. Lambert, *The Quarterly of the Department of Antiquities in Palestine*, ii (1933), pp. 1 ff., and pls. I, II; Noe², no. 429. The find consists, apart from two or three coins of Alexander, of large quantities of small silver coins of Athens, Sidon, and Tyre, and of local mints (Egypto-Arabian, Philisto-Arabian, &c.). Some Philisto-Arabian coins of this hoard were acquired by Mr. E. T. Newell and admirably studied by him in connexion with the coins published by Lambert, in 'Philisto-Arabian Series', *Num. Notes and Mon.* lxxxii (1938), pp. 47 ff. The coins of the Newell collection were minted at Ascalon or Ashdod, at Gaza, and at Shol, by a Persian governor of Palestine (about 400 B.C.). Cf. the coins found in a group of graves of various dates (seventh–third centuries B.C.) excavated in the ruins of the Crusaders' castle of 'Atlīt in Palestine, see C. N. Johns, *Quart. Dep. Ant. Palestine*, ii (1933), pp. 41 ff., esp. p. 57.

An interesting feature of the economic history of the fourth century B.C. noted in the text is the absence of Persian royal coins in the above-mentioned hoards, and the gradual disappearance of the imported Athenian coins.

They were replaced by local issues. Some of these local coins are imitations of Athenian coins and some were struck by the local representatives of the Persian government. In Palestine, for example, we meet issues of the Persian satrap Manapates, of Yehud and of Hezekiah, in Gaza of the local tyrant Batis. See for Palestine, E. L. Sukenik, *Journ. Palest. Or. Soc.*, xiv (1934), pp. 178 ff.; W. F. Albright, *Bull. Am. Sch. Or. Res.* lii (1933), pp. 20 ff.; F. M. Abel, *Rev. Bibl.* xliv (1935), p. 578 f.; O. R. Sellers, *The Citadel of Beth Zur*, 1933, p. 73 f.; E. T. Newell, *Num. Notes and Mon.* lxxxii (1938), pp. 53 ff., and for Gaza, pp. 49 ff. I shall speak of this feature later in this chapter. Cf. pl. XI.

17 Finds of pottery of pre-Hellenistic times in Palestine have been discussed recently by J. H. Iliffe, 'Pre-Hellenistic Greek pottery in Palestine', *Quarterly Dep. Ant. Palestine*, ii (1933), pp. 15 ff., pls. V–IX; cf. O. R. Sellers, *The Citadel of Beth Zur*, 1933, p. 41. A striking instance of close relations between Greece and Palestine in the Greek archaic and classical periods is furnished by the excavations of a cemetery at 'Atlīt in 1930–1; see C. N. Johns, 'Excavations at 'Atlīt (1930–1): the South-Eastern Cemetery', *Quart. Dep. Ant. Palestine*, ii (1933), p. 41 (graves of the Persian period), and ibid. vi (1937), pp. 121 ff. (archaic graves). Egyptian, Egypto-Phoenician, Phoenician, and Greek objects predominate in the graves of the sixth–fourth centuries B.C. The best pottery is Greek (mostly imported from Athens), as are some of the metal objects (e.g. mirrors), and the weapons (partly Persian, esp. the Iranian arrow-heads, p. 56, fig. 14). Similar and contemporary are the finds in the graves of Tell-Far'a and what are known as the Philistinian graves of Gezer. The wooden bed and stool found at the former place (now reconstructed in the Palestine Museum of Jerusalem) are of great interest, showing almost pure Attic forms. On these finds see J. H. Iliffe, *Quart. Dep. Ant. Palestine*, iv (1934), pp. 182 ff., cf. *Palestine Museum, Jerusalem, Bull.*, iv (1927), pl. VII (pottery); and on a hoard of Egyptian bronzes of the fourth century found with sherds of pottery, J. H. Iliffe, loc. cit. v (1935), pp. 61 ff. On the monuments and grave-finds in Palestine of the period of Persian domination in general see C. Watzinger, *Denkmäler Palästinas*, ii, 1935, pp. 4 ff.; cf. F. M. Abel, *Rev. Bibl.* xliv (1935), p. 579. On Lycia, G. Rodenwaldt, 'Griechische Reliefs in Lykien', *Sitzb. Berl. Akad.* xxvii (1933), pp. 1028 ff. Cf. the finds of Deve Huyuk in North Syria, C. L. Woolley, *Liverp. Ann. of Arch.* vii (1914–16), pp. 115 ff. On Susa and Uruk, below, n. 22.

18 For the hellenization of Phoenician art in the fifth and fourth centuries B.C. it will suffice to refer to the well-known set of Phoenician and Carthaginian anthropoid sarcophagi of this period and the famous sculptured sarcophagi of Sidon; for the flourishing state of Sidon at this time and the Iranian influences, to the beautiful remains of the palace of the Persian governor at Sidon now in the Museum of Beirut (*Syria*, iv (1923), pls. 43, 44). We look forward with expectation to the results of systematic excavations just begun at Saida (Sidon). The previous excavations of G. Contenau in 1914 (*Syria*, i (1920), pp. 16, 108, 198, 287 ff.) and of Mme de Lasseur at Tyre in 1921 (*Syria*,

iii (1922), pp. 11 ff.) revealed mostly graves and remains of later times. The systematic excavations of Byblus have not yielded very much material belonging to the later periods of the city's existence, see above, note 6.

On Cyprus during the Persian domination see the general remarks of S. Casson, *Ancient Cyprus*, 1937, pp. 192 ff., and especially the report of the excavation of the great palace of Vouni by the Swedish Expedition, E. Gjerstad, etc., *The Swedish Cyprus Expedition*, iii (1937), pp. 111 ff. (the palace), cf. pp. 76 ff. (temple of Athena). See particularly the remarks of E. Gjerstad on the date and history of the palace in the light of contemporary events, p. 286 ff., and *A.J.A.* xxxvii (1933), pp. 593 ff. Of the greatest interest are the beautiful silver bowls and gold bracelets of Persian workmanship (p. 238 f. and p. 274 f., and pls. IV, XC–XCII), and the Attic black-varnished and red-figured pottery (pp. 262 ff., pls. LXXXIII–LXXXVI).

[19] See the preliminary report of C. L. Woolley, 'Excavations at Al Mina, Sueidia', *J.H.S.* lviii (1938), pp. 1 ff., and E. S. G. Robinson, 'Coins from Al Mina (1936)', *Num. Chr.* xvii (1937), pp. 182 ff., cf. my pl. XII, 2. We may regard as trading stations similar to Al Mina the settlement in the region of Antaradus recently excavated by E. Forrer on behalf of Bryn Mawr College (communication of M. H. Seyrig) and that of Cheikh Zanab four kil. south of the mouth of Nahr-el-Kebir (Eleutherus), to which belonged the Phoenician necropolis excavated by Cap. de la Bassetière. In one of the graves of the necropolis was found a fine red-figured rhyton and several black-varnished dishes of the fifth century B.C., see C. L. Brosse, Cap. de la Bassetière, and E. Pottier, *Syria*, vii (1926), pp. 193 ff. The existence and lively trade of Ugarit is attested for the late sixth century B.C. by a coin hoard (Cl. F. A. Schaeffer, *Mél. Syr. off. R. Dussaud*, 1939, pp. 461 ff.) and for the fourth century by some graves (for example, *Syria*, xvi (1935), p. 153).

[20] Coin hoard of Beni-Hassan, J. G. Milne, *Rev. Arch.*, 1905, p. 257; *J.E.A.* 1933, p. 119; Noe², no. 144; E. S. G. Robinson, *Num. Chr.*, 1937, pp. 197 ff.; of Samanoud, Noe², no. 957; E. T. Newell, *Num. Notes and Mon.* lxxxii (1938), pp. 62 ff. Cf. the hoards of Demanhour, Noe², no. 323, and Garbier, Noe², no. 420. On the Egypto-Arabian series in general, E. T. Newell, loc. cit., p. 59.

[21] On Naucratis in general Kees, *P.W.K.* xvi. 1954 ff., cf. R. M. Cook, 'Amasis and the Greeks in Egypt', *J.H.S.* lvii (1937), pp. 227 ff. The later period of the history of Naucratis, especially in the late fifth and the early fourth centuries, has been very little studied. Many sherds of Athenian black-figured and especially late red-figured vases were found at Naucratis, see H. Prinz, 'Funde aus Naukratis', *Klio*, Beiheft vii, 1908, pp. 75 ff. Athenian coins found at Naucratis: the silversmith's hoard, Noe², no. 729 (buried about 439 B.C.), cf. Noe², no. 730. Imitations of Athenian coins at Naucratis in the fourth century B.C., E. T. Newell, *Num. Notes and Mon.* lxxxii (1938), pp. 60 ff. A beautiful red-figured crater found at Memphis, now in Cairo, C. C. Edgar, *Cairo Mus. Catal.*, Greek vases, no. 32,378, pp. 84 ff. and pl. XI.

[22] The sherds of Susa: E. Pottier, *Mém. Délég. Perse*, xiii, p. 100, and

M. Pézard et E. Pottier, *Catal. d. Ant. d. la Susiane*, Mus. Nat. du Louvre, 2nd ed., 1926, p. 234 and my pl. XII, 3. The sherd of Uruk: J. Werner, in F. Heinrich, *Abh. Berl. Akad.*, 1935, phil.-hist. Kl. ii (1935), p. 36, pl. 31, *a*. Dr. Werner assigns the sherd of the black-glazed fish-plate to the second half of the fourth century.

23 On economic conditions in Greece in the fourth century B.C. see K. J. Beloch, *Gr. Gesch.* iii, 2nd ed., i, pp. 313 ff., esp. pp. 344 ff.: H. Berve, *Gr. Gesch.* ii, pp. 76 ff., and especially G. Glotz, *Histoire grecque*, iii (1936), pp. 3 ff. The works quoted in note 25 do not discriminate sharply between the fifth and the fourth centuries, basing their statements concerning the economic situation in the classical period mainly on evidence which relates to the situation in the fourth, and especially the late fourth, century.

24 On the Greek stamped and unstamped jars and the question of containers of various forms and material used in Greece in the archaic and classical periods, see B. N. Grakov, 'Packing and storage of agricultural products in classical Greece of the sixth–fourth centuries B.C.', in *Bull. of the State Acad. of the Hist. of Mat. Civilization*, cviii (1935), pp. 147 ff., esp. pp. 175 ff. (in Russian); cf. the bibliography in *C.A.H.* viii, p. 786 and p. 791. A new attempt at dating the stamped jars found at Athens is made by Virginia Grace, *Hesp.*, iii (1934), pp. 197 ff.

25 Nobody will expect me to give a full bibliography of modern works bearing on Greek economic history. The tendency to interpret the facts from modern points of view, represented mainly by E. Meyer and K. J. Beloch, has recently found support in many articles by Schwahn. The exponents of the opposite view are mainly Bücher and Hasebroek and some of the pupils of the latter. Most of the leading scholars in the field of ancient history take a middle course: Francotte (siding to a certain extent with Bücher), Glotz, Oertel, Tod, Ziebarth (who is more inclined to side with E. Meyer and Beloch), Berve, Heichelheim, and myself. An excellent bibliography of works bearing on the economic history of Greece in the fifth century will be found appended to the lucid chapter on that subject by M. N. Tod, *C.A.H.* v, 1927, pp. 1 ff. and pp. 491 ff. For a careful discussion of the controversy see F. Oertel in Poehlmann–Oertel, *Geschichte der soz. Frage und des Sozialismus in der antiken Welt*, ii², 1925, pp. 517 ff. (with bibliography).
I will mention the most important of the more recent contributions. Prominent in the controversy is J. Hasebroek, *Staat und Handel im alten Griechenland*, 1928, and *Griechische Wirtschafts- und Gesellschaftsgeschichte*, 1931 (see my review of this book, *Zeitschr. f. ges. Staatsw.* xcii (1932), pp. 333 ff.); cf. H. Knorringa, *Emporos*, 1926, and G. M. Calhoun, *The Business Life of Ancient Athens*, 1926. Supporting the point of view of Hasebroek, K. von der Lieck, *Die xenophontische Schrift von den Einkünften*, Diss. Bonn, 1933, and H. Winterscheidt, *Aigina*, 1938. Against Hasebroek in many essential points E. Ziebarth, *Beiträge zur Geschichte des Seeraubs und Seehandels im alten Griechenland*, 1929, cf. his 'Neue Beiträge zum griechischen Seehandel', *Klio*, xxvi (1933), pp. 231 ff., esp. pp. 236 ff., where he has

listed the reviews of his book and has formulated the controversial points
under discussion. More radical in his support of Meyer–Beloch is W. Schwahn,
Demosthenes gegen Aphobos, 1929; cf. his articles 'Die xenophontischen Πόροι
und die athenische Industrie im vierten Jahrhundert', *Rh. Mus.* lxxx (1931),
pp. 253 ff., and 'Schiffspapiere', ibid. lxxxi (1932), pp. 39 ff. Against him
F. Oertel, 'Zur Frage der attischen Gross-Industrie', *Rh. Mus.* lxxix (1930),
pp. 230 ff., and F. Heichelheim, *Schmollers Jahrb.* liv (1930), pp. 181 ff. (969 ff.).
The latest contributions to the discussion are F. Heichelheim, 'Die Ausbreitung
der Münzgeldwirtschaft und der Wirtschaftsstil im archaischen Griechenland',
Schmollers Jahrb. lv (1931), pp. 37 ff. (229 ff.), 'Welthistorische Gesichtspunkte
zu den vormittelalterlichen Wirtschaftsepochen', *Festgabe für W. Sombart,
Schmollers Jahrb.* lvi (1933), pp. 181 ff. (1021 ff.); cf. his art. 'Sitos' in
P.W.K., Suppl. vi, 833 ff., and 'Monopole', ibid. v, sect. A., and *Wirtschaftsgeschichte des Altertums*, 1938. On the difficulties in applying modern terms
to the various trends of the economic life of classical Greece, see the judicious
remarks of M. I. Finkelstein, Ἔμπορος, ναύκληρος and κάπηλος, *Cl. Ph.* xxx
(1935), pp. 320 ff.

I may mention also the general treatment of Greek history by H. Berve,
Griechische Geschichte, 3rd ed., 1931–3, and by G. Glotz, *Histoire grecque*, i–iii
(1925–36), and *La Cité grecque*, 1928. It is useless to enumerate the various
books and articles dealing with the economic history of Greece written and
published in Soviet Russia. Most of them depend entirely on the so-called
'bourgeois science', which they insult vehemently, while they add no new
material or new points of view, repeating *à tort et à travers* the general remarks,
long since discarded, of Marx and Engels on the economy of 'slave-holding'
societies.

[26] The great expansion of Greek trade and the prosperity of Greece in the
fifth century are well illustrated by the historical analysis of the coin-hoards
of that century found in the various parts of the Greek world. Some remarks
on the subject will be found in the article by F. Heichelheim in *Trans. of the
Intern. Numismatic Congress*, 1936, pp. 68 ff.; cf. A. Blanchet, *Rev. Num.*
xxxix (1936), pp. 1 ff. and F. Heichelheim, *Wirtschaftsg.*, pp. 294 ff.

[27] The evidence is collected in the books and articles quoted in notes 23
and 25. K. von der Lieck in his dissertation *Die xenophontische Schrift von
den Einkünften*, 1933, has pointed out the transference of the interest of
Athens from purely political to economic questions (cf. Berve, *Gr. Gesch.*
ii, pp. 114 ff.), which began in 354 B.C. and which led to the rule of Eubulus
and became later one of the leading features of Greek politics in general. This
change was certainly due, not only to the political bankruptcy of Athens, but
also—and in a large measure—to the necessity of saving her from ruin and
her population from starvation by any possible means. That other Greek
cities were similarly situated at about the same time is shown by Ps.-Arist.
Oecon. II. The device suggested by the Ps.-Xenophontic Πόροι is, of course,
rather in the nature of political propaganda than a serious suggestion by an
experienced financier. The author himself may have believed in his remedy,

in this resembling his many successors both in the United States and in
Europe, who are suggesting equally fantastic though apparently simple plans
for solving the present economic crisis of the world. It was certainly not
Eubulus who wrote the Πόροι.

28 H. W. Parke, *Greek Mercenary Soldiers*, 1933, pp. 113 ff.

29 The famine is well attested by several statements of Demosthenes (34.
39; 42. 20 and 31) and of other contemporary writers, by the activity of
Cleomenes in Egypt (see Ps.-Arist. *Oecon.* ii. 33 e, and the comments of
Groningen), by what is known as the 'Stele dei cereali' from Cyrene, and by
many Athenian decrees in honour of various merchants who at that time
imported grain to Athens. See Schäfer, *Demosthenes*, iii, 2nd ed., 295. The
inscription from Cyrene has recently been republished by G. Oliverio, *Doc.
antichi dell'Africa Italiana*, II. i (1933), and in *S.E.G.* ix, 2 ; cf. F. M. Heichelheim, *P.W.K.*, Suppl. vi. 847, art. 'Sitos', and M. Segre, *Mondo Classico*, iv
(1934), pp. 398 ff. The Athenian decrees are quoted by Heichelheim, loc. cit.,
p. 850. The famine was not due to the changed orientation of world economics
in the early Hellenistic period, but was a heritage from the past. In the new
economic conditions of the Hellenistic period Athens very soon became prosperous again. Witness the comedies of Menander.

30 A. W. Gomme, *The Population of Athens in the Fifth and Fourth Centuries* B.C., 1933; cf. G. Glotz, loc. cit. As regards the statistical data discussed by Gomme, see the admirable remarks of G. de Sanctis, *Riv. Fil.* lxv
(15) (1937), pp. 288 ff. (in a review of Gomme's book). He points out how
contradictory and difficult to interpret are the figures given by our reliable
sources for the years 431/0 and 324/3 B.C. Cf. A. W. Gomme, and G. de
Sanctis, op. cit. lxvi (16) (1938), pp. 169 ff.

31 A. W. Gomme, loc. cit., pp. 79 ff. We may find another expression of the
depressed mood of the population of Greece in the later fourth century B.C. in
the frequency of suicides attested by the reaction of Plato and the Pytha-
goreans against it. An interesting figure is that of Hegesias, the πεισιθάνατος,
a Hedonist of the time of Ptolemy Soter, who preached suicide; the term
ἀποκαρτερεῖν invented by him to express voluntary death by hunger was
very popular in Attic comedy. The question of suicide was still a subject
of discussion in the time of Zeno and Chrysippus. See H. Diels, *Der antike
Pessimismus*, 1921, p. 24; U. von Wilamowitz-Moellendorf, *Der Glaube der
Hellenen*, ii (1932), p. 271, n. i; E. Benz, *Das Todesproblem in der stoischen
Philosophie*, 1929, pp. 54 ff.

32 See the excellent article 'Sklaverei' by W. L. Westermann in *P.W.K.*,
Suppl. vi. 902 ff. Cf. F. M. Heichelheim, *Wirtschaftsg.*, pp. 401 ff.

33 A good summary treatment of this point will be found in G. Glotz, *Hist.
gr.* iii, pp. 10 ff. (with bibliography).

34 The material is collected in the art. 'Sitos' by F. M. Heichelheim quoted
in note 29.

35 The literary evidence on this point was collected long ago by H. Blümner, *Die gewerbliche Thätigkeit der Völker des klassischen Alterthums*, 1869, and B. Büchsenschütz, *Die Hauptstätten des Gewerbefleisses im klassischen Alterthume*, 1869. Since that time a mass of new evidence, papyrological, epigraphical, and archaeological, has accumulated, but has never been brought together in full. The collections of material made by Büchsenschütz and Blümner, though old and not chronologically arranged, are of the greatest value, and a revision of the two books, with new documentation and a chronological assortment of the evidence, would provide a sound and much-needed foundation for an economic history of archaic, classical, and Hellenistic Greece. Th. Reil's *Beiträge zur Kenntnis des Gewerbes im hellenistischen Ägypten*, 1913, M. Chwostow's unfinished book, *Sketches on the Organization of Industry and Trade in Greek and Roman Egypt*, i, 1914 (in Russian), and M. Schnebel's *Die Landwirtschaft im hellenistischen Ägypten*, i, 1925, as well as A. Jardé's unfortunately unfinished work *Les Céréales dans l'antiquité grecque*, I, 'Production', 1925, may serve to a certain extent as models for a careful collection and interpretation of the material. Nothing similar to the volumes of Reil and Chwostow exists for the classical and Hellenistic period of Greece, Asia Minor, the Pontus, and Sicily and Italy. A book of the type of T. Frank's *Economic Survey of Ancient Rome*, with due attention paid to archaeological material, is much needed. A good survey of the known facts, taking account of the archaeological material, will be found in F. Heichelheim, *Wirtschaftsg.*, pp. 373 ff. and notes 33 ff.

36 See above, p. 84, and notes 16 ff. Very little has been written on Persia in the time of Artaxerxes III Ochus and Darius III, or on the second Persian domination in Egypt. For Persia see W. W. Tarn, *C.A.H.* vi, pp. 21 ff. For Egypt, H. R. Hall, ibid., pp. 151 ff., and W. Schur, *Klio*, xx (2) (1926), pp. 270 ff. The great achievements of Artaxerxes III show how strong and rich the Persian Empire was in his time. His policy in Egypt must be studied afresh. A careful collection and interpretation of the existing material, in the style of Posener's book on the first Persian domination, is much needed, and so is a more careful excavation of the ruins of Naucratis with due attention to the later period of its history.

37 On the economic history of South Russia see the bibliography to my chapter 'The Bosporan Kingdom' in *C.A.H.* viii, p. 785 f.; cf. my articles 'Olbia' and 'Panticapeo' in *Enciclopedia Italiana*, and those on Olbia, Nymphaion, and Phanagoria by E. Diehl in *P.W.K.*

38 See F. Heichelheim, art. 'Sitos' in *P.W.K.*, Suppl. vi. 838, and A. Kočevalov, *Rh. Mus.* lxxxi (1932), pp. 321 ff.; A. W. Gomme, *The Population of Athens*, pp. 28 ff.

39 On the finds made in the ruins, and on the contents of the graves, of Panticapaeum and the other Greek cities of the Bosporan kingdom, see my *Skythien und der Bosporus*, 1931, pp. 164 ff. On Olbia and its dependencies, the bibliography quoted in note 37.

40 A review of the finds made in the Scythian graves of the various periods, arranged in geographical and chronological order, is included in my *Skythien und der Bosporus*, pp. 277 ff.; cf. my *Iranians and Greeks in South Russia*, 1922, pp. 35 ff. and pp. 83 ff.

41 T. N. Knipovich, 'Tentative characterization of the settlement near Elizavetovskaja Staniza on the basis of the discoveries made in 1928 by the expedition of the State Academy of the History of Material Civilization', *Bull. of the State Acad. of Hist. of Mat. Civ.* civ (1935), pp. 111 ff., esp. pp. 137 ff. and pp. 180 ff. (in Russian).

42 On the vases of the Kertch style, K. Schefold, *Untersuchungen zu den Kertscher Vasen*, 1934. On the water colour vases, my *Skythien und der Bosporus*, pp. 182 ff.; cf. the short remarks of E. Pfuhl, *Malerei und Zeichnung*, p. 913, paragraph 1002, and M. Swindler, *Ancient Painting*, p. 357 f. K. Schefold, loc. cit., p. 137, points out that the water-colour vases were an imitation and continuation of the 'Dutzendware' of the Kertch style. He does not believe in the local production of red-figured vases of this style in South Russia. A careful study of clay, style, and forms will probably show that he is wrong. The late E. von Stern collected all the water-colour vases and prepared them for publication, but his book has never appeared.

43 On the 'Megarian' jars (more than 800 of which have been found partly in Greek cities and partly in native settlements of South Russia) see B. N. Grakov, 'Incised stamps on the necks of some Hellenistic jars', *Studies of the State Historical Museum*, i (1926), pp. 165 ff. (in Russian). Mlle Knipovich (loc. cit., pp. 157 ff.) is inclined to regard these jars, not as imported from Callatis or Heraclea (Grakov), but as Chersonesian products (it is to be noted that no such stamps are represented in the Callatian collection of stamps published by Cantacusène, see below). It is characteristic of the trade relations of the fifth and fourth centuries B.C. that at Elizavetovskaja there were found in several trial trenches: 6 fragments of Thasian stamped jars, 1 of a Rhodian jar (fourth–third century), 5 of Chersonesian jars, 11 of jars with the names of ἀστυνόμοι (very probably of Sinopic make —B. N. Grakov, *Ancient Greek pottery-stamps with the names of astynomoi*, 1929, (in Russian); cf. C. Cantacusène, 'Timbres amphoriques trouvés à Callatis', *Rev. Hist. du Sud-est Européen*, 1935, the majority being stamps with the names of *astynomoi*), and 8 of the 'Megarian' group with incised stamps. Of the unstamped jars the greater part (some are Ionian, some Thasian and Rhodian) are very similar to the group of jars with incised stamps (Knipovich, loc. cit., pp. 156 ff.).

On Chersonesus as a wine-producing country, see my article 'Chersoneso' in *Enciclopedia Italiana* and the bibliography quoted there. Recent investigations have shown that in the Roman period wine was made in some of the cities of the Bosporan kingdom, V. F. Gaydukevich, 'Ceramic building materials of the Bosporan kingdom. Bosporan tiles', *Bull. of the State Acad. of Hist. of Mat. Civ.* civ (1935), p. 215 (in Russian).

44 B. N. Grakov, 'Epigraphic documents of the royal tile-factory of Panticapaeum', *Bull. of the State Acad. of Hist. of Mat. Civ.* civ (1935), pp. 202 ff., and the substantial paper by Gaydukevich quoted in the preceding note, pp. 211 ff. (both in Russian).

45 See my chapter 'Bosporan Kingdom' in *C.A.H.* viii, pp. 582 ff., cf. Knipovich (memoir quoted in note 41), p. 177. Mlle Knipovich points out at the gold objects found in the tumuli near Elizavetovskaja Staniza have a pale colour, and show a style very different from that of the Panticapaean gold objects. Were they produced locally?

On the Panticapaean school see my books quoted in *C.A.H.* viii (bibliography). I have dealt several times with the Iranian subjects treated by the Panticapaean artists and with the Iranian elements in their composition and style, see the short summary in *Skythien und der Bosporus*, pp. 387 ff.; cf. 'L'art gréco-iranien' in *Rev. des Arts Asiat.* xxviii (1933), pp. 202 ff.; 'The great hero of Middle Asia and his exploits', *Artibus Asiae*, v (1932), pp. 99 ff.; 'Some new aspects of Iranian art', *Sem. Kond.* vi (1933), pp. 161 ff., and 'Dura and the problem of Parthian Art', p. 169 and n. 9. On the 'Pontic' animal style and its development, K. Schefold, 'Der skythische Tierstil in Südrussland', *Eurasia Septentrionalis Antiqua*, xii (1938), pp. 1 ff. Miss G. M. Richter, 'A Greek sword-sheath from South Russia', *Metr. Mus. St.* iv. i (1932), pp. 109 ff., thinks that it was Athenian artists settled in Panticapaeum during and after the Peloponnesian war who must be regarded as creators of this style.

46 *C.A.H.* viii, pp. 566 ff. and 574 ff. Cf. F. Heichelheim, *P.W.K.*, Suppl. vi. 836 ff. and *Wirtschaftsg.*, pp. 329 ff.

47 G. Kazarow, *C.A.H.* viii, pp. 559 ff., cf. his article 'The origin and the rise of the Odrysian kingdom in Ancient Thrace' in *Učiliscen Pregled*, xxxii (1933), pp. 737 ff. (in Bulgarian), cf. *P.W.K.* vi A, 421 ff. (art. 'Thrake' by Lenk, Betz, and Kazarow). The enormous wealth of the Odrysian kings was proverbial at Athens in the fourth century. See the description of the wedding-banquet of Iphicrates by Anaxandrides in his *Protesilaus* (*ap.* Athen. iv. 131; Kock, ii. 151) and the famous account by Xenophon (*Anab.* vii. 3, 21) of the symposion of Seuthes.

48 The group of tumuli-graves at Duvanlij is described and illustrated in the excellent book by B. D. Filow (in collaboration with I. Welkow and V. Mikow), *Die Grabhügelnekropole bei Duvanlij in Südbulgarien*, 1934. On Kukuva Mogila, B. Diakovitch, *Bull. de l'Institut arch. Bulg.* iii (1925), pp. 111 ff.; B. Filow, ibid. iv (1926–7), pp. 27 ff. (in Bulgarian). Bashova and Mushovitza, B. Filow and I. Welkow, 'Grabhügelfunde aus Duvanlii in Südbulgarien', *J.D.A.I.* xlv (1930), pp. 281 ff. Golemata, Lazarskata, and Arabadzijskata—B. Filow, 'Neuentdeckte Thrakische Hügelgräber von Duvanlij (Südbulgarien)', *Bull. de l'Institut arch. Bulg.* vii (1932–3), pp. 217 ff.; Dalboki—W. Prokhorow, *Bulgarian Excavations near Eski Zagora*, St. Petersburg, 1880 (in Russian); B. Filow, 'Das Antike Stein-

grab von Dalboki', *Bull. de l'Institut arch. Bulg.* vi (1930–31), pp. 45 ff. (in Bulgarian). Urukler—I. Welkow, 'Neue Grabhügelfunde aus Bulgarien', ibid. v (1928–9), pp. 25 ff. (in Bulgarian). Garčinowo—N. Fettich, 'Der Skythische Fund von Gartschinowo', *Acta Arch. Mus. Nat. Hung.* xv (1934), cf. B. Filow, 'Ein "skythisches" Bronzerelief aus Bulgarien', *Eurasia Septentrionalis Antiqua*, ix (1934), pp. 197 ff. Panagurishte, Brezovo, &c. —B. Filow, 'Denkmäler der thrakischen Kunst', *Röm. Mitt.* xxxii (1917), pp. 21 ff., and I. Welkow in *Bull. de l'Institut arch. Bulg.* viii (1934), pp. 1 ff. (a grave of the middle fifth century B.C. very similar to those of Duvanlij). An interesting grave of the fifth century with imported gold ornaments was recently discovered at Mumdzilar, G. Feher, ibid., pp. 110 ff. Cf. my *Skythien und der Bosporus*, pp. 535 ff., and Radu Vulpe, *L'Âge du fer dans les régions thraces de la péninsule balcanique*, 1930, pp. 131 ff. (with an excellent map).

An excellent analysis of some of the Bulgarian finds referred to above is contained in K. Schefold's review of Filow's book on the find at Duvanlij (*Gnomon*, xii (1936), pp. 572 ff.). In this review Schefold suggests exact dates for various graves of the Bulgarian group, and classifies the finds according to their place of origin.

[49] For the sword with an ivory handle see the Delian inventories, where the entry listing a μάχαιρα ἱππικὴ ἐλεφαντίνη προσηλωμένη ἀνάθεμα Θυμώδα τοῦ Μέντορος appears regularly (see, e.g., Durrbach et Roussel, *Inscr. de Délos*, no. 1441 A 1, l. 65).

[50] Another Tarentine bronze *situla* of the fifth to fourth centuries B.C., this one with beautiful *repoussé* bas-reliefs, was recently found at Păstrovo and published by D. Zontschew in *J.D.A.I.* li (1936), Anz., p. 411. In this article Zontschew gives a full list of other similar *situlae* found in Bulgaria; cf. the appended list of *situlae* of this type found in the Balkan peninsula and in Asia Minor by J. Werner. Note that only one of seventeen *situlae* was found in Asia Minor, the rest being discovered in the Balkan peninsula and the majority in Bulgaria. Cf. note 54.

[51] I must point out that the Thracian and Scythian graves of the sixth to fourth centuries B.C. show a far-reaching similarity in their contents. The centres from which the goods were exported were the same for both countries. It must be noted, however, that while in South Russia most of the graves even of the sixth and fifth centuries yielded a large number of Scythian objects, probably of local workmanship, in the early graves of Thrace the Scythian objects are rare and were certainly imported. The local objects show an unmistakable late-Hallstatt character and are similar to those of the graves at Trebenishte. These graves therefore certainly belonged to Thracian grandees. The graves of the later group are much more Scythian. Cf. Kazarov, *P.W.K.* vi A, 535 (an excellent list of various types of graves excavated in Bulgaria). It is also to be noted that the objects of Ionian workmanship common in South Russia are rare in Bulgaria, at least in the fifth century.

52 See my paper 'The silver vase of Voronej', *Mat. for the arch. of S. Russia*, xxxiv (1914), pp. 91 ff. (in Russian).

53 The horse-frontlet of Panagurishte, B. Filow, *Röm. Mitt.* xxxii (1917), p. 40, fig. 25; the belt of Loveč, I. Welkow, *Bull. de l'Institut arch. Bulg.* viii (1934), pp. 18 ff. On the shapes of metal belts in Italy, M. Rostovtzeff, 'Notes d'Arch. Orientale', *Syria*, xiii (1932), pp. 327 ff.; the Luristan belts, id., 'Some remarks on the Luristan bronzes', *Ipek*, vii (1931), p. 53, pl. v, 1, and R. Dussaud, 'Ceinture en bronze du Louristan', *Syria*, xv (1934), pp. 187 ff. The kettle of Gundestrup: M. Rostovtzeff, 'The Great Hero of Middle Asia and his exploits', *Artibus Asiae*, iv (1932), p. 108, n. 11. Celtization of Greek coins: R. Paulsen, *Die ostkeltischen Münzprägungen. Die Münzprägungen der Boier*, 1933; cf. *C.A.H.*, vol. of plates, iii, pp. 16, 17. The same process is noticeable in the coins of the Odrysian kings, *C.A.H.*, vol. of plates, iii, pp. 18, 19; cf. the evolution of finger-rings found in the Thracian graves, B. Filow, *Die Grabhügelnekropole bei Duvanlij in Südbulgarien*, 1934, pp. 191 ff.

54 I. Welkow, *J.D.A.I.* xlvi (1931), Anz., pp. 418 ff.; B. Filow, 'Die Kuppelgräber von Mezek', *Bull. Inst. Arch. Bulg.* xi (1937), pp. 11 ff. (in Bulgarian with German résumé) and I. Welkow, 'Die Ausgrabungen bei Mezek und Svilengrad', ibid., pp. 117 ff. (in Bulgarian with German résumé). Note especially the *candelabrum*, pp. 38 ff., figs. 37–46; the *situla* (Tarentine?), pp. 57 ff., figs. 60, 61, and the Scytho-Thracian vase and ornaments, pp. 154 ff., figs. 122–5. Cf. the grave of Lozengrad, F. W. Hasluck, *Ann. Br. Sch. at Athens*, xvii (1910–11), pp. 76 ff., and B. Filow, *Sbornik Shishmanov*, p. 46 (in Bulgarian).

55 It is a pity that none of the Greek cities of Thrace have been excavated. However, the little we know of them shows that their aspect and development were very similar to those of the Greek cities of the north coast of the Euxine. I may call the attention of the reader to the large number of stamped jars found at Bizona, Odessus and elsewhere in Bulgaria and published by K. Shkorpil, *Bull. de l'Inst. arch. bulg.* viii (1934), pp. 24 ff. As in south Russia, stamps of Thasos, Rhodes, and Sinope predominate, while Cnidian and Parian stamps appear sporadically. Besides these there are a certain number of stamped jars probably of local origin. Unfortunately no attempt was made by Shkorpil to date the stamps. Evidence of local ceramic production is furnished by the many pottery kilns discovered at Callatis, Heraclea, Odessus, and some other unidentified places (Shkorpil, loc. cit., p. 25 f.). Shkorpil has not attempted to date the kilns.

56 V. Parvan, *Dacia*, 1928, pp. 35 ff. and pp. 74 ff.; cf. Radu Vulpe, *L'Âge du fer dans les régions thraces de la péninsule balcanique*, 1930; A. Alföldi, 'Studi Ungheresi sulla Romanizzazione della Pannonia', *Gli Studi Romani nel mondo*, ii (1935), pp. 267 ff.; E. Panaitescu, 'Momenti della Civiltà Romana nella Mesia', ibid., pp. 225 ff. (with bibliography); B. Saria, 'Eine Emonenser Landmannschaft in Savaria', *Pannonia-Könyvtár*, viii (1935), pp. 5 ff.; C. Daicoviciu, *La Transylvanie dans l'Antiquité*, 1938. On the recent excavations of Istrus see, in addition to the summary by Parvan, S. Lambrino in

Rev. Ét. Lat. ix (1931), pp. 77 ff., and xi (1933), pp. 457 ff., also *Dacia*, iii–iv (1927–32), pp. 376 ff. On the archaic pottery of Istrus, M. F. Lambrino, *Dacia*, iii–iv (1927–32), pp. 362 ff. and *Les vases archaïques d'Histria*, 1938. A similar analysis of other groups of pottery will yield important material for the economic history of Greece and Rome. Very interesting for the early commercial relations between modern Rumania (especially its coast) and Greece is the rich collection of Greek vases of Kalinderu: some at least of these were found in Rumania. See E. Cotin, *La Collection des vases grecs du Musée Kalinderu*, 1937 (S. Lambrino, *Bibliothèque d'Istros*, i). The Scythian finds in Hungary and Rumania are dealt with by N. Fettich in my *Skythien und der Bosporus*, pp. 484 ff.

[57] Trebenishte—B. Filow, *Die archaische Nekropole von Trebenischte am Ochridasee*, 1927; N. Vulič, 'Ein neues Grab bei Trebenischte', *Oest. Jahresh.* xxvii (1932), pp. 1 ff., and 'Neue Gräber in Trebenischte', ibid. xxviii (1933), pp. 164 ff., id. *Rev. Arch.* vi (1934), pp. 26 ff., cf. id. *J.D.A.I.* xlv (1930), Anz., pp. 276 ff. and pp. 461 ff. On the origin of the bronzes of Trebenishte, C. Praschniker, 'Zu den neuen Funden von Trebenischte', *Oest. Jahresh.* xxvii (1932), pp. 106 ff. The attempt to attribute the bronzes to Italian workshops (E. Pernice, *Gött. Gel. Anz.* cxci (1929), pp. 445 ff., and A. K. Neugebauer, *Forsch. u. Fortschritte*, 1931, pp. 193 ff.) must be regarded as an obvious mistake. Nor do I regard as probable the suggestion of V. Čajkanović, 'Das Rätsel von Trebenište', *Rev. Internat. des Études Balkaniques*, i–ii (3–4) (1936), pp. 137 ff., that the graves at Trebenishte are those of Celts who were returning home after the capture and pillage of Delphi (which never took place!). The contents of the graves and their probable date do not support the suggestion. We should, for example, expect to find in the graves the typical La Tène military equipment (e.g. the swords); but, so far as I know, no La Tène objects were found in them. It would be still more surprising, if the graves belonged to the Hellenistic period, to find in them no coins or other objects of late classical and Hellenistic times. In the article by Čajkanović the reader will find a summary of the many conjectures as to the nationality of the men and women buried in the graves.

[58] On Illyria see the bibliography by M. Holleaux in *C.A.H.* vii, p. 932. Add, on Albania in general, M. Ugolini, *Albania Antica*, Ricerche archeologiche, i (1928), 'L'Acropoli di Fenice', ii (1932), and on Apollonia, *Albania*, i (1925)–v (1935). Cf. L. Rey, *Répertoire topobibliographique des Antiquités d'Albanie*, 1928, and 'Lettre d'Albanie', *Rev. Internat. des Études Balkaniques*, iii. i (5) (1937), pp. 301 ff. See also the periodical *Japigia*. On the relations between the Adriatic Sea and Greece before the fourth century, R. L. Beaumont, *J.H.S.* lvi (1936), pp. 162 ff. On Dionysius and his Illyrian colonies, M. Holleaux, *C.A.H.* vii, pp. 825 ff. On the texts of Theopompus and Ps.-Aristotle, Francotte, *P.W.K.* ix. 1410 and Fluss, ibid. xvi. 1742 (art. Naro).

[59] L. Marton, 'Die Frühlatenezeit in Ungarn', *Arch. Hungarica*, xi (1933); cf. A. Alföldi, quoted in n. 56.

[60] P. Jacobsthal, 'Einige Werke keltischer Kunst', *Die Antike*, x (1934), pp. 17 ff., and 'Bodenfunde griechischer Vasen nördlich der Alpen', *Germania*, xviii (1934), pp. 14 ff. ; cf. H. Hubert, *Les Celtes et l'expansion celtique jusqu'à l'époque de la Tène*, 1932, pp. 98 ff., and W. von Jenny, *Keltische Metallarbeiten aus heidnischer und christlicher Zeit*, 1935.

[61] I may quote as an example the careful collection of material in F. von Duhn, *Italische Gräberkunde*, i, 1924, and ii, 1939.

[62] A good summary in A. Della Seta, *Italia Antica*, 2nd ed., 1928 (with good bibliography).

[63] See, e. g., T. Frank, *An Economic Survey of Ancient Rome*, i, 'Rome and Italy of the Republic', 1933, where no chapter is devoted to the economic history of pre-Roman Magna Graecia, Etruria, and the rest of Italy. In vol. iii (1937) of the *Econ. Survey* V. M. Scaramuzza, in the section dealing with Sicily, begins his survey with the First Punic war. Some material (centring round Latium and Rome) will be found in T. Frank's excellent book *An Economic History of Rome*, 2nd ed., 1927, ch. ii, 'The early trade of Latium and Etruria', pp. 16 ff., cf. ch. vii, 'Industry and Commerce', pp. 108 ff. In *C.A.H.* iv one (rather meagre) chapter (ch. iv, 'The outer Greek world in the sixth century', by P. N. Ure) is devoted to the conditions of the sixth century, but special chapters have not been devoted to the evolution of Italy and Sicily from the economic and cultural point of view in the fifth and fourth centuries. Cf. F. Heichelheim, *Wirtschaftsg.*, ch. vi, where he pays due attention to the economic history of Italy.

[64] See, e. g., F. Schachermeyr's review of Hasebroek, *Griechische Wirtschafts-u. Gesellschaftsgeschichte*, 1931, in *Klio*, xxvi (1932–3), pp. 121 ff.

[65] The evidence has been repeatedly collected and illustrated, see, e. g., H. Knorringa, *Emporos*, 1926, p. 98 f. Salt fish was imported into Greece from Italy (Tarentum) by Bruttian and Campanian merchants, Euthydemus περὶ ταρίχων *ap*. Athen. iii. 116 c ; much was imported also from Cadiz (Athen. ibid., and iii. 118 d and e, from Antiphanes and Nicostratus). It remained so in later times, see the famous cookery-book of Archestratus, fr. 52, Ribbeck ; fr. 38, Brandt (Sicilian tunny).

[66] It will be sufficient to refer to Blümner, *Die gewerbliche Thätigkeit*, &c., p. 106, and to the copious bibliography on the Etruscan bronze ware in Della Seta, loc. cit., p. 465 f.

[67] Blümner, loc. cit., p. 121 f. For the Sicilian beds and cushions, Eubulus (Kock, ii. 200).

[68] Cf. the article by Schachermeyr quoted in note 64.

[69] See, e. g., the remarks of R. Hackl, 'Merkantile Inschriften auf attischen Vasen', *Münch. Arch. Studien*, 1909, p. 103. Note the large quantity of cheap Attic pottery referred to in the mercantile inscriptions and the

low prices of pottery in general. Imports of small quantities of such ware would not pay. On the Greek vases imported into Italy see the bibliography in Della Seta, loc. cit., p. 449.

[70] Much has been written recently on Tarentine art and especially on Tarentine toreutic: see E. Pernice, *Die hellenistische Kunst in Pompeji*, iv, *Gefässe und Geräte aus Bronze*, 1925; K. A. Neugebauer, 'Reifarchaische Bronzevasen mit Zungenmuster', *Röm. Mitt.* xxxviii–xxxix (1923–4), pp. 341 ff.; P. Wuilleumier, *Le Trésor de Tarente (coll. E. de Rothschild)*, 1930, cf. A. Rumpf, 'Relief in Villa Borghese', *Röm. Mitt.* xxxviii–xxxix (1923–4), pp. 446 ff.; W. Amelung, 'Studien zur Kunstgeschichte Unteritaliens und Siziliens', ibid. xl (1925), pp. 181 ff.; G. E. Rizzo, *Nuovi studi sul cratere di Buccino*, ibid., pp. 217 ff. On the Tarentine *situlae* found in the Balkan peninsula see above, notes 50 and 54. On the bronzes of Sicily see the bibliography collected by Della Seta, loc. cit., p. 450.

[71] See, e. g., Hehn, *Kulturpflanzen*, &c., 6th ed., p. 72 f., and p. 11, cf. A. Jardé, art. 'Vinum' in Daremberg et Saglio, *Dict.* v, p. 923.

[72] T. Frank, *An Economic History of Rome*, 2nd ed., 1927, p. 60 f.

[73] Della Seta, loc. cit., pp. 167 ff., and bibliography, p. 453.; cf. Courby, *Les Vases grecs à reliefs*, Paris, 1922.

[74] M. Rostovtzeff, 'Notes d'archéologie orientale, II, Les agrafes de ceintures', *Syria*, xiii (1932), p. 328 f.; cf. E. Pernice, *Die hellenistische Kunst in Pompeji*, iv, *Gefässe und Geräte aus Bronze*, p. 7, cf. 6 (on the Italian cuirass found in Africa).

[75] See F. Heichelheim's contributions quoted in notes 16 and 26.

CHAPTER III

[1] The best general accounts of the economic development of the Hellenistic world will be found in G. Glotz, *Le Travail dans la Grèce ancienne*, 1920, pp. 379 ff. (there is an English translation); U. Wilcken, 'Alexander der Grosse und die hellenistische Wirtschaft', *Schmollers Jahrb.*, xlv (2) (1921), pp. 45 ff.; F. Oertel, in R. v. Pöhlmann's *Gesch. der soz. Frage und des Sozialismus in der antiken Welt*, ii, 2nd ed., 1925, pp. 537 ff.; K. J. Beloch, *Gr. Gesch.*, iv, 2nd ed., 1925, pp. 270 ff.; W. W. Tarn, *Hellenistic Civilization*, 2nd ed., 1930, pp. 69 ff.; F. Heichelheim, 'Welthistorische Gesichtspunkte zu den vormittelalterlichen Wirtschaftsepochen', *Festgabe für W. Sombart*, 1933, pp. 181 ff. and *Wirtschaftsg.*, ch. vii. For Athens there are the excellent books of W. S. Ferguson, *Hellenistic Athens*, 1911, and S. Jebelev, *History of Athens from 229 to 30 B.C.*, 1898 (in Russian).

[2] On Alexander and his economic activity: U. Wilcken, 'Alexander der Grosse und die hellenistische Wirtschaft', *Schmollers Jahrb.*, xlv (2) (1921), pp. 45 ff., and *Alexander der Grosse*, 1931, pp. 238 ff., cf. pp. 263 ff.;

W. W. Tarn, *C.A.H.* vi, pp. 427 ff.; H. Berve, *Das Alexanderreich auf prosopographischer Grundlage*, i, 1926, pp. 291 ff. and *Griechische Geschichte*, ii, 1933, pp. 159 ff.; A. M. Andreades, Σύστημα Ἑλληνικῆς δημοσίας οἰκονομίας, i. 2, 1, 1930, of which there is a French translation; cf. his paper, 'Le montant du budget d'Alexandre le Grand', *XXIIᵉ Session de l'Institut International de Statistique, Londres, 1934* (La Haye, 1934). On the sources, E. Kornemann, *Die Alexandergeschichte des Königs Ptolemaios I. von Aegypten*, 1935, esp. pp. 159 ff. I may quote in addition some of the most recent surveys of the general policy of Alexander, including his economic policy: W. Kolbe, 'Die Weltreichidee Alexanders des Grossen', 1936 (*Freiburger Wissenschaftliche Gesellschaft*, xxv); W. W. Tarn, 'Alexander the Great and the Unity of Mankind', *Proc. Brit. Acad.* xix (1933, pp. 123 ff); U. Wilcken, 'Die letzten Pläne Alexanders des Grossen', *Sitzb. Berl. Akad.*, xxiv (1937), pp. 192 ff., (on the western plans of Alexander), and V. Ehrenberg, *Alexander and the Greeks*, 1938.

[3] Alexander and Columbus: U. Wilcken, 'Alexander der Grosse und die hellenistische Wirtschaft,' p. 50. The only resemblance I can see between the discovery of America and Alexander's conquest of the East is the increased amount of gold and silver subsequently put into circulation in western Europe and Greece respectively. I see no striking parallel between the development of the ancient world after Alexander's conquests and the evolution of the modern world.

[4] See H. Berve, *Das Alexanderreich auf prosopographischer Grundlage*, 1926, ii, pp. 169 ff., cf. pp. 193 ff.

[5] See the references in note 2. Excellent lists of Alexander's colonies will be found in H. Berve, *Das Alexanderreich*, ii, pp. 291 ff., and V. Tscherikower, 'Die hellenistischen Städtegründungen von Alexander dem Grossen bis auf die Römerzeit', 1926 (*Philol. Suppl.* xix), pp. 138 ff., cf. W. W. Tarn, loc. cit. and E. Bickermann, *Gnomon*, iv (1928), pp. 351 ff. V. Chapot, 'Alexandre fondateur de villes', *Mél. Glotz*, i, 1932, pp. 173 ff., goes too far in his endeavour to minimize the results of Alexander's colonization. On the individual colonies ascribed to Alexander see A. H. M. Jones, *The Cities of the Eastern Roman Provinces*, 1937 (Index, s.v. 'Alexander'). On Bactria, Alexander's handling of the country and the massacre there of 23,000 Greek mercenaries (Diod. xviii. 7, cf. xvii. 99. 5 f.), see W. W. Tarn, *The Greeks in Bactria and India*, p. 72. On Bactria in the early Hellenistic period, see below, Ch. IV.

[6] Much has been written on Alexander's coinage. A useful survey, based to a large extent on the masterly monographs of E. T. Newell, will be found in Ch. Seltman, *Greek Coins*, 1933, pp. 203 ff. It is very probable that Alexander chose the Attic standard not only in view of its popularity in the Aegean world but also because it was widely used alongside of the Persian in the Persian Empire, especially in Palestine—see O. R. Sellers and W. F. Albright, *Bull. Am. Sch. Or. Res.* xliii (1931), p. 10. The only standard which

competed with the Attic in Alexander's time was the Rhodian. Cf. below,
notes 38 (on the hoards of Alexander's coins) and 49.

⁷ On the pay of the Hellenistic soldiers, which included ὀψώνιον, σῖτος
or μέτρημα, σιτώνιον or σιτηρέσιον, ἱματισμός or ἐσθής, see the remarks of
Kromayer–Veith, *Heerwesen* (*Handbuch Alt.-Wiss.* iv. 3, 2), 1928, pp. 122 ff.
(with bibliography), and Rostovtzeff, *Rev. É. A.* xxxiii. (1931), p. 11, cf.
H. W. Parke, *Greek Mercenary Soldiers*, 1933, p. 233, and G. T. Griffith, *The
Mercenaries of the Hellenistic World*, 1935, pp. 264 ff.
Soldiers frequently received gratuities or payments in advance before
great battles as a kind of insurance (δόμα, δωρεαί). Money in advance (πρόδομα)
was sometimes paid to newly recruited mercenaries (Polyb. xv. 25. 16,
misinterpreted by A. Passerini, *Athen.* ix (1931), p. 263, cf. U. Wilcken, *Aktenst.
d. Th. Bank*, vi, 14 and vii, 9–10; I am indebted for this reference to Mr. G. T.
Griffith). On σιτηρέσιον and μέτρημα, see the inscriptions of Cos, Paton–Hicks,
nos. 10 and 11; A. Neppi Modona, *L'isola di Coo nell'antichità classica*, 1933
(*Mem. pubbl. a cura dell'Ist. Storico-Archeol. di Rodi*, i), p. 43—a list of subscriptions to defray the σιτηρέσιον (Paton–Hicks, 10), and the μέτρημα
(ibid. 11) to the soldiers in 201 B.C. Cf. G. Cardinali, *Riv. Fil.*, xxxv (1907), pp.
7 ff. New evidence on ὀψώνιον and σιτώνιον in Egypt, Hunt, *P.Teb.* 722 and
723; U. Wilcken, *P. Würzb.* (*Berl. Abh.*, 1933), no. 7, cf. *P. Br. Mus.* ii, nos.
219–27 (pp. 1–9); Wilcken, *U.P.Z.* i, p. 160 and p. 164; *P.S.I.* iv. 350, 4;
Wilcken, *Arch. Pap.* vii, p. 89; E. P. Wegener, *J.E.A.* xxiii (1937), p. 222,
no. vi.
For the organization of the Egyptian army, see below, Ch. IV. Large gifts
were frequently given to officers of the army as a reward for past services or
as a means of securing their loyalty. Such gifts were given, for example, to
two officers, one Cretan, the other Aetolian, of the Ptolemaic garrison of
Gaza by the kings (probably two successive kings—Euergetes I and Philopator, or more probably Philopator and Epiphanes, shortly before the
capture of Gaza by Antiochus III). They are mentioned in a funeral epigram
set up by one of the officers to his son and his grand-daughter (*S.E.G.* viii.
269, where references to previous publications and discussions will be found),
l. 9 ff.: ἦ μὴν ἀμφοτέρους γε παλαίπλουτοι βασιλῆες | Αἰγύπτιοι χρυσεαῖς
ἠγλάϊσαν χάρισιν. The χρυσεαὶ χάριτες were probably gold crowns.

⁸ See the general statement of Plutarch where he contrasts Cleomenes with
the other Hellenistic monarchs (Plut. *Cleom.* 13, 5): ἃς μὲν γὰρ οἱ λοιποὶ τῶν
βασιλέων ἐπὶ τοὺς ἀνθρώπους θήρας ἐποιοῦντο χρήμασι καὶ δωρεαῖς, δελεάζοντες
αὐτοὺς καὶ διαφθείροντες, ἀτέχνους καὶ ἀδίκους ἐνόμιζε εἶναι, κτλ. There was,
of course, not much difference in this respect between the Successors and the
later Hellenistic kings. An interesting subject for special inquiry is that of
the history and character of the δωρεαί. The origin of the later δωρεαί,
revocable grants of land to friends, high officers, distinguished philosophers
and other literary stars, courtesans, &c., whether in the East (especially
in the Persian Empire), or in the West (especially in Macedonia), is to be found
in the feudal structure of both Persia and Macedonia. It is unnecessary to

refer to the well-known δωρεαί of the Persian kings to Persians and particularly to foreigners (everybody will think in this connexion of Themistocles). More important for the history of Hellenistic δωρεαί is the immemorial practice of Macedonian kings whereby large or small holdings were granted both to Macedonians and to Greeks: see F. Hampl, *Der König der Makedonen*, 1934, p. 28 (Hegesippus [Dem.], *Halon.* 41, cf. 39), 40 f. and 45. Most of these δωρεαί lay outside Macedonia, but some of them were given by Macedonian kings to their ἑταῖροι in Macedonia proper. I may quote, for example, the bargain between Cassander and Polyperchon (Diod. xx. 28. 2 and 3) in 309 B.C.: Cassander guarantees to Polyperchon for his support τὰς προγεγενημένας κατὰ Μακεδονίαν δωρεάς. On Philip V see below, Ch. V.

The grant of personal *doreai*, feudal in its origin, became a very important political factor in the policy of Alexander and of his successors. I may recall, for example, those given to Eumenes in Asia Minor by Alexander and Perdiccas (Diod. xviii. 57. 3 f.), those granted by Antipater to Craterus in 323 B.C. (Diod. xviii. 18. 7), the treatment by Ptolemy Soter in 312 of Andronicus, the strategus of Tyre, who remained faithful to Antigonus and Demetrius during the siege and was later captured by Ptolemy (Diod. xix. 86. 2: οὐ μὴν ὅ γε Πτολεμαῖος ἐμνησικάκησεν ἀλλὰ τοὐναντίον δοὺς δωρεὰς εἶχε περὶ αὑτόν, ἕνα τῶν φίλων ποιησάμενος καὶ προάγων ἐντίμως), the many cases of political refugees receiving δωρεὰς μεγάλας καὶ συντάξεις from various Hellenistic kings of the early third century B.C., as reported by Teles περὶ φυγῆς (Hense), p. 23, &c. There was the same political motive and the same survival of Macedonian and Persian traditions in the grants of Antiochus Epiphanes, e.g. in his gift of Tarsus and Mallus to his mistress Antiochis. Later the grant of *doreai*, especially in Egypt and Syria, became one of the devices of the economic policy of the Ptolemies and Seleucids alike, see Rostovtzeff, *Studien z. Gesch. d. röm. Kolonates*, 1910, pp. 251 ff., and *A large estate in Egypt*, 1922, pp. 42 ff., and pp. 143 ff. Cf. below, Chs. IV and V.

It is difficult to decide whether we should connect with the *doreai* of this character the grants of land made by a superior power to a subordinate, e.g. the bestowal by Antigonus on Asander of his Carian satrapy δωρεάν, similar grants of land by the Romans after Magnesia to various cities and kings δωρεάν (e.g. Clazomenians, Polyb. xxi. 45. 5; Eumenes II, id. xxi. 45. 10; Rhodians, id. xxii. 5. 4, xxv. 4. 5 and 5. 1; cf. A. Heuss, 'Die völkerrechtlichen Grundlagen der röm. Aussenpolitik in rep. Zeit', (*Klio*, Beih. N.F. 18), p. 108, &c.).

I need not quote individual cases of large gifts made to various cities by the Successors. The best known are the gifts of Antigonus to Athens in 306/5 and again in 305/4 B.C. (Diod. xx. 46, 4; Plut. *Demetr.* 10, 1; *S.I.G.*³ 334). I may mention also the loan granted by Lysimachus to the city of Miletus, which was repaid with great difficulty by the city with the help of another loan furnished by some rich citizens of Cnidus (Rehm, *Milet, Erg. d. Ausgr.* i. 3, pp. 294 ff.—282 B.C.), the large gifts of grain to Rhodes by Soter, Cassander and Lysimachus during Demetrius' siege of the city (Diod. xx. 96 and 100), the well-known gifts of Lysimachus to Athens after Ipsus

(10,000 med. of grain and later 130 tal.) ; see A. M. Andreades, *A History of Greek Public Finance*, i, 1933, p. 176, and Ἡ δημοσιονομικὴ πολιτικὴ τοῦ βασιλέως Λυσιμάχου, *Hellenica*, ii (1929), pp. 257 ff. (=*Mél. P. Thomas*, 1930, pp. 6 ff.)

9 See below, Ch. IV.

10 Characteristic of the early Hellenistic kings and especially of Antigonus is the reply of the latter to one of his friends, Aristodemus, who was supposed to be the son of a cook, when Aristodemus advised him to be less lavish in his expenditure and gifts: "οἱ λόγοι σου" εἶπεν, "ὦ Ἀριστόδημε, περιζώματος ὄζουσιν" Plut. *Mor. Apophthegm.* 182 Ἀντιγόνου, D, 11. Cf. one of the many scandalous actions of Demetrius, Plut. *Demetr.* 27, 1: he ordered the Athenians to pay him 250 tal., καὶ τῆς εἰσπράξεως συντόνου καὶ ἀπαραιτήτου γενομένης, ἰδὼν ἠθροισμένον τὸ ἀργύριον ἐκέλευσε Λαμίᾳ καὶ ταῖς περὶ αὐτὴν ἑταίραις εἰς σμῆγμα δοθῆναι. Cf. also the general description of a Hellenistic court by Plut. *Cleom.* 13: its luxury, its grand air, its multitude of servants and officers.

11 The date and interpretation of the inscription at Miletus are controversial: see W. W. Tarn, *J.H.S.* xlvi (1926), pp. 158 ff.; *Hermes*, lxv (1930), pp. 446 ff.; *J.H.S.* liii (1933), p. 62, n. 50, on one side ; and W. Otto, *Beiträge zur Seleukidengeschichte*, 1928, pp. 25 ff.; *Phil.* lxxxvi (1931), pp. 400 ff. Cf. W. Peremans, *Rev. Belge*, xii (1933), pp. 49 ff. (on the date of the battle of Cos), and C. B. Welles, *R.C.*, no. 14. In accord with my view (rule of Ptolemy between 295 and 289 B.C.) P. Roussel in G. Glotz, *Hist. Gr.* iv. 1, p. 354, n. 29.

12 On the loans collected by Philocles, J. A. O. Larsen, 'Roman Greece', T. Frank, *Econ. Surv.* iv, p. 340. Larsen regards the loans collected by Philocles as contracted for payment of the tribute not to Demetrius but to Philadelphus, which I consider highly improbable. On the loans in general, below, Ch. V, n. 22. Cf. the three inscriptions from Boeotia recently published (N. G. Pappadakis, Ἀρχ. Δελτίον, viii (1923), pp. 182 ff.; W. Schwahn, 'Boiotische Stadtanleihen aus dem III. Jahrh. v. Chr.', *Hermes*, lxvi (1931), pp. 337 ff.), which relate to loans contracted by two cities of Boeotia (Charsiai and Acraiphia), the first with the city of Thisbe, and the others with two private persons, on a mortgage of all their property. None of the loans was repaid when due. The inscriptions show how serious was the financial situation of some of the Greek cities in the third century, certainly not solely as a result of the mismanagement of their finances.

13 There is no good general study of the armies of the Hellenistic period. The earlier accounts of 'Greek military antiquities' such as those of Köchly und W. Rüstow, *Geschichte des gr. Kriegswesens*, 1852; H. Droysen, *Heerwesen und Kriegführung der Griechen*, 1889; Ad. Bauer, *Griechische Privat- und Kriegsaltertümer*, 2nd ed. (*Handb. kl. Altertumswissensch.* iv. 1. 2), pay very little attention to the question of the organization of the Hellenistic armies and treat the Hellenistic age as a unit without distinguishing between the various periods (an exception is the excellently illustrated book by

P. Couissin, *Les Institutions militaires et navales des Grecs*, 1931). In this they are followed by the most modern general surveys, e.g. Kromayer–Veith, *Heerwesen*, &c., 1928, pp. 120 ff., and M. Cary, *A History of the Greek World*, 1932, pp. 231 ff.

Of the more special studies bearing on the Hellenistic armies in general I may quote here K. Grote, *Das griechische Söldnerwesen der hellenistischen Zeit*, 1913; A. Spendel, *Untersuchungen zum Heerwesen der Diadochen*, 1915; my own remarks, *Rev. É. A.* xxxiii (1931), pp. 5 ff.; H. Berve, *Das Alexanderreich*, &c., i, 1926, pp. 101 ff.; H. W. Parke, *Greek Mercenary Soldiers from the Earliest Times to the Battle of Ipsus*, 1933, esp. parts V, 'The Age of Alexander', and VI, 'The Age of the Diadochi', pp. 177 ff., and G. T. Griffith, *The Mercenaries of the Hellenistic World*, 1935. The works dealing with the armies of the individual Hellenistic States will be cited later in this book. Two documents which have been recently found, one at Amphipolis, the other at Chalcis, have a very important bearing on the regulations in force in the Macedonian armies. The first belongs certainly, and the second in all probability, to the time of Philip V, and both bear on the conditions prevailing in Macedonian garrisons. It is probable that regulations similar to those contained in these two documents were observed in the earlier Macedonian armies. One of them, that found at Amphipolis, which is fragmentary, illustrates various aspects of the life of the garrison of the city, see P. Roussel, *Rev. Arch.*, v (1934), pp. 39 ff., and M. Feyel, ibid. vi (1935), pp. 29 ff. The other, found at Chalcis, is complete and contains regulations concerning the management by the οἰκονόμοι (and φρούραρχοι) of the military storehouses, see Σ. Β. Κουγέας, Ἑλληνικά, vii (1934), pp. 177 ff. This last is a διάγραμμα of the king published by the commandant of Chalcis. The document is not dated, but the forms of the letters point to the time of Philip V. The supreme jurisdiction in the case of offences rests with the king. Cf. on these documents C. B. Welles, *A.J.A.* xlii (1938), pp. 245 ff. and E. Bikermann, *Rev. Phil.* xii (1938), pp. 295 ff. With these two documents we may compare an inscription of 221 B.C. recently found in Macedonia (Eordaia) (at a place called Κοιλάδα near Kozane) and published by Χ. Ι. Μακαρόνας, Ἐφ. Ἀρχ., 1934–5, pp. 117 ff. and C. B. Welles, loc. cit., p. 276. It contains a letter of Philip V in reply to a (fragmentary) petition of several officers and soldiers of a λόχος headed by a τετράρχης. The military titles of the soldiers and officers are of great interest. (On this document more is said below, Ch. V, n. 35 ff.)

14 Mutinies and betrayals of the Successors by their armies, or parts of them, are too familiar to students of the Hellenistic period to need support by quotations. As regards open revolts, I may quote at random that of Macedonians against Antipater (Polyaen. iv. 6, 4) and that of 3,000 Macedonian soldiers against Antigonus in Cappadocia (id. iv. 6. 6). Cf. Parke, op. cit., p. 208. The character of the soldier who receives promotion and becomes rich after having betrayed his former commander is well known to the New Comedy. Menander, Κόλαξ, 40 ff., speaks of one of them, probably a Thracian,

who changed his name *Βίθυς* into *Βίας*, a *διμοιρίτης* with quantities of money. Wondering about the origin of his wealth, Pheidias, his rival, says: *πόλ[ιν τιν' ἢ ναῦ]ν ἢ σατράπην ἢ σ[υμμάχους]* | *[προδοὺς ἐκέρδα]νέν τι δῆλός ἐστι* (the restorations are supported by the utterances of Pheidias that follow).

[15] On the relations between the cities and the rulers, and on similar relations between the armies and their commanders-in-chief, based on *συμμαχία* and *εὔνοια*, see F. Schröter, *De regum hell. epistulis*, &c., 1933, p. 44; E. Bickermann, 'Bellum Antiochenum', *Hermes*, lxvii (1932), p. 58 f., and 59, 1, cf. p. 63 f.; V. Ehrenberg, in Gercke u. Norden, *Einl.*, iii, 3, 1932, p. 83; M. Holleaux, *B.C.H.* lvii (1933), pp. 37 ff.; C. B. Welles, *R.C.*, Indices, s.v. *εὔνοια* and p. 66 f.; P. Zancan, *Il monarcato ellenistico nei suoi elementi federativi*, 1934, pp. 19 ff.; E. Bickermann, 'Alexandre le Grand et les villes d'Asie', *Rev. E. G.* xlvii (1934), pp. 346 ff.

A good summary of the views expressed by various scholars concerning the constitutional status of the Greek cities of Asia Minor in the time of Alexander and the Successors will be found in Th. Lenschau's report on Greek history in *Bursians Jahresb.*, ccliii (1936), pp. 151 ff. To this has to be added a recent treatment of the problem by V. Ehrenberg, *Alexander and the Greeks*, 1938, pp. 41 ff., (cf. W. W. Tarn, *Cl. Rev.*, lii (1938) pp. 234 f.), and also by E. Bikerman, *Institutions des Séleucides*, 1938, pp. 133 ff. (cities) and 51 ff. (army). We must sharply discriminate between the legal status of the army and the cities and the situation *de facto*. Legally the Successors were the masters of the army and the overlords of the Greek cities. *De facto* they depended almost entirely on them, and acted accordingly. On *εὔνοια* in general, as it appears in official documents of various kinds to denote a feeling which animates both the ruler and the ruled, W. Schubart, 'Das hellenistische Königsideal nach Inschriften und Papyri', *Arch. Pap.* xii (1936), pp. 8 ff. On the notion of *εὔνοια* in Greece, especially in the fourth century, and the technical political meaning of this word, E. Skard, 'Zwei religiös-politische Begriffe Euergetes–Concordia' (*Avh. utgitt av Det NorskeVidenskaps Akad.*, ii, Hist.–Filos. Kl., 1931, ii, pp. 29 ff.). As regards the cities and the subjects of the kings in general, compare also the treatise *περὶ βασιλείας* of Ecphantus (Stob. iv. 7. 64) the Pythagorean (second century B.C.?) : 'and there must exist complete goodwill (*εὔνοια*) first on the part of the king towards his subjects, and secondly on their part towards the king, such as is felt by a father towards his son, a shepherd towards his sheep, and by a law towards those who use it' (transl. by E. Goodenough, *Yale Class. Stud.* i, 1928 p. 84) ; cf. another fragment of Ecphantus (Stob. iv. 7. 65) translated by Goodenough, ibid., p. 89. On the date of Ecphantus, W. W. Tarn, 'Alexander the Great and the Unity of Mankind', *Proc. Brit. Acad.* xix (1933), p. 128.

Most instructive as regards the *de facto* relations between the cities, the army, and the king in time of danger and war is the well-known document, or rather set of documents, relating to Smyrna and to the royal soldiers stationed and settled at Magnesia (*O.G.I.* 229, Seleucus II). Smyrna whole-heartedly supported Seleucus II in his struggle with Egypt. Her relations with the king are described several times in this dossier as εὔνοια καὶ φιλία (l. 3), or εὔνοια καὶ φιλοτιμία (l. 8). In her dealings with the rebellious soldiers of Seleucus II in Magnesia, Smyrna exhorted them διαφυλάσσειν τὴν φιλίαν καὶ συμμαχίαν τῶι βασιλεῖ (ll. 15 and 18) or διατηρεῖν τὴν συμμαχίαν καὶ τὴν εὔνοιαν τῶι βασιλεῖ (ll. 37, 62, 93). On this inscription see V. Ehrenberg, *Alexander and the Greeks*, p. 48; E. Bikerman, *Inst. Sél.*, pp. 100 ff.; C. J. Cadoux, *Ancient Smyrna*, 1938, pp. 114 ff. Cf. Lysimachus' letter to Priene (*O.G.I.* 12; Welles, *R.C.*, no. 6), where Lysimachus describes his power as based on himself, his friends, and his δυνάμεις; the same expressions are used by the city of Ilium in the decree concerning King Antiochus I (*O.G.I.* 219): note esp. l. 16 where, in speaking of Antiochus' kingdom, the Ilians describe it as prosperous and brilliant μάλιστα μὲν διὰ τὴν ἰδίαν ἀρετήν, εἶτα καὶ διὰ τὴν τῶμ φίλων καὶ τῶν δυνάμεων εὔνοιαν. On the political role played by the armies of the Diadochi before the establishment of the balance of power, cf. F. Granier, *Die makedonische Heeresversammlung*, 1931, pp. 58 ff.; F. Hampl, *Der König der Makedonen*, 1934, p. 63; P. Zancan, *Il monarcato ellenistico*, &c., 1934, pp. 35 ff.

[16] I should like to recognize in the speaker of an interesting fragment of Menander's Ἁλιεῖς, 24 K., a mercenary soldier who is boasting about his wealth: εὐποροῦμεν οὐδὲ μετρίως. ἐκ Κυΐνδων χρυσίον, | Περσικαὶ στολαὶ δὲ κεῖν[τ]αι πορφυραῖ, τορεύματα | ἔνδον ἐστ', ἄνδρες, ποτήρι' [ἄλλα τ' ἀργυρώματα] | κάκτυπωμάτων πρόσωπα, τραγέλαφοι, λαβρώνια. Cf. the inventory of gifts bestowed on Apollo of Didyma by Seleucus I (*O.G.I.* 214; Welles, *R.C.*, no. 5). The life of the soldiers of the armies of the Diadochi was not dull. Bias the διμοιρίτης of Menander's Κόλαξ (293 K.) boasts of his drinking exploits: κοτύλας χωροῦν δέκα | ἐν Καππαδοκίᾳ κόνδυ χρυσοῦν, Στρουθία, | τρὶς ἐξέπιον μεστόν·γ'. (Στρουθ.) Ἀλεξάνδρου πλέον | τοῦ βασιλέως πέπωκας. (Βι.) οὐκ ἔλαττον, οὐ | μὰ τὴν Ἀθηνᾶν. (Στρ.) μέγα γε. No wonder that these rich soldiers were hated by the civilians of Athens of Menander's time (Men. Περίκειρ. 65 and 173 f. (Allinson); Κόλαξ, 40 ff. (Allinson); Σικυώνιος, 439 K.).

[17] Excellent accounts of a large moving army and of its camp will be found in the descriptions of Eumenes' army in the East by Plutarch, Diodorus, and Polyaenus: Plut. *Eum.* 9; Diod. xix. 43. 7; Just. xiv. 3, 6; Polyaen. *Strat.* iv. 6, 13. The last gives a short but very graphic description of the camp and the ἀποσκευή: Ἀντίγονος δὲ τῶν Εὐμενείων στρατιωτῶν εἰδὼς ἀπομένειν τὴν ἀποσκευήν, ἐν ᾗ γυναῖκες ἦσαν αὐτῶν καὶ τέκνα, καὶ παλλακαί, καὶ οἰκέται, καὶ χρυσός, καὶ ἄργυρος, καὶ ὅσα ἄλλα ἐκτήσαντο ἀπὸ τῆς μετὰ Ἀλεξάνδρου στρατείας. Compare the story of the death of Ceteus, the Indian στρατηγός, and of the contest between his two wives for the privilege of being burned on his funeral pyre in the camp of Eumenes, Diod. xix. 33 ff. One of these wives before dying gives away her jewels to her girl relatives and friends. Note the presence of all these women with their jewels and slaves in the camp. They all belonged to the ἀποσκευή. Similar conditions prevailed in the army of Ophelas when he moved against Carthage: Diod. xx. 40–1. 1. Cf. the ἀποσκευαί of the Autariatae who were serving in the army of Lysimachus, Polyaen. *Strat.* iv. 12. 1.

It is worthy of note that in many cases the ἀποσκευή played an important part in deciding the issue of great battles, the soldiers caring for it more than for their commander. The best known is the case of Eumenes quoted above. Compare the case of Ptolemy I in 306 B.C., Diod. xx. 47, 4. After the defeat of Menelaus' army near Salamis (Cyprus) Demetrius took 3,000 prisoners and incorporated them in his army ἀποδιδρασκόντων δ' αὐτῶν πρὸς τοὺς περὶ τὸν Μενέλαον διὰ τὸ τὰς ἀποσκευὰς ἐν Αἰγύπτῳ καταλελοιπέναι παρὰ Πτολεμαίῳ, γνοὺς ἀμεταθέτους ὄντας ἐνεβίβασεν εἰς τὰς ναῦς καὶ πρὸς Ἀντίγονον εἰς Συρίαν ἀπέστειλεν. It will be observed that Ptolemy preferred that forces serving outside Egypt should not have their ἀποσκευαί with them. Cf. U. Wilcken, Arch. Pap. viii (1927), p. 89. On the ἀποσκευαί in general, W. Schubart, G.G.A. clxxv (1913), p. 617; E. Bevan, House of Seleucus II, 1902, p. 291; Kromayer–Veith, Heerwesen, p. 126; E. Bikerman, Inst. Sél. pp. 91 ff. On the technical and juridical meaning of ἀποσκευή, M. Holleaux, Rev. E. G. xxxix (1926), p. 355; E. Kiessling, Arch. Pap., viii (1927), pp. 241 ff.; U. Wilcken, ibid., p. 88 (P. Bad. 48); H. Kortenbeutel, 'Zum Sondergericht der Aposkeuai', Aeg. xvi (1936), pp. 292 ff.; U. Wilcken, Arch. Pap. xii (1937), pp. 23 f.; cf. M. Holleaux, 'Ἡγεμὼν τῶν ἔξω τάξεων, Rev. E. G. xxxv (1922), p. 198; D. Cohen, Οἱ ἔξω τάξεων, Mnem. liv (1926), p. 82. On the ἀποσκευαί of the armies of the Successors, H. W. Parke, Greek Mercenary Soldiers, p. 207 and note 7.

[18] Diod. xx. 82–3, cf. 84. 5 and 97. 5, and the description of the navy of Demetrius in 302/1, Diod. xx. 110: ψιλικὰ δὲ τάγματα καὶ πειρατῶν παντο-δαπῶν τῶν συντρεχόντων ἐπὶ τοὺς πολέμους καὶ τὰς ἁρπαγὰς οὐκ ἐλάττους ὀκτα-κισχιλίων. On the pirates and the part which they played in the political life of this period, below, Ch. IV.

[19] Plut. Eum. 13 (cf. 2): the story of Eumenes and the three hundred talents which he was supposed to contribute to the building of Nearchus' fleet. He pretended not to have cash and to have collected the money (probably from his debtors) with difficulty through his ἐπίτροποι. However, when his tent was destroyed by fire, melted gold and silver to the amount of more than 1,000 talents was found in the ashes.

[20] Pillage: many instances, e.g. in Polyaen. iv. 6. 6; requisitions, e.g. in Plut. Phoc. 26. I am inclined to believe that the third paragraph of Suidas' article on βασιλεία (below, note 24) refers to such compulsory contributions and requisitions, as opposed to regular taxation. I cannot find in this paragraph any criticism of the Ptolemaic fiscal system; rather a concealed approval of it.

[21] See P. Jouguet, 'La politique intérieure du premier Ptolémée', Bull. de l'Inst. Fr. d'Arch. Or. xxx (1930), p. 528 f., and L'Égypte Ptolémaïque, 1934 (G. Hanotaux, Hist. de la Nation Égyptienne, vol. iii), pp. 36 ff.; cf. Cl. Préaux, 'Politique de race ou politique royale,' Chron. d'Égypte, xi (1936), pp. 111 ff. Below, Ch. IV.

22 On the veterans and invalids, H. Haessler, *Veteranenfürsorge im griechi-schen Altertum*, 1926; O. Jacob, 'Les cités grecques et les blessés de la guerre', *Mél. Glotz*, 1932, pp. 461 ff. The subject has not been treated by G. T. Griffith, *The Mercenaries of the Hellenistic World*, 1935. Cf. H. Berve, *Das Alexanderreich*, &c., i, 1926, p. 197 (on Alexander's army). On the mercen-aries who received plots of land from their employers, G. T. Griffith, loc. cit., pp. 314 ff. Cassandreia: Polyaen. vi. 7. 2. Theangela: M. Rostovtzeff, *Rev. E. A.* xxxiii (1931), p. 18 f. Aspendus: above, Ch. I, n. 7. Smyrna: *O.G.I.* 229 (cf. note 15 above). The cases of Ephesus (*S.I.G.*³, 363), of Dyme (ibid. 529), and of Pharsalus (?)—*I.G.* ix. 2. 234—are different. Cf. L. Robert, *Coll. Fröhner, I. Inscript. Gr.*, pp. 94 ff.

23 On the veterans of Alexander's army see the fine remarks of L. Robert, *Antiquité Classique*, iv (1935), p. 164. On Gorgus and Minnion of Iasus, L. Robert, loc. cit., p. 166, and W. Peek and R. Herzog, *Ath. Mitt.* lvii (1932), pp. 52 ff. On the Macedonians and other foreigners at Colophon see the decrees of the city published by B. D. Meritt, *Am. J. Ph.* lvi (1935), pp. 358 ff., and the improved reading and correct interpretation and dating of these decrees given by L. Robert, *Rev. Phil.* x (1936), pp. 162 ff., and esp. p. 162, n. 2. Whether they were Macedonian officers or not, the subscribers of Colophon became rich while in the service of Alexander or Antigonus. On Laomedon, at whose order the famous sarcophagus of Alexander found at Sidon was supposed to have been made, see H. Berve, *Das Alexanderreich*, no. 464; I. Papastavru and C. F. Lehmann-Haupt, *Amphipolis* (*Klio*, Beih. 37), 1936, pp. 88 ff. To a later time belongs the well-known Artemidorus of Perge, who after service in the army of one of the Ptolemies settled down in Thera and built there his famous τέμενος; *I.G.* xii. 3, Suppl., pp. 294 ff.; Hiller von Gaertringen, *Thera*, iii, pp. 89 ff.; U. von Wilamowitz-Moellendorff, *Der Glaube der Hellenen*, ii, 1932, pp. 387 ff. On petty tyrants in Asia Minor during the late Persian domination and the time of Alexander, my paper in *Anatol. Stud. pres. to Sir William Ramsay*, 1923, p. 373, and A. H. M. Jones, *The Cities of the Eastern Roman Provinces*, pp. 28 ff., cf. 46 ff. On Hermeias of Atarneus, D. E. W. Wormell, *Yale Class. St.* v (1935), pp. 57 ff. On the later tyrants, below, Ch. IV, n. 230.

24 This character of the rule of the Successors is well defined in the state-ment which Suidas incorporated as paragraph 2 in his article βασιλεία, the first paragraph being a definition of βασιλεία based on Chrysippus. The state-ment is apparently derived not from some treatise περὶ βασιλείας but from an historian or publicist of the early Hellenistic period. This paragraph may be quoted in full: οὔτε φύσις οὔτε τὸ δίκαιον ἀποδιδοῦσι τοῖς ἀνθρώποις τὰς βασιλείας, ἀλλὰ τοῖς δυναμένοις ἡγεῖσθαι στρατοπέδου καὶ χειρίζειν πράγματα νουνεχῶς. οἷος ἦν Φίλιππος καὶ οἱ διάδοχοι 'Αλεξάνδρου· τὸν γὰρ υἱὸν κατὰ φύσιν οὐδὲν ὠφέλησεν ἡ συγγένεια διὰ τὴν τῆς ψυχῆς ἀδυναμίαν, τοὺς δὲ μηδὲν προσήκοντας βασιλεῖς γενέσθαι σχεδὸν ἁπάσης τῆς οἰκουμένης. Cf. J. Kaerst, *Stud. z. Entw.* &c., pp. 59 ff.; W. W. Tarn, *Antigonus Gonatas*, pp. 253 ff. I cannot agree, however, with Tarn in the view that paragraph 3, which contrasts unlawful

exactions by the kings with a regular well-organized taxation, proves that 'Stoicism condemned the ordinary Hellenistic kingdoms'. There is nothing specifically Stoic in Suidas' third paragraph, and the statement cannot be directed against the Ptolemies, whose aim was to organize efficiently a regular taxation. The first paragraph may be another excerpt from the same source as that from which paragraph 2 is derived. The leading idea of paragraph 2 is similar to that of Xen. *Mem.* iii. 9. 10: the true kings and rulers are those who know how to rule; cf. Diotogenes the Pythagorean περὶ βασιλείας (Stob. iv. 7. 61), who considers the main duties of a king to be military leadership, justice, and cult.

A further development of the picture given by Suidas' source is the statement of Ael. Aristides εἰς ʽΡώμην, 27. Aristides, however, contrasts the Macedonian kingship with the real βασιλεία, though he emphasizes in the Macedonian monarchies the same point as Suidas' source, viz. the fact that the Macedonians were self-made kings: ὑφʼ ἑαυτῶν αὐτοὶ γεγενημένοι; cf. Rostovtzeff, *Ges. u. Wirtsch.* i, p. 240, n. 6. It is evident that Aristides also has in mind the Diadochi, not the later Macedonian kings.

[25] On the relations of Alexander and the Successors with the Greek cities, see the bibliography quoted above in note 15. It is known that modern scholars are not agreed on the question whether Alexander did or did not admit the cities of Asia Minor into the Corinthian League. While E. Bikerman, 'Alexandre le Grand et les villes d'Asie', *Rev. É.G.* xlvii (1934), pp. 346 ff. (cf. *Inst. Sél.*, pp. 133 ff.), insists on the latter view (supported by V. Ehrenberg, *Ost und West*, 1935, p. 227—cf. *Alexander and the Greeks*, pp. 1 ff. (Alexander) and 41 ff. (the Successors)—and by G. Radet, *J. d. Sav.*, 1935, p. 149 f. (cf. U. Wilcken, *Berl. S.B.* xxviii (1935), p. 302, n. 5), P. Zancan defends the former view (*Il Monarcato ellenistico*, pp. 8 ff.; cf. Th. Lenschau quoted in note 15 and W. Schubart, 'Das Königsbild des Hellenismus', *Die Antike*, xiii (1937), pp. 272 ff.). It must be said that though the Diadochi regarded themselves legally as masters, not as allies, of the Greek cities, they were never consistent in this respect and certainly spoke a quite different language in their propaganda. This is why so much stress is laid in their official statements and those of their subjects on συμμαχία and εὔνοια as the leading features of the relations between the king and the cities (above, note 15). Very interesting in this respect is the statement of Diodorus (Hieronymus) xix. 57. 3 (315 B.C.) about Antigonus when he was making preparations for war against the coalition of his enemies. He appealed to the ἔθνη, πόλεις, and δυνάσται and asked them for their help: τά τʼ ἔθνη καὶ πόλεις καὶ δυνάστας προσεκαλεῖτο εἰς συμμαχίαν. Did he appeal only to those tribes, cities, and dynasts who were not his subjects, or to those inside as well as outside the sphere of his domination? On the formula and the technical terms used by Antigonus (the statement of Diodorus certainly goes back to the published text of Antigonus' proclamation) see Index *s.v.* ἔθνος, and on the general political situation V. Ehrenberg, *Alexander and the Greeks*, p. 43. Cf. also A. Heuss, 'Antigonos Monophthalmos und die

griechischen Städte', *Hermes*, lxxiii (1938), pp. 133 ff., whose interesting point of view cannot be discussed here.

26 There is much that is interesting in the series of abbreviated decrees of Ephesus of the late fourth and early third centuries B.C. republished (with additions) and commented upon by J. Keil, *Jahreshefte*, xvi (1913), pp. 231 ff. They show the vicissitudes of Ephesus in the times after Alexander's death: first supporting Perdiccas (ii, *h*, *n*), then siding with Antipater (ii, *p*), still later under the overlordship of Demetrius (iii, *b*). We come next to the friendly relations with Ptolemy Soter (decree in honour of Callicrates, the friend of Ptolemy I, cf. Diod. xx. 21, 310 B.C.) and the time of Lysimachus' domination (iii, *c*—construction of the wall by Lysimachus with the co-operation of a citizen of Cyzicus; Cyzicus without doubt fell within the sphere of influence of Lysimachus, cf. below, Ch. IV). The group of decrees shows at the same time the wide range of the commercial relations of Ephesus. How great was the freedom of action of the major and minor cities in time of war is shown by the well-known story of Hieron the tyrant of Priene—the struggle of the democrats of Priene against him, and the help given to the former by Ephesus with great financial difficulty, *Inschr. v. Pr.* no. 37; *S.I.G.*³ 363; Paus. vii. 2. 10.

27 On the Corinthian alliance above, Ch. I, note 7. On the συμπολιτεῖαι and the other κοινά (the Ionian, Dorian, and Aeolian), W. Schwahn, Συμπολιτεία *P.W.K.* iv A. 1262 ff., and E. Kornemann, *Κοινόν*, ibid., Suppl. iv. 918 ff. On the κοινὸν τῶν Ἰώνων, Th. Lenschau, 'Iones', ibid. ix. 1876 ff.; U. von Wilamowitz-Moellendorff, *Berl. S.B.*, 1906, pp. 38 ff. On the Lycian κοινόν and its destinies under and after Alexander, A. H. M. Jones, *The Cities of the Eastern Roman Provinces*, pp. 99 ff. On the κοινὸν τῶν Καρῶν and the κοινὸν τῶν Χρυσαορέων, L. Robert, *Ét. Anat.*, 1937, p. 571. On the Nesiotai, A. Guggenmeier, *Die Geschichte des Nesiotenbundes bis zur Mitte des 3. Jahrh.*, Diss. Würzburg, 1929, and the articles of Schwahn and Kornemann quoted above and Schwahn, 'Nesiotai', *P.W.K.* xvii. 74 ff.; W. A. Laidlaw, *A History of Delos*, 1933, pp. 94 ff. In general, W. W. Tarn, *Hell. Civ.*, 2nd ed., p. 66, and Schwahn, *s.v.* Συμμαχία, *P.W.K.* iv A. 1129 ff. In these articles the reader will find good bibliographies. On the character of the Anatolian leagues, V. Ehrenberg, *Alexander and the Greeks*, p. 42, and H. Bengtson, *Phil.* xcii (1937), pp. 139 ff.

28 Kahrstedt, art. 'Synoikismos', *P.W.K.*, iv A, 1440 ff. On the policy of Antigonus as regards synoecism and on the synoecism of Teos and Lebedos, C. B. Welles, *R.C.*, nos. 3/4, cf. p. 8 (foundation of Antigoneia in the Troad); cf. A. Wilhelm, 'Zu König Antigonos' Schreiben an die Teïer', *Klio*, xxvii (1935), pp. 280 ff., and P .Zancan, *Il Monarcato ellenistico*, &c., 1934, pp. 28 ff. I cannot agree with Zancan that the συνοικισμός was decided upon by the two cities after the earthquake of 304/3 and was not imposed on them by Antigonus. On the date of the Tean decree (*S.E.G.* ii. 579) which may refer to the synoecism of Teos and Lebedos, A. Wilhelm, loc. cit., pp. 282 ff.

The enlargement of Colophon in the time of Antigonus (311–306 B.C.) looks very much like the synoecism of Teos and Lebedos. Antigonus does not appear in the foreground, though he was probably active behind the scenes. Noteworthy is the participation of rich foreigners in the ἐπίδοσις which, as at Teos and Lebedos, was adopted to meet the expense of the city's enlargement. See the inscription first published by B. D. Meritt, *A.J.Ph.* lvi (1935), pp. 358 ff., and subsequently discussed and dated by L. Robert, *Rev. Phil.* x (1936), pp. 158 ff. (cf. above, note 23). Like Antigonus, Lysimachus was an enthusiastic believer in synoecism. On his synoecism of Ephesus, Colophon, and Lebedos, F. Geyer, *P.W.K.* xiv. 25 ff., and on his synoecisms in general, A. M. Andreades, *Hellenica*, ii (1929), pp. 257 ff. Besides Ephesus he dealt with Smyrna, Ilium, and Alexandria Troas. Note that in three cases he took up the process where it had been left by Antigonus. Cf. V. Tscherikower, 'Die hellenistischen Städtegrundungen', &c., *Phil. Suppl.* xix (1927), pp. 154 ff.; F. Oertel, *P.W.K.*, xi. 2 ff.; A. H. M. Jones, *The Cities*, &c., pp. 41 ff.

²⁹ I will deal with the topic of the colonization of the East by the Diadochi and Epigoni in the next chapter. On the alleged colonies of Perdiccas, A. H. M. Jones, loc. cit., p. 239, and my paper, 'Le Gad de Doura et Seleucus Nicator', *Mél. syriens R. Dussaud*, 1938, pp. 281 ff. On those of Antigonus, below, Ch. IV.

³⁰ Pottery made and used at Athens in the Hellenistic period is well known from the finds on the western and northern slopes of the Acropolis (A. Watzinger, *Ath. Mitt.* xxvi (1901), pp. 67 ff., and M. Z. Pease, 'Pottery from the N. slope of the Acropolis', *Hesperia*, iv (1935), pp. 293 ff.), and from those made during the recent American excavations of the Agora (Homer A. Thompson, 'Two centuries of Hellenistic pottery', *Hesperia*, iii (1934), pp. 311 ff.). Cf. F. Courby, *Les Vases grecs à reliefs*, 1922.

³¹ South Russia: see above, Ch. II, notes 17 ff.

³² Athenian pottery at Alexandria, E. Breccia, *Bull. de la Soc. Arch. d'Alex.* viii (1905), pp. 95 ff., and *Necropoli di Sciatbi* (Catalogue Général, &c.), pp. 45 ff.; R. Pagenstecher, *Die griechisch-ägyptische Sammlung E. v. Sieglin*, ii, 3, 1913, pp. 5 ff. (Exped. E. v. Sieglin. Ausgrab. in Alexandria, ii). I cannot discuss here the problem of the Panathenaic amphorae of which fragments have been found in Alexandria, whether they were imported or local imitations. On the Hellenistic Panathenaic amphorae in general, S. Dow, 'Panathenaic Amphorae from the Hellenistic period', *Hesperia*, v (1936), pp. 50 ff. Cf. my Pl. xx.

³³ SAMARIA, G. A. Reisner, C. S. Fisher, D. G. Lyon, *Harvard Excavations at Samaria*, i, 1924, p. 274 ff. GEZER reveals the same characteristics as Samaria, R. A. Macalister, *The Excavations of Gezer*, ii, 1912, pp. 211 ff., and pl. CXXXVI, 14 (black-glazed) and 18 (West slope), as do also TANTURAH (Dora), *British School of Archaeology at Jerusalem, Bulletin*, vii (1925), pp. 82 ff. (G.M. Fitzgerald); BETH-SHAN, G. M. Fitzgerald, *The Four Canaanite Temples of Beth-Shan*, ii,

part ii, 'The pottery', 1930, pp. 15 ff. (*Publ. Pal. Sect. Mus. Pennsylv.*, vol. ii), cf. A. Rowe, *The Topography and History of Beth-Shan*, 1930 (*Publ. Pal. Sect. Mus. Pennsylv.*, vol. i), pp. 44 ff.; and BETH-ZUR, O. R. Sellers, *The Citadel of Beth-Zur (A preliminary Report*, &c.), 1933, pp. 41 ff. On the red-glazed pottery in the East, with some remarks on the Hellenistic pottery found in Syria and Palestine in general, J. H. Iliffe, 'Sigillata ware in the Near East', *Quart. Dep. Ant. Pal.* vi (1936), pp. 4 ff. The excavations at Seleuceia on the Tigris yielded mostly pottery of Parthian times (N. C. Debevoise, *Parthian Pottery from Seleuceia on the Tigris*, 1934, and a communication of Miss W. van Ingen of Michigan University of Aug. 26, 1935). The same is true of the other Babylonian cities.

The excavations of ANTIOCH have not so far yielded many finds of the early Hellenistic period, see *Antioch-on-the-Orontes*, i, 1934, pp. 67 ff. ('Pottery', by F. O. Waagé). I was able during my short stay at Antioch in 1937 to glance at the new finds, which to my mind suggest the same conclusions as the other sites. Dr. Waagé will shortly publish a new Report on the pottery found at Antioch and at Daphne. The harbour-city of Al-Mina at the mouth of the Orontes, not far from Seleuceia in Pieria, recently excavated by Sir Leonard Woolley (above, pp. 85 ff.), has not yielded much material of the late fourth century B.C. (C. L. Woolley, 'Excavations at Al Mina, Sueidia', *J.H.S.* lviii (1938), p. 26). However, Woolley states that the city was prosperous in the time of Alexander and was still importing as before large quantities of almost exclusively Attic pottery. The city ceased to exist after the foundation of Seleuceia in Pieria in 301 B.C. (above, p. 105). The evidence hitherto published relating to the other cities of Syria and Phoenicia is slight and has been very little studied. It is to be hoped that the excavators of Syrian sites will in future pay more attention to the pottery of the Hellenistic and Roman periods. A good study of the Hellenistic pottery found in the many excavations of Palestinian, Syrian, and Mesopotamian cities is urgently needed both by archaeologists and historians. The material is rich and easily accessible, though dispersed among the Museums of the Near East, Europe, and the U.S.A.

[34] DURA. Mr. F. E. Brown, a member of the Dura staff for many years and now field director of the excavations, writes as follows: 'The "Attic" black-glaze pottery with the typical metallic lustre over the glaze is the earliest imported pottery on the site and occurs along with the native wares (common ware, etc.) in the lowest levels of all the Hellenistic portions of the city. For a long time it appears to have been the only imported pottery.' It is interesting to observe that only two types of this pottery are commonly found at Dura: (1) a plate with a slight rim and a rather high, broad foot, and (2) a flat bowl with a taller, more delicate foot and sharp sides. Other black-glaze forms are exceptional. It is to be noted that no expensive Athenian ware has been found at Dura. Only comparatively cheap pottery—but this in large quantity—was imported. Of course in the later third and in the second century the black-glaze ware may have been no longer imported from

Athens but may be a Syrian imitation of it. The study by Prof. P. V. C. Baur and myself of the sherds of Hellenistic pottery now kept in the Yale Gallery of Fine Arts has confirmed Mr. Brown's statement. One sherd certainly represents the West-slope painted brand of pottery. Some black-glazed sherds may be of local Syrian make.

[35] PERGAMON, A Conze, 'Kleinfunde aus Pergamon', *Berl. Abh.*, *phil.-hist. Kl.*, 1902, pp. 1 ff., and *Alt. von Pergamon*, i (with co-operation of R. Zahn); Th. Wiegand und H. Schrader, *Priene*, 1904, pp. 394 ff. (R. Zahn); EPHESUS, J. Keil, *Jahreshefte*, xvi (1913), p. 232, I *e: Κίττωι καὶ Βακχίωι παισὶ Βακχίο Ἀθηναίοις, ἐπειδὴ ἐπαγγέλλονται τῆι πόλει τὸγ κέραμ[ογ] τὸμ μέλανα ἐργάσεσθαι καὶ τῆι θεῶι τὴν ὑδρίαν λαμβάνοντες τὸ τεταγμέν[ον] ἐν τῶι νόμωι.* The 'black ware' (perhaps used for cult purposes, like the hydria of the goddess) is in all probability the Athenian black-glazed pottery. Note its popularity and the presence of Athenians at Ephesus to carry out an important order.

[36] Conquest and reorganization of Thrace by Philip, F. Hampl, *Der König der Makedonen*, 1934, pp. 39 ff.; cf. A. Momigliano, *Filippo il Macedone*, 1934. Philip certainly founded in Thrace many new settlements of a more or less urban character. On Philippi (Crenides), P. Collart, *Philippes, ville de Macédoine*, 1937, pp. 161 ff. On Alexander's Alexandropolis, V. Tscherikower, *Die hellenistischen Städtegründungen*, 1927, p. 1, cf. A. H. M. Jones, *The Cities of the Eastern Roman Provinces*, pp. 4 ff. Alexander's organization of Thrace as a satrapy, B. Lenk, art. 'Thrake', *P.W.K.* vi A. 428 ff. Zopyrion's expedition against the Scythians and Olbia, S. Jebelev, 'Miletos and Olbia', *Bull. d. l'ac. d. Sc. de l'U.R.S.S., Classe des humanités*, 1929, pp. 447 ff. (in Russian). Zopyrion was the third governor of Thrace (after Alexander the Lyncestian and Memnon; the latter revolted against Alexander —in alliance with the Scythians?).

The fourth satrap of Thrace (after the revolt of Seuthes) was Lysimachus. On the activity of Lysimachus see Geyer, art. 'Lysimachus', *P.W.K.* xiv. 1 ff., and Lenk, art. 'Thrake', ibid. vi A. 448 ff. Cf. A. M. Andreades, *Ἡ δημοσιονομικὴ πολιτικὴ τοῦ βασιλέως Λυσιμάχου, Hellenica*, ii (1929), pp. 257 ff. In his paper Andreades has studied the economic policy of Lysimachus in all its aspects. The best testimony to his political, and especially his economic, success is afforded by his coins. On his capital Lysimacheia, Tscherikower, loc. cit., p. 162. Hoards of his coins, below, note 52. Lysimachian coins minted by various Greek cities after his death: Geyer, loc. cit., p. 27, cf. K.Regling, *P.W.K.* xv, art. 'Münzwesen', 471 and 474, and *Klio*, xxii (1922), pp. 292 ff., and E. T. Newell, 'The Alexandrine coinage of Sinope', *A.J.Num.* lii (1918), pp. 118 ff. On the occupation of the Danube by the Celts, H. Hubert, *Les Celtes depuis l'époque de la Tène et la civilisation celtique*, 1932, pp. 69 ff. Celtic imitations of Greek coins in the Eastern regions, R. Forrer, *Keltische Numismatik der Rhein- und Donaulande*, 1908, pp. 210 ff.; R. Paulsen, *Die Münzprägungen der Bojer*, 1933, cf. Hubert, op. cit., pp. 76 ff. and 308 f., and my Chs. II, n. 53 and VI, n. 30.

The wealth of Northern Greece and Thrace is attested not only by the coins but also by several rich finds of jewellery made in Thessaly, Macedonia, and Thrace, R. Segall, *Museum Benaki*, Katalog der Goldschmiede-Arbeiten, 1938, pp. 31 ff., esp. 46 ff.

[37] See the fine picture of Athenian life in the time of Demetrius of Phaleron given by W. S. Ferguson, *Hell. Athens*, pp. 65 ff. In his footnotes the reader will find references to the evidence, which therefore need not be repeated here. My interpretation, however, of the texts differs in some points from that of Ferguson. I do not think Menander wrote for aristocrats, nor do I understand what Ferguson means by this term. If he means the propertied classes in general, I am in agreement with him.

As regards the sources from which these classes derived their income, the picture drawn by Theophrastus coincides in the main with that of Menander, but is fuller. The most important passages are these. Agriculture: ii. 12; iii. 4; iv (ἄγροικος), 3 (μισθωτοὶ ἐν ἀγρῷ), 8, 10, 11 (this chapter is full of interesting evidence on the management of a rural estate by a respectable Athenian citizen); x. 8; xiv. 3. Trade: i. 5; xxi. 14; xxiii. 4; there is a delightful picture of the ἀλαζών talking of his wealth and his commercial and banking operations to foreigners in the harbour (on the mole), xxiii. 1. Moneylending: i. 5; vi. 9 (a curious enumeration of retail traders to whom Theophrastus' 'character' lent money); ix. 7; xxiii. 4. Alongside of the respectable professions there are some which are disreputable: πανδοκεῦσαι, πορνοβοσκῆσαι, τελωνῆσαι, κηρύττειν, μαγειρεύειν, κυβεύειν (vi. 5). Foreign goods and foreign dresses used extensively at Athens: Theophr. *Char.* xxi. 15; Men. *Epitr.* 272; Eubulus (Kock ii. 201). On Metrocles: Teles, περὶ πενίας καὶ πλούτου, p. 40 (Hense): τότε μὲν γὰρ ἐξ ἀνάγκης ἔδει ὑπόδημα ἔχειν, καὶ τοῦτο ἀκάττυτον, εἶτα χλανίδα, παίδων ἀκολουθίαν, οἰκίαν μεγάλην, εἰς τὸ σύνδειπνον ὅπως ἄρτοι καθαροί, ὄψον μὴ τὸ τυχόν, οἶνος ἡδύς, ὑποδοχὰς τὰς ἐπιβαλλούσας ἵνα πολυτελῶς. Cf. Men. 537 K.; Theophr. *Char.* ii. 12 and xxiii, 9; Dio Chr. *Or.* iv, p. 169 R.; G. A. Gerhard, *Phoinix*, pp. 116 ff. and 128 ff. Athens, of course, was not able to compete in the lavishness of her banquets with the 'barbarian' kings and nobles or with the Hellenistic potentates, but the menus of Athenian hosts as collected by Athenaeus from various early Hellenistic sources (Athen. iv. 130 e and ff.) are not those of paupers.

[38] Many hoards of Alexander's coins have been found in Greece (the most typical are the eight in the Peloponnese and the three in Thessaly—viz. Andritsaena, Corinth, Epidaurus, Kyparissia, Olympia, Ougri, Patras, Tripolitsa in the Peloponnese and Kililer (2) and Lamia in Thessaly) and at least six in Macedonia (the most typical the two at Pella and Salonica). Next to Greece comes Egypt, then Syria, Phoenicia and Cyprus, Asia Minor, and the West (Italy). Note also the hoard of Taxila and that of Azerbeijan. See S. P. Noe, 'A bibliography of Greek coin hoards', 2nd ed., *Num. Notes and Monogr.*, 2nd ed., lxxviii (1937), and the excellent monographs on individual Alexander coin-hoards in Greece by E. T. Newell in *Num. Notes and Monogr.* iii (Kyparissia), 1921; xxi (Andritsaena), 1924; and xxxix (Olympia), 1929. To the Greek hoards mentioned above must be added two more in the possession of E. T.

Newell, who mentions them in his book, *The Coinages of Demetrius Poliorcetes*, 1927, p. 163, n. 13.

It is interesting to find that the hoards of Greece are not so rich as those of the East, particularly those of Egypt (esp. Abu Hommos—2,800 Æ, Abukir —600 N and 20 gold medallions, Demanhur—at least 8,000 silver tetradrachms, Semenood—more than 1,000 Æ; see the remarks of E. T. Newell, *Num. Notes and Monogr.* xix, 1923), and of Syria (esp. Aleppo—3,000 Æ and the two hoards of Saida of 3,600 each; see E. T. Newell, *Dated Alexander coinage of Sidon and Ake*, 1916, p. 57, and cf. his *Tyrus rediviva*, 1923). The hoards of Greece represent probably the savings of typical Greek *bourgeois*, who never became as rich as the nabobs of the East. A larger number of hoards of Alexander's coins (81) are mentioned by Ch. Seltman, *Greek Coins*, p. 215, n. 1, who probably included in his list hoards minted after 190. It should also be noted that, according to such an acute observer of the coin market in Syria as M. H. Seyrig, stray finds of Alexandrian tetradrachms in Syria are quite common and consequently the market is full of them.

[39] See F. Heichelheim, *Preisschwankungen*, pp. 8 ff. and 41 ff.; W. W. Tarn, *Economica*, x (1930), p. 316; M. Cary, 'Sources of silver for the Greek world', *Mél. Glotz*, 1932, pp. 133 ff. Cary does not accept the view of Tarn that in the early Hellenistic period a plentiful supply of silver came to the East from Spain; cf. for the early Ptolemies, Rostovtzeff, 'Commerce of Ptolemaic Egypt', *Journ. of Ec. and Bus. Hist.* iv (1932), p. 754. Concerning the relation between gold and silver in the late fourth century B.C. the scholars most competent in this field are not agreed, see e.g. Th. Reinach, 'Du rapport de valeur des métaux monétaires dans l'Égypte aux temps des Ptolémées', *Rev. É. G.*, xli (1928), pp. 126 ff., who assigns the rate of 1–10 to the time of Philip, while Ch. Seltman, op. cit., p. 206, assigns this rate to the time of Alexander, and for the time of Philip assumes the rate 1–12. In Egypt the rate went up considerably during the reign of Ptolemy Soter. W. Giesecke, *Das Ptolemäergeld*, 1930, must be used with great care. His statements are often based on texts which have been misunderstood and mistranslated. The survey of prices prevailing at Athens in the last years of the fourth century as given by Ferguson, *Hell. Athens*, pp. 66 ff., does not take into consideration certain prices mentioned by Diogenes Laertius in his biographies of Zenon and Diogenes (vi. 35; cf. *Gnomol. Vat.* 495; vii. 106— both bearing on prices of grain) and by Teles, περὶ αὐταρκείας (Teles, ii, ed. Hense), cf. *Gnomol. Paris.* 33 Sternb.

[40] On the λιθοκόλλητα and διάλιθα see my *Iranians and Greeks in S. Russia*, p. 236, note 8. To the material quoted in this note add: Phaenias the Peripatetic in Athen. ii. 48 f (gift of Artaxerxes I to the Cretan Entimus); ibid. xv. 689 e (Antiphanes: κάλπις χρυσοκόλλητος); Clem. Alex. (Musonius?) ii. 35; Cic. *Verr.* ii. 4. 27; Plut. *Luc.* 40. 1. A good idea of a λιθοκόλλητος patera of Syrian or Iranian workmanship may be obtained not only from south Russian specimens but also from a lead patera and moulds, from which such paterae were made, found at Dura, F. Cumont, *Fouilles de Doura-Europos*,

pp. 222 ff. and pl. LXXXV, I, and P. V. C. Baur, *Dura Report*, iv, pp. 236 ff., cf. M. Rostovtzeff, *Skythien und der Bosporus*, pp. 205 ff., 248, 404, 573 ff., 602, 610. Cf. R. Segall, *Museum Benaki*, Katalog der Goldschmiede-Arbeiten, 1938 (pp. 31 ff., on the rich treasure of Thessaly), and G. H. Macurdy, *A.J.A.* xxxvi (1932), pp. 27 ff. (Persian jewels worn by Demetrius the Besieger and dedicated by Stratonice at Delos). On the clay paterae of Apulia and Bolsena which imitate gold and silver vessels, P. Wuilleumier, *Le Trésor de Tarente*, 1930, pp. 81 ff., cf. below, Ch. VIII; on Greek relief pottery in general and on the 'orfèvrerie gemmée' of Oriental origin in Italy, Wuilleumier, op. cit., p. 28.

⁴¹ F. Heichelheim, art. 'Sitos', *P.W.K.* Suppl. vi. 847 and 851 (Cyrene's help), grain trade and gifts of grain, 849 ff.; prices, 856 ff.; and table, 885 f. In this article the reader will find a full collection and an excellent interpretation of the evidence in chronological order. I may add the evidence on the crisis at Athens in 289/8 B.C. The well-known inscription of Phaedrus, *I.G.* ii². 682; lines 28–30 of this inscription which mention the embassy of Phaedrus to Ptolemy in quest of grain are assigned by B. D. Meritt, *Hesp.* vii (1938), pp. 106 ff., to 289/8 B.C. The crisis according to Meritt was not over in 288/7 (*I.G.* ii². 650, 651), in 287/6 (ibid. 653–5) or in 282/1 B.C. (ibid. 670 A). The difficulties experienced by Athens in the late fourth and early third centuries in supplying her market with foodstuffs are reflected in the jokes current all over Greece that Athens, though the recognized centre of intellectual and artistic life, was a 'hungry' city, living on good air and hopes, see Eubulus (Kock, ii. 176) and cf. Ps.-Heraclides Crit. *F.H.G.* ii. 254 ff., and below, pp. 210 ff.

⁴² The importance of Rhodes in the late fourth century and her competition with Athens are attested by many texts collected by E. Ziebarth, 'Zur Handelsgeschichte der Insel Rhodos', *Mél. Glotz*, pp. 911 ff.; cf. Hiller von Gaertringen, art. 'Rhodos', *P.W.K.*, Suppl. v. 772 ff., and my remarks in *C.A.H.* viii, pp. 620 ff. of which I am making extensive use in this sketch. On Cleomenes see below, Ch. IV, n. 34. As regards Antigonus and his policy towards Rhodes, we must not forget that Asia Minor, Syria, and Cyprus (which last was temporarily in the hands of Antigonus) produced large quantities of grain for export and were rivals of Egypt in this respect. Bion's *mot*: Diog. Laert. iv. 49 (Bion). Priene: *Inschr. v. Pr.* no. 37, ll. 65 ff.; *S.I.G.*³ 363, and note 4. Argos (278–272 B.C. ?): Vollgraff, *Mnem.* xliv (1916), pp. 219 ff. Ephesus: *S.I.G.*³ 354 (c. 300 B.C.); cf. *I.G.* xii. 7, nos. 9 and 8; *O.G.I.* 10, and R. Heberdey, *Forsch. in Eph.* ii, p. 104, no. 453.

⁴³ Evidence on the revival of Miletus will be found in Fr. Bilabel, *Die ionische Kolonisation*, pp. 137 ff., and A. Rehm, *Milet*, i. 3, nos. 136 ff.; cf. J. Röhlig, *Der Handel von Milet*, 1933, pp. 18 ff. On the political importance of Miletus in the time of the Diadochi see the texts quoted by W. W. Tarn and myself in *C.A.H.* vii, pp. 77 f., 92, 98, and 162, and more fully by Hiller von Gaertringen, art. 'Miletos', *P.W.K.* xv. 1603 ff., cf. Welles, *R.C.* 5, and comments p. 37 and no. 14 (above, note 11). The sympolity

treaties or mutual decrees of Miletus and her colonies: Olbia (*Milet*, i. 3, no. 136; cf. S. Jebelev, 'Miletos and Olbia', *Bull. Ac. of Sc. of U.R.S.S.*, 1929, pp. 421 ff., in Russian), Cyzicus (*Milet*, i. 3, no. 137), and later Cius (*Milet*, i. 3, no. 136). An inscription recently discovered at Istrus and illustrated by L. Robert, who was the first to recognize it to be a decree of Miletus, belongs to the same time as the decrees of Olbia and Cyzicus (L. Robert, *B.C.H.* lii (1928), pp. 170 ff.; cf. ibid. liii (1929), p. 151, no. 1, and S. Lambrino, *Dacia*, iii–iv (1927–32), pp. 398 ff.).

[44] The results of the excavations of Miletus are to be found in the volu-minous publication *Milet: Ergebnisse der Ausgrabungen*, which is not yet complete. The final publication of the results of the Austrian excavations in Ephesus, *Forschungen in Ephesos*, is in its earliest stage; reports on current excavations will be found in the *Jahreshefte* of the Austrian Archaeological Institute. On Priene, Th. Wiegand und H. Schrader, *Priene*, 1904; F. Hiller von Gaertringen, *Inschriften von Priene*, 1906; K. Regling, *Die Münzen von Priene*, 1927. Cf. M. Schede, *Die Ruinen von Priene*, 1934. On land-tenure in the territory of Priene, my *Kolonat*, p. 59.

[45] Inscription of Teos, *S.E.G.* ii. 579. The document has been carefully studied several times: R. Demangel et A. Laumonier, *B.C.H.* xlvi (1922), pp. 307 ff.; R. Herzog, *Koische Forschungen und Funde*, 1899, pp. 204 ff.; cf. C. B. Welles, *R.C.*, pp. 25 and 29; A. Wilhelm, *Klio*, xxvii (1934), pp. 270 ff. Exploitation of woods for the production of charcoal is typical of many Greek cities. The 'prominence' of the charcoal-burners in Athens is well known. On the charcoal law of Delos see the paper by L. Robert, *Rev. É. G.*, xlvi (1933), pp. 430 ff., and below, Ch. IV, n. 66. I fail to see how either Pergamon (W. W. Tarn, *Hell. Civ.*[2], p. 145) or Egypt (F. Heichelheim, *Wirtschaftsg.* ii, p. 1121, n. 54) could have had any influence on the organization of taxation at Teos or Theangela in the late fourth century.

[46] S. Russia: M. Rostovtzeff, *C.A.H.* viii, pp. 574 ff., and above, pp. 106 ff. On Tarentum, above, p. 113 and n. 70.

[47] One of the important points in the reorganization of the Corinthian League in 336 was the freedom of navigation, Demosth. 17. 19 καὶ μηδένα κωλύειν αὐτοὺς μηδὲ κατάγειν πλοῖον μηδένα; cf. the programme of Isocrates viii. 20 and iv. 115. It used to be the policy of Athens, Plut. *Pericl.* 17, 1.

[48] See the collection of various devices in this respect in Ps.-Arist. *Oecon.* II, which must be assigned to the time of the Successors and reflects the ideas then prevailing, above, Ch. II, note 3 and below Ch. IV, p. 440 f.

[49] On the hoards of Alexander's coins see above, note 38. On his mints, Ch. Seltman, *Greek Coins*, 1933, pp. 206 ff. and 217 (based on the excellent studies of E. T. Newell, quoted by him p. 206, n. 2). On the large number of dies used in the various mints and on the output of particular mints, ibid., p. 207, n. 1. Excellent summaries of the history of coinage in the Hellenistic period will be found (I give only a small selection) in Sir G. Macdonald, *The*

Evolution of Coinage, 1916; K. Regling, *Münzkunde*, in Gercke und Norden, *Einleitung*, ii. 1, 2, 4th ed., 1932, pp. 17 ff; id., art. 'Münzwesen', *P.W.K.* xvi. 471 ff.; J. G. Milne, *Greek Coinage*, 1931, pp. 108 ff.; Ch. Seltman, op. cit. pp. 218 ff. (all these summaries contain bibliographical references).

[50] Interruption in Athenian coinage between 322 and 229, Head, *H.N.*, 2nd ed., p. 378; cf. U. Köhler in the articles quoted by Ferguson, *Hellen. Athens*, p. 184. No interruption in the time of Antigonus Gonatas, W. W. Tarn, *C.A.H.* vii, p. 220. A short interruption at that time, Ch. Seltman, op. cit. pp. 257 ff. On Lachares' coins, W. S. Ferguson, *The Treasurers of Athena*, 1932, p. 126. The coins of the 'New Style': J. Sundwall, 'Untersuchungen über die athenischen Münzen des neueren Stiles', *Ofversigt of Finska Vetenskaps Societens Forhandinger*, xlix (1906–7), no. 9; Seltman, op. cit., p. 260, cf. below, Ch. V, n. 36. Note that in current business in the time of Demetrius Poliorcetes, and probably in the time of the Diadochi in general, transactions were effected exclusively in Athenian, Alexandrian, and Demetrian currency: see e.g. the inscription of Arcesine (Amorgos), *I.G.* xii. 7, 69, l. 21 (repayment of a loan in: [Ἀ]ττικὸν ἢ Ἀλε|[ξάνδρειον ἢ Δημητ]ρίειον).

[51] For the coinages of Greece in the early Hellenistic times, Seltman, op. cit., ch. xv, the Leagues and free cities, pp. 252 ff. The date of the latest Corinthian *poloi* is disputed. The leading numismatists are now inclined to assign the latest *poloi* to the early third century B.C., not later than 280 B.C., whereas it was customary to date their absorption by the Achaean coinage at *c.* 243–223 B.C. See O. Ravel (and E. T. Newell), 'Corinthian Hoards', *Num. Notes and Monogr.*, lii (1932), p. 24 f.; cf. O. Ravel, *Les 'poulains' de Corinthe*, i. 193 f. (on the early history of the *poloi*). I may quote in addition some cities (outside Greece proper) which were minting silver coins in the period of Alexander and of the Diadochi: Sinope, Calchedon, Cius, Heraclea Pontica, Adramyttium, Cyzicus (until 280 B.C.), Abydus (until 280), Cebren (until 280), Gargara (until 284), Ilium (until 240), Selge, Mallus, Soli, Tarsus, Thasos (after 280 for a few years), Clazomenae (until 280), Ephesus (from 280 to 258), Miletus, Samos, Cnidus, Cos, Rhodes. The list, of course, is far from complete. It is based on B.V. Head, *Hist. Num.* 2nd ed., 1911; I have not tried to bring it up to date.

Cities which struck Alexandrian and Lysimachian coins before 190 B.C.: Byzantium, Lampsacus, Calchedon, Ephesus (295–280 B.C.), Smyrna, Mangesia ad Maeandrum, Perinthus, Aenus. For this list I am again using Head, *H.N.*, 2nd ed. For the Cilician and Phoenician cities see the same work: cf., however, on the hotly debated coins of Tyre the lucid and convincing remarks of E. T. Newell, *Tyrus rediviva*, 1923, and *The Coinages of Demetrius Poliorcetes*, 1927, pp. 44 ff. (Tyre) and 48 ff. (Tarsus), and on Sidon and Ake, 'The dated Alexander coinage of Sidon and Ake', *Yale Oriental Series*, ii, 1916, by the same writer. On Argos, Seltman, op. cit., p. 256. The coinages of Cleomenes and of Nabis are imitations of Seleucid coins, ibid.

[52] On the Alexander coin-hoards see above, note 38. Lysimachus coin-hoards: Anadol (Noe 2, n. 76—1,000 *aurei*: Alexander and Lysimachus in

enormous majority (694 and 250), besides some coins of Philip II (11), Philip III (21), Demetrius Poliorcetes (2), Seleucus I (1)) ; Tuapse (Noe, n. 1116—Lysimachus alone, 90 *aurei*) ; Asia Minor (Noe, n. 74—Alexander, 172 *aurei*, Lysimachus, 56, Philip III, 1) ; Salonica (Noe, n. 896—silver tetra-drachms of Alexander, Demetrius Poliorcetes, and Lysimachus). Cf. E. T. Newell, *Tyrus rediviva*, 1923, p. 11. The Athenian decree of 448: M. N. Tod, *Gr. Hist. Inscr.*, 1933, no. 67 ; cf. D. M. Robinson, *Am. J. Ph.*, lvi (1935), pp. 149 ff ; M. Segre, *Clara Rhodos*, ix (1938), pp. 149 ff.

53 I use the term 'prosperity' to describe the general conditions of a certain period: progress in production, brisk trade, accumulation of capital. General prosperity did not necessarily mean that the working classes enjoyed toler-ably satisfactory conditions. They were the last to profit by it. This was due to various causes, of which the existence of slavery was only one.

CHAPTER IV, PART I

1 See above, ch. I, note 13.

2 G. Glotz, *J. d. Sav.*, 1913, pp. 16 ff., 206 ff., 251 ff., and *Rev. E.G.* xxix (1916), pp. 281 ff. ; A. Segré, *Circolazione monetaria e prezzi nel mondo antico ed in particolare in Egitto*, 1922 (cf. his 'Note sull'economia dell'Egitto ellenistico nell'età Tolemaica', *Bull. de la Soc. Arch. d'Alexandrie*, xxix (8) (1934), pp. 257 ff.) ; W. W. Tarn, 'The social question in the third century', in *The Hellenistic Age* (Essays by J. B. Bury, E. A. Barber, E. Bevan, W. W. Tarn) 1923 ; F. Heichelheim, *Wirtschaftliche Schwankungen der Zeit von Alexander bis Augustus*, 1930 ; J. A. O. Larsen, 'Roman Greece', in T. Frank's *Econ. Surv.* iv, pp. 379 ff. Many corrections of Heichelheim's book will be found in some substantial reviews of it which must be read alongside of the book itself: A. Segré, *Riv. Fil.* lviii (8) (1930), pp. 513 ff. ; Tenney Frank, *Am. J. Ph.* liii (1932), pp. 181 ff. ; K. Regling, *Z. N.* xli (1931), pp. 117 ff. ; M. Rostovtzeff, *Z. f. die ges. Staatswiss.* lxxxix (1930), pp. 577 ff., and especially F. Oertel, *Z. d. Sav.-Stift.* li (1931), pp. 572 ff. ; G. Glotz, *Rev. É.G.* xlv (1932), pp. 241 ff., and W. W. Tarn, *Economica*, 1930, Nov., pp. 315 ff. Cf. some additional remarks by Heichelheim himself: 'New light on currency and inflation in Hellenistic-Roman times from inscriptions and papyri', *Economic History*, iii, No. 10, 1935, pp. 1 ff., and his *Wirtschaftsg.*, p. 483 ff. and 1065, and occasional remarks by various scholars, e.g. O. Schulthess, *P.W.K.* xv. 2. 2078 ; W. Otto, *Zur Geschichte des 6. Ptolemäers*, 1934, p. 25 ; M. Cary, 'The sources of silver for the Greek world', *Mél. Glotz*, 1932, pp. 133 ff., &c. The Delian material: *I.G.* xi. 2 (1912), cf. *Fasciculi tertii tabulae* (1927) ; F. Durrbach, *Inscriptions de Délos, Comptes des Hiéropes (250–166 av. J.C.)*, 1926 and 1929, cf. F. Durr-bach et P. Roussel, *Inscriptions de Délos, Actes des fonctionnaires athéniens préposés à l'administration des sanctuaires après 166 av. J.C.*, 1935 (this last contains almost exclusively temple inventories and very little material bear-ing on prices).

3 The best treatment of the social and economic conditions of Greece and the Greek islands in the third century B.C. will be found in the brilliant surveys of W. W. Tarn, 'The social question in the third century', *The Hellenistic Age*, 1923, pp. 108 ff., and *Hellenistic Civilization*, 2nd ed., 1930, ch. iii, 'The Greek cities: social-economic conditions', pp. 73 ff., cf. *C.A.H*.vii, p. 211 f.

4 I cannot deal here with the evolution of the conception of war and peace in Greece in general. The reader will find the material collected and illustrated in many valuable books and papers, such as W. E. Caldwell's *Hellenic Conceptions of Peace*, 1919, esp. pp. 129 ff., and especially the brilliant memoir by B. Keil, Εἰρήνη, *Ber. Sächs. Ges.*, 1916, 4; cf. H. Fuchs, *Augustin und der antike Friedensgedanke*, 1926 (*Neue Phil. Unters.* iii), H. Windisch, 'Friedenbringer—Gottessöhne', *Z.f. Neutest. Wiss.* xxiv (1925), pp. 240 ff. and W. Nestle, 'Der Friedensgedanke in der antiken Welt', *Phil. Suppl.*, xxxi (1), (1938). I have not been able to procure I. H. Thiel, *Oud Griesksch oorlogsrecht*, 1927, or a short survey by F. Bender, 'Völkerrecht und Kriegführung im Altertum', *Wien. Blätter f. Freunde d. Antike*, vii (1930), pp. 56 f., 82 f., 109 ff. Cf. F. Heichelheim, Bursian's *Jahresb.* ccl. (Suppl. 1935), p. 181, and the summary by F. Lammert, art. 'Kriegsrecht' in *P.W.K.* Suppl. vi. 1351 ff.

The pacifism of Isocrates and Xenophon (or whoever was the author of Πόροι), as contrasted with the views of Thucydides, has been frequently discussed, most recently by K. von der Lieck, *Die Xenophontische Schrift von den Einkünften*, Diss. Köln, 1933, pp. 6 ff, who refers to earlier discussions of the same subject. It appears certain that the idea of peace as the chief desideratum in international relations was first formulated by Athenian publicists and philosophers of the fourth century after the bitter experiences of Athens in the first half of that century. To the same time belongs the growth of the idea that φιλανθρωπία, πρᾳότης, ἐπιείκεια, εὔνοια, εὐεργεσία and the like should be the leading principles of human conduct both in private life and in public affairs, not only within the city-state but also in the field of its external relations. See A. Elias, *De notione vocis clementia apud philosophos veteres et de fontibus Senecae librorum de clem.*, Diss. Königsberg, 1912; S. Lorenz, *De progressu notionis φιλανθρωπίας*, Diss. Leipzig, 1914; E. Skard, 'Zwei religiös-politische Begriffe: Euergetes—Concordia', Oslo, 1932 (*Avhandl. Ak. Oslo*, II, *Hist. Fil. Klasse*, 1932, no. 2), and the long series of modern discussions of the history of the idea of *humanitas*: R. Reitzenstein, *Werden und Wesen der Humanität im Altertum*, Strassburg, 1907; J. Kaerst, *Gesch. d. Hellenismus*, ii, 2nd ed., p. 120 f.; R. Pfeiffer, 'Humanitas Erasmiana', *Stud. d. Bibl. Warburg*, 1931, p. 2, note 3; H. Dahlmann, 'Clementia Caesaris', *N. J. f. Wiss.* x (1934), pp. 17 ff.; M. Pohlenz, 'Antikes Führertum', *Neue Wege z. Antike*, ii. 3, 1934; cf. the two articles of R. Harder in *Die Antike*, v (1929), pp. 300 ff., and *Hermes*, lxix (1934), pp. 64 ff., and W. Otto, 'Zur Geschichte der Zeit des 6. Ptolemäers', *Bay. Abh.*, *Philos.-hist. Abt.*, N.F. xi (1934), p. 40, note 1, p. 75 and p. 136.

5 Cynics: G. A. Gerhard, *Phoinix von Kolophon*, 1909, p. 53; D. R. Dudley, *A History of Cynicism*, 1937, pp. 59 ff.; Chrysippus: Arnim, *S.V.F.* iii, p. 27,

no. 115 (Sen. *Ep.* 66. 5), cf. Plut. *De Alex. M. f. et v.*, i. 6 and 9 (p. 329 C, 330 E). Philo, *De conf.* xii, p. 411 f.; P. Wendland, *Philo und die kynisch-stoische Diatribe*, p. 38 f. The requirement that φιλανθρωπία, &c. (see the preceding note), should be practised both in private and public life was extended by the Stoics to the whole of mankind. Almost all the philosophers of the Hellenistic period, Stoics, Cynics, Neo-Pythagoreans, Peripatetics, asserted as unquestionable the view that the ideal ruler should display these virtues both in peace and in war. This doctrine was inherited by the Romans and applied by them in their conception of the ideal Roman emperor. See the bibliography quoted in the preceding note, and, as regards the ideal ruler and his virtues, E. R. Goodenough, 'The political philosophy of the Hellenistic Kingship', *Yale Class. Stud.* i (1928), pp. 55 ff. (Goodenough quotes the earlier contributions to this question); cf. P. Zancan, *Il monarcato ellenistico nei suoi elementi federativi*, Padova, 1934, p. 16.

On the Greek theory as applied to the Roman emperors by philosophers and publicists of Roman times (Plutarch, Dio Chrysostomus, Pliny), see my *Storia Soc. ed Econ. d. Imp. Rom.*, p. 131 and pp. 138 ff. Add to the bibliography there given V. Valdenberg, 'La théorie monarchique de Dion Chrysostome,' *Rev. É. G.* xl (1927), pp. 142 ff., and the papers of M. P. Charlesworth, 'Some Observations on Ruler-cult, especially in Rome', *Harv. Theol. Rev.* xxviii. 1 (1935), pp. 37 ff., esp. 39, and 'The Virtues of a Roman Emperor', *Proc. Br. Acad.* 23 (1937). Most of the Hellenistic kings professed to follow the dictates of philosophy in their administration and in their relations with the Greek cities (see W. Schubart, *Arch. f. Pap.* xii (1936–7), pp. 1 ff., and further below, p. 268 f.), but there is no sign of the influence of philosophical theories in their method of conducting war; in this they were rather guided by traditional Greek practice. The same is true of the Greek city-states and federations.

⁶ See the papers by B. Keil, H. Fuchs, and H. Windisch quoted in note 4. A prayer to Zeus Soter very similar to that of Magnesia will be found in the famous inscription from Philadelphia in Lydia, *S.I.G.*³ 985; O. Weinreich, 'Stiftung und Kultsatzungen eines Privatheiligtums in Philadelpheia in Lydien', *S.B. d. Heid. Akad.*, x (1919), Abh. 16 (at the end of col. iv, ll. 60 ff., p. 6). Special emphasis is laid on safety on land and sea. Lists of magistrates with remarks such as that given in the text have been found at Rhodes, Tenos, Syros, and Delos. At Delos εἰρήνη appears in the formula only three times (in 261, 255 and 179 B.C.), which may not be an accident. On this class of inscriptions, besides the papers by B. Keil and O. Weinreich quoted above, see A. Wilhelm, 'Ἐπιτύμβιον *H. Swoboda dargebracht*, 1927, pp. 343 ff. and *Mélanges Glotz*, 1932, p. 903 (on δαψίλεια); M. Rostovtzeff, *Gesellschaft u. Wirtschaft*, i, p. 295; L. Robert, *Ét. Anat.*, p. 257 f. and Chr. Blinkenberg, 'Deux documents chronologiques Rhodiens', *Det Kgl. Danske Videnskabernes Selskab*, Arch.–Kunsth. Med., II, 4 (1938). p. 9.

⁷ Polyb. ii. 56 and 57, cf. 58 and 59; Plut. *Aratus*, 45, 3–6; W. W. Tarn, *C.A.H.* vii, pp. 211 and 760; cf. Plut. *Mor.* 251 ff., *Mulierum virt.* xv (story

of the tyrant Aristotimus and especially the description of the fate of women and children), and Just. xxvi. i. Earlier acts similar to the devastation of Laconia by the Aetolians mentioned below (242 B.C.) did not arouse the same degree of indignation because their victims were *perioeci*, helots, and slaves (Plut. *Cleom.* 18. 3).

[8] W. W. Tarn, *C.A.H.* vii, p. 211. Ἀσυλία has been studied quite recently in a Giessen dissertation by E. Schlesinger, *Die griechische Asylie*, 1933; cf. the articles Λάφυρον in *P.W.K.* xii. 770 ff. (by Kahrstedt), and Συλᾶν, ibid. IV A, 1038 (by Latte), and C. B. Welles, *R.C.*, p. 58. On arbitration see A. Raeder, *L'Arbitrage international chez les Hellènes*, 1912; M. N. Tod, *International Arbitration amongst the Greeks*, 1913, and *Sidelights on Greek History*, 1932, pp. 39 ff.; G. De Sanctis, art. 'Arbitrato', *Enc. Ital.* iii, pp. 995 ff., cf. L. Robert, *Rev. Phil.* xiii (65), pp. 97 ff. I doubt, however, whether all the institutions mentioned by Tarn were created mainly with the object of making war more civilized. The leagues had their own long history and there were many reasons for their existence. The new aspect that ἀσυλία assumed in the Hellenistic period will be dealt with later in this chapter. Arbitration was a long-established institution in Greece. Its rapid spread in Hellenistic times is partly due to the fact that it was often imposed on the cities from above.

[9] Cf. the well-known Athenian decree in honour of Euryclides and Micion, *I.G.* ii, 2nd ed., 79; *S.I.G.*[3] 497, l. 9, cf. 491. It testifies to a terrible devastation of the territory of Athens after 229 B.C.

[10] On piracy: H. A. Ormerod, *Piracy in the Ancient World*, 1924; E. Ziebarth, *Beiträge zur Geschichte des Seeraubs und Seehandels im alten Griechenland*, 1929.

[11] I may quote in this connexion the beautiful mosaic of Thmuis (now in the Museum of Alexandria) signed by the artist Sophilus, which seems to be a memorial of a naval victory dedicated by one of the first Ptolemies (the date of the mosaic is uncertain; but even if it be dated in the first century B.C., as has been suggested, its original is certainly much earlier). E. Breccia has adduced certain reasons for thinking that the naval exploits of the Ptolemy in question (Philadelphus or Euergetes) were connected with the repression of piracy in the Aegean: see *Le Musée gréco-romain 1925–1931*, pp. 65 and 101, pl. A, LIII, LIV, my Pl. xxxv. Cf. *S.E.G.* viii, 503 and P. Perdrizet, *C.R. Ac. Inscr.* 1934, p. 173.

[12] Two cases both concerning Thera are known. One is the famous letter of a ναύαρχος (?) in the service of Philadelphus or Euergetes to the commander of the garrison of Thera, *I.G.* xii. 3. 328 (about 260 B.C.?). The question at issue is that of the αἰχμάλωτοι, some of them in the hands of the offenders—the Allariotai (Crete)—some in those of the Egyptians. Similar is *I.G.* xii. 3. 1291 (F. Hiller von Gaertringen in *Festschrift O. Hirschfeld*, p. 91). It is a decree of Thera in honour of a citizen of Rhaucus in Crete, who was ναύαρχος

and στρατηγός in Thera, for having repelled an invasion of pirates who had captured 400 women, children, and slaves. Cf. E. Ziebarth, *Seeraub*, p. 23; W. W. Tarn, *J.H.S.* liii (1933), p. 67. Tarn dates the last inscription about 236 B.C. The two cases tend rather to show that the pirates cared little for the Ptolemies than that the Ptolemies waged war systematically and successfully on the pirates.

[13] Paus. i. 7. 3; cf. on the date the papers of Otto and Tarn quoted above, ch. iii, note 11. On Demetrius and the pirates above, ch. iii, note 18, and below.

[14] On the addiction of the Aetolians to robbery in general Polyb. iv. 16. 4. The Aetolian robberies began very early. We hear of them at the time of Demetrius' first and second occupation of Athens, see Plut. *Dem.* 40. 7–8, and the well-known *carmen ithyphallicum* (Bergk, *P.L.G.*[4], p. 674; *F. Gr. H.* 76 (Duris von Samos), fr. 13; Athen. vi, 253), esp. ll. 25 ff.: Αἰτωλὸς ὅστις ἐπὶ πέτρας καθήμενος, | ὥσπερ ἡ παλαιά (sc. Σφίγξ), | τὰ σώμαθ' ἡμῶν πάντ' ἀναρπάσας φέρει, | κοὐκ ἔχω μάχεσθαι· | Αἰτωλικὸν γὰρ ἁρπάσαι τὰ τῶν πέλας, | νῦν δὲ καὶ τὰ πόρρω (cf. R. Flacelière, *Les Aitoliens à Delphes*, pp. 73 ff.). Cf. the much later epigram in honour of Philip V, *I.G.* iv. 1372; *S.E.G.* i. 78; Geffcken, *Griech. Epigr.*, no. 174; A. Wilhelm, *Wien. Anz.*, 1921, 18, 73 ff., 5; πολλὰ μὲν Αἰτωλοῖσι κ[ακορρέκταις κακὰ ῥ]έξας. Several documents throw light on Aetolian policy at this time. Such are the decree in honour of Phaedrus of Sphettus, *S.I.G.*[3] 409, which Flacelière, op. cit., p. 74, note 3, connects with the *carmen ithyphallicum* (cf. on the date P. Roussel in G. Glotz, *Hist. gr.*, IV. 1, p. 369, n. 71) and perhaps that in honour of Aeschron, son of Proxenus (*I.G.* ii, 2nd. ed., 652, cf. A. Wilhelm, Πραγματεῖαι ᾿Ακαδ. ᾿Αθηνῶν, IV (1936), pp. 3 ff.) dated in the archonship of Diocles (288/7 B.C. ?), which testifies to an understanding between Athens and the Aetolians. On the date of this document see A. J. Reinach, *Journ. internat. d'arch. num.*, xiii (1911), p. 225; K. J. Beloch, *Gr. Gesch.* iv. 2, 2nd ed., p. 65; and W. S. Ferguson, *Ath. Tribal Cycles*, p. 22, who are inclined to date it in the archonship of Diocles I, i.e. 288/7 B.C. Cf., however, G. De Sanctis, *Riv. Fil.* li (1), (1923), p. 176 f., and W. B. Dinsmoor, *The Archons of Athens*, p. 214 f., who prefer Diocles II, i.e. 215/4 B.C. (cf. Flacelière, op. cit., p. 79, note 2). To the time of the Demetrian war belongs the raid of Bucris, *S.I.G.*[3] 535, on which more will be said presently. See in general G. Klaffenbach, *I.G.* ix, 2nd ed., p. xv; R. Flacelière, *C. R. Ac. Inscr.*, 1929, p. 146, *B.C.H.* liv (1930), p. 88, note 3, and *Les Aitoliens à Delphes, passim*; P. Roussel in G. Glotz, *Hist. gr.*, IV. 1, p. 369, n. 71. Cf. the footnote to p. 196 on Aetolian pirates in the service of Antigonus Gonatas about 276 B.C. On Aetolian naval policy and piracy H. Benecke, *Die Seepolitik der Aitoler*, 1934, esp. p. 32 (list of Aetolian *proxeni*).

[15] P. Roussel, *B.C.H.* xlvii (1923), pp. 35 ff.; R. Flacelière, *Les Aitoliens*, pp. 86, 197 f. and 212 ff. Flacelière is inclined to assign the decrees to the time of the Chremonidean war, 267/6 B.C. War-time of course afforded the best opportunities for all sorts of misdeeds; the malefactors were either the

belligerents or pirates and robbers of all kinds, some of whom might be in the service of the belligerents.

16 B. Haussoullier, *Traité entre Delphes et Pellana*, 1917, p. 20, I B, ll. 5 ff.; *F.D.* iii. i. 486 (E. Bourguet, p. 309, suggests the date 285–280); cf. R. Flacelière, *Les Aitoliens*, &c., p. 88.

17 On the two groups of inscriptions: P. Roussel, *B.C.H.* xlvii (1923), pp. 44 ff.; G. Klaffenbach, *I.G.* ix. i, 2nd ed., p. 6; H. Benecke, *Die Seepolitik der Aitoler*, 1934, pp. 17 ff. (detailed discussion of the treaties of *asylia* without discrimination between treaties protecting whole cities and those protecting only temples); R. Flacelière, *Les Aitoliens*, &c., pp. 202 ff., 228, 243, 250, 289; G. Klaffenbach, *Berl. S.B.* xx (1937), pp. 155 ff. Flacelière assigns dates to the several decrees differing to some extent from those of Roussel and Klaffenbach. The Aetolian *koinon* made use of the piracy of its citizens to promote its political interests and to enlarge the scope of its political influence. When discussing this side of Aetolian policy in *Rev. É.A.* xxxiii (1931), p. 213, I never intended to suggest that the Aetolians aimed at the establishment of a thalassocracy. They had never in the course of their history possessed a regular navy. What their political aims were is evident. In the second period of their 'imperialistic' policy the Aetolians reached the Chersonese, the Propontis, and the Bosporus, and made Lysimacheia, Cius, and Calchedon their subject cities (Polyb. xv. 23. 7–9; Flacelière, op. cit., p. 312). These three cities were probably unable to protect themselves from the dangers of Aetolian piracy. No wonder that Philip V attacked these very cities and dealt so roughly with them.

The inscriptions forming the two groups of *asylia* decrees are these. First group: Chios—*S.E.G.* ii. 258, 3–7, cf. 12–17; Delos—*I.G.* xi. 4. 1050; F. Durrbach, *Choix*, no. 41; *I.G.* ix. i, 2nd ed., 185; Tenos—*I.G.* ix. i, 2nd ed., 191; Ceos—*S.I.G.*³ 522 i; *I.G.* ix. i, 2nd ed., 169; Athens—J. Pomtow, *Klio* XV (1917–18), p. 7, nos. 35, 36. Second group: Mytilene—*I.G.* ix. i. 2nd ed., 189, 190; Teos—*I.G.* ix. i, 2nd ed., 192; Magnesia—*I.G.* ix. i, 2nd ed., 4, cf. ibid., 135 (Lusoi); Miletus (?)—G. Klaffenbach *Berl. S.B.* xx (1937), pp. 155 ff.

18 Cf. Van der Mijnsbrugge, *The Cretan Koinon*, 1931. On *I.G.* xii. 3. 254, cf. his observations, ibid., pp. 17 ff. and p. 29 f., and G. Daux, *B.C.H.* lix (1935), pp. 94 ff. (with bibliography). On Bucris and Eumaridas, W. S. Ferguson, *Hellen. Athens*, p. 209, and the references in note 24. On the treaties between Miletus and the Cretan cities, W. Felgenträger, *Antikes Lösungsrecht*, 1933, pp. 63 ff.; E. Ziebarth, *Klio*, xxvi (1933), pp. 245 ff. It is probable that the vindicators of the men who had been unlawfully enslaved were the *proxenoi* of their respective cities.

19 U. Wilamowitz, *Der Glaube der Hellenen*, ii, pp. 355 and 394. Note that the charge of ἱεροσυλία is an insult frequently hurled by Menander's characters and that the crime itself was probably more frequent even in the days of the Successors than we know it to have been; see, for example, the story of Demetrius Poliorcetes and the temple of Artemis, Plut. *Dem.* 30. 1: when

Demetrius after his fiasco in Macedonia came to Ephesus with a handful of soldiers, everybody in Ephesus believed that, being short of funds, he would plunder the temple, but he did not, says Plutarch, because he was afraid that the soldiers would not carry out his orders.

[20] *S.I.G.*³ 399, cf. for the later time *I.G.* ii/iii, 2nd ed., 1132, and *S.I.G.*³ 692 (cf. 698). Schlesinger, *Die griech. Asylie*, pp. 56 ff.; Kahrstedt, *Gr. Staatsr.* i, 1922, p. 393.

[21] Schlesinger, *Die griech. Asylie*, pp. 59 ff. and pp. 71 ff. (list of inscriptions); Welles, *R.C.* 31–4 (Magnesia) and 35 (Teos), cf. *Inscr. Cret.* i, Cnossus 8*; Ruge, art. 'Teos', *P.W.K.* v A. 547 (list of inscriptions and discussion of their dates), and A. Heuss, 'Die völkerrechtlichen Grundlagen der röm. Aussenpolitik in rep. Zeit', 1933 (*Klio*, Beiheft 18), p. 97. On Magnesia and Teos—L. Robert, *Rev. É.A.* xxxviii (1936), pp. 13 ff.

[22] Miletus—*S.I.G.*³ 590. 8–16; Antiochia in Caria (Alabanda)—*G.D.I.* 2529; *O.G.I.* 234; Calchedon—*S.E.G.* iv. 720; Cos—R. Herzog, 'Griechische Königsbriefe', *Hermes*, lxv (1930), pp. 455 ff.; Welles, *R.C.* 21, 25–8; Smyrna— *O.G.I.* 229 and 228; *F.D.* iii. i. 481 (about 242 B.C.). On these inscriptions in general, after Schlesinger see L. Robert, *B.C.H.* liv (1930), pp. 327 ff., M. Segre, *Historia*, v (1931), pp. 241 ff., Welles, *R.C.*, pp. 58 ff., and L. Robert, *Rev. É.A.* xxxviii (1936), pp. 5 ff. (with a full bibliography).

The answers to the requests are often either reticent as regards the *asylia* (while accepting the games) or contain veiled reservations (see esp. the letter of Seleucus II to Cos, Welles, *R.C.* xxvi. 25: τῶν καθ' ἡμᾶς ὄντων ἐν ἡ|συχίαι). Even the sanctuary of the Delphian Apollo felt the need, after the liberation of Delphi from the Aetolians, of having its *asylia* recognized by the Roman Senate. The documents relating to this recognition, first published by Pomtow with many mistakes, are now available in a more correct form in M. Holleaux's article, 'Le consul M. Fulvius et le siège de Samé', *B.C.H.* liv (1930), pp. 38 ff., cf. P. Roussel, 'Delphes et l'Amphictionie après la guerre d'Aitolie', ibid. lvi (1932), pp. 1 ff. (not included in Schlesinger's bibliography), and G. Daux, *Delphes au IIe et au Ier siècle*, 1936, pp. 261 ff. Since Delphi in the third century was entirely dependent on Aetolia, *asylia* granted by the Amphictions to temples and to the influential associations of *technitai*, whose co-operation was required for the celebration of the great festivals of the various temples, was almost equivalent to *asylia* granted by the Aetolians.

I have quoted above (note 20) the *asylia* granted to the Athenian Dionysiac artists by the Amphictions in 278/7 B.C. (*S.I.G.*³ 399). About 229–228 *asylia* was granted by the Amphictions to the temple of Dionysus Cadmeios at Thebes and to the Isthmian and Nemean *technitai* (*F.D.* iii. 1. 351, cf. L. Robert, *B.C.H.* lix (1935), p. 196 f., and R. Flacelière, *Les Aitoliens*, &c., p. 263, see esp. l. 21 f.: εἶναι . . . [ἄ]συλον καθάπερ καὶ τὸ ἐν Δελφοῖς), and about 200 B.C. to the sanctuary of Apollo Ptoios in Acraiphia and to its games (Ptoia) (*S.I.G.*³ 635 A, cf. G. Daux, op. cit., p. 293, note 1, and

R. Flacelière, op. cit., p. 263, note 4). It is significant, however, that about 235–234, in the troubled times of the Demetrian wars, the *technitai* of Ionia and the Hellespont and those of Isthmus and Nemea were apparently not satisfied with the protection of the Amphictions and wanted a special grant of *asylia* by the Aetolians themselves (*S.I.G.*³ 506–8; *I.G.* ix. 1, 2nd ed., 175; *F.D.* iii. 1, p. 199 and p. 402; R. Flacelière, *Les Aitoliens*, &c., p. 260 f.).

²³ Polyb. iv. 62. 2, and iv. 67. 3, cf. ix. 35. 6 (Dion and Dodona in 219 B.C., cf. Tarn, *C.A.H.* vii, p. 765): retaliation of Philip, Polyb. v. 9–12 (a detailed criticism of Philip's action, in which the historian points out that none of his predecessors had done anything similar, cf. Tarn, *C.A.H.* vii, p. 767). Cf. the speech of Lyciscus the Acarnanian at Sparta in 211 B.C.—an answer to the speech of Chlaeneas the Aetolian (Polyb. ix. 28 ff.)—in which Lyciscus gives a list of their sacrileges and brands the Aetolians as professional ἱερόσυλοι: 'Who elected and sent out such commanders as you did, men who even ventured to lay hand on inviolable sanctuaries, Timaeus having plundered those of Poseidon on Taenaron and of Artemis at Lusoi, while Pharycus pillaged the holy place of Hera at Argos and Polycritus that of Poseidon in Mantinea? And what shall we say of Lattabus and Nicostratus? Did they not violate in time of peace the sanctity of the Panboeotian festival—conduct worthy of Scythians and Gauls? No such crimes were ever perpetrated by Alexander's successors' (Polyb. ix. 34. 8–11, transl. by W. R. Paton, Loeb Library); cf. R. Flacelière, *Les Aitoliens*, &c., p. 240 (who accepts the date of Beloch, i.e. 244 B.C.) and pp. 288 ff. (221 B.C.—pillage of the sanctuary of Athene Ithonia in Boeotia, Polyb. iv. 25. 2). Note that the temple of Artemis at Lusoi was in danger of being sacked by the Aetolians a second time in 220 B.C. (Polyb. iv. 18, 9–12). Finally *asylia* was granted to Lusoi (above, note 17).

²⁴ Copious evidence relating to the αἰχμάλωτοι and their treatment by their captors and on the terms used in this connexion, especially λύτρον, &c., has been collected by A. Wilhelm, *Jahreshefte*, xiv (1911), pp. 163 ff.; *Wien. Anz.*, 1922, pp. 16 ff.; 1924, pp. 97 ff., cf. p. 117 and p. 133; cf. M. Rostovtzeff, *Rev. É.A.* xxxiii (1931), pp. 210 ff.; C. Phillipson, *The International Law and Custom of Ancient Greece and Rome*, 1911, ii, p. 262 ff., and W. Felgenträger, *Antikes Lösungsrecht*, 1933. The art. in *P.W.K.* xiv. 72 (by Lammert) ignores the Hellenistic period; the contributions of Wilhelm and Phillipson are not quoted. Cf. Latte, *P.W.K.* iv A. 1038.

To the references given in notes 18 and 22 (inscriptions relating to grants of *asylia* and testifying implicitly to the frequency of pirate raids) I may add here some inscriptions in which raids and the taking of αἰχμάλωτοι are explicitly mentioned: (1) Thera—*I.G.* xii. 3. 1291, l. 8 (c. 236 B.C.); ibid. 328 (c. 260 B.C.?); in the last case the pirates are Cretans, cf. note 18. (2) Naxos, *S.I.G.*³ 520 (third century B.C.): the pirates are Aetolians. (3) Amorgos: Aigiale—*I.G.* xii. 7. 386, 387; *S.I.G.*³ 521 (third century); Arcesine—*I.G.* xii. 7. 36 (end of third century, not listed by Ziebarth). (4) Cyprus—*G.D.I.* 5151 (Delphi): a Vaxian settled in Cyprus kidnapped by the Aetolians.

(5) Salamis—*I.G.* ii, 2nd ed., 1225; *S.I.G.*³ 454 (*c.* 252 B.C.). (6) Attica—
I.G. ii, 2nd. ed., 746 (after 240 B.C.), Aetolians. (7) Attica, Bucris' raid
—*S.I.G.*³ 535, cf. *I.G.* xi. 4. 692; *S.I.G.*³ 510; Durrbach, *Choix*, 40–2 (date
probably the Demetrian war, R. Flacelière, *Les Aitoliens*, p. 250). (8) Theangela (Caria)—*I.G.* xi. 4. 1054a; *S.E.G.* iii. 666, and my article, *Rev. É.A.*
xxxiii (1931), p. 210 ff., cf. L. Robert, *Coll. Fröhner: Inscriptions grecques*,
i, no. 53, pp. 86 ff. (second cent. B.C.). To show how greatly the prospect of
slavery was dreaded in Greece, I may quote Men. Ἐφέσιος 195 K.: ἐγὼ μὲν
ἤδη μοι δοκῶ νὴ τοὺς θεούς, | ἐν τοῖς κύκλοις ἐμαυτὸν ἐκδεδυκότα | ὁρᾶν κύκλῳ
τρέχοντα καὶ πωλούμενον.

²⁵ See next chapter, note 9.

²⁶ This point was brought out by Wilamowitz, *G.G.A.*, 1914, p. 85, cf.
Rostovtzeff, *Rev. É.A.* xxxiii (1931), pp. 210 ff. A fine example of this Greek
national solidarity is presented by the inscription of Troezen, *I.G.* iv. 750
(*c.* 287 B.C., the time of Demetrius' operations in Asia Minor). Cf. the decree
in honour of Nossicas, a Thasian, who saved and helped some Lampsacene
prisoners taken by Demetrius in a naval battle (302 B.C. ?), G. Daux, *B.C.H.*
lii (1928), pp. 45 ff.; M. Cary, *J.H.S.* l (1930), p. 253. In his comments
Daux has collected much evidence of such help given to captive soldiers.

²⁷ The raids of Skerdilaidas belong to the next period, but I mention them
here because they do not differ in any way from those characteristic of the
period we are considering. Polyb. iv. 29. 6, speaks of a treaty between
Skerdilaidas and the Aetolians during the social war, by which the booty
was to be divided between the allies. Nevertheless after the capture of
Kynaitha the Aetolians took all the σώματα and θρέμματα for themselves, cf.
Polyb. v. 95. 4 (sea raids of Skerdilaidas and his Illyrians). Philip was at
this time proceeding in exactly the same way (Polyb. iv. 86. 4, raid on the
territory of the Eleans, cf. v. 16 and 24. 10) and so were the Achaeans,
Polyb. v. 94.

²⁸ P. Petrie, ii. 29 e, an order for the care and custody of αἰχμάλωτοι who
were sent from one place to another, cf. iii. 104, a list of κλῆροι ἀνειλημμένοι
of which one (104. 2) belonged to a certain Ἀχοᾶπις τοῦ Ἀλκέτου αἰχμαλ[ώ]-
των τῶν ἀπὸ τῆς [Ἀ]σίας. P. Lille 3, iv. 64 ff., deals with grain for the
αἰχμάλωτοι. In the reigns of Ptolemy Philadelphus and Euergetes Egypt was
full of αἰχμάλωτοι taken in the Syrian wars. Ps.-Aristeas 12 ff. and 22 ff.
may serve as a good parallel, cf. U. Wilcken, *Arch. Pap.* xii (1936–7), p. 223,
and W. L. Westermann, *Am. J. Phil.* lix (1938), pp. 1 ff. See *P. Grad.* 1 and
P. Hib. 29, cf. Plaumann and Wilcken, *S.B. Heid. Akad., phil.-hist. Kl.* v
(1914), Abh. 15, and H. Lewald, *Raccolta Lumbroso*, 1925, pp. 340 ff. (cf.
Wilcken, *Arch. Pap.* viii (1927), p. 75)—documents dealing with a special tax
on the sale of slaves, established probably in connexion with sales of large
numbers of αἰχμάλωτοι. The problems presented by these papyri have been
discussed again by W. L. Westermann, *Upon Slavery in Ptolemaic Egypt*,
1929, pp. 33 ff., apropos of *P. Columbia Inv.*, no. 480 (part of a διάγραμμα τῶν

ἀνδραπόδων of about 200 B.C.) and C. Préaux *L'Économie royale des Lagides*, 1939, pp. 305 ff; cf. Wilcken, *Arch. Pap.* ix (1928–30), p. 252 f., and Westermann, art. 'Sklaverei' in *P.W.K.* Suppl. vi. 928. I deal with this subject below, p. 321 f.

It was probably Syrian αἰχμάλωτοι who formed in the third century B.C. the population of a Σύρων κώμη in the Fayûm: for the many Σύροι and Ἄραβες in general, Preisigke–Kiessling, *Wörterb.* iii, and p. 269, p. 272, and p. 330; F. Heichelheim, *Auswärtige Bevölkerung im Ptolemäerreich*, pp. 84 ff.; cf. *Arch. Pap.* ix (1928–30), pp. 47 ff., and xii (1936–7), pp. 54 ff. (s.v. Ἄραψ, Ἀσία, Σύρος); U. Wilcken, *Festg. f. A. Deissmann*, 1927, pp. 1 ff.; *Arch. Pap.* x (1931–2), p. 247 (on *P. Enteux.* 78); M. Rostovtzeff, *Aeg.* xiii (1933), pp. 493 ff.; P. Perdrizet, 'Une stèle d'Atargatis au Musée du Caire', *Ann. Inst. d. Phil. et Hist. Orient.* iv (1936), p. 890 f. (*Mél. Cumont*), cf. the superficial article of G. Vaggi, 'Siria e Siri nei documenti dell'Egitto greco-romano', *Aeg.* xvii (1937), pp. 29 ff., and the excellent volume of W. Peremans, *Vreemdelingen en Egyptenaren in Vroeg-Ptolemaeisch Egypte*, 1937.

[29] H. Swoboda, 'Zwei Kapitel aus dem griechischen Bundesrecht', *Wien. S.B.* cxcix. 2 (1924), pp. 16 ff. Against Swoboda Schwahn, *P.W.K.* iv A. 1177 (art. Συμπολιτεία). Schwahn is certainly right in insisting that some of the proxeny decrees had a purely honorary character, the rights conferred being of no practical use or value to the recipient. But Schwahn has not succeeded in proving his point by positive arguments. We do not know how Aratus acquired property at Corinth. He may have been a *proxenos* of the city. On the other hand, the fact that many Aetolians possessed land and houses at Delphi does not prove Schwahn's point, for Delphi was probably never officially a member of the Aetolian League. The Aetolians acquired property in Delphi not through any legal right but by reason of their politically dominant position. See R. Flacelière, *Les Aitoliens*, &c., pp. 220 ff. and pp. 336 ff. The isopolity that they enjoyed may have served as an excuse.

[30] Plut. *Agis*, 7: σατραπῶν γὰρ οἰκέτας καὶ δούλους ἐπιτρόπων Πτολεμαίου καὶ Σελεύκου κεκτῆσθαι πλείονα συμπάντων ὁμοῦ τῶν ἐν Σπάρτῃ βασιλέων. The wealth of the Spartan kings consisted mostly of land, Plut. *Agis*, 5. Cf. the remarks of Wilamowitz, *Der Glaube der Hell.* ii, pp. 353 ff. and pp. 358 ff. (on the poverty of Greece as shown in her religious customs).

[31] See A. Wilhelm, 'Urkunden aus Messene', *Jahreshefte*, xvii (1914), pp. 107 ff., cf. J. Lipsius, *Rh. Mus.* lxxi (1916), pp. 161 ff. The later discussions of the τίμησις bear exclusively on Athens and the τίμησις of Nausinicus of 378/7 B.C., see, e.g., A. Momigliano in *Athen.*, N.S. ix (1931), pp. 477 ff., and A. Andreades, *A History of Greek Public Finance*, i, 1933, book iv, ch. iii D, and his Ἱστορία τῆς ἑλλην. δημ. οἰκονομίας ii, 1931, pp. 155 ff.

[32] W. L. Westermann, art. 'Sklaverei', *P.W.K.* Suppl. vi. 934, thinks that the number of slaves in general was declining in Greece in the Hellenistic period as compared with the fourth century. The material he adduces in

support of his statement is to my mind unconvincing. However, we have no statistics. The question must be studied again in the light of all available evidence, especially that furnished by the few early acts of manumission, which have never been collected in full; cf. below, Ch. V, nn. 22, 27, 30. The large number of 'home-born' (οἰκογενεῖς) slaves in the second century is proof of the large number of slaves bought in the third.

[33] F. Heichelheim, *Wirtsch. Schwankungen*, p. 97, cf. W. W. Tarn, 'The social question', &c., in *The Hellenistic Age*, pp. 117 ff.

[34] On Agis and Cleomenes see the bibliography in *C.A.H.* vii, p. 885. The most recent contributions are those of W. W. Tarn in *The Hellenistic Age*, pp. 132 ff. and *Hell. Civ.*, 2nd ed., p. 113 f.; M. Hadas, 'The Social Revolution in Third-Century Sparta', *Class. Weekly*, xxvi (1932-3), pp. 65 ff. and 73 ff.; U. Kahrstedt, 'Die spartanische Agrarwirtschaft', *Hermes*, liv (1919), pp. 279 ff. The philosophical background behind the policy of Agis and Cleomenes is stressed by F. Ollier, 'Le philosophe stoïcien Sphairos', *Rev. E.G.* xlix (1936), pp. 537 ff. The extant evidence is slight and the role of Sphaerus in the reform, if any, is obscure.

The well-known meliamb of Cercidas, the contemporary of Cleomenes, poet and statesman of Megalopolis (*P. Oxyr.* 1082; J. U. Powell and E. A. Barber, *New Chapters in the Hist. of Gr. Lit.*, 1921, pp. 2 ff.; J. U. Powell, *Collect. Alexandr.*, 1925, pp. 203 ff.; A. D. Knox, *Herodes, Cercidas and the Greek Choliambic Poets*, 1929 (Loeb Library), p. 195, meliamb II; D. R. Dudley, *A History of Cynicism*, 1937, pp. 79 ff.) contains a violent attack on the unfair and unjust distribution of wealth and a veiled attack on Macedonia. The end of this poem is usually explained as a warning to the rich of a coming revolution (storm) in which they will have to disgorge their wealth. But the text is fragmentary and 'the meaning . . . is hard to fit' (Knox). In any case the meliamb vividly reflects the mood that prevailed in Greece among part of the population about the time of Cleomenes. A similar spirit is seen in the fragments of an early Greek anthology—A. D. Knox, *The First Greek Anthologist*, 1932, and *Herodes, Cercidas*, &c., pp. 229 ff. (Cercidea). Cf. the partial redistribution of land which was suggested by one party at Megalopolis in 217 B.C., after the catastrophe of 223: reinforcement of the city by new citizens and provision of land for these by the old citizens of Megalopolis, who 'should contribute the third part of their estates', Polyb. v. 93. 6.

On the γῆς ἀναδασμός and χρεῶν ἀποκοπή of the fourth century B.C., A. Passerini, 'Riforme sociali e divisioni di beni nella Grecia del IV sec. a. C.', *Athen.* viii (1930), pp. 273 ff. It is inappropriate to talk of the existence of socialism in Greece. Socialism as a theory is a creation of modern times. But social discontent was rife in Greece in the fourth and third centuries, and the poor in their struggle with the rich were fighting not so much for political rights as to get the lands of the rich divided among themselves and debts abolished. Behind this demand for γῆς ἀναδασμός and χρεῶν ἀποκοπή there was no elaborate social programme based on a special economic and social theory, as there was none behind the similar demand of the Russian peasants before the great revolution. However, γῆς ἀναδασμός and χρεῶν ἀποκοπή were inscribed on the banner of the Greek proletariat and were the nightmare of the well-to-do classes. That is why a clause repudiating these watchwords was introduced into the oath of the heliasts in 401 B.C. at Athens and into the constitution of the Corinthian League of 338 B.C. (Rostovtzeff, *St. Soc. ed Ec. d. Imp. Rom.*, p. 3, note 3). As regards the support given to Cleomenes by the proletariat as a result of their hopes, see Plut. *Cleom.* 17. 5: ἐγεγόνει δὲ κίνημα τῶν Ἀχαιῶν, καὶ πρὸς ἀπόστασιν ὥρμησαν αἱ πόλεις, τῶν μὲν δήμων νομήν τε χώρας καὶ χρεῶν ἀποκοπὰς ἐλπισάντων, τῶν δὲ πρώτων πολλαχοῦ βαρυνομένων τὸν Ἄρατον, ἐνίων δὲ καὶ δι' ὀργῆς ἐχόντων ὡς ἐπάγοντα τῇ Πελοποννήσῳ Μακεδόνας. Cf. 16. 7 on the motives of Aratus for joining Antigonus: φεύγων δὲ τὴν μάζαν καὶ τὸν τρίβωνα, καὶ τὸ δεινότατον ὧν κατηγόρει Κλεομένους, ἀναίρεσιν πλούτου καὶ πενίας ἐπανόρθωσιν. These last words give the formula of ancient socialism: abolition of wealth and redress of poverty.

[35] The picture given in this anonymous work is confirmed by some contracts for lease of land at Thespiae belonging to 245–209 B.C. These important texts have recently been revised by M. Feyel, who has prepared a memoir on the subject, *Les Fermages de Thespies au IIIme siècle*, of which a substantial summary is given by Ch. Picard in *C. R. Ac. Inscr.*, 1936, pp. 116 ff. See meanwhile A. D. Keramopoullos Ἐπιγραφαὶ Θεσπίων, Ἀρχ. Δελτ. xiv (1935), pp. 12 ff.; M. Feyel, 'Études d'épigraphie béotienne,' *B.C.H.* lx (1936), pp. 175, 389 ff., where the reader will find a list of the most important inscriptions, with an up-to-date bibliography. The Thespiae leases deal chiefly with land which belonged to two of the city's sanctuaries—that of the Muses and that of Hermes. The property of these two sanctuaries was steadily being increased by numerous gifts from private persons, mostly citizens of Thespiae, and from foreign kings, particularly the Ptolemies and the rulers of Pergamon. The chief foreign donors were Philetaerus, son of Attalus (*I.G.* vii. 1788–90: *O.G.I.* 749–50); Philopator (M. Holleaux, *Rev. É. G.* x (1897), pp. 26 ff.; *Études*, i, pp. 99 ff.) and Philetaerus, son of Eumenes (*B.C.H.* xxx (1906), p. 467). Cf. a dedication by Philetaerus, son of Attalus, A. D. Keramopoullos, loc. cit., p. 233, cf. ibid. xix (1895), p. 321. Note that Egyptian gods were worshipped in the sanctuary, *B.C.H.* xxvi (1902), p. 293: l (1926), p. 425. On the gifts to the sanctuaries of Thespiae, Fiehn, *P.W.K.* vi A, 46 f. and 49 (art. Thespeia). On the gifts of Philetaerus and his identity, M. Holleaux, *Rev. É. G.* x (1897), p. 33; xv (1902), pp. 302 ff.; *Études*, i, p. 105, ii, pp. 1 ff.; M. Rostovtzeff, *C.A.H.* viii, p. 604.

The sacred and the public lands of the city of Thespiae were well cultivated. They were rented mostly on long terms (40, 20, 10, and 6 years) to farmers, most of them citizens of the town, sometimes in groups. Some of the farmers rented large areas, for example Andreas (Keramopoullos, Ἀρχ. Δελτ. xiv (1935) A, ll. 38–45). The economic situation of the farmers seems to have been far from miserable: they paid their rents regularly, and there is no record of arrears. Note that Thespiae was able during the Demetrian war, perhaps soon after the death of Demetrius, to grant Athens an important loan

(*I.G.* vii. 1737 and 1738, with the comments of Dittenberger, cf. Fiehn, loc. cit., p. 39); see below, Ch. V, n. 22. An interesting sidelight is thrown on the economic conditions of Boeotia by a curious inscription from Acraiphia recently published by M. Feyel, *B.C.H.* lx (1936), pp. 27 ff., a list of various kinds of fish, with indication of weight and price. Feyel suggests a kind of tariff of fixed prices for fish, and recalls the well-known complaints of the Athenians about the high price of fish at Athens in the late fourth century, Athen. vi. 224 c; A. Wilhelm, *Jahreshefte*, xii (1909), p. 148, cf. A. Jardé, *B.C.H.* xlvii (1923), p. 303. The list from Acraiphia belongs, however, to a later period (second century B.C.).

[36] The fragments of the pamphlet ascribed by some scholars (on insufficient evidence) to Heraclides Criticus are anonymous and bear no title. They are published in *F.H.G.* ii, pp. 254 ff., and *G.G.M.* i, pp. 98 ff., cf. H. Hitzig, 'Die griechischen Städtebilder des Herakleides', *Festgabe f. H. Blümner*, 1914, pp. 1 ff. (with German translation). Bibliography in Christ–Schmid, *Gr. Lit.*, 6th ed., ii. 1, 1920, p. 73, note 8; cf. the acute observations on the pamphlet by W. S. Ferguson, *Hellen. Athens*, pp. 261 ff. and 464 ff. I cannot discuss here the problem of the date of the pamphlet.

[37] A bibliography of publications dealing with the individual cities of Greece proper that have been excavated would indeed be a long one and is out of the question here. Such references will be found in all the archaeological handbooks and in the numerous surveys of archaeological work done in Greece by various scientific institutions. Current reports on such work are printed in all the periodicals devoted to classical archaeology. References have been given in these notes to those publications which contain material used in this book, and the practice will be continued.

[38] The texts that support the above statements will be found in W. S. Ferguson, *Hellen. Athens*, pp. 137 ff. and pp. 188 ff. On the Demetrian war and the new epigraphical evidence bearing on the life of Athens at the time of this war, see the bibliography quoted above, Ch. I, note 12. On Delos see below, pp. 230 ff. Cf. A. Heuss, *Stadt und Herrscher*, pp. 67 ff.

[39] The evidence has been collected in full and excellently interpreted by R. Flacelière, *Les Aitoliens*, &c., pp. 226 ff. and esp. pp. 259 ff. In what follows I give a summary of his highly instructive statements.

[40] R. Flacelière, op. cit., p. 209.

[41] See note 37. What I have said there of the mainland cities holds good for the islands also.

[42] As regards food shortage I may remark that the period under review— 280 to about 230 B.C.—was not a very bad one if compared with those which preceded and followed it. Food shortage in the early and middle third century was spasmodic, not continuous. I may quote the case of Cos, M. Segre, 'Grano di Tessaglia a Coo', *Riv. Fil.* lxii (12) (1934), pp. 169 ff., and the

severe shortage at Samos relieved in part by Bulagoras (*S.E.G.* i. 366). F. Heichelheim, 'Sitos', *P.W.K.* Suppl. vi. 852 ff.

[43] The loans of Arcesine have been discussed by W. W. Tarn, 'The social question', &c., in *The Hellenistic Age*, pp. 108 ff., and E. Schlesinger, *Die griechische Asylie*, 1933, pp. 20 ff. I agree in the main with Tarn's conclusions, though I do not think that by ὑπερπόντια are meant the ships and cargoes of the metics (see note [15] in *S.I.G.*[3] 955).

[44] Sympolity of the cities of Ceos: P. Graindor, *Mus. Belge* xxv (1921), pp. 119 ff.; H. Swoboda, *Wien. S. B.* cxcix. 2 (1923), p. 38 ff., esp. pp. 50 ff.; U. Kahrstedt, *P.W.K.* iv A. 1440 (art. 'Synoikismos'); Schwahn, ibid. iv A. 1265 (art. Συμπολιτεία), and R. Flacelière, *Les Aitoliens*, &c., pp. 204, 214.

[45] W. W. Tarn, loc. cit., is right in asserting that the higher classes of the population of the islands were prosperous in this period.

[46] M. Lacroix, 'Les étrangers à Délos,' *Mél. Glotz*, 1932, pp. 501 ff. In the pre-Hellenistic period the majority of the *entrepreneurs* and contractors were foreigners, while in the third century Delians began to predominate. Lacroix is probably right in ascribing this decline in the number of foreigners to the gradual fall in the rate of wages at Delos.

[47] F. Heichelheim, *Wirtschaftliche Schwankungen*, p. 97, cf. W. W. Tarn, loc. cit.

[48] See the inscription of 290/89 (?), *I.G.* xii. 5. 2. 1004, *O.G.I.* 773, discussed above, Ch. III. p. 140. Cf. my remarks on Cos below, pp. 236 ff., and on Priene and Teos above, pp. 175 ff.

[49] On Rhodes see the books and articles quoted pp. 169 ff., note 42. On the battle of Ephesus, F. Hiller von Gaertringen, art. 'Rhodos', *P.W.K.* Suppl. v. 783 and E. Bikerman, *Rev. É. A.* xl (1938), pp. 380 ff. On the Rhodian protection of Delos after the withdrawal of the Ptolemies from the Aegean, below note 59.

[50] M. P. Nilsson, *Timbres amphoriques de Lindos*, p. 169, and fig. 2.

[51] C. C. Edgar, 'A new group of Zenon papyri', *Bull. of the John Rylands Library*, xviii (1934), p. 111 f., n. 1; cf. my paper 'Alexandrien und Rhodos' in *Klio*, xxx (1937), pp. 70 ff.

[52] On Apollonius see my *Large estate in Egypt in the Third Century* B.C., 1922, pp. 16 ff., and C. C. Edgar, *P. Michigan Zen.*, 1931, Introd., pp. 5 ff.; cf. below, pp. 419 ff.

[53] On frankincense, myrrh, &c., which Apollonius received from Palestine, South Syria, and Phoenicia, see my paper in *Journ. of Ec. and Bus. Hist.* iv. (1932), p. 746, n. 9. Lists of shipments: *P. Cairo Zen.* 59012, 59013, 59014 and 59015, cf. the very interesting lists *P.S.I.* 428 and 535, which may be lists of goods kept in Apollonius' storehouses. Cf. below, pp. 381 ff.

[54] *P. Cairo Zen.* 59075 and 59076.

[55] The lists mentioned in note 53 have never been a subject of close study.

Some points in them have been studied carefully, e.g. the organization of the customs duties as reflected in the lists, by A. Andreades, 'Des droits de douane prélevés par les Lagides sur le commerce extérieur', *Mél. Glotz*, 1932, pp. 7 ff., and their bearing on some points in the general fiscal and economic policy of Philadelphus, by W. W. Tarn, 'Ptolemy II', *J.E.A.* xiv (1928), pp. 255 ff. (cf. his *Hellen. Civ.*², pp. 153 f., 166 f.). Otherwise we find general remarks on them, e.g. E. Ziebarth, *Beiträge zur Gesch. des Seeraubs* &c., pp. 80 f., and H. Schaal, *Vom Tauschhandel zum Welthandel*, 1931, pp. 134 f. Extensive use of the lists for the purpose of describing the Mediterranean exports and imports of Ptolemaic Egypt in the third century has been made by W. Peremans in his paper 'De Handelsbetrekkingen van Egypt', &c., *Phil. St. (Kath. Un. te Leuven)*, iii (1931–32), pp. 3 ff. and pp. 81 ff. Rhodian cabbage: Athen. ix. 9, pp. 369 f., cf. my *Large Estate*, p. 105, n. 79. Cf. the remarks on the lists of shipments by V. Tscherikower, 'Palestine under the Ptolemies', *Mizraim*, iv–v (1937), pp. 24 f. It is of course possible that ships sailing from Alexandria would first go to Rhodes and afterwards on their way to Alexandria call at the harbours of Syria.

[56] On Delos, my remarks in *C.A.H.* viii, pp. 642 ff. (and bibliography) ; W. A. Laidlaw, *A history of Delos*, 1933 ; M. Lacroix, 'Les Étrangers à Délos' &c., *Mél. Glotz*, pp. 501 ff. ; J. A. O. Larsen, 'Roman Greece' in T. Frank's *Econ. Survey*, iv, pp. 334 ff. (this section of the book contains a substantial survey of the economic life of Delos, which deals not only with the time after 167 B.C. but also with the period of Delos' independence, and gives a good bibliography). On the building contracts of the time of independence, P. H. Davis, *B.C.H.* lxi (1937), pp. 109 ff. Like the other business men of Delos, the building contractors were mostly foreigners, residing in other islands. None of them worked himself, like the contractors of Athens, Delphi, and Epidaurus in the fifth and fourth centuries: they all employed hired labour. The so-called 'minor finds' of Delos (with the exception of the lamps, the portable ovens (*réchauds*), the pottery of the Hellenistic period, and the glass) are published in an exemplary way by W. Deonna, 'Le Mobilier délien', *Expl. de Délos*, xviii, 1938. For his survey of objects relating to the private life of Delos Deonna has utilized not only the actual objects found there but also the references to them in the Delian temple inventories. Especially illuminating is the chapter on jewellery. It is to be regretted that the editors of the Delian series found it impossible to print in the volume just quoted an introductory chapter by him on the commerce and industry of Delos.

[57] On the loans of money made by the temple through the city as intermediary to various cities of the Aegean in the third century, see J. Delamarre, *Rev. Phil.*, xxviii, 1904, pp. 97 ff. ; cf. J. A. O. Larsen, loc. cit., pp. 238 ff. Larsen is inclined to think that the loans repaid by the Aegean cities under the pressure of Philocles were contracted for the purpose of paying not Demetrius, but Ptolemy. The date of the repayment quoted by him as an argument against Demetrius has no bearing on the question. Repayment of debts is often a very slow affair.

[58] A decree of Delos in honour of Dionysius of Byzantium for having sold to the city 500 med. of grain at a price fixed by the city (*I.G.* xi. 4. 627; Durrbach, *Choix* 46) certainly points to commercial relations between Byzantium and Delos. The decree belongs to the time of the Ptolemaic hegemony (first half of the third century). Early friendly relations between the Rhodians and Delos as attested by the sacred embassies (*theoriai*) and dedications of Rhodes in the late fourth and early third centuries: *I.G.* xi. 2. 161, *B*, 13–18; 63–75; ibid., 287, *B*, 36–44; 84–6, and many other mentions. Such dedications and embassies were not due to piety alone, cf. the similar dedications of Alexandria and her dependency Cos.

[59] Honours bestowed on Macedonians: *I.G.* xi. 4. 679–80; Durrbach, *Choix*, 47, and *I.G.* xi. 4. 664, 665, cf. 1053; Durrbach, *Choix*, 49 (with the comments of Durrbach). Demetrius II's agent at Delos: *I.G.* xi. 4. 666; Durrbach, *Choix*, 48. Decree of Histiaea in honour of Athenodorus, the banker, citizen of Rhodes: *I.G.* xi. 4. 1055 and 1025; *S.I.G.*³ 493; Durrbach, *Choix*, 50. Good relations between Rhodes and Macedonia are attested by the inscriptions in honour of Rhodian admirals dedicated by Delos at the time when Macedonian influence was strong in Delos: *I.G.* xi. 4. 1128; *S.I.G.*³ 455, Durrbach, *Choix*, 38; *I.G.* xi. 4. 596; Durrbach, *Choix*, 39, and *I.G.* xi. 4. 1135; Durrbach, *Choix*, 40; cf. E. Bikerman, *Rev. É.A.* xl (1938), p. 381 for another view. These dedications and the relations between Delos and Aetolia (see the comments of Durrbach on no. 40, and above p. 198, note 17, cf. R. Flacelière, *Les Aitoliens* &c., p. 202) show the insecurity in the Aegean in the middle of the third century, the danger of pirate raids, and the activity of the Rhodians in combating piracy.

[60] *I.G.* xi. 4. 609, cf. 1143, and *I.O.S.P.E.* ii. 11; *I.G.* xi. 2. 287. B, 124 ff.; Durrbach, *Inscr. de Délos, Comptes des Hiéropes*, 298, 95–6, with comments. Cf. below, p. 598. The importance of the Bosporan grain on the Aegean market in the early third century B.C. may be inferred from the fluctuation of grain prices at Delos in 282 B.C. A. Jardé, *Les Céréales dans l'antiquité*, i, pp. 168 f., attributes this fluctuation to the closing or reopening of the Thracian Bosporus by Lysimachus. Cf. E. Ziebarth, *Beiträge zur Gesch. des Seeraubs* &c., p. 69, and F. Heichelheim, *Wirtschaftliche Schwankungen* &c., p. 51.

[61] See the inscriptions quoted by Durrbach, *Choix*, note to no. 46.

[62] M. Lacroix, 'Les Étrangers à Délos' &c., *Mél. Glotz*, p. 514 ff. I may mention in this connexion two prominent inhabitants of Delos who were occupied in trade and banking. One was Mnesalcus, son of Telesarchidas. About 280 B.C. (M. Holleaux, *B.C.H.* xxxi (1907), pp. 374 ff.; *I.G.* xi. 4. 1049) he helped an unidentified city, which made him its *proxenos*, in a σπανοσιτία (by redeeming the grain-ships seized by the creditors of the city) and granted it various loans, l. 9: ἀργύριόν [τε] πολλάκις τῆι πό|[λει] παρέσχηκεν εἰς ἀναγ-καίας [χρ]είας καὶ τοῦτο | [ἐκο]μίζετο εἰς ὃ ἦν ὁ δῆμος δυνατὸ[ς] ἀποδοῦναι. Mnesalcus is well known as an influential citizen of Delos through several

other inscriptions: *I.G.* xi. 4. 558, 559; Durrbach, *Choix*, 18; *S.I.G.*³ 391, cf. *I.G.* xi. 2., 161. A, 29 (279 and 278 B.C.). About 250 B.C. we meet another rich banker, this time a Chian, Eutychus by name, a contemporary of Bucris, the Aetolian (see R. Flacelière, *Les Aitoliens* &c., p. 202). In the decree in his honour (Durrbach, *Choix*, 43) he is described as οἰκῶν ἐν || Δήλωι καὶ συνερ-γαζόμενος ἀπὸ τοῦ δικαίου [τοῖς | τὴν θά]λατταν πλέουσιν (l. 4). Eutychus is known as the founder of a festival called Eutycheia (first *phiale* mentioned in 230 B.C.). Note in both cases the connexion of banking with maritime commerce and especially with the grain trade, and also that Mnesalcus was a Delian, while Eutychus came to Delos from Chios.

⁶³ *I.G.* xi. 2. 161, *A*, 25–6, and 162 A, 29–30; Schwahn, *P.W.K.* xix. 531 f., and J.A.O. Larsen, loc. cit., pp. 354 ff.

⁶⁴ Several such collection-boxes have been found in the sanctuaries of Delos and other Greek cities (for instance Cos), see W. Deonna, 'Le Mobilier Délien', *Expl. arch. de Délos*, xviii, pp. 367 ff. (with complete bibliography).

⁶⁵ On the expenditure of the temple (and the city?) for hiring actors, cithara-players, flutists, singers, dancers, poets, &c., and for providing ἆθλα for them and all sorts of requisites, W. Deonna, loc. cit., pp. 321 ff.

⁶⁶ See note 56. The full text of the ἱερὰ συγγραφή and valuable comments (with bibliography) will be found in Durrbach et Roussel, *Inscr. de Délos*, Actes des Fonct. Ath., &c., no. 1416. On the regulations regarding the local trade in charcoal (*Inscr. de Délos*, 509), cf. L. Robert, *Rev. É.G.* xlvi (1933) pp. 430 ff., and J. A. O. Larsen, loc. cit., p. 352, who does not quote Robert.

⁶⁷ On the *sitonicon* see the interesting remarks of J. A. O. Larsen, loc. cit., pp. 344 ff.

⁶⁸ See above, pp. 190 ff., and note 2.

⁶⁹ An account of the gradual growth and embellishment of the sanctuary in the third century cannot be given here. The reader must consult the books quoted in note 56, and especially P. Roussel's little book, *Délos*, 1925. On the endowments and other gifts of the Hellenistic rulers and other important persons of the time, which reflect so fully the political vicissitudes of the period, see the comments on the accounts of the *hieropoioi* by Durrbach and Roussel; Roussel, *Délos colonie athénienne*, pp. 173 ff.; and E. Ziebarth, 'Delische Stiftungen', *Hermes*, lii (1917), pp. 425 ff.

⁷⁰ I cannot give here a detailed bibliography of books and papers dealing with the various aspects of Coan life. An excellent survey of the material, with a careful bibliography, will be found in the recent book by Aldo Neppi Modona, 'L'Isola di Coo nell'antichità classica', *Mem. d. Ist. Storico-Archeolo-gico di Rodi*, i 1933 (with bibliography on pp. 11 ff.). The best contributions to our knowledge of Cos have been made, after W. R. Paton, by R. Herzog, the excavator of the Asclepieum, in many books and papers (listed in the bibliography of Modona). The Italian students of Cos have added

a good deal of new material to that collected by Paton and Herzog. The contributions of A. Maiuri, G. Jacopi, and M. Segre in particular are enumerated in part in Modona's bibliography. On the medical school of Cos, its contribution to the 'development of medical science, and the role of doctors in the public life of Cos, see R. Herzog, 'Die Asklepiosheiligtümer als Heiltätten und Gnadenorte', *Münch. Mediz. Wochenschrift*, 1933, and S. d'Irsay, 'The cult of Asclepius', *Bull. Inst. Hist. of Medicine*, iii (1935), pp. 451 ff. As regards the mimes of Herondas, I have used the edition (with French translation, fine Introduction, and some notes) of J. Arbuthnot Nairn and L. Laloy, *Hérondas Mimes*, in the *Collection de l'Assoc. G. Budé*, 1928, and the excellent German translation with Introduction and copious comments by O. Crusius and R. Herzog, *Die Mimiamben des Herondas*, 2nd ed., 1926.

[71] The best analysis of the inscription of Cos, *S.I.G.*[3] 1000, will be found in A. Andreades, *Hist. of Greek public Finance*, i, pp. 150 ff. For the income from the fisheries see *S.I.G.*[3] 1024 (Myconos). An excellent parallel to the system of taxation as it appears in the Coan inscription is furnished by an inscription of Teos of the late fourth century, *S.E.G.* ii. 579, on which see above, ch. iii, p. 181 f., n. 45, and by the accounts of the *hieropoioi* of Delos, above, pp. 190 ff., n. 2. In matters of taxation, tradition and the system that existed at this time were different in Crete: see the inscription of Gortyn, M. Guarducci, *Riv. Fil.* lviii (8) (1930), pp. 471 ff., cf. G. De Sanctis, ibid., pp. 483 ff. I cannot deal in this book with the subject of taxation in the Greek cities. The Hellenistic period did not introduce any substantial changes into the system which had been firmly established for centuries in the Greek cities and is so well known, especially at Athens during the fifth and fourth centuries B.C. On this system, which was typical of the Greek city, see in addition to the book by Andreades quoted above, Schwahn, art. Τέλη and Τελῶναι in *P.W.K.* v A. 326 ff. and 418 ff. I shall speak later of the novelties introduced in the case of those cities which were incorporated in the Hellenistic monarchies by the Ptolemies, Seleucids, and Attalids.

I may mention some peculiar sources of income utilized by the Hellenistic cities to which no reference is made in the inscriptions of Cos, Teos, and Delos. The *sale of the franchise*, for example, was an emergency measure taken from time to time in order to increase the number of taxpayers and liturgy-bearers and at the same time to get a certain amount of cash. See E. Szanto, *Das griechische Bürgerrecht*, 1892, p. 32; G. Busolt, *Griech. Staatsk.* i, p. 227, cf. M. Segre, *Aeg.* xiv (1934), pp. 267 ff., who gives a list of inscriptions in which sale of franchise is mentioned (on the inscription from Thasos see L. Robert, *Rev. Phil.* x (1936), pp. 131 ff.). It may not be out of place to refer here to the *sale of priesthoods*, another peculiar form of taxation which was in common use in many Greek cities from the fifth century B.C., especially in Asia Minor. See on this subject the papers of L. Robert, *B.C.H.* lvii (1933), pp. 467 ff., and A. Laumonier, ibid. lviii (1934), pp. 360 ff., where the reader will find the epigraphical evidence and complete bibliographical notes. Cf. M. Segre, *Rend. Ist. Lomb.* lxix (1936), pp. 811 ff. A sharp criticism of this form of taxation was included by Paullus Fabius Persicus in his famous edict concerning Ephesus, *S.E.G.* iv. 516, ll. 34 ff. (quoted by L. Robert), cf. F. K. Dörner, *Der Erlass des Statthalters Paullus Fabius Persicus*, 1935.

⁷² No mention is made in the inscription of the ἱερὰ and δαμοσία χώρα which Cos owned in Cyprus (a gift of one of the Ptolemies), G. Patriarca, *Bull. Mus. Imp. Rom.* iii in *Bull. Comm.* lx (1932), p. 6, n. 3 (first century B.C.).

⁷³ See the inscription Paton–Hicks, no. 344. Cf. the conditions of land-tenure in Chios about 239–236 B.C., B. Laum, *Stiftungen in der Gr. u. Röm. Antike*, ii, 1914, n. 62; *G.D.I.* iv. 4, pp. 894 ff. Attalus lent a sum of money to Chios. This the city in turn lent in small sums (about 300 dr.) to small landowners at a low rate of interest. Was this a form of assistance to small landowners who were in financial difficulties?

⁷⁴ J. Vanseveren, *Rev. Phil.* xi (1937), pp. 325 ff. If the lists of Chios are really lists of *proxenoi*, they certainly testify not only to social and political but also to commercial relations with other cities. On the importance of the lists of *proxenoi* for the history of commerce in general, cf. E. Ziebarth, *Klio*, xxvi (1932–3), pp. 244 ff. On the commercial importance of Chios and the activity of its harbour in later times, L. Robert, *Rev. É.G.* xlii (1929), pp. 32 ff., cf. E. Ziebarth, loc. cit., p. 246. Cf. also L. Robert, *Étud. épig. et phil.*, 1938, pp. 118 ff., on slavery in the 5th and 4th centuries B.C.

⁷⁵ No general work on Hellenistic Crete is in existence, though much has been written on Crete in this period. See the bibliography in Van der Mijnsbrugge, *The Cretan Koinon*, 1931; cf. below, Ch. V, n. 8 (with bibliography). On the Cretan *perioeci* or ὕποικοι and their status, see the divergent opinions of M. Guarducci as summarized with the help of new evidence in *Riv. Fil.* lxiv (14), 1936, pp. 356 ff., and of J. A. O. Larsen, art. Περίοικοι, *P.W.K.* xix. 828 ff. (1937).

CHAPTER IV, PART II

⁷⁶ On Macedonia in the time of Antigonus, W. W. Tarn, *Antigonus Gonatas*, 1913; *Hell. Civ.²*, pp. 58 ff.; and *C.A.H.* vii, pp. 197 ff. On Antigonus and Rhodes and Delos, my remarks in *C.A.H.* viii, pp. 623 f., and p. 642, and above, pp. 229 and 232; cf. E. Ziebarth, 'Zur Handelsgeschichte der Insel Rhodos', *Mél. Glotz*, p. 914. On tar and pitch, G. Glotz, *R.E.G.*, xxix (1916), pp. 281 ff.; W. W. Tarn, *Economica*, 1930, Nov., pp. 315 ff., and F. Heichelheim, *Wirtschaftliche Schwankungen*, pp. 54 ff. It is evident that Macedonia, though the chief producer of tar and pitch, had no monopoly in these products, since pine forests of excellent quality existed in various other regions: in Pontus, in Cilicia, in the region of the Mysian Olympus and of Mount Ida, forests which were in the hands of the Pontic and Bithynian kings, of the Seleucids (later the Attalids), and of the Ptolemies (see Theophr. *H.P.* iv. 5. 5). As masters of the Aegean, the Macedonian kings were able to dictate their own prices to the Aegean world. On the Macedonian economic structure in general, F. Hampl, *Der König der Makedonen*, 1934, pp. 66 ff., cf.

E. Kornemann, *Die Alexandergeschichte des Königs Ptolemaios I. von Aegypten,* 1935, pp. 180 ff.

⁷⁷ A short survey of the ancient sources for Ptolemaic Egypt will be found in *C.A.H.* vii, pp. 889 ff. For the abbreviations used in citing the publications of papyri see below, Index. A good survey of the history of papyrology and a useful description of the individual finds, with a good bibliography, has been recently published by K. Preisedanz, *Papyrusfunde und Papyrusforschung* 1933 (reviews of this book are enumerated in *J.E.A.* xxi (1935), p. 102). Cf. the shorter survey and characterization of the papyrological documents as material for the history of the Ptolemaic period by Claire Préaux, *L'Économie royale des Lagides,* 1939, pp. 10 ff. In the same book (p. 14, cf. 22) the reader will find references to the books and articles in which the demotic papyri hitherto published are listed (cf. Bibliography, p. 575 f.) The papyri of Gebelen have been published by various authors and in various places; see the bibliography of Mlle Préaux, loc. cit., p. 14, n. 1. The papyri of Philadelphia: N. J. Reich, 'The legal transactions of a family preserved in the Un. Mus. of Philadelphia', *Mizraim,* ii (1936), pp. 13 ff., and ibid. vii (1937), pp. 11 ff. Some useful remarks of a general character on the demotic papyri will be found in W. F. Edgerton, 'Demotica', *Papyri u. Altertumswissenschaft,* 1934, (*Münch. Beitr.,* xix), pp. 281 ff. Cf. the interesting suggestions on the connexions between Greek and Demotic papyri in E. Seidl, 'Die demotische Zivilprozessordnung und die gr. Rechtsurkunden', *Chr. d'Ég.* xiii–xiv (1932), pp. 210 ff.; 'Demotische Urkundenlehre nach den frühptolemäischen Texten', *Münch. Beitr.,* xxvii (1937), and his bibliography relating to Egyptian national law, *Krit. Vierteljahresschr.,* xxiv (1930), pp. 37 ff. and xxvii (1935), pp. 268 ff.

I may remind the reader that bibliographies of current publications of papyri and of contributions to papyrology in the broad sense of the word will be found in many periodicals, the most complete and useful being those of the *Archiv für Papyrusforschung,* the *Journal of Egyptian Archaeology, Aegyptus,* the *Revue des Études grecques,* the *Chronique d'Égypte, Byzantion,* &c. I may add here a list of the most recent contributions to our knowledge of the principal papyri and groups of papyri of the Ptolemaic period. (1) Zenon Papyri: up-to-date lists, E. Balogh, 'Bibliographie der Veröffentlichungen des Zenonarchivs' in his paper 'Die richterliche Kompetenz des Dioiketen Apollonios', *Actes du Vᵐᵉ Congrès de Papyrologie,* 1938, pp. 68 ff. and C. Préaux, op. cit., p. 10, n. 1; cf. the current 'Urkunden–Referate' of U. Wilcken in *Arch. Pap.* Excellent selections will be found in W. Schubart, 'Griechische Briefe aus Ägypten', *Die Antike,* viii (1932), pp. 113 ff., and A. S. Hunt and C. C. Edgar, *Select Papyri* i. Private affairs, 1932 (Loeb collection). (2) Directions of the *dioecetes* to the *oeconomi* of the *nomoi, Teb.* 703: K. F. W. Schmidt, *Phil. Woch.,* 1934, pp. 1307 ff. (many new readings in *Teb.* 703 are suggested in this review). On the document in general, U. Wilcken, *Arch. Pap.* xi (1933–5), pp. 148 f.; L. Wenger, *Aeg.* xiii (1933), pp. 582 ff.; E. Berneker, *Die Sondergerichtsbarkeit im gr. Recht Aegyptens* &c., 1935, pp. 69 ff.; C. Préaux, *Chr. d'Ég.* xxi (1936), pp. 163 ff. (3) Δικαιώματα of

Halle: W. Schubart, *Arch. Pap.* xii (1936–7), pp. 27 ff. New fragments of this document have been recently found and are now in Cairo.

[78] References will be found in the section of this chapter devoted to industry.

[79] There are many excellent surveys of economic and social conditions in Egypt. A full list of them cannot be given here. Of the earlier contributions I may quote the admirable book of G. Lumbroso, *Recherches sur l'économie politique de l'Égypte sous les Lagides*, 1870, and his charming general sketch *L'Égitto dei Greci e dei Romani*, 2nd ed., 1896. Of more modern studies the best and fullest are those of U. Wilcken: for example, *Griechische Ostraka aus Aegypten und Nubien*, i–ii, 1899; *Grundzüge und Chrestomathie der Papyruskunde*, 1912 (with L. Mitteis); 'Alexander der Grosse und die hellenistische Wirtschaft', *Schmollers Jahrb.*, xlv. 2 (1921), pp. 349 ff.; *Alexander der Grosse*, 1931, pp. 267 ff. Many valuable contributions to various problems will be found also in his reports on recent publications of papyri in *Arch. Pap.* and in his comments on the documents republished by him in his *U.P.Z.* Next in importance is the excellent survey by W. Schubart, *Einführung in die Papyruskunde*, 1918. Chapters and pages devoted to social and economic conditions in Hellenistic Egypt will naturally be found in the general works on the history of the Hellenistic period, such as those of Niese, Beloch, Kaerst, &c., and on the history of Ptolemaic Egypt, such as those of Bouché–Leclercq, Mahaffy–Bevan, Schubart, and Jouguet (full titles quoted above, Ch. I, n. 1). Invaluable help in understanding Ptolemaic Egypt as seen by contemporaries is furnished by the astrological texts. Some of these go back to Ptolemaic treatises on astrology and very vividly and clearly reflect various sides of Egyptian life in the third and second centuries B.C. F. Cumont has been the first to collect these texts and to illustrate them in the light of our literary and documentary evidence: see his *L'Égypte des Astrologues*, 1937. The astrological texts as we have them do not give a detailed picture of Ptolemaic Egypt: they rather reflect the conditions prevailing in the eastern part of the Roman Empire in general. But they contain several valuable data which certainly relate to the Ptolemaic period, and these data must be carefully studied by every scholar who deals with Ptolemaic Egypt. Cf. L. Robert, *Études épigraphiques et philologiques* (*Bibl. Ec. H.-Ét.*, 272), 1938, pp. 76 ff.

I may quote also some valuable recent works which deal with the subject as a whole or in part: W. W. Tarn, *Hellenistic civilization*, 2nd ed., 1930; W. Schubart, 'Verfassung und Verwaltung des Ptolemäerreichs', *Der alte Orient*, xxxv. 4 (1937), W. L. Westermann, 'The Greek exploitation of Egypt', *Polit. Science Quarterly*, xl (1925), pp. 517 ff.; F. Heichelheim, 'Welthistorische Gesichtspunkte zu der vormittelalterlichen Wirtschaftsepochen', *Festgabe W. Sombart*, 1933, pp. 185 ff. (*Schmollers Jahrb.*, lvi. 6); A. Segré, 'Note sull'economia dell'Egitto ellenistico', *Bull. de la Soc. Arch. d'Alex.* xxix (8) (1934); V. Martin and A. Calderini in *Papyri und Altertumswissenschaft*, 1934 (*Münch. Beitr.* xix), pp. 102 ff. 166 ff.; A. Andreades, 'Budgets helléniques et budgets hellénistiques', *Atti d. IV Congr. d. Pap.*, 1936, pp. 51 ff., and H. Idris Bell, 'Proposals for a Social History of Greco-Roman Egypt', ibid. pp. 39 ff. The most important recent contribution to the study of the economic and social conditions is Mlle Claire Préaux's *L'Économie royale des Lagides*, 1938, which I have had the privilege of reading in proof. Mlle Préaux seeks to show the genesis and the development of the Ptolemaic economic system and to describe the vicissitudes of its conflict with the individualistic trend of Egyptian and Greek economic life. Cf. my own sketches: 'The Foundations of Social and Economic life in Egypt in the Hellenistic times', *J.E.A.* vi (1920), pp. 161 ff., and the chapter 'Ptolemaic Egypt' in *C.A.H.* vii, pp. 109 ff. Some passages of the latter will be found reproduced in the text with slight modifications.

[80] On this point see the books and articles quoted in *C.A.H.* vii, p. 892, and above, Ch. III, nn. 13, 14. For the economic life of Egypt in earlier times, G. Dykmans, *Histoire économique et sociale de l'ancienne Égypte*, i–iii, 1936–7, and H. Kees, 'Aegypten' in W. Otto, *Handb. d. Altertumsw.* iii. 1. 3, 1933.

[81] On Egypt in the time of Soter, see the notable remarks of E. Kornemann, 'Die Satrapenpolitik des ersten Lagiden', *Racc. Lumbroso*, 1925, pp. 235 ff. (cf. his article 'Aus der Geburtsstunde eines Gottes', *Mitt. d. schles. Ges. f. Volkskunde*, xxvii (1926), pp. 1 ff.), and of P. Jouguet,' La politique intérieure du premier Ptolémée', *Bull. de l'Inst. Fr. d'arch. or.* xxx. 1 (1930), pp. 513 ff., repeated in his history of Ptolemaic Egypt in G. Hanotaux's *Histoire de la Nation Égyptienne*, iii, cf. C. Préaux, 'Politique de race ou politique royale', *Chr. d'Égypte*, xi (21) (1936), pp. 111 ff. On the native aristocracy (an obscure and controversial problem) see W. Peremans, *Vreemdelingen en Egyptenaren in Vroeg-Ptolemaeisch Egypte*, 1937 (with French résumé), pp. 97 ff. The case of an Egyptian holder of a *dorea* in the third century B.C. (*P. Lille*, i. 47) is uncertain and disputed. Cf. C. Préaux, *L'Écon. Lag.*, p. 461. On the life of the native inhabitants who were connected with temples, see the highly interesting set of Demotic documents in the University Museum of Philadelphia, N. J. Reich, 'The legal transactions of a family', *Mizraim*, ii (1936), pp. 13 ff., and his paper 'A deed of gift in 317 B.C.,' ibid., pp. 57 ff.

[82] Much has been written on Philadelphus. I cannot quote in this note all the papers and books which deal with his policy. To the bibliography quoted in note 79 I may add: W. W. Tarn, 'Ptolemy II', *J.E.A.* xiv (1928), pp. 246 ff., and the following papers of C. Préaux, 'Quelques défauts de la politique intérieure de Ptolémée Philadelphe', *Aeg.* xiii (26) (1933), pp. 547 ff.; 'Réflexions sur les droits supérieurs de l'État dans l'Égypte lagide', *Chr. d'Ég.* x (19) (1935), pp. 109 ff.; 'Difficulté de requérir le travail dans l'Égypte lagide', ibid. x (20) (1935), pp. 343 ff.; 'Politique de race' &c., ibid. xi (21) (1936), pp. 111 ff.; 'Un problème de la politique des Lagides; la faiblesse des édits', *Atti IV Congr. Pap.*, pp. 183 ff.; 'Esquisse d'une histoire des révolutions égyptiennes sous les Lagides', *Chr. d'Ég.* xi (22) (1936), pp. 522 ff.; 'La signification de l'époque d'Evergète II', *Actes du Vme Congr. Pap.*, 1938, pp. 345 ff. All these articles are summarized in her book quoted above.

[83] The constitutional and religious aspects of the Hellenistic monarchies are discussed in all the histories of the Hellenistic world quoted in Ch. I, note 1. An excellent summary will be found in W. S. Ferguson, *C.A.H.* vii, pp. 7 ff. (with bibliography), cf. V. Ehrenberg, 'Der griechische und der hellenistische Staat', in Gercke und Norden, *Einleitung*, iii. 3 (1932), pp. 72 ff., and P. Zancan, *Il Monarcato ellenistico nei suoi elementi federativi*, 1934. See also my remarks above, Ch. III, p. 145 f. and note 17. On Egypt in particular see the bibliography given above, note 79. On the royal cult in Egypt, W. Schubart, *Die religiöse Haltung des frühen Hellenismus*, 1937, and especially U. Wilcken, 'Zur Entstehung des hellenistischen Königskultes', *Berl. S. B.* xxviii (1938), pp. 308 ff.

It has often been noticed that the current Greek philosophical ideas on kingship were accepted by the Ptolemies, see E. Schwartz, *Rh. Mus.* xl (1885), pp. 254 ff.; U. von Wilamowitz-Moellendorf, *Staat und Gesellschaft der Griechen*, p. 163; Th. Mommsen, *Röm. Gesch.* v, p. 559; U. Wilcken, 'Alexander der Grosse und die hellen. Wirtschaft', *Schmollers Jahrb.* xlv (1921), p. 349, and my own remarks in *J.E.A.* vi (1920), p. 173, and *C.A.H.* vii, p. 164; cf. above, Ch. III, p. 145 f., note 15. Soter and Demetrius of Phalerum: Plut. *Apophth. reg.* 189 D. Treatises περὶ βασιλείας: *Oxyr.* 1611, ll. 38 ff. (quotation from Theophrastus περὶ βασιλείας, ii); Kunst, *Berl. klass. Texte*, vii. pp. 13 ff. ll. 34 ff. (Berl. Pap. P. 13045, 1st cent. B.C.)—fragments of a treatise, probably περὶ βασιλείας, praising monarchy in general and the Ptolemies in particular, and implicitly Alexandria. On the letter of Ps.–Aristeas, S. Tracy, 'III Maccabees and Pseudo–Aristeas: a Study', *Yale Cl. Stud.* i. 1928; E. Bickermann, *Zeitchr. für d. neutest.Wiss.* xlix (1930), pp. 286ff.; H. G. Meacham, *The oldest version of the Bible*: '*Aristeas*' *on its traditional origin*, 1932 (which contains a translation of the letter and some comments, esp. pp. 172 ff.), and *The letter of Aristeas: a linguistic study* &c., 1935 (which contains a new edition of the Greek text of the letter). To the hitherto known treatises περὶ βασιλείας must now be added that of a certain Theopompus (not the famous one) included in the list of books of the library of a gymnasium in Rhodes: see A. Maiuri, *Nuova sill. ep. di Rodi e Cos*, 1925, n. 4; M. Segre, *Riv. Fil.* lxiii (13), 1935, pp. 214 ff., and lxiv (14), 1936, pp. 40 f. An excellent collection of texts bearing on the professional philosophy of the Hellenistic kings and their assistants is made by W. Schubart, *Arch. Pap.* xii (1936), pp. 1 ff. The fundamental text in regard to the employees of the king is *Teb.* 703, ll. 257–280, cf. my Introd., p. 69.

Recently discovered fragments of Theophrastus' πῶς πόλεις ἄριστ᾽ ἂν διοικοῖντο (W. Aly, *Forsch. u. Fortschr.* xi (1935), p. 302) show that Greek post-Aristotelian philosophy required in the magistrates of a Greek city-state not only technical training (this was a standard requirement of post-Socratic philosophy), but also a high moral standing which is defined in detail by Theophrastus. These moral requirements of Theophrastus were accepted by the Hellenistic kings and applied to their own officers. This is shown by a remarkable coincidence in ideas and terminology between the statements of *Teb.* 703 and those of Theophrastus. A full publication of the text discovered by Aly is in preparation. Cf. V. Ehrenberg, *Alexander and the Greeks*, p. 93, n. 3. On the moral standing of the Ptolemies as reflected in the above sources, see W. Schubart, 'Verfassung und Verwaltung des Ptolemäerreiches', &c., *Der alte Orient*, xxxv (1937), p. 37; W. L. Westermann, 'The Ptolemies and the welfare of their subjects', *Actes du Vme Congr. Pap.*, pp. 574 ff., and *Am. Hist. Rev.* xliii (1938), pp. 280 f.; and C. Préaux, *L'Écon. Lag.*, p. 557 ff. Mlle Préaux points out the similarities between the Egyptian and the Greek conceptions of royal power. I doubt, however, whether the Ptolemies ever realized them: their ideal was purely Hellenic. On the Ptolemies' linking themselves to Alexander, see W. W. Tarn, *J.H.S.* liii (1933), pp. 57 ff.; my paper, '*Πρόγονοι*', *J.H.S.* lv (1935), p. 62, and F. Edson Jr., 'The Antigonids, Heracles, and Beroea', *Harv. Stud. in Cl. Phil.* xlv (1934), pp. 221 ff.

[84] Ownership of the state by the king does not mean, of course, that no private property in land and movable things was recognized, but the only guarantor of such property was the king. How far private property in land had developed in the pre-Ptolemaic period, it is difficult to say. In the temple territories private ownership of land by members of the temple community was a well-known institution in Saite and Persian times. From this, however, it is a far cry to the postulate that the main pillar of economic life in pre-Ptolemaic Egypt was private property, as in Greece and Rome. In a country in which the welfare of the people and the State was based on compulsory labour and where the first claim to the products of the land was the undisputed prerogative of the king, where consequently requisitions were as common as compulsory labour, it is hazardous to speak of fully developed individualism in economic and social life.

On λειτουργία in Greece and Egypt see F. Oertel, *Die Liturgie*, 1917, who does not discriminate sharply enough between the two forms of liturgy which were in use in Egypt: the native compulsory labour and the services demanded by the king from his Greek subjects (e.g. trierarchy). On these last see *P. Cairo Zen.* 59042; *Hib.* 78, and *P.S.I.* 484; E. Bickermann, *Arch. Pap.* viii (1927), p. 238, cf. *P. Cairo Zen.* 59323, U. Wilcken, *Arch. Pap.* ix (1930), p. 230, W. Peremans, *Vreemdelingen* &c., pp. 156 ff., and C. Préaux, *L'Écon. Lag.* pp. 395 ff.

[85] I shall speak of taxation and the farming system later in this chapter. On the *Urkunden* of the Ptolemies and the study of them in general (*Urkundenlehre*), U. Wilcken, 'Ueber antike Urkundenlehre', *Papyri und Altertumswissenschaft*, 1934, pp. 42 ff. On accounting, E. Grier, *Accounting in the Zenon Papyri*, 1934 (cf. C. Préaux, *Chr. d'Ég.* x (20) (1935), pp. 384 ff.), and L. Bandi, 'I conti privati', etc., *Aeg.* XVII (1937), pp. 379 ff.

[86] A good survey of the agricultural and other resources of Egypt in the pre-Ptolemaic period will be found in the works quoted above, n. 80, and during the Roman period in A. Ch. Johnson, 'Roman Egypt to the reign of Diocletian' (T. Frank, *An Economic Survey of Ancient Rome*, vol. ii), 1936, pp. 1 ff. ('The Land, I, Agricultural products'), cf. pp. 7 ff. (II, 'The Nile and Irriga-

tion'). In the main these surveys are valid for Ptolemaic Egypt also. On agriculture in general and the work of the Ptolemies in this field, M. Schnebel, *Die Landwirtschaft im hellenistischen Aegypten*, 1925. This study is the basis (apart from some additions) of later general surveys such as those of O. Krüger, 'Agricultural production in Hellenistic Egypt', *Bull. of the Ac. of Mat. Civ. of U.R.S.S.* cviii (1935) (in Russian) and N. Hohlwein 'Le blé d'Égypte', *Ét. de Pap.* iv (1938), pp. 33 ff. There are also excellent discussions of all the material bearing on the production of grain in Ptolemaic Egypt by F. Heichelheim, art. 'Sitos', *P.W.K.* Suppl. vi, and by C. Préaux, *L'Écon. Lag.*, pp. 53 ff. (les travaux publics) and pp. 117 ff. (le blé). A useful discussion of some statistical data concerning Egyptian agriculture will be found in A. Segré, 'Note sull'economia dell'Egitto ellenistico nell'età Tolemaica', *Bull. Soc. Arch. d'Alex.* xxix (1934), pp. 15 ff., and F. Heichelheim, loc. cit., 845 ff. On the irrigation system of the Fayûm, see my remarks on *Teb.* 703, ll. 29–40, and G. Caton Thompson and E. W. Gardner, *The Desert Fayûm*, i, ii, 1934; cf. C. Préaux, *Chr. d'Ég.* xi (21) (1936), pp. 200 ff., W. L. Westermann, 'A lease from the estate of Apollonius', *Mem. of the Amer. Acad. in Rome*, vi (1927), p. 6, and C. C. Edgar, *P. Mich. Zenon*, Intr., pp. 31 ff., and *P. Col. Zenon*, 54. Work on the dikes and canals and the classes of the population exempt from this work: F. Oertel, *Die Liturgie*, 1917, pp. 8 ff., cf. U. Wilcken, *U.P.Z.* 157; W. Peremans, *Chr. d'Ég.* xi (22) (1936), pp. 517 ff.; *Vreemdelingen*, &c., pp. 156 ff. and C. Préaux, *L'Écon. Lag.*, p. 395 f. On the land surveys, U. Wilcken, *Grundz.*, pp. 176 ff., cf. A. Deleage, 'Les cadastres antiques jusqu'à Dioclétien', *Ét. de Pap.* ii (1934), pp. 73 ff.

[87] The division of the land in Egypt into various classes was first studied by Grenfell and Hunt in their classical comments on the land-surveys of Tebtunis of the late second century B.C. On this study are based the remarks in my *Studien zur Geschichte des röm. Kolonates*, 1910, cf. *J.E.A.* vi (1920), p. 165 and p. 173, and U. Wilcken, *Grundz.*, pp. 270 ff., and 'Alexander' &c., *Schmollers Jahrb.* xlv (1921), p. 76 (380) f. The terminology was never strict, even in later times. In 209 B.C. the γῆ ἐν ἀφέσει is listed after the γῆ ἐν συντάξει (?) καὶ δωρεᾷ *Teb.* 705, 6 f.; cf. B. P. Grenfell, *Rev. Laws XLIII*, 11–12, and the remarks of Hunt on *Teb.* 705. Our information on the status and management of the land assigned to the Greek cities is exceedingly meagre. We know of the existence of the Ἀλεξανδρέων χώρα and of a part of it called ἀρχαία γῆ (*Edict. Tib. Jul. Al.*, l. 59). Wilcken, *Grundz.*, p. 285 f. suggests tentatively that ἀρχαία γῆ may have been the land assigned to the first settlers, the ἀρχαῖοι κλῆροι (Arist. *Pol.* vi. 4, p. 1319a, 10). Some land may also have been assigned to the city as a whole. Some information on this 'municipal' land may be derived from a very interesting document recently published by H. I. Bell and C. H. Roberts, *Merton Papyri*, no. 5, a petition to the well-known *strategos* of the Thebaid, Boethus (149–135 B.C.). Here a woman, Berenice, ἀστὴ (?) ἀπὸ Πτολεμαΐδος (?) appears in possession of a parcel of γῆ πολιτική, which she bought (?) from a certain Panas Panopolites. The same class of land appears later in Roman times in *P. Lond.* 604 B, 260, *Brit. Mus. Pap.*

iii, p. 84, and belongs to the γῆ ἰδιωτική. We must await further evidence before forming a judgement on the status of the γῆ πολιτική of Ptolemais.

[88] On γῆ βασιλική and βασιλικοὶ γεωργοί see my *Kolonat*, pp. 47 ff., 62 ff.; U. Wilcken, *Grundz.*, pp. 272 ff., and my comments on *Teb.* 703, ll. 40–63; cf. W. Peremans, *Vreemdelingen* &c., p. 109. On the πράκτορες ἰδιωτικῶν and ξενικῶν, i.e. probably those who collected payments, respectively, from those who paid them in their ἰδία (ἰδιῶται) and those who made their payments while staying in a village which was not their own, see W. L. Westermann, *Mem. Amer. Acad. in Rome*, vi (1927), p. 16, cf. *P. Col. Zen.* 54, l. 47. I may add that the interpretation of these terms is disputed. A full list of the additional taxes paid by the 'royal peasants' and other holders of land is given by C. Préaux, *L'Écon. Lag.*, pp. 131 ff. On the collection and transport of payments in grain in general, and those of the royal peasants in particular, F. Heichelheim, 'Sitos', *P.W.K.* Suppl. vi. 865 ff. and C. Préaux, *L'Écon. Lag.* pp. 129 ff., 143 ff., with full bibliographical notes. I cannot deal here with the χειρισταί and their role in the transportation of grain. The subject is controversial, see C. Préaux, l. cit., p. 146, n. 1. As regards the contracts between the royal peasants and the crown, see J. Partsch, in Sethe und Partsch, 'Demotische Urkunden zum aegyptischen Bürgschaftsrechte vorzüglich der Ptolemäerzeit', *Abh. Sächs. Ges.* xxii (1920), pp. 610 ff., cf. C. Préaux, loc. cit., pp. 437 ff. (Les contrats). Partsch is inclined to believe that documents 1–5 are regular leases of γῆ βασιλική. Since they are made for one year only, the obvious conclusion according to Partsch is that in the early Ptolemaic times royal land was managed in a very different way from that adopted in the later period. I am afraid, however, that the documents in question are special supplementary leases of the royal and other land for sowing grass after the harvest (χλωρὰ ἐπίσπορα) or in rotation, which have nothing to do with the regular leases and which were always dealt with in the same way; cf. C. Préaux, loc. cit., p. 439 who comes to the same conclusions. See next note. However, the existence of the contractual system as the basis of the relations between the king and the royal peasants is definitely attested not only by the later documents of Tebtunis (below, Ch. VI; cf. the slightly earlier and the contemporary receipts for rent (μίσθωσις) paid by the royal peasants, *Teb.* 835–837), but also for the time of Philadelphus by the documents dealing with the *laoi* of Syria, discussed below, pp. 344 ff., and n. 139. Whether or not the ἐκφόριον system (instead of a *pars quota*) was first introduced by the Ptolemies is unknown. W. W. Tarn (*J.E.A.* xiv (1928), p. 256) takes it for granted. A group of (unpublished) documents of the third century B.C. in the Yale collection (Euergetes or Philopator) from the archives of Leon, a *topogrammateus*, throw light on certain problems of the agricultural organization of Egypt. One of them is an order of the *dioecetes* to the *basilicogrammateus* to submit at a given date the διαγραφὴ σπόρου for the following year. The order was forwarded by the *basilicogrammateus* to the *topogrammateus* and by the latter probably to the village scribe.

⁸⁹ See my remarks in *J.E.A.* vi (1920), p. 174. On flax, *Teb.* 703, ll. 87–113, and especially *Teb.* 769 (cf. for new readings, some of them very doubtful, K. F. W. Schmidt, *Phil. Woch.*, 1934, p. 1315), cf. F. Heichelheim, 'Monopole', *P.W.K.* xii. 175.

⁹⁰ The character and evolution of the relations between the temples and the Ptolemies is one of the fundamental problems of the history of Egypt in the Hellenistic period. It has been treated in a masterly way by W. Otto, *Priester und Tempel in hellenistischen Aegypten*, i, 1905, and ii, 1908, who subsequently added some new suggestions in his paper 'Aegyptische Priester-synoden in hellenistischer Zeit' (in W. Spiegelberg und W. Otto, 'Eine neue Urkunde zu der Siegesfeier des Ptolemaios IV' &c., *Bayer. S.B.*, 1926, ii, pp. 18 ff.). My views on this question are set forth in my review of Otto's book in *G.G.A.* clxxi (1909), pp. 603 ff. (e.g. on the ἐπιστάτης and the selling of offices; cf. C. Préaux, *Chr. d'Ég.* xi (22) (1936), p. 547). In 1912 U. Wilcken, *Grundz.*, pp. 603 ff., summarized the problem as it then stood and expressed his own opinion on the controversial points. Since that time much new material has been accumulated, especially papyrological. Many Demotic papyri which relate to temples and priests of the Hellenistic period are of fundamental importance. A reconsideration of the question is therefore imperative. As regards the economic situation of the priests and temples, we must discriminate between two aspects of the problem. On the one hand, we have to face the question of the economic situation of the individual priests and temple 'slaves', i.e. the economic relations of each with the temples as such, and with the crown. On the other hand, we must carefully analyse the economic relations between the temples as such and the State. No comprehensive work has been done on either of these problems in recent times. On the notion of temple 'slaves', see N. J. Reich, *Mizraim*, ii (1936), p. 36. In this note Reich has quoted ample evidence from Demotic and Greek documents on the professions of these 'slaves' (peasants, herdsmen, fishermen, supervisors of work on canals) and on their civil status (they own property, buy and sell, rent and borrow), first collected by K. Sethe, *Dem. Urk. z. äg. Bürgschaftsrechte*, p. 36, § 30. U. Wilcken, *U.P.Z.*, I, pp. 46, 571, notes 3 and 5; F. Cumont, *Rev. Arch.*, VII (1936), p. 236, n. 2; *hieroduloi* as hereditary tenants, *P. Demot. Zen.* 6 (252/1 B.C.) (Spiegelberg), cf. W. Pere-mans, *Vreemdelingen* &c., p. 111.

New evidence on ἱεροδουλία will be found in the interesting set of Demotic documents in the British Museum found probably in the temple of Sobek at Tebtunis. They are dated between 195 and 137 B.C. All the documents are self-dedications by an individual (male or female), in other words, self-enslavements to the god 'for ever', in return for the protection of the god against evil spirits. Most of these devotees know their mothers but not their fathers, and are born in the temple precincts; they are evidently children of temple-prostitutes. The documents will soon be published by Sir Herbert Thompson; see his preliminary statement, *Actes du Vᵐᵉ Congr. Pap.*, pp. 497 ff. The αἰλουροβοσκοί of Bubastis, *P. Cairo Zen.* 59451.

On the economic situation of the priests, especially as landholders, W. Otto, *Priester u. Tempel*, ii, p. 200 f., and especially J. Partsch in Sethe u. Partsch, *Dem. Urk. z. äg. Bürgschaftsrechte*, pp. 626 ff., esp. pp. 633 ff.. cf. J. Partsch, 'Die griech. Publizität der Grundstückverträge im Ptolemäerrechte', *Festschr. f. O. Lenel*, 1921, p. 78, nn. 1 and 2. Important new evidence on this point has recently been brought to light. Especially illuminating are two groups of documents. One in the University Museum of Philadelphia (U.S.A.), representing the archives of a family connected with the temple of Zemi, described by N. J. Reich, *Mizraim*, ii (1936), pp. 57 ff. and pp. 13 ff.; the documents begin in 317 B.C. and go down to the time of Philopator. The other in London, a dossier concerning a lawsuit of a priestly family of Siut in the time of Epiphanes: Sir Herbert Thompson, *A family archive from Siut*, 1934, cf. E. Seidl and B. H. Stricker, *Z. Sav.-Stift.* vii (1937), pp. 272 ff. and below, Ch. V, n. 135. On the Serapeum of Memphis and the *choachytai* of Thebes as illustrated by U. Wilcken in *U.P.Z.*, see Chs. V and VI.

Still more important is the problem of the relations of the temples as such with the king and especially the problem of the γῆ ἱερά; on this question see W. Otto, *Priester u. Tempel*, ii, pp. 82 ff., and Index s.v. γῆ ἱερά; my remarks *G.G.A.* clxxi (1909), pp. 621 ff.; U. Wilcken, *Grundz.*, pp. 278 ff.; J. Partsch, *Dem. Urk.* &c., pp. 626 ff.; C. Préaux, *L'Écon. Lag.*, pp. 480 ff., cf. pp. 461 ff. Specially instructive is the Demotic document quoted and translated by E. Seidl, *Der Eid im Ptolem. Rechte*, 1929, p. 95 f., cf. *Teb.* 876 (236 B.C.?). On the gifts, U. Wilcken, *U.P.Z.* 153–5 (255/4 B.C.). On the ἀπόμοιρα, C. Préaux, *Chr. d'Ég.* xi (21) (1936), pp. 115 ff.; *L'Écon. Lag.*, pp. 171 ff., cf. *P. Ryl. Zen.* 11, 16: μετρηταὶ Ἀρσινόης (ἑξάχοοι).

Further study and a fuller collection of material is also much wanted for a better understanding of the organization of that branch of temple economy which was connected with the so-called *beneficia* of the temples (the γέρα and ἡμέραι ἁγνευτικαί in Greek terminology), which in earlier times were in hereditary possession of the priests and in the Ptolemaic period were leased to them by the kings. The problem requires a comparative study, since this source of income and a similar treatment of it appear, for example, in the Babylonian temples (see for the Hellenistic period M. Rutten, *Contrats de l'époque Séleucide*, 1935, p. 199; E. Bikerman, *Institutions des Séleucides*, pp. 174 ff.; A. Aymard, *Rev. É.A.* xl (1938), pp. 18 ff. and p. 23) and were certainly typical of other oriental temples. Cf. C. Préaux, *L'Écon. Lag.*, pp. 489 ff. In *Teb.* 88 the thirty ἡμέραι ἁγνευτικαί are one source of income of the temple and the payments of the 'royal peasants' (a free gift) are another. The king sold or leased to the managers of the temple 6 of the 30 days of service to which the temple was entitled and nothing else. It is interesting to find Greeks purchasing religious offices and ἡμέραι ἁγνευτικαί and λειτουργικαί in the Egyptian temples, *Teb.* 853. 25 (about 173 B.C.), cf. U. Wilcken, *U.P.Z.*, II, p. 7.

[91] The problem of the γῆ κληρουχική greatly needs reconsideration in the light of the new evidence. The older evidence has been collected and inter-

preted in a masterly way by J. Lesquier, *Les Institutions militaires sous les Lagides*, 1911, pp. 202 ff., cf. my *Kolonat*, pp. 6 ff.; U. Wilcken, *Grundz.*, pp. 280 ff. Valuable evidence has been contributed by *P. Freib.* 7; Hunt and Edgar, *Sel. Pap.* ii. 412 (251 B.C.), cf. J. Lesquier, *Rev. É.G.* xxxii (1919), pp. 359 ff., and by many other papyri. It has been utilized by myself, *Large Estate*, p. 138 f., by C. Préaux, *Chr. d'Ég.* xi (21) (1936), pp. 119 ff., and *L'Écon. Lag.*, p. 63 (the cleruchs and the irrigation of their plots), p. 68 (planting of oil-producing crops, *Hamb.* 24, 222 B.C.) and pp. 463 ff. (evolution of the cleruchies), and by E. Kiessling, 'Streiflichter zur Katökenfrage', *Actes du Vᵐᵉ Congr. Pap.*, pp. 213 ff., cf. U. Wilcken, *P. Würzburg*, n. 4 and 7 (*Berl. Abh.*, 1933, No. 6). The suggestion of Kiessling (who is in the main following Gelzer) that economic reasons played no part in the policy of Philadelphus as regards the cleruchies, and that the tenure of them was for short terms, is based on very slight evidence. He disregards almost entirely the documents of the Zenon correspondence, and never quotes cases which show an active participation of the holders in the management of their *cleroi*. The part taken by the cleruchs in the irrigation and improvement of their holdings is best illustrated by *P. Petrie* iii. 42 (2), and *P. Lille* i. 39–42; cf. my *Large Estate*, p. 63 f.; *P. Lille*, Intr. to 39–51; C. Préaux, *L'Écon. Lag.*, p. 63, and E. Balogh, *Actes du Vᵐᵉ Congr. Pap.*, p. 55. On σταθμοί and ἐπισταθμία, C. Préaux, *Chr. d'Ég.* xi (21) (1936), pp. 131 ff., and *L'Écon. Lag.*, pp. 387 ff. and pp. 477 ff. Cf. M. San Niccolò, *P.W.K.* vi A, 2178 ff.; U. Wilcken, *U.P.Z.* 151 (259 B.C.), and esp. *Teb.* 820 (200 B.C.) (παραχώρησις of a σταθμός). I have not been able to consult F. Smolka, 'Ptolemajska ustawa kwaterunkowa', *Arch. Towarzystwa naukowego w Lwowie*, xvi (1935), pp. 335 ff. On the σταθμοί in other Hellenistic monarchies, see Index s.v.

⁹² My *Kolonat*, pp. 13 ff.; U. Wilcken, *Grundz.*, pp. 284 ff., and his comments on the Zois papyri, *U.P.Z.* i. 114, p. 525. The conditions of land-tenure in the south of Egypt, especially at Pathyris (Gebelen), are illustrated by several groups of papyri, mostly family archives of the Πέρσαι τῆς ἐπιγονῆς. The finds are scattered and have never been studied in their entirety, see the references in C. Préaux, *L'Écon. Lag.*, p. 14, n. 1. and E. N. Adler, 'The Adler Papyri. The Archive of a family of Pathyris . . . between 134 and 88 B.C.,' *Actes du Vᵐᵉ Congr. Pap.*, pp. 12 ff., cf. F. Pringsheim, *Z. d. Sav.-Stift.* xliv (1924), pp. 419 ff., and E. Bickermann, *Arch. Pap.* viii (1927), pp. 218 ff. On private property in land in Egypt before the Ptolemies, V. Struve, *Journ. of the Board of Publ. Educ.*, 1915, Jan. pp. 1–64, and 1917, July–August, pp. 223 ff. (in Russian). I may recall in this connexion what I have said above, note 87, on the γῆ πολιτική. On the development of private land-holding in later times and on confiscated land, see below, Ch. V, note 151.

⁹³ On the live-stock economy of the Ptolemies in general see the excellent chapter 'Viehzucht' in M. Schnebel, *Die Landwirtschaft*, 1925, pp. 316 ff., cf. on poultry (pigeons, geese, and chickens) M. Cobianchi, 'Ricerche di ornitologia nei Papiri dell'Egitto greco-romano', *Aeg.* xvi (1936), pp. 91 ff.

94 On the oxen, cows, and donkeys used for agricultural work see, in addition to the remarks of Schnebel, the new information yielded by *Teb.* 703, ll. 63–70, and my remarks in *J.E.A.* vi (1920), pp. 174 ff., and my comments on this passage; cf. C. Préaux, loc. cit., pp. 207 ff. (l'élevage), and Sh. Le Roy Wallace, *Taxation in Egypt from Augustus to Diocletian*, 1938, pp. 77 ff. On the calf byres and the calves, *Teb.* 703, ll. 66–70 and ll. 183–91, and my remarks on these passages. On the treatment of the problem of livestock on the estate of Apollonius, my *Large Estate in Egypt in the Third Century* B.C., 1922, pp. 107 ff., and C. C. Edgar, *P. Mich. Zen.*, 1931, pp. 36 f. The construction of a palisade in Philadelphia to protect the pigs and other animals from the flood (with a sketch plan of the building): *P. Mich. Zen.* 84. On the pigs see my remarks in *J.E.A.* vi (1920), p. 173, and *Large Estate*, Index s.v. 'Pigs'; M. Schnebel, loc. cit., pp. 328 ff.; F. Heichelheim, 'Monopole', *P.W.K.* xii. 190, and C. Préaux, loc. cit., pp. 221 ff. Our information is derived almost exclusively from the correspondence of Zenon.

95 On the horses, my *Large Estate*, p. 167 f., cf. my 'Foreign Commerce', *Jour. Ec. and Bus. Hist.*, IV (1932), p. 730, and W. W. Tarn, *J.E.A.* xv (1929), p. 20 f., and below, p. 396; C. Préaux, loc. cit., pp. 217 ff. Very instructive is *Teb.* 743, 10–20: delivery of hay for the βασιλικοὶ ἵπποι τρεφόμενοι ἐν Κροκοδί-(λων) πό(λει) τοῦ Ἀρσινοΐτου νομοῦ.

96 See M. Schnebel, loc. cit.; my *Large Estate*, Index, s.v. 'Sheep'; C. Préaux, loc. cit., pp. 217 ff. (petit bétail). In this case again our knowledge is based chiefly on Zenon's correspondence. On the geese, my *Large Estate* p. 110; F. Heichelheim, loc. cit., 186 (χηνοβοσκία); C. Préaux, loc. cit., pp. 270 ff. I doubt very much whether the poorly preserved remains of a πρόσ-ταγμα of Philopator, *B.G.U.* 1212 D, should be interpreted as evidence of a royal monopoly of breeding geese; the ordinance probably dealt with a special case. See *Teb.* 875 (2nd cent. B.C., account), 18: ζμηνῶν, χηνῶν, ὀρνίκων βασιλικῶν καὶ ἰδιωτικῶν οὐθέν.

97 On the pigeons see the paper of Cobianchi quoted in n. 93; C. Préaux, loc. cit., pp. 238 ff.; Wallace, loc. cit., pp. 69 ff. The document mentioned in the text is *P. Sorbonne inv.* 391: M. Hombert, *Rev. Belge de phil. et d'hist.* iv (1925), pp. 652 ff. It shows that the tax on the pigeon-houses was collected by special contractors.

98 The problem of the management of pasture-land by the Ptolemies and the taxes connected with it is very complicated, and our evidence is scanty. See my remarks in *J.E.A.* vi (1920), p. 173, and my comments on *Teb.* 703, ll. 165–74; S. Avogadro, 'Alcune osservazioni sulle tasse del bestiame' &c., *Aeg.* xiv (1934), pp. 293 ff.; Préaux, loc. cit., pp. 225 ff., and for Roman times, Wallace, loc. cit., pp. 386 ff. In addition to the *ennomion* and to the payments for pasturage a tax was paid for keeping special guards in the pastures (φυλακιτικόν). On Syria and the *prostagma* of Philadelphus see below, p. 346.

99 Bee-keeping flourished on the Philadelphian estate of Apollonius: see my *Large Estate*, pp. 105 ff.; and on bee-keeping in general C. Préaux, loc.

cit., pp. 233 ff., and F. Heichelheim, loc. cit., 187. Being a Carian himself, Zenon was probably familiar with bee-keeping: we should not forget that it was one of the regular occupations of the Carian Greeks and that Carian honey was famous, see A. Wilhelm, *Jahreshefte*, xxiv (1929), p. 167, and L. Robert, *L'Antiquité Classique*, iv (1935), pp. 170 ff. Cf. F. Heichelheim, 'Monopole', *P.W.K.* xii. 187 f., and A. Andreades, *Hist. of Gr. publ. Finance*, i, p. 157, n. 7.

[100] Hunting: F. Heichelheim, loc. cit. 172 f. (θηρία), and C. Préaux, loc. cit., pp. 197 ff. On Apollonius and Zenon, my *Large Estate*, p. 112. On the sarcophagus of Alexander see e.g. Springer–Michaelis–Wolters, *Die Kunst des Altertums*, pl. XIII and fig. 701a; on the painting in Palestine, M. Swindler, *Anc. Painting*, fig. 557, cf. Watzinger, *Die Denkmäler Palästinas*, ii, pl. 25, cf. my pl. LVIII; on the dish of Trasilico, my pl. XLIV.

[101] Fishing: F. Heichelheim, loc. cit. 186 f. (ἰχθυηρά), and C. Préaux, loc. cit., pp. 201 ff. Several passages of *Teb.* 701 (235 B.C.), cf. 721, throw much light on the fishing industry. It is interesting to see that large quantities of fish from the Μικρὰ Λίμνη were put on the Egyptian market and sold at Memphis, at Alexandria, and in the χώρα. The relations between fishermen and the State were similar to those that prevailed in the linen industry. The ἁλιεῖς paid a high φόρος (30 per cent. and 40 per cent. of the produce sold, ll. 195–210) and received loans for the purchase of tackle. In addition they got ὀψώνια. The fishermen therefore may have worked for their own account as state 'contractors'. It is possible, however, that the accounts of *Teb.* 701 are those of the manager of a *dorea* which included fisheries, not of a royal *oikonomos*.

[102] On mines, quarries, &c. and their exploitation, K. Fitzler, *Steinbrüche und Bergwerke im ptolemäischen und römischen Aegypten*, 1910; F. Oertel, *Die Liturgie*, pp. 18 ff.; F. Heichelheim, loc. cit. 159 (ἅλς), 173 (μέταλλα and νιτρική), 175 (στυπτηρία), 186 (χρυσοχοϊκή), and C. Préaux, *L'Écon. Lag.*, pp. 243 ff. (les carrières) and pp. 253 ff. (les métaux), cf. A. C. Johnson, *Roman Egypt*, pp. 239 ff., and my *Large Estate*, pp. 162 ff. and my 'Foreign commerce' &c., *Journ. of Ec. and Bus. Hist.* iv (1932), pp. 732 ff. In these books and papers the reader will find references to other valuable contributions to the study of ancient and modern Egypt in this respect. Silver in Egypt—H. Kees, *Aegypten*, p. 131; in Cyprus—Cl. F. A. Schaeffer, *Mission en Chypre*, 1936, p. 98; *Mél. syr. Dussaud*, 1939, p. 476, n. 2. On the copper mines of Cyprus see J. L. Bruce, 'Antiquities in the mines of Cyprus', in E. Gjerstad, *The Swedish Cyprus Expedition*, iii (1937), pp. 639 ff. It must be observed that mines, quarries, &c., never had a special status in Egypt. They belonged to the king as part of the Egyptian soil in general. On 'Bodenrecht' and 'Berg-recht' see the admirable study of E. Schönbauer, 'Vom Bodenrecht zum Bergrecht', *Z. d. Sav.-Stift.* lv (1935), pp. 183 ff. and esp. pp. 221 ff. It is a pity that Schönbauer's article does not deal with the status of mines, quarries, &c. in the East and in the Hellenistic monarchies.

[103] It is interesting to find what exact information Theophrastus had about the vegetation of Egypt. He probably received it from Demetrius of Phalerum, i.e. through him from the botanists of the Museum who probably made—on behalf of the king?—a thorough study of the flora of the country. On the 'forestry' of the Ptolemies, see my remarks on the passage of *Teb.* 703 quoted in the text, cf. F. Heichelheim, loc. cit. 188 (ξυλική), and C. Préaux, *L'Écon. Lag.*, pp. 159 ff. (le bois). An unpublished Oxford papyrus which Mr. C. H. Roberts has kindly shown me (time of Philadelphus, 251/0 B.C.) speaks of ἐπιχώρια ξύλα being used for building warships.

[104] I refer here again to the article by F. Heichelheim, 'Monopole' in *P.W.K.* xvi, which I have quoted repeatedly in the previous notes, and to the still more detailed treatment of all the revenues of the Ptolemies in the book by Mlle C. Préaux, *L'Économie Royale des Lagides*, 1939, which I have also often quoted before. In these two studies the reader will find exhaustive citations of sources and of modern contributions to the problem. As regards the difficult question of the origin of the monopolies, see F. Heichelheim, loc. cit.; C. Préaux, loc. cit., pp. 430 ff., and especially the paper of the late A. Andreades, 'De l'origine des monopoles Ptolémaïques', *Mél. Maspero*, ii, 1934-7, pp. 289 ff. I am inclined to think—and in this I am supported by Andreades—that the most important monopolies of the Ptolemies were organized on pre-existing local patterns which were remodelled in conformity with the general needs of the Ptolemies and with their guiding economic principles. These last have been well formulated by Mlle Préaux: accumulation of wealth, reduction of expenditure, introduction of as few changes as possible in the economic structure of Egypt, and avoidance of risk. The little we know of the organization of industry in pre-Ptolemaic Egypt has been collected and discussed by H. Kees, *Aegypten*, pp. 162 ff., and especially p. 213 on textiles. The material collected by Kees shows that the artisans were divided into two groups: one working for the king directly, and another scattered among the villages and cities of Egypt which delivered part of its produce to the treasury of the king.

[105] We are very poorly informed about the organization of Egyptian guilds in general, and especially those of workmen who were in the service of the royal monopolies and were thus ἐπιπεπλεγμένοι ταῖς προσόδοις. M. San Nicolò, in his valuable book *Aegyptisches Vereinswesen z. Zeit der Ptolemäer und Römer*, i, 1913, and ii. 1, 1915, has collected the material bearing on them in the first volume, but has never attempted (in either volume) sharply to discriminate between the native guilds that the Ptolemies inherited from the past and the new Greek associations, some of them of a professional character. Nor does he distinguish between the various native guilds, those which were and those which were not in the service of the State. Finally, he does not separate material relating to the Ptolemaic period from that relating to Roman times. The problem of the various types of associations in Ptolemaic Egypt needs renewed investigation. In my opinion the native associations must not be confused with the Greek guilds and must be divided into two

groups: the free, almost exclusively religious associations, connected with the temples (a common phenomenon in the East generally), which gradually assumed a Greek character, and local groups of men working for the king in agriculture and industry and organized as such by the State into kinds of professional, probably compulsory, guilds with their own representatives and a certain amount of corporative organization. One and the same person could belong to various professional groups of this sort, the most natural combination being that of a royal peasant or landholder in general and a workman in one or other field of industry (see for example *Teb.* 833 and the lists in W. Peremans, *Vreemdelingen* etc., pp. 135 ff.). On the other hand, groups of professional men could form a religious association or an entertainment group of Greco-Egyptian character. On the religious native associations of the Ptolemaic period see C. Roberts, Th. C. Skeat, A. D. Nock, 'The Guild of Zeus Hypsistos', *Harv. Theol. Rev.*, xxix (1936), pp. 72 ff., cf. A. E. R. Boak, 'The organization of Gilds in Greco-Roman Egypt', *Tr. Am. Phil. Ass.*, lxviii (1937), pp. 212 ff., and on the professional guilds W. Peremans, *Vreemdelingen* etc., p. 88. The existence of professional associations in pre-Ptolemaic Egypt was noticed by Hecataeus of Abdera (Diod. I. 74) and Herodotus (II, 64), cf. H. Kees, *Aegypten*, pp. 164, 255. As regards the guilds in the service of royal monopolies, I may quote a papyrus of the Rainer collection at Vienna (Gr. 12922 b) mentioned by H. Gerstinger, *Atti IV Congr. Pap.*, p. 310. It is a complaint of the λινεῖφοί to Apollonius, the *strategos* and συγγενής, against outsiders who have tried to intrude into the guild. It shows that the members of the guild regarded their position as a priviliged one.

[106] In addition to the bibliography quoted by Heichelheim and C. Préaux, cf. the latter's paper in *Atti IV Congr. Pap.*, pp. 184 f., on the ἐλαϊκή and the alleged contradiction between the law and current practice, as illustrated by *P. Cairo Zen.* 59015. I must confess that I see no such contradiction, nor does C. C. Edgar in his detailed comments (*Select. Pap.* no. 75, *Ann. du Serv.* xxiii, pp. 86 ff.): import of olive-oil into Alexandria was not prohibited, and we do not know what happened to the oil imported by Apollonius after he had paid the customs duties. Cf. p. 385 and n. 184. On μάγειροι (meat-dealers and butchers), my *Large Estate*, p. 121; *P. Ryl. Zen.* 9, cf. U. Wilcken, *Arch. Pap.* xi (1935), p. 290, and vi (1927), p. 79 f. and C. Préaux, loc. cit., p. 229.

[107] Information on the retail sale of ὀθόνια may be derived from *Teb.* 733 (143/2 B.C.), if K. F. W. Schmidt, *Phil. Woch.*, 1934, p. 1313, is right in his restoration and interpretation of the fragmentary document, esp. l. 4 f.: τοῦ[ἐ]ξειλη-φότος τὴ[ν δ]ιά[θε]σιν τοῦ ⟨ὀ⟩θ⟨ονίου⟩ | αὐτῆς. Palaeographically the restoration is very hazardous. Moreover διάθεσις τοῦ ὀθονίου is hardly possible: one would expect τῶν ὀθονίων; Hunt suggests tentatively τοῦ ἐρίου. On βυσσουργοί *Teb.* 702 (260 B.C.), an interesting official letter of a man who was concerned with, and disturbed about, arrears due from the βυσσουργοί of a temple. The early date makes the text doubly interesting. The βυσσ-ουργοί were apparently under the control of the government as early as 260 B.C. The evidence on the linen production of the *dorea* of Apollonius is

contradictory and cannot be discussed here. For a detailed discussion I may refer to C. Préaux, *L'Écon. Lag.*, pp. 95 ff. Apollonius may have had in Philadelphia weaving-shops which worked in part for the king and in part supplied the needs of Apollonius himself and his household. Cf. Ch. VIII.

[108] New information on the production of woollens on the estates of Apollonius is furnished by the very interesting letters of the Zenon correspondence *P. Mich. Zen.* 13 and *P. Col. Zen.* 15 and 17, cf. the introductions of C. C. Edgar and W. L. Westermann to these papyri, and C. C. Edgar, *P. Mich. Zen.*, Intr., p. 37. I must confess that I fail to understand why Westermann is sceptical about the existence of wool factories in Philadelphia and Memphis, owned or controlled by Apollonius and Zenon. The appearance of an ἀντιγραφεύς in the letters quoted above and the fact that he was closely connected with the shops confirms me in my impression that the wool factories of Apollonius formed part of the ἐριηρά, and were under the supervision of the *oikonomos* and his *antigrapheus* and of special contractors and their *antigrapheis*. Whether the Apollonides of the letters (cf. *P. Mich. Zen.* 22 and 24) was the *antigrapheus* of the nome or the *antigrapheus* of the ὠνή cannot be said. However, we know that the *antigrapheis* of the nome and the ὠναί were both concerned with the work done in the shops. If Apollonides was the *antigrapheus* of the ὠνή, my suggestion (rejected by C. C. Edgar) that Zenon himself may have been contractor of the ἐριηρά (acting for Apollonius?) gains in probability.

A detailed account of the συρίαι and of the wool factories in the *doreai* of Apollonius will be found in C. Préaux, *L'Écon. Lag.*, pp. 106 ff. On the taxes connected with the production, management, and sale of textiles, C. Préaux, loc. cit., p. 115 f.

[109] On the production of beer, see F. Heichelheim and C. Préaux. The most instructive documents connected with brewers are several letters in the correspondence of Zenon which deal with the affairs of two successive brewers in the beer-shop of Philadelphia—Amenneus and Pais: *P. Cairo Zen.* 59199; *P. Mich. Zen.* 36; *P. Col. Zen.* 34; *P. Cairo Zen.* 59202 and 59204. On this subject see my *Large Estate*, p. 118; W. L. Westermann, *P. Col. Zen.*, pp. 84 ff.; C. Préaux, *L'Écon. Lag.*, pp. 152 ff.; E. Balogh, *Actes du Vme Congr. Pap.*, pp. 59 ff.

[110] On the salt tax and the ἁλική, in addition to Heichelheim's paragraph, L. Amundsen, *Ostraca Osloensia*, 1933, pp. 1 ff., and C. Préaux, *Les Ostraca grecs . . . Wilbour au Musée de Brooklyn*, 1935, pp. 15 ff., cf. *L'Écon. Lag.*, pp. 249 ff. There are almost no receipts of the ἁλική after Epiphanes. Retail trade in salt: *Teb.* 732 (about 142 B.C.), cf. the interesting document of Claudius' time, A. E. R. Boak, *Am. J. Ph.* lviii (1937), pp. 210 ff. The burdensome character of the salt tax is well illustrated by *P. Cairo Zen.* 59130, of 256 or 254 B.C. A special letter from Apollonius was required to protect his tenants from the collectors of the salt tax. For the Roman period, Wallace, *Taxation*, pp. 183 ff.

[111] In addition to the corresponding paragraph in Heichelheim's article, N. Lewis, *L'Industrie du papyrus dans l'Égypte gréco-romaine*, 1934, and my review of this book in *Gnomon*, xii (1936), pp. 46 ff. ; U. Wilcken, *Arch. Pap.* xi (1935), p. 286 f. ; A. Andreades, 'Τὸ μονοπώλιον τοῦ παπύρου', *Hellenica*, v (1932), pp. 245 ff. ; and C. Préaux, *L'Écon. Lag.*, pp. 187 ff. On the mentality of the Hellenistic period which made 'books' an essential item in the life of the 'intellectuals' of this period, see K. Kerenyi, 'Die Papyri und das Wesen der alexandr. Kultur', *Atti IV Congr. Pap.*, pp. 27 ff., cf. p. 497. On the prices of papyrus in Delos, G. Glotz, 'Le prix du papyrus dans l'antiquité grecque', *Ann. d'hist. éc. et soc.* i (1929), pp. 3 ff., and *Bull. Soc. Arch. Alex.* xxv (1930), pp. 83 ff., and the books and papers quoted above ; cf. J. A. O. Larsen, 'Roman Greece', pp. 396 ff.

[112] On the baths, A. Calderini, *Rend. Ist. Lombardo*, lii (1919), pp. 297 ff., and lvii (1924), pp. 737 ff. ; my *Large Estate*, p. 121 f. ; F. Heichelheim, loc. cit. 163 ; C. Préaux, loc. cit., pp. 338 ff.

[113] On myrrh (σμύρνη) and frankincense (λιβανωτός) and the perfumes made of them (στακτή), see G. Senne, 'Weihrauch u. Myrrhe', *Die Ernte*, v (1927), pp. 161 ff. ; R. O. Steuer, *Myrrhe und Stakte*, 1933 ; G. A. Wainwright, *J.E.A.* xxi (1935), p. 254 f., and especially A. Lucas, ibid. xxiii (1937), pp. 217 ff. Though we possess some documents relating to the handling of these spices in Egypt, no exact knowledge of how they were dealt with can be derived from our evidence, apart from the fact that the ownership of imported spices was the exclusive privilege of the king. See the latest discussions of the problem by F. Heichelheim, loc. cit., and C. Préaux, loc. cit., pp. 368 ff., cf. A. Wilhelm, *J.R.S.* xxvii (1937), pp. 148 ff.

[114] References to the sources which deal with retail trade in the towns and villages of Egypt are given in my comments on the passage of *Teb.* 703 quoted in the text. It is unnecessary to repeat them here.

[115] On transport, my papers 'Kornerhebung und Transport im gr.-röm. Aegypten', *Arch. Pap.* iii (1906), pp. 201 ff. ; 'Angariae', *Klio*, vi (1906), pp. 249 ff. On the postal service, Preisigke, 'Die ptolemäische Staatspost', *Klio*, vii (1907), pp. 241 ff., and Reincke, *P.W.K.* xvi. 1523, art. 'Nachrichtenwesen', cf. in general U. Wilcken, *Grundz.*, pp. 372 ff. and pp. 376 ff. ; F. Heichelheim, *P.W.K.* Suppl. vi. 874, art. 'Sitos', and C. Préaux, *L'Écon. Lag.*, pp. 143 ff. The last two give a good bibliography of the most recent contributions to the subject. For river transport cf. M. Merzagora, 'La navigazione in Egitto nell'età greco-romana', *Aeg.* x (1929), pp. 105 ff., and Stoeckle, *P.W.K.* xvi. 1906 f., art. 'Navicularius'.

Great importance attaches to the paragraph in *Teb.* 703 dealing with the transport of grain from the nomes to Alexandria (ll. 70–87), which was regulated by a special διάγραμμα of the king: cf. my comments on these lines and the suggestions of K. F. W. Schmidt, *Phil. Woch.*, 1934, p. 1307 f. The speeding up of the grain transport (ἐπισπουδασμός) is discussed by H. Henne, *Aeg.* xiii (1933), pp. 383 ff., in connexion with *P.S.I.* 901. ii. His remarks are valuable, though his correction of ἐπιδασμὸς in the document to ἐπισπουδασμὸς is unnecessary (cf. δασμός, ἀειδασμός and similar formations). On the corporations of ὀνηλάται in the third century B.C. see *P. Enteux.* 38 (Philopator). In this document a χειριστής of a bank hires from an ὀνηλάτης eighty-three donkeys to transport βασιλικὰ χρήματα. Cf. my remarks on the *naucleroi*, *Large Est.*, p. 125, and C. Préaux, loc. cit., p. 145 f. On impressing natives for service on ships, see my remarks on *Teb.* 703, ll. 215–22. Postal service connected with the hunting of elephants, below p. 384. I may note in this connexion that the practice of impressing the population for the transport service was inherited from the Ptolemies by the Romans and remained one of the most dreaded burdens. Soon after the Roman occupation we have a well-known series of orders by the Roman rulers designed to put an end to the abuses. See my *Storia soc. ed econ.*, p. 409 and p. 435, and the new edition of the edict of Cn. Vergilius Capito (49 A.D.) by P. Jouguet, *Atti IV Congr. Pap.*, pp. 4 ff., and his notes on paragraphs 1 and 2 of this edict.

[116] U. Wilcken, *Grundz.*, pp. 356 ff. cf. C. Préaux, *L'Écon. Lag.*, p. 328. On the 'purchased' grain, also called σῖτος βασιλικός, see in addition to U. Wilcken, loc. cit., my remarks in *J.E.A.* vi (1920), p. 175, and *Large estate*, p. 90; C. C. Edgar, *P. Cairo Zen.* 59001; cf. Preisigke, *Wörterb.*, *s.v.*; F. Heichelheim 'Sitos' *P.W.K.*, Suppl. vi. 869 ff.; and C. Préaux, *L'Écon. Lag.*, pp. 141 ff.

[117] On the system of Ptolemaic taxation and the classification of taxes, U. Wilcken, *Ostraca*, i, pp. 199 ff., and *Grundz.*, pp. 169 ff., cf. 'Alexander' &c., *Schmollers Jahrb.* xlv (1920), pp. 81 (385) ff. Our main source of information is the body of tax receipts on paper and sherds (*ostraca*). A complete list of publications of the Greek *ostraca* will be found in C. Préaux, *Les Ostraca grecs . . . Wilbour du Musée de Brooklyn*, 1935, p. 12 f., and *l'Écon. Lag.*, p. 575. Mlle Préaux's introduction to the publication of the *ostraca* of Brooklyn and her introductory remarks on the various groups of *ostraca* contain many interesting ideas on the character of the Ptolemaic and Roman systems of taxation in Egypt. She has, for example, made it probable that in early Ptolemaic Egypt there was no general poll-tax similar to the Roman λαογραφία, cf. *L'Écon. Lag.*, esp. pp. 382 ff., and H. I. Bell, *J.E.A.* xxiii (1937), pp. 135 ff. On Greek taxation in general cf. Schwahn, art. Τέλη and Τελῶναι, *P.W.K.* v A. 326 ff. and 418 ff. On the customs duties and other duties connected with them, A. Andreades, 'Des droits de douane prélevés par les Lagides sur le commerce extérieur', *Mél. Glotz*, 1932, pp. 7 ff. For the customs duties within Egypt, see the oath taken by a ship-captain *P. Cairo Zen.* 59289, cf. *B.G.U.* 1792 and Mitteis, *Chrest.* 340, and in general L. Fiesel, 'Geleitszölle im griechisch-römischen Ägypten,' *Gött. Nach.*, 1925, pp. 57 ff., cf. N. Y. Clauson, *Aeg.* ix (1928), pp. 240 ff. On ἐγκύκλιον, W. L. Westermann, *Upon slavery in Ptolemaic Egypt*, p. 61, cf. *Teb.* 811, and Westermann's art. 'Sklaverei', *P.W.K.*, Suppl. vi. 939.

[118] On the βασιλικοὶ γεωργοί and the ἐπιπεπλεγμένοι ταῖς προσόδοις see above, and n. 88, cf. my *Kolonat*, pp. 62 ff.; U. Wilcken, *Grundz.*, p. 248 f. and

p. 276 f.; *U.P.Z.* i, no. 110, p. 491, comm. on l. 97 (ὑποτελεῖς) and no. 119, p. 560 f., comm. on ll. 23 and 32–4, and my remarks in *J.E.A.* vi (1920), pp. 166 ff., which I do not maintain in full, cf. note 105 above (on the guilds). Cf. the sound statements regarding the freedom enjoyed by the class in question in the time of Philadelphus made by W. L. Westermann, 'Egyptian agricultural labour under Ptolemy Philadelphus', *Agricultural History*, i. 1 (1927), p. 46 f., and the judicious considerations regarding the mentality of the λαοί in Egypt advanced by C. Préaux, 'Restrictions à la liberté du travail dans l'Égypte gr. et rom.', *Chr. d'Ég.* x (20) (1935), pp. 343 ff. However, the liberty of the labouring classes in the time of Philadelphus was not complete and was bound to give way gradually to still more constraint in later times, cf. Chs. V and VI. On the λαοί and their enslavement in case of failure to satisfy fiscal claims, see the πρόσταγμα of Philadelphus for Syria and Phoenicia regarding the unlawful and lawful enslavement of Syrian λαοί, H. Liebesny, *Aeg.* xvi (1936), col. I, ll. 33 ff., and col. II, ll. I ff., and commentary, pp. 271 ff. and esp. pp. 275 ff. The only ground for legal enslavement is set forth in col. II, ll. 18 ff.: πλὴν τῶν ὑπὸ τοῦ διοικοῦντος | τὰς κατὰ Συρίαν καὶ Φοινίκην προσόδους ἐν προσ|βολῆι διδ[ο]μένων, ὧν ἡ πρᾶξις καθήκει καὶ ἐκ τοῦ | σώματος γίνεσθαι, καθότι ἐν τῶι νόμωι τῶι | ἐπὶ τῆς μισθώσεως γέγραπται. On the responsibility of the officials of various grades, especially their material responsibility, an institution which played an enormously important role in the economic and social life of Egypt, see C. Préaux, *L'Écon. Lag.*, pp. 444 ff.

[119] On the employment of slaves and their numbers in Ptolemaic Egypt, see W. L. Westermann, *P.W.K.* Suppl. vi. 932 f., art. 'Sklaverei'. I am afraid, however, that Westermann underestimates the numbers in early Ptolemaic times. The seven male Syrians who worked with their families in the vineyards of Apollonius (τοῖς πρὸς τοῖς κτήμασι γινομένοις) in *P. Cairo Zen.* 59292, ll. 52 ff. (grain account), cf. *P. Mich. Zen.* 49, were most probably slaves (see C. C. Edgar against Westermann, *Pol. Sc. Quart.* xl (1925), p. 536). To the list of slaves mentioned in the Zenon correspondence, as given by Westermann, must be added *P. Cairo Zen.* 59080 (Iollas the weaver), 59335 (runaway παιδίσκη with her child, cf. *Hamb.* 105), 59374 (Carian slave of Philammon, a ξεναγός, named Sappho), 59442 (runaway slave). These are certain cases. But it is well known that the terms δοῦλος and ἀνδράποδον were very seldom used in Ptolemaic Egypt. Σῶμα, παῖς, παιδάριον, παιδίσκη are used in Egypt in Ptolemaic times both for slaves and for free labourers. It is therefore difficult to decide which of the σώματα, &c., who appear in Zenon's accounts (see e.g. the Index to *P. Cairo Zen.* iv) are slaves and which are hired labourers. Cf. C. Préaux, *Chr. d'Ég.* xi (22) (1936), pp. 590 ff., and *L'Écon. Lag.*, pp. 303 ff.

On the brisk traffic in slaves in Syria and Phoenicia, on the enslavement of natives of these countries, and on the importation of slaves thence into Egypt, see below, pp. 341 ff. Treatment of the slaves from the juridical point of view: R. Taubenschlag, 'Das Sklavenrecht im Rechte der Papyri', *Z. d. Sav.-Stift.* l (1930), pp. 140 ff., and *Atti IV Congr. Pap.*, pp. 259 ff. Cf.

V. Arangio-Ruiz, *Persone e Famiglia nel diritto dei Papiri*, 1930, pp. 1 ff., and
E. Seidl, *Krit. Vierteljahresschrift*, xxv (1932), pp. 306 ff. On the ἐλεύθερα
σώματα treated as slaves in Egypt see W. L. Westermann, *Upon Slavery in
Ptolemaic Egypt*, p. 20 ff. (*P. Col. Inv.* 480, ll. 24–6 and 27–8), cf. his article
in *Am. J. Ph.* lix (1938), pp. 10 ff., where he compares these enslaved σώματα
ἐλεύθερα of Egypt with the σώματα λαϊκὰ ἐλεύθερα of the Vienna document
(below, p. 341). Cf. also C. Préaux *L'Écon. Lag.*, pp. 307 ff., 539 ff. It appears
very probable to me that conditions in Egypt and Syria were similar, and
that in both cases the Ptolemies dealt with various forms of bondage transformed by certain private transactions into regular slavery. The law of
slavery in pre-Ptolemaic Egypt and the relations between Greek slavery and
the various types of bondage are as little known in Egypt as they are in Syria
and Mesopotamia. Prohibition or restriction of export of slaves from Egypt:
P. Lille 29; Mitteis, *Chrest.* 369: μηθένι ἐξέστω σώματα πωλεῖν [ἐπ'] ἐξαγωγῆι . . .
The lacuna after the last word of this quotation prevents us from knowing
whether the export of slaves from Egypt was altogether forbidden or was permitted under certain conditions. Restrictions imposed on the export of slaves
from Syria: *P. Cairo Zen.* 59093. A new interpretation of this letter, which
I cannot discuss here, has been suggested by V. Tscherikower, 'Palestine under
the Ptolemies', *Mizraim*, iv–v (1937), pp. 18 ff. and pp. 68 ff. Tscherikower's interpretation has not convinced me, cf. Westermann, *Am. J. Ph.*, lix (1938), p. 18.

120 On the priests and 'sacred slaves' see above, note 90. On the ἀλειτουργία
of even the minor priests, *P. Cairo Zen.* 59451.

121 The position of foreigners in Egypt in early and late Ptolemaic times is one
of the fundamental problems of the history of Ptolemaic Egypt and is therefore
discussed by almost all the historians. Collection and discussion of evidence
bearing on the problem, begun by A. Calderini, 'Ricerche etnografiche sui
Papiri Greco-Egizî', *Studi della Sc. Pap.* iii (1920), pp. 3 ff., have been carried
on by F. Heichelheim, 'Die auswärtige Bevölkerung im Ptolemäerreich', 1925
(*Klio*, Beiheft V (xviii)), who publishes additions to his list of foreigners,
loc. cit., pp. 83 ff., in *Arch. Pap.* ix (1930), pp. 47 ff., and xii (1936), pp. 54 ff.
and by W. Peremans, *Vreemdelingen en Egyptenaren in Vroeg-Ptolemaeisch
Egypte*, 1937; cf. W. Matthes, *Prosopographie der ägyptischen Deltagaue* &c.,
1932. There are some acute and judicious remarks on the situation of the
'Hellenes' in Egypt in E. Bickermann, 'Der Heimatsvermerk und die staats-
rechtliche Stellung der Hellenen im ptolemäischen Aegypten', *Arch. Pap.* viii
(1927), pp. 216 ff.; cf. against his view E. Schönbauer, *Z. d. Sav.-Stift.* xlix
(1929), pp. 345 ff.; V. Arangio-Ruiz, *Persone e Famiglia*, &c., 1930, pp. 23 ff.,
and W. Peremans, loc. cit., pp. 9 ff. On the problem in general, C. Préaux,
'Politique de race ou politique royale', *Chr. d'Ég.* xi (21) (1936), pp. 111 ff.;
and on special problems, E. Kornemann, 'Das "Hellenentum" der Makedonen in Aegypten', *Aeg.* xiii (1933), pp. 644 ff.; A. Neppi Modona, Πέρσαι
τῆς ἐπιγονῆς 'ἀγώγιμοι', ibid., pp. 472 ff.; A. Segré, 'Note sullo status civitatis
degli Ebrei nell'Egitto Tolemaico ed Imperiale', *Bull. de la Soc. Arch.
d'Alex.* xxviii (1933), pp. 143 ff.; O. Montevecchi, 'Ricerche di sociologia'

&c., *Aeg.* xvi (1936), p. 32, cf. C. Préaux, *Chr. d'Ég.* xii (23) (1937), p. 120 (on intermarriage). On πολίτευμα, besides Bickermann and Schönbauer, W. Ruppel, 'Politeuma', *Phil.* lxxxii (1927), pp. 269 ff.; A. Wilhelm, *Arch. Pap.* ix (1930), pp. 214 ff.; P. Zancan, *Il monarcato ellenistico,* &c., p. 85; R. Taubenschlag, *Atti IV Congr. Pap.,* p. 259, note 4.

On law and jurisdiction, E. Berneker, *Die Sondergerichtsbarkeit im griechischen Recht Aegyptens,* 1935, cf. E. Balogh, *Act. Vᵉ Congr. Pap.,* pp. 21 ff. and C. Préaux, loc. cit., p. 117 f.; R. Taubenschlag, 'Die Geschichte d. Rezeption d. gr. Privatrechts in Aegypten', *Atti IV Congr. Pap.,* pp. 259 ff., cf. E. Schönbauer, ibid., pp. 434 ff., and his article 'Reichsrecht, Volksrecht und Provinzialrecht', *Z. d. Sav.-Stift.* vii (1937), pp. 309 ff., esp. pp. 315 ff. See also R. Taubenschlag, 'The ancient Greek city-laws in Ptolemaic Egypt', *Actes Vᵉ Congr. Pap.,* pp. 171 ff. The problem of law and jurisdiction that confronted the Ptolemies was very similar to that which faces the administration of modern colonies, e.g. the colonies, dependencies, and mandatory territories of France in Africa, Syria, and the Far East. In such places native laws often conflict with those of the ruling country, and the decisive word is always with the central government. Laws and orders of the French government may be compared with the νόμοι, προστάγματα, διαγράμματα, &c., of the Ptolemies (R. Taubenschlag, *Atti IV Congr. Pap.,* p. 260, note 5), see R. Maunier, *Sociologie Coloniale,* i, 1932, and ii, 1936.

On the Greek γυμνάσια in the χώρα see the remarks of H. Henne, P. Jouguet and O. Guéraud on the subject of a petition concerning a gymnasium at Samareia in the Fayûm, H. Henne, *Bull. de l'Inst. Fr. d'Arch. or.* xxii (1923), pp. 191 ff.; P. Jouguet, *Raccolta Ramorino,* 1927, pp. 381 ff.; O. Guéraud, *P. Enteux.* 8 (first year of Philopator), and the references to sources contained in these papers, cf. *S.E.G.* viii 357 (3rd/2nd cent. B.C.) and 504 (2nd cent. B.C.). On the gymnasium of Philadelphia, *B.G.U.* 1256 and *P.S.I.* 391; of Aphroditopolis, P. Roussel, *Mél. Maspero,* ii (1934), pp. 33 ff. (*Mem. Inst. Fr. Arch. Or. du Caire,* lxvii), *S.E.G.* viii. 531 (57/6 B.C.). On that of an unknown place, the inscription *S.B.* 7246, *S.E.G.* viii. 694 (third–second century B.C.), discussed by Henne, loc. cit. On the gymnasia of the villages in general, W. Zucker, Γυμνασίαρχος κώμης, *Aeg.* xi (1931), pp. 485 ff. Cf. on the gymnasium of Ptolemais (?) H. Kortenbeutel, *Arch. Pap.* xii (1936), pp. 44 ff., *S.E.G.* viii. 641 (104 B.C.), and on the earliest known gymnasiarch of Alexandria. *S.E.G.* ii. 864. On the gymnasia of Ptolemaic Egypt in general, T. A. Brady, 'The Gymnasium in Ptolemaic Egypt', *Univ. of Missouri St.* ii. (1936), pp. 9 ff. Gymnasia and other corporations of Alexandria owning land in the *chora: Teb.* 700. Οἱ ἐκ τοῦ γυμνασίου: *S.E.G.* viii. 504, 531, 641, 694. On the Greek and native clubs and associations, M. San Nicolò, *Aegyptisches Vereinswesen zur Zeit der Ptolemäer und Römer,* i, ii, 1913, 1915, cf. his article 'Zur Vereinsgerichtsbarkeit im hellenistischen Aegypten' in 'Επιτύμβιον H. Swoboda, 1927, pp. 255 ff., and the comments of C. Roberts, Th. C. Skeat and A. D. Nock, *Harv. Theol. Rev.* xxix (1936), pp. 39 ff., on a fragment of a νόμος of a religious κοινόν of the time of Auletes (69–58 B.C.), esp. pp. 72 ff. On the native guilds cf. above, note 105, and below, Ch. VIII.

I cannot enter here into a discussion of the question which appears to modern scholars the fundamental problem of Ptolemaic history: Was the policy of the Ptolemies 'royal policy' or 'racial policy'? I am afraid that this antinomy is almost wholly imaginary. The policy of the Ptolemies was chiefly a personal and dynastic policy. Egypt was their οἶκος and their base, and they endeavoured, without theoretical preconceptions, to establish their personal power in Egypt firmly and to make it as strong as possible, using all the means at their disposal as circumstances required. If they had racial *feelings*, they never allowed them to influence their *policy*.

122 The correspondence of Zenon is a mine of information on this point. I cannot here treat in detail the important problem of the relations between 'clients' and 'patrons' in the early Ptolemaic time. They were, at least in part, a heritage of the past (H. Kees, *Aegypten*, p. 214). I may quote e.g. *P. Cairo Zen.* 59322, where Criton protects a certain Democrates before Moschion (probably an official of high standing) giving as his reason, l. 9: ἔστιγ γὰρ παρ' ἡμῶν. There are many such cases, referring mostly to the relations between Greeks of higher and lower standing. Another aspect of patronage is the protection (σκέπη) lent by various higher or lower officials to men who were working for them or were otherwise bound to them, see e.g. the famous letter of Apollonius, *P. Cairo Zen.* 59130, in which he protects his farmers from the collectors of the salt-tax, or the petition of the cat-feeders, 'sacred slaves' (ἱερόδουλοι) of Bubastis, *P. Cairo Zen.* 59451, in which they protest against a liturgy imposed on them because those who had to perform it were protected by an official, cf. *P. Cairo Zen.* 59307; *P. Hib.* 35. 8, and 95. 9. The problem as regards early Ptolemaic times needs careful investigation. Some acute remarks on it will be found in C. Préaux, 'Réflexions sur les droits supérieurs de l'État dans l'Égypte Lagide', *Chr. d'Ég.* x (19) (1935), pp. 109 ff. On later times see below, Chs. V and VI.

123 See the interesting calculations of A. Segré and C. Préaux (*L'Éc. Lag.*, pp. 133 ff.) relating to the moderate income of a 'royal peasant' from his plot of land as compared with the considerable profit made—at the expense of the actual labourers—by the owners of *doreai* from their cultivated land.

124 See the famous decree of the priests of Egypt (*stele* of Pithom) in honour of Philopator, published by H. Gauthier and H. Sottas, *Un Décret trilingue en honneur de Ptolémée IV*, 1925, and by W. Spiegelberg und W. Otto, *Bay. S.B.*, 1925, 4, cf. H. Sottas, *Rev. de l'Ég. Anc.* i (1927), pp. 230 ff., and the translation by E. Bevan in *History of Egypt under the Ptolemaic Dynasty*, 1927, pp. 388 ff. (Fr. transl. *Histoire des Lagides*, 1934, pp. 263 ff.). The passage I have in mind says: 'he (the king) has incurred huge expense for his military expedition, giving gold crowns to his army to the amount of 300,000 gold pieces'. For the inscription at Gaza, above, Ch. III, n. 7.

125 On tax-farming in Egypt, my *Geschichte der Staatspacht*, &c., 1902 (*Philol.*, Suppl. ix), and U. Wilcken, *Ostraca*, i, pp. 650 ff., and *Grundz.*, pp. 182 ff.; cf. my remarks in *Woch. f. kl. Phil.* xvii (1900), pp. 115 ff. The subject has been

treated again recently by G. McLean Harper Jr., 'Tax-contractors and their relations to Tax-collection in Ptolemaic Egypt', *Aeg.* xiv (1934), pp. 49 ff., and 'The relation of ἀρχώνης, μέτοχοι and ἔγγυοι to each other', &c., ibid., pp. 269 ff.; cf. R. Taubenschlag, 'Die societas negotiationis im Rechte der Papyri', *Z. d. Sav.-Stift.* lii (1932), pp. 64 ff., and A. Steinwenter, 'Aus dem Gesellschaftsrecht der Papyri', *Studi Riccobono*, i 1932, pp. 487 ff. See also the art. 'Manceps' by A. Steinwenter, *P.W.K.* xiv. 987 ff. and those of Schwahn, Νόμος τελωνικός, ibid. xvii. 843 f., and Τελῶναι, ibid. v a. 418 ff. On the development of the institution in Egypt C. Préaux, *L'Écon. Lag.*, pp. 450 ff. (la ferme). Cf. the general sketch on tax-farming by L. Walter, *Bay. S. B.*, 1935, pp. 33 ff.

[126] A. Segré, 'Note sull'economia dell'Egitto ellenistico nell'età Tolemaica', *Bull. Soc. Arch. Alex.* xxix (1934), pp. 265 ff. I cannot agree with his calculation of the strength of the Greek part of the army at Raphia. Quoting Polybius (v. 65), he says that the army at Raphia consisted of 77,000 Greek horse and foot and of 20,000 Egyptians 'which presupposes a population of 70,000 adult male Greeks in Egypt able to carry arms'. Now the first of these figures is wrong. According to Polybius the army consisted of the following Greek detachments resident in Egypt: ἄγημα 3,000, πελτασταί 2,000, φάλαγξ 25,000, ἱππεῖς περὶ αὐλὴν 700, Θρᾳκες καὶ Γαλάται κάτοικοι καὶ ἐπίγονοι 4,000, in all 34,700. The ten thousand Greek mercenaries were in part recently recruited in Greece, while the rest, before being summoned to Egypt, probably formed the garrisons of the Ptolemaic cities outside Egypt—ἔξω πόλεις. They were not residents in Egypt. Add to these 3,000 Cretans and 2,000 recently recruited Thracians and Galatians. The rest were Libyans and Egyptians. The maximum of 'the male adult Greeks able to carry arms' (incidentally a misleading expression, since we do not know how many such Greeks there were who were not κληροῦχοι and thus exempt from military service) will therefore be half the figure given by Segré. Moreover, he does not take into consideration that many modern scholars interpret the figures of Polybius in a quite different way from that formerly current. J. P. Mahaffy (*Hermathena*, x (1897–9), pp. 140 ff.), followed with some modifications of his views by W. W. Tarn (*C.A.H.* vii, p. 730), and G. T. Griffith (*The Mercenaries of the Hellenistic world*, 1935, p. 122) are inclined to regard the two phalanxes of Polybius—the Greek and the Egyptian—as one and the same, consisting of 20,000 Egyptians and 5,000 Greco-Macedonians. It is difficult otherwise to explain why the victory of Raphia should be ascribed to the Egyptian phalanx. If this is the right interpretation, we must deduct 20,000 from our figure, which leaves about 15,000 Macedonian and Greek soldiers settled in Egypt. To these may be added some Macedonians and Greeks left in Egypt on military duty and a certain number of mercenaries settled in Egypt.

[127] On the foreign dominions of the early Ptolemies, D. Cohen, *De magistratibus Aegyptiis externas Lagidarum regni provincias administrantibus* (no date) and my remarks, *C.A.H.* vii, pp. 126 ff.; cf. V. Ehrenberg, 'Der griechische und der hellenistische Staat' (Gercke u. Norden, *Einl.* iii. 3), pp. 85 ff. Some

scattered remarks on the subject will be found in P. Zancan, *Il monarcato ellenistico* &c., 1934, and in A. Heuss, *Stadt und Herrscher*, 1937.

[128] On Cyrene my *Storia Econ. e Soc. d. Imp. Rom.* 1933, pp. 361 ff. An interesting inscription bearing on the organization of villages in Cyrenaica has been recently published by G. Oliverio, *Doc. ant. dell'Africa Italiana,* ii, Cirenaica, i 1933, p. 126, n. 135, cf. P. Roussel, *Mél. Navarre,* 1935, pp. 375 ff. and *S.E.G.* ix. 354 (1st cent. B.C.). The κώμη had an administration and liturgies of its own and a large storehouse for grain (σιτών). In general Cyrenaica was a country of many villages and very few cities. So it was in Hellenistic times and so it remained until the Byzantine period, see the comments of Oliverio on the decree of Anastasius, *Doc. ant. dell' Afr. Ital.,* ii, Cirenaica, ii, 1936, p. 161; *S.E.G.* ix. 356. On the χώρα βασιλική our evidence is confined to Roman times, Oliverio, ibid., ii, 1, pp. 128 ff.; *S.E.G.* ix. 352 and 360.

I cannot deal here with the relations between the kings of Egypt and the cities of Cyrenaica, esp. Cyrene itself. See the well-known inscriptions found at Cyrene: the so-called constitution of Cyrene (*S.E.G.* ix. 1), the 'testament' of Euergetes II (*S.E.G.* ix. 7), and the edicts of Augustus (*S.E.G.* ix. 8)— a full bibliography of these three famous inscriptions will be found in *S.E.G.*— and finally the inscription of the late 2nd cent. B.C. (*S.E.G.* ix. 5) dealt with below, ch. VI, n. 157.

[129] The inscriptions of the time of Philometor found at Thera have been published by F. Hiller von Gaertringen, *I.G.* xii. 3. 327 (and addenda) and 466, 467 (=*O.G.I.* 59, 102 and 110); cf. *I.G.* xii. 3. 468; *O.G.I.* 112. The financial administration of Thera was closely connected with its military organization. Thus in *I.G.* xii. 3. 327, the king grants the soldiers the income from some confiscated estates. This is done by an order given to the *dioecetes* of Alexandria, the confiscation being carried out by the local *oeconomus*. In *I.G.* xii. 3. 466, cf. 467, the *oeconomus* of Thera is next in authority to the military governor of the island (ὁ τεταγμένος ἐπὶ Θήρας). He is at the same time the secretary of the garrison, his functions extending also to Crete and to Arsinoe in the Peloponnese: ὁ γραμμα[τεὺ]ς τῶν κατὰ Κρήτην | καὶ Θήρα[ν κ]αὶ ᾿Αρσινόην | τὴν ἐν [Πε]λοποννήσωι | στρατιω[τ]ῶν καὶ μαχίμων | καὶ οἰκον[όμ]ος τῶν αὐτῶν τόπων. On the date of these inscriptions, cf. F. Hiller von Gaertringen, *Klio,* xvii (1920–1), p. 94, and U. Wilcken, *U.P.Z.* i, p. 496. In general see Hiller von Gaertringen, *Die Insel Thera,* p. 168 f., 173, and my *Staatspacht,* p. 361 (33), n. 59, cf. Hiller von Gaertringen, 'Thera', *P.W.K.* v A. 2296 ff.

On Crete see the inscriptions from Itanus, *S.E.G.* ii. 512 (265 B.C.), cf. *O.G.I.* 45; *G.D.I.* 5059; *S.I.G.*³ 463 (about 246 B.C.); *O.G.I.* 119; M. Guarducci, *Hist.* v (1931), pp. 226 ff. (time of Epiphanes). Methana: Hiller von Gaertringen, ᾿Εφ. ᾿Αρχ., 1925–6, pp. 68 ff.

A garrison was kept by the Ptolemies in the island of Samos until 192 B.C.: see the inscriptions discussed by L. Robert, *Études épigr. et phil.* 1938, pp. 113 ff. The well-known decree in honour of Bulagoras (*S.E.G.* i. 366) mentions the dispatch of *theoroi* to Alexandria in the time of Euergetes I and the expenses connected with this mission (travelling expenses of the *theoroi*, sacrificial animals, crowns).

130 On the Ptolemaic navy see my remarks in *C.A.H.* vii, p. 118, and C. Préaux, *L'Écon. Lag.*, pp. 37 ff. (with bibliography). On trierarchy, *P. Cairo Zen.* 59036; Hunt–Edgar, *Sel. Pap.* ii. 410, with the comments on this document by U. Wilcken, 'Zur Trierarchie im Lagidenreich', *Racc. Lumbroso*, 1925, pp. 93 ff. Cf. my paper 'Πλοῖα Θαλάσσια on the Nile', *Ét. déd. à la mém. d'André Andreades*, 1940, pp. 367 ff.

131 A different interpretation of the two documents quoted in the text has been offered by A. Heuss, *Stadt und Herrscher*, p. 130 (Halicarnassus) and p. 92 (Samothrace). As regards Halicarnassus he is at a loss to find a probable explanation of the request of the city, while the acts of the governor of Samothrace he regards as φιλάνθρωπα, benefactions conferred on the city by the king and his governor Hippomedon. In my opinion the request of Halicarnassus is easily explained. The reorganization of the gymnasia involved the city in great expense and forced it to have recourse to a compulsory loan from its own citizens. Since these citizens were responsible for the payment of taxes to the crown (see below), it was natural that the agents of the crown should be concerned about the matter and should have reported it to Alexandria. Cf. A. Wilhelm, *Jahreshefte*, xi (1908), pp. 53 ff., and E. Ziebarth, *Aus d. griech. Schulwesen*, 2nd ed., 1914, pp. 49, 68 ff. In the case of Samothrace, the inscription says explicitly that the city received from the kings the right to import corn and the remission of customs duties, ll. 36, ff.: καὶ σίτου ἐξαγωγὴν καὶ ἀτέλειαν δοῦν[αι | τ]ῆι πόλει (ἐκ) Χερρονήσου καὶ ἄλλοθεν ὅθεν αὐτῶι εὔκαιρον φα[ί]|νηται εἶναι...), a right which it apparently did not possess. This dependence on the king in such a vital matter was certainly an important limitation of the economic freedom of the city.

131a New evidence on Ptolemy, son of Lysimachus, and a full discussion of the problem of his identity and of the history of Telmessus in Ptolemaic and later times, with a complete bibliography, will be found in two recent articles by M. Segre, *Atti IV Congr. Pap.* 1936, pp. 359 ff., and *Clara Rhodos*, ix (1938), p. 179 ff. A fragmentary decree of Telmessus of the time of Philadelphus (between 265 and 257) in honour of a certain Leimon, a friend of Ptolemy, son of Lysimachus (*Clara Rhodos*, ix (1938), p. 183, fig. 1), shows that Ptolemy, son of Lysimachus, was connected with Telmessus long before 240 when he was appointed by Euergetes dynast of the region of which it was the capital. At that time he was probably the holder of a *dorea* in the region of Telmessus, which had been granted to him by Philadelphus (the later *ager Ptolemaei Telmessii*, Liv. xxxvii. 56. 4). The document also makes it probable that Ptolemy was the son of Lysimachus, the king of Thrace, and of Arsinoe, the sister and later queen of Philadelphus. On the later destinies of Telmessus, see below, Ch. V. On Lycia as a Ptolemaic province, M. Segre, *Aeg.* xiv (1934), pp. 253 ff.; cf. above, Ch. I, n. 7 and Ch. III, n. 22.

131b On the inscription see my *Kolonat*, pp. 278 ff., cf. the bibliography in *T.A.M.* ii. 1 and on the enigmatic μετροῦντας νατα (the latter word corrected to (ἔ)νατα), E. Kalinka, *Wien. St.*, 1936, pp. 148 ff.

132 On the story of Josephus see my remarks in *Staatspacht* (*Phil.* Suppl. ix, 1907), pp. 32 (360) ff., cf. E. Meyer, *Ursprung und Anfänge des Christentums*, ii, 1921, pp. 128 ff., 32, and 462, and A. H. M. Jones, *The cities* &c., pp. 240 and 448, note 18 (no use is made of the Vienna papyrus).

132a Important information on the relations between the cities of Caria and Apollonius is contained in *P. Cairo Zen.* 59037 (Halicarnassus), cf. 59036 and esp. 59056. The Apollodotus of these letters was probably the οἰκονόμος or perhaps the local *dioecetes* of Caria. Cf. the well-known inscription from Halicarnassus *O.G.I.* 46; *Gr. Inscr. in the Br. Mus.* iv. 897; A. Wilhelm, *Jahreshefte*, xi (1908), p. 60 f.; see also *Gr. Inscr. in the Br. Mus.* iv. 906 and 907; *O.G.I.* 16; N. Greipl, *Phil.* lxxxv (1929–30), pp. 159 ff.; U. Wilcken, *Arch. Pap.* ix (1928–30), pp. 223 ff. Caunus and Alexandria: *P. Cairo Zen.* 59045 and *P. Col. Zen.* 11, cf. U. Wilcken, *Arch. Pap.* xi (1935), p. 287 f. Calynda: *P. Cairo Zen.* 59036 and 59341.

133 See T. B. Mitford, *Actes du Vme Congrès Pap.*, 1938, pp. 291 ff.; cf. *Arch. Pap.* xiii (1938), pp. 32 ff. Several other new Ptolemaic inscriptions from Cyprus have been published by him: *J.H.S.* lvii (1937), pp. 28 ff.; *Mnemosyne* vi (1938), pp. 103 ff.; and *Arch. Pap.* xiii (1938), pp. 13 ff. Most of them give interesting evidence about the strong contingents of the Ptolemaic army and navy stationed in the island; a few relate to the municipal life of its Hellenized cities. Cf. the inscriptions discussed by L. Robert, *Rev. Phil.* xiii (65) (1939), pp. 153 ff., which testify once more to the important role played by the high officials of the Ptolemies in the social and religious life of the Cyprian cities. On the archaeological aspect of Cyprus in Hellenistic times A. Westholm, *The temples of Soli*, 1936.

134 On Zenon in Palestine and his correspondence with Syria see my *Large Estate*, pp. 24 ff.; G. McL. Harper Jr., *Am. J. Ph.* xlix (1928), pp. 1 ff.; C. C. Edgar, *P. Mich. Zen.* Introd., pp. 15 ff., W. L. Westermann, *P. Col. Zen.* 2 and 3, cf. C. C. Edgar, *Arch. Pap.* xi (1935), p. 219, n. 1; V. Tscherikower, 'Palestine under the Ptolemies', *Mizraim*, 4–5 (1937), pp. 9 ff.

135 H. Liebesny, 'Ein Erlass des Königs Ptolemaios II Philadelphos über die Deklaration von Vieh und Sklaven in Syrien und Phönikien' (*P.E.R.*, Inv. Nr. 24,552 gr.), *Aeg.* xvi (1936), pp. 257 ff.; cf. W. L. Westermann, 'Enslaved persons who are free', *Am. J. Ph.* lix (1938), pp. 1 ff., V. Arangio-Ruiz, *Riv. Fil.* lxv (15), p. 274 f.; U. Wilcken, *Arch. Pap.* xii (1937), p. 223; C. Préaux, *Chr. d'Ég.* xii (24) (1937), pp. 275 ff. and *L'Écon. Lag.*, pp. 312 ff., 540 ff.

136 On the hyparchies, K. J. Beloch, *Gr. Gesch.* iv. 1, p. 394 (cf. iv. 2, p. 364), and my remarks *C.A.H.* vii, p. 166, and *Yale Class. Stud.* ii (1931), pp. 43 ff.; cf. U. Kahrstedt, 'Syrische Territorien in hellenistischer Zeit', *Gött.*

Abh., N. F., xix (1926), ii, pp. 34 ff., esp. pp. 42 ff.; W. W. Tarn, 'Seleucid-Parthian Studies', *Proc. Br. Ac.* xvi (1930), pp. 128 ff.; *Hell. Civ.*, 2nd ed., p. 121; *The Greeks in Bactria and India*, pp. 1 ff. On the Syrian possessions of the Ptolemies, U. Kahrstedt, loc. cit.; W. Otto, 'Beiträge z. Seleukiden-geschichte', *Bay. Abh.* xxxiv (1928), i, pp. 30 ff.; A. H. M. Jones, *The cities* &c., pp. 239 ff. (written without using the Vienna document); and for the earlier administrative division of Syria, O. Leuze, 'Die Satrapieneinteilung in Syrien' &c., *Schr. d. Königsb. Gelehrten Ges.* xi. 4, 1935. Cf. V. Tscherikower, loc. cit., pp. 36 ff.

[137] On the meaning of the term 'Hellenes' in Syria, see below, Ch. VI, n. 130. The λαοί of Syria and Phoenicia are frequently mentioned in the Vienna document. The meaning of the term is under discussion. Soldiers are mentioned in the same document, right col., ll. 12 ff. Philocles of Sidon: Durrbach, *Choix*, pp. 26 ff.; *S.I.G.*³ 390 and 391. On the Hellenized Sidonian aristocracy, see above, p. 227, and my paper in *Klio*, xxx (1937), pp. 70 ff. and E. Biker-man, *Mél. syr. R. Dussaud*, 1939, pp. 91 ff.

There is evidence of four πολιτεύματα in Sidon in the well-known painted Hellenistic *stelae* of the city, showing figures of soldiers and corresponding inscriptions on them: those of Caunians of Caria, of Termessians of Pisidia, of Pinareans of Lycia, and one which cannot be identified. The *stelae* are not dated; the form of letters and the style do not exclude a date as early as the second half of the third century, and the *ethnica* suggest that the soldiers represented on the *stelae* are more probably Ptolemaic than Seleucid mercenaries. However, it is possible that the Seleucids, in the time of Antiochus III and later, used the former Ptolemaic dominions as their recruiting ground. On the character and date of the Sidonian *stelae*, E. Bikerman, *Inst. Sél.*, pp. 88 ff., with bibliography; Griffith, *The Mercenaries &c.*, does not mention the Sidonian *stelae*. The πολιτεύματα of Sidon may have been associations of soldiers, or groups of foreigners in general which were joined by the soldiers who came from the respective cities, see W. Ruppel, 'Politeuma', *Philol.*, lxxxii (1926–7), pp. 310 ff.; cf. L. Robert, *B.C.H.*, lix (1935), p. 428 f. The Sidonian πολιτεύματα are not mentioned by A. H. M. Jones, *The cities* &c. Colonies of Hellenized Sidonians in Palestine: *C.A.H.* vii, p. 191 f., cf. the new interpretation of the name 'Sidonians' by E. Bikerman, *Rev. Hist. Rel.* cxv (1937), pp. 203 ff. This interpretation does not account for *O.G.I.* 593.

[138] See the discussion of this problem in the papers quoted above, n. 135, cf. n. 119. On the purchase of slaves by Zenon, below, n. 140. On the oriental forms of slavery and their connexion with bondage, see above n. 119. On Babylonia see below, Section C. On India, B. Brelocz, *Kauṭalīya-Studien*, ii (1928), pp. 11 ff.

[139] A village contractor is known in Palestine at Bethanath from a letter in Zenon's correspondence *P.S.I.* 554. 13, where he is acting in connexion with some dues in kind (grain or wine) payable by the peasants. In Egypt at Tebtunis (*Teb.* 183) a complaint of a royal peasant is addressed to him. The

rarity of the mention of κωμομισθωταί in Egypt may perhaps be accounted for by assuming that such contractors were an innovation in Egypt, possibly borrowed from the organization of Syria and Palestine. On the κωμομισθωτής, V. Tscherikower, *Palestine* &c., p. 46. On the terms νόμος, διάγραμμα, πρόγραμμα &c., C. B. Welles, *A.J.A.* xlii (1938), pp. 257 ff.

140 I may mention that a προσαγγελία of slaves is referred to in a very interesting letter of Zenon's correspondence (*P. Cairo Zen.* 59093). This registration may have been of a purely fiscal nature and may have been carried out before the customs officers, or it may have been the same registration as is mentioned in the Vienna papyrus. The problem has been discussed recently by W. L. Westermann, *Am. J. Ph.* lix (1938), p. 18, and by V. Tscherikower, loc. cit., pp. 18 ff. and pp. 68 ff. I cannot deal with it here: see above, n. 119. On Zenon's dealings in slaves in general (in Syria and Palestine), V. Tscherikower, loc. cit., pp. 16 ff.

141 Cities of the Ptolemies in Palestine: G. Hölscher, 'Palästina in der persischen und hellenistischen Zeit', 1903 (*Quellen u. Forsch. z. alt. Gesch. u. Geogr.*), pp. 58 ff.; Th. Reinach, *L'Hellénisation du Monde Antique*, 1914, pp. 335 ff.; E. Meyer, *Urspr. u. Anf. d. Christ.* ii (1921), p. 3; A. H. M. Jones, 'The Urbanization of Palestine', *J.R.S.* xxi (1931), pp. 78 ff.; V. Tscherikower, *The Jews and the Greeks in the Hellenistic period*, Tel Aviv, 1930 (in Hebrew), cf. his *Palestine* &c., pp. 43 ff.; A. H. M. Jones, *The cities* &c., pp. 241 ff., and note 20. On Beth Zur, O. P. Sellers, *The Citadel of Beth Zur*, 1933. On Sidonian colonies in Palestine (e.g. Marissa), above n. 137. The general economic features of Judaea are described in the well-known letter of Ps.-Aristeas, 112 ff. The wealth of Palestine is slightly exaggerated, but there is no reason to doubt that the description is true in the main.

142 On the administrative subdivisions of Palestine, A. H. M. Jones, *The cities* &c., p. 241 and note 19, cf. Tscherikower, *Palestine* &c., pp. 32 ff. Μερίδες and μεριδάρχαι: Jos. *A.J.* xii. 5. 5 (258 ff. Niese): I Macc. x. 65; E. Bikerman, *Rev. Hist. Rel.* cxv (1937), pp. 188 ff.; *Inst. Sél.*, p. 198.

143 On Tubias and his family and on the role of the Tobiads in the earlier and later history of Palestine, E. Meyer, *Urspr. u. Anf. d. Christ.* ii, pp. 128 ff., cf. p. 32 and p. 462; G. McL. Harper Jr., *Am. J. Ph.* xlix (1928), pp. 7 ff. (with bibliography), where no use has been made of Meyer's book. Cf. C. Watzinger, *Die Denkmäler Palästinas*, ii (1935), pp. 13 ff.; V. Tscherikower, loc. cit., pp. 49 ff., and E. Bikerman, *Inst. Sél.*, pp. 171 ff.

144 Cf. the important part played at Ascalon by Jewish τελῶναι in the time of Alexander Jannaeus: D. A. Schlatter, *Geschichte Israels von Alexander d. Gr. bis Hadrian*, 3rd ed., 1925, p. 158 f.

145 Taxation of Palestine in the time of the Ptolemies, E. Meyer, *Urspr. u. Anf. d. Christ.* ii, p. 126. On the Seleucid times, see below, p. 467 f.

146 My *Staatspacht*, p. 479 (151) f. The τελῶναι in Egypt and in Palestine: ibid., p. 343 (15), cf. Preisigke, *Wörterb.* s.v., esp. *Teb.* 43, 26 and 36, and

below, note 208 on μηνυταί. Μηνυταί in the Vienna document, l. col. 29 ff., r. col. 6 f. and 24 f., cf. *P. Hib.* 29, ll. 5–6. On the τελῶναι in Syria cf. F. Heichelheim, 'Roman Syria', T. Frank, *Econ. Surv.* iv, p. 233 f., and on the τελῶναι in general the popular sketch by H. C. Youtie, 'Publicans and Sinners', *Mich. Alumnus*, Quart. Rev. xliii (1937), pp. 650 ff.

147 For a different view, W. W. Tarn, *Hell. Civ.*², pp. 183 f., 201 f. He thinks that the aristocracy of Palestine was opposed to the Ptolemies, while the common people favoured Egypt. As evidence of the attitude of the common people, he quotes Polybius v. 86. 10. In this passage, however, Polybius speaks of Coele Syria, not of Palestine, and apparently of the population of the cities (honours bestowed on Ptolemy IV, such as στέφανοι, θυσίαι καὶ βωμοί, are typical of the cities.) The attitude of the author of *Ecclesiastes* may be explained with Tarn as reflecting a temporary rift between Philopator and one group of the Jewish hellenized aristocracy.

148 See the bibliography in note 134.

149 The estate (κτῆμα) of Bethanath in Palestine is mentioned in *P.S.I.* 594, a letter of Nicanor about ξένια which he is sending to Apollonius (esp. wine and other foodstuffs). In col. iii we find the entries: τὰ παρὰ Μέλανος ἐκ τοῦ | ἐν Βαιτανάτοις κτήματος, κτλ. Melas appears again in a long letter (*P.S.I.* 554) dealing with peasants and vineyards and written by somebody else in his name, cf. *P. Lond. Inv.* 2358A; *P. Cairo Zen.* 59004, 59019. It seems certain that the κτῆμα at Bethanath was a vine-growing estate and that it belonged to Apollonius. Nicanor was probably one of the horsemen and cleruchs of Tubias, and was at the same time a business agent of Apollonius, see *P. Cairo Zen.* 59003, 59093, 59012 and *P.S.I.* 495. An estate of Apollonius in Cyprus (?), *P.S.I.* 428, col. v, 56: ἐνεβαλόμεθα ἐκ τῆς Τετταφου (?) (C. C. Edgar, *P. Cairo Zen.* 59016, note to l. 9, suggests Πάφου, cf. *P.S.I.* 505. 6, and U. Wilcken, *Arch. Pap.* vi (1918–20) p. 394).

A detailed discussion of the estate of Bethanath will be found in V. Tscherikower, loc. cit., pp. 45 ff. I cannot, however, accept the far-reaching conclusions which he draws from the scanty material. He takes for granted that Bethanath was a *dorea* (in *P.S.I.* 594 it is called κτῆμα); from that he infers that a *dorea* must be a part of the χώρα βασιλική; and accordingly he assumes that a large, if not the largest, part of the land in Palestine was royal land. None of these statements is supported by the contents of the few documents in the correspondence of Zenon that deal with Bethanath. The κτῆμα may have been bought by Apollonius, and the κωμομισθωτής who deals with the peasants of the village is better interpreted as being, not an official in charge of the letting of royal land, but a village tax-farmer; see above, n. 139.

150 On vineyards and their cultivation in Ptolemaic Egypt, M. Schnebel, *Landwirtschaft*, pp. 239 ff. For vine-planting in general and especially on Apollonius' estate, see my *Large Estate*, pp. 93 ff., and C. C. Edgar, *P. Mich. Zen.*, Introd., p. 35 f. The legal character of the planted land: my *Kolonat*,

pp. 14 ff., and *Large Estate*, p. 94. On all these aspects of vine-growing, C. Préaux. *L'Écon. Lag.*, pp. 165 ff. Control of the government and taxes: C. Préaux, loc. cit., pp. 177 ff., where the reader will find a fine analysis of the *apomoira* section of the *nomoi telonikoi* of Philadelphus and bibliographical references to modern works dealing with this question, cf. above, n. 90. On the protective or compensatory customs duties, see the paper by Andreades quoted above, n. 117. Not all the cleruchs paid the tenth of the produce as *apomoira*. In the second century the new set of cleruchs, *machimoi* with reduced *cleroi*, paid the usual one-sixth. See *P. Ryl.* iv (in preparation), an elaborate contract of a lease of a vineyard in 170 B.C. (*passim*). I am indebted to Dr. F. Heichelheim for making me acquainted with this document.

151 On this subject see Ch. Dubois, 'L'olivier dans l'ancienne Égypte', *Rev. Phil.* xlix (1925), p. 60 (in which hardly any use is made of Zenon's correspondence) and M. Schnebel, *Landwirtschaft*, pp. 302 ff., cf. A. S. Pease, *P.W.K.* xvii. 2004 and 2454 ff. On the treatment of ἐλαϊκὰ φορτία imported into Alexandria from the χώρα, see *R.L.* col. 53; cf. Edgar, *Sel. Pap.* no. 75 (*Ann. du Serv.* xxiii, p. 90). Against my interpretation of *P. Col. Zen.* 14 we have the fact that we know nothing of an ἐμπόριον and storehouses at the river-harbour, while we know a good deal about the ἐμπόριον at the sea-harbour, A. Calderini, *Diz. dei nomi geografici* &c., 1935, s.v. Ἀλεξάνδρεια. However, an argument *ex silentio* is never valid, and the river-harbour of Alexandria, which was situated πρὸς τῶι ἐν Ῥακώτι Σαραπιείωι, is mentioned in a very interesting declaration of an ἐπίπλους in charge of two river boats. This document, which Dr. F. Heichelheim has shown me, will be published in *P. Ryl.* iv.

152 Fruit trees in general: M. Schnebel, *Landwirtschaft*, pp. 292 ff. and pp. 311 ff.; on the estate of Apollonius, my *Large Estate* p. 104; C. C. Edgar, *P. Mich. Zen.*, Intr., p. 35. On the pistachio tree see the ingenious syntheses of M. Wellmann, 'Die Georgika des Demokritos', *Berl. Abh.*, 1921, iv, p. 19. His remarks on the persea tree are more hazardous.

153 Livestock: M. Schnebel, *Landwirtschaft*, pp. 316 ff.; U. Wilcken, 'Alexander', &c., *Schmollers Jahrb.*, xlv (1921), p. 107 (411); my *Large estate*, pp. 107 ff.; C. C. Edgar, *P. Mich. Zen.*, Intr., p. 36 f. Horses: my *Large Estate*, p. 167 f. Camels: Sir Herbert Thompson, *A family Archive at Siut*, 1934; it appears from these documents that Tephope, a priest, started a lawsuit in 174/3 B.C. and that at this time 'Dionysius was his herd and Har his camel-keeper'. In later times these camels were used (along with horses) for postal service, *Teb.* 252 (description) of 95/4 or 62/1 B.C.; U. Wilcken, *Grundz.*, p. 373.

154 On the irrigation work see the books and articles quoted in note 86. A study of the names of settlements in the Fayûm, provided the whole evidence is collected and published, will greatly help us to understand better the work done by the first Ptolemies in the Fayûm and in other parts of Egypt. A rudimentary list of the inhabited places of the Fayûm will be

found in *Teb.* ii, and of Egypt in general in Preisigke-Kiessling, *Wörterbuch*, iii. A. Calderini has recently begun the publication of his dictionary of geographical names in Egypt, *Dizionario dei nomi geografici e topografici dell'Egitto greco-romano*, i. I, *A–'Αλικαρνασσεύς*, 1935.

155 Use of iron in general on Apollonius' estate: E. Grier, *Accounting in Zenon Papyri*, 1934, p. 54, and nn. 78–81, and M. Schnebel, *Landwirtschaft*, *passim* (on the σκαφεῖα p. 105), cf. C. Préaux, *L'Écon. Lag.* pp. 265 ff.

156 On the irrigation machines, M. Schnebel, *Landwirtschaft*, pp. 73 ff.; O. Krüger, *Agricultural production*, pp. 37 ff. (quoted in full above, n. 86). Krüger, pp. 38 ff., endeavours to show on insufficient grounds that Archimedes was not the inventor of the 'snail'. See against this view A. Rehm, 'Zur Rolle der Technik in der gr.-röm. Antike,' *Arch. f. Kulturg.* xxviii. 2, p. 146, n. 28: 'die archimedische Schraube .. ist als Erfindung des Mannes, dessen Namen sie trägt, so gut bezeugt wie nur möglich'. In his paper quoted above Rehm gives an interesting general survey of the part played by technique in the Graeco-Roman world and excellent bibliographical references.

157 M. Schnebel, *Landwirtschaft*, p. 131 and pp. 175 ff.; O. Krüger, loc. cit., pp. 86 ff., in dealing with threshing machines gives an interesting interpretation of *B.G.U.* vii. 1507 (third century B.C.), which, if accepted, establishes the fact that the *norag* was used in the early Hellenistic period.

158 On oil- and wine-presses, A. G. Drachmann, *Ancient Oil Mills and Presses*, 1932 (*Det Kgl. Danske Videnskabernes Selskab, Arch.-Kunsth. Meddelelser*), pp. 50 ff., and in *J.H.S.* lii (1932), pp. 116 ff., and lvi (1936), pp. 72 ff. Cf. A. Hug, art. *Μύλη*, *P.W.K.* xvi. 1064 ff., and E. G. Kagarow, 'Agricultural machines in Ancient Rome', *Probl. of the History of Mater. Civilization*, vii–viii, 1933 (in Russian).

159 On water-mills H. Blümner, *Technologie und Terminologie* &c., I² 1912 pp. 46 ff.; L. Lindet, 'Les origines du moulin à grains', *Rev. Arch.* xxxv (1899), pp. 413 ff.; xxxvi (1900), pp. 17 ff.; R. Bennett and J. Elton, *History of corn-milling*, ii, 1899; A. Baudrillart, art. 'Mola' in Daremberg et Saglio, *D. A.*; Hug, art. *Μύλη*, *P.W.K.* xvi. 1067; M. Bloch, 'Avènement et conquêtes du moulin à eau', *Ann. d'Hist. Écon. et Soc.* vii (1935), pp. 538 ff. (bibliography p. 561 f.). On the water-mill of the Athenian agora and other remains of Roman water-mills, A. W. Parsons, 'A Roman water-mill in the Athenian Agora', *Hesp.* v (1936), pp. 70 ff.

160 On the system of two crops a year see R. Johannesen, 'Ptolemy Philadelphus and scientific agriculture', *Cl. Phil.* xviii (1923), pp. 156 ff.; H. A. Thompson, 'Syrian wheat in Hellenistic Egypt', *Arch. Pap.* ix (1928–30), pp. 207 ff.; O. Krüger, loc. cit., p. 51; A. Segré, 'Note sull'economia dell'Egitto Ellenistico', *Bull. de la Soc. Arch. d'Alex.* xxix (1934), pp. 28 ff., and the remarks of C. C. Edgar on his last edition of Apollonius' letter in *P. Cairo*

Zenon, 59155, against the sweeping conclusions of M. Schnebel, *Landwirt-schaft*, pp. 145 ff. Practice of διαπορεῖν in south Arabia and India: Strabo xvi. 4. 2, p. 768.

[161] O. Krüger, loc. cit., pp. 50 ff.; A. Segré, loc. cit., pp. 15 ff., who discusses and tabulates the statistical data bearing on the relative importance of various crops cultivated in Egypt, cf. F. Heichelheim, 'Sitos', *P.W.K.* Suppl. vi. 847 f. Foreign kinds of wheat acclimatized in Egypt, C. Préaux, *L'Écon. Lag.*, p. 120. Wheat of Calymna, Etym. Magn., *s.v.* Κάλυμνος p. 486, 25; Steph. Byz., s.v. M. Wellmann, 'Die Georgika des Demokritos' (*Berl. Abh.* 1921, iv), p. 19.

[162] A. Segré, loc. cit., pp. 35 ff.; F. Heichelheim, loc. cit.

[163] Alexandria and Egypt in general have yielded a large quantity of pottery, either found in dated graves or dated by inscriptions painted on the vases themselves. Specially important in this respect are the finds made in the early Hellenistic necropolis of Shiatby, see E. Breccia, *La necropoli di Sciatbi*, 1912 (*Catal. Gén. d. Ant. Ég., Musée d'Alexandrie*), pp. 45 ff., cf. *Bull. Soc. Arch. Alex.* viii (1905), and of Hadra, E. Breccia, *Bull. Soc. Arch. Alex.* xxv (N.S. 7. 1) (1927), pp. 99 ff.; *Le Musée gréco-romain 1925–1931*, published in 1932, pp. 23 ff.; ibid. 1931–1932, published in 1933, pp. 9 ff. Cf. those made in the recently excavated necropolis of Mustafa Pasha, A. Adriani, *Ann. Mus. gr.-rom. 1933–4, 1934–5* (published in 1936). An excellent classification, dating, and illustration of the pottery discovered in Alexandria will be found in R. Pagenstecher, *Die griechisch-ägyptische Sammlung E. v. Sieglin*, ii. 3 (1913), pp. 21 ff., cf. F. Courby, *Les vases grecs à reliefs*, 1922. The 'Megarian' bowls were the most popular brand of pottery in the Hellenistic world in the late third and in the second century B.C. The early development of the Megarian bowls in one or more leading centres of production, and their later production in various other places (below, Ch. V, n. 17) are matters of dispute. I am inclined to agree in the main with the views expressed by R. Zahn, who regards Egypt and Alexandria as the centre where the 'Megarian' bowls first received the typical form and decoration that made them popular over the whole Hellenistic world. The same form and a similar decoration may have been used independently in some parts of northern Greece. See R. Zahn, in Wiegand and Schrader, *Priene*, 1904, pp. 401 ff., and *J.D.A.I.* xxiii (1908), pp. 45 ff.; also his contribution to C. W. Lunsingh Scheurleer's book, *Grieksche Ceramiek*, 1936, cf. Pagenstecher, loc. cit., pp. 64 ff., and Courby, loc. cit., pp. 277 ff. The views of Zahn as regards the origin of the 'Megarian' bowls have been recently confirmed by the discovery of a bronze bowl of 'Megarian' form and 'Megarian' decoration at Ras Shamra in Syria (C. F. A. Schaeffer, *Syria*, xvi (935), p. 153, pl. xxx, 4). The bowl was found in a grave dated by coins and pottery as belonging to the second half of the fourth century and was certainly imported into Syria from Egypt. Cf. on some early 'Megarian' bowls made probably at Tarentum, P. Wuilleumier, *B.C.H.* lvi (1932), pp. 399 ff., and my remarks on the Megarian bowls in

A.J.A. xli (1937), pp. 86 ff. The comparative rarity of Megarian bowls in Egypt is shown by the statistics of discoveries, such for example as those made in the necropolis of Mustafa Pasha in Alexandria—see A. Adriani, *Ann. Mus. gr.-rom.*, 1933–4, 1934–5, pp. 145 ff. (on the Megarian bowls)—and by the fact that very few bowls of this class are exhibited in the Museums of Alexandria and Cairo. Cf. below on the finds made at Canopus. On these bowls see also I. Noshy, *The Arts in Ptolemaic Egypt*, 1937, pp. 129 ff.

On the incense-burners, W. Deonna, 'Brûle-parfums en terre cuite', *Rev. Arch.*, 1907, ii, pp. 245 ff.; P. Wuilleumier, 'Brûle-parfums en terre cuite', *Mél. d'Arch. et d'Hist.* xlvi (1929), pp. 42 ff., cf. W. Deonna, 'Le mobilier délien', in *Expl. de Délos*, xviii (1938), pp. 371 ff. The same purpose was served by the little portable altars, on which see W. Deonna, 'Mobilier délien', *B.C.H.* lviii (1934), pp. 381 ff., and *Expl. de Délos*, loc. cit., pp. 373 ff. The charcoal ovens of Delos, similar to those of Priene and other Hellenistic cities, still await publication. In style and ornamentation they are similar to Megarian bowls and such products of relief-pottery as the clay *situla* of Olbia, E. von Stern, *Bull. de la Comm. Imp. Arch.* iii (1902), pp. 93 ff., pls. XIV–XV (in Russian). The Alexandrian origin of the prototypes of these products of ceramic industry is of course far from certain. The problem needs further study.

On the Hadra vases, Pagenstecher, loc. cit., pp. 33 ff. (many assigned to the early third century B.C.) and the reports of Breccia and Adriani quoted at the beginning of the note, cf. Ch. Picard, *Bull. Soc. Arch. Alex.* xxxii (N.S. 10, 1), 1938, pp. 3 ff., and bibliography, p. 5, n. 1. Add to this bibliography my paper in *Monuments of the Museum of Fine Arts . . . in Moscow*, i–ii (1912), pp. 61 ff., pl. XI (Hadra urn with the representation of a δρόμος ὁπλίτης), cf. E. von Stern, *Zapiski of the Soc. of Hist. and Antiquities of Odessa*, xxviii (1910). On the bas-relief vases with light background produced outside Alexandria (*hellgrundige Reliefvasen*), Pagenstecher, loc. cit., pp. 70 ff., cf. R. Zahn, 'Scherben antiker Tongefässe mit mehrfarbigem Reliefschmuck', *Bulletin van de Vereeniging tot Bevordering det Kennis van de Antieke Beshaving*, ii.i (1927), pp. 4 ff. Faienceware: R. Pagenstecher, loc. cit., pp. 118 ff. F. Courby, loc. cit., pp. 501 ff.; E. Breccia, *Le Musée gréco-romain*, 1931–1932, p. 19, pl. VI, 23–4 (two *askoi*); *Allard Pierson Museum, Algemeene Gids*, 1937, pp. 176 ff. (note the faience plaques, similar to those of glass, below, n. 167, for the adornment of walls or furniture, ibid., p. 53, nos. 506 and 507, pl. XXVII); on the technique, A. Lucas, 'Glazed ware in Egypt, India and Mesopotamia', *J.E.A.* xxii (1936), pp. 141 ff. For the Arsinoe–Berenice *oenochoai*, E. Breccia, *Inscr. greche e latine*, 1911 (*Catal. Gén.*), pp. v ff.; F. Courby, loc. cit., pp. 509 ff.; J. Noshy, loc. cit., p. 129; there are beautiful fragments of such vases in the Louvre and in the Allard Pierson Museum in Amsterdam, *Allard Pierson Museum, Algemeene Gids*, p. 177, no. 1633, pl. LXXXII. Many of the above-mentioned products of Alexandria, especially the Hadra vases and the faience, were exported mostly to the Ptolemaic dominions, e.g. Crete (for the use of Egyptian garrisons?) and to Italy. Canopus is similar to Alexandria in respect of the pottery found there, see E. Breccia, *Mon. de l'Égypte gréco-romaine*, i (1926), pl. XLIII, and pp. 77 ff.

Note the fragment of a Gnathia vase, pl. XLIII, 3, of an excellent Megarian bowl, pl. XLIII. 1, of a faience *cantharos* adorned with bas-reliefs in imitation of metal, pl. XLIII. 6, of a similar *rhyton*, pl. XLIII. 2, of a Berenice-*oinochoe*, pl. XXXVI. 9, and of many faience vases. My pls. XLI and XLII.

¹⁶⁴ On glass industry in Egypt in the Hellenistic period, A. Ippel, 'Das griechische Kunstgewerbe', in Th. Bossert, *Geschichte des Kunstgewerbes*, iv, 1930, pp. 240 ff. Glass vases of moulded and chiselled glass or cut from blocks of solid glass in imitation of metal-ware: M. Rostovtzeff, *Iranians and Greeks*, p. 127 and p. 233; and *Skythien und der Bosporus*, p. 550, p. 554 f. and p. 566 f.; cf. below. A beautiful specimen of this type of glass, found in South Russia and now in the Berlin Museum, may be dated about 200 B.C. It is an amphora which consists of two parts (an upper and a lower) fitted together. The two parts were cut from blocks of solid glass. The junction is concealed by a bronze band adorned with ivy. The top of the cover and the spout are like-wise of bronze; the latter has the form of a Silenus holding a wine-skin. See R. Zahn, *Amtl. Ber. K. Kunstsamml.* XXXV. 3 (1913), pp. 113 ff.; my pls. XLIII and LXVI. The vase of the same type said to have been found in China (in Honan) and now in the Museum of Toronto (D. M. Robinson and C. G. Harcum, *Catal. of Greek vases in the Royal Ontario Museum*, 1930, no. 626 (p. 269), pl., 99) which is regarded as an Alexandrian product of the early Hellenistic age, is thought by some competent scholars to be of modern manufacture. Ἀ ὑελοῦς πίναξ διπηχύς που τὴν διάμετρον, ἐν θήκῃ κατακείμενος ἀργυρᾷ πλήρης ἰχθύων ὀπτῶν is mentioned as one of the gifts of the wealthy Macedonian Caranus to his guests (early third century B.C.), Athen. iv. 129 d. Delian inventories: see next note.

¹⁶⁵ On the glass vases with gold ornaments, see A. Kisa, *Das Glas*, iii, 1908, p. 838, who assigns them to the Roman period. I was the first to point out their Hellenistic date and Alexandrian origin and to publish one specimen of this class certainly found in Egypt: M. Rostovtzeff, 'Painted glass vases of late Hellenistic art', *Bull. Comm. Arch. de Russie*, 1914, pp. 22 ff., pls. III and VIII (in Russian), cf. Morin-Jean, *Rev. Arch.*, 1917, i, pp. 310 ff.; M. Rostovtzeff, *Hellenistisch-römische Architekturlandschaft (Röm. Mitt.* xxvi (1911), and sepa-rately), p. 65, fig. 38. To the same class belongs a fine cup found in Italy (Trasilico in Calabria) and now in the Museum of Reggio in Calabria. It is adorned with two figures of hunters, one on horseback, recalling a similar figure in the well-known painted grave at Marissa (my pls. XLIV and LVIII, cf. C. Watzinger, *Denkmäler Palästinas*, ii (1935), pp. 18 ff.; Watzinger regards the style of the Marissa paintings as Alexandrian). I think that the cup is early Hellenistic and of Alexandrian or Syrian make (published by G. Moretti, *Boll. d'Arte*, 1913, p. 226; P. Orsi, *Arch. Storico della Calabria*, i (1912–13), p. 638; R. Delbrück, *J.D.A.I.* xxix (1914), Anz., col. 199, fig. 9; R. Paribeni, *Le Terme di Diocleziano e il Museo Nazionale Romano*, 1932, p. 299, No. 1027; and recently by E. Galli, 'Riflessi di pittura Ales-sandrina in Calabria', *Riv. R. Ist. Arch. e St. dell'Arte*, vi (1937), pp. 32 ff., together with other objects found presumably in the same grave).

The most beautiful specimen of a glass bowl with gold ornaments (not covered with a layer of glass), which is an imitation of Megarian bowls or of their metal prototypes, was found in Palestine and was kept in the collection of the late E. Rothschild. It certainly belongs to the third century B.C.; see P. Wuilleumier, *Le Trésor de Tarente*, 1930, pp. 29 ff., pls. XI–XII. Of the same type are the bowls in the British Mus. and in the Mus. of Geneva (all from S. Italy), Wuilleumier, loc. cit., pl. x. 5, and W. Deonna, *Rev. É.A.* xxvii (1925), pp. 15ff. All these bowls remind one strikingly of the beautiful specimen of Megarian bowls found in Alexandria, R. Pagenstecher, *Samml. Sieglin*, iii, p. 72, fig. 83. 4, pl. XXII. 1, and p. 196; Courby, loc. cit., p. 398, fig. 84, cf. the Megarian bowl from Canopus, E. Breccia, *Mon. de l'Égypte gréco-romaine*, 1926, pl. XLIII. 1. Mentions of glass vessels and other glass objects partly adorned with gold in the Delian inventories, esp. in the inventory of the temple of Aphrodite : βωμί[σκον ὑάλι]νον π[ερικ]εχρυσω[μέ]νον βάσιν ἔχον[τα ἐξ] ἐλέφαντος καὶ θ[ύας], Durrbach–Roussel, *Inscr. de Délos*, 1429 A ii. 24 ; ἐξάλειπτρον . . . ὑάλινον ἐν πλινθείῳ, ibid., 1417 A ii. 12 ; φωκαιΐδια ἐν ὑαλίνω(ι) ποτηρίωι, ibid., 1429 B i. 68; 1432 A b ii. 41; 1450 A 92; cf. σκύφους ὑαλίνους ἐγ κιβωτίωι δύο, ibid. 1439 A b c i. 64; 1441 A i. 77; 1450 A 53. Cf. Callixeinus' description of the πομπή of Philadelphus (Athen. v. 199 f.): in the procession figured glass cups, ὑάλινα, described as διάχρυσα. See my pl. XLIII.

[166] See my articles quoted in the preceding note. The transition from the glass vases with gold ornaments to the painted vases is illustrated by a fragment of a bowl in the Metropolitan Museum of New York (combination of gold and painted ornaments) (my pl. XLIII. 4), and by a beautiful jug of green colour with floral ornaments of gold foil attached to its outer surface in the Berlin Antiquarium, R. Zahn, *Die Antike*, v (1929), pp. 45 ff. A similar small cup was found, it is said, at Olbia and is now in the Metropolitan Museum.

[167] Ornamental glass plaques: E. Breccia, *Le Musée égyptien*, iii, 1915, p. 25, pl. XIII, figs. 14–15 ; M. Rostovtzeff, 'Painted glass vases of late Hellenistic time', *Bull. Comm. Arch. de Russie*, 1914, p. 11, pl. VI. 1–3 (in Russian); a beautiful specimen in the Museo delle Terme at Rome, C. Ricci, *Boll. d'Arte*, 1914, p. 273. Italian imitations are common and will be found in almost all the museums of ancient art. My pl. CX. 2. Glass beads imported from Alexandria into China, or imitated there, were found recently at Lo Yang: *Ill. Lond. News*, 1933, Oct. 28, Nov. 4, Dec. 9, cf. W. Yetts, ibid., 1934, May 12. For the jewels adorned with plaques of multi-coloured glass, see for example the finds in the Artjukhov Kurgan in the Kuban district (late third and early second centuries B.C.), Rostovtzeff, *Skythien und der Bosporus*, p. 248; L. Stephani, *C. R. de la Comm. Arch.*, 1880, Beilage, pl. I. 13 and 17; E. H. Minns, *Scyth. and Greeks*, p. 431, fig. 321. Absence of any allusion to glass in the papyri: Th. Reil, *Beitr. z. Kenntnis d. Gewerbes im hell. Äg.*, 1913, pp. 47 ff. Even after the invention of blown glass glass-ware remained unpopular in Egypt, D. B. Harden, *Roman glass from Karanis*, 1936, pp. 38 ff.

[168] Find at Toukh el Qarmous: C. C. Edgar, *Le Musée égyptien*, ii, 1907, pp. 57 ff. ; P. Wuilleumier, *Le Trésor de Tarente*, 1930, pp. 48 ff., esp. pp. 52 ff.,

cf. the contemporary silver jug, *Allard Pierson Museum, Algem. Gids*, n. 882, pl. xlii. My pl. XLVII. The find at Mendes—wrongly assigned to Thmuis, W. v. Bissing, *Metallgefässe*, 1901 (*Catal. gén.*), pl. III—is now assigned to the fifth or fourth century B.C., C. Watzinger, *Denkmäler Palästinas*, 1935, ii, p. 10. Cf. in general H. B. Walters, *Catal. of silver plate in Br. Mus.*, 1921, and *The Art of the Greeks*, 1937, p. 264. Ptolemaic jewels made in Alexandria are not uncommon in our museums, especially in that of Alexandria. They have never been collected in full and studied. A group of excellent Ptolemaic jewels of the second half of the third century (dated by a coin of Euergetes I of 235–222 B.C.) was found in 1931, probably somewhere in the Fayûm. They are certainly of Alexandrian workmanship. A set of jewels forming part of this find is now in the Metropolitan Museum, New York. See Ch. R. Clark, *Bull. Metr. Mus.* xxx (1935), pp. 161 ff. On a group of ear-rings in all probability of Egyptian origin, R. Zahn, 'Zur hellenistischen Schmuckkunst', *K. Schumacher-Festschrift* (hrsg. v. d. Direction des röm.-germ. Zentralmuseums in Mainz), 1930, pp. 202 ff., and in *Ant. Denkm.* iv, pl. 42.

169 Mit-Rahineh: O. Rubensohn, *Hellenistisches Silbergerät in antiken Gipsabgüssen* &c., 1911 (Pelizaeus-Museum); G. Roeder und A. Ippel, *Die Denkmäler des Pelizaeus-Museums zu Hildesheim*, 1921, pp. 139 ff.; Courby, loc. cit., p. 336 f.; A. Ippel, 'Guss und Treibarbeit in Silber. Untersuchungen z. antiken Modellabgüssen des Pelizaeus-Museums', *Winckelmannspr.* xcvii, 1937, cf. A. Adriani, *Bull. Soc. Arch. Alex.* xxxii (10. 1) (1938), pp. 189 ff. The latter contribution of Ippel contains a careful analysis of some technical devices used by the ancient toreutic artists. In the same pamphlet he publishes a set of casts of metal medallions, which according to him are much later than the bulk of the Mit-Rahineh casts (first century A.D.). On the plaster cast of an *emblema* with the busts of Soter and Berenice—a splendid product of early Hellenistic art—A. Adriani, *Bull. Soc. Arch. Alex.* xxxii (10.1), pp. 77 ff. On the moulds from Mit-Rahineh and other places, C. C. Edgar, 'Greek Moulds', *Catal. Gén. Ant. égypt. du Musée du Caire*, 1903; G. Roeder und A. Ippel, *Die Denkm. d. Pelizaeus-Museums*, &c., pp. 149 ff. On the stone models of helmets, ibid., p. 163, nos. 1101, 1851–4, 1808. The finds of Hermupolis assigned by E. Pernice, 'Hellenistische Silbergefässe im Antiquarium der Kön. Museen', *Winckelmannspr.* lviii, 1898, to the second century B.C. are now, in the light of later finds and on the basis of careful stylistic analysis, tentatively dated considerably later by A. Adriani, 'Le Gobelet en argent des Amours vendangeurs du Musée d'Alexandrie', *Soc. R. d'Arch. d'Alexandrie*, Cahier I (1939). On Hellenistic toreutic art in general, A. Ippel in T. Bossert, *Gesch. d. Kunstgewerbes*, iv, pp. 233 ff. Cf. my pls. XLV. 1 and XLVIII.

170 Goblet found in Egypt in the style of the Megarian bowls: H. Wallis, *Egypt. Ceramic Art*, 1898, i, pl. XXVI. 2. 'Megarian' bronze bowl of Ras Shamra: above, note 163. Imitation in other materials of Alexandrian metal vases found in Egypt: C. C. Edgar, *Le Musée égyptien*, ii, 1907, pp. 57 ff.; E. Breccia, *Necropoli di Sciatbi*, p. 29, no. 40, pl. XXXVII. 46, and *Le Musée gréco-romain 1925–31*, 1932, pl. XLVI, fig. 61.

[171] P. Wuilleumier, *Le Trésor de Tarente*, pp. 28 ff., and pl. II. 2 (pyxis lid); pp. 68 ff., and pl. x. 3, 4 (Città Castellana bowls). Several silver vases of similar style have been found in south Russia and in Greece, the most important in the Artjukhov Kurgan in the Kuban district, see my *Skythien und der Bosporus* pp. 248 ff.; its date (early second century B.C.) is certain: it is supported by the coin of Paerisades and by the presence in the grave of Megarian bowls and Anatolian *terra sigillata*. They may have been Anatolian or Greek imitations of Greco-Egyptian originals. For other references see Wuilleumier, loc. cit.

[172] Jug and pan from Egyed in Hungary: A. Hekler, *J.D.A.I.* xxiv (1909), pp. 28 ff.; R. Zahn, 'Glaskännchen im Berliner Antiquarium', *Die Antike*, v (1929), pp. 48 ff.

[173] A. Ippel, *Der Bronzefund von Galjûb* (Modelle eines hellenistischen Goldschmieds), 1922. Mystharion's workshop: *B.G.U.* iv. 1065; Th. Reil, *Beitr.*, p. 59; U. Wilcken, *Arch. Pap.* iv (1907–8), p. 561.

[174] Below, Ch. V, n. 118.

[175] It is unnecessary to quote the passage in which Callixeinus speaks of gold and silver vessels displayed in the πομπή of Philadelphus. In the banqueting tent the gold vessels were exhibited on a special κλίνη: ἃ δὴ πάντα χρυσᾶ τε ἦν καὶ διάλιθα, θαυμαστὰ ταῖς τέχναις, Athen. v. 197 c. The weight of all the silver and gold plate in the tent was 10,000 tal. The long description of Ps.-Aristeas will be found in his *Epist. ad Philocr.* 51–82. It would be useful to collect in full the texts referring to dedications by the first Ptolemies of gold and silver plate in various sanctuaries. The texts of Callixeinus and Aristeas have been analysed by Pernice in his monograph on the find at Hermupolis quoted above, n. 169. I may add that silver plate (ἀργυρώματα) is frequently mentioned in the correspondence of Zenon (e.g. *P. Cairo Zen.* 59038, 59044, 59327) and that frequent references to jewels and to silver and gold plate are found in the few marriage contracts of Ptolemaic times, see O. Montevecchi, 'Ricerche di sociologia' &c., *Aeg.* xvi (1936) pp. 4 ff. Cf. C. Préaux, *L'Écon. Lag.*, p. 265. It need hardly be mentioned that the first to ascribe the leading role in toreutics in the Hellenistic period to Alexandria was Th. Schreiber, *Die alexandrinische Toreutik*, 1894. His views have been often criticized by various scholars. It was Schreiber also who insisted upon the Hellenistic origin of the so-called landscape reliefs found in large quantities in Italy, and on their dependence, as regards technique and composition, on Alexandrian toreutics. This view, challenged by many prominent scholars and almost generally abandoned, has been recently revived by prominent specialists such as G. Méautis, H. Lippold, and Ch. Picard (see the bibliography in Ch. Picard, 'Observations sur l'origine et l'influence des reliefs pittoresques dits alexandrins', *Mél. Maspero*, ii, pp. 313 ff., and cf. A. Adriani, *Bull. Soc. Arch. Alex.* xxxii (1938), pp. 191 ff.).

[176] On the linen industry and its organization (the ὀθονηρά) see above, pp. 305 ff. On the workshops where wool was woven into various stuffs, and

especially where mattresses (στρώματα) and pillows (προσκεφάλαια) and blankets (περιστρώματα) were made, see my *Large Estate*, pp. 115 ff. ; cf. Heichelheim, *P.W.K.* xii. 175 ff. Important additional evidence will be found in some recently published papyri of Zenon's correspondence referring to various articles produced in the workshops of Apollonius, *P. Mich. Zen.* 13, 22, 24; *P. Col. Zen.* 15, 17, cf. *P. Cairo Zen.* 59060 and 59092. On export cf. C. Préaux, *L'Écon. Lag.*, p. 110 f.

177 Couches covered with mattresses, pillows, and rugs are reproduced in several painted tombs of the necropolis of Alexandria. The best preserved are those of Suk el Wardian, Sidi Gaber, and Mustafa Pasha. For descriptions and coloured reproductions of these couches see E. Breccia, 'La tomba dipinta di Such el Wardian', *Le Musée égyptien*, ii, 1907, pp. 63 ff., and in *Le Musée gréco-romain 1925–1931*, 1932, pl. XXVII; H. Thiersch, *Zwei Antike Grabanlagen bei Alexandria*, 1904, pls. II and III, and A. Adriani, 'La Nécropole de Moustafa Pacha', *Ann. du Musée gréco-romain*, 1933/4– 1934/5, pp. 101 ff., and pls. XXXIII and D. It is striking how painstakingly the funeral couches reproduced the couches used in the richer households of Alexandria. Adriani points out how closely the description of Callixeinus (Athen. v, p. 197a–b) fits the funeral couches of Mustafa Pasha. Note especially the mention of ψιλαὶ Περσικαί, which served as hangings on the front of the couches. On such embroidered bed-hangings cf. Theophr. *H. P.* iv. 2. 7. On the rugs which were used for covering the sarcophagi and the funerary tents of Ptolemaic Egypt and their occasional reproductions, M. Rostovtzeff, *Ancient decor. wall-painting in S. Russia*, 1913, pp. 62 ff., pls. XXV and XLVIII. 2 (in Russian) ; R. Pagenstecher, *Nekropolis*, 1919, p. 181. The famous Egyptian ὑφάντης Παθυμίας, rival in reputation of the great artists of Cyprus Ἀκεσᾶς and Ἑλικών, Athen. ii. 48 b ; cf. one of the fragments of Plato's comedies, Kock i. 654 (Phoenician and Sardian beds and bed-rugs). My pl. XLVI.

178 The most interesting and the earliest mosaic of Alexandria, which very probably imitates a rug, was found in the earliest necropolis of Alexandria, that of Shiatby, see E. Breccia, *Bull. Soc. Arch. Alex.* xix (5) (1923), pp. 158 ff., pl. V. 2, cf. his observations in *Mon. de l'Égypte gréco-romaine*, 1926, p. 82, and *Le Musée gréco-romain 1925–1931*, 1932, pl. LV. Later is the beautiful mosaic made by Sophilus, ibid., pl. A and pl. LIV (above, n. 11), which, as is shown by the border ornament, is an imitation of a rug (on this pattern see Rostovtzeff, *Anc. dec. wall-painting*, p. 62). The mosaic of Shiatby is very similar in style and technique to the pebble mosaics of the fourth century B.C. at Olynthus and Olbia, see D. M. Robinson *A.J.A.* xxxix (1936), pp. 210 ff., and *Die Antike*, xi (1935), pp. 284 ff., cf. H. Payne, *J.H.S.* liv (1934), p. 193, G. Karo, *J.D.A.I.* l (1935), Anz. col. 218 f., and F. V. Lorentz, *Röm. Mitt.* lii (1937), pp. 165 ff.

179 Rugs in the banqueting tent of Philadelphus: Athen. v, 196 b, c and esp. f; 197 b, cf. F. Studniczka, 'Das Symposion Ptolemaios II.', *Abh. Sächs. Ges.* xxx (1914) ; Jacoby, 'Kallixeinos', *P.W.K.* x. 1751 ff. ; A. Frickenhaus,

'Griechische Banketthäuser', *J.D.A.I.* xxxii (1917), pp. 118 ff. Purple αὐλαῖαι in the tent-like room of the θαλαμηγός of Philopator, Athen. v. 206 a (note that the room was very similar to the funeral tents mentioned in note 177), and the *byssos* sail reinforced by a purple topsail, ibid. 206 c; see F. Caspari, 'Das Nilschiff Ptolemaios IV.', *J.D.A.I.* xxxi (1916), pp. 1 ff.; A. Köster, 'Die Thalamegos des Ptolemaios', *Klio*, Beih. xxxii (1934), pp. 20 ff. An excellent idea of such rugs may be derived from the beautiful one represented as extended over the ceiling of the gorgeous Aula Isiaca on the Palatine (time of Caligula). See G. E. Rizzo, *Pittura ellenistico-romana*, iii, Roma, fasc. ii. 'Le pitture dell'Aula Isiaca di Caligola', 1935, pls. I and II, and pp. 20 ff. This rug should be compared with that represented as spread over the vault of the early Hellenistic grave in south Russia, see my *Anc. dec. wall-painting*, pls. xiv and xv; cf. my pl. xlvi. 2 and n. 177. I see no reason to doubt that the painting of the ceiling represents a rug, and if so, in an *Aula Isiaca* (which the room certainly was) the rug must be Alexandrian. Cf. Lumbroso, *Recherches*, pp. 107 ff.

[180] I. Noshy, *The Arts of Ptolemaic Egypt*, 1937, pp. 83 ff.; F. Poulsen 'Gab es eine alexandrinische Kunst?' in *From the Collections of the Ny Carlsberg Glyptothek*, ii (1938); G. Kleiner, *Bull. Soc. Arch. Alex.* xxxii (N.S. 10, 1), 1938, pp. 41 ff. (grave sculpture); and Adriani, ibid., pp. 76 ff. (portraits).

[181] On the foreign trade of the Ptolemies see my paper, 'Foreign commerce in Ptolemaic Egypt', *Journ. of Econ. and Bus. Hist.*, iv (1932), pp. 728 ff., many passages of which I reproduce in the text. Cf. E. Leider, *Der Handel von Alexandreia*, 1934.

[182] My 'Foreign commerce', &c., p. 732 f., and my *Ges. u. Wirtsch. im röm. Kaiserreich*, pp. 31 ff. Gold mines: in addition to the references given in my 'Foreign commerce', H. Kees, *Aegypten*, pp. 128 ff. (history of gold-mining in Pharaonic Egypt); C. Préaux, *L'Écon. Lag.*, pp. 253 ff. Philadelphus' African policy: H. Kortenbeutel, *Der ägyptische Süd- und Osthandel in der Politik der Ptolemäer und römischen Kaiser*, Diss. Berlin, 1931, pp. 16 ff.

[183] On the elephants, H. Kortenbeutel, loc. cit., pp. 23 ff., my 'Foreign commerce' &c., pp. 740 ff., cf. L. Amundsen, *Ostr. Osl.*, No. 2; U. Wilcken, *Arch. Pap.* xi (1933–5), p. 139, n. 1; A. S. Hunt, *J.E.A.* xx (1934), p. 125. On the cost of the elephants cf. C. Préaux, loc. cit., pp. 34 ff.

[184] Trade with Syria is best illustrated by the numerous documents of Zenon's correspondence that date from the time when he was Apollonius' agent in Palestine, Syria, and Phoenicia, and those later ones which resulted from his stay abroad. On these documents much has been written. See G. McL. Harper Jr., 'A study in the commercial relations between Egypt and Syria in the Third Century B.C.', *Am.J.Ph.* xlix (1928), pp. 1 ff.; H. Schaal, *Vom Tauschhandel zum Welthandel*, 1931, pp. 131 ff.; W. L. Westermann, *P. Col. Zen.* 2 and 3; C. C. Edgar, *Arch. Pap.* xi (1935), p. 219, n. 1; V. Tscherikower, *Palestine* &c., pp. 15 ff. On the goods imported from Syria and Palestine to Alexandria, W. Peremans, 'De Handelsbetrekkingen van Egypte

met het Middellandsche-Zeegebied in de 3ᵉ eeuw v. C.: De verhandelde Waren', *Phil. Stud.* (Kath. Univ. te Leuven), iii (1931-2), pp. 3 ff. and pp. 81 ff. On the importation of Syrian olive-oil and the protection of the Egyptian oil monopoly, see A. Andreades, paper quoted in n. 117, and C. Préaux, *L'Écon. Lag.*, pp. 83 ff. (with full use of other modern contributions), cf. V. Tscherikower, loc. cit., pp. 20 ff. Freedom of trade in grain in Egypt, Syria and Palestine: C. Préaux, loc. cit., pp. 149 ff., and V. Tscherikower, loc. cit. Trade with the Nabataeans: V. Tscherikower, loc. cit., pp. 25 ff., and C. Préaux, loc. cit., pp. 362 ff.

[185] Much has been written on the southern and eastern trade of Egypt in the time of the Ptolemies. I cannot give here a full bibliography. The standard work still is the Russian book by M. Khwostow, *History of the Oriental trade of Graeco-Roman Egypt*, Kazan, 1907, cf. my summary of this book and some supplementary remarks in *Arch. Pap.* iv (1908), pp. 298 ff., and ibid., v (1909), p. 181, and my paper 'Foreign commerce', quoted above. Of more recent date are the lucid presentations in U. Wilcken, 'Alexander', &c., *Schmollers Jahrb.* xlv (1921), p. 63 (367); W. Schubart, *Aegypten von Alexander dem Grossen bis auf Mohammed*, 1922, pp. 1 ff.; H. Kortenbeutel, *Der äg. Süd- und Osthandel*, &c., and C. Préaux, *L'Écon. Lag.*, pp. 353 ff., cf. W. W. Tarn, 'Ptolemy II and Arabia', *J.E.A.* xv (1929), pp. 9 ff. All the histories of the Hellenistic period and those of Ptolemaic Egypt contain, of course, substantial chapters dealing with the southern and eastern trade of Egypt. For some other modern contributions see the preceding notes. The inscriptions of the few known merchants: N. Rhodokanakis, *Zeitschr. f. Semitistik*, ii (1924), p. 113; W. Schwarz, 'Die Inschriften des Wüstentempels von Redesiye', *Jahrb. f. kl. Phil.* cliii (1896), p. 157, n. 9. The date of the Nabataean expedition and of the founding of Berenice is in dispute. I accept the earlier date of Tarn, see C. Préaux, loc. cit., p. 357.

[186] W. W. Tarn, *J.E.A.* xiv (1928), p. 258.

[187] See above, note 113.

[188] Export of grain: my 'Foreign commerce' &c., pp. 728 ff.; A. Segré, loc. cit., pp. 35 ff.

[189] Prices of grain at Delos: F. Heichelheim, *Wirtsch. Schwankungen*, pp. 51 ff.; in Egypt, pp. 56 ff. Cf. J. A. O. Larsen, 'Roman Greece' (T. Frank, *Econ. Surv.* iv), pp. 383 ff.

[190] F. Heichelheim, 'Sitos', *P.W.K.*, Suppl. vi. 852 f.

[191] See the paper of W. Peremans quoted above, note 184.

[192] See preceding note.

[193] On the western commerce of Egypt see my 'Foreign commerce' &c., pp. 752 ff., cf. U. Wilcken, 'Alexander', &c., *Schmollers Jahrb.* xlv (1921), pp. 114 ff.

[194] On the relations between Rome and Philadelphus see M. Holleaux, *C.A.H.* vii, p. 823 (with bibliography), and W. Otto, 'Zur Geschichte der

Zeit des 6. Ptolemäers, *Bay. Abh.* xi (1934), pp. 38 ff., 56, 81, 90 f., 133, 136. If we take into consideration what is said below on the commercial relations between Italy and Egypt, we shall not be astonished to find a 'Roman' in the army of Philadelphus, H. I. Bell, *Arch. Pap.* vii (1926), pp. 17 ff.; *Lond. Inv.* 2243, l. 12 (252/1 B.C.). Dinnus, of course, is as much and as little a Roman as his contemporaries of Italian origin in Greece.

195 On the coins, C. Seltman, *Greek Coins*, p. 248. Hiero II and Philadelphus, my *Kolonat*, pp. 233 ff.; J. Carcopino, *La loi d'Hiéron et les Romains*, 1914; T. Frank, *C.A.H.* vii, p. 796, and *Economic History of Rome*, 2nd ed. 1927, p. 90; A. Schenk Graf von Stauffenberg, *König Hieron II von Syrakus*, 1933.

196 S. Gsell, *Histoire de l'Afrique*, iv, p. 166, cf. ii, p. 322. Timosthenes: Strabo ii. 1. 39 ff., pp. 92 ff.; iii. 1. 7, p. 140; xvii. 3. 6, p. 827, cf. ix. 3. 10, p. 421, and xii. 2. 5, p. 618; Ptol. i. 15. 3 (ed. Müller, p. 40); Gsell, loc. cit., iv, p. 120. It was the same Timosthenes who explored Central Africa, H. Kortenbeutel, loc. cit., p. 18. Ptolemaic coins found in Tunisia: A. L. Delattre, *Carthage : Nécropole punique de la colline de St Louis*, 1896, p. 79. Carthaginian coins: Seltman, loc. cit., p. 249.

197 Sulphur is very seldom mentioned in the papyri, see Preisigke, *Wörterb.*, s.v. θεῖον. On its extensive use in agriculture and especially in viticulture see the texts quoted by Blümner, *P.W.K.* ii A. 796 ff., art. 'Schwefel', esp. Cato, *R. R.* 95; Plin. *N. H.* xvii. 264; *Geop.* xiii. 7. Egypt is mentioned as a consumer of sulphur in connexion with the new technique of niello (above, n. 172), Plin. *N. H.* xxxiii. 131; Blümner, loc. cit., p. 800.

198 Gnathian ware in Alexandria and Alexandrian ware in Apulia, A. Pagenstecher, *Samm. Sieglin*, ii. 3, pp. 120 ff. It is worthy of note that the production of pottery in Italy was as flourishing in the early third century as it had been in the fourth. On some products of S. Etruria and Latium which belong to this time, see R. Zahn, 'Aus dem Antiquarium', *Ber. aus den Preuss.Kunstsamml.* lv (1934), pp. 2 ff. This S. Etrurian pottery is closely related to the Gnathian ware. Cf. the Tarentine brand of early Megarian pottery, P. Wuilleumier, *B.C.H.* lvi (1932), pp. 399 ff. Alexandrian glass in Italy, above, n. 165. The renewal of an active import of Greek goods into Italy, after a comparatively long interruption in the late fifth and fourth centuries, is one of the phenomena that mark the end of the isolation of Italy from Greece in the fields of politics and economics and in that of culture. The new Hellenization of Italy was not only due to Pyrrhus' expedition and to the conquest of part of Sicily in the first Punic War; it was also the result of the commercial and political endeavours of the Ptolemies. This is shown, e.g., by the appearance of Italian stories in the Αἴτια of Callimachus, as has been proved by the recently found Διηγήσεις of Callimachus (see, e.g., F. Altheim in *Die Welt als Geschichte*, ii (1936), pp. 75 ff., and pp. 90 ff.), and by the exact information on Italian vegetation that Theophrastus incorporates in his treatises (e.g. *H. P.* v. 8. 1 ff., on the forests of Corsica).

[199] For a long time it was the common opinion of archaeologists and of historians of ancient art that the earliest mosaics of Pompeii, especially some choice pieces in the Casa del Fauno, were imported to Pompeii from Alexandria and must be assigned to the early Hellenistic period, see for instance O. Elia, *Pitture murali e mosaici nel Mus. Naz. di Napoli*, 1932. But recently several scholars have confidently maintained that almost all the mosaics of the house of the Faun were made in Pompeii either in the second century B.C. or still later (about the time of Sulla) and have no connexion with Alexandria; see the interesting study of H. Fuhrmann, *Philoxenos von Eretria*, 1931 (cf. the review by A. Ippel, *Gnomon*, x (1934), pp. 75 ff.) and E. Pernice, 'Pavimente und figürliche Mosaiken', *Die hellenistische Kunst in Pompeji*, vi, 1938. I cannot discuss here this complicated problem which is closely connected with the history of the building of the house. I refer also in this connexion to the other volumes of the series *Die hellenistische Kunst in Pompeji* by E. Pernice. Pernice is inclined to minimize Alexandrian import into Pompeii and Alexandrian influence on it in Hellenistic times.

[200] I have spoken above of Apollonius' trade relations with Palestine, Syria, and Phoenicia. His commercial business in Egypt itself was not less active. He had many commercial agents on his staff, some of them perhaps slaves, see e.g. *P. Mich. Zen.* 28, cf. *P.S.I.* 302 and 427 (Sosus selling wine and wheat, and buying hides); *P. Cairo Zen.* 59446 (two men buying wine wholesale); 59375 (Addaius selling wine); *P.S.I.* 859 and 860 (transport of large quantities of wine); *P. Cairo Zen.* 59516 (honey); 59470 (flax). After Apollonius' death Zenon was trading in grain and wine, *P. Cairo Zen.* 59363, 59522. In *P. Cairo Zen.* 59509 a guard of the storehouse is busy buying grain from military settlers and is reluctant to do so from crown peasants.

[201] On Ptolemaic coinage, besides the classical work of Svoronos, W. Schubart, *Z.N.* xxxiii (1922), pp. 68 ff.; J. G. Milne, 'Ptolemaic coinage in Egypt', *J.E.A.* xv (1929), pp. 150 ff.; Th. Reinach, *Rev. É.G.* xli (1928), pp. 121 ff.; W. Giesecke, *Das Ptolemäergeld*, 1930; C. Préaux, *L'Écon. Lag.*, pp. 267 ff.; J. G. Milne, 'The currency of Egypt under the Ptolemies', *J.E.A.* xxiv (1938), pp. 200 ff, and the general works quoted in note 79. The limited area within which the Ptolemaic coins circulated is shown by the fact that no hoards of them have been found in Greece, Asia Minor, or the Seleucid kingdom. Even hoards containing occasional Ptolemaic coins are unknown in Asia Minor and the Seleucid kingdom. Such hoards are confined to Greece proper: Mycenae (S. P. Noe, *A Bibliography of Greek Coin Hoards*, 2nd ed. (*Num. Notes and Monographs*, lxxviii), 1937, no. 716), Olympia (Noe², no. 754), Sophikon (Noe,² no. 997) and Sparta (Noe², no. 1004). It is to be observed that the Ptolemaic coins found in these hoards belong exclusively to the reign of the first three Ptolemies. I am inclined to explain the occurrence of these early coins in Greek hoards and some stray finds of them in Asia Minor as a result of the political ascendancy of the kings in some parts of Asia Minor and in Greece, especially the Peloponnese, in the reigns of Philadelphus and Euergetes I. The same political influence explains

the circulation both at Corinth and at Nemea of comparatively large quantities of copper coins of Euergetes I, see *Corinth* VI, 'Coins', by K. M. Edwards, 1933, p. 73, n. 468, and A. R. Bellinger, *The Excavations of Nemea in 1924–5, 1926–7* (Univ. of Cincinnati) (in preparation). In the West, on the other hand, hoards of Ptolemaic coins are not unknown (Aisaros' bank, Calabria, Noe², no. 25, and the find in Britain, my 'Foreign commerce', *Journ. Econ. & Bus. Hist.* iv (1932), p. 757), and stray finds of such coins (e.g. at Carthage) are frequent.

As regards the policy pursued by the Ptolemies of forcing their coinage on their foreign dominions, I may remind the reader that autonomous coinage regularly ceased in Greek and Phoenician cities under their control. This was so in Cyprus and Phoenicia and also in Asia Minor with possibly a few minor exceptions (we may assume, though it is not certain, that Ephesus minted from 258 to 202 B.C.; Miletus did not stop minting during the Ptolemaic overlordship; Lebedus (Ptolemais) issued some bronze coins of a semi-municipal character between 266 and 203 B.C.; there were issues by Caunus in Caria, which remained in the hands of the Ptolemies from 309 to 189 B.C., perhaps by Halicarnassus and Telmessus—for references Head, *H. N.*, 2nd. ed., s.vv.); cf. E. T. Newell, *Tyrus Rediviva*, 1923, p. 19 and A. Heuss, *Stadt und Herrscher*, p. 197. Finds of Ptolemaic coins in Palestine: Samaria— G. A. Reisner, C. S. Fisher, D. G. Lyon, *Harvard Excavations at Samaria*, i, 1924, pp. 252 ff.; Beth Zur—O. R. Sellers, *The Citadel of Beth Zur*, 1933, pp. 69 ff.; in general, W. F. Albright, *Bull. Amer. Schools of Or. Res.* xliii (1931), October, pp. 10 and 12.

Demetrius' letter, with an important correction by Th. Reinach, *Rev. É.G.* xli (1928), p. 191: *P. Cairo Zen.* 59021; W. Schubart, *Gr. Pap.* no. 2; Hunt–Edgar, *Sel. Pap.*, no. 409. Cf., besides the works quoted at the beginning of this note, U. Wilcken, *Schmollers Jahrb.* xlv (1921), p. 84 (388) f.; *Arch. Pap.* vii (1926), p. 76; E. Ziebarth, *Beitr. zur Geschichte des Seeraubs*, &c., p. 84; F. Heichelheim, *Wirtschaftl. Schwankungen*, pp. 10 ff.; and 'Monopole' in *P.W.K.* xvi. 174 f.; C. Préaux, loc. cit., pp. 271 ff.; A. Heuss, *Stadt und Herrscher*, p. 195 (inadequate and antiquated). In this letter the ἔμποροι who play such an important part in the business life of Egypt are not exclusively merchants from the Ptolemaic foreign dominions but foreign merchants in general; cf. the distinction made between ξενικὸν and Σύρον ἔλαιον in *R. L.* col. 52, 25 f.: ὅσοι δὲ τῶν ἐμπόρων | ἐκ Πηλουσίου ξενικὸν ἔλαιον ἢ Σύρον παρακο- μίζ[ω]σιν εἰς ['Αλ]εξάνδ[ρ]ειαν. The measure of Philadelphus was probably a new device. Earlier in his reign and under Soter foreign coins circulated in Egypt. I must, however, note that the reminting of worn-out and obsolete coins was not an unusual practice in the ancient world. For the Hellenistic world I may cite the reminting on a large scale of obsolete and unpopular coins into coins of Alexandrine type by Antiochus I, at Susa, E. T. Newell, 'The coinage of the Eastern Seleucid mints', *Num. St.* i (1938), pp. 127 ff. There is little doubt, moreover, that the Ptolemaic coins which came in to the hands of the Seleucids were reminted. The compulsory reminting of foreign coins and the novelty of coined money in Egyptian life may have led to the creation of special 'inspectors' or 'checkers' of coins, δοκιμασταί, who were supposed to receive and inspect all payments in money inside and outside the τράπεζαι, see *U.P.Z.* 156 (259 B.C.), cf. *P. Hib.* 41, 106, 107, 109 and the comments of U. Wilcken, ibid.; cf. also R. Herzog, *Aus der Geschichte des Bankwesens im Altertum: Tesserae nummulariae*, 1919, p. 27. It is doubtful, however, whether the measure of Philadelphus remained in force in Egypt under his successors. In *Teb.* 739. 23 (163 or 145 B.C.) a Phocaean gold stater caused some difficulties but was not rejected altogether.

[202] On barter and the use of money, see the remarks of U. Wilcken, 'Alexander,' &c., *Schmollers Jahrb.* xlv (1921), pp. 78 (382) ff.; E. Grier, *Accounting in the Zenon Papyri*, 1934, pp. 36–45 (money accounts) and pp. 46–55 (accounts of raw material, &c.). On the rate of interest in Egypt in Ptolemaic times, A. Segré, 'Il mutuo e il tasso d'interesse nell'Egitto greco-romano', *Atene e Roma*, v (1924), pp. 119 ff.; C. Préaux, loc. cit., p. 282 f. For the rate of interest in Greece, F. Heichelheim, *Wirtsch. Schwank.*, p. 126 f., and J. A. O. Larsen, 'Roman Greece', pp. 368 ff. I do not think that such a high rate as 24 per cent. was maintained in Egypt for the sake of attracting foreign capital thither. There is not the slightest evidence to show that foreigners actively participated in business in Egypt, except in the field of trade. Nor do I regard it as very probable that the rate was fixed in the interests of the king—the chief money-lender—though this may have played a secondary part. Cf. Ch. VIII.

[203] Banks: U. Wilcken, loc. cit., W. L. Westermann, 'Warehousing and Trapezite Banking in Antiquity', *Journ. of Econ. and Bus. Hist.* iii (1930), pp. 30 ff.; E. Ziebarth, 'Hellenistische Banken', *Z.N.* xxxiv (1923), pp. 36 ff.; F. Heichelheim, 'Monopole', *P.W.K.* xvi. 181 ff. (with bibliography), and *Wirtschaftsg.*, pp. 562 ff.; C. Préaux, *L'Écon. Lag.*, pp. 280 ff. (Les banques). Egyptian bankers (3 out of 25, the rest being Greeks), W. Peremans, *Vreemdelingen* &c., p. 52. Many important problems regarding the banks still await solution. For example, should we discriminate between the βασιλική τράπεζα, treasury office, and the βασιλική τράπεζα, royal bank? Were the two departments managed separately, the first being run by government officials, the second by concessionaires, and if so, what were the relations between the two? Did the banks take any part in investing the money of their customers? For the answer to these and other questions we must await the accumulation of further evidence. It may be noted that branches of the royal bank existed not only in Egypt proper but in the dominions as well. See *P. Cairo Zen.* 59036 relating to Halicarnassus, where the royal bank works in close connexion with the city treasury and takes action as ordered by a royal officer (probably the *oeconomus*). Temples issuing their own money in the Ptolemaic times: C. Préaux, loc. cit., p. 273 f. Temples as banks, ibid., pp. 293 ff. Cf. Ch. VIII.

[204] On the *thesauroi* see the preceding notes and A. Calderini, Θησαυροί, *St. d. Scuola Papir.* iv. 3, 1924; F. Preisigke, *Girowesen im griech. Aegypten*

&c., 1910; F. Heichelheim, 'Sitos', *P.W.K.* Suppl. vi. 871 ff.; C. Préaux, loc. cit., p. 142.

205 On the date of the *pompe* of Philadelphus, see above ch. iii, note 11, esp. W. Otto, 'Beitr. z. Seleukidengesch.', *Bay. Abh.* xxxiv (1928), i, pp. 5, 8, 88, and *Phil.* lxxxvi (1930–1), p. 414, n. 27, and W. W. Tarn, *J.H.S.* liii (1933), pp. 59 ff. On the description of it by Callixeinus, F. Caspari, 'Studien zu dem Kallixeinosfragment Athenaios 5, 197c–203b', *Hermes,* lxviii (1933), p. 400 (note especially on p. 405 the parallel drawn between Philadelphus' *pompe* and those of the Indian kings, Strabo xv. 1. 69, p. 718.). Caspari's comparison of the Hellenistic *pompe* with the Roman triumphal processions of the period succeeding the great victories over the Hellenistic monarchs is further discussed by A. Bruhl, 'Les influences hellénistiques dans le triomphe romain', *Mél. d'Arch. et d'Hist.* xlvi (1929), pp. 77 ff. On the meaning of the chariot with Alexander, Soter, and the Greek cities, V. Ehrenberg, *Alexander and the Greeks,* 1938, pp. 2 ff. (cf. W. W. Tarn's review of this book, *Cl. Rev.* lii, 1938, p. 234 f.).

206 On Theocritus' 'Ptolemaios', U. von Wilamowitz-Moellendorf, *Hell. Dichtung,* ii, 1924, p. 130 ff., esp. pp. 134. On the date of Teles' statement, W. S. Ferguson, *Hell. Athens,* p. 177, n. 2, cf. p. 202, n. 2. The view of Athenaeus was a commonplace in Roman times, see *Oxyr.* 1796, l. 8 f. (A. Körte, *Arch. Pap.* vii (1923–4), p. 118), and the song of the Nile sailors, *Oxyr.* 425. Cf. Parmeno, *Iambi,* 3 (J. U. Powell, *Collect. Alex.*, p. 237). The epigram of Gaza: *S.E.G.* viii. 269, cf. above, ch. iii, n. 7, and the sepulchral epigram, *S.E.G.* viii. 768 (second century B.C.), l. 25 f.: εἰμὶ γὰρ εὐέρκτης [Ἀπολ]-λώνιος, ὃν βασιλῆε[ς] κρίναντες φιλία[ις αἶσι κατηγλάϊσαν. The passage of the third hymn of Madinet Madi and the two mosaics quoted in the text are discussed in my article 'Καρποί' in *Mél. G. Radet.* I may note in this connexion that the Nile is called χρυσορόας both in the passage of Athenaeus (v. 203 c) cited above and in the second hymn of Isidorus (*S.E.G.* viii. 549, 17). The cult of the Nile was very popular with the Greeks of Egypt, see *S.E.G.* viii. 453 (220–215 B.C.), engraved on the base of a statue of Arsinoe dedicated by a man (name erased) who was ὁ τοῦ Νείλου ἱερεύς; cf. a statue of the Nile found in Egypt, E. Breccia, *Bull. Soc. Arch. Alex.* xxvi (N.S. 7), pp. 258 ff., pl. xxv. It is needless to remind the reader how popular in the Greco-Roman world were statues of the deified Nile, first created by Greek artists of Alexandria (the famous statue of the Vatican).

207 On Zenon's private affairs see my *Large Estate,* pp. 158 ff., and C. C. Edgar, *P. Mich. Zen.*, Intr., pp. 43 ff.

208 See my remarks, *Large Estate,* Index, s.v. 'Strikes'. A full collection of material will be found in W. Peremans, 'Ptolémée II Philadelphe et les indigènes égyptiens', *Rev. Belge,* xii (1933), pp. 1005 ff., and 'Égyptiens et étrangers en Égypte au IIIe siècle avant J.C.', *Chr. d'Ég.* xi (21) (1936), pp. 151 ff., cf. C. Préaux, *L'Écon. Lag.*, pp. 515 ff. The instances are many and various, and they show how difficult it was for Philadelphus to break down

the silent resistance of the natives to his new system. On the informers (μηνυταί), *P. Cairo Zen.* 59489 (alleged theft of σίπνον), 59484 (one weaver denouncing another as being στασιαστής), 59499, l. 87 (a γεωργός being στασιασταί (*sic*); cf. Ps.-Aristeas, 25, and above, note 146. Cf. O. Schulthess, art. *Μήνυσις*, *P.W.K.* Suppl. vi. 298 ff.

209 W. L. Westermann, 'Egyptian agricultural labour under Ptolemy Philadelphus', *Agricultural History*, i (1927), pp. 34 ff.; F. Heichelheim, *Wirtsch. Schwank.*, pp. 101 ff. The conclusions of these two scholars (Westermann's article remained unknown to Heichelheim), based on the same statistical material, do not coincide. Westermann, who did not compare the Delian conditions with those of Egypt, takes a less favourable view than Heichelheim. Cf. E. Grier, *Accounting in the Zenon Papyri*, 1934, p. 51; and C. Préaux, *Chr. d'Ég.* x (20) (1935), pp. 384 ff. A comparison of *P. Cairo Zen.* 59569, l. 135-6, of 246 B.C., with *P. Cairo Zen.* 59562 of 253 B.C. led Miss Grier to believe that between 253 and 246 B.C. the payments in kind made by the *dorea* of Apollonius (grain regularly portioned out) and effected by Heracleides, the supervisor of agricultural work, increased by 60 per cent. But her interpretation of these two documents, as Prof. C. B. Welles has pointed out to me, is rather doubtful: what is listed in the first document is a payment made by Heracleides, while in the second it is a payment made to him. As regards the calculations of Heichelheim we must bear in mind that it is far from certain that hired hands on the estate of Apollonius were occupied throughout the whole year without intermission.

210 On the inconsistencies in the new system of the Ptolemies and the reaction of the population to them see the papers of C. Préaux, cited in note 82. Some of her observations are incorporated in what I have said in the text.

211 The role played by Euergetes I in Greek affairs is illustrated by his active policy on the mainland of Greece (see above, ch. I, p. 39) and by such documents as the set of inscriptions found at Cos and studied by R. Herzog, *Hermes*, lxv (1930), pp. 463 ff.; cf. the decree of Samothrace in favour of Euergetes' governor Hippomedon, *S.I.G.*³ 502 (228-225 B.C.). On Philopator see Ch. V.

212 On the native revolt in Egypt in the time of Euergetes, *Teb.* 703, Introduction (this document is our richest source of information for the conditions that prevailed in Egypt in the second half of the third century). Μάχιμοι and ναῦται: *Teb.* 703 (of the time of Euergetes I or Philopator), l. 215, cf. *U.P.Z.* 157, ll. 30 ff.; misconduct of officers: *Hib.* 59, 245 B.C.; *Ent.* 87 (25th year of Euergetes I); royal peasants exhausted by ἐκφόρια, *Teb.* 703, ll. 60 ff.; flight of men pressed into service and ἀναχώρησις, *U.P.Z.* 157, ll. 33-4 (Euergetes I?); in this document among the groups which were not available for the work on the dikes are listed: 37 φυγάδες; 21 χοαχύται ὡσαύτως; total 58. In *Teb.* 703, l. 217, is quoted the ὑπόμνημα περὶ τῶν ἀνακεχωρηκό[τ]ων σωμάτων ἐκ τῶν | ἔργων. *Hib.* 71 (245-244 B.C.), a letter of Antiochus to Dorion,

l. 5: περὶ τ[ῶν] ἀνακεχωρηκότων σωμάτων ἐκ τῆς ἐ[ν] Κεφαλαῖς λατομίας. In *Teb.* 701 (235 B.C.) a village becomes ἔρημος because many of the villagers are imprisoned. Cf. above, n. 208.

It is, of course, possible that some of the oppressive measures of Euergetes' time were temporary, caused as they were by the great strain of the Syrian war, which lasted until 240 B.C. (*U.P.Z.* 157 is assigned with probability to 241 B.C.). The same may be true of *Teb.* 703, of which the exact date is unknown (see l. 236: ἀκολούθως τοῖς περιέχουσι καιροῖς). On the other hand, we may note the admonitions of the *dioecetes* to his οἰκονόμοι in *Teb.* 703 to treat the population kindly and justly (cf. *Hib.* 59. 9), and the great care taken by the king and the *dioecetes* to increase the productivity of the country (*Teb.* 769, ll. *27* ff. and ll. *72* ff.). However, the γεωργός in *Teb.* 769 warns the government that the unjust treatment to which he has been subjected may deter others from renting and planting the royal land; and the admonitions of *Teb.* 703 suggest that a different treatment of the population was the rule. The explanation of the mood of the native population of Egypt suggested in the text and in this note develops ideas that I have frequently expressed, e.g., in my *Kolonat* and in my 'Foundations of Social and Economic life', *J.E.A.* vi (1920), pp. 170, 178. My ideas accord with the point of view of Mlle C. Préaux, emphasized by her in many of her papers (see note 84), especially in 'Esquisse d'une histoire des révolutions égyptiennes sous les Lagides', *Chr. d'Ég.* xi (22) (1936), p. 522. This paper came into my hands long after I had written this section of my book. I am glad to state that our conclusions, drawn from the same material, agree in all essential points. I must emphasize, however, that Mlle Préaux underestimates the influence on the natives of the fact that their rulers were foreigners.

²¹³ It is highly probable that Euergetes took back the *dorea* granted by Philadelphus to Apollonius, see my *Large Estate*, p. 20, cf. p. 170 f. The same is true of the *dorea* mentioned in *Teb.* 773, l. 1, and 780, l. 7–8; cf. in addition the evidence quoted in *Large Estate*, loc. cit.; *B.G.U.* vi, 1238. 13 (third century); 1504. 4; 1540. 3 (Philopator); *Pap. Rev. Belge*, iv, 8 ε 3 (third century), and *P. Mich.* 182 (182 B.C.), cf. 193 and 200 (note the payments to the king of rent for land which belonged to a *dorea*). Taxes granted as a *dorea*: *P. Col.* 480; Hunt, *Sel. Pap.* 205. l. 7 f. (and note of Westermann); J. G. Tait, *Greek Ostraka in the Bodl. Libr.*, 1930, no. 32 (232 B.C.); C. Préaux, *Les Ostraca grecs . . . Wilbour au Musée de Brooklyn*, 1935, no. 2, and her interesting remarks on this text. For later times see below, chs. v and vi. A *dorea* in operation is seen, in my opinion, in *Teb.* 701 (the interpretation of Hunt is different).

²¹⁴ A copious collection of the evidence relating to Alexandria in general— its history, topography, social, economic, and religious life, &c.—has been assembled by A. Calderini in his *Dizionario dei nomi geografici* &c., 1935, s.v. Ἀλεξάνδρεια. General descriptions of Alexandria are numerous (a full list will be found in Calderini's article). I may mention the still not antiquated book by G. Lumbroso, *L'Egitto dei Greci e dei Romani*, 1895, and his posthumous

book (in course of publication), *Testi e commenti concernenti l'antica Alessandria*; the excellent guide by E. Breccia, *Alexandrea ad Aegyptum*, Eng. ed. 1922, and the very good paper by H. I. Bell, 'Alexandria' in *J.E.A.* xiii (1927), pp. 171 ff., the last two with copious bibliography. I have not seen G. Dijkmans, 'Une économie ancienne: alexandrie des Ptolémées', *Rev. d. Sciences écon.* vii (Liége, 1933), pp. 109 ff. On Alexandria as reflected in her art and industry: F. Poulsen 'Gab es eine alexandrinische Kunst?' in *From the Collections of the Ny Carlsberg Glyptothek*, ii (1938), and I. Noshy, *The Arts in Ptolemaic Egypt*, 1937; cf. above on Egyptian industry, and on the Pompeian paintings my article 'Die hellenistisch-römische Architekturlandschaft', *Röm. Mitt.* 1911, p. 47 f., figs. 26–8. Pharos: new evidence in Ibn Al-Sayj's description of the Pharos of 1165–6 (with measurements): M. Asin Palacios, 'Al-Andalus', *Rev. de las Escuelas de Estudios árabes* &c., i (1933), pp. 241 ff. cf. ibid. iii (1935), pp. 185 ff., and L. Otero, ibid. i. (1933), pp. 293 ff. (reconstruction); cf. also R. Vallois, *R.É.G.* xlix (1936), pp. 167 ff., and *Rev. Arch.* vii (1936), pp. 104 ff. Alexandria and the *Adoniazusai*: A. S. F. Gow, *J.H.S.* lviii (1938), pp. 180 ff.; the 'Zoo': H. M. Hubbell, *Class. Journ.* xxxi (1935), pp. 68 ff. Alexandria as an autonomous city appears in such documents as the temple inventories of Delos, e.g., Durrbach–Roussel, *Inscr. de Délos*, no. 1403 B *a* I, gifts brought by the θεωροί of the king and of Alexandria; ll. 65 and 75: θεωρῶν τ[ῶν παρὰ βασιλέως Πτολε]μαίου καὶ τῆς πόλεως τῶν Ἀλεξανδρέων. The epigrams describing the fountain and the shrine of Homer: O. Guéraud et P. Jouguet, *Publ. Soc. ég. Papyrologie*, ii (1938). On the *Boule* of Alexandria in the early Ptolemaic period: M. Segre, *Bull. Soc. Arch. Alex.* xxxii (N.S. 10) (1938), p. 135.

[215] On Apollonius see my preliminary remarks in my *Large Estate*, and those of C. C. Edgar in *P. Mich. Zen.*, Introduction. It will be of great importance, after all the Zenon papyri have been published, to collect the complete evidence about Apollonius' official, economic, and domestic life. Delayed payment of wages and salaries, e.g., *P. Cairo Zen.* 59043 and E. Grier, *Accounting* &c.

[216] On the *dorea* of Apollonius see the papers quoted in the preceding note; cf. my *Out of the Past of Greece and Rome*, 1932, pp. 92 ff. On the houses: N. Lewis, 'New light on the Greek house from the Zenon papyri', *A.J.A.* xxxvii (1933), pp. 397 ff., and A. R. Schütz, *Der Typus des hellenistischägyptischen Hauses im Anschluss an Baubeschreibungen griechischer Papyrusurkunden*, Diss. Würzburg, 1936 (see especially the quotations from the Zenon correspondence, pp. 1 ff.). Zenon's correspondence contains many details about houses in process of construction and decoration. On Philadelphia, P. Viereck, *Philadelpheia*, 1928 (*Morgenland*, Heft 16).

[217] On this subject more will be said in Ch. VIII.

[218] On Syria: my chapter 'Syria and the East', *C.A.H.* vii, pp. 161 ff., esp. pp. 173 ff. (with bibliography); W. W. Tarn, *Hellen. Civ.*, 2nd ed., pp. 116 ff., and *The Greeks in Bactria and India*, 1938, pp. 1 ff.; E. Bikerman, *Institutions des Séleucides*, 1938. For the political history and administration

of Syria in the third century B.C. see the chapters of *C.A.H.* relating thereto, with the bibliographies ; cf. n. 230.

²¹⁹ It is unnecessary to give here a list of inscriptions bearing on the Seleucid Empire. The most important of them will be quoted and discussed later in this section.

²²⁰ A good list of publications in which the cuneiform business documents of the Seleucid period are transcribed, translated, and discussed will be found in the dissertation of O. Krückmann, *Babylonische Rechts- und Verwaltungsurkunden aus der Zeit Alexanders und der Diadochen,* 1931, cf. M. San Nicolò, *Beiträge zur Rechtsgeschichte im Bereiche der keilschriftlichen Rechtsquellen,* 1931. A full publication of the cuneiform texts by San Nicolò and Krückmann is in preparation. To the bibliography of Krückmann may be added M. Rutten, *Contrats de l'Époque séleucide conservés au Musée du Louvre,* 1935, with an excellent bibliography and a survey of the history of Uruk ; cf. A. Aymard, 'Une ville de la Babylonie séleucide d'après les contrats cunéiformes', *Rev. É. A.* xl (1938), pp. 5 ff. (p. 7, n. 4, gives a list of documents published in transcriptions only and p. 9, n. 4, a similar list of translated documents). On the dates of the tablets, E. Cavaignac, *Rev. Assyr.* xxviii (1931), pp. 73 ff., and xxxiv (1937), pp. 140 ff., and A. T. Olmstead, *Cl. Phil.,* xxxii (1937), pp. 1 ff.

²²¹ Parchments and papyri of Dura : F. Cumont, *Fouilles de Doura-Europos,* 1926, pp. 281 ff. ; J. Johnson, *Dura Studies,* 1932, pp. 35 ff., and the lists by myself, C. B. Welles, and E. T. Silk, *Excav. at Dura-Europos,* Prel. Rep. ii, pp. 201 ff., v, pp. 295 ff., vi, pp. 416 ff., and vii–viii, pp. 426 ff. ; cf. the reports of C. B. Welles and myself, *Münch. Beitr. z. Papyrologie,* xix (1934), pp. 351 ff. Individual parchments are published and illustrated by A. R. Bellinger and C. B. Welles, *Yale Class. Stud.* v (1935), pp. 95 ff., and by C. B. Welles, *Z. d. Sav.-Stift.* lvi (1936), pp. 99 ff., and *Archives de l'Hist. du droit oriental,* i (1937), pp. 261 ff. Parchments of Avroman, E. H. Minns, *J.H.S.* xxxv (1915), pp. 22 ff. ; P. Meyer, *Jurist. Papyri,* 1920, p. 120 ; A. Cowley, *J.R.A.S.,* 1919, p. 147 ; H. S. Nyberg, *Le Monde oriental,* xvii (1923), pp. 182 ff. Bullae and seals of Orchoi and Seleuceia : my 'Seleucid Babylonia', *Yale Class. Stud.* iii (1932), pp. 26 ff., and R. H. McDowell, *Stamped and Inscribed Objects from Seleucia on the Tigris,* 1935, cf. F. E. Brown, *A.J.A.* xlii (1938), pp. 607 ff.

²²² On the Seleucid coinage see below, notes 243 ff.

²²³ I shall not be expected to give a full list of the publications in which the ruins of the above cities and the discoveries made in them have been recorded, studied, and illustrated. A good partial survey of recent work done by Germany in Asia Minor and elsewhere will be found in G. Rodenwaldt, 'Neue deutsche Ausgrabungen', *Deutschtum und Ausland,* 23–4, 1930. Cf. W. Otto, *Handbuch der Archäologie,* i, 1937 : F. Koepp, 'Geschichte der Archäologie', pp. 11 ff., and Th. Wiegand, 'Die Denkmäler' &c., pp. 71 ff., and the relative articles in *P.W.K.* For the inscriptions cf. J. J. E. Hondius, *Saxa loquuntur,* 1938.

[224] On the ruins of Syria see my sketch 'La Syrie romaine' in *Rev. Hist.* clxxv (1935), pp. 1 ff., cf. F. F. Cumont, *C.A.H.* xi (1936), pp. 613 ff. (with bibliography). Nothing similar to the work of Watzinger (see following note) exists for Syria. On Antioch on the Orontes, G. W. Elderkin and others, *Antioch-on-the-Orontes*, i, 1934, and R. Stilwell and others, ii, 1938. Reports on the current excavations in this city are published from time to time in *A.J.A.* and in *Syria*. The last of them (*A.J.A.* xlii (1938), pp. 205 ff.) reports on the work of 1935-6. No Hellenistic monuments, except some sherds, coins, and other minor objects have yet been discovered.

[225] C. Watzinger, *Denkmäler Palästinas*, i, ii, 1933 and 1935; cf. on Petra and some other Nabataean sites, G. and A. Horsfield, 'Sela–Petra' &c., *Quart. Dept. Ant. Pal.* vii (1938), pp. 1 ff. On Gerasa, C. Kraeling and others, *Gerasa*, 1938, and N. Glueck, *A.J.A.* xli (1937), pp. 361 ff. and viii (1938), pp. 87 ff.

[226] Hellenistic temples at Orchoi: J. Jordan, 'Uruk–Warka', *Wiss. Veröff. d. d. Orient-Ges.* li (1928), and the yearly 'Vorläufige Berichte' on the excavations of Uruk published by J. Jordan, E. Heinrich, and A. Nöldeke and their assistants in the *Berl. Abh.* (phil-hist. Kl.) from 1930. A highly interesting Parthian temple which presents quite a Hellenistic aspect has been recently unearthed at Orchoi, see E. Heinrich, 'Sechster vorl. Ber.' &c., *Berl. Abh.*, 1935, no. 2, pp. 33 ff. On the history of the city and its excavation see the short report of M. Rutten, *Contrats de l'Époque séleucide conservés au Musée du Louvre*, 1935, pp. 25 ff., cf. A. Aymard, *Rev. É.A.* xl (1938), pp. 5 ff.

[227] Seleuceia: L. Waterman, *Prelim. Rep. upon the Excav. at Tel Umar*, i, 1931, ii, 1933; cf. for bibliography the book by R. H. McDowell quoted in note 221 and his *Coins from Seleuceia on the Tigris*, 1935. The results of the last two campaigns at Seleuceia will shortly be published by C. Hopkins.

[228] Dura: F. Cumont, *Fouilles de Doura-Europos*, 1926; *Excavations at Dura-Europos*, Preliminary Reports, i–vii/viii, 1929–39, cf. M. Rostovtzeff, *Caravan Cities*, 1932, pp. 153 ff. (more complete in the Italian edition, 1934), and *Dura-Europos and its Art*, 1938. On the date of the capture of Dura cf. A. Alföldi, 'Die Hauptereignisse der Jahre 253–61 n. Chr. im Spiegel der Münzprägung', *Berytus* iv (1937–8), pp. 41 ff.

[229] The monuments of India and Bactria of the Hellenistic period are collected and illustrated in many books of which I give here a small selection. On Bactria: W. W. Tarn, *The Greeks in Bactria and India*, 1938; cf. on the excavations of Kapisa below, p. 544, n. 317. On India: Sir John Marshall, *Cambr. Hist. of India*, i, 1921, p. 621; V. Smith and K. de B. Codrington, *A History of Fine Art in India and Ceylon*, 2nd ed., 1930, pp. 28 ff.; Sir John Marshall, *A Guide to Sanchi*, 2nd. ed., 1936, pp. 9 ff. (cf. the forthcoming book by him and M. A. Foucher, *The Monuments of Sanchi*); N. G. Majumdar, *A Guide to the Sculptures in the Indian Museum*, i, *Early Indian School*, 1937, pp. 54 ff.; all with copious bibliographies. On Taxila: Sir John Marshall,

A Guide to Taxila, 3rd ed., 1936, pp. 26 ff.. and his forthcoming book on Taxila. I shall return to the problem of the relations between India, Bactria, and the Hellenistic world at the end of this section. Less work has been done on the monuments of the Iranian plateau belonging to the Hellenistic period. On the temple of Persepolis built at the foot of the terrace of the palace and the Greek dedications to Iranian gods under Greek names found in this Iranian temple, see E. Herzfeld, *J.R.A.S.*, 1934, p. 232; id., *Archaeological History of Iran*, 1935, pp. 44 ff.; J. Sturm, *P.W.K.* xix. 1273. Since the ruins and the inscriptions are not yet published, I must reserve my judgement concerning the date of the temple and of the votive inscriptions assigned by Herzfeld to the time shortly after Alexander. On the columns of Istakhr (the city that succeeded Persepolis) and the temples of Kangawar and Khurha see Herzfeld, *Arch. Hist.*, pp. 48 ff. (cf. pl. vi). The dates of these monuments are uncertain. The results of the excavations of Susa are published in the volumes of the French *Délégation en Perse : Mémoires*, vols. i–xxv (1900–34); on the early history of Susa and Elam cf. G. G. Cameron, *History of Early Iran*, 1936.

[230] The history of the Iranian satrapies of the Seleucid kingdom is but imperfectly known and is consequently controversial. On the independence of Persis, which is attested by coins minted by local kings early in the third century, probably soon after the death of Seleucus I, E. T. Newell, 'The coinage of the eastern Seleucid Mints' (*Num. Studies*, i), 1938, p. 160 f. On the foundation of the Parthian kingdom and the secession of Parthia under Andragoras and of Bactria under Diodotus, see the judicious analysis of our literary and numismatic evidence by J. Wolski, 'Arsaces I the founder of the Parthian State', *Eos*, xxxviii (1937), pp. 492 ff., and xxxix (1938), pp. 244 ff. (published also separately as a Krakow dissertation) (in Polish), and his forthcoming paper 'Diodotos I and the foundation of the Greco-Bactrian kingdom', in *Eos* (in Polish), cf. the review of E. Bikerman, *Rev. Phil.*, 1939, and N. Debevoise, *A political history of Parthia*, 1938. The early tyrannies of Caria, Ionia, and Lycia: Eupolemus of Iasus (?) (end of the fourth century)—my paper, *Rev. É.A.* xxxiii (1931), p. 23, and L. Robert, *L'Antiquité Class.* iv (1935), pp. 157 ff., and *Coll. Froehner*, i, *Inscr. gr.*, no. 52, pp. 65 ff.; Timarchus of Miletus—Just. *prol.* xxvi; App. *Syr.* 65; tyrants of Apollonia in Lycia (?) (early third century B.C.)—Zolotas in 'Ἀθηνᾶ, xx (1908), p. 233; M. Segre, *Athen.* xii (1934), pp. 3 ff.; L. Robert, *Villes de l'Asie Mineure*, 1935, p. 56, n. 3; Docimus, general of Antigonus, founder of the city of Docimium in Phrygia—Imhoof–Blumer, *Kleinas. Münzen*, pp. 223 ff.; W. Peek, *Ath. Mitt.* lvi (1931), p. 124, no. 8; A. Wilhelm, *Sitzb. Berl. Akad.*, 1932, p. 851; L. Robert, *Rev. É.G.* xlv (1932), p. 203, n. 2 and *Rev. Phil.* viii (1934), pp. 267 ff.; H. Bengtson, 'Die Strategie in der hell. Zeit, i', *Münch. Beitr.* xxvi (1937), p. 199; A. H. M. Jones, *The Cities* &c., p. 49 and n. 33; perhaps Themison, the favourite of Antiochus II, founder of Themisonium (?) in S. Phrygia—A. H. M. Jones, loc. cit.; W. Ruge, *P.W.K.* v A, 1638 ff., cf. F. Schachermeyer, ibid. 1632, no. 3. For the later tyrants in various parts

of Asia Minor, Ernst Meyer, *Die Grenzen* &c., pp. 69 ff. and pp. 138 ff.; *C.A.H.* vii, pp. 183 ff.; W. W. Tarn, *Hell. Civ.* 2nd. ed., p. 120; A. H. M. Jones, loc. cit., pp. 48 ff. Especially interesting are Lysias and Philomelus in Phrygia (M. Holleaux, *Rev. É.A.* xvii (1915), pp. 237 ff.; P. Roussel and G. Nicole, *Rev. É.G.* xxix (1916), pp. 452 ff., cf. A. Wilhelm, *Wien. S. B.* clxvi (1910–11), pp. 48 ff.), and still more Olympichus in Caria (M. Holleaux, *Rev. É.A.* v (1903), pp. 223 ff., and *Rev. É.G.* xii (1899), pp. 20 ff.). New information regarding Olympichus is contained in the decree of the city of Alinda in honour of two officers of his civil staff (δια]τρίβοντες | [π]αρ᾽ Ὀλυμπίχωι στρατηγῶι ἐν τῶι ἐπιστολογραφίωι), A. Laumonier, *B.C.H.* lviii (1934), pp. 291 ff. Pisidia and Cilicia were always countries of petty tyrants, tribal and temple States. On the temple-state of Olba, J. Keil and A. Wilhelm, *M.A.M.A.* iii, 1931, pp. 44 ff.; M. Schede, *Gnomon*, x (1934), pp. 584 ff.; A. H. M. Jones, loc. cit., pp. 210 ff. On Ptolemy of Telmessus, above, p. 336 f. On the tyrannies in general, cf. E. Bikerman, *Inst. Sél.*, pp. 166 ff.

231 A careful analysis of the character of the royal power of the Seleucids will be found in E. Bikerman, op. cit., pp. 3 ff., chs. i and ii; on the royal cult, ibid., pp. 236 ff., cf. my articles, *J.H.S.* lv (1935), pp. 56 ff., *C.R. Ac. Inscr.*, 1935, pp. 290 ff., *Mél. syr. R. Dussaud* 1939, pp. 281 ff. On the descent of Seleucus I from Apollo, Stähelin, *P.W.K.* ii A. 1232; L. Robert, *Ét. Anat.*, pp. 172 ff.; E. Bikerman, loc. cit., p. 253, n. 1. On the royal power of the Successors in general, see above, Ch. III.

232 Note that in Hellenistic times Syria produced a remarkable group of philosophers of various creeds, especially Stoics. Stoicism from the outset was closely connected with the Semitic conception of life and remained congenial to the hellenized Semites and semitized Greeks of the Seleucid kingdom. I cannot cite here the numerous papers that deal with this subject. It will be sufficient to refer to J. Bidez, 'La cité du Monde et la cité du Soleil chez les Stoiciens', *Bull. Ac. Royale de Belgique*, 5ᵐᵉ sér. xviii (1932), pp. 244 ff. (and separately). I may, however, point out that in the time of the Roman Empire the most widely read treatises of Stoic philosophy were those produced by philosophers of eastern origin. Such were the famous Chrysippus of Soli and the great Posidonius of Apamea. Such also were Diogenes, native of Seleuceia, surnamed Βαβυλώνιος, successor of Zeno, and his pupils Persaeus of Citium, Boethus from Sidon, and Antipater from Tarsus. See the list of 'useful' books 'bearing on life' given in the notable letter of Theon addressed to Heracleides the philosopher, recently found in Egypt (first–second century A.D.), A. Vogliano, *Dal Iᵒ vol. dei Papiri d. R. Univ. di Milano*, 1935, no. 2; cf. the other lists of books quoted by him, especially that published by G. Manteuffel, *Pap. Varsov.* no. 5, which contains fragments of the section dealing with books on philosophy: these are almost exclusively books by Stoics, and the list is very similar to that contained in Theon's letter.

233 On the attitude of the Seleucids towards the various gods of their

kingdom, see the brief general remarks of E. Bikerman, *Inst. Sél.*, pp. 250 ff., cf. p. 123.

[234] Reconstruction of Esagila and Ezida by Antiochus I: E. Schrader, *Keilinschriftliche Bibliotek*, iii. Hälfte 2, pp. 136 ff. (F. E. Peiser) ; F. H. Weissbach, *Die Keilinschriften der Achämeniden*, 1911, pp. 132 ff. ; C. F. Lehmann-Haupt, 'Neue Studien zu Berossos', *Klio*, xxii (1928), p. 132. On the work done under Alexander, O. Krückmann, *Bab. Rechts- und Verwaltungsurk.*, &c., p. 70 f. Prof. F. J. Stephens of Yale draws my attention to the fact that Antiochus I never did any work in Esagila; he confined himself to the temple of Nabu in Borsippa—the Ezida. He says so in his inscription. However, he regards himself as trustee of the two temples—'Pfleger von Esagila und Ezida' (so now translated by F. Weissbach instead of ' Ausschmücker von Esagila und Ezida')—and professes in his inscription the desire to rebuild Esagila also. The temple of Esagila has been excavated by German archaeologists. No texts or remains testifying to the activity of Alexander or Antiochus I have been found, and the reconstruction by Alexander is not mentioned by the excavators in their report: see E. Wetzel und F. H. Weissbach, 'Das Hauptheiligtum des Marduk in Babylon, Esagila, und Entemenaki', *Ausgr. d. d. Or. Ges. in Babylon*, vii (1938). Gift of Antiochus I: Sidney Smith, *Babylonian historical texts*, 1924, pp. 156 ff. Royal gifts of land and valuables which finally appear in the possession of the temples of Babylon: C. F. Lehmann-Haupt, *Zeitschr. f. Ass.* vii (1892), pp. 330 ff.; W. Otto, *Beitr. z. Seleukidengesch.*, p. 72, n. 3; O. Krückmann, loc. cit., p. 8. The tablet that contains the document published by Lehmann-Haupt is much in need of revision and republication. Unfortunately this tablet, which at the time of its publication was in New York, having been brought from Babylonia by Rev. W. H. Ward and having been copied in London by Pinches and Lehmann-Haupt, has never been seen since. Cf. in general A. Aymard, *Rev. É.A.* xl (1938), p. 20, n. 2, and E. Bikerman, *Inst. Sél.*, p. 176. On the temple-money (?) of Babylon, Susa, and Ecbatana, E. T. Newell, 'The coinage of the eastern Seleucid Mints' (*Num. St.* i), 1938, p. 106, n. 14 (Babylon), pp. 117 f. and 122 (Susa), and p. 171 (Ecbatana). The friendly relations of Alexander and his successors with the leading temples and cities of Babylonia were in fact a continuation of the policy of the Assyrians and Persians, and they must be explained as a recognition of the great influence which the temples and the sacred cities had on the people of Babylonia. For Assyrian times see the interesting paper of F. M. Th. Böhl, 'Der babylonische Fürstenspiegel', *Mitt. Altor. Ges.* xl (1937), 3.

[235] The history of the Hellenistic temples of Uruk is derived from various documents found both in the early excavations of that city and in those still being carried on (by a German expedition). The activity of Anu-uballit I-Nicarchus in Bît-rêš is attested by the clay cylinder of the Yale collection, A. T. Clay, *Yale Or. Stud., Babyl. Texts*, i, 1915, pp. 81 ff. That of Anu-uballit II-Kephallon in the Wuswas is attested by his bricks from the temple of Anu and Antum (J. Jordan, 'Uruk Warka', *Wiss. Ver. d. d. Or. Ges.* li,

pp. 40 ff.). The date of these bricks, first read by Schroeder as 130 Sel.—which date was inconsistent with the name of the ruling king Antiochus recorded on the bricks (in 182 B.C. the king was Seleucus IV, see W. W. Tarn, *Hell. Civ.*, 2nd ed., p. 118 f. and p. 141; M. Holleaux, *B.C.H.* lvii (1933), p. 30, n. 2; my *Seleucid Babylonia*, p. 6 f.)—has been corrected by E. Heinrich, 'Fünfter vorl. Ber.', *Berl. Abh.*, 1933, phil.-hist. Kl. v (1934), p. 25, n. 1, who reads 110 Sel. instead of 130. Finally, the activity of the same man in the 'Südbau' is recorded in a long inscription on blue glazed bricks which decorated the cult niche of the temple. The inscription is not yet fully deciphered but certainly testifies to the building activity of Anu-uballit-Kephallon; see the note of O. Krückmann in A. Nöldeke &c., 'Siebenter vorl. Ber.', *Berl. Abh.*, 1935, phil.-hist. Kl. iv (1936), pp. 36 ff. On the status of the temples of Uruk in general and on the liberal policy of the Seleucids towards them, as illustrated by the cuneiform tablets, see the paper of A. Aymard quoted above, pp. 18 ff. and p. 23, and E. Bikerman, *Inst. Sél.*, pp. 174 ff.

236 Inscriptions of the temple of Nanaia in Susa, *S.E.G.* vii, 1 ff., esp. nos. 15 ff. (manumissions), cf. L. Robert, *Rev. Phil.* x (1936), pp. 137 ff.; F. Cumont, *C.R. Ac. Inscr.* 1937, pp. 313 ff. and 1938, pp. 305 ff. Cf. below, n. 270. It is interesting to note in this connexion the gold stater of Seleucus I minted at Susa. It shows the head of Apollo on the obverse and on the reverse, in place of the usual Athena, the image of Artemis shooting an arrow from a chariot driven by two elephants. E. T. Newell, 'The coinage of the eastern Seleucid Mints' (*Num. St.* i), 1938, p. 124, no. 329, suggests that this image may represent hellenized Nanaia identified with the Artemis *archegetis* of Seleucus.

237 O. Schroeder, *Vorderasiat. Schriftdenkmäler der k. Mus. z. Berlin*, xv, 1916, no. 16; M. Rutten, *Contrats de l'Époque séleucide*, p. 52. Remains of a bronze statue of one of the Seleucids and of some other similar statues have been recently found by Sir Aurel Stein in the ruins of a temple in a secluded valley of Elam near the small village of Shami in Khuzistan. Was it a temple of the ruling king and of his πρόγονοι or a temple of a local god in which the ruling king and his 'house' were *synnaoi theoi*? See the preliminary report of Sir Aurel Stein, *Geogr. Journ.* xcii, 4 (1938), pp. 325 ff., fig. 9 (my pl. x. 1).

238 See the material collected in my paper 'Kleinasiatische und syrische Götter im röm. Aegypten', *Aeg.* xiii (1933), pp. 508 ff., cf. my 'Dura and the Parthian Art', *Yale Class. Stud.* v (1935), pp. 206 ff., my *Dura-Europos and its Art*, 1938, pp. 58 ff., and F. Cumont, *Mél. syr. R. Dussaud*, 1938, pp. 6, nn. 1 and 8.

239 On the cult of Atargatis and Hadad, of Astarte and Adonis, in the Hellenistic and Roman periods, F. Cumont, *Les Religions orientales*, 3rd ed. 1929, pp. 160 ff. and pp. 180 ff.; on the iconography of Atargatis and Hadad, cf. P. V. C. Baur, *Excav. Dura-Europos*, Prel. Rep. iii, 1932, pp. 100 ff., and C. Hopkins, ibid. v, 1934, pp. 172 ff., and pl. xiv. Cf. my paper 'Le Gad

de Doura et Seleucus Nicator', *Mél. syr. R. Dussaud*, 1938, p. 281 ff., and F. E. Brown, *Dura Rep.* vii–viii, 1939, pp. 153 ff. On the cult of Syrian and Phoenician gods in Egypt, see my paper quoted in the preceding note. On Adonis in Egypt see the masterly paper by G. Glotz, 'Les fêtes d'Adonis sous Ptolemée II', *Rev. É.G.* xxxiii (1920), pp. 169 ff., cf. above, n. 214. A careful collection and study of the material bearing on Syrian, Phoenician, and Anatolian cults in Ptolemaic Egypt would certainly yield important results.

240 *O.G.I.* 214 (Seleucus I and Antiochus I, 288/7 b.c.) cf. *Milet*, i. 7 (1924), p. 283. 3 ; Welles, *R.C.* 5, and Hiller von Gaertringen, 'Miletos', *P.W.K.* xiv. 1604 f. Cf. E. Bikerman, *Inst. Sél.*, pp. 123 f. and 152, and L. Robert, *Ét. Anat.*, p. 450 ff.

241 E. Bikerman, *Inst. Sél.*, 1938, ch. iii: L'Armée, ch. iv: Le Fisc séleucide, ch. v: Organisation du Royaume. Our information on the organization of royal courts is rapidly increasing. In addition to the material collected by Bikerman, pp. 207 ff. (cf. A. Heuss, *Stadt und Herrscher* &c., p. 88), I may mention the role which royal judges played in Europus-Dura in Parthian times as illustrated by two documents: *D. Perg.* 20 and 40 (a.d. 87) ; see the remarks of C. B. Welles, *Z. d. Sav.-Stift.* lvi (1936), pp. 105 ff., and *Dura Rep.* vii–viii, pp. 427 ff. The institution seems to have been in use in all the Hellenistic monarchies: Eumenes appointed judges in Cappadocia (Plut. *Eum.* iii. 20) ; royal (?) judges are attested for Ptolemaic Palestine (*P. Cairo Zen.* 59006 and 59003, l. 18), and judges of the same type appear in the *diagramma* of Philip V (of 167 b.c.) found at Thessalonice (S. Pelekides, 'Ἀπὸ τὴν πολιτεία κτλ., τῆς ἀρχαίας Θεσσαλονίκης, 1934, p. 6, l. 23, cf. M. Hollaux, *Études* i, p. 268, n. 3). Additional evidence on the χρεοφυλάκια and χρεοφύλακες at Susa will be found in F. Cumont, *C.R. Ac. Inscr.*, 1937, pp. 313 ff., and on the municipal γραμματοφυλάκια and χρεοφυλάκια in Asia Minor in L. Robert, *Ét. Anat.*, pp. 453, 457 ff., and 486 ff.

242 See the bibliography quoted in Ch. III, n. 1. As regards the date of Ps.-Arist. *Oecon.* ii, E. Bikerman draws my attention to the fact that while in Persian times and under the rule of Antigonus (Diod. xix. 55) the satrap was in charge of financial administration also, in Seleucid times (Bulagoras' inscription, *S.E.G.* i. 366) this was no longer the case. But of course we do not know when exactly this change was introduced.

243 On the Seleucid coinage see the bibliography in *C.A.H.* vii, p. 879, and the more copious bibliography in R. H. McDowell, *Coins from Seleucia on the Tigris*, 1935, p. xiii f. An excellent summary will be found in J. G. Milne, *Greek Coinage*, 1931, pp. 108 ff. Cf. E. T. Newell, 'The coinage of the eastern Seleucid Mints from Seleucus I to Antiochus III', *Num. St.* i, 1938, and 'The Pergamene mint under Philetaerus', *Num. Notes and Mon.* lxxvi (1936), pp. 10 ff. Cleomenes III and Nabis: C. T. Seltman, *Greek Coins*, p. 256 f. Cf. the lucid pages on Seleucid coinage in E. Bikerman, *Inst. Sél.*, pp. 211 ff. Byzantium and Callatis and imitation of Seleucid types

at Istrus: K. Regling, *P.W.K.* xvi. 475. Circulation of Seleucid coins in Asia: I have quoted the statement of Milne, but I must point out that no large quantities of Seleucid coins have ever been found in India—a striking contrast to the frequency of Roman coins in the Roman imperial period, especially in southern India. I have found no Seleucid coins in the collections in the various museums of India, especially in that of Calcutta. Sir John Marshall (in a letter of March 16, 1937) confirms my impression: 'Seleucid and Parthian coins', he says, 'turn up occasionally in the Indian bazaars at Peshawar, Rawalpindi, &c., but I have never known of them being found in any large quantities in India.' The absence of Seleucid coins among those found at Taxila is especially striking.

[244] On gold in Bactria and India, W. W. Tarn, *The Greeks in Bactria and India*, pp. 104 ff.

[245] On the copper minted in the Greek cities of Asia Minor in Seleucid times, see my paper, 'Some remarks on the monetary and commercial policy of the Seleucids and Attalids', *Anatolian Studies presented to W. H. Buckler*, 1939, pp. 277 ff. On the bronze coinage of Syria and Mesopotamia, E. Bikerman, loc. cit., pp. 223 ff. The exclusive circulation of Seleucid coins in the cities of the empire is attested by the coin finds. In Palestine, for example, there were no other coins in circulation after Antiochus III. See G. A. Reisner, C. S. Fisher, and D. G. Lyon, *Harvard Excavations at Samaria*, i, 1924, pp. 252 ff. At Samaria pre-Hellenistic coins are rare. Then there appears a continuous set of Ptolemaic coins from Ptolemy I to Ptolemy V, with issues of Ptolemy II prevailing. From the time of Antiochus III Ptolemaic coins disappear, and Seleucid coins reign supreme until about 96 B.C., the most numerous being those of Antiochus III and IV. Almost exactly the same is true of Beth Zur (O. R. Sellers, *The Citadel of Beth Zur*, 1933, pp. 69 ff.). Here again after the Ptolemaic coins (the last being those of Ptolemy VI) we have none but the Seleucid, again with those of Antiochus III prevailing, until 96 B.C. In the last years of the Seleucid rule we have concurrently with the Seleucid issues some Maccabaean coins. Cf. below, n. 248 on Seleuceia and Dura (on the mint of Dura below, p. 489) and E. Bikerman, loc. cit., pp. 211 ff., who quotes also the examples of Sardis and Lysimacheia. A. Heuss, *Stadt und Herrscher*, p. 195, denies on insufficient grounds the existence of any monetary monopoly in the Seleucid Empire.

[246] On the coin hoards see the volume by Sydney P. Noe, *A Bibliography of Greek Coin Hoards*, 2nd ed., 1937, and K. Regling, 'Hellenistischer Münzschatz aus Babylon', *Z.f.N.* xxxviii (1928), pp. 92 ff.; cf. my article quoted in the preceding note. Occasional stray finds of Ptolemaic coins in Asia Minor do not contradict the above statement. Ptolemaic silver was of course good, and Ptolemaic coins would not be refused if occasionally offered in payment.

[246 a] E. T. Newell, 'The coinage of the eastern Seleucid Mints', pp. 126 ff.

247 O. Krückmann, *Babyl. Rechts- u. Verwaltungsurk.* &c., p. 68. See, e.g., M. Rutten, *Contrats de l'Époque séleucide*, no. ii (sale of land), l. 12: 'pour 15 sicles d'argent pur . . . en statères d'Antiochus de bon poids', and many other documents where the same stereotyped expression is used.

248 On the coins of Alexander and of the Seleucids discovered in Seleuceia between 1927 and 1931 see the excellent monograph of R. H. McDowell, *Coins from Seleucia on the Tigris*, 1935. On the coins of Europus-Dura see the chapters on the finds in *Excav. of Dura-Europos*, Prel. Rep., by A. R. Bellinger, esp. vol. iii, pp. 139 ff., and vol. iv, pp. 259 ff., cf. vol. vii–viii, pp. 391 ff., and my *Dura-Europos and its Art*, ch. i, n. 7 (A. R. Bellinger), cf. above, n. 245.

249 On the weights, measures, and coins of Babylonia in Seleucid times, A. Aymard, *Rev. É.A.* xl (1938), p. 23, n. 4; cf. E. Bikerman, loc. cit., p. 228.

250 The bronze weight of Babylon: A. Dumont, *Rev. Arch.* xx (1869), pp. 191 ff. *Mél. d'arch. et d'épigr.*, 1892 (pp. 134 ff.); E. Babelon, 'Inv. Coll. Wadd.', *Rev. Num.* ii (1898), p. 635, no. 7466; F. Lehmann-Haupt, *P.W.K.*, Suppl. iii. 607 ff.; O. Viedebantt, 'Zur hebräischen, phönizischen und syrischen Gewichtskunde', *Z. d. d. Pal. Ver.* xlv (1922), p. 15, no. 101; R. H. McDowell, *Stamped and inscribed objects from Seleucia on the Tigris*, p. 146 and p. 256 f.; E. Bikerman, *Inst. Sél.*, p. 214. The bronze weight of Seleuceia: R. H. McDowell, loc. cit., pp. 256 ff., cf. F. E. Brown's review of the book in *A.J.A.* xlii (1938), pp. 607 ff. It is interesting to see that at Seleuceia in the Parthian period it was the municipal *paraphylax* who was in charge of the control of weights and measures. So it was in Asia Minor in Roman times (McDowell, loc. cit., weight in the British Museum). This function of the *paraphylakes* was pointed out by myself (*Stor. Ec. e Soc.*, p. 491) but is not mentioned by L. Robert, *Ét. Anat.*, pp. 98 ff., and T. R. S. Broughton, 'Roman Asia Minor' (T. Frank, *Econ. Surv.* iv), p. 868. The existence of the same practice in Parthian Seleuceia and Roman Asia Minor points to a common, probably Seleucid, origin. The *paraphylax* may have been an associate or a subordinate of the *agoranomos*.

251 No corpus of Hellenistic weights found in various parts of the Hellenistic world is in existence. (For the weights of Athens, E. Pernice, *Griechische Gewichte*, 1894, and for those of Delos, W. Deonna, 'Le Mobilier délien', *Délos*, xviii, 1938, pp. 172 ff., cf. S. Reinach, *Traité d'épigraphie grecque*, p. 464 and L. Robert, *Rev. Phil.* xiii (65) (1939), pp. 185 ff.; see also my general remarks in Ch. VIII on the policy of the Hellenistic kings as regards weights and measures.) All the inscribed weights of Syria, Phoenicia, and Palestine will be published by P. R. Mouterde; cf. his remarks in *Mél. Univ. St.-Joseph*, xvii (1933), p. 246. I am indebted to him for permission to use his preliminary catalogue in manuscript, and I am also indebted to M. H. Seyrig for kindly sending me his notes on, and photographs of, the Syrian weights which have come to his notice. There are, however, some

useful collections of part of the material. The article 'Pondus' by E. Michon in Dar. et Saglio, *D. d. A.* is excellent; cf. F. Lehmann–Haupt, *P.W.K.*, Supp. iii. 607 ff., and O. Viedebantt, 'Zur hebräischen, phönizischen und syrischen Gewichtskunde', *Z. d. d. pal. Ver.* xlv (1922), pp. 1 ff. Publications of single examples with useful comments will be found, for instance, in Babelon–Blanchet, *Cat. d. Br. de la Bibl. nat.*, pp. 674 ff.; A. Dain, *Inscr. gr. du Musée du Louvre. Textes inédits* 1933, pp. 197 ff., nos. 237–45; E. Michon, *Mém. Soc. Ant. Fr.* li (1890), pp. 20 ff.; *Bull. Soc. Ant. Fr.*, 1906, p. 193; *Rev. Num.* 4ᵐᵉ sér. xvii (1913), pp. 314 ff.; *Rev. Arch.* v (1935), pp. 264 ff.; E. Pernice, *Griechische Gewichte*, p. 73. I reproduce some specimens of royal weights and of those of Antioch and Seleuceia on pls. liv and lv. On the control of weights by the Seleucid government, R. H. McDowell, *Stamped and inscribed objects from Seleucia on the Tigris*, pp. 151 ff. I may note in this connexion the curious weight of Athens (one of twelve weights of the same type) published by E. Pernice, loc. cit., p. 21 and no. 158, p. 106. This weight shows a countermark, the horned helmet of Seleucus I. Was it not an Attic weight used in the Seleucid Empire and counter-stamped by the royal office of weights and measures? There is no section on weights and measures in Broughton's 'Roman Asia Minor'. A further point to be noted is that the numerous weights styled in the inscriptions Σελεύκεια or 'Αντιόχεια μνᾶ or Σελεύκειον or 'Αντιόχειον διμναῖον, ἡμίμνουν, τέταρτον, ὄγδοον, ἐκκαιδέκατον, &c., may be explained, not as standard royal weights of Seleuceia and Antioch, but as those of king Seleucus or Antiochus. This was suggested in a private letter by H. Seyrig. In support of his view he quotes such expressions as Σελεύκειον δίδραχμον in *I.G.* xii. 2, 203 B 22 (270/69 B.C.), cf. E. Babelon, *Traité des monnaies*, i, p. 486, and E. Bikerman, *Inst. Sél.*, p. 4. I may add that expressions like 'Αλεξάνδρειον, Δημητρίειον, &c., ἀργύριον are common in Hellenistic and later documents, see above, Ch. III, n. 50, and my article in *Anat. St. W. H. Buckler*, p. 297, n. 1. M. Seyrig's suggestion is very attractive, but before forming a final judgement on this and many other problems regarding the 'royal' weights of the Seleucids, we must await the full publication of the copious material.

²⁵² On the expeditions of Demodamas and Patrocles, M. Cary et E. Warmington, *Les Éxplorateurs de l'Antiquité*, 1932 (or its English original), pp. 213 ff. In this book the authors deal with exploration, but commercial relations are occasionally referred to. Cf. the hopelessly antiquated and incomplete but useful book by R. Henning, *Terrae incognitae*, 1936, pp. 172 ff. and pp. 182 ff. These two books also discuss the relations between India and the Hellenistic world from the point of view of its exploration. On Demodamas and Patrocles cf. the interesting remarks of W. W. Tarn, *The Greeks in Bactria and India*, pp. 488 ff.

²⁵³ While the eastern and southern trade of the Ptolemies has been made the object of special study by many modern scholars, very little has been written on the trade of the Seleucids with India and Arabia. See my sketches: *C.A.H.* viii, pp. 651 ff., and vii, pp. 155 ff., and *Caravan Cities*, pp. 1 ff., and

W. W. Tarn, *Hell. Civ.*, 2nd ed., pp. 209 ff. The best and fullest treatment of
the subject in its various aspects will be found in W. W. Tarn, *The Greeks
in Bactria and India*, 1938, esp. pp. 112 ff., and Appendix 14, also *passim* for the
later development. Tarn (pp. 66 f., 261, 367, and Appendix 12) has very much
to say about the importance of the eastern sea route for the Seleucid commerce
with India. He may be right for later times, but hardly for the third century
B.C. On Gerrha see Tarn, loc. cit., Index, *s.v.* Gerrha, and the short but excellent article of Tkač, *P.W.K.* vii. 1270 ff. The regular commercial relations
between India and the Seleucid Empire are attested by the finds at Taxila.
In the Hellenistic period this city was in close relations both with the Bosporan kingdom (through the Sacians and later the Sarmatians) and with
Seleucid Syria. The first connexion is proved by the jewellery of the Sacian
period found at Taxila, which shows the same forms and ornamentation as
the jewellery of the same and of earlier date in South Russia. The second we
may infer from the many Hellenistic objects, in all probability of Syrian
workmanship, found at Taxila. It was without doubt the Parthians who,
after the middle of the third century B.C., acted as intermediaries between
Seleucid Syria and Northern India. See Sir John Marshall, *Guide to Taxila*,
3rd ed., 1936, and his forthcoming book on Taxila. On Seleuceia see above
note 227. Cf. P. R. Mouterde, *Mél. Univ. St.-Joseph*, xix (1935), p. 119 f.
(an inscription of Seleuceia illustrating the constitution of the city). On
the Seleucid mints in the eastern part of the empire see E. T. Newell's
book quoted in n. 243. A careful investigation of the many faience and glass
beads found in China (mostly local imitations of western originals) might
materially assist us to form some idea of the development of trade relations
between China and the western world. According to C. G. Seligman and H. C.
Beck, *Bull. Mus. Far Eastern Ant.* (Stockholm), x (1938), pp. 1 ff., such
local beads appear in the Far East from the fourth century B.C. We know
very little of the attention paid by the Seleucids to the development and
maintenance of their roads. A general idea of them may be derived from
· the sketch map by W. W. Tarn, *C.A.H.* vii, facing p. 155. Seleucus I inherited a good system of roads from Persia and its satraps and vassal
kings (e.g. Ps.-Ar. *Oecon.* ii. 14, on Condylus, the hyparch of Mausolus)
but he certainly added a good deal of his own. Ὁδοὶ βασιλικαί, for instance,
are several times mentioned as boundaries of the estate of Laodice (*O.G.I.*
225; Welles, *R.C.* 18, l. 4, and 20, ll. 10, 16, 17), cf. σταθμὸς βασιλικός near
the Tigris not far from Babylon, Diod. xix. 92. 3. On the routes across
the Syrian desert in ancient and modern times, Chr. Ph. Grant, *The Syrian
Desert Caravans, Travel, Exploration*, 1937.

²⁵⁴ On the earthquake, and the royal and other gifts to Rhodes, and Polybius' detailed account, M. Holleaux, *Rev. É.G.* xxxvi (1923), pp. 480 ff.;
on the gift of Seleucus, ibid., p. 485; F. Hiller von Gaertringen, *P.W.K.*,
art. 'Rhodos', 785; E. Bikerman, *Inst. Sél.*, p. 119. I cannot discuss here the
chronological problem. Polybius explicitly states that Seleucus, the donor,
was the father of Antiochus III. The ship or ships of Seleucus I: see the

Tab. Hierop. 442 B 31; 161 B 78, and later, e.g., *Inscr. de Délos* 1432 A b 11, 55; 1441 A 11. 91; 1450 A 174. Cf. W. Deonna, 'Le mobilier délien', *Délos*, xviii, 1938, p. 197 (little votive ship pl. III, 21, and p. 199 fig. 234). W. W. Tarn, *Antig. Gon.*, p. 81, thinks that the ship or ships were dedicated by Seleucus after his marriage with Stratonice in memory of the naval victories of her father Demetrius. I am inclined to connect them with a naval victory of Seleucus himself. Offerings of Stratonice can be traced in Delos from 279 B.C. (*Tab. Hierop.* 161 A 91, cf. B 15 and note, where the other gifts are listed); cf. on Stratonice W. W. Tarn, *Antig. Gon.*, pp. 349 ff.; Geyer, *P.W.K.* iv A, 319 ff., no. 8. The Stratonicea were probably organized by Antigonus Gonatas in honour of his sister Stratonice, wife of Antiochus I, or by Antiochus II, but I must note that the identity of the Stratonice in whose honour the Stratonicea were founded is disputed. I cannot here discuss this question which has no direct bearing on the subject of this book (see, e.g., W. W. Tarn, *C.A.H.* vii, pp. 715 and 722; Geyer, loc. cit., no. 9; Durrbach, *Choix*, 16; E. Bikerman, *Rev. É.A.* xl (1938), pp. 374 f., and the other books and articles on the history of the Hellenistic world in the middle of the third century quoted above, Ch. I, n. 12).

255 On the system of taxation of the Seleucids in general, see E. Bikerman, *Inst. Sél.*, pp. 106 ff. (Fisc séleucide). On the land-taxes of the Seleucids in Asia Minor and on the different forms of land-tenure in Asia Minor under the Seleucids, my *Staatspacht*, p. 356 f., and my *Kolonat*, pp. 240 ff., cf. *C.A.H.* vii, pp. 176 ff.; W. W. Tarn, *Hell. Civ.*, 2nd ed., p. 127 f., and E. Bikerman, loc. cit., pp. 176 ff. My views do not always coincide with those of Bikerman. I cannot, however, enter here into a detailed discussion of the various controversial points. See also A. Heuss, *Stadt und Herrscher*, pp. 105 ff. Φόροι of the χώρα around Teos and Lebedus are regarded by Antigonus as the natural source of supply for the cities in its neighbourhood, Welles, *R.C.* 3, ll. 83 ff., and his note on the passage. It is evident that these φόροι were paid in kind. On the other hand, the payments of the Laodice estate were calculated in money, ibid. 18, l. 10, and there is no mention in the Laodice documents of payments in kind, while the peasants of the village of Baetocaece paid their dues in kind, ibid. 70. 9: καὶ σὺν τοῖς ἐνεστῶτος ἔτους γεν[ν]ήμασιν ὅπως ἡ ἀπὸ ταύτης πρόσοδος, κτλ. The statement of the Mnesimachus inscription of Sardis (*Inscr. Sardis*, i, col. 1, ll. 12–13), τῶν ἀγγείων τῶν οἰνηρῶν καὶ τοῦ φόρου τοῦ ἀργυρικοῦ καὶ τοῦ λητουργικοῦ καὶ τῶν ἄλλων τῶν γενομένων ἐκ τῶν κωμῶν καὶ χωρὶς τούτων ἔτι πλέον, gives the impression that several payments both in kind and money were made by the inhabitants of the villages, though in general the φόροι from the various parts of the estate of Mnesimachus are calculated in cash. Remission of δεκάτη to the settled soldiers: *O.G.I.* 229, ll. 100 ff.

256 On Palestine see the bibliography in *C.A.H.* vii, p. 901, cf. below, Ch. VII, n. 103.

257 Rabbi J. Newman, *The agricultural life of the Jews in Babylonia*, 1932, pp. 161 ff. It was Dr. F. M. Heichelheim who drew my attention to this

book. He will deal with the problem of Parthian and Sasanian taxation in his forthcoming book, *The Public Finances of the Hellenistic Empires.*

[258] On the salt revenue in Egypt, above, p. 309 and note 110. On the same revenue in the Seleucid kingdom F. Heichelheim, *P.W.K.*, art. 'Monopole', 190. 2; my paper 'Seleucid Babylonia', *Yale Class. Stud.* iii (1932), pp. 82 ff.; R. H. McDowell, *Stamped and inscribed objects from Seleucia on the Tigris*, 1935, pp. 179 ff., and the review of this book by F. E. Brown in *A.J.A.* xlii (1938), pp. 607 ff.; E. Bikerman, *Inst. Sél.*, pp. 112 ff. I cannot discuss here the various interpretations of the same scanty evidence suggested by the above-named scholars.

[259] On the taxes of the Seleucids, E. Bikerman, *Inst. Sél.*, loc. cit. In this book the reader will find references to the ancient sources.

[260] See the preceding note, and cf. W. L. Westermann, 'Sklaverei', *P.W.K.*, Suppl. vi. 931. It is well known that slave labour was extensively used in Babylonia in the Persian and Seleucid periods: see I. Mendelssohn, *Legal Aspects of Slavery in Babylonia, Assyria and Palestine*, 1932; O. Krückmann, loc. cit., pp. 18 ff.; B. Meissner, 'Warenpreise in Babylonien', *Berl. Abh.*, 1936, i, pp. 36 ff. Note that among the slaves there were privileged classes, those who could not be bought and sold on the market. Such are the *širku* of the temples—the ἱερόδουλοι (see P. Koschaker, 'Über einige gr. Rechts-urkunden aus dem östl. Randgebieten des Hellenismus', *Abh. Sächs. Akad.* xlii (1931), pp. 76 ff.), the mysterious *šašanu*, but especially the royal slaves and slaves in the service of the army. These facts show how large were the numbers of slaves in Seleucid Babylonia and how many of them were in the service of the kings. We are reminded of the large numbers of slaves owned by the Roman emperors. See M. Rutten, *Contrats de l'Époque séleucide*, pp. 135 ff., cf. E. Bikerman, loc. cit., p. 176, and A. Aymard, *Rev. É.A.* xl (1938), p. 35, n. 4. The few parchments and papyri found at Europus-Dura (above, note 221) show that there were many slaves there in Parthian and Roman times. The same is attested for Asia Minor by the Mnesimachus inscription (above, note 255). There is no doubt that slavery was much more prevalent in the Seleucid kingdom than in Egypt, in spite of the existence of serfdom in the former. See above, n. 236 and below, n. 270 on the manu-missions of Susa. However, a special study of the slaves and the 'Sklaven-recht' of Babylonia is much needed. It is particularly important to dis-tinguish between the various forms of serfdom and real slavery in the Greek sense of the word. A very interesting instance is furnished by the manu-missions of Susa mentioned above. Prof. C. B. Welles points out to me that slaves manumitted by the Greek soldiers are all women of about 30 years of age. According to him they may have been their concubines, like the Phoenician λαϊκὰ σώματα, concubines of Greek soldiers mentioned in the Vienna papyrus discussed above (p. 343, and n. 138).

[261] On the expenditure of the Seleucids, E. Bikerman, op. cit., pp. 122 ff.

[262] I avoid the word 'urbanization' which I made use of in my *Social*

and Economic History of the Roman Empire, in order to avoid conveying the idea that the two processes—that of the Hellenistic period and that of the Roman Empire—were identical in their form and purpose. Roman urbanization consisted mainly in the introduction of urban life and urban mentality of the Greco-Italian type into areas of almost purely tribal and village life, while the building of Greek cities by the Seleucids had many and various purposes set out below, among which the substitution of city life for tribal life on a large scale was not included. The object of Greco-Macedonian colonization was first and foremost military and political; the urbanization of the Roman Empire had no military object at all, and its political *raison d'être* was much less prominent than its social, economic, and cultural purpose. Real urbanization had been achieved in Syria, Babylonia, and Mesopotamia long before the conquest of Alexander.

[263] The *locus classicus* on Dura-Europus and its founder Nicanor is Isidorus of Charax, i, cf. *Cosm. Rav.* ii, 13, p. 82, ed. Parthey and Pinder. A discussion of the problem with references to the ancient sources and modern contributions will be found in my article: 'The foundation of Dura-Europos on the Euphrates' in *Ann. Inst. Kondakov*, x (1938), volume in honour of A. A. Vasiliev, pp. 99 ff. It is unnecessary to repeat here the contents of this paper. Cf. A. H. M. Jones, *The Cities* &c., pp. 216 ff., and H. Bengtson, *Die Strategie in der hell. Zeit*, i, 1937, pp. 184 ff., who have been led independently by the same evidence to somewhat similar conclusions.

[264] The following are some of the best summaries of our information regarding the colonization of the Seleucid Empire: E. R. Bevan, *House of Seleucus*, 1902, chs. 11–13; K. J. Beloch, *Gr. Gesch.* iv, 2nd ed., pp. 251 ff.; E. Meyer, *Blüte und Niedergang des Hellenismus in Asien*, 1925; Ernst Meyer, *Die Grenzen der hellenistischen Staaten in Kleinasien*, 1925; F. Cumont, *Fouilles de Doura-Europos*, 1926, pp. xv ff.; V. Tscherikower, *Die hellenistischen Städtegründungen* &c., *Philol.*, Supp. xix (1927); W. W. Tarn, *Hell. Civ.*, 2nd ed. pp. 130 ff., and the map in *C.A.H.* vii, facing p. 155; G. T. Griffith, *The Mercenaries* &c., 1935, pp. 147 ff.; A. H. M. Jones, *The Cities*, &c., 1937, esp. pp. 216 ff. and pp. 227 ff., cf. also his chapter on Asia Minor. Quite recently W. W. Tarn, *The Greeks in Bactria and India*, 1938, pp. 1 ff., has given an interesting survey of the Seleucid colonization of the Near East in connexion with a fine description of the general policy of Seleucus I and his successors. Cf. E. Bikerman, *Inst. Sél.*, pp. 78 ff. The *locus classicus* about the Macedonian colonization is App. *Syr.* 57.

[265] See preceding note and U. Kahrstedt, 'Syrische Territorien in hellenistischer Zeit', *Abh. Gött. Ges.*, N.F., xix. 2 (1926); W. Otto, 'Beiträge zur Seleukidengeschichte', *Bay. Abh.* xxxiv. 1 (1928); E. Honigmann, 'Syria', *P.W.K.* iv A, esp. 1610 ff.; F. Schachermeyr, 'Mesopotamia', *P.W.K.* xv, esp. 1140 ff., and A. H. M. Jones, *The Cities* &c., pp. 242 ff. I cannot accept Mr. Jones's redistribution of the four satrapies of the Seleucids, which contradicts the clear statement of Posidonius and is based on no reliable evidence.

A more thorough archaeological exploration of the Seleucis will certainly yield new evidence on the Hellenistic period of its history. The existence of Parapotamia on the Euphrates as a separate satrapy to which for administrative purposes the Arabian tribes of the Syrian desert were attached is well attested by Polybius (v. 48. 16, cf. v. 69. 5), Isidorus of Charax (according to whom Parapotamia began to the south of Nicephorion, *G.G.M.* i, p. 247), and Strabo (xvi. 2. 11). This literary evidence is supported and completed by documents recently discovered. *D. Perg.* 10 (*Yale Class. Stud.* ii (1931), p. 6) of A.D. 120 shows that at this time a governor-general ruled in the name of the Parthian king over Mesopotamia and Parapotamia and was at the same time *Arabarches*. Certain other documents acquaint us with the official names of Dura-Europus, which were Εὐρωπὸς ἐν Παραποταμίᾳ (*D. Perg.* 21, l. 3 and 40, l. 3, both of A.D. 87, C. B. Welles, *Z. d. Sav.-Stift.* lvi (1936), p. 101 ; *Exc. Dura-Europos*, Prel. Rep., vi, 1936, p. 420, n. 3) and later Εὐρωπὸς πρὸς 'Αραβίᾳ (*D. Perg.* 23, l. 4, A.D. 180 ; C. B. Welles, *Papyri und Altertumsw.*, 1934, p. 382 ; *Exc. Dura-Europos*, loc. cit., p. 429). The name of Εὐρωπὸς πρὸς 'Αραβίᾳ occurs of course in Roman times only, but it must be remembered that in *D. Perg.* 10 the governor of Mesopotamia and Parapotamia is at the same time *Arabarches*. Pliny's statement concerning the Parapotamia on the Tigris (*N.H.* vi. 131) may be exact, though the existence of a Parapotamia on the Tigris is not attested elsewhere. See my comments on *D. Perg.* 10 in *Yale Class. Stud.* ii (1931), pp. 42 ff. As regards Parapotamia I agree with B. Niese, *Gesch. d. gr. u. mak. St.* ii, p. 94, and Lehmann-Haupt, *P.W.K.* ii A, 168, art. 'Satrap', against K. J. Beloch, *Gr. Gesch.*, 2nd ed., iv. 2, p. 358.

266 On the *cleroi* of the city of Antioch, see my *Storia Soc. ed Ec. d. Imp. Rom.*, p. 312, n. 19. On Antioch, the bibliography ibid., p. 157, n. 3, cf. above and, on the other cities of the Tetrapolis and on Syria in general, ibid., p. 161, note. On the 'territory' of Antioch and Apamea, E. Littman, *Ruinenstätten und Schriftdenkmäler Syriens*, 1917 ; P. J. Mattern, 'À travers les villes mortes de Haute Syrie', *Mél. Univ. St.-Joseph*, xvii. 1. 1933, and my paper 'La Syrie Romaine', *Rev. Hist.* clxxv (1935), pp. 1 ff. Cf. W. W. Tarn, *The Greeks in Bactria and India*, p. 7 and n. 4, and F. Cumont, 'The Population of Syria', *J.R.S.* xxiv (1934), pp. 187 ff., and *C.A.H.* xi, pp. 613 ff.

267 On Seleuceia in Pieria see the admirable paper of M. Holleaux, 'Une inscription de Séleucie-de-Piérie', *B.C.H.* lvii (1933), pp. 6 ff. (the last work of this great and much regretted student of Hellenistic history). The inscription of Seleuceia interpreted by Holleaux plays a large part in the discussion of the problem of the relations between the Seleucids and the cities of their kingdom in general. See above, Ch. III, n. 15, and below, p. 489. Seleuceia on the Tigris above, notes 227 and 253.

268 I cannot enter here into a detailed discussion of the thesis almost universally accepted by the leading modern scholars, that the Seleucid foundations with geographical Macedonian names were military colonies, κατοικίαι, not cities, πόλεις, of the Greek type; that they therefore had no

city constitution and no territory assigned to them; and that some of them later received new dynastic names, which meant that they were promoted to the rank of Greek cities. I doubt very much whether we have sufficient material for such bold generalizations. I prefer therefore to describe some of the best known colonies, i.e. to set out what little we know of their social and economic conditions. For finer distinctions and more detailed discussion I may refer to the books quoted in note 264 and especially to the recent book by W. W. Tarn, some of whose suggestions, however, I do not regard as very probable. In my opinion the Seleucid work of colonization was highly diversified and presented different aspects in the various satrapies. Moreover, we must sharply distinguish between those cities which had a long history behind them and where the Macedonian or Greek colony was superimposed on a community possessing immemorial traditions—whether Iranian, Indian, Elamitic, Babylonian, Aramaean, or Phoenician—and those little hamlets and fortresses of natives which were transformed into Greco-Macedonian cities or perhaps κατοικίαι. Excavation alone may in time enable us to give a general picture of the colonization of the East by the Seleucids. Cf. below, pp. 491 ff.

²⁶⁹ Constitution and social and economic conditions of Dura-Europus: F. Cumont, *Fouilles de Doura-Europos*, Introduction, and the short summaries that I have published of the results of the recent excavations: *Città Carovaniere*, 1934, pp. 141 ff.; *C.A.H.* xi, pp. 115 ff., and *Dura-Europos and its Art*, 1938, ch. i. On the royal judges and the χρεοφύλακες, above, note 241; on the dynastic cult of the Seleucids, above, note 231; subdivision of the territory into villages, C. B. Welles, *Arch. de l'Hist. du Droit orient.* i (1937), pp. 271 ff., and *Excav. Dura-Europos*, Prel. Rep. v, p. 310, cf. vii–viii, pp. 433 ff. According to the documents of Parthian and Roman times the territory of the Greek city of Europus was very large. On the north it certainly extended to the Khabur river. The fact that many Εὐρωπαῖοι are recorded in the later documents as οἰκοῦντες in a village seems to indicate that their ancestral *cleroi* belonged to the territory of some village in the territory of Europus. A good parallel to the royal law or order on inheritance is furnished by the mention of the 'orders ("data") of the king which are recorded as regards the deposits' in a cuneiform tablet containing a contract of deposit of the time of Antiochus III (218 B.C.), J. N. Strassmaier, *Zeitschr. f. Ass.* iii (1888), p. 137, no. 13; O. Krückmann, *Babyl. Rechts- u. Verwaltungsurk.*, p. 68. On the mint of Dura see the forthcoming paper of A. R. Bellinger and E. T. Newell.

²⁷⁰ F. Cumont, *C.R. Ac. Inscr.*, 1930, p. 214; 1931, pp. 238 ff.; 1937, pp. 313 ff. and 1938, pp. 305 ff.; W. W. Tarn, *Mél. Glotz*, 1932, pp. 831 ff.; A. Wilhelm, *Gött. Nachr.*, Fachgr. i, N.F., i. 4 (1935), pp. 79 ff.; W. W. Tarn, *The Greeks in Bactria and India*, pp. 27 ff. On the manumissions, L. Robert, *Rev. Phil.* x (1936), pp. 137 ff., cf. above, n. 236. The ingenious restoration by Robert of the document in *S.E.G.* vii. 15 shows that the document is a regular Greek manumission. Note that the manumittor is a certain Βάχχιο[s . . . φάμενος] | εἶναι τῆς Εὐάνδρο[υ ἱππαρχίας (?)], i.e. a soldier. On the constitution

and social life of Seleuceia in Parthian times, see my remarks in *C.A.H.* xi, p. 119 f.

271 On the parchments of Avroman, above, note 221, cf. C. B. Welles, *Yale Class. Stud.* v (1935), pp. 118 ff.

272 Rural Macedonian settlements in Asia Minor: H. Swoboda, K. F. Herrmann, *Lehrbuch*, i. 3, 6th ed., 1913, pp. 199 ff.; Oertel, *P.W.K.* xi. 3 ff., art. Κάτοικοι (with bibliography), cf. the remarks of L. Robert, *Rev. Arch.* 6me sér. iii (1934), pp. 88 ff., esp. p. 91, and A. H. M. Jones, *The Cities*, &c., p. 115. A revised list of the Macedonian κατοικίαι and some remarks on the character of these rural settlements will be found in E. Bikerman, *Inst. Sél.*, pp. 80 ff.

273 Cf. the following letters nos. 39 and 40 and A. Wilhelm, *Wien. Anz.* lvii (1920), pp. 40 ff. Note that *O.G.I.* 236 testifies to the activity of Zeuxis in Asia Minor.

274 On the Seleucid management of the χώρα βασιλική, my *Kolonat*, pp. 246 ff. On the estates assigned to various persons by the king, in addition to my *Kolonat*, see E. Kornemann, 'Domänen', *P.W.K.*, Suppl. iv. 234 ff. The inscription of Mnesimachus is discussed by W. H. Buckler and D. M. Robinson, *A.J.A.* xvi (1912), pp. 11 ff., cf. p. 533 f. A new revision of the text with some comments in *Sardis*, vii, *Gr. and Lat. Inscr.* 1 (complete bibliography, ibid., p. 7), cf. E. Bikerman, *Inst. Sél.*, p. 181 f. Babylonian tablets: above, n. 234. On the policy of the Seleucids in general, W. W. Tarn, *Hell. Civ.*, 2nd ed., pp. 122 ff. and E. Bikerman, *Inst. Sél.*, pp. 176 ff.

275 On the number of Macedonians and Greeks in Egypt and Syria, A. Segré, 'Note sull'economia dell'Egitto ellenistico nell'età Tolemaica', *Bull. Soc. Arch. Alex.* xxix (1934), pp. 257 ff., and the discussion of his calculations, above, p. 331 f., n. 126. Cf. below, Ch. VIII. On the size of the armies of the Seleucids, G. T. Griffith, *The Mercenaries of the Hellenistic World*, pp. 143 ff. and E. Bikerman, *Inst. Sél.*, pp. 51 ff.

276 F. Cumont, 'The population of Syria', *J.R.S.* xxiv (1934), pp. 187 ff. cf. F. M. Heichelheim, 'Roman Syria', T. Frank, *Econ. Surv.* iv, pp. 158 ff. On Antioch: St. John Chrysostom, *Homil. in Ignat.* 4 (*Patr. Gr.* l, p. 591) and *Homil.* 85 (86) (*Patr. Gr.* lviii, p. 762). Note that in Roman times the city of Apamea occupied an area of 618 acres. Note also that in much later times the territory of Cyrrhus occupied 1,600 square miles and contained 800 Christian parishes and about 200,000 orthodox inhabitants, Theodoret. *Epist.* 42 and 113 (*Patr. gr.* lxxxiii, pp. 1217 and 1220 and 1316). Cf. below, Ch. VIII.

277 The standard formula was extensively used and in such a way that it is difficult to decide whether it applies to independent communities alone, or to these and to self-governing bodies within the kingdom. The earliest mention of the formula in the Hellenistic period is, so far as I know, the statement of Diod. xix. 57. 3 (314 B.C.) about Antigonus: τά τ' ἔθνη καὶ πόλεις

καὶ δυνάστας προσεκαλεῖτο εἰς συμμαχίαν. Next comes the well-known inscription *O.G.I.* 229, l. 11, where Seleucus II writes in regard to the *asylia* of Smyrna: πρὸς τοὺς βασιλεῖς καὶ τοὺς δυνάστας καὶ τὰς πόλεις καὶ τὰ ἔθνη, cf. *S.I.G.*³ 590, l. 11, about 196 B.C. (recognition of ἀσυλία of Didyma by ἔθνη, πόλεις, and βασιλεῖς). The terminology was still the same in the time of Sulla and Caesar, *S.I.G.*³ 760—Caesar (with the note by J. Keil), and *O.G.I.* 441, l. 130—Sulla. Cf. in general E. Meyer, *Blüte und Niedergang des Hellenismus*, p. 43, n. 1, and Ernst Meyer, *Die Grenzen* &c., p. 138. It was C. B. Welles who suggested to me the interpretation of ἔθνη as including some κοινά. J. Keil regards ἔθνη as meaning tribes, not yet organized as *poleis* and *demoi*. E. Bikerman quotes in support of Keil's opinion Jos. *A.J.* xii, 142.

²⁷⁸ On the native tribes and dynasts, see above, note 230 and below, p. 516.

²⁷⁹ I have dealt with the temples of Asia Minor in detail in my *Kolonat*, pp. 269 ff., and I have very little to add to the evidence that I have collected and illustrated in that book. In fact very little new material has been added to the evidence available in 1910, and very little work has been done on the subject. Cf. W. W. Tarn, *Hell. Civ.*, 2nd ed., pp. 124 ff.; E. Bikerman, *Inst. Sél.*, pp. 172 ff; T. R. S. Broughton, 'Rom. Asia Minor' (T. Frank, *Econ. Survey*, iv), pp. 641 ff., 676 ff.

²⁸⁰ A good list of sanctuaries in Asia Minor that owned land or villages in Hellenistic and Roman times will be found in T. R. S. Broughton, loc. cit., p. 676. On the village temples and villages which belonged to temples of the Roman period see H. Swoboda, 'Kome', *P.W.K.* Suppl. iv. 963 ff.; my *Storia Ec. e Soc.*, p. 304, n. 5, and Broughton, loc. cit., pp. 641 ff. On the sanctuary of Apollo Laerbenus, *M.A.M.A.* iv. pp. 96 ff., and L. Robert, *Ant. Class.* iv (1935), p. 461, and *Villes d'Asie Mineure*, 1935, pp. 127 ff., cf. Broughton, loc. cit., pp. 681 ff.

²⁸¹ On the temples of Olba and the Plutonium of Nysa above, p. 439. I shall deal later with the temples of Pontus, Cappadocia, and Armenia. The hypothetical temple-state of Commagene was probably not very different from the later Commagenian monarchy as reflected in the well-known inscriptions of Nimrud Dagh, *O.G.I.* 383; L. Jalabert et R. Mouterde, *Inscr. . . . de la Syrie*, i, nos. 1 ff., esp. 47, cf. my paper 'Πρόγονοι' *J.H.S.* lv (1935), pp. 63 ff., and below, Ch. VI, nn. 121 and 131.

²⁸² See my *Kolonat*, pp. 269 ff. We know for example that the village of the god of Baetocaece was given to a high official of one of the Seleucids (Welles, *R.C.* 70) and that a part at least of the land that belonged to the temple of Aezani was divided among the soldiers of the Seleucid army (*O.G.I.* 502). *Asylia*: the Plutonium of Nysa, above, p. 439, and the temple of Amyzon, Welles, *R.C.* 40. Δεκάτη paid by a temple (?), Welles, *R.C.* 41 (temple of Seleuceia-Tralles). A tax on sheep was paid by the high priest and the κάτοικοι of the temple of Apollo Tarsenus to the Pergamene kings (Welles, *R.C.* 47), cf. E. Bikerman, *Inst. Sél.*, p. 114. On the κάτοικοι of the temple territories, Welles, *R.C.*, p. 345.

283 Other still more doubtful cases are quoted in my *Kolonat*, pp. 275 ff., cf. T. R. S. Broughton, *Roman Asia Minor*, pp. 642 ff. The epigraphical evidence relating to the temple of Men Ascaënus, which yielded a large crop of inscriptions, or rather to the two temples of this god connected with the city of Antioch, has been collected and revised by H. Kasten, *Bursian*, 253 (1936), pp. 64 ff. On Stratonicea, W. W. Tarn, *Hell. Civ.*, 2nd ed., p. 136, and W. Ruge, *P.W.K.* iv A, 322 ff. Oppermann, ibid. Suppl. v. 453 f., and L. Robert, *Villes d'Asie Mineure*, p. 81 f., and *Ét. Anat.*, passim (Index s.v. Stratonicée de Carie).

284 On the question whether *baris* is an Anatolian word see E. H. Sturtevant in Welles, *R.C.*, p. 320. It is surprising to find the word used by a Semite in Transjordan. Another Anatolian word, according to Prof. E. H. Sturtevant (private letter), is *tyrsis*. Cf. my 'Notes on the econ. policy of the Pergamene kings', *Anat. Stud. pres. to Sir William Ramsay*, p. 374, n. 1.

285 I have dealt with the λαοὶ βασιλικοί and with the κάτοικοι and πάροικοι of the cities and temples in my *Kolonat*, pp. 258 ff., cf. Swoboda, *P.W.K.*, Suppl. iv. 961 ff., art. 'Kome'; Oertel, *P.W.K.* xi. 3 ff., art. 'Κάτοικοι'; Kornemann, *P.W.K.*, Suppl. iv. 234 ff., art. 'Domänen', cf. my paper in the *Anat. Stud. pres. to Sir William Ramsay*, pp. 371 ff., and E. Bikerman, *Inst. Sél.*, pp. 176 ff. On the temple *katoikoi*, above, note 282.

286 On the history of Damascus and her ancient remains see J. Sauvaget, 'Esquisse d'une histoire de Damas', *Rev. Ét. Islam.*, 1934, pp. 422 ff.

287 Welles, *R.C.* 70, 9: ὅπως ἡ ἀπὸ ταύτης (i.e. τῆς κώμης) πρόσοδος ἀναλίσκηται εἰς τὰς κατὰ μῆνα{ς} συντελουμένας θυσίας καὶ τἆλλα τὰ πρὸς αὔξησιν τοῦ ἱεροῦ συντείνοντα ὑπὸ τοῦ καθεσταμένου ὑπὸ τοῦ θεοῦ ἱερέως ὡς εἴθισται (quoted in this connexion by E. Bikerman, loc. cit., p. 174).

288 On the villages of Syria in Roman times see the bibliography quoted in my *Storia Soc. ed Econ.*, pp. 315 ff.; cf. my paper 'La Syrie romaine', *Rev. Hist.* clxxv (1935), esp. pp. 27 ff., and F. Cumont, *C.A.H.* xi, pp. 613 ff. On the villages of Mesopotamia see the parchments and papyri of Dura, above, n. 221.

289 See the remarks of W. W. Tarn based on material supplied by Dr. Sidney Smith (*Hell. Civ.*, 2nd ed., p. 118).

290 O. Krückmann, *Babyl. Rechts- und Verwaltungsurk.* &c.; P. Koschaker 'Keilschriftrecht', *Zeitschr. d. d. Morgenl. Ges.* lxxxix (N.F. 14) (1935), pp. 1 ff.; A. Aymard, *Rev. É.A.* xl (1938), pp. 11 ff., and E. Bikerman, *Inst. Sél.*, pp. 174 ff.

291 See my remarks on this problem in my *Seleucid Babylonia*. The private seals of the bullae have never been collected, described, and published in full. Some are reproduced in the works quoted in note 221 (at the end). Cf. M. Rutten, *Contrats de l'Époque séleucide*, pp. 114 ff., esp. pp. 120 ff., and two plates, and A. Aymard, loc. cit., p. 38. The impressions should be studied

side by side with the intaglios of the same time and with the contemporary terracottas and pottery which are found in large quantities in the ruins of the Babylonian cities, especially in Seleuceia see my 'Dura and the Problem of Parthian Art', *Yale Class. Stud.* v, pp. 179 ff.

292 The texts relating to Nicarchus and Kephallon are cited in note 235. W. W. Tarn and M. Holleaux (quoted in the same note, cf. W. W. Tarn, *The Greeks in Bactria and India*, p. 26, n. 1) think that Kephallon was either the *epistates* or the *strategos* of Uruk. They may be partly right. For the king, Kephallon was probably a magistrate equivalent rather to the Greek *strategos* than to the Greek *epistates*, while there may have been in the city a Greek *epistates*. We have evidence of two men in charge of a Greco-Oriental city, one a Greek, Antiochus, the other an Iranian, Phraates, probably agents of the Parthian king, in the well-known inscription of Seleuceia on the Eulaeus (*S.E.G.* vii. 1; Welles, *R.C.* 75, cf. W. W. Tarn, *The Greeks in Bactria and India*, p. 27 and M. Engers, *Mnem.* vii (1938–9), pp. 136 ff.). The office of the 'city-lord' may have been hereditary at Uruk as the office of the *strategos* and *epistates* was later in Parthian Dura. On the status of Uruk in the Seleucid period, A. Aymard, loc. cit., p. 33, n. 2. He comes to the same conclusions as myself.

293 On the double names in Uruk in general, A. Aymard, loc. cit., pp. 30 ff. (with bibliography), cf. H. Bengtson, *Die Welt als Gesch.* v (1939), p. 180, and on the double names in general W. Otto, *Kulturgeschichte des Altertums*, p. 100, n. 201, and E. Bikerman, *Rev. Hist. Rel.* cxv (1937), pp. 215 ff. Note that a complete change of name was not allowed in Egypt (*B.G.U.* 1213 and 1250; cf. above, n. 121 and below, Ch. VIII). It is well known that double names are very common in Hellenistic and still more in Roman times throughout Syria, Palestine, and Mesopotamia. For the first two, P. Dhorme, *Rev. Bibl.*, 1925, p. 292; for the second C. B. Welles quoted in the following note.

294 A. Aymard, loc. cit., p. 32, is inclined to minimize the numbers of the Greek residents at Uruk. This I regard as a *petitio principii*. The assumption of a second Babylonian name by a Greek is, of course, less probable and common, especially in early Hellenistic times before the policy of association became a leading feature of the policy of the Seleucids, than the assumption of a Greek name by a Babylonian (on the later times C. B. Welles, *Dura Rep.* vii–viii, p. 431). However, the use by an individual of a Greek name only, especially if the name of the father is also Greek, is to my mind almost conclusive. The deed of Nicanor, son of Democrates, A. Aymard, loc. cit., p. 35, n. 4 (with bibliography).

295 Above, pp. 469 ff.

296 In a document of 218 B.C. which deals with a *depositum irregulare* we read 'according to the law of the king which is written about the depositum', F. E. Peiser, *Keilinschr. Bibl.* iv, pp. 316 ff., l. 9 f.; M. San Nicolò, *Beitr. z. Rechtsg. im Ber. der Keilschr. Rechtsquellen*, 1931, p. 84.

[297] The treasury of Bel at Babylon was managed in the reign of Antiochus IV by a royal officer in exactly the same way as the finances of the temple of Sardis were managed by a royal *neokoros* in the time of Eumenes II, A. T. Olmstead, *J. Am. Or. Soc.* lvi (1936), p. 247, cf. E. Bikerman, *Inst. Sél.*, p. 174.

[298] E. Bikerman, *Inst. Sél.*, pp. 170 ff.

[299] All works on Hellenistic history deal with the basic problem of the hellenization of the Seleucid kingdom. It is unnecessary to quote them here. A good summary will be found, e.g. in E. Meyer, *Blüte und Niedergang des Hellenismus in Asien*, 1925. Cf. note 293 and Ch. VI, n. 130, and the pages devoted to this topic in W. W. Tarn, *The Greeks in Bactria and India*, pp. 67 ff. On the hellenized Sidonians of the time of the Ptolemies see above, p. 341, and n. 137. Especially illuminating is the inscription from Sidon recently republished and illustrated by E. Bikerman, *Mél. syr. R. Dussaud*, 1939, pp. 91 ff., which may belong to the last years of the rule of the Ptolemies or to the first of that of the Seleucids. A Greek settler in Marissa in Palestine, pl. LVIII (with description). I may mention in addition a man bearing a Greek name and descended from a father and grandfather with Greek names who in 47 B.C. was president (archon) of an association of cutlers (μαχαιροποιοί) at Sidon, below, Ch. VIII. It is very probable that the family was a family of hellenized Phoenicians and the association an oriental hellenized guild.

[300] On the gradual orientalization of the Greeks in the Seleucid kingdom see my paper 'L'Hellénisme en Mésopotamie', *Scientia*, 1933, Febr., pp. 110 ff., cf. my *Dura-Europos and its Art*, ch. i. W. W. Tarn, *The Greeks in Bactria and India*, pp. 34 ff., 67 ff., minimizes the influence of the East on the Greek settlers. Intermarriage for him is a negligible factor, and he thinks that religious aspirations were of little importance. Dura he regards not as typical but as exceptional, and he eliminates it without discussion. On the temple of Zeus Olympius in Dura see my *Dura-Europos and its Art*, ch. ii, p. 36, and on this temple and the semi-oriental image of Zeus Olympius, my paper 'Le Gad de Doura et Seleucus Nicator', *Mél. syr. R. Dussaud*, pp. 281 ff.

[301] I cannot deal in detail with the complicated and controversial problem of the relations between the Seleucids and the Greek cities, nor can I produce all the material relating to this question. A full collection of it and a detailed discussion will be found in the works quoted in ch. III, note 16, especially in the books of P. Zancan, *Il Monarcato ellenistico*, pp. 55 ff. ; V. Ehrenberg, *Der gr. und der hell. Staat*, 1932, p. 82, and *Alexander and the Greeks*, 1938, pp. 41 ff. ; A. Heuss, *Stadt und Herrscher*, 1937, (cf. the review of E. Bikerman, *Rev. Phil.* xiii (1939), pp. 335 ff.), and especially E. Bikerman, *Inst. Sél.*, pp. 106 ff., 133 ff. My point of view as briefly presented in the text coincides in the main with that of Bikerman.

[302] Inscription of Polycritus, Zolotas, 'Ἀθηνᾶ, xx (1908), pp. 195 ff., ll. 30 ff. Τὰ συμφέροντα is of course a technical term. On the historical circumstances

of the decree in honour of Polycritus and of that in honour of the στρατηγοί (*S.I.G.*³ 410), see below, note 304.

303 Above, Ch. III, pp. 173 ff., and notes 43 and 44.

304 *S.I.G.*³ 410 (decree in honour of the *strategoi*) and Zolotas, 'Aθηνâ, xx (1908), pp. 195 ff. (decree in honour of Polycritus of Erythrae). On the date and the interpretation of these decrees: K. J. Beloch, *Gr. Gesch.* iv. 2, p. 343; G. de Sanctis, *Atti Acc. Torino*, xlvii (1911–12), pp. 793 ff., cf. Rostovtzeff, *C.A.H.* vii, p. 179 (on the inscription *O.G.I.* 223), A. Wilhelm, *Mél. Glotz*, p. 903, and L. Robert, *B.C.H.* lvii (1933), p. 479, note. We have the same situation at Cyzicus, helped by Philetaerus (*O.G.I.* 748; M. Segre, *Athenaeum*, viii (1930), pp. 488 ff.), and other cities of Asia Minor, see F. Stähelin, *Geschichte der kleinasiatischen Galater*, 2nd ed., 1907; W. W. Tarn, *C.A.H.* vii, p. 105; Hiller v. Gaertringen, 'Miletos', *P.W.K.* xv. 1605; A. Wilhelm, 'Επίγραμμα ἐκ Λυκίας, Πρακτικὰ τῆς 'Ακαδημίας 'Aθηνῶν, vi (1931), pp. 322 ff. In this paper Wilhelm has given a masterly interpretation of a well-known epigram in honour of Neoptolemus, Ptolemy's general, who fought gallantly against the Galatians and their allies, the Paeonians and Agrianes.

305 On Priene, Pergamon, and the other centres of ceramic production in Asia Minor see A. Conze, *Alt. v. Perg.* i. 2, pp. 254 ff. (with contributions of R. Zahn); R. Zahn, *Priene*, pp. 394 ff.; S. Loeschke, *Ath. Mitt.* xxxvii (1912), pp. 344 ff.; F. Courby, *Les Vases grecs à reliefs*, 1922, pp. 451 ff.; H. A. Thompson, *Hesperia*, iii (1934), pp. 471 ff.; F. O. Waagé in *Antioch-on-the-Orontes*, i, pp. 68 ff.; D. Burr, *Terra-cottas from Myrina*, 1934. On the types of Hellenistic pottery found in South Russia see M. Rostovtzeff, *Skythien und der Bosporus*, 1931, pp. 153 ff. There is no type of early Hellenistic pottery that is not represented in South Russia. Among the specimens of these various types found there many were imported, chiefly from Asia Minor, but a large number were produced locally. This is certain as regards some examples of relief pottery, and especially the Megarian bowls, R. Zahn, *J.D.A.I.* xxiii (1908), pp. 45 ff. (my pl. LXVIII. 2); perhaps as regards the 'lagynoi', of which a large number have been found in South Russia (G. Leroux, *Lagynos*, 1913; C. Picard, *Rev. Arch.* xxii (1913), pp. 167 ff.; E. Pfuhl, *Malerei und Zeichnung* 1000; H. Thompson, *Hesperia*, iii (1934), p. 450 f.); and quite certain as regards what are known as the water-colour vases found almost exclusively in South Russia (a corpus of these last was prepared for publication by the late E. von Stern, but never published). Cf. above, Ch. II, pp. 108 ff., and notes 41 ff. The finds made in the systematic excavations of Istrus during recent years show *mutatis mutandis* the same picture as those of south Russia. The Hellenistic pottery found in this place has not yet been published, but Mme Lambrino has kindly informed me in a private letter that most of the imported Hellenistic pottery was made, in all probability, in Asia Minor.

306 The same conclusion may be drawn from some stray inscriptions which illuminate for a moment the economic situation of Miletus and of some

other cities. We may assign to about the end of the third century B.C. (228?) an interesting correspondence between Cius and Miletus, in which each city complains of the wars and of the expenses entailed thereby, and of the poor harvests of which they are the cause (A. Rehm, *Milet, Erg. d. Ausgr.* i. 2, no. 141). We have a similar illustration at Samos. In the inscription in honour of Bulagoras (*S.E.G.* i. 366) the Samians bitterly complain of mal-treatment by the φίλοι of Antiochus II, of lack of money, and of a severe famine which was somewhat relieved by the intervention of Bulagoras.

307 Sidney Smith, *Babylonian historical texts*, 1924, pp. 150 ff., cf. M. Segre, *Athenaeum*, viii (1930), p. 495 f. The crisis is reflected in the coinage issued by the mint of Seleuceia at the time. See E. T. Newell, 'The coinage of the eastern Seleucid Mints', pp. 60 ff. It is interesting to find that the people complain that they had to use 'copper coins of Greece'. This means pro-bably that silver disappeared from circulation and that they had to use copper coins to which they were not accustomed, since it was an innovation of the Greeks. On the date of the first Syrian War, above, Ch. I, n. 12 and Ch. III, n. 11.

308 L. C. West, *Trans. Am. Phil. Ass.* lv (1924), pp. 159 ff., cf. F. Heichel-heim, 'Roman Syria', in T. Frank, *Econ. Survey*, iv, 1938, pp. 127 ff.

309 B. Meissner, *Babylonien und Assyrien*, i, p. 367 (prices of real estate in Babylonia), and 'Warenpreise in Babylonien', *Berl. Abh.*, 1936, 1, cf. *Berl. Sitzb.*, 1937, pp. 5 ff. The general conclusions of the author, p. 40 (pros-perity of Uruk in the Seleucid period and low prices in general), contradict his own statements on p. 6 regarding the price of grain, which was a little lower in 274/3 and 233/2 than in Persian times, and on p. 9 regarding the rise of the price of sesame oil between 274/3 and 233/2, but they are supported by Heichelheim (*Wirtschaftsg.*, p. 443). On prices, and especially on the prices of houses at Uruk, see also F. M. Heichelheim, *Wirtschaftliche Schwankungen*, p. 88 (not quoted by Meissner) and *Wirtschaftsg.* p. 443 f. and n. 5. Cf. in general O. Krückmann, *Babylonische Rechts- und Verwaltungsurkunden aus der Zeit Alexanders und der Diadochen*, 1931, and A. Aymard, *Rev. É.A.* xl (1938), pp. 23 ff.

310 Contracts of sale of slaves by private persons, for example, M. Rutten, *Contrats de l'époque Séleucide*, pp. 134 ff. Cf. above notes 260 and 290. On the manumissions of Susa, above, notes 260 and 270.

311 No comprehensive comparative study of Hellenistic pottery found in Palestine, Phoenicia, and South Syria on the one hand, and in North Syria and Mesopotamia on the other, has ever been carried out. For the former we have careful records of the finds at Gezer, Samaria, Beth-Shan, and Beth-Zur: R. A. S. Macalister, *The Excavations of Gezer*, ii, 1912, pp. 211 ff., pl. CXXXVI, cf. pl. CLXXXIV; G. A. Reisner and others, *Harvard Excavations at Samaria*, i, 1924, p. 274, cf. pp. 310 ff. and p. 18 f.; Fitzgerald, *Beth-Shan Excavations 1921–3*, iii, 1931, p. 39, and pl. XXXIV; O. R. Sellers, *The Citadel*

of Beth-Zur, 1933, pp. 37 ff. The development on all these sites is almost exactly the same: black glazed pottery imported and home-made, Megarian bowls, 'Pergamene' and 'Samian' ware. Note the presence of Egyptian or imitated faience. Cf. J. H. Iliffe, 'Sigillata wares in the Near East', *Quart. Dep. Ant. in Palestine*, vi (1936), pp. 4 ff. The situation is much the same as regards North Syria and Mesopotamia: *Antioch-on-the-Orontes, I, The Excavations of 1932*, 1934, pp. 67 ff., pls. XIII ff.: 'Pottery' by F. O. Waagé: (1) Athenian and imitated black glazed pottery, (2) moulded Megarian bowls, (3) 'Pergamene' ware. The pottery collected in the Museum of the American University at Beirut fits admirably into this scheme: Sir Leonard Woolley, *Guide to the Arch. Mus. of the Am. Un. of Beirut*, 1921, pp. 16 ff., esp. p. 18. Exactly the same picture is presented by Dura. I may add that in respect of pottery Hellenistic Cyprus is exactly like Syria: A. Westholm, *The Temples of Soli*, 1936, pp. 114 ff. In Mesopotamia the moulded 'Megarian' bowls and the so-called 'Pergamene' or 'Anatolian' ware had to compete with the Mesopotamian faience. The date of the first appearance of this ware and its relation to the similar wares of Egypt, Asia Minor, and China are disputed. I shall speak of this later. See A. Lucas, 'Glazed ware in Egypt, India, and Mesopotamia', *J.E.A.* xxii (1936), pp. 141 ff. There is certainly a connexion between the Mesopotamian faience and the Hellenistic relief pottery. Numerous Megarian bowls of Syrian provenance are scattered over many museums of Europe and America, and there are many of them in the museums of Palestine, Beirût, and Damascus. A full collection of these will probably show how early in the third century this industry started in Syria and Palestine. My pl. LX, 1, 2.

[312] No collection of early Syrian glass has ever been made. The later blown glass is comparatively well known. The glass bowl from Ephesus now in the British Museum has been recently illustrated by P. Fosling, 'Drinking bowls of glass and metal from the Achaemenian time', *Berytus*, iv (1937), pp. 121 ff. (published in 1939, cf. next note). On the cut or cast glass found in South Russia (my pls. XLIII. 1 and LXVIII. 3) and mentioned in the Delian inventories and in some literary texts, above, p. 370 f., nn. 164, 165. Cast and chiselled glass may have been made in Achaemenid times both in Egypt and in Phoenicia, and the manufacture may have continued in both places in the Hellenistic period.

[313] On the Achaemenid toreutic art see the article by P. Fosling quoted in the previous note and H. Luschey, 'Achaemenidisch-persische Toreutik', *J.D.A.I.* liii (1938), Anz., pp. 761 ff.; cf. his forthcoming article in the *Zeitschr. f. Assyr.*, and his Munich dissertation *Die Phiale*, 1938. I was surprised to find no reference in the Anzeiger article to the splendid discoveries in Cyprus mentioned above, Ch. II, n. 18. Nor has Mr. Luschey taken account of my papers dealing with the influence of Achaemenid art on the Panticapaean Greek artists, above, Ch. II, n. 35. I have quoted above, Ch. III, n. 16, some passages of Menander which mention τορεύματα brought to Greece from the East by mercenary soldiers, and I have referred to the popularity of λιθοκόλλητα and διάλιθα, which were certainly of oriental origin

or imitations of oriental work, in the early Hellenistic age (above, Ch. III, n. 40). For the bowls or cups found in Siberia and Persia see M. Rostovtzeff, 'Some new aspects of Iranian art', *Sem. Kond.* vi (1933), pp. 161 ff. The find of Nihavand: E. Herzfeld, 'The hoard of Karen Pahlavs', *Burl. Mag.* lii (1928), pp. 21 ff., figs. A–B and D–E, cf. O. M. D[alton], *Br. Mus. Q.* ii (1928), pp. 88 ff. The bowls of the Nihavand find and the other bowls of the same style will be published and illustrated by R. Zahn (to whose kindness I owe the privilege of reading his article in manuscript). Zahn is inclined to regard the bowls from Nihavand as imported into Persia and of Greek workmanship. I am inclined to think that the bowls were made by a Greek artist residing in Syria. See my pls. LX. 2 and LXI. 3. On the date, H. U. v. Schönebeck, *Ein hellenistisches Schalenornament*, 1938, pp. 57 ff. Through Syria Persia also received the beautiful silver *emblema* of Tarentine work-manship belonging to the Coll. Loeb (now in Munich), which also formed part of the treasure of Karen Pahlavs, see R. Zahn, 'Silber-Emblem der Samml. Loeb', *Festschr. J. Loeb*, 1930, pp. 131 ff. Very similar to the Niha-vand objects are those found somewhere in Syria and incorporated in the collection of Prince L. Czartoryski, viz. the three silver-gilt *emblemata* of the third century B.C., two adorned with repoussé figures (Bacchant and Satyr on one and Heracles and Methe (?) on the other), and one with scrolls of acanthus very similar to those of the Megarian bowls, J. de Witte, 'Monuments d'argent trouvés en Syrie', *Gaz. Arch.*, vi (1880), pp. 138 ff., and pls. 23 and 24, cf. G. Lippold, *P.W.K.* vi A 1767. In this article Lippold points out that among the gifts of Seleucus I to the temple of Didyma was a special vase called Seleucis, cf. *P.W.K.* ii A. 1200, no. 5. The elephant *emblema*, my pl. LIII. 1.

[314] For bibliography, M. Rostovtzeff, 'Dura and the problem of Parthian Art', *Yale Class. Stud.* v (1935), p. 220, n. 78.

[315] Papyrus in Syria: Theophr. *H.P.* iv. 8. 4, cf. ix. 7. 1; in Babylonia: Plin. *N.H.* xiii. 73. See the discussion of these texts by N. Lewis, *L'Industrie du papyrus dans l'Égypte gréco-romaine*, 1934, pp. 5 ff., and C. B. Welles, *Arch. de l'hist. du Droit oriental*, i (1937), p. 261 ff.

[316] W. W. Tarn, *The Greeks in Bactria and India*, 1938. The reader will find references to the sources and to modern contributions in this masterly book: they need not be repeated here. My conclusions, though based on the same material, do not always coincide with those of Tarn. Cf., for the early political and economic history of Bactria, the contributions of E. T. Newell and J. Wolski quoted above, n. 230.

[317] On the archaeological exploration of Afghanistan, J. Hackin, *L'Œuvre de la Délégation archéologique française en Afghanistan*, Tokio, 1933. On the recent excavations at' Kapisa near Begram, J. Hackin, *C.R. Ac. Inscr.*, 1938, pp. 59 ff. On the situation and importance of Kapisa, A. Foucher, 'Notes sur l'Itinéraire de Hiuan–Tsang en Afghanistan', *Études Asiatiques*, 1925, i, pp. 266 ff. (with map), and W. W. Tarn, in the book quoted in the

preceding note. From the political and commercial point of view the city was second to Bactra only. On Alexandria, J. Hackin, *Rev. É.A.* xli (1939), pp. 267 ff.

318 On Taxila, Sir John Marshall, *A Guide to Taxila*, 3rd ed., 1936 (Tarn has used the second edition). A full account of the excavation of Taxila and a catalogue of the finds will be given by Sir John Marshall in his forthcoming book on Taxila.

319 See my articles: 'Sarmatian and Indo-Scythian antiquities', *Rec. Kondakov*, 1926, pp. 355 ff., and 'Some aspects of Iranian art', *Sem. Kondak.* vi (1933), pp. 161 ff. Cf. my remarks on the 'Sarmatian' art in *C.A.H.* xi, pp. 102 ff., and bibliography, p. 876. The jewels of Taxila of the Saca period: Sir John Marshall, *Arch. Surv. of India*, Ann. Rep., 1926–7 (published in 1930), pls. XXVI–XXVIII, and ibid., 1929–30 (published in 1935), pp. 55 ff. and pls. XVI–XIX. See my pl. LXII.

320 On the Arthašāstra and the problems connected with this treatise, B. Breloer, *Zeitschr d. d. Morgenl. Ges.* lxxxviii (1934), pp. 130 ff.; lxxxix (1935), pp. 40 ff. and *Kautaliya Studien*, i–iii, 1 (1927–34), cf. F. Heichelheim, 'New light on the influence of Hellenistic financial administration in the Near East and India', *Economic History*, iii (13) (1938), pp. 1 ff.

CHAPTER IV, PART III

321 On Pergamon see my 'Notes on the Economic Policy of the Pergamene kings', *Anat. Stud. pres. Sir William Ramsay*, 1923, pp. 359 ff.; and my chapter 'Pergamum' in *C.A.H.* viii, pp. 590 ff. (with bibliography). Cf. H. E. Stier, *Aus der Welt des Pergamonaltars*, 1932 (a general survey of the chief aspects, other than social and economic, of the Hellenistic period); W. Zschietzschmann, *P.W.K.* xix. 1235 ff. (a useful survey of the monuments excavated at Pergamon) and W. v. Massow, *Führer durch d. Pergamonmuseum*, 2nd ed., 1936 (with bibliography). On the recent excavations of the Asclepieum, a building of the fourth cent. B.C., twice rebuilt by the Attalids, O. Deubner, *Das Asklepieion von Pergamon*, 1938.

322 On Philetaerus see, in addition to the papers quoted in the preceding note, W. Hoffmann, *P.W.K.* xix. 2157 ff. Apart from scattered literary evidence, we may form an idea of the policy of Philetaerus from several inscriptions: his loan to Pitane for the purchase of land from Antiochus I, *O.G.I.* 335, l. 135; his reverence for Apollo Chresterius, whose sanctuary stood between Myrina and Cyme, ibid. 312, cf. C. Schuchhardt, *Alt. v. Perg.* i. 1, p. 98; his relations with Cyzicus, his neighbour and perhaps ally, *O.G.I.* 748, F. W. Hasluck, *Cyzicus*, 1910, p. 265; Philetaerus and Delos, Durrbach, *Choix*, 31, cf. the Philetaereia organized by Eumenes I at Delos, *I.G.* xi. 2, 287 B, l. 119; *Inscr. d. Délos* 298 A, 95; 346 B, 14; 442 B, 54; his gifts to the temple of the Muses at Thespiae, above, n. 35; honoured by the Delphians, M. Holleaux, *Rev. É.A.* xx (1918), pp. 9 ff.; R. Flacelière, *Les*

Aitoliens &c., p. 220. On the temple of Demeter near the upper gymnasium, W. Zschietzschmann, loc. cit., 1251 f. The organization of the army goes back probably to Philetaerus and Eumenes I, and was completed by Attalus I during his great wars. I cannot refer here to certain peculiarities in this respect shown by the Pergamene *dynasteia* as compared with Egypt and Syria. See my remarks in *C.A.H.* viii, p. 596, cf. G. T. Griffith, *The Mercenaries* &c., pp. 171 ff., and below, Ch. VI, n. 82 ; and on the inscriptions of Delphi relating to the soldiers of Attalus I stationed at Lilaia in 208 B.C., R. Flace-lière, *Les Aitoliens* &c., p. 301, cf. L. Robert, *Coll. Fröhner,* i, *Inscr. Gr.*, 1936, p. 96, n. 2. The presence in the Pergamene army of Pergamene citizens and of many Mysians and Masdyenes, alongside of strong contingents of mercenaries, should be noted.

323 On the territory of Pergamene *dynasteia* see my remarks in *Anat. Stud.*, pp. 362 ff. The *dynasteia* of Philetaerus was probably as large as the satrapy of Orontes. Note how strongly Orontes' role in the history of Pergamon is emphasized in the official chronicles of Pergamon (*Inschr. v. Perg.* 613; *O.G.I.* 264). Cf. E. Meyer, *Die Grenzen der hell. Staaten in Kleinasien*, 1925, pp. 94 ff., and A. H. M. Jones, *The Cities* &c., p. 47.

324 On the date of the altar see the remarks of W. Zschietzschmann, loc. cit., 1256, and especially the restoration of the building inscription suggested by him; cf., however, W. von Massow, *Führer*, p. 51, who represents the common opinion.

325 A stray ray of light illuminates, for example, the history of the city of Temnus and the conditions of life prevailing there in the third century B.C. In a fragmentary decree of Temnus found at Smyrna (published and illustrated by L. Robert, *Ét. Anat.*, pp. 90 ff. ; the exact date is unknown), a decree passed in reply to one of Smyrna, we see the city of Temnus in close relations with the latter and acting as an independent body politic. The decree contains no hint of any dependence of Temnus on the dynast of Pergamon (cf. E. Meyer, *Die Grenzen* &c., pp. 95 and 101). The conditions of life in the neighbourhood of Temnus, in the districts around Mt. Sipylus, appear to have been far from peaceful and safe. Some citizens of Smyrna, captured by brigands, were rescued by the city of Temnus and restored to Smyrna. It is to be noted that Smyrna at that time was a Seleucid city (L. Robert, *Rev. É.A.* xxxviii (1936), pp. 23 ff.).

326 I have given a list of temples in the territory of the *dynasteia* in *Anat. Stud.*, pp. 370 ff., cf. T. R. S. Broughton, 'Roman Asia Minor' (T. Frank, *Econ. Survey*, iv), p. 676 f. I am now inclined to think that temple territories in the Pergamene *chora* were not as a rule independent territorial units for administrative purposes. This, of course, is a conjecture, and there were probably many exceptions to the rule. There is perhaps evidence of one of these in the inscription relating to the temple of Apollo Tarsenus in the upper Caicus valley, C. B. Welles, *R.C.* 47 (185 B.C.?, on the date, below, Ch. V, n. 62).

327 The lists of ephebes: W. Kolbe, *Ath. Mitt.* xxxii (1907), pp. 415 ff.; P. Jacobsthal, ibid. xxxiii (1908), pp. 384 ff., and H. Hepding, ibid. xxxv (1910), pp. 416 ff. A complete revised republication of these basic texts is urgently needed. I have discussed in a few lines the meaning of *topoi* in *C.A.H.* viii, p. 598 and p. 602 f., cf. A. H. M. Jones, *The Cities* &c., p. 48, and n. 31, and L. Robert, *Villes de l'Asie Mineure*, 1935, pp. 79 ff. It is evident that *topoi* were territorial subdivisions. The analogy to the Ptolemaic τοπαρχίαι is striking.

328 Land was, for example, purchased from the king through his agents by soldiers—*Inschr. v. Perg.* 158; C. B. Welles, *R.C.* 51, ll. 18 ff.: τῶ[ν δὲ ... κα]ὶ τῶν ἄλλων ἐγγαίων ὧν ἀπέδοτο Δή|μαρ[χ]ο[ς ὁ παρ᾽ ἡμῶν, ἐὰν δὲ κ]αί τινες ἄλλοι τῶν τὰ βασιλικὰ πραγματευ|[ομένων ἄλλους ἐγγαίους μετὰ] ταῦτα πωλῶσιν, ἔσονται αἵ τε κτήσεις κύ|[ριαι . . . κατὰ τὰ συγχωρη]θέντα ἑκάστοις. The supplements are not certain, but the meaning of the passage is clear. The text proves the existence (alongside of royal land, cleruchic land, and the *doreai*) of a category of land which in Ptolemaic Egypt was designated by the name γῆ ἰδιόκτητος. Unfortunately we know nothing of the status of this land, i.e. whether it became the irrevocable property of the purchasers.

329 *Pars quanta* paid by the landholders: App. *Bell. Civ.* v. 4, where Antony's statement in his speech at Ephesus that the Romans did not impose taxes in accordance with an assessment of property (πρὸς τιμήματα) probably refers to the Attalid system of taxation. It is not, however, clear whether in speaking of the Attalids Antony means that this system was applied to all the land in their kingdom—in which case the statement is notoriously incorrect (see further below, on the *dekate*)—or has in mind certain categories of land only, perhaps land and other property belonging to citizens and other inhabitants of Greek cities. See next chapter. *Dekate* or *eikoste* was paid on their land by military settlers, the cleruchs, *Inschr. v. Perg.* 158; C. B. Welles, *R.C.* 51, ll. 17 ff. Perhaps a *dekate* (Ps.-Arist. *Oecon.* ii. 1. 4: ἀπὸ τῶν βοσκημάτων, ἐπικαρπία τε καὶ δεκάτη καλουμένη) was paid by the κάτοικοι of the temple of Apollo Tarsenus in the upper Caicus valley in respect of their sheep; see the letter of Attalus, the brother of Eumenes II, of 185 B.C., by which exemption from this tax was granted to *katoikoi*, C. Schuchhardt, *Ath. Mitt.* xxiv (1899), pp. 212 ff.; C. B. Welles, *R.C.* 47. On the date see below, Ch. V, n. 62.

330 There is evidence of a large production of grain, cattle, and horses in the gifts made by the Attalids to cities, sanctuaries, &c., of Asia Minor and Greece, see for example Polyb. xviii. 16; Liv. xxxii. 40. 8 (Sicyon); Polyb. xxxi. 31. 1. The gifts of Philetaerus to the people of Cyzicus are very interesting (*O.G.I.* 748): in 280/79 B.C. he gave them money and 50 horses εἰς φυλακὴν τῆς χώρας (cf. Diog. L. iv. 6. 30); in 279/8 he granted them ἀτέλεια for cattle which they exported from his territory; in 276/5, during the war against the Galatians, he gave them large quantities of wheat and barley (was he, too, taking part in this war, and is not this the war that was glorified at Delos,

F. Durrbach, *Choix*, 31?). The inscription shows how efficiently agriculture and pasturage were organized by Philetaerus. We may compare an inscription from Ilium, a letter of Attalus II (?) to the sanctuary of Athene at Ilium announcing a gift of cattle with their herdsmen, L. Robert, *B.C.H.* liv (1930), pp. 348 ff.; C. B. Welles, *R.C.* 62. The king gave also a piece of land which he had bought and which obviously lay in the territory of Ilium (cf. the case of Sicyon above). The similarity of this gift to that which Philomelus, son of Lysias, tyrant of Phrygia, bestowed on the temple of Didyma—ten pairs of mules and five drivers—is striking, L. Robert, loc. cit., p. 350.

331 On the organization of industry in the Pergamene State, see my remarks in *Anat. Stud.*, pp. 379 ff. On parchment see above, p. 540 f., and Bilabel, *P.W.K.* xv, 596 ff., art. 'Membrana'. I regard it as certain that it was not Eumenes II, as Varro suggests (Plin. *N.H.* xiii. 70), who began the manufacture of parchment at Pergamon. Pergamon belonged to a part of the world that had used parchment as writing-material for centuries before the Hellenistic age. Eumenes probably increased its production in connexion with the creation of his library. Metal ware (silver plate) of Pergamene manufacture in the third cent. B.C.: G. Lippold, *P.W.K.* vi A. 1767, cf. my pl. LXXII.

332 On slaves in the Pergamene economy, see Chs. V and VI. On the Pergamene workmen and artists at Delphi at the time of Attalus I, Eumenes II, and Attalus II, see the Delphian inscriptions quoted in the text and G. Daux, *Delphes au IIe et au Ier siècle* &c., 1936, pp. 497 ff.; cf. Appendix X, pp. 682 ff., and L. Robert, *Ét. Anat.*, pp. 87 ff. On slaves employed by the kings at Pergamon, *O.G.I.* 338, 20 ff.: εἰς δὲ τοὺς παροίκους μετατεθῆναι τοὺς ἐκ [τῶν] | ἐξελευθέρων καὶ βασιλικοὺς τούς τε ἐνήλικα[ς] | καὶ τοὺς νεωτέρους, κατὰ τὰ αὐτὰ δὲ καὶ τὰς γυναῖ|κας πλὴν τῶν ἠγορασμένων ἐπὶ τοῦ Φιλαδέλφου | καὶ Φιλομήτορος βασιλέων καὶ τῶν ἀνειλημμένω(ν) | ἐκ τῶν οὐσιῶν τῶν γεγενημένων βασιλικῶν, κατὰ τα[ὐ]τὰ δὲ καὶ τοὺς δημοσίους. Slaves tending the royal cattle: C. B. Welles, *R.C.* 62, and above, note 330.

333 Gifts of the Attalids: G. Cardinali, *Il regno di Pergamo*, 1906, pp. 199 ff., and my remarks, *C.A.H.* viii, p. 604, cf. L. Robert, *Ét. Anat.*, pp. 84 ff. and 201.

334 W. Ruge and E. Meyer, *P.W.K.* iii. 507 ff., art. 'Bithynia'; Th. Reinach, *Numismatique ancienne: Trois Royaumes d'Asie Mineure*, 1888; J. Sölch, 'Bithynische Städte im Altertum', *Klio*, xix (1924), pp. 140 ff.; W. Ruge, *P.W.K.* xvii. 468 ff., art. 'Nikomedeia'; F. Geyer, ibid., 493 f., art. 'Nikomedes'; G. Cardinali, 'Bitinia', *Enciclopedia Italiana*; A. H. M. Jones, *The Cities* &c., pp. 148 ff. L. Robert, *Rev. Phil.* xiii (65), 1939, p. 168 f. (Astacus and Nicomedia, Cromna and Amastris).

335 R. Herzog, *Ath. Mitt.* xxx (1905), pp. 173 ff.; *S.I.G.*³ 456; Welles, *R.C.* 25. On the date (about 240 B.C., which is more probable than 250 B.C.) Welles, loc. cit. A large part of the letter is devoted to the assurance of safety

given to the merchants, ll. 33 ff.: καὶ τῶν | πλειόντων τὴν θάλασσαν | ὅσοι ἂν τυγχάνωσι τῶν ὑμε|τέρων προσβάλλοντες τοῖς | τόποις ὧν ἡμεῖς κρατοῦμεν (thus Ziaëlas did not hold all the coast which harboured the pirates) φροντίζειν ὅπως ἡ ἀσφάλει[α] | αὐτοῖς ὑπάρχῃ· κατὰ ταὐτὰ [δὲ] | καὶ οἷς ἂν συμβῇ πταίματός [τι-]|| νος γενομένου κατὰ πλοῦν | προσπεσεῖν πρὸς τὴν ἡμετέ[ραν], | πᾶσαν σπουδὴν ποιεῖσθαι ἵν[α] | μηδ᾽ ὑφ᾽ ἑνὸς ἀδικῶνται. The passage quoted shows that cases of piracy and of robbery of shipwrecked people were of frequent occurrence and that the Bithynian coast was not safe for Greek merchants. The hostility of the inhabitants to foreigners, their μισοξενία, may have been a reaction of the Thracian population of Bithynia to the philhellenic measures of their kings.

[336] My chapter 'Pontus and its neighbours', *C.A.H.* ix, pp. 211 ff. (with bibliography). The best and fullest survey of all the available material is still Th. Reinach, *Mithridate Eupator*, 1890, and the German translation of this book (1894); cf. A. H. M. Jones, *The Cities* &c., pp. 153 ff., and my article 'Ponto', *Enciclopedia Italiana.*

[337] F. Cumont and others, *Studia Pontica*, iii, 1910, Inscriptions &c., no. 95 a. On the eparchies, my note in *C.A.H.* ix, p. 215, n. 2.

[338] The standard work on the Galatians is still F. Stähelin, *Geschichte der kleinasiatischen Galater*, 2nd ed., 1907. On the economic and social life of the Galatians see the fine remarks of J. G. C. Anderson, 'Exploration in Galatia cis Halym', part ii, *J.H.S.* xix (1899), pp. 312 ff. For the later period, J. Keil, *C.A.H.* xi, pp. 597 ff., and bibliography, p. 917.

[339] On the Celtic expansion and civilization in the long period of their independent political life, see J. M. de Navarro, *C.A.H.* vii, pp. 41 ff., and copious bibliography, pp. 871 ff., and especially the excellent posthumous work of H. Hubert, *Les Celtes*, i and especially ii, 1932 (H. Berr, *L'Évolution de l'humanité*, I. iv. 6), also with exhaustive bibliography. It is needless to supplement the above-quoted bibliographies by references to some more recent contributions. For the later period, *C.A.H.* xi, chs. xii and xiii, with corresponding bibliographies, and T. Frank, *Economic Survey*, vol. iii, 1937, part iv, pp. 379 ff. (A. Grénier).

[340] M. Rostovtzeff, *Iranians and Greeks*, pp. 138 ff., *Artibus Asiae*, iv (1933), pp. 99 ff., and *Skythien und der Bosporus*, p. 488, note. On Celtic metal-work in general, W. A. von Jenny, *Keltische Metallarbeiten aus heidnischer und christlicher Zeit*, 1935.

[341] See, for example, the letters of Eumenes II and Attalus II to Attis, priest of the temple of Cybele of Pessinus, Welles, *R.C.*, nos. 55–61. Attis was a cult-name. His brother's name mentioned in the letters was Aiorix. He was therefore a Galatian. Cf. below, Ch. V.

[342] Galatian mercenaries were numerous in the Hellenistic armies of the third and early second centuries B.C. See G. T. Griffith, *The Mercenaries*, pp. 118 ff. and p. 137 (for Egypt), p. 166 (for Syria), cf. Index s.v. 'Gauls'.

In Egypt a unique set of painted *stelae* of the third century B.C. from the necropoleis of Hadra and Shiatby and some funeral vases from the same graves give us a good idea of the names and appearance of Galatian mercenaries. See A. Reinach, 'Les Galates dans l'art alexandrin', *Mon. et Mém. Piot*, xviii (1910), pp. 40 ff., esp. pp. 57 ff., and 'Les Gaulois en Égypte', *Rev. É.A.* xiii (1911), pp. 33 ff.; cf. on the supposed Galatian horsemen R. Pagenstecher, *Nekropolis*, 1919, pp. 65 ff., esp. p. 69, and E. Breccia, *La Necropoli di Sciatbi*, 1912; ii, pls. XXII–XXIV; M. H. Swindler, *Ancient Painting*, 1929, p. 344. For the later period our information is scanty. Besides certain literary allusions, we have only some graffiti of Abydus (A. Reinach, loc. cit.). The papyri and inscriptions of this period are silent about the Galatians, see J. Lesquier, *Inst. mil.*, 1911, pp. 109 ff. and pp. 122 ff.; F. Heichelheim, *Die ausw. Bevölkerung*, p. 75, notes 4 and 7, cf. his articles in *Arch. Pap.* ix (1930), p. 49, and xii (1936), pp. 54 ff. It is not till the first century B.C. that the Galatians appear again: first in the inscriptions of Hermupolis of 80–78 B.C. in the lists of the members of a military κοινόν (one Galatian out of 823 names; note that the Thracians are much more numerous)—see F. Zucker, 'Doppelinschrift spät-ptolemäischer Zeit aus der Garnison von Hermupolis Magna', *Abh. Berl. Akad.* cxxi (1938), p. 53, cf. *Aeg.* xviii (1938), pp. 279 ff. and *S.B.* 8066—and later as soldiers of Gabinius. These last, of course, are not mercenaries but recruits. It is to be noted that all the Galatians mentioned in the inscriptions and in the literary texts (with one exception) were in active service and so were not soldiers of the territorial army. Our information, it is true, is haphazard, but this fact—note that settled soldiers of other 'nationalities' are comparatively often mentioned—may point either to the reluctance of the Ptolemies to settle those wild men in Egypt, or to the desire of the Galatians to return to their own country, or to both. I may add that, according to M. Segre, the Cardaces settled by Antiochus III in Lycia (below, Ch. V, nn. 60, 61) were Galatians.

[343] Phylarchus, Frg. 2, *F. Gr. Hist.* 81 (Athen. iv. 34, p. 150 d), and the comments of Jacoby.

[344] F. Miltner, 'Die Meerengenfrage in der griechischen Geschichte', *Klio*, xxviii (1935), pp. 1 ff.

[345] F. W. Hasluck, *Cyzicus*, 1910; W. Ruge, *P.W.K.* xii. 228 ff.

[346] On the Cyzicenes, K. Regling, *P.W.K.* xii. 224 f., art. 'Kyzikener', and 'Der griechische Goldschatz von Prinkipo', *Z.f.N.* xli (1931), pp. 1 ff.

[347] Siege by Arrhidaeus: Diod. xviii. 51; Athen. xi. 509 a; *Marm. Par.* B, 12 (Jacoby, *F. Gr. Hist.* 239). Philetaerus and Cyzicus: *O.G.I.* 748, and above, n. 330. The well-known inscription concerning Laodice's estate situated near the territories of Zeleia and Cyzicus (*O.G.I.* 225; Welles, *R.C.* 18–20) does not imply that Cyzicus and Zeleia were subject cities of Antiochus II, as Ruge suggests. However, we know very little of the history of Asia Minor in the early Hellenistic period. A kind of suzerainty of Lysimachus, perhaps of

Seleucus I and Antiochus I and Antiochus II, over the city, might be suggested if we accept the idea of Babelon that some coins of Lysimachus, Antiochus I, and Antiochus II, bear the mint-mark of Cyzicus (F. W. Hasluck, loc. cit., p. 174, cf. E. Babelon, *Rois de Syrie*, p. lvi f., and B. Niese, *Gesch. d. griech. u. maked. Staaten*, ii. p. 85, n. 1, and p. 135, n. 7). But this, if it is a fact (which is doubtful), does not mean that Cyzicus was one of their subject cities.

[348] On the territory of Cyzicus, Diod. xviii. 51, and the inscription discussed by F. W. Hasluck and myself, see my *Kolonat*, p. 263, n. 1, and Hasluck, *J.H.S.* xxiv (1904), p. 21, n. 4; ibid. xxvi (1906), p. 29; and *Cyzicus*, p. 272, n. 23, and p. 50, cf. p. 255 (on the village administration). The purely agricultural character of life in the region of which the territory of Cyzicus forms a part is attested by numerous dedications to Zeus Olbios, the divine protector of the peasants, found somewhere south of Lake Manyas, probably on the site once occupied by the temple of this god. See L. Robert, *Coll. Fröhner*, i, *Inscr. gr.*, pp. 58 ff., nos. 47–8, and *Rev. Phil.* xiii. (65) (1939), p. 190. Cf. his comments, loc. cit. and *Ét. Anat.*, p. 205 f., pl. xxviii, 4. The inscription of the Thrakiokometai and the funeral inscription of Moirocles: G. Mendel, *Cat. Sculpt. Mus. Constantinople*, iii, 1912, no. 1074. Zeleia: *S.I.G.*³ 279; my *Kolonat*, p. 260.

[349] Cf. the decree in honour of Antonia Tryphaena, in the time of Tiberius, *S.E.G.* iv. 707. It gives a vivid picture, probably not less true of an earlier age, of the merchants 'from the whole of the civilized world' (ἀπὸ τῆς οἰκουμένης) and of the 'foreigners' (ξένοι), who gathered at Cyzicus at the time of the fair (πανήγυρις). On the products of Cyzicus, F. W. Hasluck, *Cyzicus*, p. 171.

[350] Bürchner, *P.W.K.* xii. 590 ff. On the Lampsacenes, K. Regling, ibid. 589 f., art. 'Lampsakener' (with bibliography). Cyzicus and Lampsacus at Delos: *I.G.* xi. 4. 562 (Cyzicus) and 571 and 708 (Lampsacus); F. Durrbach, *Choix*, p. 275.

[351] H. Merle, *Die Geschichte der Städte Byzantion und Kalchedon*, diss. Kiel, 1916.

[352] On Heraclea see the valuable programmes of J. H. Schneiderwirth, *Heraclea am Pontus*, 1882, and *Das pontische Heraclea*, 1885; G. Busolt, *Griechische Staatskunde*, 3rd ed., 1920, pp. 402 ff.; K. J. Beloch, *Gr. Gesch.* iii. 1, 2nd ed., 1922, pp. 137 ff., cf. p. 302, and iii. 2, pp. 94 ff. Cf. U. von Wilamowitz-Moellendorf, *Staat u. Gesellschaft der Griechen*, 2nd ed. 1923, p. 39 (on the use made of Heraclea in the speculations regarding the best form of government), and R. Laqueur, art. 'Nymphis', *P.W.K.* xvii. 1608 ff. (on the early history of Heraclea). On the situation of Heraclea and her excellent harbour, see the remarks of L. Robert, *Ét. Anat.*, pp. 251 ff. On some coins of Geta, Gordian, and Gallienus there is represented a high tower-like building with a fire burning on the top. This building L. Robert regards as a lighthouse. If he is right, the lighthouse may be regarded as a construction of Roman imperial times or

as an Hellenistic imitation of the Alexandrian Pharos, cf. my *Storia Soc. ed Econ.*, p. 202, n. 34.

353 Heraclean navy. In the war between Ceraunus and Gonatas (280 B.C.) Heraclea supported the former (Memnon 13; Just. xxiv. 1. 8). The Heraclean squadron was the strongest in the fleet of Ceraunus; it consisted of ἑξήρεις, πεντήρεις, ἄφρακτοι καὶ ὀκτήρης μία; the last, which was doubtless the last word in naval construction and the pride of the Heracleotes, is described in detail by Memnon. The ship, with its 1,600 rowers, 1,200 soldiers, and two κυβερνῆται, was certainly a brilliant illustration of Heraclea's power. In the war between Antiochus I and Antigonus, when Antiochus I was fighting Nicomedes I of Bithynia, Heraclea, the ally of Antigonus, sent a squadron of 13 τριήρεις to help Nicomedes (Memnon 18). In the war between Antiochus II and Byzantium Heraclea sent 40 τριέρεις to the support of Byzantium (Memnon 23). When the Galatians appeared on the horizon of Asia Minor and pillaged the territory of Byzantium, Heraclea helped the latter materially, contributing 4,000 staters to the cost of war (Memnon 19). Later, when the Galatians invaded Pontus in the first year of the rule of Mithridates III and the army of the king was short of supplies (about 255 B.C.), Heraclea sent grain to Amisus (Memnon 24). In retaliation the Galatians invaded the territory of Heraclea; they were bought off by a ransom of 5,000 staters, besides individual payments to each of the Galatian chiefs of 200 staters (Memnon 24; F. Stähelin, *Gesch. d. kleinas. Galater*, 1907, p. 17).

354 Chersonesus and Heraclea: my article 'Chersoneso' in *Enciclopedia Italiana*. The keen interest shown by Philadelphus in the cities of the Pontic coast is noteworthy. I shall speak of Sinope presently. The relations of Philadelphus and those of Soter with Heraclea were as close as with Sinope. Memnon, 25, mentions that Philadelphus sent Heraclea 500 *artabae* of grain and built a temple of Proconnesian marble on the city's acropolis for its chief god, Heracles. On the regular communications between the Black Sea, the Sea of Azov, Rhodes, and Alexandria see the well-known statement of Diod. iii. 34. 7. It took 14 days to reach Alexandria from the Sea of Azov, i.e. probably from Panticapaeum. Heracleans at Athens: the Index to *I.G.* ii (period from Euclides to Augustus) shows among the metics of Athens 89 Heracleans, and the Supplement adds another 12. For the Roman period the Index to *I.G.* iii registers 81 names, W. S. Ferguson, *Hell. Ath.*, p. 316, n. 4. It is highly probable that most of the Heracleans buried at Athens were Pontic Heracleans. But many may have been citizens of other cities of the same name, especially Heraclea ad Latmum in Asia Minor or Heraclea Trachinia. Note that in the list of *proxenoi* of Thermus the two Pontic Heracleans are specifically characterized as such, *I.G.* ix, 2nd ed., 31, 44 and 112 (223/2 B.C. and 205/4 B.C.) and that the number of Milesians at Athens was very large both in the Hellenistic and in the Roman period. The funeral inscriptions of Athens are not dated. Most of the Heracleans of the pre-Augustan times belong probably to the second–first centuries B.C., but of course not all of them.

355 On Amisus, G. Hirschfeld, *P.W.K.* i. 1839 f.; F. Cumont and others, *Studia Pontica*, ii, 1906, pp. 111 ff., and iii, 1910, pp. 1 ff. Amisenes at Athens: Index to *I.G.* ii. On the necropolis of Amisus, my *Skythien und der Bosporus*, p. 148. Jewels found at Amisus, Amasia, and Sinope: L. Pollak, *Klassisch-antike Goldschmiedearbeiten im Besitze . . . A. J. von Nelidow*, 1903, nos. 142, 160, 175, 390, 523 (Amisus); 219, 251, 282, 325, 367, 498 (Amasia); 192 (Sinope). Specimens of Amisene pottery and terracottas: my pls. LXIV, LXV, and LXVII, 2. The pottery of Greek and Hellenistic times has never been carefully studied. Specially interesting are the painted (black and red) *rhyta* and *askoi* with fore-parts of various animals (bulls, goats, rams, horses), which go back to Minoan and 'Hittite' prototypes, but may be ascribed to the fourth and third centuries B.C. Some of them are Greek, others Iranian in style. On 'Cappadocian' pottery in general, H. de Genouillac, *Céramique cappadocienne*, 1926; on the pottery of the later period, ibid. i, p. 64, and especially nos. 171 and 173 of his catalogue (vol. ii, pl. 14 and pl. 15). Cf. against his dates, Sir Arthur Evans, *Palace of Minos*, Index under 'Eski Samsun' (p. 46) and 'Bull heads' (p. 21). I owe my acquaintance with this pottery and the bibliographical references to the kindness of Prof. R. Zahn, who regards the specimens reproduced in our pls. LXIV. 1, 2 and LXVII. 2 as certainly Hellenistic in date. On some monuments (of archaic date) excavated by Macridy Bey at Samsun: Macridy Bey, 'Une citadelle archaïque du Pont', *Mitt. Vorderas. Ges.* xii (1907), no. 4.

356 On Sinope, D. M. Robinson, *Ancient Sinope*, 1906 (cf. *Am. J. Ph.* xxvii (1906) pp. 125 ff., 245 ff., and 447 ff., and *A.J.A.* ix (1905) pp. 294 ff.); W. Ruge, *P.W.K.* iii A. 252 ff. Descriptions of the city: Strabo xii. 3. 11, p. 545 f.; Polyb. iv. 56. The Sinopians at Athens: the Index to *I.G.* ii enumerates 21 or 22 funeral inscriptions, and the Index to the Supplement another two. Cf. the Sinopian *proxenoi* at Oropus, *S.E.G.* i. 104, and a Sinopian as *proxenos* at Thermus in Aetolia, *I.G.* ix, 2nd ed., 25, l. 22 (245–236 B.C.). Commercial relations between Sinope and Panticapaeum, above, ch. ii, n. 43. The contradictory evidence about the Sarapis statue has repeatedly been collected and discussed. I cannot deal with the question here. See, e.g., Roeder, *P.W.K.* i A. 2404 ff. Coins of Sinope: E. S. G. Robinson, *Num. Chr.* 4th ser. xx (1920), pp. 1 ff., and 5th ser. x (1930), pp. 1 ff. The importance of the mint of Sinope is reflected in the well-known story of Diogenes the Cynic; see the ingenious combination of numismatic data with this story, Ch. Seltman in D. R. Dudley, *A History of Cynicism*, 1937, pp. 20 ff. and pp. 54 ff.

357 Callatis: N. Vulić, *P.W.K.* x. 1610 ff. Istrus: Vulić, *P.W.K.* ix. 2268 f. All the cities of the western coast submitted to Lysimachus after the war mentioned in the text. Their history in the third century is a blank. With the second century we see more clearly; below, Chs. V and VI. B. Lenk, *P.W.K.* vi A. 433 ff., art. 'Thrake', does not deal with the Greek cities.

358 On Olbia my article 'Olbia' in *Enciclopedia Italiana* (with bibliography).

359 Bosporan kingdom: my chapter 'The Bosporan kingdom', *C.A.H.*

viii, pp. 561 ff., cf. my article 'Panticapeo' in *Enciclopedia Italiana* (both with bibliography). I cannot repeat here the references to ancient sources and modern contributions which the reader will find in that chapter and article.

[360] See my chapter 'The Sarmatae and the Parthians' in *C.A.H.* xi, pp. 91 ff., and bibliography, p. 876.

[361] The decline of the Scythian power is illustrated by the archaeological evidence furnished by the tumuli of the South Russian steppes. I have tried to classify and to date the most important groups of Scythian and other burials in South Russia in my book *Skythien und der Bosporus*. The dates which I there assigned to the different groups and to single burials have been discussed several times since by competent scholars. Their general tendency is to assign the most splendid and important burials, which I attributed to the period when the Bosporan kingdom reached the zenith of its prosperity (fourth to early third centuries B.C.), to a somewhat earlier time, none of these graves being in their view later than Alexander and some of them belonging to the end of the fifth century. See for example G. M. Richter, 'A Greek sword-sheath from South Russia', *Metr. Mus. St.* iv. 1, 1932, pp. 109 ff., and especially K. Schefold, 'Der skythische Tierstil in Südrussland', *Eur. Sept. Ant.* xii (1938), pp. 3 ff. This important question cannot be discussed here. From the historical point of view I see no reason for an abrupt disappearance of Scythian princely graves in the late fourth century. The dates assigned to the various burials are derived from a purely stylistic analysis of some of the objects found in these graves, which leads individual scholars to widely divergent conclusions (for example, the Chertomlyzk burials are very differently dated by Miss Richter and by Schefold). Schefold's dating of the latest Scythian graves cannot therefore be regarded as final. Some of them may belong to the early third century B.C.

[362] I cannot here enter into a discussion of the contents of the Sacian and Sarmatian graves and of the new style of jewellery and toreutic art which they brought with them from their Asiatic home and to which they remained attached for many centuries. See my papers: 'Sarmatian and Indo-Scythian antiquities', *Rec. Kondakov*, 1926, pp. 255 ff., and 'Some new aspects of Iranian art', *Sem. Kond.* vi (1933), pp. 161 ff., cf. *C.A.H.* xi, pp. 102 ff., and bibliography, p. 876. See also the recent remarks on this subject by A. Salmony, *Eur. Sept. Ant.* ii (1937), pp. 91 ff., and K. Schefold, ibid. xii (1938), p. 63. I am inclined to regard the Hellenized version of the new animal style as a creation of Bactrian artists; above, p. 546. The contents of the royal graves of the tumulus at Karagodeuashkh should be restudied in the light of the new evidence discovered since their excavation. See my *Skythien und der Bosporus*, pp. 323 ff., esp. p. 328; cf. pp. 547 ff. on the graves closely connected with Karagodeuashkh, and Schefold, loc. cit. Cf. my pl. LXVIII.

CHAPTER V

1 Cf. Liv. xxxii. 33–4. On the conference at Nicaea: De Sanctis, *Stor. d. Rom.* iv. 1, 1923, p. 81 f.; M. Holleaux, *C.A.H.* viii, p. 171.

2 G. De Sanctis, *Stor. d. Rom.* iv. 1, p. 71 f.; M. Holleaux, *C.A.H.* viii, p. 151. The main account will be found in Polyb. xv. 21–3, cf. xviii. 3. 11–12. Destruction of Phthiotic Thebes and sale of its population into slavery, Polyb. v. 100. 8 (it was E. Bikerman who reminded me of this case).

3 Täubler, *Imp. Rom.* i, pp. 430 ff.; M. Holleaux, *C.A.H.* viii, p. 125. Cf. the arrangements with Attalus in 209/8 B.C., M. Holleaux, loc. cit., p. 130.

4 Pol. ix. 42. 5 (209 B.C.); M. Holleaux, loc. cit., p. 128.

5 J. Carcopino, *Points de vue sur l'impérialisme romain*, 1934, p. 38; M. Holleaux, *C.A.H.* viii, pp. 126 ff.

6 M. Holleaux, *C.A.H.* viii, p. 194. In Ch. IV, note 44 I have quoted the articles by Harder which try to prove that the Roman Senate and aristocracy in their international relations were guided by principles of *Humanitas, Justitia, Clementia*, and *Fides*, cf. A. Heuss, 'Die völkerrechtlichen Grundlagen der röm. Aussenpolitik in republ. Zeit', *Klio*, Beiheft xxxi (xviii), 1933, pp. 18 ff. I am inclined to regard these principles of action attributed to the Roman aristocracy, as formulated by Cic. *De off.* i, esp. 34–40 (*bellica officia*), as pure theory borrowed by the Romans from the Greeks or rather formulated for them by Greek philosophers, esp. Panaetius. See M. Pohlenz, 'Antikes Führertum. Cicero *de officiis* und das Lebensideal des Panaitios' (*Neue Wege z. Antike*, ii. 3), 1934, cf. H. Dahlmann, 'Clementia Caesaris', *Neue Jahrb. f. Wiss.* x (1934), pp. 17 ff., and especially U. Knoche, 'Magnitudo animi', *Phil. Suppl.* xxvii. 3 (1935), pp. 74 ff. Knoche draws attention to Polyb. xxxi. 10. 7, where he maintains that the Roman pretence of acting as εὐεργέται was a mere political weapon in dealing with the Hellenistic World: πολὺ γὰρ ἤδη τοῦτο τὸ γένος ἐστι τῶν διαβουλίων παρὰ ʿΡωμαίοις, ἐν οἷς διὰ τῆς τῶν πέλας ἀγνοίας αὔξουσι καὶ κατασκευάζονται τὴν ἰδίαν ἀρχὴν πραγματικῶς, ἅμα καὶ χαριζόμενοι καὶ δοκοῦντες εὐεργετεῖν τοὺς ἁμαρτάνοντας. Cf. W. Otto, 'Zur Geschichte der Zeit des 6. Ptolemäers', *Bay. S.B.* xi (1934). In any case no trace of the influence of these ideas of humanity, &c., will be found in the Roman methods of conducting war in such highly civilized countries as Greece. For the Romans, as for the Greeks, the ideas of *humanitas, fides, clementia* remained pure theory so far at least as concerned the practice of war.

7 Kahrstedt, art. Λάφυρον, *P.W.K.* xii. 772, says that the right of others than the heads of the State to appropriate booty was recognized exclusively by the Aetolians, who permitted their citizens to carry out private raids and acquire booty. Kahrstedt quotes in support of his statement the well-known speech of Philip in which he characterizes the methods of warfare of the Aetolians (above, n. 1). He omits, however, to quote the practice of Philip, the commissions given by him to Demetrius of Pharos and then to Dicaearchus

and his companion, and the interesting description by Plutarch of the early activity of Philopoemen (Plut. *Philop.* 4). Philopoemen began his career by taking part in πολιτικαὶ στρατεῖαι, ἃς ἐποιοῦντο κλωπείας ἕνεκα καὶ λεηλασίας εἰς τὴν Λακωνικὴν ἐμβάλλοντες. The private character of these raids is emphasized by the statement that Philopoemen spent the income derived from them on horses, armour, and weapons, and λύσις αἰχμαλώτων. This makes it certain that they were not public raids. On Nabis see V. Ehrenberg, art. 'Nabis' in *P.W.K.* xvi. 1471 ff., and below, note 14. It is unfortunate that the regulation about the distribution of booty among the soldiers of Philip's army, a paragraph in a general regulation for the Macedonian army, is so badly preserved; see P. Roussel, 'Un Règlement militaire macédonien', *Rev. Arch.*, 6 sér., iii (1934), pp. 39 ff., col. III, and M. Feyel, ibid., 6 sér., vi (1935), pp. 29 ff., cf. G. De Sanctis, *Riv. Fil.* lxii (12) (1934), p. 519; C. B. Welles, *A.J.A.* xlii (1938), p. 245 f. It appears that the booty was distributed by a special χειριστής, and that disputes were settled by a commission of King's friends, cf. Polyb. iv. 80. 16. The technical term for booty in this document is ὠφέλεια, cf. J. Schweighäuser, *Lex. Polybianum*, 1822, s.v. The new fragment of this regulation published by Feyel belongs in part to the chapter on booty and prescribes rules for the treatment of small parties of soldiers sent out on a raid and bringing back a certain amount of spoil (see the comments of Feyel). It is possible that another paragraph of the same chapter treated of the αἰχμάλωτοι and that there was a section regarding the burning of corn (or corn-fields) and the destruction (?) of vines, which are regarded as ἀτάκτημα. Was it because the section related to these acts when committed elsewhere than in enemy country? Or were there regulations about devastating enemy country?

[8] On the Cretan κοινόν, M. von der Mijnsbrugge, *The Cretan Koinon*, New York, 1931; M. Holleaux, *C.A.H.* viii, pp. 292 ff. (sketch of the history of Cretan piracy in the late third and early second century). The fundamental treatises on the political activity of Crete in Hellenistic times are still those of G. Cardinali, 'Crete e le grandi potenze ellenistiche sino alla guerra di Litto', *Riv. d. Stor. Ant.* ix (1904), pp. 69 ff.; 'La guerra di Litto', *Riv. Fil.* xxxiii (1905), pp. 519 ff.; and 'Creta nel tramonto dell' ellenismo', ibid. xxxv (1907), pp. 1 ff., and the two excellent memoirs of M. Holleaux, *Rev. É. G.* xxx (1917), pp. 88 ff., and xxxiii (1920), pp. 223 ff.

[9] A. Neppi Modona, 'L'isola di Coo', 1933, pp. 43 ff. (*Mem. d. Ist. St. Arch. di Rodi*, i); M. Segre, Κρητικὸς πόλεμος, *Riv. Fil.* lxi (11) (1933), pp. 365 ff. The Κρητικὸς πόλεμος—war between Rhodes and Crete (205/4)—is mentioned (together with the next war) in *S.I.G.*³ 569 and 568; alone in *S.I.G.*³ 567 (Calymna) and in one of the inscriptions published by Segre; the war between Philip and the Rhodians (from 201 B.C.), in *S.I.G.*³ 568, 569 and in the subscription list Paton–Hicks, no. 10, cf. 11. We may connect with one of these wars, or with the activity of pirates in general in the first decades of the second century, the decree of the Athenian cleruchs of Imbros in honour of Lysanias, a brave and distinguished man who is praised for the

services he rendered during an ἐπιβουλή of the λῃσταί, Michel, 157; *I.G.* xii. 8, 53 (before 166 B.C.). I again recall the fact mentioned above that most of the Greek islands were fortified against the pirates: the rural population were protected against them by περιπόλια and πύργοι, H. A. Ormerod, 'Towers in the Greek islands', *Ann. of Arch. and Anthrop.* xi (1924), pp. 31 ff., cf. G. Jacopi, *Clara Rhodos*, vi–vii (1932–33), p. 423, no. 43; M. Segre, loc. cit., p. 385; M. Rostovtzeff, *Anatolian Stud. presented to Sir William Ramsay*, p. 374 f.; and esp. the excellent article by A. Bon, 'Les Ruines antiques dans l'île de Thasos', *B.C.H.* liv (1930), pp. 147 ff., esp. p. 179 and pp. 184 ff., cf. Y. Béquignon, 'Les Pyrgoi de Teos', *Rev. Arch.* 5 sér., xxviii (1928), pp. 185 ff., and W. Ruge, 'Teos', *P.W.K.* v A. 554 f., see also L. Robert, *Ét. Anat.*, p. 531, n. 2.

[10] *S.I.G.*³ 594 (about 195 B.C.).

[11] On Antiochus and sea-robbery cf., in addition to the statement of Livy quoted in the text, Polyb. xxi. 12; Livy xxxvii. 27. 5 ff. On the Delphian *theoroi* and Chersonesus, *S.I.G.*³ 604 (192/1 B.C.); E. Schwyzer, *Dial. gr. ex. epigr. pot.* 1923, no. 333. The inscription has been revised and reprinted with comments by G. Daux, *Delphes au II* *e* *et au I* *er* *siècle*, &c., pp. 658 ff., cf. p. 25 f. See below, n. 88.

[12] On Hybristas, B. Niese, *Gesch. Griech. u. Mak. Staaten*, ii, p. 729, 2.

[13] See the letters of Sp. Postumius Albinus to the Delphians and to the Amphictions and the appended S.C., and the letter of C. Livius Salinator to the Delphians: M. Holleaux, *B.C.H.* liv (1930), pp. 39 ff., and the comments on these documents by M. Holleaux, loc. cit., pp. 1–36; P. Roussel, ibid. lvi (1932), pp. 1–36, and G. Daux, *Delphes au II* *e* *et au I* *er* *siècle*, &c., pp. 262 ff. No doubt the Delphians were not accusing the Aetolians of having assassinated their ambassadors, and the Romans did not mention the Aetolians in this connexion. Nevertheless the complaints of the Delphians were mainly directed against the Aetolians, and we may see in their request for investigation a veiled reference to them.

[14] On the social and economic conditions of Greece at the end of the third century, see the masterly picture by M. Holleaux, *C.A.H.* viii, p. 146 f. On Aetolia, R. Flacelière, *Les Aitoliens*, &c., 1937, p. 310 f. On Nabis, V. Ehrenberg, *P.W.K.* xvi. 1481 ff., art. 'Nabis'. On Boeotia, B. Haussoullier, *Traité entre Delphes et Pellana*, 1917, pp. 106 ff. On Thessaly, Livy xxxiv. 51. 4 ff. (194 B.C.), and xlii. 5. 7 f. (173 B.C.), cf. the paper of R. V. Schmidt quoted in n. 30, pp. 104 ff. The earlier discussions of the subject are quoted in the above-mentioned works. Quite recently A. Passerini, 'I moti politico-sociali della Grecia e i Romani', *Athen.* xi (1933), pp. 309 ff., has given a general survey of the political and social conditions of Greece in the second century. He is certainly right in emphasizing the support that the Romans gave (until the Achaean war) to the disruptive forces in Greece, viz. the opponents of order and of the propertied classes, the men whose dream was redistribution of land and abolition of debts. The adroit Roman propaganda is excellently illustrated by the well-known manifesto of the Romans against

Perseus addressed probably to the Amphictions and published at Delphi, *S.I.G.*³ 643, cf. Liv. xlii. 13. 3. In his article 'La τρυφή nella storiografia ellenistica', *Stud. Ital. d. Fil. Cl.* xi (1934), p. 52, Passerini interprets Polybius' statements regarding Boeotia and Aetolia, which I have used above, as a set of current commonplaces, as τόποι about τρυφή, ὄχλου κολακεία, and ὕβρις applied mechanically by the authority on whom Polybius drew (a Hellenistic historian of the common type) to Boeotia and Aetolia. Such is not my impression. In those passages Polybius meant, not to perorate about the τρυφή in general, but to give realistic pictures of Boeotia, Aetolia, &c., and he succeeded in his endeavour. It was not his fault that there was a good deal of τρυφή, κολακεία, and ὕβρις in the Greek life of this period.

¹⁵ I cannot quote here all the modern discussions of the subject. I will confine myself to those contributions which deal with the conditions in the second century B.C.: B. Haussoullier, *Traité entre Delphes et Pellana*, 1917, pp. 102 ff.; L. Robert, *B.C.H.* liii (1929), pp. 156 f. I cannot quote here the many new inscriptions found after the publication of Robert's paper.

¹⁶ This brief sketch is based on the Delphian inscriptions, which have been admirably interpreted by P. Roussel, *B.C.H.* lvi (1932), pp. 1 ff.; R. Flacelière *Les Aitoliens*, &c., pp. 333 ff. (on the *epimeletai*), and G. Daux, *Delphes au IIᵉ et au Iᵉʳ siècle*, &c., pp. 225 ff. (M. Acilius Glabrio and his donations), pp. 259 ff. 'Delphes contre l'Amphictionie', and pp. 473 ff.: 'Arbitrages et tribunaux étrangers'; cf. G. Klaffenbach, *Gnomon*, xiv (1938), pp. 6 ff.

¹⁷ On Hellenistic pottery in general, C. W. Lunsingh Scheurleer, *Grieksche Ceramiek*, 1936. On the Megarian bowls of the third century B.C., see note 163 of the preceding chapter and Index s.v.; cf. H. Thompson, 'Two centuries of Hellenistic pottery', *Hesp.* iii (1934), pp. 351 ff. The later centres: Delos (?)—F. Courby, *Les Vases gr. à reliefs* 1922, pp. 392 ff.; Sparta—M. B. Hobling, *Ann. Br. Sch. Athens*, xxvi (1923–4, and 1924–5), pp. 277 ff.; Calydon in Aetolia—E. Dyggve, F. Poulsen, K. Rhomaios, 'Das Heroon von Kalydon', 1934, pp. 419 ff. (*Mém. de l'Ac. r. d. Sc. et d. Lett. de Dan.*, sér. 7, vol. iv. 4). Special attention should be paid to the many finds of Megarian bowls in Macedonia, see, e.g., those made in Heraclea Lyncestis, A. D. Keramopoullos, *Eph. Arch.*, 1932, pp. 65 ff. On the clay censers and portable charcoal ovens (*réchauds*) see Ch. IV, n. 163. From one or several early centres of production they spread far and wide over the Hellenistic world and were soon made locally. The same is certainly true of the terracotta figurines, F. Winter, *Die Typen der figürlichen Terrakotten*, 1903. Alexandria—E. Breccia, *Terracotte figurate greche e greco-egizie del Museo d'Alessandria*, vols. i and ii, 1930–34; Babylon and Uruk—M. Rostovtzeff, 'Dura and the problem of Parthian Art', *Yale Class. Stud.* 5 (1935), p. 180 f.; Reports on the excavations of Warka, *Berl. Abh.*, Fifth Rep., 1933, pls. XIX, XX, XXI; Sixth Rep. 1935, pl. XXX; Seventh Rep. 1935, pl. XXXVIII; Eighth Rep. 1936, pl. XLVI, fig. K, and pl. LVII; Seleuceia on the Tigris—C. Hopkins, *Michigan Alumnus Quart. Rev.* 1937, no. 10, pp. 28 ff.; N. C. Debevoise, *Asia*, xxxviii (1938), pp. 746 ff.; W. von Ingen, 'Figurines from Seleucia on the Tigris' (*Un. of Mich. St.*, Hum. Ser., xlv), 1939

Myrina—E. Pottier et S. Reinach, *La Nécropole de Myrina*, 1886–88 ; D. Burr *Terracottas from Myrina in the Mus. of Fine Arts, Boston*, 1934 (on p. 79 f. a good bibliography). Amisus—above, p. 592. Tarsus—*P.W.K.* iv A. 2437 ; *A.J.A.* xxxix (1935), pp. 528 ff., and xli (1937), p. 286. Cf. in general, J. Charbonneaux, *Les terres cuites grecques*, 1936 (bibliography p. 24).

[18] For tabulations of war indemnities and booty, see the lists in W. Kroll, *Die Kultur der Ciceronischen Zeit*, i, 1933, p. 88, and notes, and T. Frank, *Econ. Surv.* i, 1933, pp. 127–38. The most detailed is that of J. A. O. Larsen, ibid. iv, 1938, pp. 313 ff. I regret that Larsen, in speaking of the economic bearing on Greece of the Roman wars with Macedonia, has not collected the evidence on the methods of conducting war used by the Romans and by both the allies and the enemies of Rome. This would help him to understand better the economic status of Greece in the early second century B.C.

[19] W. S. Ferguson, *H.A.*, 1911, pp. 287 ff.

[20] Production of grain in various Hellenistic States, F. Heichelheim, art. 'Sitos', in *P.W.K.* Suppl. vi. 845 ff. Export of grain from Egypt to Athens at the time of the 'Social' war, *I.G.* ii.² 845 A and B ; A. Wilhelm, Πραγματεῖαι τῆς Ἀκαδημίας Ἀθηνῶν, iv (1936), pp. 25 ff. (the sender was Aeschron the Aetolian, probably a grandson of Aeschron the Aetolian, who saved some Athenians from robbers in the early third century B.C., *I.G.* ii². 652. see above Ch. IV, n. 14) ; South Russia to Rhodes, Delos, and Delphi, *C.A.H.* viii, pp. 580 and 581, and pp. 629 and 630, cf. p. 642 ; Numidia to Delos, Athens, and Rhodes, Heichelheim, loc. cit. 856. Export of grain from Carthage to the East—a new though not surprising fact—is attested by an inscription of the early second century B.C. found at Istrus, S. Lambrino, *Dacia* iii–iv (1927–32), pp. 400 ff. (decree of the city in honour of a Carthaginian who imported grain and sold it to the city). The importation of grain (made very expensive by the cost of transport) from far distant Carthage to Istrus, a neighbour of Thrace and Olbia, and almost a neighbour of Panticapeum, shows how irregular were the production and export of Thracian and S. Russian grain, and how precarious from time to time was the situation even of the Greek cities of the western and northern shores of the Black Sea (a fact mentioned by Polybius iv. 38. 5). It may be suggested that the Carthaginian of the inscription referred to was engaged in trade in general, and that the grain he sold was not produced in Carthage, resembling in this one of his compatriots who was occupied in the Egyptian trade with Somaliland (see the well-known papyrus, U. Wilcken, *Z. f. äg. Spr.* lx (1925), pp. 86 ff.). But this suggestion is highly improbable. The export of grain from Carthage shows that my idea that an agricultural revival took place there after the Second Punic war may be correct ; see against it T. Frank, *Econ. Hist. of Rome²*, 1927, p. 115, and *Econ. Survey of Anc. Rome*, i. *Rome and Italy*, 1933, p. 203 ; cf. R. M. Haywood, ibid. iv, pp. 7 and 16, and my *Storia Econ. e Soc.*, p. 20 f.

[21] Problem of grain supply: F. Heichelheim, art. 'Sitos' in *P.W.K.* Suppl. vi. 854 ff. (trade), 856 ff. (prices), and esp. 875 ff. (grain supply of the Greek

cities; the material is fully collected but is unfortunately not presented in chronological order). In Heichelheim's article the reader will find an excellent and up-to-date bibliography.

²² TAXATION: above, Ch. IV, p. 241 n. 71 and ch. III, p. 182 and no. 75. For the attitude of the population towards the *telonai* in the early third century B.C., Her. *Mim.* vi. 63 ff. It never changed in later times. There exists no good account of the history of LITURGIES in the Hellenistic period and of the role which they played in the economic life of the cities. J. Oehler, art. 'Liturgie' in *P.W.K.* xii. 1875 ff. gives a mere list of inscriptions of the fourth century B.C. to the fourth century A.D. in which the word liturgy occurs. In Egypt (F. Oertel, *Die Liturgie,* 1917) 'liturgy' played quite a different part in the life of the State and of the individual. A general work on the liturgies in the Hellenistic period is very much needed. The oppressive part played by them in the life of the cities is illustrated by many decrees of the Hellenistic age granting exemption from them to individuals and groups, see, e.g., *I.G.* vii. 2413/14 (middle of the second century B.C.; privileges given to the Dionysiac artistes of Thebes by a Roman magistrate), l. 5 f.: ὑμᾶς παντάπα]σιν [ἀ]λειτουργήτους εἶναι καὶ ἀνεπισταθ[μεύτους καὶ ἀτελ]εῖς καὶ ἀν[ει]σφό[ρ]ους πάσης εἰσφορ[ᾶς], cf. Ch. VI, n. 18. DONATIONS. In most of the cases the contributions of the magistrates appear as free gifts, and are recorded in decrees by which the city confers honours and privileges on the donors. It is impossible to quote even a selection of such decrees. In some cases, however, it is more than probable that the free gifts of the magistrates are disguised liturgies. One example out of many will suffice. We possess a long set of decrees of Arcesine and Minoa (Amorgos) in honour of the magistrates in charge of the Itonia who contributed to the celebration of this festival (*I.G.* xii. 7, 22, 24, 25, 32, 33, 35, 241; J. Vanseveren, *Rev. Phil.* xi (1937), p. 317, no. 3). The magistrates honoured in these decrees defrayed the expense of the sacrifices and of feeding during the celebration a large group (500 in one case) of citizens and other residents in the city and guests. The regularity of these decrees suggests that the donations of the magistrates were practically a liturgy. EXTRAORDINARY TAXATION (εἰσφορά: see below, n. 20 and Ch. VII *passim*). SUBSCRIPTIONS: A. Kuenzi, ᾽Επίδοσις, 1923. In this valuable book the author deals chiefly with Athens of the fourth century, and in an appendix gives a list of the texts mentioning subscriptions in other Greek cities. The material was not complete at the time when the list was prepared. Since then many new texts have been found. I do not propose in this short note to bring Kuenzi's list up to date. I may, however, without aiming at completeness, quote some of the more important texts discovered since the publication of his book. For the early period I may mention the interesting fragmentary text from Colophon (probably of 311–306 B.C.) recording a public subscription for rebuilding and extending the city walls, B. D. Merritt, *Am.J.Ph.* lvi (1935), pp. 358 ff., cf. L. Robert, *Rev. Phil.* x (1936), pp. 158 ff. Very illuminating are some inscriptions from Chios. Some of them relate to the reinforcement of the walls and may be connected

with a donation for this purpose by a certain Attalus, whose identity is disputed. We may assign this reconstruction of the walls to the time after the
siege of the city by Philip V in 202 B.C. See M. Zolotas, Ἀθηνᾶ, xx (1908),
p. 163, no. 3 (cf. A. Plassart and Ch. Picard, *B.C.H.* xxxvii (1913), p. 211)
(donation of Attalus); Zolotas, ibid., p. 212, no. 11, and p. 200, no. 7 (cf.
A. Plassart and Ch. Picard, *B.C.H.* xxxvii (1913), p. 212 f.); L. Robert, *B.C.H.*
li (1933), p. 509, and J. Vanseveren, *Rev. Phil.* xi (1937), pp. 321 ff. On the
ἐπιδόσεις of Chios in general, L. Robert, loc. cit., pp. 505 ff. and p. 536 f.
Cf. the inscriptions of Samos (*S.E.G.* i, no. 367) and of Iasus (A. Wilhelm,
Σιτομετρία, *Mél. Glotz*, 1932, pp. 899 ff.). See also the inscription of Crannon
in Thessaly (before 168 B.C.) which speaks of an ἐπίδοσις organized by the
city for the purpose of repaying her debts contracted during the Antiochian
war, Y. Béquignon, *B.C.H.* lix (1935), pp. 36 ff. In the article quoted above
Wilhelm has collected a large amount of new epigraphical evidence on
subscriptions for the organization of food supply (ἐπιδόσεις εἰς σιτωνίαν or
σιτομετρίαν). Note also two lists of subscriptions, one from Rhodes and another
from Cos, for the purchase of books for the library, probably of the gymnasia
of the two cities, M. Segre, *Riv. Fil.* lxiii (13) (1935), pp. 214 ff., cf. ibid.
lxiv (14) (1936), p. 40, and L. Robert, *B.C.H.* lix (1935), pp. 421 ff. (second
century B.C.). Very interesting are also the many inscriptions which mention
ἐπιδόσεις of members of associations and clubs chiefly for building temples
and shrines. A short list is given in Kuenzi, loc. cit., p. 74, n. 1. One of the
most illuminating inscriptions of this kind is that recently found at Callatis,
Th. Sauciuc-Saveanu, *Dacia*, I (1924), pp. 126 ff., and pp. 317 ff.; B. Haussoullier, *Rev. Arch.*, 5 sér., xxii (1925), pp. 62 ff.; G. Glotz, *C. R. Acad.
Inscr.* 1925, p. 287; A. Wilhelm, *Wien. Anz.* lxv (1928), pp. 129 ff. It is a
pity that the inscription is not exactly dated (third century B.C.?). It
shows that the city was enjoying some measure of prosperity at the
time of the ἐπίδοσις. LOANS: W. W. Tarn, in *The Hellenistic Age*, 1923,
pp. 108 ff.; cf. his *Hell. Civ.*² pp. 107 ff.; A. Andreades, 'Die öffentlichen
Anleihen', *Vierteljahresschr. f. Soc. u. Wirtschaftsg.* xx (1927–8), pp. 283 ff.;
id., *A History of Greek Public Finance*, i, 1933, pp. 168 ff.; B. Laum,
'Anleihen', *P.W.K.* Suppl. iv. 23 ff.; cf. the inscription from Crannon
quoted above and also Ch. III, note 12; J. A. O. Larsen, 'Roman Greece' in
T. Frank, *Econ. Surv.* iv, 1938, pp. 338 ff., 368–79; F. Heichelheim, *Wirt-
schaftsg.*, pp. 558 ff. FOUNDATIONS: B. Laum, *Stiftungen in der gr. u. röm.
Antike*, 1914, cf. L. Robert, *B.C.H.* lix (1935), p. 483; J. Vanseveren, *Rev.
Phil.* xi (1937), p. 314, no. 1; and J. A. O. Larsen, 'Roman Greece', pp. 361 ff.
SALE OF FRANCHISE AND OF PRIESTHOODS, above, Ch. IV, n. 71, especially M.
Segre, 'Osservazioni epigrafiche sulla vendita di sacerdozio', *Rend. Ist. Lomb.*
xx (3) (1937), pp. 83 ff. The sale of priesthoods appears to have been a peculi-
arity of Asia Minor; no inscriptions bearing on it have been found in Greece.

23 On the depopulation of Greece, see the admirable remarks of W. W.
Tarn, *Hell. Civ.*², pp. 92 ff.; cf. A. Landry, 'Quelques aperçus con-
cernant la dépopulation dans l'antiquité gréco-romaine', *Rev. Hist.* clxxvii

(1936), pp. 1 ff. The statement of Polybius as noted in the text is fully supported as regards the Greek population of Greece, i.e. the citizens of the cities, by several inscriptions collected and interpreted by Tarn, loc. cit., p. 92. The data of the inscriptions must be interpreted in the light of similar modern phenomena. The material collected by Landry, loc. cit., shows that, if we allow for the higher mortality in ancient Greece as compared with modern times, the birth-rate of Hellenistic Greece, as shown by the size of an average Greek family ascertained from the material collected by Tarn, meant the rapid depopulation of the country. Tarn is inclined to think that the decrease was limited to the citizens of the cities, and was compensated by the increase in the number of slaves, freedmen, and foreign immigrants. I cannot accept this view. Our information on the number of slaves in Greece in the time of Polybius is scanty (see below, notes 27 and 30). I doubt very much whether the increase in the number of slaves, if there was any increase, was sufficient to compensate for the rapid decrease of the free population. The supply of slaves was large but purchasing power of Greece was low. On the other hand, home-born slaves were few, i.e. the size of slave families was not and could not be large. Nor can we assume the existence of large numbers of immigrants. From the economic point of view Greece was not a very attractive place for immigrants. Finally, the statement of Polybius (xxxvi, 17. 5) is explicit. He speaks not of the depopulation of the cities only but of the depopulation of Greece in general. He says: ἐπέσχεν ἐν τοῖς καθ' ἡμᾶς καιροῖς τὴν Ἑλλάδα πᾶσαν ἀπαιδία καὶ συλλήβδην ὀλιγανθρωπία δι' ἣν αἵ τε πόλεις ἐξηρημώθησαν καὶ ἀφορίαν εἶναι συνέβαινε. It is evident that he refers both to the cities, as social and economic units, and to the land, the χώρα, which remained untilled, certainly because of lack of labour. On the exposure of children, G. Glotz, *Études sociales et juridiques sur l'antiquité grecque*, 1906, pp. 187 ff.; and his arts. 'Expositio' and 'Infanticidium' in Dar. et Sagl., *Dict. d. A.*; W. S. Ferguson, *H.A.*, pp. 80 ff., 374; Weiss, art. 'Kinderaussetzung, *P.W.K.* xi. 463 ff.; W. W. Tarn, *Hell. Civ.*², pp. 92 ff.; A. Cameron, 'The exposure of children and Greek Ethics', *Cl. Rev.* xlvi (1932), pp. 105 ff. (revulsion of Greek public opinion against the exposure of children); C. Lécrivain, *Mél.Glotz*, 1932, pp. 531 ff. (legal aspect). On the Roman period, my *Stor. Ec. e Soc.* p. 550, cf. P. Collart, *Mél. Glotz*, pp. 243 ff.

[24] Poseid. Hermaphroditus, fr. 11 (Kock III, 338); Men. *Perik.* 380 ff. (Körte); 688 ff. (Loeb); Ferguson, *H.A.*, pp. 81 ff.

[25] e.g. W. W. Tarn, *Hell. Civ.*², pp. 91 ff.

[26] G. T. Griffith, *The Mercenaries of the Hellenistic World*, 1935. Civil emigration to the Greek cities of Asia Minor is well attested as regards Miletus by many inscriptions: Hiller von Gaertringen, art. 'Miletus', *P.W.K.* xv. 1607; cf. A. Rehm, *Milet, Erg. d. Ausgr.* i. 3, 1914, p. 227, n. 4. Miletus at this time was practically an independent city.

[27] On slavery in Hellenistic times in general and on the increase in the number of slaves in the period under review, see W. L. Westermann, *P.W.K.*

Suppl. vi. 928 ff. and 933–4 (correct in the last column the disturbing mis-print 251 B.C. for 201 B.C. in the dating of the Delphian manumissions), cf. J. A. O. Larsen, in T. Frank, *Econ. Surv.* iv, pp. 414 ff. (based on Wester-mann) and F. Heichelheim, *Wirtschaftsg.*, pp. 640 ff. Strictly speaking, the Delphian acts of manumission, which do not begin before 201 B.C., cannot support the thesis that the number of slaves increased in the late third and early second centuries B.C. We have no statistics for the period before 201 B.C. similar to those of the period after that date. It may have been that, while the number of slaves at Delphi was decreasing, manumissions were increasing (G. Glotz, *Le Travail dans la Grèce ancienne*, 1920, p. 420, cf. pp. 231 ff.). However, there is no doubt that the supply of slaves in the late third and early second centuries B.C. was abundant (cf. above, note 23 and below, note 30). On the Delphian manumissions (900 acts of manumission are known, of which about one-third, some of them published in various periodicals, others unpublished, will not be found in the fine collection of Collitz, *G.D.I.* ii, cf. *F.D.* iii, pt. 3, nos. 1–60), see G. Daux, *Delphes au IIe et au Ier siècle*, &c., 1936, pp. 46 ff., and App. I (with complete bibliography and exact dating of the priesthoods). On the numbers of manumitted slaves during the several priesthoods, see the tabulation of Collitz, *G.D.I.* ii, pp. 635 ff., on which all the later calculations are based. More accurate than the tabulation of Calderini is that of M. Bloch, *Die Freilassungsbedingungen der delph. Freilassungsinschriften*, 1914, pp. 16 ff. His tabulation shows that in the third century B.C. about one-third of the slaves who were bought were Greeks. In my calculations I disregard the early years, because the publica-tion of the acts was not carried out systematically during the first priesthood. A set of manumissions, very similar to, though less numerous than, the Delphian set, is that of the sanctuary of Asclepius at Buttos (near Naupactus), see E. Nachmanson, *Ath. Mitt.* xxxi (1907), pp. 1 ff., cf. G. Klaffen-bach, *Berl. Sitzb.*, 1935, pp. 693 ff. The Buttos manumissions are dated between 170 and 146 B.C. They present the same picture as those of Delphi. About one fourth of the bought slaves are of Greek origin. The number of slaves is not so large as at Delphi, but the set of documents is not complete, as it is at Delphi. Cf. also the manumission acts of Naupactus, *I.G.* ix. 1, 359 ff. The set starts, as at Delphi, in 195/4 B.C.

[28] W. S. Ferguson, *H.A.*, pp. 373 ff.

[29] Very little is known of Corinth in this period: see the volumes of the Reports of the American Excavations at Corinth and F. J. de Waele, *P.W.K.* Suppl. vi. 182 ff. and 1350 ff. Cf. Rhys Carpenter, *Ancient Corinth: a guide to the Excavations and Museum* (last edition). Corinth is one of the rare instances of modern excavation where due attention has been paid to the coins discovered. Unfortunately those published and illustrated by K. M. Edwards, *Corinth*, vi. 1933, are rather disappointing. The number of the pre-Roman coins is small, their dating uncertain, especially in the case of the local small change which represents the bulk of the finds (see the remarks of A. Bellinger in the forth-coming volume *The Excavations of Nemea, 1924–7, by the Univ. of Cincinnati*).

Judging by the small coins in circulation, the early Hellenistic time was a more or less prosperous period in the life of Corinth, more prosperous than the second century B.C. The same picture is presented by Nemea, see A. Bellinger's description of the coins in the volume on Nemea just mentioned. In the Hellenistic period the Corinthian *Pegasi*, formerly the predominant currency of the Corinthian Gulf and of S. Italy and Sicily, were no longer minted. The date of the last *Pegasi* is controversial. The date of a hoard of coins of the latest style found at Arta is determined by some coins of Philip II (posthumous), i.e. it cannot be later than 280 B.C. See O. Ravel, 'Corinthian Hoards', *Num. Notes and Mon.* lii (1932) (the reader will find here the summary of other dates suggested as regards the latest *Pegasi*).

Typical of the conditions of the Achaean League in general is the situation of Sicyon in 197 B.C. Attalus I twice helped the city: once he ransomed their sacred land for them, another time he gave them gifts of money and grain (Polyb. xviii. 16; Liv. xxxii. 40. 8). About ten years later Eumenes II offered the Achaeans 120 tal. in order to provide, out of the interest of this sum, for the payment of the members of the Boule. The offer was rejected for political and perhaps social reasons, Polyb. xxii. 7. 3 ff.; W. Schwahn, *Rh. Mus.* lxxix (1930), pp. 178 ff. On Demetrias and its prosperity in the third century and the decline of this prosperity after the Second Macedonian war, see F. Stählin, E. Meyer, A. Heidner, *Pagasai und Demetrias*, 1934, pp. 194 ff. (prosperity of the city in the third century), and pp. 195 ff. (conditions after 196 B.C.). Cf. the decree of Iolcos in honour of Antigonus Gonatas, Ernst Meyer, *Rh. Mus.* lxxxv (1936), pp. 367 ff. After 146 B.C. at Demetrias, as in other cities of Greece, the well-to-do ruling class consisted of a small group of men and families, F. Stählin, *Ath. Mitt.* liv (1929), p. 202. Nor was it different in other parts of Thessaly. The famous letters of Philip to Larissa (*I.G.* ix. 2, 517; *S.I.G.*³ 543; Dessau *I.L.S.* 8763) show that the citizen population was decreasing at Larissa in 219–214 B.C. and that the fields were not cultivated. I see no reason for regarding conditions at Larissa as exceptional. Philip favoured the lower classes and tried to find a remedy for depopulation by liberal grants of franchise. Later, after 196 B.C., Larissa, like Demetrias, was ruled by a small group of well-to-do people (F. Stählin, *Das hell. Thessalien*, 1927, p. 95) who were fairly prosperous. The same conditions prevailed in other Thessalian cities (Stählin, loc. cit., passim; add to the material quoted by him the inscription from Crannon (above n. 22) of the time after the Antiochian war; hard pressed by the war the city resorted to borrowing and, after the war, organized a subscription in order to repay at least a part of its debts, Y. Béquignon, *B.C.H.* lix (1935), pp. 36 ff., cf. M. N. Tod, *J.H.S.* lvii (1937), p. 189).

[30] On the Delphian and Aetolian manumissions, see above, note 27. Abundant though it is, the Delphian material is not conclusive. We know only that the number of manumissions is greater in the period 201–140 than in the later period. But it is not certain that all the manumissions were published in the later period, while it is more or less certain that they were in the

earlier. As regards the significance of 8–9 manumissions per year, I must observe that this number does not help us to form an accurate idea of the part played by slavery in the economic life of Delphi. We do not know what the population of Delphi was, nor what frequency of manumissions implied, whether prosperity or the reverse. The only thing that the documents teach us is the part played by wars and piracy in the history of slavery, which is demonstrated by the prevalence of bought slaves of various origin over the home-born. The conditions in Thessaly are interesting. At Larissa (*I.G.* ix. 2, 539–68) there are no manumissions in the third century B.C., there are three in the second century, nine in the first, while the bulk (17) fall in Imperial times; F. Stählin, *Hell. Thess.*, 1927, p. 95, n. 10. It is regrettable that the whole of the rich Thessalian material has never been studied from the historical point of view, the valuable dissertation of G. Rensch, *De manumissionum titulis apud Thessalos*, diss. Hal. xviii. 2, 1911, dealing mostly with the legal and economic aspect of the manumissions. Some rather superficial remarks on slavery and manumissions in Thessaly from the historical point of view will be found in R. V. Schmidt, 'From the History of Thessaly', *Bull. Ac. Hist. Mat. Civ.* ci (1934), pp. 109 ff. (in Russian).

[31] We have some information on the standard of life in the Hellenistic period and on the requirements of the population as regards comfort and recreations. But our literary, epigraphical, and archaeological evidence is scattered over the whole Hellenistic world and the whole period. The literary texts, except those dealing with Athens of the late fourth and early third centuries, the descriptions of cities in the mimes of Herondas, and the illustrations of Alexandria by Theocritus, refer mostly to striking and therefore exceptional cases of luxury and extravagance. The epigraphical material is scanty and unevenly distributed. The same must be said of the archaeological material. Of Hellenistic cities, i.e. cities which were laid out in the Hellenistic period and retained this aspect in later times, very few have been excavated, and of these none are in Greece. At Athens the periods that left an indelible mark on the city were the classical on the one hand and the Roman on the other. And so it was at Corinth, at Sparta, and at the great pan-Hellenic sanctuaries of Olympia and Delphi. The minor cities that were prominent in the Hellenistic period have never been excavated. Of the islands Delos was in the main a Hellenistic city. But it was a city *sui generis*, a city of wealthy merchants, mostly of foreign origin, a city not typical of Hellenistic Greece. We have fuller knowledge of some cities of Asia Minor: Pergamon, the capital of the Attalids, the only Hellenistic capital that has been thoroughly excavated (pp. 659 ff.); the two larger commercial and industrial cities, Ephesus and Miletus, of which Miletus, as excavated, was in the main a creation of the Hellenistic period; and finally the agricultural city of Priene (above, pp. 177 ff.), built by Alexander and embellished in the second century by means of the famous Orophernes' fund. It is principally Delos and the cities of Asia Minor that help us to form our ideas of the general aspect of Hellenistic city life. We must not forget, however, that the latter cities are typical of

Asia Minor and provide no basis for the reconstruction of the life that prevailed in Greece proper at the time in question. As regards the establishment
of new games and the revival of old religious ceremonies, we must bear in
mind, besides what I have said in the text, that the Greeks were a profoundly
religious people and were deeply attached to traditions (below, Ch. VIII).
The first thing, for example, they did after the peace of Naupactus was to
' revive their traditional sacrifices and festivals and various local religious
rites' (Polyb. v. 106). And yet in the same passage Polybius describes the
ruinous effect on the Peloponnese of the period preceding Naupactus. Cf.
S. Dow, *Harv. St. Cl. Phil.* xlviii (1937), pp. 124 ff.

[32] On the prices see the books and articles quoted above, Ch. IV, p. 190, n. 2,
and below, note 110, especially F. Heichelheim, *Wirtschaftsg.*, pp. 451 ff.
I cannot follow Heichelheim in his explanation of a short interruption in the
rise of prices at Delos in the decade between 190 and 180 B.C., a time of violent
political convulsions in the Hellenistic world, especially in Asia Minor and
Syria. The causes were probably of a local, not of a general character.

[33] On the Achaean coinage, Ch. T. Seltman, *Greek Coins*, 1933, p. 255 f.,
cf. K. Regling, *P.W.K.* xvi. 472 and 475, and M. Crosby and E. Grace, 'An
Achaean League Hoard', *Num. Not. and Mon.* lxxiv (1936); S. P. Noe, 'A
bibliography of Greek Coin Hoards', 2nd ed., *Num. Not. and Mon.* lxxviii
(1937), no. 60. Note that, to judge from the coin hoard of Arcadia published
by Crosby and Grace, some of the cities of the Peloponnese, of Euboea, and of
Greece in general, including the Aetolian and the Arcadian Leagues, participated in the revival of silver coinage that was a characteristic feature of Asia
Minor and the islands after Cynoscephalae and Magnesia, cf. E. T. Newell,
'Five Greek bronze coin hoards', *Num. Not. and Mon.* lxviii (1935), p. 17
—abundant bronze coinage of Carystos, Chalcis, and Euboea after 197 B.C.;
and p. 19—silver emitted after Magnesia by Euboean cities along with the
cities of Asia Minor (note three Eretrian tetradrachms in the Babylonian
hoard, on which further below).

[34] The inscription of Prytanis of 226/5 B.C.: B. D. Meritt, *Hesp.* iv (1935),
pp. 525 ff., no. 39; L. Robert, *B.C.H.* lix (1935), p. 436, and P. Roussel, ibid.,
pp. 520 ff. The decree in honour of Cephisodorus: B. D. Meritt, *Hesp.* v
(1936), pp. 419 ff. Note that at the time of his management of the *sitonia* the
price of grain was very high in Egypt, see F. Heichelheim, *Aeg.* xvii (1937),
pp. 63 ff. (he quotes *B.G.U.* vi. 1266).

[35] The evidence regarding the relations of Athens with the leading powers
of the time is fully collected in the books of S. Jebelev, *History of Athens*,
1898, pp. 198 ff. (in Russian), and W. S. Ferguson, *Hellenistic Athens*, pp.
298 ff. On Pharnaces see my chapter 'Pontus' in *C.A.H.* ix, p. 220, n. 3, cf.
on the date of his death, S. Dow, *Hesp.* iv (1935), p. 91 (Delian inscr., F. Durrbach, *Choix*, 73). Massinissa: *I.G.* ii. 968, 44, cf. on his Rhodian and Delian
relations (in 179 B.C.) *Inscr. de Délos*, 442 A, 100 ff., and inscriptions in his
honour put up at Delos by Hermon son of Solon, his friend (Durrbach, *Choix*,

68; *S.I.G.*³ 652), and by Charmylas son of Nicarchus, a Rhodian (Durrbach, *Choix*, 69; *I.G.* xi. 4. 1116); cf. the instructive note of Durrbach on these inscriptions. Pontic (?) merchant in grain and oil and his relations with Athens in 175/4 B.C., *S.I.G.*³ 640, cf. the decree of Oropos in honour of two Sinopians, *S.E.G.* i. 104 and 107 (end of the third or beginning of the second century), and D. M. Robinson, *Ancient Sinope*, 1906, pp. 269 ff. Note that in the war against Philip the Athenian navy co-operated with the Rhodians and the islanders, *S.I.G.*³ 582, cf. below, n. 94.

³⁶ On the reform of Athenian coinage in 180 B.C., J. Sundwall, *Untersuch. über die Ath. Münzen des neueren Stiles*, 1906–7, pp. 106 ff.; B. V. Head, *H. N.*², pp. 378 ff.; P. Roussel, *Délos, colonie athénienne*, 1916, p. 4. In general cf. M. L. Kambanis, 'Notes sur le classement chronologique des monnaies d'Athènes (Série avec noms des magistrats)', *B.C.H.* lvi (1932), pp. 37 ff.; lviii (1934), pp. 101 ff., cf. also his articles, ibid. lix (1935), pp. 101 ff., lx (1936), p. 101 ff. and lxii (1938), pp. 60 ff.

³⁷ Our information about the administrative and economic activity of Philip V and Perseus, though poor in general, is nevertheless gradually increasing. The evidence, however, has never been collected in full, modern historians being mainly interested in the foreign policy of the two kings and in the history of their wars. Very important new evidence regarding the organization of PHILIP'S ARMY is now available in the fragments of Philip's military regulations found at Amphipolis, P. Roussel, *Rev. Arch.*, 6 sér., iii (1934), pp. 39 ff., and M. Feyel, ibid., 6 ser., vi (1935), pp. 29 ff., cf. M. Segre, *Riv. Fil.* lxiii (13) (1935), pp. 222 ff., and S. B. Kugeas, Ἑλληνικά, viii (1935), p. 149 f., and the well preserved *stele* from Chalcis which contains regulations about the food supply of the Macedonian garrisons, S. B. Kugeas, in Ἑλληνικά, vii (1934), pp. 177 ff., cf. *Rev. É.G.* xlix (1936), p. 363, and K. Kuruniotes, Ἑλληνικά, viii (1935), pp. 173 ff. Cf. the letter of Philip V of 181 B.C. (?) found on the slopes of the Scopus near modern Cozani (in Eordaia), a reply to the petition of a group of officers and soldiers of his army concerning the assignment to them for cult purposes of land in the territory of Greia which formerly belonged to a certain Corragus, a Macedonian, see Ch. I. Macaronas, *Eph. Arch.* 1934–5, pp. 117 ff. (published in 1936), cf. *A.J.A.* xl (1936), p. 534, and C. B. Welles, ibid. xlii (1938), pp. 246 ff. The inscription contains new evidence on the structure of the Macedonian army. It needs careful revision and renewed study. The letters and διαγράμματα of Philip and his officers concerning the cities of Macedonia, Thessaly, and the foreign dominions of the king, as enumerated in the above-cited paper of Macaronas (cf. C. B. Welles, loc. cit., p. 245, n. 1): Thessalonice (S. Pelekides, Ἀπὸ τὴν πολιτεία καὶ τὴν κοινωνία τῆς Ἀρχαίας Θεσσαλονίκης. Ἐπιστημονικὴ Ἐπετηρὶς τῆς Φιλοσοφικῆς Σχολῆς (Πανεπιστήμιον Θεσσαλονίκης) 2 (1934), παράρτημα, pp. 6 ff. (a διάγραμμα of Philip V of 187 B.C. regarding the Sarapeum of the city forwarded, with an order to publish it, by Andronicus the *epistates* of the city); Larissa (*S.I.G.*³ 543, above note 29); Gonnoi (*Arch. Eph.* 1913, pp. 25 ff., nos. 165 ff., esp. p. 36—fragments of a large dossier concerning a dispute about land between

Gonnoi and Heracleia); Abae (Phocis, *S.I.G.*³ 552); Nisyros (*S.I.G.*³ 572);
Paros (*I.G.* xii. 5. 1, 125); Chalcis (*S.I.G.*³ 561); Magnesia on the Maeander
(*Inschr. v. Magn.* no. 24). On these documents in general cf. C. B. Welles,
A.J.A. xlii. (1938), pp. 245 ff., and E. Bikerman, *Rev. Phil.* xii (1938), pp.
295 ff. On Demetrias, above note 29. On Thessalonice, above and E. Oberhummer, *P.W.K.* vi A. 145 ff.; Geyer, ibid. xiv. 768. On the role of Thessalonice under the earlier Macedonian kings, above, Ch. IV, p. 253. Philip's
activity after Tempe: P. V. M. Benecke, *C.A.H.* viii, p. 253, and Geyer,
P.W.K. xiv. 757.

³⁸ The settlement of Thracians in Macedonia and in the territories of the
early Macedonian colonies was traditional in the economic and social policy
of the Macedonian kings. See the fragmentary letter of Alexander recently
found at Philippi (unpublished, see the preliminary report of Ch. Picard, *Rev.
Arch.*, 6 sér., xi (1938), pp. 334 ff.), cf. P. Collart, *Philippes, ville de Macédoine*,
1937, p. 179; L. Robert, *Rev. Phil.* xiii (1939), p. 146. According to Picard,
Alexander in his reply to an embassy from Philippi 'annonçait là des dis-
positions pour la mise en valeur par les Thraces de certaines terres incultes; il
prévoit aussi un nouveau barrage'. We should like to know what was the
status of these Thracians, whether military colonists, πάροικοι, or *laoi*. As
regards the measures of Philip, I am inclined to follow Livy xxxix. 24: 'ut
vero antiquam multitudinem hominum, quas belli cladibus amissa erat, resti-
tueret, non subolem tantum stirpis parabat cogendis omnibus procreare atque
educare liberos, sed Thracum etiam magnam multitudinem in Macedoniam
traduxerat', the report of Polybius xxiii. 10. 4 being apparently biased.

³⁹ The existence of large estates belonging to the kings and their capitalistic
exploitation are attested, not in the passages of Livy and Polybius quoted
above, but by the well-known statements of Livy concerning the measures
taken by Aemilius Paulus after the war with Perseus (Liv. xlv. 18. 3). In that
passage he refers to the prohibition of the leasing (*locationes*) of the mines and
praedia rustica for exploitation. Since the measure was probably directed
against Macedonian and Roman capitalists, the *praedia rustica* must be
understood to be royal estates, managed under Philip and Perseus as large
agricultural concerns. The care taken by Philip of the royal land is illustrated by the inscription of Cozani quoted in note 37. The land assigned by
him to his officers and soldiers belonged formerly to Corragus (as a *dorea*?)
and was probably taken back by the crown. It was ψιλὴ γῆ. The statement
in l. 6: ἕως ἂν συντε|λῶσιν τὰς θυσίας ἐ[ν τῶι 'Απ]ελλαίωι μηνί implies that the
land was granted to the soldiers for an indefinite time—'as long as they perform the sacrifices in the month Apellaeus' (I prefer this translation of
ἕως ἂν to the two other alternative translations which grammatically are as
correct as that which I am suggesting, viz. 'until they' or 'in order that
they'). The intention of the king was probably not only to safeguard the
performance of the sacrifices but also to have the land cultivated.

⁴⁰ Coinage of Philip: H. Gaebler, *Die ant. Münzen Nordgriechenlands*, iii,
Makedonia und Paionia, 1 (1906), pp. 1 ff., pp. 26 ff., and 2 (1935), pp. 1–7,

and *Z.N.* xxxvi (1926), pp. 113 ff. (municipal coinage of Thessalonice, Pella, Amphipolis, and the coinage of the five Macedonian districts). On Philip's silver and bronze coinage, A. Mamroth, ibid. xl (1930), pp. 277 ff., and xlii (1932), pp. 219 ff.; Perseus' coinage, ibid. xxxviii (1928), pp. 1 ff.

[41] The evidence regarding the army and the resources of Perseus before and during the war will be found in J. A. O. Larsen, 'Roman Greece', T. Frank, *Econ. Surv.* iv, p. 292 f.

[42] On Pergamon see the bibliography above, p. 553, n. 321. On the political events of the time under review above, pp. 52ff.

[43] I may quote in this connexion some inscriptions from the neighbourhood of Smyrna which testify to the existence of a special city-army at Smyrna and to the defence of the city's territory by fortresses and garrisons. The inscriptions found at Bel Kave and at Ak Kaya record honours bestowed each on a στρατηγός by οἱ συνστρατευσάμενοι καὶ ταγέντες ὑφ᾽ ἑαυτὸν ἐν τῷ χωρίῳ καὶ συνδιατηρήσαντες. It is evident that there was a war between Smyrna and an enemy who tried to invade its territory. The date of the inscriptions is unfortunately unknown. The example of Miletus shows that the war may have been purely local, and not one of the great wars of the second century (e.g. that of the time of Seleucus II, see C. J. Cadoux, *Ancient Smyrna*, 1938, p. 119 note). See A. Seylaz, *Jahreshefte*, xxviii (1933), Beibl., pp. 121 ff., and the remarks of J. Keil, ibid., p. 123 f. Cf. Keil–Premerstein, iii, *Reise*, p. 6, and the inscription of Dyme, *G.D.I.* 1612; E. Schwyzer, *Dial. gr. ex. epigr.* 1923, no. 426; L. Robert, *Coll. Fröhner*, I, Inscr. gr., 1936, p. 96, n. 5.

[44] On Antiochus III's policy towards the cities of Asia Minor, his granting of autonomy to Amyzon, Alabanda, Iasus (Welles, *R.C.* 38; *O.G.I.* 234, 237) E. Bickermann, 'Bellum Antiochicum', *Hermes*, lxvii (1932), p. 58 f. The inscription of Corragus: *S.E.G.* ii. 663; M. Holleaux, *B.C.H.* xlviii (1924), pp. 1 ff. (*Ét. d'Épigr. et d'Hist. gr.* ii, pp. 73 ff.); G. de Sanctis, *Riv. Fil.* liii (3) (1925), pp. 68 ff.; M. Rostovtzeff, *C.A.H.* vii, pp. 178 ff.; viii, p. 605; M. Segre, *Clara Rhodos*, ix (1938), p. 195; E. Bikerman, *Inst. Sél.*, p. 135 and passim. In my opinion the expression ὑπὸ τὴν παράληψιν τῆς πόλεως cannot refer to the simple taking over of the city by Corragus from his predecessor; it implies that the city was in the hands of somebody else and was handed over to Corragus, in his capacity of royal governor, by its temporary master. Now the city appears in the inscription as having suffered much during a war and as having lost its privileges at this time. The city therefore had probably supported its former master and resisted the efforts of his enemy, who finally got possession of it and punished it severely by taking away its privileges. These privileges the city now recovers from a Pergamene king. All this accords with the vicissitudes of several cities of the Pergamene kingdom, which did not surrender to Antiochus III, were captured by him, and were afterwards restored by the Romans to Eumenes II. This happened in the case of Lampsacus, Smyrna, Alexandria Troas, and probably some other cities, App., *Syr.* 2 (for Lampsacus and Smyrna). The fragmentary inscription found at Sardis, and now lost or destroyed, which I have quoted in the text is very difficult to restore

and to date. It may be an order of a king or a decree of a city whose name began with T. It may belong to the time of Eumenes II or to the earlier reign of Antiochus III. See W. H. Buckler and D. M. Robinson, *Sardis*, vii. 1, n. 2; E. Bikerman, *Rev. Ét. juives*, c (1935), p. 34, n. 1, and *Inst. Sél.*, p. 136, n. 1; L. Robert, *Rev. Arch.* 6 sér., vii (1936), p. 234; M. Segre, *Clara Rhodos*, ix (1938), p. 192. The similarity of the situation as described by this inscription to that which we find in the inscription of Corragus is striking. See below, p. 642. Similar was the situation at Theangela (?) as attested by a fragmentary decree (not dated) recently attributed to that city and restored by L. Robert, *Coll. Fröhner*, I, Inscr. gr., 1936, pp. 98 ff. For the methods of waging war adopted by Antiochus and the Romans I may refer to the descriptions of the war by Polybius and Livy. Note that Antiochus profited by the good offices of the cities, which willingly furnished foodstuffs for his navy and army (Liv. xxxvii. 27. 3), while the Romans pressed hard on the cities (Liv. xxxvii. 9. 2 (Phocaea): 'gravia hiberna navium erant, grave tributum, quod togae quingentae imperatae erant cum quin-gentis tunicis, gravis etiam inopia frumenti, propter quam naves quoque et praesidium Romanum excessit') and were forced to rely upon shipments from Italy, their main stores being located at Chios (Liv. xxxvii. 27).

⁴⁵ Decree of Telmessus, G. Jacopi, *Clara Rhodos*, ii (1932), pp. 172 ff., no. 3; M. Segre, *Riv. Fil.* lx (10) (1932), pp. 446 ff. L. Robert, *B.C.H.* liv (1930), pp. 332 ff., and *Rev. Phil.* viii (1934), p. 284, cf. id., *Étud. Anat.*, 1937, p. 73, n. 1, has brought forward some very important considerations which make it probable that the title of Soter was given to Eumenes II not in 166, as most modern scholars believe, but after the war against Prusias and Ortiagon, i.e. in 183 B.C. It was probably at this time that Eumenes II and the city of Pergamon sent out embassies to various Greek cities and leagues requesting the grant of inviolability to the sanctuary of Athena Nikephoros and recognition of the games Nicephoria, *S.I.G.*³ 629 (*I.G.* ix². 1, 179), and G. Daux, *Delphes au IIᵉ et au Iᵉʳ siècle*, 1936, pp. 299 ff. (Aetolia); *S.I.G.*³ 630, and G. Daux, loc. cit., pp. 293 ff. (Delphi); Welles, *R.C.* 49 and 50 (letters to Iasus (?) and Cos and the corresponding decrees of the two cities). The Delphian decree is a text of great historical importance. It shows how Eumenes and those who supported him justified his acts in the eyes of Greece. Note the emphasis laid on Eumenes' philhellenism and his lavish gifts to Greek cities. On the date Welles, loc. cit.; G. Daux, *Mél. Glotz*, 1932, pp. 289 ff.; L. Robert, *Rev. Phil.* viii (1934), p. 284 (note). On the political importance of the Delphian decree, which repeats the letter of Eumenes, G. Daux, *Delphes*, &c., pp. 293 ff.

⁴⁶ On this war see my chapter 'Pontus' in *C.A.H.* ix, p. 220, and p. 217, n. 1, cf. Chr. M. Danov, *Bull. Inst. Arch. Bulg.* xii (1939), pp. 225 ff. and 255 f., cf. A. Salač, *Eunomia* i (1938), pp. 3 ff.

⁴⁷ On the administrative divisions of the new Pergamene Empire P. Ghione, 'I comuni del regno di Pergamo', *Mem. Acc. Torino*, lv (1905), pp. 67 ff., and M. Holleaux, *B.C.H.* xlviii (1924), pp. 13 ff. (*Ét. d'Ép. et d'Hist.*

3261.3   **M**

gr. ii, pp. 85 ff.). We may think that the new accessions were divided into *strategiai* as they had been under the Seleucids (E. Bikerman, *Inst. Sél.*, pp. 197 ff.), and we may recognize in the officials who figure in some inscriptions, for instance in the inscription of Telmessus (?) (M. Segre, *Clara Rhodos*, ix (1938), p. 192), the district governors of the Attalids, cf. Segre, loc. cit., p. 195. But I much doubt whether the old *dynasteia* was included in this division either as one *strategia* or several. I cannot here discuss this problem in detail. On the direct relations between the Attalids and the cities of their realm, A. Heuss, *Stadt u. Herrscher*, 1937, p. 22, cf. P. Zancan, *Il Monarcato ellenistico*, 1934, pp. 102 ff.

⁴⁸ I may mention that, in dealing with some temples which formerly belonged to the Seleucids, the later Attalids refer to and confirm the acts of their predecessors: οἱ πρὸ ἐμοῦ βασιλεῖς, see the two letters of Attalus III, one to the temple of the Persian goddess in Lydia (*O.G.I.* 333; Welles, *R.C.* 68), the other to the κάτοικοι of the Carian Hiera Kome (Welles, *R.C.* 69). Cf. above, Ch. IV, n. 282.

⁴⁹ Much has been written on the Roman settlement of Asia Minor after the treaty of Apamea. I follow the lucid discussion of the problem by E. Bikerman, 'Notes sur Polybe', *Rev. É. G.* l (1937), pp. 217 ff., cf. the list of cities, ibid., pp. 235 ff.

⁵⁰ I quote a few examples; Miletus, below, note 76; Chios, G. Zolotas, ᾿Αθηνᾶ, xx (1908), pp. 163 ff., cf. *B.C.H.* xxxvii (1913), p. 211, and *G.D.I.* iv. 4, pp. 894 ff. (loans or endowments for building the city walls, heating the gymnasium, &c.), on the date, J. Vanseveren, *Rev. Phil.* xi (1937), p. 323 f.; Colophon Nova, M. Holleaux, *B.C.H.* xxx (1906), pp. 349 ff. (*Ét. d'Ép. et d'Hist. gr.* ii, pp. 51 ff.) (in honour of Athenaeus, fourth son of Attalus I); on the relations of Claros to the Attalids in general, see Ch. Picard, *Ephèse et Claros*, 1922, pp. 647 ff.; Iasus (?), Welles, *R.C.* 49. Cf. the decrees of Greek cities in answer to the invitation to recognize the Nicephoria, especially the decree of Delphi (above, n. 45) in which the benefactions of Eumenes II in general to the Greek cities of Asia and Europe are so highly praised. A complete list of benefactions conferred by the Attalids, in the form of donations or edifices, on various Greek cities, both within and without the Pergamene *dynasteia* and kingdom, will be found in L. Robert, *Ét. Anat.*, 1937, pp. 84 ff., cf. p. 153 (Colophon).

⁵¹ Under 'subject cities' are included both tributary cities and cities received as a gift from the Romans. It is probable that there were differences of detail in the treatment of these two classes by the kings, but evidence is lacking. A. Heuss, *Stadt und Herrscher*, pp. 178 ff., esp. p. 185 f., apparently sees no difference between the subject and the 'allied' cities, and regards their relations with the king not as sharply distinguished in two types but as organized according to circumstances.

⁵² See, e.g., *O.G.I.* 331. iv; Welles, *R.C.* 67. 13: κρίνομεν ... τὰ γραφέντα ὑφ' ἡμῶμ προστάγματα ἐν τοῖς ἱεροῖς νόμοις φέρεσθαι παρ' ὑμῖν; *O.G.I.* 329, a decree

in honour of Cleon, the governor of Aegina : in speaking of the judicial activity of Cleon the decree emphasizes his skill in reconciling the parties (συλλύειν) and proceeds, 12 : τοὺς δὲ μ[ὴ] συλλυομένους ἀναπένπον[τος] | ἐπὶ τὰ καλῶς καὶ δικαίως νενομοθετημένα ἡμῖν ὑπὸ τῶ[ν βα]σιλέων κατά τε τὰ εἰς [τινα χρ]όνον (the restoration of this passage by Dittenberger is far from certain) κεχρημα-τισμένα π[ροσ]|||τάγματα καὶ τοὺς νόμους, which shows the large part played in the life of the city by the royal laws and orders. On Cleon's decree, cf. A. Heuss, *Stadt und Herrscher*, pp. 35, 76 f., 83 f., and 131 f., and on διάγραμμα and νόμος, ibid., pp. 78 ff., and in general, pp. 124 ff. ; I cannot agree with Heuss in his interpretation of this decree ; on the relations between διάγραμμα and νόμος, C. B. Welles, *A.J.A.* xlii (1938), pp. 275 ff. and E. Bikerman, *Rev. Phil.* xii (1938), pp. 295 ff.

⁵³ Keil–Premerstein, ii, *Reise*, p. 13, no. 18, a dispute between Hiero-caesarea and Thyatira about their boundaries decided *regiis con[stitutionibus]*, i.e. by προστάγματα of the kings ; *Inschr. v. Priene*, 27 ; Welles, *R.C.* 46 : a letter of an Attalid to Priene ordering the acceptance of the decision of Smyrna in a boundary dispute between Priene and Miletus ; the date is unknown. In the first document there is mention of measurement of the land by the agents of the king.

⁵⁴ On the inscription of Amlada, besides the comments of J. Keil, see A. H. M. Jones, *The Cities* &c., p. 131 f., and notes 15, 16. Cf. below, n. 55. On the inscription of Teos see the remarks of L. Robert, *Ét. Anat.*, pp. 39 ff., and esp. pp. 42 ff. A similar clause appears in the Pergamene decree of 130–100 B.C. regarding the priesthood of Asclepius *S.I.G.*³ 1007, l. 20 : εἶναι δ]ὲ καὶ ἀτέλειαν Ἀσκληπιάδηι πάντων [ὧν] ἡ πόλις κυρία. It must be noted that similar statements appear in several much older honorary decrees, and the stereotyped clause was therefore a creation of the early Hellenistic period. See the important set of honorary decrees found in the ruins of Iasus, *C.I.G.* 2672–8, cf. E. L. Hicks, *J.H.S.* ix (1888), pp. 340 ff., nos. 2–4, and Michel 463–5. On the date of these documents (late fourth—early third centuries B.C.) and the identity of the persons honoured, L. Robert, *Antiquité Class.* iv (1935), pp. 159 ff., and id., *Coll. Fröhner*, I, Inscriptions gr., 1936, pp. 73 ff., cf. A. Heuss, *Stadt und Herrscher*, &c., p. 113 (the contributions of Robert remained unknown to him). Cf. E. Bikerman, *Inst. Sél.*, p. 110 f.

⁵⁵ On the problem of royal taxation in the Hellenistic period see the chap-ter 'Monarchische Steuerverwaltung und Stadt' in A. Heuss, *Stadt und Herrscher*, &c., pp. 105 ff. It is to be regretted that the author tends to treat the problem as a whole, without discriminating between the different Hellen-istic kingdoms. My method of treatment is quite different. It is evident that the theory and practice of taxation were not uniform throughout the Hellen-istic world, but varied according to the historical past of a given country and according to the type and history of a given city. For example, the relations between the kings and the ancient Greek cities are not to be confused with those between the kings and the cities newly created by them. As re-gards extraordinary contributions the inscriptions of Amlada and of the

unidentified city T . . . show that the kings did not hesitate to impose contributions of this kind on their subject cities in addition to regular taxes. We probably have instances of such extraordinary contributions in the 9,000 drachmas which the city of Amlada was unable to pay and in the χρήματα which are mentioned in the Sardis inscription (ll. 11–12 and 23; the word is partly restored). Much interest in this respect attaches to the decree of Apamea on the Maeander in honour of Cephisodorus (between 188 and 159 B.C.). Cephisodorus was a rich man. He erected the statues of Eumenes II and his brother Attalus in the city. During one of the wars of Eumenes II he lent 3,000 drachmas to a magistrate of the city who had to deliver grain to the soldiers. It is evident that the city was expected to feed the soldiers who probably camped near or in it. See W. H. Buckler, *J.H.S.* lv (1935), pp. 71 ff.; *M.A.M.A.* vi, no. 173. (Cf. Addenda at the end of this book.) We may connect with this last inscription one from Attuda, *M.A.M.A.* vi, no. 68—a honorary inscription for Solon, son of Attalus, φίλος πρῶτος (court title), who apparently remitted to the city (and paid from his own income?) a certain amount of corn ([ἀ]νέντα σεῖτ[ον] | ὑπὲρ πα[τρίδος καθ' αὑτοῦ (?)]| [πρ]όθεσιν). His son Attalus was a citizen of Tabae and was highly honoured by this city, *M.A.M.A.* vi, no. 164. It is interesting to see members of the Anatolian aristocracy in the service of and perhaps related to the Attalids. Cf. *M.A.M.A.* vi, no. 165 (Tabae)—honorary inscription for Antipater, son of Pyrrhus. This Macedonian may have been the son of the high official of Eumenes II, C. B. Welles, *R.C.*, no. 47, l. 19.

⁵⁶ *O.G.I.* 329 (Cleon, governor of Aegina at the time of Eumenes II and Attalus II), cf. 281 (Attalus I); *S.I.G.*³ 642 (Hicesias, another governor of Aegina, one of the predecessors of Cleon). The inscription in honour of Cleon, the governor of the island has been dealt with frequently (see above, n. 52). See especially ll. 11 ff. (quoted above n. 52). Of course Cleon acted as judge only in cases where the city and the citizens had recourse to him. The tenor of the inscription, however, suggests that in fact his judicial activity became quite *regular* and that he served as a kind of established supreme judge, royal ἀρχιδικαστής (on the δικασταί and ἀρχιδικασταί see above, Ch. IV, n. 241, and Heuss, loc. cit., p. 88).

⁵⁷ Th. Sauciuc, *Andros*, 1914, pp. 85 ff.

⁵⁸ It is very desirable that a careful collection should be made of all the material bearing on the activity of the Attalids, and especially the later Attalids, in building cities. The subject has been repeatedly studied (see the bibliography quoted above, Ch. IV, n. 321, but never in full and never from a historical point of view, with the utilization of all the available material and in connexion with historical topography. See the remarks of L. Robert, *Rev. Arch.*, 6 sér., iii(1934), pp. 88 ff., esp. p. 91. How greatly the patient and laborious work hitherto done needs revision is shown by Robert's book, *Les Villes de l'Asie Mineure*, 1935, and especially by his remarks on Apollonis (pp. 31 ff.), Stratoniceia on the Caicus (p. 43 ff., a foundation of Antiochus I according to him, pp. 49 ff.), Dionysopolis (pp. 131 ff.), the two (?) Eumeneias (in Caria

and in Phrygia, pp. 151 ff.), and the military κατοικίαι (pp. 75 ff.). On the various types of κατοικίαι (some of them native villages), L. Robert, *Ét. Anat.*, pp. 191 ff. On the synoecism of Apollonis and similar συνοικισμοί of Antiochus III and other kings in Asia Minor and elsewhere, see E. Bikerman, 'La charte séleucide de Jérusalem', *Rev. Ét. Juives*, c (1935), pp. 4 ff., and L. Robert, *Coll. Fröhner*, I, Inscr. gr., pp. 98 ff., cf. A. Heuss, *Stadt u. Herrscher*, pp. 99 ff. There is a useful list of cities of Asia Minor at the end of the Roman Republican period (note that, with the exception of Pompey, the Romans contributed very little to the urbanization of this country) compiled by T. R. S. Broughton, 'Roman Asia Minor', T. Frank, *Econ. Surv.* iv, pp. 700 ff.

⁵⁹ The inscription is published by M. Segre, *Clara Rhodos*, ix (1938), pp. 190 ff., and figs. 5 and 6, cf. L. Robert, *Ét. Anat.*, p. 375, n. 1. In the article by Segre will be found a detailed commentary on the inscription.

⁶⁰ M. Segre, loc. cit., pp. 181 ff., and the historical resumé on p. 208.

⁶¹ I realize of course that many points in the letter of Eumenes and in the history of the family and *dorea* of Ptolemy, son of Lysimachus, are obscure and their interpretation by Segre, accepted in the main in the text, doubtful. I may quote some instances. Prof. C. B. Welles draws my attention to the fact that in a document of 204 B.C. (Welles, *R.C.* 36) Ptolemy, son of Lysimachus, appears as still alive, and suggests that Lysimachus, his son, might have been his co-regent. Though it is very probable that the Cardaces were settled in the region of Telmessus by Antiochus, the history of the estate of Ptolemy and of the purchase of part of this estate by the Cardaces is far from certain. Was the estate of Ptolemy returned to him after Apamea or was it made *ager publicus*? Ptolemy, of course, was alive at that time but the meaning is not necessarily that he received his estate back, unless, as I have suggested in the text, he had rendered some services to Rome during the war. It is not certain that Ptolemy sold part of his land to the Cardaces before Apamea.

The document of 193 which followed the letter of Eumenes on the stone may have been, as Segre suggests, the deed of sale of this land, but it may have been something else. In spite of the material produced by Segre (loc. cit., p. 198) it appears very strange that Eumenes should remit to the Cardaces the price of a piece of land which did not belong to him, and that at a time when the owner of the land was still alive and again in possession of it. May he not have died between 188 and 181 and his land have passed to Eumenes? The point about the poll-tax (Segre, loc. cit., pp. 199 ff.) is likewise conjectural. On the poll-tax in the Seleucid kingdom see, in addition to the works quoted by Segre, E. Bikerman, *Inst. Sél.*, pp. 111 ff.; on Egypt below, p. 708 f.

⁶² Temples: see my remarks in *Anat. Stud. pres. to Sir William Ramsay*, 1923, pp. 387 ff. and *Sardis, Gr. and Lat. Inscr.*, no. 4 (about 155 B.C.); cf. in general A. Heuss, *Stadt u. Herrscher*, pp. 45 ff., and T. R. S. Broughton, 'Roman Asia Minor', T. Frank, *Econ. Surv.* iv, pp. 641 ff. Cf. above, Ch. IV, notes 280 ff. In the letter about the immunity of the sheep which belonged

to the temple of Apollo Tarsenus (dated by E. Boehringer, *Alt. v. Perg.* ix, 1937, p. 92, wrongly in the time of Attalus I—230/29 B.C., not in that of Eumenes II) the man to whom this letter is addressed by Attalus may be the *neocoros* of the temple. Ephesus: Strabo, xiv. p. 642, cf. p. 641. As regards the land of Zeus of Aezani, I see no reason to believe with Broughton (loc. cit., p. 644, cf. p. 682) that the *cleroi* into which part of the land of the god was divided by the kings remained the property of the god, see my review of *Econ. Surv.* iv, in *Am. J. Ph.* lx (1939), pp. 363 ff.

[63] We have practically no information about the villages of the Pergamene kingdom which did not belong to city or temple territories, or about the management by the Pergamene kings of forests, mines, salt-pans, fisheries, and pastures. Most of the evidence belongs to earlier and later times. On the role of villages in the social and economic life of Asia Minor see above, Ch. IV, p. 560, cf. T. R. S. Broughton, 'Roman Asia Minor', pp. 627 ff., esp. p. 646 f. It is very regrettable that Broughton has not added to his lists of temples, large estates, and cities a list of villages in the style of his other lists and of his short tabulation of the known *koina* or unions of villages, mostly of Hellenistic date, in Caria and some other parts of Asia Minor (loc. cit., p. 702).

[64] What are known as the 'small finds' of Pergamon have never been published in full, nor have they been interpreted in the light of the finds made in other places in Asia Minor, Greece with the islands, Italy, and Sicily. The same is true of almost all the other cities excavated in Asia Minor with one exception—Priene (above, pp. 175 ff.). There is a general survey of the minor finds of Pergamon with short descriptions in A. Conze, 'Kleinfunde', *Berl. Abh.*, 1902, and id., *Alt. von Pergamon*, i, 1913, pp. 248 ff. (in collaboration with R. Zahn), cf. E. Böhringer und F. Krauss, *Alt. v. Perg.* ix, 1937, esp. pp. 100 ff.

[65] The best study of Pergamene toreutics is that of H. Winnefeld, 'Hellenistiche Silberreliefs im Antiquarium der K. Museen', *Berl. Winckelmannspr.* 86 (1908), cf. G. Lippold, *P.W.K.* vi A. 1767. It is based on the study of two silver *emblemata* found at Miletopolis near Pergamon. In the same study Winnefeld has shown how strikingly similar are the silver *emblemata* from Miletopolis to some medallions on the bottoms of red-glazed vases of the second and first centuries B.C. One (found in South Russia) shows a portrait of a Hellenistic ruler who has been identified with Orophernes or with one of the Seleucids. On the origin of the Hellenistic 'terra sigillata', see the Excursus by F. O. Waagé at the end of this book. Pergamene bronze plate found in S. Russia: C. Griniewicz, 'Bronze vase of the tumulus of Courdjips', *Bull. de la Comm. arch.* lxv (1918), pp. 45 ff. (in Russian), cf. F. Courby, *Les vases grecs à reliefs*, 1922, pp. 473 ff.

[66] Eastern red-glazed pottery: R. Zahn, *Priene*, Kleinfunde, pp. 410 ff.; Conze-Zahn, *Alt. v. Pergamon*, i. 2, pp. 254 ff.; S. Loeschke, *Ath. Mitt.* xxxvii (1912), pp. 345 ff.; R. Pagenstecher, *Die gr.-äg. Sammlung E. v. Sieglin*, ii. 2, 1913, pp. 100 ff.; F. Courby, *Les vases grecs à reliefs*, 1922, pp. 451 ff.;

H. A. Thompson, 'Two centuries of Hell. pottery', *Hesp.* iii (1934), pp. 471 ff. ; F. O. Waagé, in *Antioch-on-the-Orontes*, i, 1934, pp. 67 ff. (pottery), cf. his articles in *Hesp.* ii (1933), pp. 291 ff., and 'Vasa Samia', *Antiquity*, xi (1937), pp. 46 ff. Waagé discriminates between the so-called Pergamene and the Samian ware, the latter being of much later date, while J. H. Iliffe, 'Sigillata ware in the Near East', *Quart. Dep. Ant. Pal.* vi (1936), pp. 11 ff., cf. *J.H.S.* lvi (1936), pp. 234 ff., expresses doubts about this division into two classes. Cf. in general T. R. S. Broughton, 'Roman Asia Minor', p. 831 (good collection of texts of Roman writers where *vasa Samia* are mentioned). The mention of Pergamene goblets in Pliny suggests that he was referring to the ornamental ware of Pergamon (see my pl. LXXIII), while what he calls Samian ware was the cheap table ware. Finds in Pergamon: above, n. 64; in South Russia : T. Knipowitsch, 'Die Keramik römischer Zeit aus Olbia', *Mat. z. röm.-germ. Keramik*, iv. 1, 1929; in Syria: the above-quoted papers of Iliffe and Waagé; in Mesopotamia: the finds made at Seleuceia on the Tigris and at Dura are not yet published. Collection of Greek and Roman stamps: the paper of Iliffe quoted above and H. Comfort, *J. Am. Or. Soc.* lviii (1938), pp. 30 ff. Thanks to the courtesy of Dr. Waagé and Mr. R. J. Braidwood I have had an opportunity of studying the fine collections of Hellenistic pottery (among them intact specimens of red-glazed dishes and lamps) found at Jedeideh and Chatal Hüyük (still unpublished) in Syria, cf. the finds at Alishar Hüyük, H. H. v. d. Osten, *The Alishar Hüyük*, Seasons of 1930–32, p. iii, pp. 74 ff.

[67] A. Oxé, Arretinische Reliefgefässe vom Rhein', *Materialien z. römisch-germanischen Keramik*, v, 1933; H. Dragendorff, 'Arretina', *Sitzb. d. Heid. Akad.* xxvi (1935/6), 2 Abh.; 'Darstellungen aus der augusteischen Geschichte auf arretinischen Kelchen', *Germania*, xix (1935), pp. 305 ff., and 'Firmen-stempel und Künstlersignatur auf arretinischen Reliefgefässen', *Festschrift für August Oxé*, 1938, pp. 1 ff.; cf. the bibliography in the article by H. Comfort quoted in the preceding note.

[68] The deposit of Rhodian stamped jars found at Pergamon testifies in all probability to close commercial relations between Pergamon and Rhodes in the years between 220 and 180 B.C. (approximately). See C. Schuchhardt, in *Die Inschriften von Pergamon*, ii, pp. 423 ff., cf. F. Bleckmann, *De inscriptioni-bus quae leguntur in vasculis Rhodiis*, 1907, pp. 14 ff., and *Klio*, xii (1912), pp. 249 ff.; F. Hiller von Gaertringen, art. 'Rhodos', *P.W.K.* Suppl. v. 835 ff.; V. Grace, *Hesp.* iii (1934), pp. 214 ff. After 180 B.C. Pergamon probably emancipated itself from Rhodes and may have organized its commerce on different lines. It is possible that the Attalids were now using mainly the Delian harbour as the clearing-house for their export goods. The large quantity of Megarian bowls of a special type found at Delos, bowls very similar to those found at Pergamon, and the distribution of these bowls over a very large area (below, Ch. VI, n. 63) may suggest, since Delos was never an important centre of ceramic production, that the so-called Delian brand of Megarian bowls was produced in Asia Minor, but distributed by the merchants

of Delos. This idea was suggested to me by Dr. Deubner Jr., who is preparing a comprehensive work on the relief vases of Pergamon.

[69] K. Regling, art. 'Münzenwesen', *P.W.K.* xvi. 471 and 475. Note how the resumption of coinage by various cities of Asia Minor after Magnesia influenced the mainland. The leading cities of Euboea—Carystos, Chalcis, and Eretria—started, probably in 192 B.C., their own silver coinage, E. T. Newell, 'Five Greek bronze coin hoards', *Num. Notes and Mon.* lxviii (1935), pp. 17 ff., and the coinage of the Greek Leagues was never more abundant (above, n. 33). Note also how the action of Rome influenced both Philip V, who, as mentioned above (n. 40), after the conference of Tempe (187 B.C.) gave permission to Thessalonice, Pella, Amphipolis, and to whole districts of his kingdom to mint their own silver, and Antiochus IV, who gave the right to eighteen cities of his kingdom to mint coins for the empire, E. Babelon, *Rois de Syrie*, pp. ci ff., and B. V. Head, *H.N.*², p. 763. A list of cities of Asia Minor and of the larger islands which coined Alexandrian and Lysimachian tetradrachms after 190, incomplete as it is, may illustrate the general tendency as stated in the text (the list is based on Head, *H.N.*²): Myrina, Temnus, Methymna, Mytilene, Clazomenae, Colophon, Erythrae, Magnesia ad Maeandrum, Phocaea, Priene, Smyrna, Teos, Chios, Samos, Alabanda, Antiocheia ad Maeandrum, Mylasa, Stratoniceia, Astypalaea, Cos, Sardis, Aspendus, Side, Sillyon. The distribution of these cities within the sphere of influence of the Attalids and Seleucids will be noted.

[70] On the *cistophori*, Head, *H.N.*², p. 534; K. Regling, art. 'Kistophoren', in *P.W.K.* xi. 524 ff.: fourteen cities of Asia Minor, all of them depending in one way or another on Pergamon, took part in this coinage. It began probably about 200 B.C. Cf. T. R. S. Broughton, 'Roman Asia Minor', pp. 555 ff. (here will be found a list of cistophoric cities). Posthumous Alexanders and Lysimachi coined in various cities of Asia Minor and *cistophori* minted in the above mentioned cistophoric cities of Asia Minor were the main coinage of the Attalids in the second century B.C. The first (of the Attic standard) circulated almost exclusively in Syria, the second (of the Rhodian standard) in Asia Minor and in Greece. This is attested by the coin hoards and by the above-mentioned (n. 18) lists of booty and indemnities taken by the Romans during and after the Syrian war. Two kinds of coins are mentioned in these lists: the *cistophori* and the Attic tetradrachms. These last were, in all probability, the posthumous Alexanders and Lysimachi of Attic standard minted in Asia Minor. See my paper quoted in the next note.

[71] I have listed and studied these hoards in my article 'Some remarks on the monetary and commercial policy of the Seleucids and Attalids' in *Anatolian Studies presented to W. H. Buckler*, 1939. The pages that follow in the text represent an abstract of the article slightly modified in view of some remarks of E. Bikerman which he had the kindness to communicate to me in a private letter. Most important is his observation that the cities which emitted the international currency were free, not subject, cities. Cf. his remarks in his *Inst. Sél.*, p. 212, on the existence of a monetary convention

between the Seleucids and Aspendus, Phaselis, and Selge. Such a convention I regard as little probable. Countermarks of Tryphon appear on the coins of Lebedus and Heraclea in Ionia, E. T. Newell, *Num. Notes and Mon.* lxxxii (1938), pp. 21 ff.

[72] On the city of Pergamon above, pp. 557ff. For the palaces with their mosaics, the *heroon* (?) and the arsenal and storehouses, G. Kawerau und Th. Wiegand, *Alt. v. Perg.* v. 1, 1930; E. Böhringer und F. Krauss, ibid. ix, 1937; Áskos von Szalay (†) und E. Böhringer, ibid. x, 1938. On the Arsenal, F. Lammert, 'Die Arsenale und die Geschütz-Kugeln von Pergamon', *Z. f. hist. Waffenkunde*, vi (1937–38), pp. 155 ff. On the Library, B. Götze, 'Antike Bibliotheken', *J.D.A.I.* lii (1937), pp. 225 ff., and C. Wendel, 'Neues aus alten Bibliotheken', *Zentralbl. f. Bibliothekswesen*, liv (1937), pp. 585 ff., and lv (1938), pp. 641 ff. On the famous Asclepieion near the city rebuilt by the Attalids, O. Deubner, Das Asklepieion von Pergamon, 1938.

[73] On the cities of the Pergamene kingdom see P. Ghione, 'I communi del Regno di Pergamo', *Mem. Acc. Torino*, lv (1905), pp. 67 ff., cf. my article in *Anatolian Studies presented to Sir W. Ramsay* quoted above. On Myrina, E. Pottier et S. Reinach, *La Nécropole de Myrina*, 1886–88; W. Ruge, art. 'Myrina' in *P.W.K.* Suppl. vi. 615 ff., and D. Burr, *Terracottas from Myrina in the Museum of Fine Arts, Boston*, 1934, pp. 3 ff. On Teos, W. Ruge, art. 'Teos' in *P.W.K.* v A. 539 ff., and Poland, art. 'Technitai', ibid. 2473 ff., cf. G. Daux, 'Craton, Eumenes II et Attale II', *B.C.H.* lix (1935), pp. 210 ff. Note that Craton was a typical representative of the rich Anatolian *bourgeoisie* of his time.

[74] For the modern surveys of the history of the minor monarchies I refer to the pertinent notes on Ch. IV. The ancient sources are quoted in the text.

[75] Practically nothing is known of the organization by Prusias I of his new cities. Bithynian inscriptions of the Hellenistic period are extremely rare. The literary sources are silent. Quite recently L. Robert, *Ét. Anat.* 1937, pp. 228 ff., was fortunate enough to find in the Museum of Brûssa a fragmentary honorary decree of Prusa on Mount Olympus. The date is uncertain. The document may belong to the time of Prusias I or may be later. I cannot deal with this inscription at length. It has no direct bearing on my subject. It is interesting, however, to find a royal *epistates* of the city rendering it certain services of a financial character: loans of money without interest (?), money for μισθοί (?). The inscription seems to be a document very similar to the inscriptions (previously mentioned) of Corragus, of Cleon of Aegina, of Hippomedon of Samothrace, of Epinicus of the same place (*Am.J.Ph.* lx, pp. 452 ff.), of the unidentified city T ..., all decrees in honour of royal *strategoi* or *epistatai*. It seems therefore probable that the relations of Prusias with his Greek cities were of the same character as those of the Ptolemies, Attalids and other Hellenistic kings with the cities of their kingdoms. See above on the Permagene kingdom, and A. Heuss, *Stadt und Herrscher*, &c., pp. 17 ff. Cf. an inscription of Nicomedia restored by

L. Robert, *Ét. Anat.*, pp. 235 ff., which speaks of ambassadors sent by a king Prusias, one of whom has the court title τῶμ φίλων.

[75a] New evidence on the policy of Pharnaces I is supplied by the fragmentary inscription of Odessus (modern Varna) recently found and published, see Chr. M. Danov, 'Die Beziehungen des Pontischen Reiches zur linken Schwarzmeerküste', *Bull. Hist. Soc.* (of Bulgaria), xiv (1938), pp. 54 ff.; A. Salač, *Eunomia*, i (1938), pp. 3 ff. (Prague), and Chr. M. Danov, *Bull. Inst. Arch. Bulg.* xii (1939), p. 226 f. The inscription is not exactly dated. It is a decree of the city of Odessus which mentions an embassy to king Pharnaces I probably in order to ask for help in difficult times. The fragmentary inscription requires renewed study.

[76] The evidence for the facts quoted in the text will be found in the excellent article 'Miletos' by Hiller von Gaertringen in *P.W.K.* xv. 1607 ff. The article on Magnesia on the other hand is rather poor. On the *bouleuterion* of Miletus, *Milet. Erg. d. Ausgr.* i. 2, 1908, p. 100, nos. 1, 2, cf. pp. 95 ff., where all the evidence on Timarchus and Heracleides is collected; cf. also E. Bikerman, *Inst. Sél.*, p. 123, n. 9.

[76a] On the ἐρημοφυλακία collected in Egypt in Roman times and attested by many receipts S. L. Wallace, *Taxation in Egypt*, 1938, pp. 272 ff. It was a tax for the support of the desert police but was levied from those only who were in need of their protection, exporting and importing goods from or to Egypt. Several similar sections of the police force were known in Ptolemaic Egypt (I have mentioned them above, Ch. IV, p. 317, cf. Ch. VI; they were all probably supported by special taxes. On the police and gendarmes of the Hellenistic States in general, below, Ch. VIII.

[77] On the τράπεζα δημοσία of Miletus see A. Rehm, *Milet. Erg. d. Ausgr.* i. 3, no. 141, l. 51; no. 145 passim, and no. 147, l. 54; Th. Wiegand, *VII Bericht*, (*Berl. Abh.* 1911), p. 28, l. 24 (ἐμπορικὰ δάνεια). All the data concerning the city bank of Miletus are collected and carefully studied in the light of parallel evidence by E. Ziebarth, 'Hellenistische Banken', *Z.N.* xxxiv (1924), pp. 26 ff., cf. id., art. 'Trapeza' in *P.W.K.* vi A. 2200. Note that the city bank of Miletus was not created before the end of the third century.

[78] On the markets, A. von Gerkan, 'Der Nordmarkt und der Hafen an der Löwenbucht', *Milet, Erg. d. Ausgr.* i. 6, 1922, pp. 87 ff., and H. Knackfuss, 'Der Südmarkt und die benachbarten Bauanlagen', ibid. i. 7, 1924. I cannot give here a detailed description of these two splendid buildings, see pl. LXXV and fig. 6. Note that the North market was rebuilt in connexion with the construction of the *bouleuterion* (175–164 B.C.) about the time of Antiochus IV, and served as a connecting-link between the political (*bouleuterion*) and the religious (*Delphinion*) centres of the city. From the economic point of view the South market was much more important than the North market. Road from Pidasa to Ionopolis: A. Rehm, *Milet. Erg. d. Ausgr.* i. 3, no. 149, ll. 44 ff.; ferry service in the Latmian gulf, ibid., no. 150, ll. 99 ff. (*S.I.G.*³ 633). Cf. J. Röhlig, *Der Handel von Milet*, 1933, p. 62.

[79] A. Rehm, loc. cit., no. 150, ll. 86 ff.; *S.I.G.*³ 633: in the treaty between Miletus and Heraclea a whole paragraph is devoted to the runaway domestic, i.e. private, slaves.

[80] The history and monuments of Priene, above, pp. 175 ff. On Orophernes, C. B. Welles, *R.C.* 63.

[81] The location of the Milesian Pidasa, which ought not to be confounded with the two localities of more or less the same name, is discussed by Ruge, *P.W.K.* xix. 27 ff., cf. L. Robert, *Villes d'Asie Mineure*, 1935, p. 55 (where he refers to a full treatment of the Milesian inscription in his forthcoming 'Recherches en Carie') and p. 62, n. 7. See also id., *Collection Fröhner*, I, Inscr. Gr., p. 79.

[82] On Mylasa and Olymus see W. Ruge, *P.W.K.* xvi. 1046 ff., and xvii. 2510, cf. 1061 on the fertility of the territories of Mylasa, Olymus, and Euromus, and on the marble quarries of Mylasa. In these two articles Ruge gives lists of inscriptions found in the two places. The documents which I have in mind —the contracts of sale and lease—have never been completely collected and adequately published. A *corpus* and a comprehensive study of them would be of great service to the students of economic and legal history. The inscriptions are incorporated in the lists of W. Ruge quoted above and are separately listed by T. R. S. Broughton, 'Roman Asia Minor', p. 560, cf. p. 680, see also L. Robert, *Études épigr. et phil.* 1938, p. 175 and p. 225. Some of these inscriptions are printed and discussed in *Inscr. Jur. Gr.* i, no. xiii, quater, A.B.C., p. 243, cf. p. 258 (list of texts) and p. 272 (comments and bibliography) (not quoted by Broughton). On the banking operations of the temples controlled by the corresponding cities and in some cases perhaps by officers appointed by the kings, see A. M. Andreades, *Hist. of Gr. Publ. Fin.* i, 1933, p. 180 ff.; J. A. O. Larsen, 'Roman Greece', pp. 357 ff.; T. R. S. Broughton, 'Roman Asia Minor', pp. 888 ff., cf. p. 559. The activity of the temple of Ephesus in this respect is illustrated by Dio Chrys. xxxi. 54 ff. The mention in this passage of δῆμοι and βασιλεῖς as depositors in the bank may point to a Hellenistic source which Dio was using. Cf. the well-known 'Ephesian debtor law' of 85 B.C., *S.I.G.*³ 742.

[83] On the trade of Ephesus, above, p. 173, cf. M. Cary and E. Warmington, *Les explorateurs de l'Antiquité*, 1935, p. 220 and n. 138. On its banking see the preceding note.

[84] The evidence for the war against Byzantium will be found in Hiller von Gaertringen, art. 'Rhodos' in *P.W.K.* Suppl. v. 785 f. Our main source is Polyb. iv. 37 ff. (on the tribute, iv. 46. 4; and on the role of Cavarus in making peace, iv. 52). On the part which Byzantium took in the war against Philip, Polyb. xvi. 2. 10. The decree of Athens in honour of Heris the Byzantine, two trierarchs, and a treasurer, *S.I.G.*³ 580. On Cavarus and the kingdom of Tyle, Chr. M. Danov, *Bull. Inst. Arch. Bulg.*, xii (1939), pp. 214 ff. and 253 ff. (in Bulgarian with German résumé).

[85] E. Bickermann, 'Rom und Lampsacus', *Phil.* lxxxvii (1931), p. 277, and 'Bellum Antiochicum', *Hermes*, lxvii (1932), pp. 47 ff.

[86] On the conditions of the Pontic cities, those of the 'left Pontus', in the second century B.C. see my remarks in *Gnomon*, x (1934), pp. 3 ff. and the article of Danov (pp. 235 ff.) quoted above, n. 84, cf. the same article, pp. 218 ff., on the trade relations of the cities of the Western shore of the Euxine.

[87] Rhodes and the Crimea: my remarks in *Gnomon*, x (1934), pp. 3 ff., and *C.A.H.* viii, pp. 628 ff. and p. 641. On the Pontic slaves: Scythian (1) *I.G.* xii. 1. 526; *G.D.I.* 4061, (2) *I.G.* xii. 1. 527; *G.D.I.* 4062, (3) A. Maiuri, *Nuova Silloge* no. 233, (4) ibid., no. 421; Sarmatian, *I.G.* xii. 1. 525; *G.D.I.* 4060; Maeotian, Maiuri, *N.S.* no. 229, cf. *I.G.* xii. 1. 514. Free (?) Bosporan at Rhodes, Maiuri, *N.S.* no. 166. Borysthenite, Maiuri, *N.S.* no. 95. Olbian, *S.E.G.* iii. 676. 17 (Ὀλβ]ιαπολίτας).

[88] Bosporus, Chersonesus, and Delphi: see above, n. 11, and G. Daux, *Delphes au II*e *et au I*er *siècle*, pp. 21, 25, 658 ff. (decree of Delphi for the Chersonesites), and 520 (decree for Paerisades and Camasarye), cf. B. Latyschev, Ποντικά, 1909, pp. 298 ff. Panticapaeum and its relations with Miletus: B. Haussoullier, *Ét. sur l'hist. de Milet*, 1902, pp. 202, no. 2855, 29 f., and p. 206, no. 5, l. 6, cf. pp. 168 ff., 212, and 222.

[89] I have already mentioned that Delos was in active commercial relations with South Russia in the third century B.C. Note that in 276 three φιάλαι were dedicated by Chersonesus at Delos and the festival of the *Chersonesia* was created. After 250 the φιάλαι were deposited in the temple of Apollo and are thereafter mentioned regularly. No new dedications, however, were made either by the Chersonesites or by the Bosporan kings. See F. Durrbach, *Comptes des Hiéropes*, *I.G.* xi, nos. 164 B, l. 6 (276 B.C.); 439 A, 14–15 (181 B.C.); 442 B, 16–17, cp. his note to no. 442, p. 164. Cf. E. Schulhof, *B.C.H.* xxxii (1908), p. 126.

[90] Pergamon and South Russia: above, notes 65, 66. Export from Alexandria to South Russia: glass, my *Skythien und der Bosporus*, 1931, pp. 248, 425; faience figurines used mostly as amulets, some of Hellenistic times, B. Touraïeff, 'Objets égyptiens et égyptisants trouvés dans la Russie Méridionale' *Rev. Arch.* xviii (1911), pp. 20 ff.; A. V. Schmidt, *The New Orient* (in Russian), xiii–xiv (1926), pp. 342 ff.; my article 'Greek sightseers in Egypt', *J.E.A.* xiv (1928), p. 14. I have dealt with some antiquities found in South Russia and Bulgaria which testify to trade relations between the Sacians (successors of the Scythians and predecessors of the Sarmatians in South Russia) and northern India through Bactria in my paper 'Sarmatian and Indo-Scythian Antiquities', *Recueil N. P. Kondakov*, 1926, pp. 239 ff. (in Russian with résumé in French), cf. 'Some new aspects of Iranian Art', *Sem. Kondak.* vi (1933), pp. 161 ff. Cf. on the Sacians W. W. Tarn, *C.A.H.* ix, p. 582 f., and id., *The Greeks in Bactria and India*, 1938, pp. 79 ff., cf. Index, s.v. Sacas and my remarks, *C.A.H.* xi, p. 94 f.

[91] On Rhodes see my chapter 'Rhodes', &c., *C.A.H.* viii, pp. 619 ff., from which I freely quote, and the excellent art. 'Rhodos' by Hiller von Gaertringen in *P.W.K.* Suppl. v. 731 ff. Cf. E. Ziebarth, 'Zur Handelsgeschichte der Insel Rhodos', *Mél. Glotz*, 1932, pp. 909 ff., and on the new inscriptions from Rhodes, M. N. Tod, *J.H.S.* lv (1935), p. 201 f., and lvii (1937), p. 196 f.

[92] Rhodes and Sinope, Polyb. iv. 56, cf. D. M. Robinson, *Ancient Sinope*, 1906 (*Am. J. Phil.* xxvii (1906), p. 250), and *C.A.H.* viii, p. 625. I do not believe that Rhodes made such a large gift to Sinope. It was probably a loan, like the much earlier loans of Rhodes to Priene (*S.I.G.*³ 363, and n. 4) and to Argos (W. Vollgraff, *Mnem.* xliv (1916), pp. 219 ff.), cf. *C.A.H.* viii, p. 623. About 230–220 B.C. a Rhodian banker, resident in Delos, enabled the Histiaeans to purchase grain by granting them a loan, *S.I.G.*³ 493; F. Durrbach, *Choix*, 50; cf. *C.A.H.* viii, p. 626. An unpublished decree of Sinope found at Cos attests that the latter through an ambassador took a prominent part in the action in favour of the Sinopians (date 220 B.C.). It shows the solidarity of Rhodes and Cos and even a certain dependence of Cos on Rhodes in matters of foreign policy. R. Herzog, *J.D.A.I.* xviii (1903), Anz. p. 198; id., *Ath. Mitt.* xxx (1905), p. 182.

[93] There is no good comprehensive publication of stamped jar-handles found in the Greek cities of the western coast of the Black Sea. See meanwhile the general remarks of V. Parvan, *Dacia*, 1928, p. 101, cf. G. Cantacuzène, 'Timbres amphoriques trouvés à Callatis', *Rev. Hist. du Sud-Est européen*, xii (1935), pp. 298 ff., cf. V. Parvan, *Getica*, 1926, p. 796 f. (French résumé), and the Index, s.v. 'amfore' (and *'amphorae'*), 'Rhodes', 'Rhodieni', 'Rhodiens', 'Rhodos', and the article of Danov (pp. 227 ff.) quoted above, n. 84.

[94] After the downfall of the Ptolemaic hegemony in the Aegean and the *de facto* dissolution of the Island League, Rhodes, as I mentioned above, became practically the only official protector of the safety of the Greek islands and of commerce in the Aegean. This is shown by the well-known Delian inscription of the middle of the third century B.C., a decree in honour of Antigenes, the Rhodian admiral (Durrbach, *Choix*, 39; *I.G.* xi. 4. 596; E. Bikerman, *Rev. É. A.* xl. (1938), p. 381). This position was still held and the same policy pursued by Rhodes during the war against Philip. A Delian text (*S.I.G.*³ 582), which mentions an order (διάγραμμα) issued by the Rhodian admiral Epicrates in favour of Delos, shows how seriously Rhodes took this task. It is in this sense, i.e. as a measure which was intended to protect and neutralize Delos and probably the other important harbours of the Aegean, that I am inclined to interpret (with Bikerman) the somewhat obscure words of the order of Epicrates: ὅπως οἱ πει[ρατεύον]τες τοὺς πολεμίους ὁρ[μηθῶσιν] ἐκ τῶν ἰδίων λιμένων, τῶ[ι δὲ ἐν Δήλωι μ]ηθεὶς ὁρμητηρίωι χρή[σηται]. See the interpretation of this order by E. Bikerman, *Rev. Phil.* xii (1938), p. 300.

[95] We derive our information about the leading role of Rhodes in the grain commerce in the late third and early second centuries B.C. from some Delian texts. The most important is the decree of Histiaea in honour of the Rhodian

banker Athenodoros for having helped the *sitonai* of Histiaea to provide their city with grain (Durrbach, *Choix*, no. 50, of 230–220 B.C.). The Rhodian appears here as a financier, while the actual transaction was carried out at Delos. A Rhodian appears again in the same capacity of intermediary and financier in one of the two inscriptions dedicated at Delos to king Massinissa (Durrbach, *Choix*, nos. 68, 69, of 179 B.C.) in recognition of a gift of grain which he made to the city of Delos. Cf. the comments of Durrbach on the texts quoted above, and n. 35 to this chapter.

[96] The turnover of Rhodian trade in the early second century B.C. has been calculated from the statement of the Rhodian ambassadors in Rome in 170 B.C. that the income of the city of Rhodes from its harbour dues amounted before this date to one million drachmas a year (Polyb. xxx. 31. 10–12 [xxxi. 7. 12]). If by ἐλλιμένιον Polybius meant customs duties (this identification is generally accepted by modern scholars) and these last were the customary 1/50 (*pentekoste*), i.e. 2 per cent. of the value of the merchandize, the turnover of the trade in the Rhodian harbour must be calculated at about 50 million drachmas (the sum named by the Rhodian ambassadors was of course a round one). Such is the calculation of K. J. Beloch, *Gr. Gesch.* iv. 1, 2nd ed., p. 291, n. 4, p. 299 f., cf. pp. 289 ff. On the emendation of the text of Polybius and the calculations based on this emendation see the bibliography in J. A. O. Larsen, 'Roman Greece', T. Frank, *Econ. Surv.* iv, 1938, p. 356. Unfortunately we have no corresponding figures for the other commercial cities of that and earlier times which would enable us to estimate the real comparative importance of Rhodian commerce.

[97] On Rhodian jars see the bibliography in *C.A.H.* viii, p. 790, 1, 2, b (supplement to the bibliography in M. P. Nilsson, *Timbres amphoriques de Lindos*, &c., 1909), cf. F. Hiller von Gaertringen, 'Rhodos', *P.W.K.* Suppl. v. 835 ff., and on the chronology of Rhodian stamps in general V. Grace, *Hesp.* iii (1934), pp. 214 ff. See also F. Heichelheim, *Wirtschaftsg.*, p. 471 f., and n. 12. He announces a special article on the chronology and distribution of Rhodian jars. I am afraid that in view of the mass of unpublished material stored in the museums his conclusions based on statistics of published stamps are not convincing. To the list of publications of finds of Rhodian stamped jar-handles given in *C.A.H.* may be added: Athens (Agora), V. Grace, loc. cit.; Samos (with large admixture of Sinopian handles), W. Technau, *Ath. Mitt.* liv (1929), pp. 58 ff.; Carthage, S. Gsell, *Histoire de l'Afrique*, iv, 1920, p. 154, n. 1; Palestine, Beth Zur, O. R. Sellers, *The Citadel of Beth Zur*, 1933, pp. 52 ff.; Transjordan, Jerash (Gerasa), C. H. Kraeling, *Gerasa*, 1938. Inscriptions (C. B. Welles), nos. 241–7; Babylonia, Seleuceia on the Tigris, R. H. McDowell, *Stamped and Inscribed Objects from Seleucia on the Tigris*, 1935, pp. 250 ff., cf. my review of this book, *J.H.S.* lv (1935), pp. 251 ff., and Uruk (Warka), A. Nöldecke, vii, *Vorl. Ber.*, *Berl. Abh.*, 1935, p. 35, pl. xxxvii, b, c; Elam, Susa, F. Cumont, *C.R. Ac. Inscr.* 1937, p. 316 (cf. id., *Syria*, viii (1927), pp. 49 ff.); Syria, Antioch on the Orontes (unpublished); Mesopotamia, Dura-Europus (several Rhodian stamps and one Thasian). On

the Danubian lands, above note 93; S. Russia, above, p. 109, n. 43 and *C.A.H.* viii, p. 629. It is certain that Nilsson's list and my own are incomplete. I know of none which is complete. There is scarcely a single excavated place where Rhodian jars have not been found. We expect from Miss V. Grace and Mrs. Silva Lake a comprehensive study of the Rhodian stamps.

⁹⁸ A certain idea of the general aspect of Rhodes may be derived from the better preserved and carefully excavated ruins of its sister city Lindos. The buildings of the Acropolis of Lindos have been partly restored by the Italian Service of Antiquities. No comprehensive work on the history and ruins of the city is in existence. A short survey with excellent bibliography will be found in F. Hiller von Gaertringen's article 'Rhodos' in *P.W.K.* Suppl. v, pp. 746 ff., cf. the Reports on the Danish excavations by Chr. Blinkenberg and K. F. Kinch, *Expl. Arch. de Rhodes*, vols. i ff. (in course of publication).

⁹⁹ I cannot discuss here the importance of the Rhodian school in the development of Greek art in the Hellenistic period. Chapters devoted to it will be found in all the histories of Greek art. The sculptures (statues and bas-reliefs) found on the island of Rhodes and in Cos and kept in the Museum of Rhodes and in the Antiquarium of Cos are reproduced and discussed by L. Laurenzi, *Clara Rhodos*, ix. (1938), pp. 9 ff. A list of Rhodian artists and of artists of non-Rhodian origin active in Rhodes has been compiled by F. Hiller von Gaertringen, art. 'Rhodos', *P.W.K.* Suppl. v, pp. 827 ff. (with bibliography).

¹⁰⁰ On the Rhodian army and navy, *C.A.H.* viii, pp. 635 ff. I reproduce this section here with some modifications based on new material and renewed treatment of the subject in recent years, relating mostly to the navy: G. Jacopi, *Clara Rhodos*, ii (1932), pp. 169 ff.; M. Segre, *Riv. Fil.* lx (10) (1932), pp. 452 ff. (inscription about 260–250 B.C. which mentions ξένοι and μισθοφόροι, cf. F. Hiller von Gaertringen, *G.G.A.* cxcv (1933), pp. 16 ff.; M. Segre, *Clara Rhodos*, viii (1936), pp. 227 ff., a fine study of the organization of the Rhodian navy, and Chr. Blinkenberg, 'Triemiolia' (Lindiaka VII), *Det Kgl. Danske Videnskabernes Selskab*, Arch.-Kunsth. Medd. ii. 3 (1938), who, in discussing the typical Rhodian τριημιολίαι, reprints and studies several of the inscriptions bearing on the organization of the Rhodian navy.

¹⁰¹ The καθήμενοι or παρακαθήμενοι occur in another inscription besides that quoted in the text, F. Hiller von Gaertringen, *Ath. Mitt.* xx (1895), pp. 222 ff.; *S.I.G.*³ 1225. They may have been oarsmen.

¹⁰² On the Rhodian trierarchy A. Maiuri, *N.S.*, 18, cf. 21; M. Segre, *Clara Rhodos*, viii (1936), pp. 227 ff.

¹⁰³ Real mercenaries (see the treaty between Hierapytna in Crete and Rhodes, *S.I.G.*³ 581, ll. 40–5) of foreign origin are rarely attested. A statement by Livy (xxxiii. 18. 3) suggests that, along with detachments of allies, the Rhodian army consisted chiefly of units recruited in the Peraea, cf. M. Holleaux, *B.C.H.* xvii (1893), p. 60 f.; E. Meyer, *Die Grenzen der hell. Staaten*,

1925, p. 54, and the fragmentary inscription A. Maiuri, *Ann. Sc. Ital.* iv–v (1924), pp. 482 ff. Cf. G. T. Griffith, *The Mercenaries*, 1935, &c., p. 90 f.

[104] A. Maiuri, *N.S.* 22 ; F. Hiller von Gaertringen, *Gnomon*, ii (1926), p. 197 ; my pls. LXXVII and LXXVIII.

[105] The inscription of Polycles is typical, A. Maiuri, *N.S.* 18 ; *C.A.H.* viii, p. 638.

[106] Cf. U. von Wilamowitz-Moellendorff, *Textgeschichte der griech. Bukoliker*, 1906, p. 119 ; W. Leaf in G. M. Calhoun, *The Business Life of Ancient Athens*, 1926, pp. 105 ff. E. Ziebarth, *Beiträge zur Gesch. d. Seeraubs*, &c., 1929, p. 87, and Anhang ii, no. 77.

[107] H. Kreller, 'Lex Rhodia', *Zeitschr. f. d. ges. Handelsrecht u. Konkursrecht*, lxxxv (1921), pp. 257 ff.

[108] On Delos, above, Ch. IV, pp. 230 ff.; cf. on the recent epigraphical evidence M. N. Tod, *J.H.S.* lv (1935), pp. 200 ff., and lvii (1937), pp. 195 ff. Dependence of Delos on Rhodes, above notes 94 and 95, cf. the next note. Delos and South Russia, above, n. 89 ; Delos and the Ptolemies, *Inscr. de Dél.* 1525–39 (Philopator, Epiphanes, Philometor), cf. W. A. Laidlaw, *A History of Delos*, 1933, p. 109. I may refer again in this connexion to the difficulties that Delos experienced especially in the early second century in providing its population with sufficient and not too expensive corn, above, p. 235 and J. A. O. Larsen, 'Roman Greece', pp. 344 ff.

[109] Statistics about finds of stamped jar-handles at Delos, *C.A.H.* viii, p. 629. My conclusions based on these statistics I now regard as wrong: Cnidus (V. Grace, *Hesp.* iii (1934), pp. 241 ff.) cannot be considered as a rival of Rhodes in the early second century B.C., since it was at this time a dependency of Rhodes, Ernst Meyer, *Die Grenzen*, p. 72 and p. 140, cf. Bürchner, *P.W.K.* xi. 920. I must, however, repeat here what I said before, that the dates of many of the stamped jar-handles are uncertain and that the problem of dating needs careful comparative study. The fact stressed by Larsen, loc. cit., pp. 392 ff., points in the same direction. It is interesting to see that in this period Delos bought for the sacred ceremonies exclusively Cnidian and Coan wine, that is to say, wine produced in the two wine-growing States politically dependent on Rhodes.

[110] Prices at Delos, F. Heichelheim, *Wirtsch. Schwank.*, pp. 48 ff. ; *Wirtschaftsg.*, pp. 452 ff. ; Larsen, loc. cit., pp. 380 ff., cf. above, n. 32. I must emphasize again that the fluctuations of prices at Delos, valuable as is the light they throw on the economic vicissitudes of this island, are often not easy to explain, and have been in fact interpreted in various ways. I need only refer to the different interpretations of the same material in the careful studies of Heichelheim and Larsen quoted above. General political conditions played an important but not an exclusive part in the fluctuation of prices in Delos. Our knowledge is unfortunately very limited and we must not base sweeping generalizations on insufficient material not always easy to interpret.

¹¹¹ Rise of rents at Delos, Larsen, loc. cit., pp. 400 ff. Relations between Syria and Delos as reflected in the honorary inscriptions of Delos, P. Roussel, *Délos. col. athén.*, 1916, p. 88, n. 3; *Inscr. de Délos*, 1540–53, cf. Durrbach, *Choix*, 59 (Antiochus III), 71, 72 (Seleucus IV), 70 (Laodice, daughter of Seleucus IV), 87 (Antiochus IV). On the Poseidoniasts of Berytus in Delos in 178 B.C., Ch. Picard, *B.C.H.* xliv (1920), pp. 297 ff.; cf. on the history of the Poseidoniasts of Berytus and the Heracleists of Tyre Ch. Picard, *Rev. Arch.*, 6 sér., viii (1936), pp. 191 ff. New evidence on the Poseidoniasts, M. N. Tod, *J.H.S.* liv (1934), pp. 140 ff.; *Inscr. de Délos*, 1520, cf. the remarks of Ch. Picard, *Rev. Arch.*, 6 sér., viii (1936), pp. 188 ff.

¹¹² On Tenos, Fiehn, 'Tenos', *P.W.K.* v A. 515 ff. On Thasos, F. v. Hiller, ibid. 1320 f. Cf. the curious fragments of a harbour regulation, M. Launey, *B.C.H.* lvii (1933), pp. 394 ff.

¹¹³ On Cos, A. Neppi Modona, *L'isola di Coo nell'antichità classica*, 1933; cf. the new inscriptions found after the appearance of Modona's book in M. N. Tod, *J.H.S.* lv (1935), p. 203, and lvii (1937), p. 197 f. Cf. above, Ch. IV, n. 72. The situation became easier and more peaceful after Philip's defeat by the Romans. See L. Robert, *B.C.H.* lix (1936), p. 421: donation of a library, books, and money by two donors (early second century B.C.). Taxation of Cos in the second century B.C., *S.I.G.*³ 1000, and above, p. 241. Carpathos and its Ephesian benefactor (second century B.C.), M. Segre, *Historia*, vii (1933), p. 577.

¹¹⁴ F. v. Hiller, 'Thera', *P.W.K.* v A. 2296 ff. (on Artemidorus the Ptolemaic veteran, col. 2297, and on Epicteta, col. 2299, and ibid., on the Aleipterion of Procleidas).

¹¹⁵ See my remarks in *C.A.H.* vii, p. 163, and E. Bickermann, *Der Gott der Makkabäer*, 1937, pp. 66 ff., and his *Inst. Sél.*, p. 121 f. On Antiochus IV and the temple of Nanaia see W. W. Tarn, *The Greeks in Bactria and India*, p. 214 and pp. 463 ff. (Appendix 7: Antiochus IV and the temple of Nanaia). Tarn rejects the version that Antiochus plundered the temple. I do not regard this version as impossible. He may have enforced his demand by the same means as he used in Jerusalem.

¹¹⁶ M. Rostovtzeff, *Caravan Cities*, 1932, cf. M. Cary and E. Warmington, *Les explorateurs de l'Antiquité*, 1932, pp. 108 ff, and pp. 220 ff. Cf. the remarks of E. T. Newell, 'The Coinage of the Eastern Seleucid Mints', *Num. St.*, i (1938), p. 96 f., on the revival and consolidation at this time of the trade of Seleuceia on the Tigris as expressed in its coinage.

¹¹⁷ See for example a Parthian coin (Phraates III) found in a Panticapaean grave, my *Skythien und der Bosporus*, p. 209. The necropolis of Bori in the Caucasus plundered by an amateur excavator yielded several interesting objects of the late Hellenistic and early Roman Imperial times. Among them were several coins. The earliest—Sacian imitation of gold staters of Alexander—date probably from the second century B.C. Next come coins of

Phraates IV (37–2 B.C.) and Gotarzes (A.D. 50–51) of Parthia and many coins of Augustus (mainly of 2 B.C.). The necropolis was in use until the early third century A.D. The objects found in the graves are mostly Greek and Italian, but many were certainly imported from the East, presumably from Indo-Scythia (for example bracelets with inlaid stones), and perhaps Parthia. A Parthian source may be assigned to some silver-plated parts of wooden couches or chairs (especially legs) which show great similarity with bronze objects of the same forms and style found at Shami in Susiana (unpublished), see Sir Aurel Stein, 'An Arch. Journey in Western Iran', *Geogr. Journ.* 92 (1938), pp. 324 ff. Moreover, I am inclined to regard the silver dish with the figure of a standing horse and an altar before it as a product of Hellenistic Mesopotamian art. The figure of the sacred horse reminds me of the cave sanctuary of Heracles on Mount Sanbulos (Karafto) in Kurdistan described by Tacitus (Ann. xii. 13), see Sir Aurel Stein, loc. cit., p. 336 and fig. 21, cf. *S.E.G.* vii. 36. The find of Bori was published and discussed by E. Pridik, *Mat. Arch. of Russia*, xxxiv, 1914, pp. 94 ff. (in Russian). Fragments of couches, pls. IV, 1–6, and V; silver dish, p. 100, pl. I, 3. Syrian green-blue glazed amphora (see note 120) found in South Russia, A. Strelkoff, *J.D.A.I.* (1935), Anz., pp. 58 ff.

[118] The πομπή of Antiochus IV, Athen. v, 194 c–195 f., esp. 195 b: τὸ δὲ τῶν χρυσωμάτων καὶ ἀργυρωμάτων πλῆθος οὕτως ἄν τις ὑπονοήσειεν ὅσον ἦν. ἑνὸς γὰρ τῶν φίλων Διονυσίου τοῦ ἐπιστολογράφου χίλιοι παῖδες ἐπόμπευσαν ἀργυρώματα ἔχοντες, ὧν οὐδὲν ἐλάττον᾽ ὁλκὴν εἶχεν δραχμῶν χιλίων. βασιλικοὶ δὲ παῖδες παρῆλθον ἑξακόσιοι χρυσώματα ἔχοντες· ἔπειτα γυναῖκες ἐκ χρυσῶν καλπίδων μύροις ἔρραινον εἰς διακοσίας, cf. ibid. c: ἐν τῷ γυμνασίῳ πάντες ἐκ χρυσῶν ὁλκείων ἠλείφοντο κροκίνῳ μύρῳ. Note that Polybius in his brilliant characterization of Antiochus IV says about him (Athen. v, 193 d): μάλιστα δὲ πρὸς τοῖς ἀργυροκοπείοις εὑρίσκετο καὶ χρυσοχοείοις εὑρησιλογῶν καὶ φιλοτεχνῶν πρὸς τοὺς τορευτὰς καὶ τοὺς ἄλλους τεχνίτας. This shows how high was the artistic reputation of the toreutic artists of Antioch. I may also mention the various dedications, made at Miletus and Delos by Seleucus I and Stratonice, of gold and silver plate, some of it inset with stones, *O.G.I.* 214; Welles, *R.C.* 5. 21 ff., and the Accounts of the hieropes of Delos, *Inscr. de Délos*, no. 287, with the note, and the earlier and later inventories. I may recall in conclusion the well-known passage in one of the Verrines of Cicero in which gold vessels adorned with precious stones appear as a distinctive feature of the life of the Seleucids; Cic. *Verr.* iv. 62: 'poculo ex auro, quae, ut mos est regius et maxime in Syria, gemmis erant distincta clarissimis', cf. E. Bikerman, *Inst. Sél.*, p. 35, n. 14. It is to be regretted that our archaeological evidence in this respect is so poor. I know of no metal ware which could be assigned to Syria in the period under discussion. Scarcity of silver and gold in Syria may be to a certain extent responsible for this. Expensive silver and gold plate was kept for the living, and did not easily find its way into the graves. Cf., however, below, Ch. VI, n. 143.

[119] Ordinary wreaths of myrrh and frankincense branches are not very

comfortable to wear. The bushes from which the two substances are extracted are thorny. What Posidonius has in mind are wreaths of a peculiar
type often represented in Hellenistic and Roman paintings. These were
crowns and garlands which either consisted of flowers strung on threads or of
the same flowers packed tight in a net or a bag. These crowns and garlands
are always adorned with the long fillets described by Posidonius. This type
of garland is, for example, represented in some Panticapaean graves, see my
'Ancient Dec. Wall-painting', *J.H.S.* xxxix (1919), pls. VII, 2, and IX (nets),
and on some painted glass vases, see my article 'Painted glass vases', &c.,
Bull. Comm. Imp. Arch. 1914, pls. I, II, and XII (in Russian), cf. my *Anc.
Dec. Wall-painting in South Russia*, 1914, Index s.v. 'Garland' (in Russian).
For myrrh and frankincense wreaths, nets or bags were probably used.

[120] On the Mesopotamian glazed pottery see above, Ch. IV, n. 311. The most
recent study is N. C. Debevoise, *Parthian Pottery from Seleucia on the Tigris*,
1934. The abundant and in some instances exactly dated finds of Dura will
be illustrated by N. P. Toll in the Final Report on the excavation of Dura.
Beautiful specimens of this ware in the Metropolitan Museum (some of them
alleged to have been found in the neighbourhood of Homs-Hemesa) were
published and discussed by G. M. Richter, *Bull. Metr. Mus.* xi (1916), pp.
64 ff.; xix (1924), p. 94 f.; xxxiii (1938), pp. 240 ff. See description of pl.
LXXX. It may be noted in this connexion that a glazed funeral *hydria* of
the Mesopotamian type was found in Alexandria in the necropolis of Hadra
in a grave of the Ptolemaic period (no exact date was assigned to this grave
by the excavators), see E. Breccia, *Le Musée gréco-romain*, 1931–1932
(1933), p. 19, pl. V, 22.

The coin hoard of Susa was published by J.-M. Unvala, *Rev. Num.* xxxviii
(1935), pp. 155 ff., pl. V. I owe to the kindness of M. R. de Mecquenem and
J.-M. Unvala a photograph of the pot in which the hoard was found.

[121] My chapter 'Rhodes', &c., *C.A.H.* viii, pp. 619 ff.

[122] Above, notes 66 and 71.

[123] Above, n. 111. Syrian mosaicists and other artists at Delos, J. Chamonard, 'Les mosaïques de la maison des Masques', *Expl. Arch. de Délos*, xiv.
(1933), cf. id., *B.C.H.* lvii (1933), pp. 98 ff. Cf. Ch. Picard, *Syria*, xiv (1933),
pp. 318 ff., and *Berytus*, ii (1935), pp. 11 ff. Syrian ephebes, P. Roussel,
B.C.H. lv (1931), pp. 438 ff., esp. p. 447. Foreign sanctuaries in Delos, below,
Ch. VI, n. 62.

[124] On the Oriental merchants in Greece see Durrbach, *Choix*, p. 207 f.,
and my papers: 'Foreign commerce of Ptolemaic Egypt', *Journ. of Ec. and
Bus. History*, iv (1931–32), p. 745, and *C.A.H.* viii, p. 640 and p. 647, cf. W. A.
Laidlaw, *A Hist. of Delos*, 1933, p. 200, n. 29. Many inscriptions attest the
close relations in which these merchants stood to Delos and to other centres
of international commerce in the Mediterranean. The most ancient of them
belong to the second century B.C., to the time of Epiphanes and of the gradual
disintegration of the Seleucid Empire after his death. Most interesting is the

group which appears in the Delian inventories. At the head of this group we find the Bactrian Hyspaosines who first appears in 179 B.C. (*Inscr. de Délos*, 442 B, l. 109) and twice later (ibid. 1432 A a II, 26 and 1450 A, 136) as dedicant first of a λέοντος προτομή and later of an ἐκτύπωμα ʿΥρκανοῦ κυνός. We may identify this Hyspaosines or at least connect him with the well-known founder of Charax in Babylonia and of the dynasty of Mesene, perhaps a former satrap of Epiphanes, see W. W. Tarn, *C.A.H.* ix, p. 578. He or his successors emitted in 125/4 B.C. their own silver money which copies the reverse type of Euthydemus I of Bactria (G. Hill, *B.M.C., Arabia*, &c., p. cxcvi f.). A bronze issue of his coins was overstruck by Mithradates II in 122/1 B.C. (E. T. Newell, *Num. Notes and Mon.*, xxvi, 1925). Prof. A. R. Bellinger has found among the coins of Dura a bronze of Hyspaosines of hitherto unknown type, which is to be dated according to him in 140 B.C. since it copies a type of Demetrius II struck in Seleuceia on the Tigris just before his defeat and capture in 140/39 B.C. At about the same time we meet in the inventories of Delos an Αὖλος Γερραῖος, *Inscr. de Délos*, 1439 A b c ii, 24 ff.; 1449 A a b ii, 28, and a Τημάλλατος Γερραῖος, ibid., 1442 A, 82 and B, 57, 58; 1444 A a, 45 and 51; 1449 A a b ii, 60 f; 1450A, 119 (the last 140–39 B.C.), cf. a bilingual dedication of two Minaeans to their god Ouadd, *Inscr. de Délos* 2320. Contemporary are also the Petraean Arabs at Tenos, P. Graindor, *Mus. Belge* 1910, pp. 34 ff., no. 16, cp. p. 45 f., no. 23 (cf. *I.G.* xii. 5, 845, a Phoenician merchant at Tenos) and at Rhodes, *S.E.G.* iii. 674. 34 (cf. Chalce, *I.G.* xii. 1. 963). I may recall in this connexion the embassy of Moschion of Priene to the Nabataeans *Inscr. v. Pr.* 108 (of approximately the same time). Several dedications at Delos are probably of a later date: a Petraean (?) Arab, *Inscr. de Délos*, 2321; men from Hadramaut, ibid. 2319, cf. 2315 and 2322. I may mention finally the well-known inscriptions of Puteoli, *I.G.* xiv. 842 a. Prof. G. Levi Della Vida has published quite recently two very interesting bilingual inscriptions discovered on the island of Cos: one Greco-Nabataean and another Greco-Palmyrene; see G. Levi Della Vida, 'Una bilingue greco-nabatea', *Clara Rhodos*, ix (1938), pp. 139 ff. and *Mél. syr. R. Dussaud*, vol. ii (in print). Whatever their date may be (the Nabataean probably belongs to the time of Aretas IV 9 B.C.–40 A.D.), they testify to established and uninterrupted direct relations between Syrian and Nabataean merchants and the Aegean.

[125] My conception of the policy of Epiphanes coincides in many points with the brilliant characterization of his activity in Judaea by E. Bickermann, *Der Gott der Makkabäer*, 1937. The bas-relief from Dura is reproduced and discussed by F. E. Brown, *Report* VII–VIII, pp. 258 ff., and by myself in *Dura-Europos and its Art*, 1938, p. 78 and p. 84, cf. my article 'Le Gad de Doura et Seleucus Nicator', *Mél. syr. R. Dussaud*, 1938, pp. 281 ff. On the statues of Zeus Olympius and Epiphanes in the *temenos* of Zion, Porphyrius in Hier. *ad Dan.* viii. 5, cf. viii. 13, viii. 14, and xi. 37; Bickermann, loc cit., p. 102, cf. Posidonius, *F. Gr. Hist.* 87, fr. 109, 4; Bickermann, loc. cit., p. 106. I am inclined to think that the author of 1 Macc. (i. 41) was right in his account of the general trend of Epiphanes' policy. He of course simpli-

fies and generalizes it, but the general tendency was unmistakable for one who may have been an eye-witness of the events. As regards the activity and mood of Epiphanes after the Egyptian expedition I agree with the views expressed by W. W. Tarn, *The Greeks in Bactria and India*, pp. 182 ff. (against W. Otto, *Zur Geschichte der Zeit des 6. Ptolemäers*); Tarn gives a brilliant picture of Epiphanes as a king of great ideas and great strength. That Epiphanes acted in concert with Eucratides is very probable, though Tarn's reasons for representing Eucratides as an agent and general of Epiphanes are not convincing. The greatest difficulty in accepting Tarn's view is that Eucratides appears in Bactria as a completely independent king.

A valuable survey of modern conceptions of the character and activity of Epiphanes and some general considerations on the trend of his policy will be found in F. Reuter, *Beiträge zur Beurteilung des Königs Antiochos Epiphanes*, Diss. Münster, 1938. I cannot, however, agree with the author's contention that the policy of Epiphanes was utterly different from that of Seleucus IV, the latter endeavouring to create a Panhellenistic alliance against Rome, the former trying to establish a *modus vivendi* between his Asiatic kingdom and Rome and to remodel his kingdom on Roman lines. The evidence is too scanty to support this view.

[126] On Philopator's rule see E. Bevan, *A History of Egypt*, 1927, pp. 217 ff.; P. Jouguet, *L'Égypte ptolémaïque*, 1933, pp. 61 ff., cf. S. L. Wallace, 'Census and Poll-tax in Ptolemaic Egypt', *Am. J. Ph.* lix (1938), pp. 418 ff.

[127] See the article by Wallace quoted in the preceding note. No new fiscal devices can be detected in the letter of Theogenes, *dioecetes* of Philopator (cf. *Teb.* 705), found at Edfu (Apollinopolis) and recently published, J. Manteuffel, *Fouilles franco-polonaises* (of Edfu), 1939, ch. iii, p. 140, and pl. xviii (P. Edfou no. 5), cf. C. Préaux, *Chr. d'Ég.*, xxviii (1939), pp. 386 ff.

[128] The earliest reference to the ἴδιος λόγος will be found in *Teb.* 874 of 179 B.C.; before the publication of this document the earliest mention of it was to be found in *B.G.U.* 992; Wilcken, *Chrest.* 162 (of 162 B.C.), cf. *S.B.* i. 4512, 5, 6 (167–134 B.C.). On the chief of this department, who also was known as ἴδιος λόγος, and his sphere of activity, U. Wilcken, *Grundz.*, pp. 146 ff.; G. Plaumann, *P.W.K.* ix. 882 ff., and *Berl. Abh.* 1918, no. 17 (published in 1919). Ἴδια as *terminus technicus* designating the *res privata* of the king, below, n. 151.

[129] On the civil war of the time of Philopator see the careful study of C. Préaux, 'Esquisse d'une histoire des révolutions égyptiennes sous les Lagides', *Chr. d'Ég.* xxii (1936), pp. 526 ff. On the attitude of the temples during the revolt, W. Otto, *Priester und Tempel*, ii, 1908, pp. 307 ff., and especially the decree of Rosetta, *O.G.I.* 90, l. 27, cf. the decree of Memphis quoted in the following note. Mlle Préaux gives in her article a full survey of the sources and a complete bibliography.

[130] See the trilingual decree of the priests of Egypt voted at Memphis, of 217 B.C.; fragments of two copies of it have been recently found and

published, *S.E.G.* viii, 467 and 504 a (with bibliography). The decree of 217 B.C. is based on a royal proclamation issued after the war and the victory of Raphia. From this document the priests quote freely. We have such a quotation without doubt in the passage to which I refer in the text, *S.E.G.* viii. 467, l. 19 f.; after mentioning the gifts to temples the priests say: καίπερ | πολλῆς αὐτῶι δαπάνης γεγενημέ||νης ἐν τῆι στρατείαι καὶ ἐστεφανω|κότος αὐτοῦ τὰς δυνάμεις χρυσῶν | μυριάδων τριάκοντα. The document certainly attests the great consideration shown by the king for the priests. His gifts to them were lavish. They included some new revenues: πρόσοδοι χωρὶς τῶν προανακειμένων. But no essential privileges were granted to them. Such concessions were reserved for his successors. In his proclamation the king certainly gave an account of his campaigns in the Pharaonic style. Mention of rich booty could not be omitted in such an account: it was a *locus communis*. Cf. the fragmentary πρόγραμμα, *B.G.U.* 1212 c, of Philopator which refers to an earlier one of Euergetes I, and the other fragmentary royal orders copied on this sheet of papyrus, perhaps also of Philopator.

[131] Another cause of the gradual decline in the revenue derived by Egypt from its foreign commerce may have been the impoverishment of Greece, the main buyer of corn, its rapidly decreasing buying capacity of which I spoke earlier in this chapter, cf. A. Segré, *Bull. Soc. Arch. Alex.*, xxix (N.S., viii, 3) (1934), pp. 302 ff. Copper standard and inflation: F. Heichelheim, *Wirtsch. Schwank.*, pp. 19 ff. Cf. Mickwitz, 'Inflation', *P.W.K.* Suppl. vi, pp. 127 ff., and the reviews of Heichelheim's book quoted above in Ch. IV, n. 2. I repeat that the evidence on the deterioration of Philopator's silver coinage is slight. Cf. *P. Mich.* iii. 173, and *B.G.U.* 1012, and the dating and interpretation of these documents by F. Heichelheim, *Aeg.* xvii (1937), pp. 61 ff. Valuable evidence on the consequences of Philopator's monetary policy will be found in *Teb.* iii. 1 and 2. See for example the accounts of 210 B.C., *Teb.* 884, and of 200 B.C., *Teb.* 885, cf. 1062 (207 or 190 B.C.) and the later bank accounts of the second century B.C. (the exact date is unknown), *Teb.* 890. The last show that gold and silver coins were treated as bullion and were rated according to the state of preservation of the individual coins.

[132] On Epiphanes' rule see E. Bevan, *A History of Egypt*, 1927, pp. 252 ff.; P. Jouguet, *L'Égypte Ptolémaïque*, pp. 117 ff. On the civil war, the paper of Mlle Préaux quoted in note 129, pp. 532 ff.

[133] *O G.I.* 90, cf. *S.E.G.* viii. 463 and 784, cf. C. Préaux, *Écon. Lag.*, p. 180 f.

[134] I have discussed this topic in a special memoir ' Πλοῖα θαλάσσια on the Nile', *Ét ded. à la mém. d'André Andréades*, 1940, pp. 367 ff., where I have quoted the documents. See especially *Teb.* 856, ll. 11 ff. (171 B.C.), and 890 (second century B.C.), ll. 20, 34, 93, and the later documents *B.G.U.* viii. 1744–6 and 1755, and those published by H. Zilliacus, *Aeg.* xix (1939), pp. 59 ff. On the ναυκληρομάχιμοι below, p. 721. On Comanus and his ship, W. L. Westermann, *Arch. Pap.* xiii (1938), pp. 1 ff. The earliest occurrences of πλοῖα θαλάσσια on the Nile and of ναυκληρομάχιμοι are dated in the

reign of Philometor, but they certainly had ceased to be a novelty at this time. They may go back to Philopator or even to earlier times.

[135] Sir Herbert Thompson, *A family Archive from Siut*, 1934, pp. 26 ff. (deed of apportionment of 174/3 B.C.) and pp. 37 ff. (deed of apportionment of 181/0 B.C.). Take, e.g., item 6. It is described in the early version as : 'together with the ⅓ share of the house which is in the necropolis of Siut with its grounds', while in the later version it is said: 'together with the ⅓ share of the house which is in the necropolis of Siut, which was formerly built (but) which is ruined to-day'. Or item 12: 'the garden open land' (early version) and 'the garden waste land' (the later). Cf. E. Seidl and B. H. Stricker, *Z. d. Sav.-Stift.* lvii (1937), pp. 272 ff.

[136] *S.B.* 5675, cf. U. Wilcken, *Z. d. Sav.-Stift.* xlii (1921), p. 132; my remarks, *Teb.* 703, Intr., p. 69, and E. Berneker, *Die Sondergerichtsbarkeit im griechischen Recht Aegyptens*, 1935, p. 61, cf. C. Préaux, *Écon. Lag.*, p. 522, cf. 549, 555.

[137] *U.P.Z.* 110, ll. 155 ff. On Hippalus, W. Otto, *P.W.K.* viii. 1657, and *Teb.* 895, cf. T. C. Skeat, *Arch. Pap.* xii (1937), pp. 40 ff.; C. Préaux, loc. cit., p. 527. The same man is mentioned in several other documents: *Teb.* 750, 19 (187 or 175 B.C.), 853, 17, and 920, 15. It is interesting to note that in *Teb.* 750 Hippalus appears as an influential man whose σκέπη (patronage) several persons enjoyed, cf. (for σκέπη) the almost contemporary *Teb.* 758. In *Teb.* 895 Hippalus is granting πίστεις (safe conducts) to debtors of the crown. Both σκέπη and πίστεις though of earlier origin (the earliest mention of πίστεις is in 187/6 B.C., *Teb.* 741) played a very important part in the life of Egypt in the second and first centuries B.C., cf. below, Ch. VI, p. 904 f. Note in *U.P.Z.* 110, ll. 159 ff., the description of the motives of those who were supposed to help the government in its evil plight: οἷς ὀφειλόμενόν ἐσ|τι διὰ τὴν πρὸς τὰ πράγματα εὔνοιαν ἀσμένως ἐπιδέξασθαι τὸ προτεινόμενον; cf. the similar expression in *Teb.* 124, 3 ff., and *B.G.U.* 1185, l. 2, and cf. also *Teb.* 703, 134 ff. with my note, and in general on εὔνοια as one of the principal motives supposed to animate the ruler and his assistants in their relations with the ruled and *vice versa*, W. Schubart, *Arch. Pap.* xii (1936–37), pp. 8 ff., and above, Ch. III, n. 15. The practice of Hippalus survived under Philometor and later, though in general more efficient and less gentle methods were used at that time. See *Teb.* 734, two fragments of official reports, one of 141 another of 139 B.C., concerning two cases of ἐπιβολή. In both cases not compulsion but persuasion was used: in one case the cultivation of unproductive land was taken up by βασιλικοὶ γεωργοί of Dinnys, in the other by some grandees (ἐν ὑπεροχῇ ὄντων) of Arsinoe.

[138] Assignment of uncultivated land to new κληροῦχοι or κάτοικοι in the second century, C. Préaux, loc. cit., pp. 470 ff. Renting of substantial pieces of such land (which probably belonged to the class γῆ ἱερά) to temples for long terms, *Teb.* 737 (136 B.C.): χέρσος ἀφορολόγητος and ἄλλος ὑπόλογος rented for a term of 20 years on emphyteutic conditions: five years without rent

(ἀφορί), another five years for a nominal rent, and the last ten years for a higher rent, cf. for later times the inscription of Magdola of 95/4 B.C., *S.B.* 7259; *S.E.G.* viii. 466: piece of land ἱερ[ᾶς] γῆς ἀχρήστων and αἰγιαλός. The case of 136 B.C. was of course not the first of its type. *Doreai*—below, n. 150ᵃ.

[139] C. B. Welles, *A.J.A.* xli (1937), p. 509, cf. *Teb.* 886 (about the same year, 182 B.C.), account of agricultural expenditure in which wages paid to the labourers are still calculated at the rate 1 to 60, cf. *P. Mich.* iii. 200. The years about 182 B.C. were apparently decisive years in the history of inflation, cf. the bank accounts, *Teb.* 890.

[140] On Antiochus IV in Egypt see the fragment of his edict (πρόσταγμα), *Teb.* 698, cf. U. Wilcken, *Arch. Pap.* xi (1935), p. 146; K. Fr. W. Schmidt, *Phil. Woch.* liv (1934), p. 1304, and esp. W. Otto, 'Zur Geschichte der Zeit des 6. Ptolemäers', *Bay. Abh.* xi (1934), pp. 54 ff.; and C. Préaux, loc. cit., pp. 491 ff. On the devastation of Egypt by the soldiers of Antiochus IV, probably during his second campaign, *Teb.* 781, cf. Wilcken, loc. cit., p. 147. See also Hier. *ad Dan.* xi. 21, and Otto, loc. cit., p. 57. Cf. A. Passerini, 'Roma e l'Egitto durante la terza guerra Macedonica', *Athen.* xiii (1935), pp. 317 ff., and F. Hampl, *Gnomon,* xii (1936), pp. 30 ff. On the time of Philometor in general, P. Jouguet, 'Les débuts du règne de Ptolémée Philométor etc.' *Rev. Phil.* xi (63) (1937), pp. 193 ff., and 'Eulaeos et Lenaeos', *Bull. Inst. d'Égypte,* xix (1937), pp. 157 ff.

[141] The date of the revolt of Dionysius Petosarapis and its character, W. Otto, loc. cit., p. 3, n. 6, and pp. 71 and 91. On the revolt in the Thebaid of 165/4 B.C., Diod. xxxi. 17 b. Two graffiti found in the temple of Abydos, of which one mentions the (Nubian) king Hurgonaphor, may be assigned not to the reign of Epiphanes, but to the time of the joint rule of the two kings and of the queen, i.e. to 164/3 B.C., see P. Lacau, *Études de Pap.* ii (1934), pp. 229 ff., and P. Jouguet, *Mél. O. Navarre,* 1935, pp. 265 ff.

[142] The ἐντολαί of Herodes and the accompanying documents, U. Wilcken, *U.P.Z.* 110, with excellent introduction and comments, cf. my *Kolonat,* pp. 55 ff., and C. Préaux, *Écon. Lag.,* pp. 504 ff., cf. 565, n. 4. The reduction of rent mentioned in l. 28 may be compared with the κουφισμός of the rent of royal land granted by the *hypodioecetes* Sarapion (*U.P.Z.* 22, cf. *Teb.* 807) in 162 B.C. (Sarapion may have become *dioecetes* some years later, *Teb.* 732 and 743) and the *dioecetes* Ptolemy, *Teb.* 72. 443 ff., to the cultivators of royal land in the Fayum, cf. my *Kolonat,* pp. 33 ff. On the ἀποσκευαί, above, Ch. III, n. 17. The attitude of the population towards various forms of liturgy imposed both on the Greeks and the natives: *B.G.U.* 1256; Hunt-Edgar, *Sel. Pap.* ii. 275 (lampadarchy imposed on a cleruch), and *Teb.* 731 dating 153 or 142 B.C. (γενηματοφυλακία). Escaping the liturgies by becoming soldiers, *U.P.Z.* 110, l. 161: μηδεὶς ἐαθῇ στρατεύεσθαι. On the μάχιμοι after Raphia, J. Lesquier, *Inst. mil.* &c., pp. 7 ff.; U. Wilcken, loc. cit., Introd. and note to ll. 10–23; *Teb.* 703, ll. 215 ff., and my comments; G. T. Griffith, *The mercenaries* &c., pp. 112 ff. Lesquier was still of the opinion that μάχιμοι of the usual type of

non-Egyptian origin, i.e. 'Greeks', do not appear in Egypt before the first century B.C. But Pamphylian horse styled μάχιμοι (with Greek names) appear in an unpublished document of 170 B.C., soon to be published by Dr. F. M. Heichelheim in *Ryl.* iv. The document shows that after Raphia Philopator and his successors made little distinction between native and foreign settled soldiers, provided they could have them at a low cost. See below, n. 150.

[143] On the first of these documents see the remarks of C. Préaux, loc. cit., pp. 492 and 496 ff. It is possible that Ammonion of Moeris was not a purely Egyptian sanctuary but the sanctuary of Zeus Ammon, the great god of Alexander.

[144] P. Baraize published by P. Collart et P. Jouguet, *Ét. de Pap.* ii (1934), pp. 23 ff., cf. U. Wilcken, *Arch. Pap.* xi (1935), p. 292 f. The case of the house which once belonged to Ptolemy, the father of the famous Hermias, was probably similar. During the revolt of the Thebaid under Epiphanes the house was destroyed and the ruins occupied or bought from the new government by an Egyptian family, see U. Wilcken, *U.P.Z.* ii. 1935, p. 44.

[145] On Ptolemy the recluse and his father and brothers see U. Wilcken, *U.P.Z.* i. pp. 104 ff., cf. A. Calderini, *Aeg.* xiii (1933), pp. 674 ff., and N. J. Reich, *Mizraim*, i (1933), pp. 9 ff. I cannot discuss here the difficult problem of the ἐγκάτοχοι. It is certain that they were god-possessed devotees of Sarapis who lived in the sanctuary of the god and were 'bound' by Sarapis, i.e. confined to the περίβολος of the sanctuary for the time of their κατοχή. The history of the problem will be found in U. Wilcken, *U.P.Z.* i. pp. 52 ff. cf. p. 295 against F. von Woess, 'Das Asylwesen Aegyptens' &c., 1923 (*Münch. Beitr.* 5), and p. 651, reply to F. von Woess, *Z. d. Sav.-Stift.* xlvi (1926), pp. 56 ff. Cf. G. Heuser, *Die κατοχή im Serapieion bei Memphis*, 1935. See also L. Wenger, *Arch. f. Kulturgeschichte*, xxviii (1938), pp. 114 ff., and F. Cumont, *L'Égypte des Astrologues*, 1937, pp. 148 ff.

The theory of Wilcken seems to be now generally accepted, see e.g. A. D. Nock, *Conversion*, 1933, p. 80 and p. 153 and L. Wenger, loc. cit. It is interesting to note, as a clue to the psychology of Ptolemy, that Apollonius, his younger brother, became an ἐγκάτοχος for a short time just before he became an active soldier. To become either ἐγκάτοχος or soldier was perhaps the choice open to those who sought for more or less security in life. Apollonius chose first the former alternative, then the latter. Had he a free choice? He and Ptolemy made every possible effort to obtain the appointment. Was it the appointment itself that they aimed at or permission for Apollonius to be a soldier and at the same time to remain a resident of the Sarapeum? See U. Wilcken, *U.P.Z.* i, pp. 113 ff. On the anti-Greek attitude of the Egyptians residing in the Sarapeum, during and soon after the ἀπόστασις, *U.P.Z.* 7, 13 (163 B.C.), and 8, 14 (161 B.C.), cf. 15, 17 (158 B.C.). An eloquent testimony to the difficult situation in which many highly educated men of the privileged class found themselves in the troubled times of Philometor's reign will be found in the copy of a letter, *U.P.Z.* 144. The author of the letter, addressed to an unfaithful friend, speaks of poverty and bad luck, almost of hunger. He hopes for better times, 40 ff.: μετὰ τὴν | τῶν πραγμάτων νυνεὶ ἀποκατάστασιν.

¹⁴⁶ *U.P.Z.* 111, cf. the Delian decree, *O.G.I.* 116; M. Holleaux, *Arch. Pap.* vi (1918), p. 10 f.; Durrbach, *Choix*, p. 157 (remarks on the decree *O.G.I.* 116 apropos of a similar decree connected with the same events, Holleaux, loc. cit., pp. 9 ff.; Durrbach, *Choix*, 92; *Inscr. de Délos* 1517). Cf. *Teb.* 739, 40; W. Otto und H. Bengston, 'Zur Geschichte des Niederganges des Ptolemäer-reiches', *Bay. Abh.* xvii (1938), p. 26, n. 4.

¹⁴⁷ P. Collart, *Atti IV Congr. Pap.*, p. 70, mentions an unpublished papyrus of the Sorbonne of the fifth year of Euergetes II relating to συγγεγραμμένοι [ἐν τ]οῖς ἐν τῆι Ἀραβίαι φρουρ[ίοις]. Were the φρούρια frontier posts of a military character or a chain of gendarmes' posts with military and police functions?

¹⁴⁸ The position of the tax-farmers and of their ἔγγυοι (guarantors) is illustrated by the so-called Zois papyri (*U.P.Z.* 114, 150–148 B.C.). We see how easily a tax-farmer became bankrupt, and the consequences of his bankruptcy for his guarantors.

¹⁴⁹ I have collected the material bearing on these measures (mostly from the land registers of Cerceosiris, *Teb.* vol. i) in my *Kolonat*, pp. 30 ff. Since the publication of this book new material has constantly accumulated, material mostly of an earlier or of a later time than the land registers of Cerceosiris. This new material has been fully used by Mlle Préaux, *Écon. Lag.*, pp. 491 ff. I have quoted above (p. 717, n. 137) some of the documents on ἐπιβολή and κουφισμός, on the renting κατὰ τὴν ἀρετήν or ἐξ ἀξίας (cf. *Teb.* 710), and on emphyteutic (cf. *Teb.* 807) and long term leases sometimes taken by temples collectively (n. 138). The reader will easily find supplementary material in *Teb.* iii. 1 and 2. On ἀρετή as a technical term, *Teb.* 5, 146 and 165, cf. 787, 9.

¹⁵⁰ On the evolution of the *cleruchy* C. Préaux, *Éc. Lag.*, pp. 463 ff., cf. U. Wilcken, *Grundz.*, p. 385. On the μάχιμοι and their *kleroi* above, note 142. We cannot date exactly the practice of granting land to the new μάχιμοι. There is, however, very little doubt that the first to do so was Philopator. *U.P.Z.* 110 shows that at the time of Philometor the number of settled μάχιμοι was large and that their *kleroi* had long been in their possession. It is natural that in the difficult times of Epiphanes and Philometor many λαοί should have been added to the number of those who held *kleroi* in the time of Philopator, i.e. that it should have been a constant practice of the government to increase the native settled army.

¹⁵⁰ᵃ On the *doreai* see the valuable remarks of W. L. Westermann on *P. Col. Inv.* 228 (in the forthcoming volume *P. Columbia*, iv), by W. L. Westermann, C. W. Keyes, and H. Liebesny, and his tabulation and study of the money-*doreai* of Ptolemaic Egypt. Among them he lists the *dorea* of *Teb.*

773. Cf. the interesting documents *P. Mich.* 182 (182 B.C.), cf. 183, 193, and 200 which require renewed study (land ἐν βασιλικῆι καὶ [ἐν] δωρεᾶι).

[151] Important information on the growth of private property in Egypt was yielded recently by the Columbia papyrus quoted in the preceding note. I cannot enter here into a discussion of this interesting papyrus. Its date is uncertain. Between the two dates suggested by the editors: Euergetes I or Epiphanes, I am inclined to choose the latter. The document is a *prostagma* of the king, apparently supplementary to one previously published. It deals in my opinion with declarations of property for the collection of a tax of 2 per cent. imposed on the owners of οὐσίαι (land in private property?) in and around Alexandria and in the *chora* and levied in money. The income of this tax went as *dorea* in Alexandria to the priests, perhaps of a new dynastic cult, in the *chora* to other holders of the *dorea*. The rapid growth of private land property was at the time of the *prostagma* apparently a new phenomenon. The question of taxation of this land was a new problem. It was solved by the introduction of a new and rather heavy tax assessed on the basis either of the income yielded by the property or of the total value of the estate.

The first inscription, that of Psenamosis: E. Breccia, *Bull. Soc. Arch. Alex.* xxvi (*N.S.* vii. 1) (1929), pp. 66 ff.; *S.B.* 7457; *S.E.G.* viii. 529. The second, that of Psenemphaia: O. Guéraud, *Bull. Soc. Arch. Alex.* xxxii (*N.S.* x. 1) (1938), pp. 21 ff. The third: *Arch. Pap.* v (1913), p. 162, no. 8, cf. p. 227. Cf. *Mém. Inst. Fr. Arch. Or.* lxvii (1934–7), p. 40, n. 5, and *B.G.U.* 1188. It seems to me very probable that the συγγέωργοι of Psenamosis were owners of vine-estates. This is suggested by the term κτήσεις and by the fact that they chose the time of vintage for a special celebration (ἐν τῶι Μεσορὴ ἐπὶ τοῦ τρυγήτου). I do not think that the owners of these κτήσεις were modest farmers residing in the above-named villages and enlivening their dull peasant lives with common banquets and celebrations (this is the opinion of Guéraud, loc. cit., p. 26). In the present case I am rather inclined to assume that the συγγέωργοι were residents in Alexandria who had invested part of their money in land, especially in vine-estates. In an inscription of 69 B.C. (unpublished) is mentioned a σύνοδος γεωργῶν ἰδίων. Dr. F. M. Heichelheim, who has shown me this inscription and will publish it, compares ἰδίων (ἐδαφῶν) with the ἴδια (private possessions of the king) mentioned in Ps. Arist. *Oecon.* ii (above, p. 444). The γεωργοί of the inscription would then be tillers of the land privately owned by the king. I am rather inclined to connect ἰδίων with γεωργῶν, some γεωργοί, i.e. landowners (like the συγγέωργοι or γεοῦχοι of the neighbourhood of Alexandria), having formed a club or association. Cf. the club of the god Sobk at Tebtunis, *P. Cairo dem.* 30618, col. i (138/7 B.C.); M. San Nicolò, *Aeg. Vereinsw.* ii, 1, 1915, p. 166. Similar to the γεοῦχοι and perhaps classed with them were the landowners in the South, at Pathyris, of whom I spoke above, Ch. IV, p. 257. Their economic life and social standing have been recently illuminated by the find of the records of one of them and his family, Horus, son of Nechontes, a thoroughly egyptianized 'Perses' or 'Ionian', for a long time in the military service. He was born in the middle of the second century, and after the end of his military service became a hereditary tenant of the γῆ ἱερά of this region. We can follow his and his family's economic life, concentrated on the cultivation of the aforesaid sacred land for several years. See Addenda to Ch. IV n. 92 at the end of this book.

152 On the inflation of the time of Philometor, F. M. Heichelheim, *Wirtsch. Schwank.*, pp. 29 ff. Heichelheim and Oertel, *Z. d. Sav.-Stift.* li (1931), p. 573, are inclined to ascribe this inflation to the Roman activity in the East; against this view, T. Frank, *An Econ. Survey of Ancient Rome*, i, p. 147, and W. Otto, *Bay. Abh.* xi (1934), pp. 25 ff. Otto suggests that the inflation was due to the mismanagement of Egypt by Eulaeus and Lenaeus. I regard this explanation as too narrow. On the profit drawn by the Government from its policy of inflation, see Heichelheim, pp. 32, 104. The contention is based on the few cases of *adaeratio* of the military salary, esp. on the case of Apollonius, brother of Ptolemy the recluse (*U.P.Z.* 14, cf. *Theb. Akten.* vi, and *Teb.* 723, 6–7). It must be noted, however, that Ptolemy in his requests insisted upon the fact that Apollonius' appointment would be of great assistance to himself, for Apollonius would then be able to support him. Why should he say this if the salary of Apollonius was insufficient even to save him from hunger? ('Beträchtlich unterhalb des von uns angesetzten kulturellen Existenzminimum', says Heichelheim.) Or was he concealing his real aims? There are some factors in the case of Apollonius which we do not fully understand. Silver and gold coins were still in circulation in Egypt in the second century B.C., e.g. *Teb.* 735, 739, 743, 809, and esp. the bank account 890, but were treated as bullion. Note that in 739 (163 or 145 B.C.) a gold stater of Phocaea was offered, together with silver, in payment for taxes collected from catoecic land, cf. J. G. Milne, *J.E.A.* xx (1934), pp. 193 ff. The situation as we find it in Egypt in the second and first centuries B.C. appears to me very similar to that which is characteristic of modern China. Not being a specialist in modern currency problems, I consulted the late Prof. James Harvey Rogers of Yale University, formerly special representative of the United States Treasury in China, Japan, and India. He was kind enough to formulate for my use some fundamental facts bearing on the question. I quote his letter of November 26, 1938: 'While well-documented cases are difficult to find, many of the war-lords of China seem to have pursued monetary policies of the following kind:

(1) The currency of sections of the country conquered by the war-lord has been debased by reducing the fineness of the standard silver coins.

(2) The weight has been reduced.

(3) The silver has frequently been displaced by circulating notes.

In each case the profit taken has gone largely to the coffers of the war-lord himself.

Fractional silver coins have frequently been treated in the same way, and minor coins, which in the beginning have almost always been issued at a profit (i.e. the weight of the metal included in them has been worth less as metal than as coin), have usually been increased by the war-lord to such an extent as to cause them to decline greatly in value with respect to the silver coins.'

CHAPTER VI

1 The material relating to the Roman method of conducting war in the struggle against Perseus and to the treatment of Greece after that war will be found in G. Colin, *Rome et la Grèce de 200 à 146 av. J.C.*, 1905, pp. 406 ff. (conduct of war) and pp. 447 ff. (measures taken by the Romans after the war). On the treatment of Aetolia, Epirus, and Acarnania, ibid., pp. 448 ff. Cf. A. Nikitsky, *Journ. of the Board of Publ. Educ.*, 1906, April, pp. 174 ff. (in Russian) and the short remarks of Larsen, 'Roman Greece', p. 291 f. Haliartus and Coronea in Boeotia—note the two Coronean girls manumitted at Delphi about 148 B.C., *F.D.* iii. 3 (1932), no. 5, and *G.D.I.* ii. 2288, cf. Liv. xlii. 63; Strabo, ix. 2. 30, p. 411; also the Aetolian girl, *F.D.* iii. 3, no. 9 (about 157 B.C.), and *G.D.I.* ii. 2167, 2172; Westermann, *P.W.K.* Suppl. vi. 930)— many villages in Greece, Chalcis in Euboea (Liv. xliii. 7), Abdera (Liv. xliii. 4) fell victims to the greed and indiscipline of the Roman commanders and Roman soldiers. I remind the reader also of the heavy contribution imposed on Athens (above, p. 629 f.). It should be noted that the Senate as a rule was not in sympathy with such measures. It tried, for example, to undo the ruthless measures taken against Coronea and Abdera. The case of Abdera and its neighbour the Thracian king Cotys is well known. After the war there was a dispute between king Cotys and Abdera which was discussed before the Senate, Abdera being represented by its ambassadors, Teians by origin (Teos was the metropolis of Abdera). Who emerged victorious from the conflict we do not know. See the decree of Abdera in honour of the ambassadors *S.I.G.*³ 656; *I.G.R.* iv. 1558, discussed at length by Colin, loc. cit., pp. 493 ff., and others, the last and best discussion being that of L. Robert, *B.C.H.* lix (1935), pp. 507 ff. (with full bibliography).

2 Polyb. xxx. 15; Liv. xlv. 34; Plut. *Aem. Paul.* 29; Cross, *Epirus*, p. 99 f.; Holleaux, *C.A.H.* viii, p. 272 f.; Larsen, 'Rom. Greece', p. 302, who endeavours to minimize the effects of Roman pillage. The results—devastation and depopulation of the country—are described by Strabo, vii. 7. 8–9, p. 327, esp. 9: νῦν δὲ τὰ πολλὰ μὲν ἐρημία κατέχει, τὰ δ' οἰκούμενα κωμηδὸν καὶ ἐν ἐρειπίοις λείπεται.

3 A detailed analysis of the sources will be found not in the art. 'Korinthos', *P.W.K.* Suppl. iv. 1003 (Lenschau), but in Münzer's article 'Mummius' (7 a in the Nachträge), ibid. xvi. 1197 ff. Cf. the short remarks of Larsen, op. cit., pp. 203 ff., who does not quote the article by Münzer. The behaviour of the soldiers and commanders during and after the Achaean war was no better than during and after the Persean war, see G. Colin, *Rome et la Grèce*, pp. 625 ff.

4 For the results and the social and economic background of the Achaean war I may remind the reader of the well-known descriptions of Diodorus and Polybius. Diod. xxxii. 26. 2 and 3 (146 B.C.): οἱ δὲ [οἱ Ἀχαιοί] ἐν ὀφθαλμοῖς ἰδόντες συγγενῶν καὶ φίλων σφαγὰς καὶ πελεκισμοὺς καὶ πατρίδων ἁλώσεις καὶ

ἁρπαγὰς καὶ πανδήμους μεθ᾽ ὕβρεως ἀνδραποδισμούς, καὶ τὸ σύνολον τὴν ἐλευθερίαν καὶ τὴν παρρησίαν ἀποβαλόντες, μεγίστων ἀγαθῶν ἠλλάξαντο τὰς ἐσχάτας συμφοράς. Diodorus ((drawing on Polybius) lays the blame on the στρατηγοί and their demagogic line of action: καὶ χρεῶν ἀποκοπὰς εἰσηγοῦντο, καὶ πολλοὺς τῶν ἀπόρων χρεωφειλετῶν ἔχοντες συνεργοὺς ἀνέσειον τὰ πλήθη, τινὲς δὲ καὶ δι᾽ ἀφροσύνην ἐνέπεσον εἰς ἀπεγνωσμένους διαλογισμούς. Polybius (xxxviii. 15) gives approximately the same picture and emphasizes especially the compulsory supply of twelve thousand adult male slaves 'home-born and home-bred' (τῶν οἰκογενῶν καὶ παρατρόφων) to the army by the city *bourgeoisie* of the Achaean League. This limitation to home-bred slaves was dictated by the desire to have in the army not barbarians or half-barbarians but thoroughly hellenized men. The twelve thousand represented of course a small minority of the slaves in the possession of the *bourgeoisie*. The rest naturally, in view of the prospect of liberation, did not keep quiet and made the situation of the well-to-do classes, oppressed by heavy contributions, uncertain and dangerous.

[5] On Athens' situation after the Persean war see Jebelev, *H.A.*, pp. 187 ff., and Ferguson, *H.A.*, pp. 312 ff., chs. viii: 'Athens and Rome', and ix: 'Athens and Delos'. Cf. J. Hatzfeld, *Les Trafiquants italiens dans l'Orient hellénique*, 1919, pp. 41 ff.

[6] As is well known, the best and fullest picture of Delos after the Persean war was drawn years ago by P. Roussel, *Délos, colonie athénienne*, 1916, and still holds good. Cf. a summary in W. A. Laidlaw, *A History of Delos*, 1933, pp. 169 ff., and a still shorter one in *C.A.H.* viii, pp. 643 ff. (with bibliography). Interesting evidence on the early period of the Athenian cleruchy has been discussed by P. Roussel, *B.C.H.* lviii (1934), pp. 96 ff. On the pottery found at Delos, above, Ch. V, n. 68 and below n. 63. It is not certain that the Megarian bowls, portable ovens, incense-burners, &c., found in large quantities at Delos are of local manufacture. However, even if they were imported, it was not from Athens that they came.

[7] On the coinage of Athens, Ch. Seltman, *Greek Coins*, p. 261, J. P. Shear, *Hesp.* ii (1933), pp. 255 ff. and M. L. Kambanis' articles quoted above, Ch. V, n. 36, cf. Larsen, 'Rom. Greece', pp. 326 ff. On the coins which were in use in Delos in the time of her independence, see P. Roussel, *Délos, col. ath.*, pp. 168 ff., and Durrbach–Roussel, *Inscr. de Délos*, 1432 B b. i, 1–62, and B a. ii, 1–26 (note of the editors p. 122). The reserve fund of the period of independence was still intact after 167 B.C. No attempt was made to replace by Athenian currency the various coins (mostly Histiaean and Rhodian) kept in the στάμνοι which contained this old reserve fund. The new gifts which were contributed by the pilgrims after 167 B.C., and were taken out of the θησαυροί (collection boxes) every year, consisted of all sorts of coins: Athenian coins of the new style (see M. N. Tod, *J.H.S.* liv (1934), p. 155), Alexandrian, Ephesian, συμμαχικά, Roman, &c. (some of these coins cannot be identified), see *Inscr. de Délos*, 1432 C, cf. 1421 A b. i, 1–15. This gives us an excellent idea of the variety of coins which circulated in Greece after 167 B.C. However, the Athenian government changed into its own currency

the coins which it took out of the θησαυροί to keep as reserve capital. In general the Athenian magistrates did not encourage the circulation of foreign coins in Delos. This is shown by the many coin-hoards found at Delos: the majority of them consist of Athenian coins of the new style (Noe², nos. 303–6, 308–13, 315, 316, 318, 319; cf. P. Roussel, *Délos, col. ath.*, p. 48, n. 4). Interesting is the much later hoard, Noe², no. 307 (cf. J. N. Svoronos, *Journ. Int. Arch. Num.* ix (1906), p. 302) which consisted of one denarius of Juba I and 649 Roman Republican denarii.

[8] On the coin circulation in Syria under Epiphanes and his immediate successors, see above Ch. V, pp. 665 ff., n. 71 and my article in *Anatolian Studies pres. to W. H. Buckler* quoted above. The most characteristic hoard is that of Til Barsib, Thureau-Dangin et Dunand, *Til Barsib*, p. 81, with several Athenian 'owls' (not listed in Noe). On the Arabian imitations of Athenian 'owls' of the new style, G. F. Hill, *B.M.C., Arabia,* &c., pp. liv ff.; Ch. Seltman, *Greek Coins*, p. 262. Cf. my article in the volume in honour of Buckler.

[9] Hoards of Athenian 'owls' of the new style: Noe² lists: Carystos (Euboea) (no. 212), Halmyros (Thessaly) (no. 478), Hierapytna (Crete) (no. 433, cf. E. J. P. Raven, *Num. Chr.* lxxi (1938), pp. 133 ff.), unknown place in Crete (no. 282), unpublished hoard from Crete (Raven, loc. cit., p. 152, n. 37), Salonica (Macedonia) (no. 1184, cf. M. L. Kambanis, *B.C.H.* lviii (1934), pp. 131 ff., and ibid. lix (1935), pp. 101 ff., 108 ff.). The Aenianes of Hypata in Thessaly 'produced (about 168 B.C.) a copy of the Pheidian Athena head on their didrachms', Seltman, loc. cit., p. 262. The Amphictionic law of the end of the second century B.C., *S.I.G.³* 729, and *F.D.* iii. 2. 139; text and translation but no comments in Larsen, 'Rom. Greece', p. 382. The standard work on this law is still Th. Reinach, 'L'Anarchie monétaire et ses remèdes chez les anciens Grecs', *Mém. de l'Ac. d. Inscr.* xxxviii. 2, pp. 351 ff., cf. B. Keil, *Z.N.* xxxii (1915), pp. 56 ff. In his paper Reinach gives a general picture of the monetary circulation of the Hellenistic world in the first century B.C. According to Keil, the Amphictionic law was directed especially against the competition of Roman currency with the Athenian. Against Keil and the date 96–95 B.C., G. Daux, *Delphes au IIᵉ et au Iᵉʳ siècle*, pp. 387 ff. It is tempting to compare with the Amphictionic law about the Athenian currency the well-known Athenian decree regulating Athenian weights and measures, *I.G.* ii². 1013 (copy of Fourmont), cf. B. D. Meritt, *Hesp.* vii (1938), pp. 127 ff., no. 27—a fragment of another copy of the same decree (new restorations). O. Viedebantt, *Hermes*, li (1916), pp. 120 ff., esp. pp. 143 ff., has pointed out the similarity of the two measures, and in fact it is more than probable that the Athenian law was a direct outcome of the Athenian commercial policy of the time. It was in the interest of Athens that its weights and measures both in internal and in external trade should be as reliable as its coinage. Some changes in the standard may be explained by the desire to facilitate the use of Athenian weights and measures by the Italian merchants. Cf. below, n. 14.

Reverting to the part played by the 'owls' in the economic life of Greece during the first century B.C., I may quote again the hoard of Hierapytna mentioned above (on which see E. J. P. Raven, *Num. Chr.* lxxi (1938), pp. 133 ff.). It gives an excellent idea of the circulation of coins in the late second and the early first century B.C. down to the time of the civil wars. In this rich hoard alongside of Cretan silver, including imitations of Athenian coins (a revival of Cretan coinage due to the share taken by the Cretans in the piracy of the time), the leading currencies are the Athenian silver of the new style, the *cistophori*, and the Roman *denarii*, together with some remnants of the Achaean silver. The Cretan imitations of Athenian silver may have been partly due to a certain shortage of the latter owing to the slave revolt of about 100 B.C. and later to the siege by Sulla, but in the main they furnish evidence of the popularity of the Athenian 'owls' on the Aegean market. Another proof of this is the minting in Greece by Lucullus and Sulla in 87 B.C. of silver tetradrachms of Athenian type, the so-called Λουκούλλειον νόμισμα or πλάτη Λευκόλλεια (below, Ch. VII, n. 7).

[10] Rhodian stamped jar-handles found at Athens in the excavations of the Agora: V. Grace, *Hesp.* iii (1934), pp. 200 ff., cf. M. Rostovtzeff, *C.A.H.* viii, p. 629. The Cnidian stamped jars have been little studied. Their chronological sequence is little known. According to Miss Grace, loc. cit., pp. 241 ff., the majority of the Cnidian jars found at Athens belong to the late third and early second centuries B.C. (66 types as contrasted with 11 types of the second–first centuries B.C.). At this time Cnidus was no longer in the hands of the Ptolemies but formed part first of the sphere of influence and later of the dominions of Rhodes. Above, Ch. V, n. 109. Cf. Addendum to this note.

[11] It is interesting to compare the circulation in the northern Balkan lands of the Thasian and Maronean coins with that of the Athenian. I have listed the hoards of Athenian coins above (n. 9). Much longer is the list of hoards of Macedonian, Thasian, and Maronean coins and their local imitations found in the northern regions of the Balkan peninsula. I cannot produce it here, but the reader may consult the Index to the second edition of Noe's book. Most of them were found in Bulgaria (I have counted 26 hoards). Next comes Rumania (with 12 hoards), then Hungary, Serbia, and Turkey. Still larger are the numbers of Macedonian, Maronean, and Thasian coins found in the ruins of the cities of the Danubian countries and of the northern Balkan lands in general, see V. Parvan, *Dacia*, 1928, pp. 98 ff. On the Macedonian coins see Larsen, 'Rom. Greece', p. 328 (no mention of the Thasian and Maronean coins). On the Thasian and Maronean coins, Head, *H.N.*[2], pp. 251 and 263; F. Hiller von Gaertringen, *P.W.K.* v A. 1318 ff.; K. Regling, ibid. xv. 475 ff. On the Thracian and Celtic imitations, R. Forrer, *Keltische Numismatik der Rhein- und Donaulande*, 1908 (cf. below, n. 30.) On the *cistophori*, above, Ch. V, n. 70; on the Rhodian modest drachmas subsequent to 166 which followed its pretentious coinage after 189 B.C., Head, loc. cit., p. 640.

[12] Some facts may be quoted to illustrate the part played by commerce in the life of Athens in the late second century B.C. An Athenian inscription of 112/1 B.C. (*S.I.G.*[3] 706) shows that the foreign ναύκληροι and ἔμποροι of Athens

were influential enough to have their own Athenian πρόξενος, who at the same time was ἐπιμελητὴς ἐπὶ τὸν λιμένα, and to honour him, with the approval of the βουλή of the city. The foreign shipowners and merchants of Athens formed a religious σύνοδος, a curious combination of professional and religious association similar to those of Delos. The economic dependence of the leading families of Athens on the rich foreigners of Delos is reflected in an interesting fact. The strongly nationalistic government of Athens insisted for a long time on admitting as Athenian ephebes Athenian citizens only. The lists of ephebes of 128/7 B.C. (S. Dow, *Hesp.* iv (1935), pp. 71 ff., n. 37) and of 123/2 (*I.G.* ii.² 1006) show no admixture of foreigners. It is in 119/8 B.C. that the first group of 17 foreigners appears in the list (*I.G.* ii². 1008), and from that time foreigners are regular members of the Athenian epheby. See W. S. Ferguson, *H.A.*, pp. 415 ff., esp. p. 418; O. W. Reinmuth, *The Foreigners in the Athenian Ephebia*, 1929, and S. Dow, loc. cit. It is evident that the Athenian aristocracy was forced to yield to the pressure of the Delian plutocracy of Syrian and Italian merchants. Note the presence (temporary or permanent) of many Italians at Athens in the period under review, J. Hatzfeld, *Les Trafiquants* &c., pp. 41 ff.

¹³ On the find of Mahdia: A. Merlin et L. Poinssot, 'Cratères et candélabres de marbre trouvés en mer près de Mahdia', *Notes et Documents publiés par la Dir. des Ant. et Arts*, Gouv. Tunisien, vol. ix, 1930. The authors date the sinking of the ship shortly after 86 B.C. (the date of the capture and sack of Athens by Sulla). In discussing the candelabra and *crateres* of Mahdia they quote identical and similar objects found in Italy and elsewhere. Cf. the publication of the Attic inscriptions of this find by A. Dain, *R.E.G.* xliv (1931), pp. 290 ff., and *Inscriptions grecques du Musée du Bardo*, 1938, pp. 9 ff. On the find of Anticythera, O. Rubensohn, 'Parische Künstler', *J.D.A.I.* l (1935), pp. 50 ff. In this article will be found a good bibliography. Add to it Ch. Picard, *Sculpture antique*, ii, 1926, p. 218, and W. Deonna, in Dar. et Saglio, *Dict. des Ant.* iv, p. 1501. A. Köster, *Das antike Seewesen*, 1923, pp. 196 ff., speaks of a much later date (third century A.D.) without quoting the evidence on which his statement is based. Cf. on the date (late first century B.C.) G. Leroux, *Lagynos*, 1913, p. 102. Similarly the wreck off Cape Artemision (N. Euboea) yielded the splendid bronze statues of Poseidon (or Zeus) and of a 'jockey' on horseback (the latter Hellenistic), now in the National Museum of Athens, H. G. Beyen, *La statue d'Artémision*, 1930, cf. R. Herbig, *Gnomon*, v (1929), p. 636 f. The date of this shipwreck is supplied by the abundant pottery found in the ship, especially late Hellenistic *sigillata* (first century B.C.?). The vessel probably sailed from Thessaly or Macedonia. There is no necessity to assume that the ships of Mahdia, Anticythera, and Artemision were transporting Roman war booty or goods seized by pirates. We may connect them with the events of the Mithridatic or civil war. But they may have been transporting goods which had been bought in Greece by merchants who intended to sell them in Italy. On the export of products of art from Greece to Italy in the second and first centuries B.C. in general, H. Fuhrmann, *Philoxenos von*

Eretria, 1931, pp. 216 ff., cf. H. U. von Schoenebeck, *Festgabe Th. Wiegand*, 1938, p. 62, n. 1. The many Greek sculptures and paintings found in Pompeii, Herculaneum, and Rome, and signed by Athenian, Parian, Samian, Rhodian, and other artists may, of course, have been imported or may have been made in Italy by sculptors and painters of Greek origin, see pls. LXXXV and LXXXVI. However, the well-known mosaic of Dioscurides of Samos, for example, was probably not made in Pompeii but imported, Fuhrmann, loc. cit. Revival of the prosperity and of the industrial and artistic activity of Paros in the late second and in the first century B.C., O. Rubensohn, loc. cit. Note that products of Athenian workmanship penetrated as far as Lyons in Gaul. These may have been imported before Lyons became a Roman colony, directly from Athens, or at a later date, and, if so, probably from Italy, see H. Dragendorff, 'Der Altar der Roma und des Augustus in Lugdunum', *J.D.A.I.* lii (1937), pp. 117 ff., and Fig. 5.

[14] It may be noted in this connexion that in the period under review the Athenian law on weights and measures effected the equalization of the Athenian mina with the Roman weights and measures, O. Viedebantt, *Hermes*, li (1916), pp. 141 ff., and above, n. 9.

[15] The best and the fullest treatment of the problem will be found in S. A. Jebelev, 'Ἀχαϊκά,, 1903, pp. 1 ff.; this book contains a full bibliography, cf. Th. Reinach, *Mithridate Eupator* (Germ. transl., 1895), p. 128 f. Nothing essential has been added since, see the short statements and the bibliographical references in the general histories of the Hellenistic period quoted above and in Larsen 'Rom. Greece', pp. 306 ff. On the relations between Greece and the governor of Macedonia, V. Costanzi, *Riv. Fil.* xlv (1917), pp. 402 ff. On the dissolution and later reconstitution of the κοινά, G. Daux, *Delphes au II⁰ et au I⁰ʳ siècle*, p. 354, with bibliographical references and Larsen, loc. cit., p. 309.

[16] Corinth—Cic. *De leg. agr.* i. 2. 5, cp. ii. 19. 51; Boeotia—Cic. *De nat. deor.* iii. 19. 49; S.C. concerning the sanctuary of Amphiaraus, *S.I.G.*³ 747; Euboea— Plut. *Sulla*, 23; S.C. de Asclepiade, *C.I.L.* i². 588.

[17] App. *Mithr.* 54; Plut. *Sulla*, 19. 12; Paus. ix. 7. 5–6, cf. G. F. Hertzberg, *Hist. de la Grèce*, i (Fr. transl., 1887), pp. 339 f.; on the date, G. Daux, *Delphes*, &c., pp. 398 ff. Cf. below, p. 940.

[18] References in note 16. Grants to the Isthmian and Nemean Dionysiac artistes of Thebes, *I.G.* vii. 2413 and 2414; for a better reading and for the date and circumstances of the grants, G. Klaffenbach, *Symbolae ad hist. coll. art. Bacchiorum*, 1914, pp. 24 ff., cf. Poland, *P.W.K.* v A. 2475 and 2491; G. Daux, *Delphes*, &c., p. 358. Such grants to the *technitai* were of course not new. We possess many Amphictionic decrees conferring ἀσυλία, ἀσφάλεια and ἀτέλεια on the various associations of Dionysiac artistes: the Athenian, the Isthmian, the Ionian. With Delphi vied the Hellenistic kings and the great cities; see the inscription of Craton, L. Robert, *B.C.H.* lix (1935), pp. 193 ff. and G. Daux, ibid., pp. 210 ff. Later, more detailed and specific grants

were common. On those of Sulla and Antony to the Ionian artistes, below, Ch. VII, nn. 17 and 117 ; cf. above, Ch. IV, n. 22.

¹⁹ J. Hatzfeld, *Les Trafiquants italiens*, pp. 67 ff. (Boeotia and Euboea) and pp. 73 ff. (Corinth). Note the Italians settled in the rich agricultural territory of Thespiae, Cic. *Ad fam.* xiii. 22. 1 ; *I.G.* vii. 1862 (1st cent. B.C.), cf. 1826 and 1827. It was certainly agriculture, not commerce, that attracted Italians to Thespiae. Naturally no less popular with the Roman settlers than the Isthmus, Boeotia, and Euboea were the rich agricultural and grazing districts of the province of Macedonia and of Epirus. See further, below.

²⁰ A. Wilhelm, 'Urkunden aus Messene', *Jahreshefte*, xvii (1914), pp. 1 ff. Inscription I is an honorary decree for the collector of the εἰσφορά, Aristocles (*I.G.* v. 1. 1432 ; Wilhelm, pp. 2 ff.) ; inscription II (*I.G.* v. 1. 1433 ; Wilhelm, pp. 48 ff.) gives accounts of the εἰσφορά; inscription III (*I.G.* v. 1. 1532 ; Wilhelm, pp. 86 ff.) is a fragmentary list of taxpayers with indication of their census ; and inscription IV (*I.G.* v. 1. 1434 ; Wilhelm, pp. 116 ff.) contains a list of arrears owing by Romans in respect of the same or a similar εἰσφορά. Inscription III has been republished by M. N. Tod, *B.S.A.* 1926/27, pp. 151 ff., who has shown that it does not belong to the same group. Prof. Sterling Dow, who is preparing a new edition of this inscription, regards it as earlier than the first century B.C. (Larsen, 'Rom. Greece', p. 420). The results of Wilhelm's analysis and the analogous material collected by him have been extensively used by later writers in describing Greek economic life during the Hellenistic period in general, e.g. W. W. Tarn, *Hell. Civ.*², pp. 95 ff. ; R. Cohen, *La Grèce et l'Hellénisation du Monde Antique*, 1934, p. 545 ff. ; Larsen, 'Rom. Greece', pp. 419 ff. Cf. below, Ch. VIII, n. 85 on a different view of some modern scholars concerning the economic interpretation of the inscriptions of Messene.

²¹ *I.G.* v. 1. 1379 (second–first centuries B.C.) ; L. Robert, *B.C.H.* lii (1928), pp. 426 ff. On the slaves in the Peloponnese at the time of the Achaean war, above, note 4.

²² Religious renascence of Athens: A. Wilhelm, *Jahreshefte*, xvii (1914), pp. 84 ff. On the splendid Pythiads sent to Delphi by Athens in 138, 128, 106, and 98, Colin, *F.D.* iii. 2, pp. 12 ff. ; P. Roussel, *B.C.H.* lviii (1934), pp. 92 ff. ; G. Daux, *Delphes*, &c., pp. 540 ff. Cf. P. Roussel, loc. cit., p. 93, on the numerous inscriptions of the *thiasoi* of the same time. See above (Ch. V, n. 31) on a similar revival of cults and celebrations in the Peloponnese after Naupactus. Renascence of self-confidence and glorification of Athens as the home of civilization and progress, as expressed in the Amphictionic decree of 125 B.C.: *S.I.G.*³ 704 E, 1 ff. ; *F.D.* iii. 2, 69 ; *I.G.* ii². 1134 ; A. Wilhelm, *Wien. Anz.* lix (1922), p. 25 f. ; G. Daux, *Rev. É. G.* xlvii (1934), p. 177, and *Delphes*, &c., pp. 369 ff., cf. the decree of 97 B.C., Daux, *Delphes*, &c., p. 566. On the historical importance of the decree, R. Herzog, *Berl. S. B.* xxxii (1935), p. 974. The statements in the decree are, of course, merely repetitions of ancient *topoi*.

On the Heroon of Calydon and its date (before 100 B.C., probably middle of the second century), E. Dyggve, F. Poulsen, K. Rhomaios, *Das Heroon von Kalydon*, 1934, pp. 397 ff. (109 ff.), esp. p. 406 (118). I may quote in this connexion the group of Hellenistic painted graves in Aegina dating about 144 B.C., which show that the island enjoyed a certain prosperity under Pergamene rule, G. Karo, *J.D.A.I.* xlvi (1931), Anz., pp. 274 ff. I may also remind the reader that the national revival of Greece, by which I mean the revival of self-consciousness, was not confined to Greece proper and to the islands. We shall find it expressed in the the same forms in Asia Minor. It was the answer of Greece to the final loss of political independence.

²³ On the political situation in Athens at the end of the second and the beginning of the first century, see the detailed surveys of S. Jebelev, *H.A.*, pp. 292 ff., and W. S. Ferguson, *H.A.*, pp. 425 ff., cf. J. Carcopino, *Hist. Rom.* ii, p. 417, and G. Daux, *Delphes*, &c., p. 561. The Delphian affair of 125 B.C.: G. Colin, *B.C.H.* xxvii (1903), pp. 104 ff.; *S.I.G.*³ 826, cf. *F.D.* iii. 4. 43; G. Daux, *Delphes*, &c., pp. 372 ff.

²⁴ A. Passerini, 'Moti politico-sociali della Grecia e i Romani', *Athen.* xi (1933), pp. 309 ff. On the two slave revolts in Attica, S. Jebelev, *H.A.*, pp. 217 ff., and W. S. Ferguson, *H.A.*, pp. 379, 428, cf. W. L. Westermann, *P.W.K.* Suppl. vi, 944 and 957 (where the two revolts are merged into one). The revolt which took place among the slaves in the Laurium mines may be responsible for a certain shortage of the 'owls' in the Aegean market in the early first century B.C., see E. J. P. Raven, *Num. Chr.* lxxi (1938), pp. 150 ff. On the slave revolts in general: K. Bücher, *Die Aufstände der unfreien Arbeiter*, 1874, and R. Pöhlmann, *Gesch. d. Soz. Fr.* i, pp. 403 ff. Cf. the remarks of U. Kahrstedt, *G.G.A.* clxxxviii (1926), pp. 97 ff., and 1928, pp. 484 ff.; F. Oertel, *N.J.Kl. Alt.* iii (1927), pp. 1 ff., and W. W. Tarn, *Hell. Civ.*², p. 115. On the revolts in the West: J. Carcopino, *Hist. Rom.* ii, pp. 176 ff., 332 ff., cf. 512 ff., and H. Last in *C.A.H.* ix, pp. 11 ff., and pp. 153 ff. (with bibliography p. 913 f.), cf. on the war of Spartacus ibid., pp. 329 ff. See also Westermann, loc. cit. On Aristonicus see below, p. 808, on Saumacus, leader of the Panticapaean bondmen and probably ally of the Crimean Scythians, S. Jebelev, 'L'abdication de Pairisadès et la révolution scythe dans le royaume du Bosphore', *Rev. É. G.* xlix (1936), pp. 17 ff. For the sympathy of the rural proletariat and small landowners with the slaves of Sicily, Diod. xxxiv–xxxv. 48 (first war); Diod. xxxvi. 6 (second war): οὐ γὰρ οἱ δοῦλοι μόνον, ἀλλὰ καὶ τῶν ἐλευθέρων οἱ ἄποροι πᾶσαν ἁρπαγὴν καὶ παρανομίαν ἐργαζόμενοι &c. Note the antagonism between the city *bourgeoisie* and the rural proletariat, ibid.: διὸ καὶ πάντες οἱ κατὰ τὰς πόλεις ὑπελάμβανον τὰ μὲν ἐντὸς τειχῶν μόλις εἶναι ἴδια, τὰ δ' ἐκτὸς ἀλλότρια καὶ δοῦλα τῆς παρανόμου χειροκρασίας, cf. Diod. xxxvi. 11: plunder and slaughter by ἐλεύθεροι οἱ τὰς ἐπὶ χώρας κτήσεις οὐκ ἔχοντες.

²⁵ The date of the inscription is disputed. I am inclined to accept that suggested by the first editors (see G. F. Hertzberg, *Gesch. Griech.* i, 1866, p. 322 f., n. 7 b), and approved by G. Colin, *Rome et la Grèce de 200 à 146 av.*

J.C., 1905, p. 654 f., and M. Holleaux, *Hermes*, xlix (1914), p. 583, n. 4. Cf. id. Στρατηγὸς Ὕπατος, 1918, p. 17 ff. Cf. the brief comments on the inscription of Hertzberg, loc. cit., Colin, loc. cit., and S. Jebelev, Ἀχαϊκά, 1903, pp. 24 ff. I cannot however, accept Colin's interpretation of one of the most important sentences of the document—ll. 14–15. Here Fabius speaks apparently of the revolutionaries having abolished all the συναλλάγματα (contracts of all sorts) and debts and so created conditions irreconcilable with the freedom of Greece and the guiding principles of Fabius' policy. It is evident that the συναλλάγματα were private contracts (to a large extent documents concerning loans, mortgages, &c.) partly relating to landed property. The passage quoted above is fragmentary and has not been correctly restored. A short summary dealing with 'Prosperity, Poverty and the Problem of population' in Greece from 200 to 30 B.C. will be found in Larsen, 'Rom. Greece', pp. 418 ff. In this summary Larsen does not discriminate between the periods from 200 to 146 B.C. and from 146 B.C. to the time of Sulla.

[26] On Macedonia after the Persean war Geyer, *P.W.K.* xiv. 751 ff. esp. 762 ff. On the measures of Aemilius Paulus see the principal histories of the Hellenistic period and of Rome, especially B. Niese, *Gesch. d. Gr. u. Mak. St.* iii, pp. 189 ff., and J. Carcopino, *Hist. Rom.* ii, pp. 128 ff., cf. Larsen, 'Rom. Greece', pp. 294 ff., 312, 418 ff.; V. Ivanov, 'De societatibus vectigalium publicorum P. R.', *Zapiski of the Classical Section of the Imp. Russ. Arch. Society*, vi (1910), p. 97 f., and T. Frank, *Econ. Survey*, i, p. 156. The interpretation of these measures is controversial. P. V. M. Benecke, *C.A.H.* viii, p. 273, regards them as quite reasonable and beneficent for the population.

[27] On the wars of the second half of the second century, *P.W.K.* vi A. 438 ff. The inscription of Lete: *S.I.G.*³ 700 (cf. A. Wilhelm, *Glotta*, xxiv (1936), pp. 133 ff.) and 701. M. Minucius and his victory: *S.I.G.*³ 710, cf. F. Münzer, *P.W.K.* xv. 1962 ff., n. 54. An inscription in his honour set up by the city of Europus recently found at Asiclar (Europus) has been published, with important comments, by S. B. Kugeas, *Hellenica*, v (1932), pp. 5 ff. He is right in suggesting that the great victory of Minucius was won near Europus.

[28] On Thessalonice, Oberhummer, *P.W.K.* vi A. 145 ff. The inscriptions of the Apustii were first published by Ch. Avezou and Ch. Picard, *B.C.H.* xxxvii (1913), pp. 125 ff. The text has been improved by M. Holleaux, ibid. xxxviii (1914), pp. 63 ff., and A. Wilhelm, *Jahreshefte*, xvii (1914), pp. 105 ff., and especially *Wien. S.B.* clxxxiii (published in 1924), pp. 21 ff., and *Hermes*, lxiii (1928), pp. 229 ff. The inscription of Perinthus: G. Seure, *B.C.H.* xxxvi (1912), p. 614. M. Apustius Agrippa πραγματικός of this inscription was either an agent and freedman of the Thessalonican Apustii or a member of their family. It is tempting to connect the Apustii of Thessalonice with the plebeian senatorial family of Apustii. One of them, L. Apustius, was in 200 B.C. legate of P. Sulpicius Galba during the Macedonian war (Liv. xxxi. 27; Zonar. ix. 15). In 190 B.C. he was legate of L. Cornelius Scipio (Liv. xxxvii. 4. 2) and died in Lycia (ibid. 16. 12). There is no doubt that the Apustii resided in Thessalonice. In decree IV the son is called (l. 2) γινόμε[νος διάδοχος

τῆς πατρι]κῆς ἐργασίας, which Wilhelm corrects into τραπεζιτι]κῆς. I think, however, that ἐμπορι]κῆς is the more probable alternative for πατρι]κῆς. On Abdera after the Persean war and her conflict with Cotys before the Roman Senate, see above, n. 1.

[29] The standard work on the Italians in Greece is the excellent volume of J. Hatzfeld, *Les Trafiquants italiens dans l'Orient hellénique*, 1919. It fully deserves a new edition in revised form. On the early Italian expansion, see pp. 20 ff., where the reader will find quoted the texts relating to this period; on the time between the middle of the second century and the Mithridatic war, pp. 31 ff. Cf. also the list of Italian families resident in the East at the end of the book. The Romans in Messene: A. Wilhelm, *Jahreshefte*, xxii (1914), pp. 4 ff. (inscr. I, l. 32) and 48 f. (inscr. II, ll. 8, 14, 47); cf. pp. 116 ff., pp. 56 ff. A large estate belongs to the Italian Nemerios, inscr. II, l. 26, above, p. 753. On the formation of large estates of Romans in Greece and Asia Minor after the first Macedonian war and later, cf. M. Rostovtzeff, *Kolonat*, p. 286 and below, Ch. VII, nn. 34 and 35.

[30] On the coins of Macedonia, Maronea, and Thasos see above, n. 11, and on Macedonia H. Gaebler, *Z.N.* xxiii (1902), pp. 141 ff., and *Die Antiken Münzen Nord-Griechenlands*, III, Makedonien und Paionia, 1 (1906), pp. 3 ff., cf. 2 (1935), pp. 1–7. Cf. K. Pink, 'Die Münzprägung der Ostkelten und ihrer Nachbarn', *Diss. Pannonicae*, ii. 15, 1939, pp. 119 ff. (with excellent bibliography; Pink announces in his book a study by Prof. Jónás on the Thasian coins). Th. Reinach (quoted in n. 9) is probably right in regarding the Maronean and Thasian coinage of the late second century (after 148 or 146 B.C.) as a kind of Roman provincial coinage. The Romans were aware of the great popularity which Macedonian, Thasian, Maronean, and Abderite coins had enjoyed in Thrace in the past. It is probable that in the second century these early coins and their imitations, alongside of the coins of Philip II, Alexander, and Lysimachus and their imitations, were still in circulation in the Celtic and Thracian regions of the Balkan peninsula. See G. Kazarow, *C.A.H.* viii, pp. 556, 558 f. No wonder that the Roman government should be ready and willing to allow Maronea and Thasos to provide the reviving trade between Greece and the Northern Balkans with currency that was familiar to the customers of Greece. On the Celtic imitations of the silver tetradrachms of Philip II see above, Ch. III, p. 161, and n. 36. Pink in his study quoted above in this note endeavours to prove that all the Macedonian kings until the end of the dynasty coined large masses of posthumous Philippi (both gold staters and silver tetradrachms) to pay their Celtic mercenaries and for their commerce with the North Balkan lands. It was not until this coinage ceased that the Celtic imitations of these coins were minted both by the West and the East Celts. As I was not convinced by his argument and suspected that posthumous silver tetradrachms of Philip II ceased to be coined after the beginning of the third century B.C., and that it was at this time that the East Celtic and Thracian imitations of them began, I consulted Dr. E. T. Newell, who has informed me that while

posthumous gold Philippi were coined by some Greek cities as late as the second century B.C., the issue of silver tetradrachms came to an end after the reign of Cassander. It is natural, he thinks, that the barbaric imitations of these coins should have begun in the Balkan peninsula as soon as their issue was suspended in Macedonia. The history of the gold staters was different. These were never imitated by the Eastern Celts, but became in the second century the standard coinage of the Western Celts. I cannot go here into details. It is to be hoped that Dr. E. T. Newell will soon publish his study on the posthumous Philippi and their barbaric imitations.

31 On the general conditions of the Balkan peninsula in the second century B.C., C. Patsch, *Beiträge zur Völkerkunde von Südosteuropa*, 5. 1: Bis zur Festsetzung der Römer in Transdanubien, 1932 (*Wien. S.B.* ccxiv. 1) ; B. Lenk, *P.W.K.* vi A. 438 ff. ; for Transylvania, C. Daicoviciu, *La Transylvanie dans l'Antiquité*, 1938. Cf. above, n. 27. On the Greek cities, M. Rostovtzeff, *Gnomon*, x (1934), pp. 3 ff. and above, Ch. V, p. 674, n. 86.

32 The dating of all the inscriptions mentioned in the text is controversial. None of them bears a certain date, the forms of the letters are not a certain guide, and the political, economic, and military situation of the cities remained the same for a long time. The much later set of inscriptions which may be grouped around the well-known and precisely dated inscription of Acornion (Dionysopolis near Odessus–Varna) of 48 B.C.—*S.I.G.*³ 762, cf. *Gnomon*, x (1934), p. 6—are written in exactly the same style and reflect an almost identical situation: see, e.g., the inscription of Tomi quoted above and compare it with that of Mesembria (G. Seure, *Rev. Arch.* xviii (1911), pp. 423 ff.). Cf. also the inscription of Apollonia, *A.E.M. aus Oest.* x (1886), p. 163, no. 1. It is not surprising that L. Robert, *B.C.H.* lix (1935), p. 504 f., does not discriminate between the various groups of these inscriptions in his useful remarks about them. On *S.I.G.*³ 707, see S. Lambrino, *Bull. Soc. Nat. Ant.* 1933, p. 80 (who suggests that the inscription belongs to Tomi or Istrus).

33 I may refer in this connexion, though I am not dealing here with the 'barbarians', V. Parvan, 'La pénétration hellénique dans la vallée du Danube', &c., *Ac. Roum., Bull. de la Sect. Hist.* x (1923), pp. 21 ff. On the Thasian and Maronean coins and their circulation, see above, notes 11 and 30. On the Western currents of trade, E. Gohl, 'Verkehr griechischer Münzen in Ungarn', *Numism. Közlöny* for 1902, 1922, and 1923 (in Hungarian, quoted and used by A. Alföldi, 'Studi ungheresi sulla Romanizzazione della Pannonia', *Studi Rom. nel Mondo*, ii (1935), pp. 267 ff.). Cf. the careful studies of C. Patsch

34 On the relations between the leaders of the Pontic Greek cities and the 'barbarians', V. Parvan, 'La pénétration hellénique dans la vallée du Danube', &c., *Ac. Roum., Bull. de la Sect. Hist.* x (1923), pp. 21 ff. On the Thasian and Maronean coins and their circulation, see above, notes 11 and 30. On the Western currents of trade, E. Gohl, 'Verkehr griechischer Münzen in Ungarn', *Numism. Közlöny* for 1902, 1922, and 1923 (in Hungarian, quoted and used by A. Alföldi, 'Studi ungheresi sulla Romanizzazione della Pannonia', *Studi Rom. nel Mondo*, ii (1935), pp. 267 ff.). Cf. the careful studies of C. Patsch

on the circulation of the coins of Apollonia and Dyrrachium, and other contributions to the same problem quoted by L. Robert, *B.C.H.* lix (1935), p. 496, n. 5, and my remarks on the economic history of the Dalmatian coast, *Storia Ec. e Soc. d. Imp. Rom.*, pp. 272 ff. See also C. Daicoviciu, *La Transylvanie dans l'Antiquité*, 1938, pp. 26 ff.

[35] On South Russia in the years before Mithridates, M. Rostovtzeff, *C.A.H.* ix, pp. 227 ff. On the revolt of Saumacus, S. Jebelev, 'L'Abdication de Pairisadès et la revolution scythe dans le royaume du Bosphore', *Rev. É.G.* xlix (1936), pp. 17 ff. Prof. Jebelev is right in pointing out the similarity between the revolt of Saumacus and that of Aristonicus. But his contention that Saumacus was the leader of a Scythian slave revolt and he himself a slave is not convincing. Saumacus is not called θρεπτός (houseborn slave) of Pairisades in the inscription of Diophantus (*I.O.S.P.E.* i² 352, l. 34). The inscription speaks of Pairisades as τὸν ἐκθρέψαντα αὐτόν, which does not necessarily mean that Saumacus was his slave. Moreover, it is hard to believe that if Saumacus was really a slave, the Chersonesites would have mentioned it in such a veiled form. Besides, we know nothing of slavery being a prominent feature in the economic life of Bosporus, while serfdom is well attested. And, finally, the bulk of the serfs of the Bosporan kingdom certainly did not consist of Scythians—the rulers of the Crimea, a group of warriors, lords and masters of the native population. Close relations between the dynasties of Bosporus and of the Scythians are well attested, and the system of hostages was very common in the Hellenistic world. On the various meanings of the term θρεπτός, so frequent in the inscriptions of Asia Minor, A. Cameron, *Anat. St. pres. to W. H. Buckler*, 1939, pp. 27 ff. Cf. above, n. 24.

[36] The bibliography on Rhodes given in Ch. V, n. 91 need not be repeated here. A complete enumeration of all the facts concerning the history of Rhodes that are stated in our sources will be found in Hiller von Gaertringen, art. 'Rhodos', *P.W.K.* Suppl. v. 796 ff. On the large income derived by Rhodes from its dominions and obtained, at least in part, by imposing on its dependent cities an elaborate system of taxation, see above, Ch. V, p. 619, n. 22, and cf. the inscription of Hyllarima, A. Laumonier, *B.C.H.* lviii (1934), pp. 360 ff. On the customs duties, above, Ch. V, n. 96.

[37] On this Cretan war of 155–153, Polyb. xxxiii. 15. 3; 16 and 17, cf. 4; Diod. xxxi. 37 f., cf. 43 f. Plundering of Siphnos by the Cretans, Diod. xxxi. 45. On the war in general, M. Segre, Κρητικὸς πόλεμος, *Riv. Fil.* lxi (11) (1933), pp. 379 ff. Segre publishes in his article a new inscription of Carpathos bearing on this war; cf. *S.I.G.*³ 570, and the subscription list, *G.D.I.* iii. 3590. The inscriptions *I.G.* xii. 8. 53 and 159 (Imbros and Samothrace) are probably earlier.

[38] Cf. the somewhat similar endeavour of Eumenes II during his war against Pharnaces of Pontus (184–179 B.C., see above, p. 636) to become master of the mouth of the Hellespont in order 'to prevent the entrance of vessels bound for the Euxine', which was checked by the Rhodians, Polyb.

xxvii. 7. 5. This Rhodian intervention was the beginning of misunderstandings between Eumenes II and the Rhodians. On the war between Attalus II and Prusias II, see B. Niese, *Gesch. d. Gr. u. Mak. St.* iii, pp. 326 ff., *C.A.H.* viii, p. 282, and L. Robert, *Ét. Anat.* pp. 111 ff.; cf. *O.G.I.* 327 (with the comments of Dittenberger). The last time that Bithynian kings interfered with the freedom of the Straits was in 88; this was one of the causes of the first Mithridatic war. Cf. below, n. 71.

[39] The Delphian copy of the law concerning piracy, *S.E.G.* iii. 378 (with bibliography); G. Colin, *F.D.* iii. 4, pp. 34 ff., cf. J. Carcopino, *Mél. Glotz*, i, pp. 117 ff. and *Hist. Rom.* ii, p. 341 f. Rhodian initiative and participation, *S.E.G.* iii. 378 B. 12 f.: γράμματα [πρὸς] τοὺς βασιλεῖς κατὰ τὸν νόμον τοῦτον ἀποστελ[λόμ]ενα τοῖς ἀ[πὸ | ῾Ρ]οδίων πρεσβευταῖς [ὅταν μέλλωσιν εἰς τὴν ἑαυτῶν πατρίδα ἀναχωρήσειν ἀποδότω. Access of Rhodian ambassadors to the Senate for report son the law, ibid. B. 17 ff. Acts of kings favourable to the pirates, ibid. 10 f.: μὴ ἐκ τῆς βασιλείας αὐτ[ῶν μήτε] τῆ[ς] | χώρας ἢ ὁρίων πειρατὴ[ς μηδεὶς ὁρμήσῃ, μηδὲ οἱ ἄρχοντες ἢ φρούραρχοι οὓς κ]αταστήσουσιν τ[οὺς] πειρατὰς ὑποδέξωνται.

[40] Hiller von Gaertringen, loc. cit., pp. 801 ff.

[41] Decree of Ceramus, E. Hicks, *J.H.S.* x (1891), pp. 114 ff.; Michel 458, discussed by L. Robert, *Villes d'Asie Mineure*, 1935, pp. 60 ff. On Mylasa and Euromus—the decree for Moschion, Le Bas–Waddington, v. 394; Michel 472. The result of the συμπολιτεία between Mylasa and Euromus was according to L. Robert an appeal to Rome (?) and the Rhodians (Hula-Szanto, *Wien. S.B.* cxxxii (1895), p. 9). On the two last inscriptions, see the comments of L. Robert, loc. cit., p. 59 f. On the φρούρια of the Rhodians and those of the Attalids, which protected the cities from the hill-robbers, my remarks in *Anat. St. pres. to Sir William Ramsay*, p. 375 (with bibliography). On the character of the Carian plateau, L. Robert, loc. cit., pp. 231 ff.

[42] Above, note 10.

[43] On the chronology of the Rhodian stamps, see above, n. 10 and especially the sound remarks of V. Grace, *Hesp.* iii (1934), pp. 214 ff.

[44] Above, p. 767.

[45] Cf. J. Hatzfeld, *Les Trafiquants italiens*, &c., p. 154 f.

[46] On Delos, see the bibliography quoted in note 6. On Delos after 166 the standard works are P. Roussel, *Délos, colonie athénienne*, 1916, and F. Durrbach, *Choix d'inscriptions de Délos*, I, Textes historiques, 1921, pp. 113 ff., a marvellous collection of the most important texts bearing on the history of Delos with exhaustive comments, cf. F. Durrbach et P. Roussel, *Inscriptions de Délos. Actes des Fonctionnaires Athéniens*, &c., après 166 av. J. C., 1935, and P. Roussel et M. Launey, *Inscriptions de Délos. Décrets postérieurs à 166 av. J. C.; dédicaces postérieures à 166 av. J. C., and Textes divers, &c., postérieurs à 166 av. J. C.*, 1937 (in two parts). Cf. Larsen, 'Roman Greece', pp. 334 ff.

[47] Note, e.g., the large number of Syrian slaves at Minturnae, J. Johnson, _Excavations at Minturnae_, II, Inscriptions, part I: Republican Magistri, 1933, pp. 106 ff.; W. L. Westermann, art. 'Sklaverei', _P.W.K._ Suppl. vi. 952.

[48] Inscriptions mentioning the redemption of αἰχμάλωτοι in the second century B.C.: _I.G._ ix. 2. 66 (Thessaly, probably time of the Persean war, cf. Polyb. xxvii. 14. 1); ibid. 1211; Michel 423 (decree for Aratocritus who redeemed several war prisoners). On _I.G._ xii. 8. 53 (Imbros) and 159 (Samothrace) see above, note 37. It is a great pity that the most interesting inscription of Astypalaea, _I.G._ xii. 3. 171, cannot be exactly dated; the text has been splendidly restored by A. Wilhelm, _Ath. Mitt._ xxviii (1903), pp. 449 ff., and reprinted in this improved form in _I.G._ xii. 3, Suppl. 1286, and _I.G.R._ iv. 1029. Hiller regards it as belonging to the second century B.C., while the editors of _I.G.R._ are inclined to assign it to the time of the Mithridatic war (about 85 B.C.). The inscription gives a dramatic picture of a piratic raid on the coast of Asia Minor. The pirates invaded the Pygelis (part of the territory of Ephesus) and from here pillaged the temple of Artemis Munichia and the adjacent χωρία, abducting free men and slaves and robbing them of their σκεύη (Wilhelm) or ἔπιπλα (myself). The Astypalaeans received information about it from the Ephesians, sailed out, attacked the pirates with great valour and conquered them with great difficulty and danger. The captured pirates were punished, the Ephesians and their children who were rescued by the Astypalaeans were treated kindly by them 'as if they were their own children'. No _symmachia_ between the Ephesians and the Astypalaeans (its existence was suggested by Carcopino, see n. 53) is mentioned in the inscription, and we do not know who the pirates were. However, since the Astypalaeans had a treaty of alliance with Rome (_I.G._ xii. 3. 173, and Suppl. p. 278), renewed in 105 B.C. (a little before the Romans began to fight the pirates), it is probable that it was the obligation of the Astypalaeans towards the Romans that lay behind their assistance (ἐπικουρία, as restored in the Astypalaean inscription, l. 3) to the Ephesians. The situation is well explained if we assume the later date for the Astypalaean inscription, that of 85 B.C. It is well known that Ephesus went over to the Romans during the Mithridatic war and lived through a period full of dangers, see the well-known Ephesian decree, _S.I.G._3 742, and below, Ch. VII. Nevertheless the earlier date is equally acceptable. Note the tone of the inscription which testifies to the deep indignation which the Greeks felt when facing piratic raids on centres of Greek life.

[49] Diod. xxxvi. 3 (the reply of Nicomedes), cf. J. Carcopino, _Hist. Rom._ ii, p. 332. Our information on the activity of land robbers in Asia Minor in the Hellenistic period is scanty. It has been recently collected by L. Robert, _Ét. Anat._, pp. 90 ff. A decree of Temnus published by Robert (loc. cit.) speaks of some citizens of Smyrna being kidnapped by the robbers. Still more interesting is a metrical epitaph of an officer from Apamea in Bithynia (late Hellenistic period), who in his early career Ἀσίδο[ς] ἐν γυάλοις ἤ[μο]ς [λ]ῃστῆρας ἀλαλκών | σκῦλα δοριδμητ[ῶν ἐ]πραθον ἐνδαπίων _S.E.G._ viii. 497. In the

Seleucid and Pergamene kingdoms the bondsmen, βασιλικοὶ γεωργοί, probably could not be sold into slavery by the owners of the estates on which they resided, even if the owners were the kings or the temples. The situation of the λαοὶ βασιλικοί in those kingdoms was probably similar to that of the λαοί who lived in the territories of Greek cities in Asia Minor. The classical example is that of the Mariandyni in the territory of Heraclea Pontica (Posidonius, Fr. 8, *F. Gr. Hist.* 87). However, the conditions of the serfs (royal, private, and temple serfs) in Bithynia, Pontus, Pamphylia, Cappadocia, and Galatia were probably different, being similar in all probability to those of the πελάται in the Bosporan kingdom. These more primitive relations between landowners and serfs are perhaps illustrated by the reliable information which we have about the relations between masters and serfs in the northern part of the Balkan peninsula: Illyrian masters and Thracian serfs (Theopompus *Phil. II*, quoted by Athen. x. 443 b; Fr. 40, *F. Gr. Hist.* 115), and the Dardanians and their serfs (Agatharchides Cnid. Fr. 17, *F. Gr. Hist.* 86). Note that Strabo (xii. 2. 9, p. 539), in speaking of the fortified castles of the Cappadocian kings and of the similar castles of the feudal aristocracy of Cappadocia, says that these castles gave safety to their owners and to their σώματα and χρήματα. Of the λαοὶ βασιλικοί in Asia Minor we know very little, see my *Kolonat*, pp. 247 ff., esp. 258 ff. (Seleucids); p. 280 f. (Attalids, cf. *Anat. St. pres. to Sir William Ramsay*, p. 375, and *C.A.H.* viii, pp. 609 ff.); pp. 281 ff. (Cappadocia, Armenia, Iberia, cf. *C.A.H.* ix, pp. 213 ff.). I see nothing to prevent the kings, the chief priests, or the feudal lords of Bithynia, Pontus, Cappadocia, Galatia, and Paphlagonia from selling under one pretext or another some of their serfs to an agent of the Roman *publicani* or to a Delian slave dealer. A lively traffic in Phrygian slaves is attested for the middle of the first century B.C. by an inscription of Acmonia, *M.A.M.A.* vi. 1939, no. 260. Sornatius, who dedicated to the city the στατάριον, was probably a Roman slave dealer.

On the date of *O.G.I.* 345, G. Daux, *B.C.H.* lvii (1933), p. 77. It is very probable that the comparatively large number of Syrian and Anatolian slaves on the Greek market, as attested by the manumission acts of Delphi for 201–50 B.C., should be connected with the lively trade in slaves which began before the activity of the Cilician pirates and was fully developed in the middle of the second century B.C. According to the statistics of A. Calderini, *Manomissione*, &c., 1908, pp. 408 ff., and W. K. Westermann, *P.W.K.* Suppl. vi. 934 (which need, however, careful revision and must be supplemented by the acts of manumission published after the appearance of Calderini's book), in the acts there are named 47 slaves from Greece and the islands, 46 from the Balkan lands (especially numerous were the Thracians), 10 from the shores of the Black Sea, while 37 came from Asia Minor, and 53 from the rest of the Near East, 38 being Syrians, 4 Jews, 3 from Egypt. The acts published since Calderini wrote give approximately the same picture. I take *exempli causa* the acts published in the *F.D.* iii. 3; we find in them 5 Syrian slaves, 3 from Asia Minor, 1 from Thrace, 1 Sarmatian, 1 Dardanian and one from Alexandria (most of the acts belong to the middle of the second century B.C.). The same is true of the manumissions of the temple of Asclepius at Buttos (near Naupactus) and of Naupactus (above Ch. V, n. 27) dated between 170 and 146 B.C. The numerous acts of manumission in Thessaly give no information on the nationality of the manumitted slaves. Cf. in general what has been said above, Ch. V, nn. 27 and 30, and on the numbers of slaves in Achaea during the Achaean war, above, n. 4. On the Cappadocian and Pontic slaves of the early and late Roman Empire, T. R. S. Broughton, 'Roman Asia Minor', p. 636.

[50] Cretan mercenaries in the Syrian wars of that time are well known. The fact is confirmed by several Cretan coins restruck on the coins of Antiochus IX (114–95 B.C.). J. N. Svoronos, *Numismatique de la Crète ancienne*, 1890, p. 78, no. 99; E. J. P. Raven, *Num. Chr.* lxxi (1938), p. 151.

[51] On Cilician piracy, Ormerod, *C.A.H.* ix, pp. 350 ff. (with bibliography). Collection of texts relating to this piracy and a short account of its development: E. Ziebarth, *Beiträge zur Geschichte des Seeraubes und Seehandels im alten Griechenland*, 1929, pp. 32 ff. and 110 ff., nos. 88 ff. Part taken by Syrians and Jews in piratic raids before and after Pompey: J. Dobiaš, 'Les premiers rapports des Romains avec les Parthes', &c., *Arch. Orient.* iii (1931), pp. 244 ff. Strabo's mention of the Roman embassy of 139 B.C. in connexion with the pirates (xiv, p. 669) is obscure. The context shows that the inquiry was not meant seriously. The whole passage of Strabo bearing on piracy needs careful study. How many αἰχμάλωτοι were scattered all over Syria is illustrated by a passage in the well-known letter of Demetrius I (152 B.C.) by which he granted to the Jews among other privileges: καὶ πᾶσαν ψυχὴν Ἰουδαίων τὴν αἰχμαλωτισθεῖσαν ἀπὸ γῆς Ἰούδα εἰς πᾶσαν βασιλείαν μου ἀφίημι ἐλευθέραν δωρεάν, 1 Macc. x. 33, and Fl. Jos., *A.J.* xiii. 2. 3 (52). I cannot here discuss the difficult question of the genuineness of Demetrius' letter, see in general E. R. Bevan, *C.A.H.* viii, pp. 710 ff., and E. Bikerman, art. Makkabäer, in *P.W.K.* xiv. 785, 786 (both with bibliography). I personally agree with E. Meyer, *Ursprung und Anfänge des Christentums*, ii (1921), pp. 255, n. 1, and 454 ff., and E. Bikerman, loc. cit. (cf. his recent book *Der Gott der Makkabäer*, 1937), that the documents inserted in 1 and 2 Macc., especially the Seleucid letters, are genuine. There are still, however, scholars who regard the documents as partial or complete forgeries: H. Willrich, *Urkundenfälschungen in der hellenistisch-römischen Literatur*, 1924; H. Volkmann, *Klio*, xix (1925), pp. 373 ff.; E. R. Bevan, loc. cit., cf. R. Laqueur, *H.Z.* cxxxvi (1927), pp. 247 ff. The attitude of the Phoenician cities towards Cilician piracy is illustrated by Strabo's remark about Aradus (xvi. 2. 14, p. 754). Having the right of *asylia*, Aradus gave refuge to all sorts of people. However, ὁρῶντές τε τοὺς γειτονεύοντας Κίλικας τὰ πειρατήρια συνισταμένους οὐδ' ἅπαξ ἐκοινώνουν αὐτοῖς τῆς τοιαύτης ἐπιτηδεύσεως, which probably implies that the other cities had a different policy, see J. Dobiaš, loc. cit., p. 249.

[52] See App. *Sic.* 6; Diod. xl. 1. 3; Plut. *Pomp.* 29, cf. Flor. iii. 6. On the Cretan coinage of the late second and the first century B.C., on the Cretan hoards, and on the prosperity of Crete due to co-operation with Cilicia, see E. J. P. Raven, *Num. Chr.* lxxi (1938), pp. 133 ff., esp. 148 ff. On the excavations of Amnisus, S. Marinatos, *J.D.A.I.* li (1936), Anz. pp. 215 ff.

⁵³ J. Carcopino, *Hist. Rom.* ii, p. 334, has quoted three texts which according to him attest the early extension of Cilician activity to the Aegean Sea:
the inscription of Astypalaea quoted in note 48, an inscription of which the
date and the connexions are disputed; the famous passage of Cass. Dio,
xxxvi. 20 ff., relating to the pirates about the time of Pompey (no mention is
made by Dio of ransom money or tribute paid by the cities of Asia Minor);
and finally the well-known Delian dedication made by Damon, son of
Demetrius, an Ascalonite merchant, Δίι Οὐρίωι καὶ Ἀστάρτηι Παλαιστινῆι
Ἀφροδίτηι Οὐρανίαι in gratitude for his escape from pirates (σωθεὶς ἀπὸ πειρατῶν),
which unfortunately is not dated and may belong to the time of the Mithridatic war (Clermont–Ganneau, *C.R. Ac. Inscr.* 1909, pp. 308 ff.; *Explor. arch.
de Délos*, ii. 1909, p. 58; P. Roussel, *Les Cultes égyptiens à Délos*, 1916, p. 152;
Inscr. de Délos, 2305).

⁵⁴ On M. Antonius' expedition against the pirates, see the principal histories
of Rome, e.g., J. Carcopino, *Hist. Rom.* ii, p. 334. On the so-called piratic law
found at Delphi, above, note 39.

⁵⁵ On the foreigners at Delos in the period of independence, A. Lacroix,
Mél. Glotz, pp. 501 ff.

⁵⁶ Athens' commercial relations with the East have been mentioned before;
here it will suffice to remind the reader, *exempli gratia*, of the ἔμποροι of
Citium who are attested as residents in Athens in 333/2 (*S.I.G.*³ 280, cf. *I.G.*
ii.² 4636; note that Zenon, the founder of the Stoic school, was a native of
Citium), and of those of Egypt (*S.I.G.*³ 280, l. 44–5). At the time of the commercial renascence of Athens in the late third and especially in the second
century B.C. (above, pp. 628 ff. and 744) foreigners, and in particular Orientals,
played again a certain part in the life of Athens, see W. S. Ferguson, *H.A.*,
p. 316, cf. S. Dow, 'The Egyptian cults in Athens', *Harv. Theol. Rev.* xxx
(1937), pp. 183 ff.

⁵⁷ The inscriptions of the Italian religious associations discovered mostly
in the Italian *Pastas* and in the *agora* of the Competaliasts will be found in
Inscr. de Délos, nos. 1730–71. Professional organizations almost certainly
Italian, ibid. 1711 (οἰνοπῶλαι), 1712 (*olearii*), 1713 and 1714 (ἐλαιοπῶλαι). On
the Italian associations in general, P. Roussel, *Délos, col. ath.*, pp. 76 ff., and
the bibliography quoted above in notes 6 and 46.

⁵⁸ On the Heracleists and Poseidoniasts, see the bibliography given in
n. 46, cf. Ch. V, n. 111. The decree of the Heracleists of Tyre, *Inscr. de Délos*,
1519; that of the Poseidoniasts of Berytus, ibid. 1520. On the *fonduq* of the
Berytians, Ch. Picard, *B.C.H.* xliv (1920), pp. 263 ff.; *Explor. arch. de Délos*,
vi. 1921; *Rev. Arch.*, 6 sér., viii (1936), pp. 188 ff. The inscriptions found in the
house of the Berytians: *Inscr. de Délos*, 1772–96. The application to the
various rooms of the excavated building of the names of its constituent
parts found in the inscriptions, apart from the ἱερόν, is controversial. On
the *fonduq* of Dura, M. Rostovtzeff and F. E. Brown, *C.R. Ac. Inscr.*, 1935,

pp. 290 ff.; M. Rostovtzeff, *Dura-Europos and its Art*, 1938, p. 44 (and passim), pl. VII, and fig. 8; F. E. Brown, *Rep. vii–viii*, 1939, ch. v.

⁵⁹ On the Alexandrian ἐγδοχεῖς, see my paper 'Foreign Commerce of Ptolemaic Egypt', *Journ. of Ec. and Bus. Hist.* iv (1932), pp. 762 ff., and *Inscr. de Délos*, 1528, 1529, cf. 1526.

⁶⁰ *O.G.I.* 344; Durrbach, *Choix*, 103; *Inscr. de Délos*, 1705.

⁶¹ The Hellenistic kings honoured at Delos after 166 B.C.: *Inscr. de Délos*, 1525–39 (Ptolemies); 1540–53 (Seleucids); 1554 (Attalus II of Pergamon, cf. 1575); 1556–74 (Pontus: Mithridates V and Mithridates VI); 1575 and 1576 (Stratonice, daughter of Ariarathes IV, and Ariarathes VII of Cappadocia); 1577–80 (Bithynia). Cf. the comments of Durrbach, *Choix*, on many of these inscriptions.

⁶² On the cults, P. Roussel, *Délos, col. ath.*, pp. 249 ff. W. A. Laidlaw, *A History of Delos*, pp. 217 ff., gives a useful summary, though he omits the cults of the associations and of private people. The inscriptions of the sanctuaries of the foreign and minor gods worshipped at Delos will be found collected in full in *Inscr. de Délos*. See especially 2037–219 (dedications to Egyptian gods); 2220–304 (Syrian gods) ; 2305–27 (other Oriental gods); 2328–33 (presumably Jewish). Especially numerous and illuminating are the dedications found in the Sarapieia of Delos (P. Roussel, *Les Cultes égyptiens à Délos*, 1916) and those found in the temple of Hadad and Atargatis (P. Roussel, *Délos, col. ath.*, pp. 252 ff.). On the minor sanctuaries of Mount Cynthos, A. Plassart, *Expl. arch. de Délos*, xi. 1928, 'Sanctuaires et cultes du Mt. Cynthe.'

⁶³ We may regard as evidence of lively commercial relations between Delos on the one hand and the mainland of Greece, the islands of the Aegean, and the northern part of the Balkan peninsula on the other, the numerous finds in these regions of Megarian bowls of types which are regarded as characteristic of the special Delian brand of Megarian bowls. In addition to the regions mentioned above, bowls of the same type have also been found in S. Russia, Asia Minor, Egypt, and Italy. See F. Courby, *Les Vases grecs à reliefs*, pp. 395 ff.; on the bowls found at Alexandria, cf. A. Adriani, 'La Nécropole de Moustafa Pacha', *Ann. du Mus. Gréco-Romain* (Alexandria) (1933/4–1934/5), pp. 145 ff., and on those found on the lower Danube, V. Dumitrescu, *In memoria lui Vasile Parvan*, 1934, pp. 121 ff. In my opinion, however, the facts quoted by Courby are not conclusive. The Delian origin of the Megarian bowls of the so-called Delian type is not certain (see Ch. V, n. 68). Trade relations between Delos and the Crimea seem to be attested for the late second century B.C. by *S.I.G.*³ 1126 (105/4 B.C.); *Inscr. de Délos*, 2128—a dedication to Zeus Urius and the Egyptian gods by a merchant of Nymphaeum (near Panticapaeum) for his own and his son's safety καὶ ὑπὲρ τῶν πλοϊζομένων πάντων. Slave trade? Cf. Ch. V, n. 89.

⁶⁴ M. N. Tod, *J.H.S.* liv (1934), p. 150 f. (*Inscr. de Délos*, 1520), cf. Durrbach, *Choix*, p. 213. τραπεζιτεύοντες or τραπεζῖται ἐν Δήλῳ are frequently

mentioned at Delos, Durrbach, *Choix*, 132 and 138; *Inscr. de Délos*, 1715–29. In one case they act as a group, *Inscr. de Délos*, 1715, cf. 1729.

[65] See the calculations of P. Roussel, *B.C.H.* lv (1931), pp. 438 ff.

[66] On the general aspect of the city, P. Roussel, *Délos, col. ath.*, pp. 284 ff., cf. W. A. Laidlaw, loc. cit., pp. 232 ff., and the works quoted by him.

[67] *C.A.H.* viii, p. 649.

[68] On the sculptures found at Delos and the signatures of the artists, see P. Roussel, *Délos, col. ath.*, pp. 287 ff., and *Inscr. de Délos*, nos. 2489 ff., and 'Numéros de rappel', p. 330, cf. F. Mayence and G. Leroux, *B.C.H.* xxxi (1907), pp. 389 ff.; L. Bizard and G. Leroux, ibid., pp. 504 ff. (choregic monument of Carystius), and C. Michalowski, *Expl. arch. Délos*, xiii, 1932: 'Les portraits hellénistiques et romains'. On mural paintings, M. Bulard, 'Peintures murales et mosaïques de Délos', *Mon. et Mém. Piot*, xiv. 1908; 'Description des Revêtements peints à sujets religieux', *Expl. arch. Délos*, ix. 1926; and *La Religion domestique dans la colonie italienne de Délos*, 1926, cf. M. Swindler, *Ancient Painting*, pp. 342 ff., and Ch. Picard, *Rev. Art ancien et mod.*, 1928, ii, pp. 255 ff. On mosaics, M. Bulard, loc. cit.; J. Chamonard, *Expl. arch. Délos*, xiv. 1933: 'Les mosaïques de la maison des Masques'. It is to be noted that some of the artists who made the mosaics and some of the statues were Orientals, especially Syrians (above, Ch. V, n. 123).

[69] What I have said in the text is based on the careful study of O. Rubensohn, 'Parische Künstler', *J.D.A.I.* l (1935), pp. 50 ff. Note that we have many signatures of Parian artists. It is needless to mention that the dates of the various artists of Paros are far from certain.

[70] The Galatian war of Eumenes II (168–166 B.C.): Liv. xlv. 19. 3; Polyb. xxx. 1–2; Polyaen. iv. 8. 1; Diod. xxxi. 13. The war was bloody and cruel. It is noteworthy that many αἰχμάλωτοι were sacrificed by the Galatians to their gods. The cities of Asia Minor suffered severely and were in great terror. See, for Sardis, *O.G.I.* 305. 11; for the Ionian League, the letter of Eumenes II, *O.G.I.* 763; Rehm, *Milet, Erg. d. Ausgr.* i. 9, No. 306; C. B. Welles, *R.C.* no. 52; for Amlada, the three letters—of an unknown person, of Attalus III, and of Attalus II—in which an attack of the Galatians on Amlada is mentioned: *O.G.I.* 751, C. B. Welles, *R.C.* no. 54 (for the second letter), and H. Swoboda, J. Keil, F. Knoll, *Denkmäler aus Lykaonien, Pamphylien und Isaurien*, 1935, pp. 33 ff., nos. 74–5 (for all three letters and their dates). On the political status of Selge and the vicissitudes of the city, cf. A. H. M. Jones, *The cities* &c., pp. 131 ff., and notes 15 and 16 (the author quotes the new publication of the letters but makes no use of it). In this war Eumenes was certainly a benefactor not only of the cities of his own kingdom but also of those of all Asia Minor, just as he had been during the Ortiagon-Galatian war of 184 B.C. See the inscription of Telmessus quoted above, Ch. V, n. 45: ἀναδεξάμενος τὸν πόλεμον, says the inscription, οὐ μ[όνον ὑπ]ὲρ τῶν ὑφ' αὑτὸν τασσομένων, ἀλλὰ καὶ | [ὑπὲρ ἄ]λλων τῶν κατοικούντων τὴν Ἀσίαν.

[71] Bithynian wars, B. Niese, *Gesch. d. Gr. u. Mak. St.* iii, pp. 326 ff. On the wars of Attalus II and III, ibid., pp. 359 ff., cf. above, n. 38. On the war with Selge see the comments of J. Keil on the inscriptions of Amlada quoted in the preceding note. On the war waged for the sake of Orophernes' money left in deposit at Priene and claimed by Ariarathes V, the protégé of Attalus II, Polyb. xxxiii. 6; Diod. xxxi. 32. The sorry plight of Priene at this time, repeated lack of money for urgent needs, and threatening famine are mentioned in the well-known decree for Moschion, who helped the city by repeated gifts and loans of money and sales of grain for less than the market price, see *I. v. Pr.* 108. Unfortunately his various benefactions cannot be exactly dated (above, Ch. V, n. 124). With the unhappy state of Priene at this time were connected the repeated embassies of Moschion, in search probably of help, to Syria, to Egypt, and to the Nabataeans. Correspondence of Eumenes II and Attalus II with the chief priest of Pessinus: C. B. Welles, *R.C.*, nos. 55–61, pp. 241 ff. On the Thracian war, see the inscription *O.G.I.* 330; on its date (145 B.C.), L. Robert, *B.C.H.* lii (1928), pp. 438 ff., cf. the Menas inscription of Sestus, *O.G.I.* 339 (the inscription of Bizye is not connected by Robert with the same expedition, see *Rev. É. G.* xlviii (1935), p. 333, and *Villes de l'Asie Mineure*, 1935, p. 77). On the Hellespontine and Thracian province of the Attalids, M. Holleaux, *B.C.H.* xlviii (1924), pp. 14 ff. Celebration by Attalus II of his military successes in general: *O.G.I.* 328. The war and victory of Attalus III: *O.G.I.* 332. The wars were certainly a great burden on the cities of the kingdom, which had to feed the armies: see above, Ch. V, n. 55.

[72] On the urbanization of the Pergamene kingdom see my remarks above, Ch. V, n. 58. L. Robert (*Rev. Arch.* 6, sér. iii (1934), pp. 88 ff., esp. p. 91) insists on the agricultural, not military, character of this colonization.

[73] Athens—*I.G.* ii², 3171, cf. *O.G.I.* 318. Delphi—*S.I.G.*³ 671 and 672 (for the date, G. Daux, *B.C.H.* lix (1935), pp. 222 ff.), cf. *I.G.* ii². 953, and *S.I.G.*³ 670 and 682, and in general G. Daux, *Delphes, &c.*, pp. 497 ff. Κοινὸν τῶν Ἰώνων—Rehm, *Milet, Erg. d. Ausgr.* i. 9, no. 306, pp. 144 ff., cf. ibid., no. 307; C. B. Welles, *R.C.* 52; donation of money for buying grain, Th. Wiegand, *Milet, VII. Bericht*, pp. 27 ff.; B. Laum, *Stiftungen*, ii, pp. 159 ff., no. 129 b (full bibliography, G. Daux, *B.C.H.* lix (1935), p. 226, n. 5; and ibid., pp. 226 ff., on the date of this document). Calaureia—*O.G.I.* 297. Cos—Sacrifice calendar of Cos, Paton–Hicks, 43 b. 5 and 18 f.; A. Neppi-Modona, *L'isola di Coo*, 1933, p. 46, n. 8. The date is controversial. Paton and Hicks think of Eumenes I and Attalus I, while Neppi-Modona is inclined to identify the kings with Eumenes II and Attalus II. Ephesus—Strabo, xiv. 1. 24, p. 641. I cite again (see above, Ch. V, nn. 22 and 50) the inscription of Chios, which is of earlier date (Attalus I (?)), because it is a typical instance of the use of loans by the kings (?) as a means of binding independent cities to themselves.

[74] An interesting text (*O.G.I.* 331; C. B. Welles, *R.C.*, nos. 65–7)—three letters of Attalus II written on behalf of Sosander and Athenaeus, distant

relatives of the king—show the exalted position enjoyed by such relatives in the Pergamene kingdom (cf. above, Ch. V, n. 55). On the high officials of the crown see, e.g., the decree of Pergamon for a σύντροφος τοῦ βασιλέως (Attalus II), who was entrusted with an embassy to Rome, *O.G.I.* 323, the somewhat similar decree of Aegina in honour of Cleon, governor of the island under Attalus II, and the decree of Sardis in honour of Timarchus, a former *rhiscophylax* of the king, W. H. Buckler and D. M. Robinson, *Sardis*, vii. 1, no. 4, cf. no. 89.

[75] The inscriptions which speak of these wealthy people of Asia Minor will be quoted and discussed presently. On Craton, whose life is known from ten complete or fragmentary inscriptions, see G. Daux, 'Craton, Eumène II et Attale II', *B.C.H.* lix (1935), pp. 210 ff. Pasparus was evidently a very rich man. L. Robert, *Ét. Anat.*, pp. 45 ff., is right in pointing out that the honours paid to him by Pergamon were bestowed as a recognition chiefly of his great service to the city, his embassy to Rome. However, unless he had considerable wealth and intimate relations with powerful Roman friends, which again required substantial means, Pasparus would certainly have been helpless at Rome. Besides, the gifts which he bestowed on the city of Pergamon are not less valuable than those of Menas and show him to have been a real nabob (an expression which I used in my *Soc. and Ec. Hist.*), a typical product of the time.

[76] On the social conditions of the Pergamene kingdom see above, p. 564 f. All over Asia in Hellenistic times there were certainly large numbers of slaves (beside serfs) who were employed in cultivating the fields and gardens of the (mostly absentee) landlords. This is attested for the Seleucid period by the well-known Sardis inscription, W. H. Buckler and D. M. Robinson, *A.J.A.* xvi (1912), p. 13, col. i, cf. p. 56, cf. *Sardis*, vii. 1, no. 1, and by some inscriptions of Priene (*I. v. Priene*, 18; *O.G.I.* 215, l. 24: Larichus receives from the city ἀτέλειαγ καὶ τῶ[γ] | κτηνῶγ καὶ τῶν σωμάτων ὅσα ἂν ὑπάρχηι ἔν τε [τ]οῖς ἰδίοις κτήμασ[ι] | καὶ ἐν τῆι πόλει). For the period we are considering see *O.G.I.* 351; *I. v. Priene*, 39: Ἀριαράθης τὴν Πριηνέων] πόλιν πολιο[ρκήσας] | [καὶ κ]τήματα σ[υλήσας, πλεῖστα] δὲ καὶ σώματα [ἰδιωτικά τε καὶ | δημό]σια ἀπ[αγαγών] (155 B.C.). Cf. Polyb. xxxiii. 6. 6 ff. and my *Kolonat*, pp. 250 ff. On royal slaves, above, Ch. IV, n. 332. For private people, see, e.g., the slaves whom Craton bequeathed to the Dionysiac artistes, *O.G.I.* 326 (Attalus II). These references will suffice. For Strabo and Diodorus the Pergamene kingdom was as much a State based on slave labour as was contemporary Sicily, see Strabo xiv. 1. 38, p. 646: εἰς δὲ τὴν μεσόγαιαν ἀνιὼν (Aristonicus) ἤθροισε διὰ ταχέων πλῆθος ἀπόρων τε ἀνθρώπων καὶ δούλων ἐπ' ἐλευθερίᾳ κατακεκλημένων οὓς Ἡλιοπολίτας ἐκάλεσε; Diod. xxxiv–xxxv. 1. 26: τὸ παραπλήσιον δὲ γέγονε καὶ κατὰ τὴν Ἀσίαν κατὰ τοὺς αὐτοὺς καιρούς, Ἀριστονίκου μὲν ἀντιποιησαμένου τῆς μὴ προσηκούσης βασιλείας, τῶν δὲ δούλων διὰ τὰς ἐκ τῶν δεσποτῶν κακουργίας συναπονοησαμένων ἐκείνῳ καὶ μεγάλοις ἀτυχήμασι πολλὰς πόλεις περιβαλόντων. It is perhaps not too hazardous to connect with the war of Aristonicus the funeral epigram of Demetrius found in Amyzon and dated

to the second century B.C. Demetrius was murdered by his slave, and his house was burnt. The slave was crucified by the citizens of Amyzon, *Greek Inscr. Br. Mus.* iv. 2. 1036; L. Robert, *Ét. Anat.*, p. 389. In any case the inscription reflects well one aspect of the relations between slaves and masters in Asia Minor in the second century B.C.

[77] We must of course discriminate between the privileges granted by the Pergamene decree to the higher classes of the time of Attalus III (πάροικοι, soldiers, military κάτοικοι) and to the lower classes. By this act the former became citizens and as such would fight with the other citizens in the troubled times after the death of Attalus III; the latter, of whom part had already fled from the city and were ready to join an organized revolt (ll. 25 ff.), were invited to come back to their ἰδία and to resume peaceful work under changed and more privileged conditions. *Mutatis mutandis* the situation was the same as in Egypt. The motives of the city in passing its decree of φιλάνθρωπα are clearly emphasized in ll. 8 ff.: ἀναγκαῖ]όν τέ ἐστιν ἔνεκα τῆς κοινῆς ἀσ[φ]αλείας καὶ τ[ὰ ὑποτετα]|γμένα γένη μετέχειν τῆς πολιτείας. See the discussion of the decree by M. Segre, *Athen.*, xvi (1938), p. 123 f.

[78] The best accounts are those of B. Niese, *Gesch. d. gr. u. mak. St.* iii, pp. 360 ff.; U. Wilcken, art. 'Aristonicus', *P.W.K.* ii. 962 ff., and G. Cardinali, 'La morte di Attalo III e la rivolta di Aristonico', *Saggi di St. Ant. e di Arch.*, 1910, pp. 269 ff., cf. H. Last, *C.A.H.* ix, pp. 102 ff., and T. R. S. Broughton, 'Roman Asia Minor', pp. 505 ff.

[79] The decree of Pergamon (rather than Elaea, see M. Segre, *Athen.* xvi (1938), p. 128) about the συμμαχία with Rome, *S.I.G.*³ 694 (130/29 B.C.), in describing the war speaks of μεγάλοι κίνδυνοι [κ]αὶ κατὰ γῆν καὶ κ[ατὰ θ]άλασσαν. The *foedus* of Rome with Methymna (*S.I.G.*³ 693) may be explained as a preventive measure taken by Rome against the naval aims of Aristonicus. Note that Methymna was devastated by Prusias II in the first Bithynian war. Was Aristonicus helped by the pirates? Such help is not attested; but the pirates supported Perseus and later Mithridates. It is difficult to believe that under the last Attalids the Ephesians had their own navy. Ephesus was their second capital, and *cistophori* were coined there. It would hardly have been allowed to have its own navy.

[80] The war is mentioned in the following inscriptions. (I) PERGAMON: the numerous inscriptions in honour of Diodorus, son of Heroides, Pasparus (mostly of 125 B.C.). The most important was first published by Hepding, *Ath. Mitt.* xxxii (1907), pp. 243 ff., no. 4, cf. *I.G.R.* iv. 292. The parts which bear on Aristonicus' war have been recently restored by A. Wilhelm, *Wien. S.B.* ccxiv. 5 (1932), pp. 21 ff., where will be found a complete list of the Pasparus inscriptions and a full bibliography. On the date, L. Robert, *B.C.H.* liv (1930), pp. 337 ff. A paper by the same author on Pasparus (announced loc. cit.) has not yet been published, cf. his *Ét. Anat.*, pp. 45 ff. Cf. the interesting, though fragmentary, votive epigram to Athena of one who was saved by her during the war of Aristonicus, *I. v. Perg.* 14; F. Hiller von

Gaertringen, *Hist. gr. Epigramme*, 1926, no. 111. (2) PERGAMON or ELAEA (above, n. 79): *S.I.G.*³ 694. (3) METHYMNA, Lesbos: decree of the νέοι, *S.E.G.* iii, 710, cf. *S.I.G.*³ 693 (*foedus* between Rome and Methymna). (4) CYZICUS: decree for Machaon, *I.G.R.* iv. 134. (5) SESTUS: decree for Menas, *O.G.I.* 339. (6) PRIENE: decree for Moschion, *I. v. Priene*, 108, 223 ff., and for Herodes, ibid. 109, 92. (7) BARGYLIA, Caria: decree for Poseidonius, M. Holleaux, *Rev. É. A.* xxi (1919), pp. 1 ff., and another one (dated at the beginning of the war and mentioning hardships of the city and a miraculous intervention, ἐπιφάνεια, of Artemis Kindyas), L. Robert, *Ét. Anat.*, pp. 459 ff., cf. T. R. S. Broughton, *Cl. Phil.*, xxix (1934), pp. 252 ff., and L. Robert, *Villes d'Asie Mineure*, 1935, p. 48. (8) HALICARNASSUS: *C.I.G.* 2501; A. Wilhelm, *Jahreshefte*, xi (1908), pp. 69 ff. Cf. BYZANTIUM, Tac. *Ann.* xii. 62. (9) STRATONICEA: decree in two fragments, *B.C.H.* xliv (1920), p. 70 f., and ibid. xi (1887), p. 161 f., cf. P. Roussel, *B.C.H.* lv (1931), p. 70, no. 1, and A. Wilhelm, *apud* A. Schober, *Der Fries des Hekateions von Lagina*, 1933, p. 13. Reprinted and discussed by L. Robert, *Ét. Anat.*, p. 461 f., in connexion with a discussion of the decree of Bargylia. (10) As regards the attempt of a group of supporters of Aristonicus to hand over Pergamon to him, see the decree for Pasparus, *I.G.R.* iv. 292; Wilhelm, loc. cit., ll. 11 ff.: ἀνεκτήσα]|το δὲ καὶ τοὺς βίους τῶν ἀνειρημένων ὑπὸ Μιθραδ[άτου καὶ τῶν ἄλλων τῶν . . . .] | ἐν τῶι πολέμωι, ἐξ ὧν ἀφόρητος ἐπηκολούθει τῆι πόλει κί[νδυνος. It is difficult to accept the restoration ἀποθανόντων in the lacuna of l. 12. I prefer ἀποστάντων or ἀφεστακότων, and translate the sentence as follows: 'He secured (for the city) the estates of those who were killed (or executed) by Mithridates and of the rest of those who rebelled during the war, men whose action threatened the city with intolerable danger.' I cannot go into details. Suffice it to say that the interpretation of this passage by Wilhelm is rather vague and involved. I see that H. Last interprets the passage in the same way as I do, *C.A.H.* ix, p. 105. L. Robert, *Ét. Anat.*, pp. 45 ff., deals with other parts of the same decree. Cf. Addendum to this note.

[81] I cannot enter here into a detailed discussion of the Hellenistic Utopias and especially of that of Iambulus. A good treatment of these, with complete bibliographical references, will be found in W. W. Tarn, 'Alexander the Great and the Unity of Mankind', *Proc. Brit. Acad.* xix, 1933, pp. 9 ff. (141 ff) (he has proved that Iambulus' work is not a product of Stoic philosophy), cf. pp. 43 ff. on Euhemerus' Panchara (I still believe in a connexion between Euhemerus and Ptolemaic Egypt). On the solar religion of the Orient and its influence on Greece and especially on Stoicism, J. Bidez, 'La Cité du monde et la cité du soleil chez les stoïciens', *Bull. de l'Ac. Royale de Belgique*, 5 sér. xviii (1932), pp. 244 ff. On the Sun God as master, liberator, and guardian of justice, ibid., pp. 275 ff., and the papers by F. Cumont in *Rend. Pontif. Acc. Rom. Arch.* i (1925), pp. 65 ff., and v (1927), pp. 69 ff. See also A. Dölger, *Antike und Christentum*, v (1936), pp. 138 ff. Cf., on the θεοὶ Ὅσιοι καὶ Δίκαιοι of Asia Minor associated with Zeus Bronton, the Sun and the Moon, and with other gods, L. Robert, *Rev. Phil.* xiii (65) (1939), pp. 202 ff., and pl. 1. As

regards "Ἥλιος Δικαιοσύνης compare the contemporary cult-name Δικαιοσύνη, associated posthumously with Ptolemy Philometor by Cleopatra II in 139 and then assumed by Cleopatra III, W. Otto and H. Bengtson, 'Zur Geschichte des Niederganges des Ptolemäerreiches', *Bay. Abh.* xvii (1938), pp. 43 f., 140 f., 143 f., and 150, cf. L. Robert, *Mél. Syr. R. Dussaud,* ii (1940), p. 731. I cannot here discuss this cult-name and the cult-name Δίκαιος adopted by Commagenian, Bactrian, and Parthian kings.

[82] On the organization of the Pergamene army see my chapter 'Pergamon' in *C.A.H.* viii, pp. 594 ff., cf. G. T. Griffith, *The mercenaries of the Hellenistic world,* 1935, pp. 171 ff. C. A. Forbes, *Neoi,* 1933, p. 51, denies that military training was ever given to the ephebes and *neoi* of Pergamon and the other cities of the Pergamene kingdom, and L. Robert, *Rev. É.G.* xlviii (1935), p. 333 (review of Forbes's book), agrees with him. But although ἀκοντισμοί and τοξεῖαι mentioned in the Menas inscription and οἱ διὰ τῶν ὅπλων ἀγῶνες in one of the inscriptions relating to Pasparus of Pergamon (*O.G.I.* 764, l. 24; *I.G.R.* iv. 294) are not uncommon in other cities as part of the physical training of young men, the peculiar conditions of Sestus and Pergamon lead me to think that in this case the training was intended to make the young men fit for military service. Note in the Menas inscription (*O.G.I.* 339, l. 71 f.) his general remark on the aim of the training: ἐξ ὧν αἱ τῶν νεωτέρων ψυχαὶ πρὸς ἀνδρείαν ἁμιλλώμε|ναι καλῶς ἄγονται τοῖς ἤθεσιν πρὸς ἀρετήν (observe the Stoic ideas), cf. *I. v. Priene* 112, 74 f.: δι' [ὧν μὲν] τὸ σῶμα βουλόμενος ἄοκνο[ν] τυγχάνειν, δι' ὧν δὲ τ[ὰς ψυχ]ὰς πρὸς ἀρετὴν καὶ πάθος ἀνθρώπινον προάγεσθαι. Cf. my remarks on the *iuvenes, Stor. Ec. e Soc. d. I.R.,* pp. 54, 120, 125, 148, 268, 379, 500, and 501. The date of the organization of the *neoi* at Pergamon is not known. It may have existed before 147 B.C. Cf. *O.G.I.* 748; *S.E.G.* ii. 663. 9–12 ; Welles, *R.C.* no. 51, l. 24.

[83] The decree of the city which followed the death of Attalus III and preceded the war of Aristonicus, *O.G.I.* 338 ; the ratification of the contents of the king's testament by the Senate, *O.G.I.* 435, of unknown date. The most recent discussions of the problems concerning the decree of the city and the testament of Attalus III are those of M. Segre, *Athen.* xvi (1938), p. 123 f., and T. R. S. Broughton, 'Roman Asia Minor', p. 508. Cf. above, n. 77.

[84] A brilliant treatment of the gradual development of the methods of rule used by the Roman government in the provinces in general will be found in J. Carcopino, *Hist. Rom.* ii. 117 ff. That of G. H. Stevenson in *C.A.H.* ix, pp. 437ff. (with bibliography) is more antiquarian than historical. For the later time J. M. Cobban, *Senate and Provinces, 78–49 B.C.,* 1935 (with bibliography, which supplements in some points that given by Stevenson). On the province of Asia, V. Chapot, *La Province romaine proconsulaire d'Asie,* 1904, pp. 14 ff. ; T. Frank, *An economic history of Rome,* 2nd ed., 1927, pp. 141 ff., and T. R. S. Broughton, 'Roman Asia Minor', pp. 535 ff., cf. A. Passerini, *Athen.* xv (1937), pp. 277 ff.

[85] Cf. my *Kolonat,* p. 283. On the *lex Sempronia,* Cic. *Verr.* ii. 3. 6. 12, cf. Schol. Bob., p. 259 (Orelli) ; Diod. xxxiv–xxxv. 25 ; Fronto *ad Ver.* ii. 1.

[86] On the *senatus consultum* and the praetor's decree of 129 B.C., F. Miltner and Selahattin Bey, *Türk Tarih, Arkeologya ve etnografya Dergisi*, ii (1934), pp. 240 ff., cf. p. 301; A. Passerini, *Athen.* xv (1937), pp. 252 ff.; M. Segre, ibid. xvi (1938), pp. 119 ff. In his article A. Passerini discusses the passage of Appian in the light of the new evidence, without quoting the inscription of Pasparus. M. Segre in his discussion takes for granted that the *chora* of Pergamon was immune. The new date assigned by Passerini to the S.C. is based on the names of the consuls in part restored; before the new fragment was found the inscription was dated 110 B.C., see F. Münzer, *P.W.K.* xv. 618, who now accepts the new date (private letter). The wording of the S.C. of Adramyttium is very similar to that of the *S.C. de Oropiis* (73 B.C.), *S.I.G.*³ 747, which makes it probable that in the case of Pergamon also temple interests were at stake. I may add that the letter of Julius Caesar engraved on the same stone as the Smyrnaean copy of the S.C. (M. Segre, loc. cit.), though certainly dealing with the territory of Pergamon, its status at the time of Attalus III, its frontier towards the territory of Elaea, mentions also *asylia* and something which somebody 'consecrated to the gods'. Cf. the inscription published by M. Segre, *Il Mondo classico*, iii (1933), pp. 485 ff., and ibid. iv (1934), p. 71—an ἐπίκριμα of P. Servilius Isauricus concerning the *asylia* of the Asclepieum and its 'sacred laws'.

[87] Cic. *De lege agr.* ii. 15. 39 and esp. 18. 50 and 19. 52.

[88] I have dealt with the history of the χώρα βασιλική after the Attalids in my *Kolonat*, pp. 283 ff. Against my point of view, T. Frank, 'Dominium in solo provinciali', *J.R.S.* xvii (1927), pp. 141 ff., and *An econ. hist. of Rome*, 2nd ed., 1927, pp. 141 ff. His theory that the *dominium in solo provinciali* was a late product of juridical thought has not been accepted *in toto* by other scholars; see for bibliography the German and Italian editions of my *Soc. and Ec. Hist.*, ch. vii, n. 1. Cf. J. Carcopino, *Hist. Rom.* ii, pp. 131 ff. Frank's ideas have been developed by T. R. S. Broughton, 'Roman Land-holding in Asia Minor', *Tr. Am. Phil. Ass.* lxv (1934), pp. 207 ff., cf. his 'Roman Asia Minor', pp. 509 ff. For Frank and Broughton the decisive argument against the *ager publicus* theory is the absence of the χώρα βασιλική of the Attalids in the list of regions which were offered by the law of Servilius Rullus for sale in Asia Minor (see note 87). I regard this argument as fallacious, like all arguments *ex silentio*. The law of Rullus did not propose to offer for sale *all* the *ager publicus* that was owned by the State. There were tracts of *ager publicus* '*extra Italiam*' which the law intended to subject to a *pergrande vectigal*. The Attalid χώρα βασιλική may have been one of those tracts. Or Caesar may have had reasons of a political nature for not including it in the list of lands offered for sale. The silence of the law is equally puzzling if we accept the theory that the *agri regii* were private estates of the kings. Some private estates of the Attalids, and especially of Attalus III, certainly existed. See *I. v. Priene*, 111, l. 112; cf. on the estates confiscated by Attalus III *O.G.I.* 338, ll. 20 ff.; G. Cardinali, 'La morte di Attalo III', &c., pp. 269 ff., and my paper in *Anat. Stud.*, p. 376. What happened to them? They

disappeared, says Broughton. How and why? I must emphasize the fact that, if we accept the theory of Frank and Broughton, it is hard to understand why in the case of Asia Minor the Romans departed from their established practice, a practice which they regularly followed, where similar conditions existed, in their other provinces both in the East and in the West earlier and later, see for example above, p. 748, on Greece, and below, on Bithynia, Ch. VII, n. 65. I may add that in the absence of positive evidence one may suggest (if the treatment of Asia *was* exceptional) the following possibility. We may suppose that the *chora* of the Attalid kingdom (if distinct from the *chora basilike*) was already treated as *ager stipendiarius* by the Seleucids and the Attalids, and paid a *decuma* (δεκάτη), while the *laoi* of the *chora basilike* paid rents and dues. In this case the Romans would not have introduced any changes except perhaps the extension of the system of the δεκάτη—applied in the past possibly also to the military *cleroi* and temple land (?)—to the city territories. It may be noted that it is possible to interpret in this sense the documents quoted by L. Robert, *Ét. Anat.*, p. 159 f. (*O.G.I.* 488 and *I.G.* ii. 3059 and 3233), where the village of Castolos appears as the place of origin of its inhabitants resident in Attica. But the solution of the problems indicated above must await the discovery of further evidence.

[89] The few cases of encroachment of the *publicani* on temple land included in the territory of a city are listed in my *Kolonat* p. 284, cf. Broughton, loc. cit., p. 220, n. 72. They are: Ilium, *O.G.I.* 440 (89 B.C.); Priene, *I. v. Priene*, III, ll. 112 ff., cf. ibid. 117 (first century B.C.); Thyatira, *I.G.R.* iv. 1211. Cf. the S.C. of Adramyttium and Smyrna, above, n. 86. On Ephesus, Strabo, xiv. 1. 26, p. 642.

[90] On temple-states in Asia Minor, my remarks in *Kolonat*, pp. 273 ff.; *Anatol. Stud.*, pp. 369 ff.; *C.A.H.* ix, pp. 214 ff.

[91] On Attalus III, B. Niese, loc. cit. iii, pp. 363 ff., and the paper of G. Cardinali quoted in note 78.

[92] It is to be noted that in the speech *pro Flacco* (7. 17) Cicero in quoting a *psephisma* of the city of Pergamon, voted at the instigation of Mithridates of Pergamon, says that the voters were *sutores* and *zonarii*, which testifies to the great importance of the textile industry in Pergamon in 62 B.C. Most of the cities of Asia Minor were at this time centres of trade and industry. In the same speech (8. 18) Cicero designates the members of the popular assemblies of the cities of Asia Minor as *opifices* and *tabernarii*.

[93] On the *publicani* and their activity in Asia Minor and on the feelings of the provincials towards them, see the books and articles quoted in the following Chapter, note 45. The few texts relating to the period before Sulla are discussed by J. Carcopino, *Hist. Rom.* ii, pp. 74 ff., and esp. 134 f. On the Romans in Pergamon see the lists of ephebes found in the Gymnasium of Pergamon, W. Kolbe, *Ath. Mitt.* xxxii (1907), pp. 415 ff.; P. Jacobsthal, ibid. xxxiii (1908), pp. 384 ff.; H. Hepding, ibid. xxxv (1910), pp. 422 ff., esp. 424. In the list *Ath. Mitt.* xxxii (1907), p. 438, no. 303, the Romans form a

special group. Cf. C. A. Forbes, *Neoi*, 1933, for the *neoi* (with the dates of the single lists as established by Hepding); T. Frank, *Econ. Survey*, i, p. 277, and Broughton, 'Roman Asia Minor', pp. 535 ff., and 543 ff.

94 On Rutilius Rufus, F. Münzer, *P.W.K.* i A. 1273 ff.; stay in Asia as legate of Q. Mucius Scaevola 94 B.C., trial 92 B.C. On his literary activity and on his personal character, G. L. Hendrickson, 'The Memoirs of Rutilius Rufus', *Class. Phil.* xxviii (1933), pp. 153 ff. On Scaevola and his government, F. Münzer, *P.W.K.* xvi. 437 ff. Cf. on the date of Scaevola's governorship, J. P. V. D. Balsdon, *Cl. Rev.* li (1937), pp. 8 ff. It was during his governorship that there occurred the ταραχή, ἔχθρα, and διαφορά between Ephesus and Sardis which apparently led to a regular war, accompanied by σύλησις and ἀδικίαι. A σύλλυσις was achieved by Scaevola: *I.G.R.* iv. 297; *O.G.I.* 437. However futile and unconnected with the activity of the *publicani* the reasons for this local ταραχή may have been, the fact of the ταραχή shows how excited the cities of Asia Minor were on the eve of Mithridates' war.

95 On the *negotiatores*, J. Hatzfeld, *Les Trafiquants*, &c., pp. 44 ff.

96 The honorary inscriptions found in the ruins of the Stoa of Orophernes will be found in *I. v. Priene*, 107–30, cf. 131–9. On the Stoa, M. Schede, *Die Ruinen von Priene*, 1934, pp. 49 ff., esp. 55.

97 On the Μούκιεια, Pfister, *P.W.K.* iii A. 1229. 5 (s. v. 'Soteria'), and F. Münzer, ibid. viii. 1146. On the cult of P. Servilius Isauricus, the son of the famous conqueror of the pirates, P. Servilius Vatia Isauricus (triumph in 74 B.C.), F. Münzer, *Römische Adelsparteien*, 1921, p. 356 f. (14 inscriptions for him and his relatives), cf. id. *P.W.K.* ii A. 1800.

98 I have dealt with some of the families mentioned in the text in two papers (both first published in Russian): 'Queen Dynamis of Bosporus', *J.H.S.* xxxix (1919), pp. 88 ff., and 'Caesar and the South of Russia', *J.R.S.* vii (1917), pp. 27 ff. The evidence about the family of CHAEREMON is collected in the notes to *S.I.G.³* 741. On Pythodoris and her connexion with Antony, Th. Mommsen, *Eph. Ep.* i, pp. 270 ff.; against his view, H. Dessau, *Eph. Ep.* ix (1913), p. 691, but see W. W. Tarn, *C.A.H.* x, p. 112, n. 5. MITHRIDATES OF PERGAMON. His biography has often been written by various scholars, mostly in connexion with his relations with Caesar and with the Galatian royal family: G. Hirschfeld, *Hermes*, xiv (1879), p. 474 f.; Th. Reinach, *Mithr. Eup.*, p. 292 f.; F. Stähelin, *Gesch. d. kleinas. Galater*, 2nd ed., 1907, pp. 92 ff., and 118; Geyer, *P.W.K.* xv. 2205 f., no. 15. The epigraphical evidence bearing on him and found at Pergamon, *I. v. Perg.* 213 and 247; *I.G.R.* iv. 1682; H. Hepding, *Ath. Mitt.* xxxiv (1909), pp. 329 ff., and ibid. xxxv (1910), p. 471, n. 55; P. Jacobsthal, ibid. xxxiii (1908), p. 407, n. 36, cf. my paper quoted above, *J.R.S.* vii (1917), p. 30 f., and L. Robert, *Ét. Anat.*, p. 53, n. 3. Cf. the letter of Julius Caesar (part of the dossier regarding the *chora* of the Pergamenes, above, p. 813, n. 86) in which Mithridates is mentioned as Pergamene ambassador to him. The letter first published by A. Passerini, *Athen.* xv (1937), pp. 252 ff., has been discussed in the light of the other

presented to W.H. Buckler, 1939, pp. 227 ff. As regards Pergamon, Mithridates
evidence by M. Segre, ibid. xvi (1938), pp. 119 ff., cf. L. Robert, *Anat. Stud.*
was the real successor of the great Pasparus. The identity of Mithridates of
Pergamon with the Mithridates mentioned by Cicero (*pro Flacco* 17 and 41:
in the last passage he is called *columen accusationis*) was pointed out by A.
Du Mesnil in 1883 in his edition of the speech (p. 82), though rejected by
Orelli (*Onom. Tull.*). Contemporaneously and independently the same conclusion was reached by B. Niese, 'Straboniana', IV, *Rh. Mus.* xxxviii (1883),
p. 593, n. 2. The identification, however, has never been mentioned and
discussed by later modern biographers of Mithridates. I regard it as highly
probable. It suits so well the picture of Mithridates as revealed by the
inscriptions and the description of him in *Bell. Alex.* 26, which ultimately goes
back to Caesar: . . . 'Mithridates Pergamenus magnae nobilitatis domi
scientiaeque in bello et virtutis, fidei dignitatisque in amicitia Cæsaris' . . . .
A descendant of his (βασιλεὺς Μιθριδάτης) may have edited the collection of the
letters of Brutus (*Epistol. gr.*, Hercher, pp. 177–91), see R. Herzog, *H.Z.* 125
(1922), p. 211, n. 1. HIERON, ZENON, and POLEMON, Strabo, xii. 8. 16, p. 578,
and xiv. 2. 24, p. 660, cf. Philostr. *Vit. Soph.* i. 25 (530). H. Dessau, *Röm.
Kaiserzeit*, ii, p. 618 and p. 621, n. 1, has very little to say of Zenon and
Polemon, except to place Zenon's home once at Laodicea and a few pages
below at Nysa, cf. my paper in *J.H.S.* quoted above. EUTHYDEMUS and
HYBREAS, Strabo, xiv. 2. 24–5, pp. 659–60. CALLISTUS and THEOPOMPUS of
Cnidus. On Callistus, *S.I.G.*³ 761 A and B, with the notes; G. Daux,
Delphes, &c., pp. 407 ff. On Theopompus, F. Münzer, *P.W.K.* v. 2174,
and E. Bux, ibid., cf. G. Daux, loc. cit. The abundant epigraphical evidence
from Cnidus is collected in Pomtow's notes to *S.I.G.*³ 761 C, cf. my paper
in *J.R.S.* quoted above, p. 35 f. THEOPHANES and POTAMON of Mytilene
(Lesbos). On the former, *S.I.G.*³ 753 and 755, and notes; R. Laqueur, *P.W.K.*
v A. 2090 ff., who points out his close friendship with Pompey, and F. Hiller
von Gaertringen, *Gött. Nachr.*, Fachgr. I, vol. i. 6 (1936), pp. 107 ff. On
Potamon and his family and descendants, *S.I.G.*³ 754 and 764, cf. *I.G.* xii.
2. 35, and *I.G.R.* iv. 33; L. Robert, *B.C.H.* lix (1935), pp. 471 ff., and my
paper in *J.R.S.* vii (1917), pp. 32 ff., cf. F. Hiller von Gaertringen, loc. cit.,
p. 121. NICIAS of Cos: R. Herzog, 'Nikias und Xenophon von Kos', *H.Z.*
cxxv (1922), pp. 189 ff.; A. Neppi Modona, *L'Isola di Coo*, 1933, pp. 50 ff.

⁹⁹ Cf. M. Schede, *Die Ruinen von Priene*, 1934, p. 8 f.

¹⁰⁰ Vitruv. iii. 2. 3. On the Artemision, J. Kothe, in *Magnesia a. M.*,
Bericht über die Ergebn. der Ausgr., 1904, pp. 39 ff.; A. von Gerkan, *Der
Altar des Artemistempels in Magnesia*, 1929; M. von Massow, *Führer
durch das Pergamon Museum*, 2nd ed., 1936, pp. 28 ff. On the other
temples of Hermogenes and his school and especially on the temple of Hekate
in Lagina, A. Schober, *Der Fries des Hekateions von Lagina*, Istanbuler
Forschungen, ii (1933), pp. 16 ff. and 26, cf. L. Robert, *Ét. Anat.*, pp. 552 ff.
On the inscription, L. Robert, loc. cit., p. 461 f. Robert (*Ét. Anat.*, p. 427, n.
2) is inclined to assign, with J. Chamonard, *B.C.H.* xix (1895), pp. 260 ff., a

later date to the temple—after the Mithridatic war. My impression is that Schober is right. To the same group belong, according to Schede and Krencker, the Hellenistic temple of Ancyra, later rebuilt as a temple of Rome and Augustus, but originally constructed by the Attalids (like the temple of Pessinus, Strabo, xii. 5. 3, p. 567). Though this point cannot be proved, the statement of Strabo and the temple of Ancyra show that Galatia shared in the prosperity of Asia Minor both in late Pergamene and in Roman times. See D. Krencker and M. Schede, *Der Tempel in Ankara*, 1936, p. 50.

[101] B. Haussoullier, *Milet et le Didymeion*, 1902, pp. 220 ff., and on the rich citizens of Miletus, p. 235; F. Hiller von Gaertringen, art. 'Miletos', *P.W.K.* xv. 1611 ff.

[102] On the minting of *cistophori* in Asia Minor after 133 B.C., see the books and articles dealing with the *cistophori* quoted above, Ch. V, no. 70, esp. T. R. S. Broughton, 'Roman Asia Minor', pp. 555 ff. The minting of these coins testifies to the continued exploitation of the rich silver mines of Asia Minor and to the need of a currency which would be equally familiar to Asia Minor and Greece, on the one hand, and to Italy, on the other; cf. the hoard of Hierapytna in Crete, E. J. P. Raven, *Num. Chr.* lxxi (1938), pp. 133 ff. If we accept Broughton's theory that the cessation of the minting of *cistophori* in some leading cities of Asia Minor between about 67 B.C. and 58 B.C. is to be explained by the shortage of silver in Rome at this time, we must assume that Rome regarded herself as the owner of Anatolian mines, free to use the output as she liked.

[103] On Prusias' war against Attalus II, above, nn. 38 and 71.

[104] On the last three Bithynian kings and on the literary evidence relating to them, Th. Reinach, 'Un nouveau roi de Bithynie', *Rev. Num.*, 1897, pp. 247 ff. (and *L'Histoire par les Monnaies*, 1902, pp. 167 ff.). Reinach was the first to insert Nicomedes III Euergetes between Nicomedes II Epiphanes and Nicomedes IV Philopator and to regroup the literary evidence about the last kings who bore the name Nicomedes. His starting-point was the Delphian inscription *O.G.I.* 345, republished recently in a more complete form by G. Colin in *F. D.* iii. 4, no. 77. The date of the accession of Nicomedes III is supplied by *I. v. Priene*, 55, and a dedication of Delos *O.G.I.* 346; Durrbach, *Choix*, 101; *Inscr. de Délos*, 1579, cf. A. Plassart, *B.C.H.* xxxvi (1912), pp. 407 ff. Reinach also gave a fine survey of the leading features of the reign of Nicomedes III. On the Bithynian kings named Nicomedes, F. Geyer, *P.W.K.* xvii. 493 ff.

[105] NICOMEDES II EPIPHANES. Inscription of Delos (dedication of Nicomedes II in honour of Massinissa), Durrbach, *Choix*, 93; *Inscr. de Délos*, 1577 and 1577 bis, cf. 1578. Decree of the Ionian κοινόν: *I. v. Priene*, 55. Temple dedicated to his mother Apame: *I.G.* ii.² 3172, cf. A. Wilhelm, *Jahreshefte*, xi (1908), pp. 75, 79 ff. NICOMEDES III. Delian inscriptions: *O.G.I.* 346; Durrbach, *Choix*, 101; *Inscr. de Délos*, 1579 (127/6 B.C.); *O.G.I.* 342; Durrbach, *Choix*, 102; *Inscr. de Délos*, 2038 (110–109 B.C.), cf. *O.G.I.* 344; Durrbach,

Choix, 103; *Inscr. de Délos*, 1705 (merchants dealing with Bithynia). Delphian inscription: see above, p 783. Argos—*I.G.* iv. 558, and A. Wilhelm, loc. cit., (115/14 B.C.); Epidaurus—*I.G.* iv². 591, cf. A. Wilhelm, loc. cit. NICOMEDES IV (before his accession) *O.G.I.* 343; Durrbach, *Choix*, 104; *Inscr. de Délos*, 1580 (105/4–103/2 B.C.). The references in the Sacrifice calendar of Cos, Paton–Hicks, 35, to king Nicomedes (τᾶι αὐτᾶι] ἀμέραι καὶ βασιλεῖ Νικομή[δει) is assigned by R. Herzog on the ground of the lettering of the extant modern copy of the text (the stone itself is lost) to the time of Nicomedes I (R. Herzog, *Ath. Mitt.* xxx (1905), p. 180; cf. A. Neppi Modona, *L'Isola di Coo*, 1933, p. 183).

[106] Granius Licinianus, xxxv, pp. 28 and 29, cf. Th. Reinach, loc. cit. Note the characterization of Nicomedes: 'nam postquam Nicomedes Euergetes, ⟨qui⟩ est ita dictus quod beatos egentes faciebat multosque beneficiis alliciebat'.

[107] The preface to the *Periegesis* of Ps.-Scymnus gives interesting evidence of the mood of the population of Asia Minor in the first years of the existence of the Roman province. The author pays reverence to the great city of Rome, vv. 231 ff. Rome is to him ἄστρον τι κοινὸν τῆς ὅλης οἰκουμένης. But his real sympathy is with the glorious kings of Pergamon, the great heroes of the Greek population of Asia Minor (vv. 16 ff.: τοῖς ἐν Περγάμῳ | βασιλεῦσιν, ὧν ἡ δόξα καὶ τεθνηκότων | παρὰ πᾶσιν ἡμῖν ζῶσα διὰ παντὸς μένει). The Bithynian dynasty is the true successor of the Attalids (v. 50 f.: ἐγὼ δ' ἀκούων διότι τῶν νῦν βασιλέων | μόνος βασιλικὴν χρηστότητα προσφέρεις) protected as they were by the great god of Greek Asia Minor, Apollo of Didyma. In his summary Ps.-Scymnus lays great emphasis on the part of his *Periegesis* that deals with the barbarian tribes and stresses the point that his work is not only interesting but also useful. He does not fail to emphasize that he gives a list τῶν ἐμπορίων ὅσα τ' ἐστιν εὐτυχέστατα (v. 86). The interest of Nicomedes III in didactic poetry, in learned handbooks, is paralleled by the interest which Attalus III had in treatises on agriculture. On the identity of the king and on the date of the publication of the treatise, L. Pareti, 'Quando fu composta la periegesi del pseudo Scimno', *Saggi di St. ant.*, &c., *dedic. a G. Beloch*, 1910, pp. 133 ff.; cf. A. Plassart, *B.C.H.* xxxvi (1912), p. 409, n. 2, and G. Daux, *B.C.H.* lvii (1933), pp. 77 ff. On the character of the work and its sources, my *Skythien und der Bosporus*, 1933, pp. 28 ff., cf. Gisinger, *P.W.K.* v A. 685 ff. Add to my bibliography p. 28, n. 1, U. Höfer, 'Die Periegese des sog. Skymnos', *Rh. Mus.* lxxxii (1933), pp. 78 ff.

[108] Help to Rome: Memnon, 29. On the Heracleans at Athens, above, Ch. IV, p. 592, n. 354.

[109] On Cyzicus, above, Ch. IV, pp. 587 ff., nn. 345 ff. History of Cyzicus in the late Hellenistic period, F. Hasluck, *Cyzicus*, 1910, p. 175 f.

[110] On Sinope and its commerce see above, Ch. IV, pp. 593 ff., n. 356. B. N. Grakov in his *corpus* of stamps with the names of the astynomi (B. N. Grakov, *Ancient Greek ceramic stamps with the names of the Astynomi*, Moscow, 1929 (in Russian)) has dealt with their chronology. It is very probable that in

Roman times the jars were no longer stamped, and it is evident from the author's lists that there was no notable decline in the Sinopian commerce in the second century B.C. As regards the Sinopians at Athens, above, Ch. IV, loc. cit. Cf. Chr. M. Danov, *Bull. Inst. Arch. Bulg.* xii (1939), pp. 225 ff. (in Bulgarian with French resumé).

[111] Delian honours to Laodice, the sister of Pharnaces I and sister-wife of Mithridates IV Philopator Philadelphus, Durrbach, *Choix*, 74; *Inscr. de Délos*, 1555–6; to Mithridates V Euergetes, *Inscr. de Délos*, 1557 and 1558; Durrbach, *Choix*, 99 (129 B.C.), cf. Durrbach, *Choix*, 100; *Inscr. de Délos*, 1559. See also the agonistic catalogue of Chios in which among the victors in the horse-races appears Mithridates Euergetes: M. Segre, *Il Mondo class.* ii (1932), pp. 132 ff. (who suggests Eupator, but see L. Robert, *B.C.H.* lix (1935), pp. 453 ff.). Delian honours to Mithridates Eupator, *O.G.I.* 369; Durrbach, *Choix*, 113; *Inscr. de Délos*, 1560: statues of Eupator and of his brother Chrestus dedicated in 115 B.C. by a former gymnasiarch; Durrbach, *Choix*, 114; *Inscr. de Délos*, 1561: dedication to Zeus Urius, the great protector of maritime commerce and especially Pontic commerce, for the safety of Eupator and Chrestus (same date). Relations between Pontus and Athens before and after the accession of Mithridates: W. S. Ferguson, *H.A.*, pp. 437 ff.; Durrbach, *Choix*, p. 216. Coins of Mithridates, Head, *H.N.*[2], p. 501; Th. Reinach, *Mithridate Eupator*, pp. 476 ff. (German transl.); Babelon–Reinach, *Rec. Gén.* i. 1[2], 1925; Ch. Seltman, *Greek Coins*, p. 273 f., cf. L. Laffranchi, 'Nuovi testi numismatici sulle vittorie Romane nel Ponto', *Hist.* ix (1935), pp. 39 ff., and F. Imhoof–Blumer, *Num. Z.* xlv (1913), pp. 169 ff. (for the municipal bronze coinage of the time of Mithridates VI).

[112] The Heroon of Mithridates: F. Chapouthier, 'Le Sanctuaire des Dieux de Samothrace', *Expl. Arch. Délos*, xvi, 1935. The inscriptions, revised by the same writer, ibid., pp. 32 ff. Cf. Durrbach, *Choix*, 133–6, and *Inscr. de Délos*, 1562–74. For the building and its sculptural decoration, E. Dyggve, F. Poulsen, K. Rhomaios, *Das Heroon von Kalydon*, 1934, pp. 95 ff. On Helianax, son of Asclepiodorus, see note to *Inscr. de Délos*, 1552. On the possible connexions of his family with Rhodes, ibid., note to 1556.

[113] Note that it was an Amisene who set up at Delos a statue of an Athenian holder of a court-title of Mithridates Euergetes, Durrbach, *Choix*, 100; *Inscr. de Délos*, 1559. In his note to this inscription Durrbach quotes the funeral epigram of the two brothers Pharnaces and Myron, probably Amisenes, who were driven by a storm to Seriphos, where they were taken for pirates and killed by the peasants, Kaibel, 214. Protus, who built them a cenotaph on Rhenea, was an Amisene himself, probably resident in Delos, where his four sons erected his statue, *Inscr. de Délos*, 1984, cf. 2598, l. 23. A. Wilhelm, *Jahreshefte*, iv (1901), Beibl., p. 17, and *B.C.H.* xxix (1905), pp. 410 ff., is right in assuming the existence of a numerous Amisene group of merchants at Delos. Cf. Ch. IV, note 355 on the Amisenes at Athens. It is interesting to find that no Sinopians are attested at Delos and none are found among the friends of Helianax while they were so numerous at Athens. Was this

because Sinope was mainly a centre of transit trade and Amisus was the chief harbour for the products of the country itself including the slaves?

[114] Durrbach, *Choix*, 137 and note; *Inscr. de Délos* 2039, 2040.

[115] On the policy of Mithridates VI see, besides the classical work of Th. Reinach, *Mithridate Eupator*, 1890 (and German translation), my chapter 'Pontus' in *C.A.H.* ix, pp. 225 ff. (with bibliography); J. Carcopino, *Hist. Rom.* ii, pp. 402 ff. New light on the expansion of Mithridates' protectorate over the Greek cities of the 'left' Pontus has been recently shed by a fragmentary inscription of Apollonia Pontica, a decree of the city in honour of a commander of a military detachment sent by Mithridates to help (?) the city, see Chr. M. Danov, *Jahreshefte*, xxx (1936), Beibl., pp. 87 ff.; id., *Bull. Hist. Soc. Sofia*, xiv (1937), pp. 65 ff., and id., *Bull. Inst. Arch. Bulg.* xii (1939), pp. 237 ff. Cf. the inscription of Olbia, below, Ch. VII, n. 13.

[116] On the history of Galatia in the second century B.C., F. Stähelin, *Gesch. der Kleinasiatischen Galater*, 2nd ed., 1907, p. 49 (Heraclea and Lampsacus) and 50 ff., cf. Bürchner and Brandis, *P.W.K.* vii. 519 ff. and 534 ff. On the decree of Lampsacus (*S.I.G.*³ 591) see M. Holleaux, *Rev. É.A.* xviii (1916), pp. 1 ff., *Rome et la Grèce, &c.*, pp. 53 ff., and *C.A.H.* viii, p. 179; E. Bickermann, *Phil.* lxxxvii (1932), pp. 277 ff.; L. Robert, *B.C.H.* lix (1935), p. 498, n. 1. Galatian slaves on the Greek market: Stähelin, loc. cit., p. 47, n. 3; Westermann, *P.W.K.* Suppl. vi, 934 (based on A. Calderini, *La Manomissione &c.*, 1908). Hellenization and Phrygianization of Galatia, J. G. C. Anderson, *J.H.S.* xix (1899), pp. 312 ff. Funeral barrows of the family of Deiotarus: Remzi Uguz, 'Karalar Hafrivati', *Türk Tarih, Arkeologya ve etnografya Dergisi*, ii (1934), pp. 102 ff., and French résumé, p. 308, cf. Remzi Oguz Arik et J. Coupry, 'Les tumuli de Karalar et la sépulture du roi Deiotaros II', *Rev. Arch.*, 6 sér., vi (1935), pp. 133 ff.

[117] Above, pp. 571 ff; cf. A. H. M. Jones, *Cities* &c., pp. 175 ff., and Fr. Cumont, *C.A.H.* xi, pp. 606 ff.

[118] Ariarathes V and Athens: W. S. Ferguson, *H.A.*, p. 300 f. Decree of Dionysiac artistes: *O.G.I.* 352; *I.G.* ii², 1330; *B.C.H.* l (1926), p. 497 f.; A. Wilhelm, *Jahreshefte*, xxiv (1929), pp. 184 ff.; L. Robert, *Ét. Anat.*, p. 449. Statue of Carneades, *I.G.* ii². 3781. Ariarathes VII and Delos, Durrbach, *Choix*, 136 g.; *Inscr. de Délos* 1576, cf. 1575.

[119] K. Regling, 'Dynastenmünzen von Tyana, Morima und Anisa in Kappadokien', *Z.N.* xlii (1932), pp. 1 ff.

[120] On the urbanization of Cappadocia, A. H. M. Jones, loc. cit. Ariaratheia was still a Greek city in the second century B.C., *I.G.* ii.² 980, cf. Jones, loc. cit., p. 430, n. 1, and 431, n. 12. But, like many Hellenistic capitals, it sank into insignificance after the transfer of the capital to another place. The equation Nyssa-Nysa suggested by Jones is very doubtful. On Tyana, Jones, loc. cit., p. 430, n. 9. The foundations of Archelaus were either unknown to Strabo as not mentioned by his source, or appeared to him not

worth mentioning. Inscription of Anisa, Michel, 546 (after Curtius *Ges. Abh.*
ii. 1894, pp. 271 ff., 429 ff.). It has been discussed recently by F. Cumont,
Rev. É.A. xxxiv (1932), pp. 135 ff. (cf. *C.A.H.* xi, p. 608), and K. Regling,
loc. cit., p. 11, cf. W. Ruppel, Πολίτευμα, *Phil.* lxxxii (1927), p. 443 f.;
A. H. M. Jones, loc. cit.; W. W. Tarn, *The Greeks in Bactria and India*, p. 19;
and L. Robert, *Rev. Phil.* xiii (65) (1939), p. 211. Ruppel assigns the inscription to Roman times and regards the πολίτευμα as a 'griechische Landmannschaft', perhaps a military colony (J. Oehler, *Monatsschr. f. Gesch. d. Judent.*,
xvii (1909), p. 529, suggests Jewish settlers). I see no reason for dating the
inscription in the Roman period, i.e. after Pompey. Even if it were so, it
is improbable that a quasi-urban constitution was granted to Anisa by
Pompey.

[121] On the history of SYRIA after Epiphanes see the summary of E. R.
Bevan in *C.A.H.* viii, pp. 518 ff., and ix, pp. 397 ff. (bibliography, viii, pp.
778 ff.), cf. Honigmann, art. 'Syria', *P.W.K.* iv A. 1618 ff. PARTHIA—W. W.
Tarn, *C.A.H.* ix, pp. 574 ff.; R. H. McDowell, *Coins from Seleucia on the
Tigris*, 1935, esp. pp. 201 ff. N. C. Debevoise, *A political history of Parthia*,
1938. ARMENIA—bibliography, *C.A.H.* xi, p. 880, cf. E. T. Newell, *Num.
Notes and Mon.* lxxxii (1938), pp. 25 ff. JUDAEA—I cannot quote the
enormous bibliography concerning the Maccabees. Excellent short summaries
of the events will be found in E. Bickermann, *Die Makkabäer*, 1935, *Der
Gott der Makkabäer*, 1937, and *Inst. Sél.*, p. 168. On the progress made by the
NABATAEANS before and after 130 B.C. and on the Arab states in Syria,
U. Kahrstedt, 'Syrische Territorien in hellenistischer Zeit', *Gött. Abh.*, N.F.
xix. 2 (1926), pp. 86 ff.; E. Bikerman, *Inst. Sél.*, p. 168. HEMESA—Strabo
xvi. 2. 10, p. 753, cf. Benzinger, *P.W.K.* v. 246 f., and A. H. M. Jones,
Cities &c., pp. 258, 261 f. On EDESSA—my chapter 'Parthia' in *C.A.H.* xi,
p. 115, and bibliography p. 881, cf. A. H. M. Jones, loc. cit., p. 221. CHALCIS
and the Ituraeans—Benzinger, *P.W.K.* iii. 2091 f.; A. H. M. Jones, 'The
Urbanization of the Ituraean Principality', *J.R.S.* xxi (1931), p. 265, and
Cities &c., p. 255. COMMAGENE—Honigmann, *P.W.K.* Suppl. iv. 987 ff.;
A. H. M. Jones, *Cities* &c., pp. 243 ff.; and F. Cumont, *C.A.H.* xi, p. 608,
cf. E. T. Newell, loc. cit., pp. 30 ff., and G. Jacopi, *Dalla Paflagonia alla
Commagene*, 1936.

[122] Half-independent satraps—Diod. xxxiii. 28. Local dynasts: LYSIAS—
Strabo xvi. 2. 10, p. 753 (46–44 B.C.), and Jos. *A.J.* xiv. 40 (63 B.C.); Honig-
mann, *P.W.K.* xiii. 2530, no. 5. BEROEA—Posid. Fr. 24, *F. Gr. Hist.* 87;
Pomp. Trog. *Prol.* 39; Jos. *A.J.* xiii. 365; Strabo xvi. 2. 7, p. 751; W. Otto,
P.W.K. viii. 511, n. 3; Honigmann, *P.W.K.* xii. 192 f. Otto thinks that it
was Dionysius, son of Heracleon, who founded the tyranny. STRATON—Jos.
A.J. xiii. 384. On the tyrannies in the Phoenician cities and in Transjordan,
G. Hölscher, *Palästina in der persischen und hellenistischen Zeit*, 1903, pp. 83 ff.,
and U. Kahrstedt, 'Syrische Territorien', &c., pp. 91 ff., cf. A. H. M. Jones,
Cities &c., p. 257, and n. 40. It is not always possible to discriminate
between Greek city tyrants and petty Arab dynasts. On the city tyrannies

in the Seleucid Empire in general, above, Ch. IV, n. 230 and E. Bikerman, *Inst. Sél.*, pp. 106 ff.

[123] On the granting to the cities of the status of ἱερά, ἄσυλος, and αὐτόνομος, see U. Kahrstedt, 'Syrische Territorien,' &c., pp. 73 ff., and especially the fine remarks of E. Bikerman, *Inst. Sél.*, pp. 149 ff. (p. 153, list of the cities ἱεραὶ καὶ ἄσυλοι) and 232 ff. (on the right of coinage). Cf. A. H. M. Jones, *Cities* &c., pp. 227 ff. and the interesting paper by H. Seyrig, *Syria*, xx (1939), pp. 35 ff. (cf. E. Bikerman, *Rev. Phil.* xiii (1939), p. 339). E. Schlesinger, *Die griechische Asylie*, and A. Heuss, *Stadt und Herrscher*, do not mention the *asylia* of the Syrian cities.

[124] Seleuceia in Pieria. Ptolemies—*S.I.G.*³ 475 (about 229 B.C.). Seleucus IV—*S.E.G.* vii. 62; C. B. Welles, *R.C.* 45; M. Holleaux, *B.C.H.* lvii (1933), pp. 6 ff. Demetrius and Tryphon—U. Wilcken, *Hermes*, xxix (1894), pp. 436 ff.; V. Chapot, *Mém. de la Soc. d. Ant.*, lxvi (1907), pp. 172 ff.; C. B. Welles, *R.C.* 71 and 72. Grypus—*O.G.I.* 257; C. B. Welles *R.C.* loc. cit., cf. E. Bikerman, *Inst. Sél.*, pp. 140, 192. Coins—E. T. Newell in C. B. Welles, *R.C.*, p. 292, n. 3, cf. Head, *H.N.*², p. 783; *B.M.C.*, Galatia, &c., Intr., p. lxxi. Tetrapolis—*B.M.C.*, Galatia, &c., Intr., p. lviii, and pl. XVIII, 5–8; E. Bikerman, *Inst. Sél.*, p. 234. Autonomous copper of most of the Syrian cities, Head, *H.N.*², pp. 778 ff.; U. Kahrstedt, loc. cit.; A. H. M. Jones, loc. cit., pp. 246 ff., 255, and E. Bikerman, *Inst. Sél.*, p. 234 f.

[125] *Asylia* of Aradus, Strabo xvi. 2. 14, p. 754. On the coinage of Aradus and Marathus, Head, *H.N.*², pp. 788 ff., 792 ff., cf. G. F. Hill, *B.M.C.*, Phoenicia, Intr., pp. xxxii ff. On Marathus, Honigmann, *P.W.K.* xiv. 1435 ff. Cf. U. Kahrstedt, loc. cit.; A. H. M. Jones, *Cities* &c., p. 239 f., 251, and 257, and E. Bikerman, *Inst. Sél.*, p. 140. On the coins of Aradus and the Phoenician cities in general, J. G. Milne, 'The coinage of Aradus in the Hellenistic period', *Iraq*, v (1938), pp. 22 ff., cf. W. Otto, 'Beitr. z. Seleukideng.', 1928, pp. 15 ff.

[126] Autonomy of Tyre, *S.E.G.* ii. 330; A. Wilhelm, *Wien. Anz.* lix (1922), pp. 11 ff. (letter of Tyre ἱερᾶς καὶ ἀσύλου to Delphi, probably about the recognition of its liberty). Cf. the decree of Teos, *S.E.G.* iv. 601. On the *asylia* of Tyre, Wilhelm, loc. cit.; none of these documents nor the autonomy of Tyre are mentioned in the book by W. B. Fleming, *The History of Tyre*, 1915, pp. 65 ff. Money paid by Tyre for its autonomy, Strabo xvi. 2. 23, p. 757: οὐχ ὑπὸ τῶν βασιλέων δ' ἐκρίθησαν αὐτόνομοι μόνον μικρὰ ἀναλώσαντες ἀλλὰ καὶ ὑπὸ τῶν Ῥωμαίων βεβαιωσάντων τὴν ἐκείνων γνώμην. The procedure was probably the same as in the case of Seleuceia. The king informed Rome about his grant. Rome endorsed it and probably maintained the autonomy of the city after the annexation of Syria. Coinage of Tyre, Head, *H.N.*², pp. 799 ff.; E. Bikerman, *Inst. Sél.*, p. 235, and especially E. T. Newell in C. Kraeling, *Gerasa*, 1938, p. 375; *Num. Notes and Mon.*, lxxxii (1938), pp. 39 ff., and *Dura Report*, vii–viii, 1939, pp. 443 ff., cf. J. G. Milne, *Iraq*, v (1938), pp. 22 ff. According to E. T. Newell, the high reputation of Tyrian

coins was established in the second century B.C. Under Alexander Balas and his successors the city issued an enormous amount of new coins, mostly of the Ptolemaic standard, with the head of the reigning king on one side and the Ptolemaic eagle on the other. From 124 B.C. to A.D. 59, the period of autonomy, Tyre coined its own abundant money on the same standard and with similar types: eagle on the reverse and Heracles on the obverse. These coins enjoyed a great reputation and are found all over Palestine, Phoenicia, Syria and the Farther East (hoard of Teheran, Noe², no. 1081). Most of them were shekels (tetradrachms) and half-shekels (didrachms), with some drachms (quarter of a shekel). When the Romans put an end to this coinage they began to strike similar coins at Antioch. This Roman coinage was regarded throughout Syria and Mesopotamia as a continuation of the Tyrian and shared its éclat. This accounts for the name ἀργύριον Τυρίου κόμματος or ἀργύριον Τύριον given to it in many documents of the first and second centuries A.D. This name cannot be interpreted as meaning 'silver of Tyrian standard', because the standard was not exactly the same. The history of the Tyrian coinage sketched above, which is paralleled by that of the coinage of other Phoenician cities and of Seleuceia in Pieria, is highly characteristic of the economic life of the period. It shows how strong the cities were in the late second and the early first century B.C. and the important part they played in the commerce of the time, being practically rivals, not subjects, of the kings. It is very instructive to compare the coinage of Tyre with that of Ptolemais-Ake recently illustrated by E. T. Newell in his masterly monograph 'Late Seleucid mints in Ake-Ptolemais and Damascus', *Num. Notes and Mon.* lxxxiv (1939). It must be noted that Ptolemais-Ake never became autonomous and was used by the Seleucids as a minting-place until *c.* 106 B.C.

¹²⁷ War between Aradus and Marathus, Diod. xxxiii. 5; Strabo xvi. 2. 12, p. 753, cf. Honigmann, *P.W.K.* xiv. 1432 f.

¹²⁸ Posid. Fr. 2, *F. Gr. Hist.* 87, cf. ii C, p. 164 (142 B.C.). Cf. E. Bikerman, *Inst. Sél.*, pp. 72, 79.

¹²⁹ Strabo xvi. 2. 18 and 20, p. 755, cf. 2. 8: Γίνδαρος ἀκρόπολις τῆς Κυρρηστικῆς καὶ λῃστήριον εὐφυές. On the robberies which persisted after Pompey, J. Dobiaš, 'Les premiers rapports des Romains avec les Parthes &c.', *Arch. Orient.* iii (1931), pp. 247 ff.

¹³⁰ On the Hellenes in Syria, W. Otto, *Phil. Woch.*, 1926, pp. 39 ff., esp. 42, cf. W. Graf Uxkull-Gyllenband, *B.G.U.* v. 2 (1934), p. 27, and E. Bickermann, *Die Makkabäer*, 1935, and *Der Gott der Makkabäer*, 1937.

¹³¹ Commagene—above, note 121. On the mentality of the kings see my article Πρόγονοι in *J.H.S.* lv (1935), p. 63, cf. my paper 'Dura and the problem of Parthian art', *Yale Class. Stud.*, v (1935), p. 241 f., H. Schaeder, *Vortr. d. Bibl. Warburg*, iv, 1924-5, pp. 137 ff., H. Junker, *Wörter und Sachen* xii (1929), pp. 155 ff. and A. D. Nock, Σύνναος θεός, *Harv. Stud.*, xli (1930), p. 27. On the social and economic structure of Commagene, my *Soc. and Ec. Hist. of the R. E.*, ch. vii, n. 7 (Italian edition). For the inscriptions of Antiochus, besides the

comments of Jalabert and Mouterde, see A. Wilhelm, 'Zu der Inschrift König Antiochos I von Kommagene aus Samosata', *Wien. Stud.* xlvii (1929), pp. 127 ff., and F. Krüger, 'Orient und Hellas in den Denkmälern und Inschriften des Königs Antiochos I von Kommagene', 1937 (*Greifsw. Beitr. z. Lit. und Stilfr.*, 19). New fragments of inscriptions of Antiochus, of the same type as that of Nimrud Dagh, from Samosata and Palas, G. Jacopi, *Dalla Paflagonia alla Commagene*, 1936, pp. 21 ff. For the feudal structure, Jalabert and Mouterde, *Inscr.* i, no. 47, col. iv, 5, and no. 51, l. 14.

[132] Coins of Ptolemy the tetrarch and his son Lysanias, *B.M.C.*, Galatia, &c., Intr., p. lxxiii, cf. pl. LIV; Head, *H.N.*², pp. 783 ff.

[133] Mount Hermel—P. Perdrizet, 'Le Monument de Hermel', *Syria*, xix (1938), pp. 47 ff. The Mausoleum of Sampsiceramus of Hemesa: C. Watzinger, 'Das Grabmal des Sampsigeramos von Emesa', *Kunsthistoriske Sällskapets Publikation*, 1923, pp. 18 ff., and *Denkmäler Palästinas*, ii, 1935, p. 37. Inscription, *O.G.I.* 604.

[134] The Hellenistic elements in the life of Palestine before the Maccabees and the Hellenistic character of the monarchy of the Hasmonaeans have been stressed recently in E. Bickermann's two books, *Die Makkabäer*, 1935, and *Der Gott der Makkabäer*, 1937. Cf. the Greek inscriptions and paintings in the hypogees of Marissa, one of which (*O.G.I.* 593) mentions an Ἀπολλο-φάνης Σεσμαίου, ἄρξας τῶν ἐν Μαρίσηι Σιδωνίων. On the meaning of the term 'Sidonians', see E. Bickermann, *Rev. Hist. Rel.* cxv (1937), pp. 203 ff., who takes it as equivalent to South Phoenicians. Whether South Phoenicians or real Sidonians, the Sidonians of Marissa were completely hellenized. The archaeological evidence has been collected, dated, and carefully studied by C. Watzinger, *Denkmäler Palästinas*, ii, 1935, pp. 10 ff.: Hasmonaean coins—p. 23; Mausoleum of Jonathan—p. 22; late Hellenistic graves—pp. 59 ff.; Marissa —pp. 17 ff. and A. Reichenberg, *Denkmäler der judischen Antike*, 1937, pls. 10 ff. Cf. my pl. LVIII.

[135] The Nabataeans and Petra: A. Grohmann, *P.W.K.* xvi. 1453 ff.; my *Caravan cities*, 1932, pp. 37 ff., esp. 51 ff.; N. Glueck, 'A newly discovered Nabataean temple &c.,' *A.J.A.* xli (1937), pp. 361 ff. (early first century A.D.), cf. ibid. xliii (1939), pp. 381 ff.; G. and A. Horsfield, 'Sela-Petra &c.', *Quart. Dep. Ant. Pal.* vii (1938), pp. 1 ff. (careful excavation and description of rock-cut houses); G. Hölscher, *P.W.K.* ix. 1170 ff. (history of the city; topography and monuments are not discussed). Coins: G. F. Hill, *B.M.C.*, Arabia &c., 1922, Intr., pp. xi ff. Nabataean coinage begins with Aretas III, the Philhellene (87–62 B.C.), who added Damascus to his caravan-state and minted coins in imitation of late Seleucid coins both in his own capital and at Damascus, with his own portrait and Greek legends. On his bronze coins of Damascus the reverses show the figure of the Tyche of that city (E. T. Newell, *Num. Notes and Mon.*, lxxxiv (1939), pp. 92 ff.). His successor Obodas II, however, who was no longer in possession of Damascus, substituted Aramaic for Greek legends. El Khazne is dated by C. Watzinger, *Denkmäler Palästinas*, ii, p. 77, in the

time of Aretas IV Philopatris and Philodemus (9 B.C.–A.D. 40) and interpreted as the Heroon of this king. To him he ascribes also the building of the Hellenistic city. I do not think that the hellenization of the city started so late. The question, however, can only be solved by systematic excavations. Nabataean pottery: J. H. Iliffe, *Quart. Dep. Ant. Pal.* vi (1936), pp. 12 ff., cf. iii (1934), p. 132. Nabataean sculpture, as represented by the finds made by Glueck, certainly goes back to Hellenistic sculpture in general. Cf. Ch. Picard, *Rev. Arch.* x (1937), pp. 244 ff. and *C.R. Ac. Inscr.* 1937, pp. 440 ff.

[136] The find in S. Arabia: H. Schlobies, *Forsch. und Fortschr.* x (1934), p. 242 f. The head in the British Museum: R. P. Hinks, *B.M.Q.* xi (1937), pp. 153 ff., cf. my pl. xcvi and description (for the date and interpretation). Strong Hellenistic influences are shown by another find made in S. Arabia, in the ruins of Ukhadud, viz. the two bronze lion heads, now in the British Museum, published by Sydney Smith, *B.M.Q.* xi (1937), pp. 154 ff., and pl. XLII, and assigned by him to the period before A.D. 50. On S. Arabia's economic life A. Grohmann, 'Südarabien als Wirtschaftsgebiet' i, *Osten und Orient* i. 4, 1922 and ii, *Schr. Philos. Fak. Deutsch. Univ. Prag*, xiii. 1933.

[137] Parthia: above, n. 121, cf. W. W. Tarn, *The Greeks in Bactria and India*, chs. i and ii, esp. p. 30; M. Rostovtzeff, *C.A.H.* xi, pp. 104 ff., and N. C. Debevoise, *A Political History of Parthia*, 1938, pp. 28 ff. and 70 ff.

[138] On Armenia, above, n. 121. Tigranes I—F. Geyer, *P.W.K.* v A. 969 ff. On the coinage of Tigranes I, E. T. Newell, *Num. Notes and Mon.* lxxxiv (1939), pp. 95 ff.

[139] On Dura in Seleucid and Parthian times, my remarks in *C.A.H.* xi, pp. 115 ff. (with bibliography), cf. above, pp. 482 ff. The inscriptions of Dura-Europus: *S.E.G.* vii, nos. 331 ff. (with bibliography), cf. the annual Reports, v, vi, vii–viii. The parchments and papyri of Seleucid, Parthian, and Roman times: F. Cumont, *Fouilles de Doura-Europos*, 1926, pp. 281 ff., and in the annual Reports: ii, pp. 201 ff., v, pp. 295 ff., vi, pp. 416 ff., vii–viii, pp. 426 ff.; *Münch. Beitr. z. Pap.* xix (1934), pp. 351 ff. (Rostovtzeff) and 379 ff. (Welles); cf. A. R. Bellinger and C. B. Welles, 'A third-century contract of sale from Edessa in Osrhoene', *Yale Class. Stud.* v (1935), pp. 95 ff.; C. B. Welles, *Z. d. Sav.-Stift.* lvi (1936), pp. 99 ff., and 'Dura Papyrus 101', *Archives d'Hist. du Droit orient.* i (1937), pp. 261 ff. Cf. above, Ch. IV, n. 221. Archaeological material of the Parthian time: M. Rostovtzeff, 'Dura and the problem of Parthian art', *Yale Class. Stud.* v (1935), pp. 157 ff., and *Dura-Europos and its Art*, 1938. My pl. xcvii.

[140] On Seleuceia on the Eulaeus, the memoirs of Cumont quoted in *C.A.H.* xi, p. 116, and Rostovtzeff, *C.A.H.* xi, pp. 115 ff. All the inscriptions found at Seleuceia are reprinted in *S.E.G.* vii, 1–33, see especially 1, 3 (Nicolaus, the gymnasiarch), 6, 12, 13, 14, 25, cf. F. Cumont, *C. R. Ac. Inscr.*, 1937, pp. 313 ff. and 1938, pp. 305 ff. Several new restorations and interpretations of the two metrical inscriptions *S.E.G.* vii, 13 and 14, A. Wilhelm, 'Drei griechische Epigramme aus Susa und aus Heliopolis-

Baalbek', *Gött. Nach.*, Fachgr. I, N. F., i. 4 (1935), pp. 79 ff. Manumissions and their purely Greek character, L. Robert, *Rev. Phil.* x (1936), pp. 137 ff. Babylonia in the Seleucid and Parthian period, M. Rostovtzeff, 'Seleucid Babylonia', *Yale Class. Stud.* iii (1932), pp. 3 ff., and *C.A.H.* xi, pp. 115 ff., cf. M. Enger, *Mnem.* vii (1938), pp. 136 ff. Gymnasium at Babylon, *S.E.G.* vii. 39.

¹⁴¹ Sir Aurel Stein, 'An Archaeological Journey in Western Iran', *Geogr. Journ.* xcii (1938), pp. 324 ff., cf. the forthcoming full account of the careful work of excavation done by the author, which will soon be published by Macmillan & Co. On the statue of the Parthian dignitary, A. Godard, 'Les statues Parthes de Shami', *Athar e Iran*, ii (1937), pp. 285 ff. My pl. XCVIII.

¹⁴² See, e.g., Strabo, xvi. 2. 4, p. 749(Seleucis) ; 9, p. 751 f. (Laodicea) : εἶτα Λαοδίκεια, ἐπὶ τῇ θαλάττῃ κάλλιστα ἐκτισμένη καὶ εὐλίμενος πόλις, χώραν τε ἔχουσα πολύοινον πρὸς τῇ ἄλλῃ εὐκαρπίᾳ· τοῖς μὲν οὖν Ἀλεξανδρεῦσιν αὕτη παρέχει τὸ πλεῖστον τοῦ οἴνου, τὸ ὑπερκείμενον τῆς πόλεως ὄρος πᾶν κατάμπελον ἔχουσα μέχρι σχεδόν τι τῶν κορυφῶν (note the flourishing export of wine to Alexandria) ; 10, p. 752 (Apamea) : καὶ χώρας εὐπορεῖ παμπόλλης εὐδαίμονος; 16, p. 755 (Coele-Syria) : διαρρεῖται δὲ ποταμοῖς ἄρδουσι χώραν εὐδαίμονα καὶ πάμφορον; 20, p. 756 (Damascus) : ἡ Δαμασκηνὴ χώρα διαφερόντως ἐπαινουμένη κτλ. It is certain that Strabo took much of his information from his Hellenistic sources.

¹⁴³ Posid. Fr. 9, *F. Gr. Hist.* 87 ; E. Bikerman, *Inst. Sél.*, pp. 91 and 95, who gives details about Sidetes' army and quotes some other passages bearing on the organization of the train (ἀποσκευή) of Seleucid armies. I may quote in this connexion an interesting silver *emblema* published by A. Sambon, *Le Musée*, iii (1906), pp. 75 ff., pl. XII. This *emblema* is adorned with the portrait head of Antiochus VII Sidetes covered with a Parthian bashlik and with a torc round the neck. This Parthian garb may mean that Antiochus after his victories over the Parthians is here represented as the king of his conquered enemies. The dish, bowl, or cup to which the *emblema* originally belonged might be one of those which Antiochus distributed to the officers and soldiers of his victorious army in memory of their exploits (see the following note). The *emblema* is a fine product of Seleucid artists and testifies to the flourishing state of the toreutic art in Syria in the late Seleucid period (cf. above, Ch. IV, n. 313, and Ch. V, n. 118.)

¹⁴⁴ Posid. Fr. 13, *F. Gr. Hist.* 87. On the date, F. Jacoby, *F. Gr. Hist.* ii c, p. 167 f. The banquet may have been given to Himerus either as Parthian governor or during the time of his independent rule (124–122 B.C. according to the coins, R. H. McDowell, *Coins from Seleucia on the Tigris*, 1935, p. 202 f., 219).

¹⁴⁵ Posid. Fr. 24, *F. Gr. Hist.* 87 ; E. Bikerman, *Inst. Sél.*, p. 95.

¹⁴⁶ Strabo xvi. 2. 23, p. 757 (Tyre) and 24 f. (Sidon), cf. above, n. 126. I cannot enter here into the history of blown glass. The basic text, a 'pocket

history' of glass manufacture, is Pliny, *N.H.* xxxvi. 190–9. An interpretation of this text and a technical and stylistic analysis of the earliest specimens of blown glass (with bibliographical references) will be found in the valuable papers of D. B. Harden, 'Romano-Syrian glasses with mould-blown inscriptions', *J.R.S.* xxv (1935), pp. 163 ff., and *Bull. Metr. Mus.* xxxi (1935), p. 193; cf. W. A. Thorpe, 'The prelude to European cut glass', *Journ. Soc. of Glass Technology*, xxii (1938), pp. 5 ff. I may point out in this connexion that Pliny in the passage quoted above does not mention gold glass and painted glass. The great demand for 'Murrine' glass in Italy begins according to another statement of Pliny (*N.H.* xxxvii. 18; Thorpe, loc. cit., p. 11) at about the same time, *c.* 60 B.C. My pls. CIX and CX.

[147] Strabo xvi. 2. 19, p. 756, cf. W. S. Ferguson, *H.A.*, p. 391; P. Roussel *Délos, col. ath.*, p. 92, n. 1. There cannot be any doubt that Tryphon took and damaged Berytus. For a while Berytus may have been in decay. However, it is probable that the city was one of the mints of the Seleucids and coined its own autonomous money (under the name of Laodicea in Phoenicia) later than Tryphon. Unfortunately these coins cannot be exactly dated, G. F. Hill, *B.M.C.*, Phoenicia, Intr., p. liii.

[148] On the goods exported from Syria in the Roman Imperial period, L. C. West, 'Commercial Syria under the Roman Empire', *Trans. Am. Phil. Ass.* lv (1924), pp. 159 ff., cf. R. Mouterde, *Mél. Un. St. Joseph*, xii (1927), p. 288, and F. Heichelheim, 'Roman Syria', T. Frank, *Econ. Surv.* iv. 1938, pp. 203 ff. Export of wine to Alexandria, above, n. 142. Relations between Tyre and the other Phoenician cities and Alexandria as attested by the Phoenician standard of their autonomous coins, above, n. 126. Some ancient trading houses of Phoenicia still busy in 150 B.C., R. Eisler, *Zeitschr. d. Morg. Ges.* lxxviii (1924), pp. 61 ff.

[149] On the trade of Seleucid Syria with India and perhaps a sporadic trade with China in the third century B.C., above, p. 455 ff. On the report of Chang K'ien, known in two versions, those of Ssu-ma Ch'ien (99 B.C. or somewhat later) and Pan-Ku (A.D. 92), W. W. Tarn, *The Greeks in Bactria and India*, pp. 513 ff., cf. 280 ff. On the silk-route, A. Herrmann, *Das Land der Seide und Tibet im Lichte der Antike*, 1938, pp. 27 ff. (Quellen u. Forsch. z. Gesch. d. Geogr. u. Völkerk. i). The uninterrupted commercial intercourse between Syria and Parthia is attested by many coin-hoards found in modern Persia. In these hoards, belonging to the time of Parthian domination, Seleucid silver and copper are fairly well represented alongside of Parthian and Bactrian coins, see for example the hoards of Ardabil (Noe², 63) and of Kermanshah (Noe², 547). (The hoards of Kuh-i-Taftan, Noe², 583, and that of an unknown place in Persia, Noe², 809, contained only Seleucid and Bactrian coins; they testify to trade between Syria and Bactria in the second century B.C.) I may note in this connexion that at Dura Seleucid currency was still in circulation long after Dura became Parthian; see the note of A. R. Bellinger in my *Dura-Europos and its art*, p. 138, n. 7. Cf. the interesting remarks of C. G. Seligman on the Chinese bull-headed rhyton, which he with

probability derives from similar rhytons of Seleucid or Parthian workmanship, C. G. Seligman, *Custom is King: Essays presented to Dr. R. R. Marett*, 1936, cf. id., *Antiquity*, xi (1937), p. 20.

[150] Relations between Italy and Syria are attested by many facts, especially by the role played by Oriental merchants in the life of Puteoli (R. Annecchino, 'Pozzuoli antica nei traffici di Roma con l'Oriente', *Atti IV Congr. Naz. St. Rom.* i (1938), pp. 224 ff., with bibliography) and by the activity of Syrian merchants at Delos (above, Ch. V, notes 123 and 124). It is an interesting observation of Ch. Picard (*Syria*, xiv (1933), pp. 318 ff.) that the symbolical figures of the trident and of the trident and dolphins which occur both in the late Hellenistic Syrian mosaics of Delos and on some later mosaics of Pompeii and Hadrumetum may be regarded as invented by the Phoenicians and borrowed from them by the merchants of Pompeii. I may quote in addition the hoard of 40 silver coins found at Campli near Battaglia in Picenum (Italy). The majority were *cistophori*, but among them there were, besides a late tetradrachm of Lysimachus, tetradrachms of Demetrius I Soter, of Eucratides and of Tyre, the last dated 77/6 B.C. The hoard was therefore buried after 77 B.C., Noe², 130; K. Regling, *Z.N.* xxxviii (1928), p. 98. The find is a brilliant illustration of what I have said on the orientation of trade in the sections dealing with the Pergamene kingdom and with Delos. Asia Minor and Syria were the lands which provided Italy with the most important merchandise, especially slaves.

[151] Strabo xvi. 1. 27, p. 748, note especially his description of the φύλαρχοι: οἱ γὰρ παροικοῦντες ἑκατέρωθεν τὸν ποταμὸν φύλαρχοι, χώραν οὐκ εὔπορον ἔχοντες, ἧττον δὲ ἄπορον νεμόμενοι, δυναστείαν ἕκαστος ἰδίᾳ περιβεβλημένος ἴδιον καὶ τελώνιον ἔχει, καὶ τοῦτ' οὐ μέτριον. χαλεπὸν γὰρ ἐν τοῖς τοσούτοις καὶ τούτοις αὐθάδεσι κοινὸν ἀφορισθῆναι μέτρον τὸ τῷ ἐμπόρῳ λυσιτελές. In this section, describing the caravan route, Strabo certainly confuses Hieropolis-Bambyce with Edessa. That the caravans after having crossed the Euphrates should recross it again in order to reach Bambyce is out of the question. On the location of Scenae see Weisbach, art. Σκηναί in *P.W.K.* v A. 470.

[152] Palmyra: see bibliography in my *Caravan Cities*, pp. 224 ff., and my remarks, pp. 31 ff., cf. D. Schlumberger, 'Études sur Palmyre', *Berytos*, ii (1935), pp. 149 ff.; A. von Gerkan, 'Die Stadtmauer von Palmyra', ibid., pp. 25 ff. and Z. Sęczykowski, 'Recherches sur la reconstruction du plan de l'ancienne Palmyre', *Biuletyn historii sztuki i kultury*, vi (1938), pp. 271 ff. (in Polish with French résumé). On the status of Palmyra in the time of Augustus, D. Schlumberger, *Syria*, 1939, xx, pp. 43 ff. Pre-Augustan remains of the temple of Bel at Palmyra have been revealed by the careful excavations of the still extant temple by the Syrian Service des Antiquités. The remains will soon be published and studied by M. H. Seyrig. On the trade routes in the Syrian desert, Père Poidebard, *La Trace de Rome dans le désert syrien*, 1934, cf. id., *C.R. Ac. Inscr.* 1934, p. 26, and the review of his book by Sir Aurel Stein, *Geogr. Journ.* 1935, Jan., pp. 66 ff. Cf. the remarks

of H. Seyrig, 'Commerce maritime de Palmyre', *Ann. de l'Inst. de Philol. et d'Hist. Or.* iv (1936), pp. 397 ff. Cf. Addendum to this note.

[153] The *rayonnement* of Nabataean commerce may be inferred from the distribution of the Nabataean inscriptions as listed in *P.W.K.* xvi. 1457 ff. (A. Grohmann). Grohmann's article does not contain a section dealing with the development of Nabataean trade. It is interesting to note that many of the Nabataean inscriptions were found between Forat and Dumaetha and at Dumaetha itself (Musil, *Arabia Deserta*, pp. 195, 301, 303, 470, 494, 515). Note also the comparatively numerous Nabataean inscriptions in Egypt. Relations between the Nabataeans and Sabaeans, J. H. Mordtmann, 'Ein Nabatäer im Sabäerlande', *Klio*, xxv (1932), pp. 429 ff., cf. above, notes 135 and 136. On the merchants from the great trading centres of Arabia in Delos and elsewhere in Greece, above, Ch. V, n. 124.

[154] See above, pp. 781 ff. and my article in *Anatol. Stud. pres. to W. H. Buckler.* On the Phoenician standard in Seleucid coinage, Head, *H.N.*², pp. 764 ff., and above, notes 126 and 148.

[155] J. Dobiaš, 'Les premiers rapports des Romains avec les Parthes', &c., *Arch. Orient.* iii (1931), pp. 258 ff.

[156] J. Dobiaš, loc. cit., pp. 215 ff., against Th. Mommsen, *R.G.* iii, p. 143, and F. Cumont, *Syria*, vi (1925), p. 282, n. 1, and id., *Fouilles de Doura-Europos*, 1926, p. xxviii, n. 2. We must not forget that the great successes of Mithridates II of Parthia were quite recent and showed that the weakness of Parthia was a temporary phenomenon favourable to Rome and so to be made use of.

[157] On the political history of Egypt under Euergetes II and the two Cleopatras see the excellent monograph by W. Otto and H. Bengtson, 'Zur Geschichte des Niederganges des Ptolemäerreiches. Ein Beitrag zur Regierungszeit des 8. und des 9. Ptolemäers', *Bay. Abh.*, N.F. xvii (1938), pp. 22–194. In this study the reader will find all the available sources quoted and analysed. I may, however, in this note mention some basic documents which bear directly on the subject of this book. The first proclamation of peace of Euergetes II of 145/4 B.C. is known, in the form in which it was published in Egypt, exclusively from quotations: *U.P.Z.* 161, col. 3, 57 ff.; 162, col. 5, 21, and col. 9, 21, cf. col. 7, 18 and U. Wilcken's comments on these documents pp. 60 and 83; *Teb.* 699; *Ostr. B.G.U.* 1311; *P. Neut.* 1, 24, cf. U. Wilcken, *Arch. Pap.* xi (1933), p. 147 and W. Otto and H. Bengtson, loc. cit., pp. 26 and 46. On the decree of Cyprus, below, n. 193, and Otto and Bengtson, loc. cit. The decree of about 139 B.C. in favour of the priests quoted in *Teb.* 6, 40, is discussed by Otto and Bengtson, loc. cit., p. 38. It hardly formed part of a general amnesty decree of the type of those of 145/4 and 118 B.C. The attitude of the Greeks of Alexandria towards Euergetes II during the *amixia* is illustrated by the king's order of 124 B.C. partly preserved in *Teb.* 700. By this order all the gymnasia, politeumata (?), and other associations of Alexandria were summoned to declare, under penalty of death, their

land property in the _chora_. This property was then sold, certainly—at least in part—for the profit of the king's κεχωρισμένος λόγος. On this document see Otto and Bengtson, loc. cit., pp. 67 ff. I may note in this connexion that my interpretation of two passages in _U.P.Z._ 196 quoted in the text does not coincide with that given by Otto and Bengtson, loc. cit., p. 130. With the disturbances of the time of Euergetes (or Philometor?) may be connected the services rendered to the city of Heracleopolis by Archippus, son of Zoilus, a Macedonian, probably a military commander (_strategos_?) mentioned in his funeral epigram, _S.E.G._ viii, 370; _S.B._ 7803. On the φιλάνθρωπα of Soter II (108 B.C.) mentioned by Diod. xxxiv–v. 20, see the same authors, p. 171. They were very probably included in a general amnesty decree of this king. The inscription of Cyrene of 109/8 (?): G. Oliverio, _Doc. ant. d. Africa Italiana_, ii. 2, no. 538; _S.E.G._ ix. 5; cf. the interpretation of this inscription by Oliverio, loc. cit., V. Arangio-Ruiz, _Riv. Fil._ lxv (15) (1937), pp. 266 ff., Otto and Bengtson, loc. cit., pp. 122 ff. and 174 f., and P. Roussel, _Rev. É.A._ xli (1939), pp. 5 ff. Roussel tentatively assigns the document either to the time of Philometor or to that of Euergetes II, cf., however, W. Otto, _Bay. S.B._, 1939, 3, pp. 16 ff. See below, nn. 186, 192. Shorter summaries of the events of the time of Euergetes II and the two Cleopatras and narratives of those subsequent to the death of Cleopatra III will be found in E. R. Bevan, _History of Egypt_, &c., pp. 306 ff., and P. Jouguet, _L'Égypte Ptolémaïque_, pp. 155 ff., cf. on the role of Euergetes II and its significance C. Préaux, 'La signification de l'époque d'Euergète II', _Actes Vᵉ Congr. Pap._, 1938, pp. 345 ff., and on the gradual decline of Greek civilization in Egypt in the late Ptolemaic period F. Oertel, 'Der Niedergang der hellenistischen Kultur in Aegypten', _N. Jahrb. Kl. Alt._ xxiii (1920), pp. 361 ff.

On the civil and dynastic wars in Egypt during the period we are considering see the remarks of C. Préaux, _Chr. d'Ég._ xi (21) (1936), p. 118, and ibid., xi (22) (1936), pp. 542 ff. On the meaning of ἀμιξία—a term repeatedly used by contemporary sources to designate the civil war of the time of Euergetes, while the term ταραχή is used in a more general sense and especially for the troubles of the time of Epiphanes and Philometor (P. Collart et P. Jouguet, _Ét. de Pap._ ii (1933), p. 33)—see Preisigke, _Wört._; Liddell and Scott (new ed.); C. Préaux, _Chr. d'Ég._ xi (21) (1936), p. 543, and Otto and Bengtson, loc. cit., p. 65. On _P. Lond._ ii. 401, 20 (p. 12), of 111 B.C., and the _amixia_ mentioned in it, Otto and Bengtson, loc. cit., p. 160. To the letters relating to the revolt of the Thebaid in 88 B.C., reproduced by Wilcken, _Chr._ 12, and Hunt–Edgar, _Sel. Pap._ ii. 417 and 418, add some more letters of Platon, P. Collart, _Rec. Champollion_, 1922, pp. 273 ff., and _P. Bouriant_ 10, 11, and 12; O. Krüger, _Racc. G. Lumbroso_, 1925, pp. 316 ff., and _P. Ross.-Georg._ ii, 1929, no. 10; _P. Bad._ 16; cf. the report of a village scribe of the Pathyrites nome speaking of an invasion of a region in the Latopolites and Pathyrites nomes by some of the 'rebels', W. Spiegelberg, _Zeitschr. f. Aeg. Spr._ lxv (1930), pp. 53 ff. Cf. C. Préaux, loc. cit., p. 548. At Hermupolis we find in 79/8 B.C. a strong garrison which consisted of a detachment of mercenary soldiers, to a large extent men from Syria and Idumaea, F. Zucker, 'Doppelinschrift spätptolemäischer Zeit aus der Garnison von Hermopolis Magna', *Berl. Abh.*, phil.-hist. Kl. vi (1937, published in 1938), cf. *Aeg.* xviii (1938), pp. 279 ff. (a group of soldiers of this detachment is styled οἱ παρεφεδρεύοντες ἐν ῾Ερμοῦ πόλει ξένοι ᾿Απολλωνιᾶται &c.). In 64/3 B.C. in the Heracleopolite nome were stationed οἱ παρεφεδρεύοντες ἐν τῶι νομῶι ἱππεῖς (*B.G.U.* viii, 1747, 1748) and οἱ ἀποτεταγμένοι τ[ῶι στρατηγῶι] Θηβαῖοι πεντάρουροι (*B.G.U.* viii, 1749, 1750), and in addition some πλοῖα θαλάσσια at the disposal of the *dioecetes* (*B.G.U.* viii, 1744–6). On this last, my paper in *Ét. Andréades* (above, Ch. V, n. 134). Cf. the document of the first century B.C. concerning the transport of grain to Alexandria, H. Zilliacus, *Aeg.* xix (1939), pp. 59 ff. and U. Wilcken, *Arch. Pap.* xiii (1939), pp. 223 ff. The cornships according to this document were protected by special soldiers styled οἱ [περὶ τὴν] διοίκησιν μαχαιροφόροι καὶ ἔπιπλοι (l. 19 f.).

[158] *Teb.* 5, cf. Wilcken, *Chr.*, nos. 65, 260, 307, and 339 (sections of the decree reproduced in the various chapters of the *Chrestomathy*), and Hunt–Edgar, *Sel. Pap.* ii. 210 (the best-preserved parts of the decree with some improved readings). On the general character of the document, F. Preisigke, 'Die Friedenskundgebung des Königs Euergetes II.', *Arch. Pap.* v (1913), pp. 301 ff.; U. Wilcken, *U.P.Z.* i, pp. 498 ff., and W. Schubart, *Arch. Pap.* xii (1936), pp. 10 ff. Cf. C. Préaux, *Chr. d'Ég.* xi (22) (1936), pp. 545 ff.

[159] The name φιλάνθρωπα is often used for our documents, especially in quotations (e.g. *Teb.* 73, 3, and 124, 7, and 36: προπεφιλανθρωπη[μένους], cf. 739, 40), see Preisigke's paper quoted in the preceding note and U. Wilcken, *U.P.Z.* i, pp. 498 ff. One may be inclined to find the full and official name of the documents in such quotations as *Teb.* 73, 3 (113–11 B.C.): κατ[ὰ] τὸ ἐκκεί-μενον τῶν φι[λα]νθρώπων πρόσταγμα or *B.G.U.* 1156, 24 f. (16 B.C.), and *B.G.U.* 1053; Mitteis, *Chr.* 105, ii, 4 ff. (13 B.C.): πρόσταγμα φιλανθρώπων καὶ ἐργασίας, cf. *P. Oxy.* 785 (A.D. 1), especially if one accepts the correction εὐεργεσία for ἐργασία suggested by F. von Woess, *Das Asylwesen Aegyptens*, &c., 1923, pp. 97 ff., cf. C. Préaux, *Chr. d'Ég.* x (19) (1935), p. 114. However, Woess's correction is not necessary. Πρόσταγμα ἐργασίας was probably a special order regulating compulsory work. In this case πρόσταγμα φιλανθρώ-πων probably means an order which contains a φιλάνθρωπον, a grant. It is more appropriate therefore to use for the combination of ἀφέσεις and προσ-τάγματα, which the documents under review represent, the general name φιλάνθρωπα under which the documents were known in Egypt. The names 'amnesty decree' and 'peace proclamation' are modern. A list of φιλάνθρωπα will be found in U. Wilcken, *U.P.Z.* i, pp. 498 ff., cf. on the decrees of Euergetes II, above, n. 157, and on that of Auletes, U. Wilcken, *Arch. Pap.* vi (1920), pp. 405 ff. On the Ptolemaic *mandata* see my Introduction to *Teb.* 703, and the contributions of various scholars quoted above, Ch. IV, n. 77.

[160] On the archives of Menches see especially M. Engers, *De Aegyptiarum κωμῶν administratione*, &c., 1909, cf. my *Kolonat*, pp. 1 ff. A good picture of Menches as he appears in the light of the documents contained in his archives will be found in G. McLean Harper Jr., 'Menches, *komogrammateus* of Ker-keosiris', *Aeg.* xiv (1934), pp. 14 ff.

[161] Some of these documents have been studied by W. Kunkel, *Arch. Pap.* viii (1927), pp. 187 ff., and *Z. d. Sav.-Stift.* xlviii (1928), pp. 285 ff.

[162] An interesting specimen of a thoroughly hellenized Egyptian, perhaps of the priestly caste, or an egyptianized Greek or Thracian, a man who was thoroughly familiar with Egyptian religion and history and at the same time received an excellent Greek education, is afforded by Isidorus, who compiled in the first century B.C. four long poems in Greek praising the great goddess Hermuthis-Isis. The poems have been engraved on the pillars of the vestibule of the temple of the goddess in one of the villages (Ibion Eicosipentaruron) near Tebtunis. They were found and published by A. Vogliano, *Primo Rapporto degli scavi . . . nella zona de Mādīnet Mādī,* 1936, cf. *S.B.* 8138–41; *S.E.G.* viii. 548–51. Cf. my remarks above, p. 410, and in the forthcoming *Mél. Radet,* and W. Otto and H. Bengtson, loc. cit., pp. 81 ff., and passim. We can hardly discover the national identity of Isidorus: he has a high regard both for the Egyptians and for the Greeks and Thracians, that is to say, for the constituent elements of the population of his village. Typical representations of the Greco-Egyptian intellectual aristocracy of the Greek villages are furnished by the many basalt and granite statues of priests and 'presidents' of various sanctuaries of the Fayûm, mostly of the late Ptolemaic and early Roman times. See pl. c. As an example of an Egyptian who played an important political and military role in the time of Euergetes II, I may quote the famous Paos, a general of the king in the Thebaid at the time of the *amixia.* The evidence which concerns him has been collected several times, most fully by Otto and Bengtson, loc. cit., pp. 69 ff.; cf. Phommus, the *epistrategos* and *strategos* of the Thebaid of III B.C., ibid., pp. 8 and 161. I may also cite Tatas, an Egyptian or Anatolian, a 'royal doctor' (βασιλικὸς ἰατρός) who is mentioned in the lawsuit of Hermias as having quoted in his report (προσαναφορά) to the *strategos* the order of the king concerning the ταριχευταί of Thebes. Tatas need not necessarily be regarded as a personal doctor (*Leibarzt*) of the king. He may have been an Egyptian doctor in the royal service (like the βασιλικοὶ δικασταί, &c.), perhaps in the charge of the sanitary side of the operations performed on the bodies of the deceased by the various corporations connected with the embalming of corpses (*U.P.Z.* 162, col. 2, 25, and the note by Wilcken). Cf. Ch. VIII.

[163] The family which I have quoted in the text is known from several Demotic documents (U. Wilcken, *U.P.Z.* ii, nos. 163–9), which were found apparently in the same grave in which the Theban χοαχύται buried or kept their archives (*U.P.Z.* ii, p. iv), among them the acts of the famous lawsuit of Hermias (*U.P.Z.,* nos. 160–2). On these documents and on the Greco-Egyptian family of Hermias and Apollonius see *U.P.Z.* ii, p. 43 (the genealogy of the family) and p. 95 (character of the family). Similar was the family of Horus from the Pathyrites nome, the egyptianized Persian or Ionian, a former soldier, E. N. Adler, J. G. Tait, F. M. Heichelheim, F. Ll. Griffith, *The Adler Papyri,* 1939, cf. C. Préaux, *Chr. d'Eg.* xiv (28) (1939), pp. 393 ff., and U. Wilcken, *Arch. Pap.* xiii (1939), p. 218.

[164] On *U.P.Z.* 148 see C. Préaux, 'Lettres privées grecques d'Égypte relatives à l'éducation', *Rev. Belge*, viii (1929), pp. 767 ff. (with bibliography). On the use of two languages in Ptolemaic Egypt cf. W. Peremans, *Ant. Class.* iv (1935), pp. 403 ff. The fact that a Greek was invited to teach in an Egyptian family of which the members apparently did not speak Greek (otherwise why should the prospective teacher learn Αἰγύπτια γράμματα?) is significant. It is an interesting observation of Edgar and Smyly that in 171 B.C. most of the commanders and owners of river boats which transported grain to Alexandria have good Greek names, 'whereas in the list of ordinary boats carrying goods and passengers in Petr. iii. 107, the names are almost entirely Egyptian'. Does this mean that gradually the transport business was concentrated in the hands of the Greek *bourgeoisie* of Egypt, that is to say, that the Greeks progressively became the wealthier part of the population, or that the Greek names of the shipowners prove nothing more than a thorough amalgamation of the Greek and Egyptian *bourgeoisie*, the formation of a new class which was neither Greek nor Egyptian? On the problem of Macedonian, Greek, Semitic, Thracian, and other foreign names and Egyptian names, see the bibliography quoted in the articles by F. Zucker quoted above, n. 157, and L. Robert, *Rev. Phil.* xiii (65) (1939), p. 179. The role of the κάτοικοι in the life of a provincial city is further illustrated by an inscription of Aphroditopolis, dated 57/6 B.C., set up by οἱ ἐκ τοῦ γυμνασίου to their gymnasiarch, who was at the same time ἱππάρχης ἐπ' ἀνδρῶν κατοίκων ἱππέων, S.E.G. viii. 531, cf. B.G.U. 1188 (15/14 B.C.), 2 ff.: παρὰ Κάστορος [γ]υμν[ασι]άρχου Κόμα καὶ τῶν ἄλλων [τῶ]ν ἐν τῆι κώμηι κατοίκων καὶ τῶν ἄλλων γεωργῶν καὶ τῶν βασιλικῶν γεωργῶν τ[ῶν] ἐν τῆι κώμηι κατοικούντων. The κάτοικοι may have been of various origin. Some of them were but slightly hellenized (the Jews especially kept strictly to their religion, names, and mode of life, see *Teb.* 817, 818, and the other papyri quoted in 817, Intr., cf. 882) but socially they belonged to the upper class, that of the Greeks. On the relations between Greeks and natives in general, below, Ch. VIII. I may quote as proof of the 'superiority complex' the tone in which Hermias, the ἡγεμὼν ἐπ' ἀνδρῶν of Omboi in Upper Egypt, speaks of the Theban χοαχύται, a group of lower priests highly esteemed by the natives, in his complaints against them. Cf. Addendum to Ch. IV, pp. 263, &c.

[165] On the relations between priests and temples and the Ptolemies see above, Chs. IV and V. The comparison between the inscription of Canopus and that of Rosetta was first drawn by U. Wilcken, *Grundz.*, p. 95, cf. W. Spiegelberg, *Priesterdekrete von Kanopus und Memphis*, 1922; W. Otto, 'Siegesfeier des Ptolemaios IV. und Priestersynoden', *Bay. S.B.*, 1926, 2, p. 32 f. On the γῆ ἱερά above, Ch. V, n. 130. On the gifts and especially the γῆ ἀνιερωμένη, see my remarks, *G.G.A.* clxxi (1909), p. 623, and Wilcken's comments on *U.P.Z.* 153–5. Most scholars (for example C. Préaux, *Écon. Lag.*, pp. 486 ff.) regard the concessions of Euergetes II to the priests in 118 B.C. as a real surrender, as a grant to the priests of complete immunity and freedom in the management of the γῆ ἱερά, in addition to full recognition of their rights to the γῆ ἀνιερωμένη. I doubt this. The paragraphs of the

φιλάνθρωπα dealing with the grants to the temples (*Teb.* 5, ll. 57 ff.) are in a very confused state. In my opinion what we have is not the original text, but an abbreviation. Hence the seemingly chaotic character of these paragraphs. Brief as they are, they do not suggest to me that the priests received from Euergetes complete immunity. I see remission of some taxes and nothing more. The lines interpreted as dealing with the γῆ ἱερά, ll. 60 ff.: μηδ]ὲ τὰς ἱερὰς [ἀρούρας] σκε[υ]άζειν | παρε[υ]ρ[έ]σι μηδεμιᾷ, ἐὰν δὲ διὰ τῶν ἱερέ[ων . . . . δ]ιοικεῖσθαι appear in the φιλάνθρωπα at the end of the paragraph which deals with the ἀνιερωμένα. I am therefore inclined to regard them as referring to the latter, not to the γῆ ἱερά. The γῆ ἱερά was dealt with in the first lines of the section of the φιλάνθρωπα which referred to the temples. The statement of the king about the γῆ ἱερά is of a confirmatory, not a reformatory, charac- ter. No essential changes were introduced by it, l. 50: [προσ]τετάχασι δὲ κ[αὶ τὴν ἱερ]ὰν γῆν καὶ τ[ὰς ἄ]λλας ἱερ[ὰς προσόδους | τ]ὰς ὑπαρχούσας τοῖς ἱεροῖς [[. .]] μένιν [κυρί]ως. The temples were merely protected against unlawful acts of the officials. No wonder that in the documents belonging to the archives of Menches the γῆ ἱερά is managed in the traditional way by the officials of the crown. Quite different was the problem of the γῆ ἀνιερωμένη. Though the γῆ ἀνιερωμένη was not a new feature in the life of the temples, probably no strict rules existed about it. The officials of the crown, in order to stop the growth of these 'private estates' of the temples, tried to wrest from them as much of this land as was possible. The rest they wanted to treat as pieces of γῆ ἱερά. The priests resisted. The struggle was acute. In the struggle Euergetes took the side of the priests.

[166] A careful collection of the evidence relating to this class is much desired. On the tax-contractors, their sureties, and the officials of the crown connected with tax-collection, see above, p. 328 f.

[167] The germs of liturgy which were inherent in the organization of the state-contracts by the Ptolemies have been pointed out in my *Gesch. der Staatspacht*, pp. 336 ff., and U. Wilcken, *Ostraka*, i, pp. 513 ff., cf. his *Grundz.*, pp. 182 ff., and my review of the *Ostraka* in *Woch. f. kl. Phil.*, 1900, pp. 124 ff. Cf. also on the liturgy of the Ptolemaic period F. Oertel, *Die Liturgie*, 1917, pp. 26 ff.

[168] My *Kolonat*, pp. 6 ff.; J. Lesquier, *Les institutions militaires de l'Égypte sous les Lagides*, 1911, pp. 230 ff.; C. Préaux, *Chr. d'Ég.* xi (21) (1936), pp. 122 ff., and *Écon. Lag.*, pp. 468 ff. The fact is attested by official regulations and by the wills of the κληροῦχοι, e.g. *B.G.U.* 1185 and 1285, 5.

[169] W. Kunkel, *Z. d. Sav.-Stift.* xlviii (1928), pp. 285 ff., cf. U. Wilcken, *Arch. Pap.* ix (1930), p. 237, and C. Préaux, *Écon. Lag.*, pp. 470 ff. *Teb.* 124, I repeat, is very fragmentary and its interpretation is difficult. Especially difficult are ll. 30–36. The main problem is whether others than soldiers were allowed to acquire the κλῆροι κατοικικοί from their former holders, probably with the obligation of military service. L. 32: ἕτεροι δὲ ἐξ ἰδιοκτη[μόνων] καὶ ἐξ ἄλλων εἰδῶν μεταβεβή[κασιν] εἰς τὴν κα[τοικίαν] hardly justifies the conclusion

that the ἰδιοκτήμονες and other men who changed their status for that of a κάτοικος did so by purchasing a κλῆρος κατοικικός (cf. ll. 37 ff.). They may only have changed their status. However, the problem is obscure and we must await new evidence.

¹⁷⁰ See for example the famous letter of 1 B.C. written by Hilarion, a hired hand, who worked in Alexandria, to his wife Alis, who remained at home (at Oxyrhynchus) and was expecting a child (*Oxy.* 744; Hunt and Smyly, *Sel. Pap.* 105). In this letter Hilarion instructs his wife to expose the baby if it be a girl. The letter has been discussed several times, most recently by F. Zimmermann, *Act. Vᵉ Congr. Pap.* 1938, pp. 583 ff., who points out that Hilarion was acting under the pressure of poverty and need. Cf. W. L. Westermann, *P.W.K.* Suppl. vi, 903, and Preisigke, *Wört.*, s.v. ἀναιρέω: exposure of children as one of the sources of slavery attested in Egypt since the time of Augustus. I may point out in this connexion that a fragment of Musonius Rufus' treatise Εἰ πάντα τὰ γινόμενα τέκνα θρεπτέον, which advocates large families and combats abortion, &c., has been recently found in Egypt, J. Enoch Powell, *Arch. Pap.* xii (1937), pp. 175 ff.

¹⁷¹ V. Martin, 'Les papyrus et l'histoire administrative de l'Égypte gréco-romaine', *Münch. Beitr. z. Pap.* xix (1934), pp. 128 ff., who has collected some evidence on the part which fiscal interests played in determining the actions both of government officers and of taxpayers and workmen. Cf. W. Schubart, *Arch. Pap.* xii (1936), pp. 18 ff. For a different view, W. L. Westermann, *Am. Hist. Rev.* xliii (1938), p. 284.

¹⁷² I cannot discuss in this book the administrative jurisdiction of the royal officials. I have dealt with it *en passant* in my *Kolonat*, pp. 67 ff. Since that time excellent work has been done in this field. The fundamental study is that of H. Berneker, 'Die Sondergerichtsbarkeit im griechischen Recht Ägyptens,' &c., *Münch. Beitr. z. Pap.* xxii (1935). See the useful summary in C. Préaux, *Écon. Lag.*, pp. 547 ff., and E. Balogh, *Act. Vᵉ Congr. Pap.* 1938, pp. 21 ff.

¹⁷³ For this list cf. my *Kolonat*, pp. 71 ff. I shall discuss some of the features of the activity of the officials in the light of other documents presently. Here may be given some evidence concerning those features which I do not intend to discuss at greater length in the text. On the σταθμοί (*Teb.* 5. 168 ff.) and their role in the life of Egypt, above, p. 285 f., cf. C. Préaux, *Écon. Lag.*, pp. 387 ff., 477 ff. and *Teb.* 933 (third century). The paragraph of *Teb.* 5. 221 ff., dealing with the exaction of State debts from the *laoi* and *hypoteleis* by the *practores*, has been corrected and interpreted by E. Schönbauer, *Z. d. Sav.-Stift.* xlvi (1926), p. 206, cf. H. Liebesny, *Aeg.* xvi (1936), pp. 275 ff.; V. Arangio-Ruiz, *Riv. Fil.* lxv (15) (1937), pp. 266 ff.; C. Préaux, *Écon. Lag.*, p. 542. We may infer from this paragraph of *Teb.* 5 that the power of the officials of the crown as regards the *laoi* and *hypoteleis* who were crown debtors—powers which under Philadelphus still included the right of selling the debtor into slavery—were restricted by Philadelphus' successors and

limited to the mere arrest of them. Even this seems to have been forbidden by Euergetes II. As regards *Teb.* 5. 231 ff. I may remark that the habit of pawning the working tools for debts is known to have existed since the early Ptolemaic times, *Petr.* ii. 13 (1), and *P. Cairo Zen.* 59633, 20. This was still done in 111 B.C. in one of the villages of the Fayûm, *Teb.* 878. In this case the debtors of the crown were not royal peasants.

[174] G. McLean Harper Jr., *Aeg.* xiv (1934), p. 29 f. It is interesting to compare the role played by Menches at Cerceosiris with that of Herieus, the *topogrammateus* of Pois in S. Egypt (Coptite nome) at about the same time (116 B.C.). Petenephotes, a humble *paraschistes* of Thebes, describes his position and influence in the following words (*U.P.Z.* 196, col. ii, 54 ff.; A. Wilhelm, *Wien. Anz.* lxxiv, 1937, pp. 71 ff.): καὶ τρόπον τινὰ ὄντ[ος τού]του τὰ ὅλα | τῆς Πώεως καί τινων ἄλλ[ω]ν τῶν | ἐμοὶ ἀποδιεσταλμένων κωμῶν | καὶ μάλιστα τῶν ἐν τῆι Πώει πραγμα|τικῶν καὶ τὸ πρεσβεῖον ἔχοντος | παρὰ τοὺς ἄλλους τοὺ[ς] ἐν τῆι κώμηι | κατοικοῦντας καὶ ἅπαντι διαφέροντος, i.e. 'he was the centre of life (the whole of it) in Pois and certain other of the villages assigned to me and especially of the officials of Pois, the most honoured man among the residents of the village, a man for whom everybody cared much'. It is to be noted that Herieus died in his office, which he probably held for a long time.

[175] *Teb.* 10; U. Wilcken, *Chr.* 160, and Introduction; Hunt–Edgar, *Sel. Pap.* 339; G. McLean Harper, Jr., *Aeg.* xiv (1934), pp. 16 ff., cf. my *Kolonat,* p. 35 f. Cf. the case of the οἰκονόμος τῶν σιτικῶν at Dimeh, who in 98 B.C. was ordered by the king to pay a certain amount of corn to the temple of this place, *O.G.I.* 177, 179; U. Wilcken, *Chr.* 168; C. Préaux, *Écon. Lag.,* p. 531.

[176] On the *doreai*, above, Ch. IV, pp. 289, 414 f. and 420 f., and notes 213 and 215 ff.; Ch. V, p. 731 f. and n. 150 a. The habit of assigning the proceeds of certain taxes to higher officials was probably inherited by the Ptolemies from the Egyptian past and from Persia, and was in all probability not confined to Ptolemaic Egypt. The practice furnishes evidence of the widespread conception of the taxes as part of the private income of the king. Δωρεαί, in the form of the right to collect taxes, are frequently attested in Egypt, especially since the reign of Euergetes I. Those who profited by them were sometimes prominent personalities: Dicaearchus in the time of Philopator, the well-known Agathocles. To the evidence collected above add *B.G.U.* 1834, 51/50 B.C., which shows that the institution was in full vigour under the last Ptolemies.

[177] V. Martin, 'Les papyrus et l'hist. adm.', *Münch. Beitr. z. Pap.* xix (1934), pp. 138 ff., and C. Préaux, *Écon. Lag.,* pp. 514 ff.: 'Les conséquences de la responsabilité des fonctionnaires'. Mlle Préaux has collected and discussed in this chapter ample evidence bearing on the relations between the government and the officials on the one hand and between the officials and the population on the other. She rightly regards the material responsibility of

the officials as the root of the evil. But it must be kept in mind that this material responsibility was not an innovation of the Ptolemies. An earlier example of an official inspection is *Teb.* 788 (C. Préaux, loc. cit., p. 521).

[178] My *Kolonat*, pp. 53 ff., cf. above, pp. 717 ff. I cannot enter here into the discussion of the legality of torture either for extorting the truth from a person suspected of some crime or even from a witness or as punishment. The mention of torture *expressis verbis* in the complaints quoted above shows that, though probably legal, torture was not commonly applied to free men. A good treatment of the problem of torture in Roman law (without mention of the Hellenistic period) will be found in A. Ehrhardt, art. 'Tormenta', *P.W.K.* vi A. 1775 ff. Cf. for Ptolemaic Egypt in addition to the documents quoted in the text (*Teb.* 5, l. 58, and *Amh.* 31, l. 11—πειθανάγκη, which probably is an euphemism for torture; *Teb.* 789—στρέβλαι and *B.G.U.* 1847, l. 16 —βάσανος), *P. Lille* 29, l. 22 (βάσανος applied to slaves in the third century B.C.).

[179] An excellent treatment of the ἀναχωρήσεις, especially for the Roman period, will be found in V. Martin, loc. cit., pp. 144 ff.; cf. C. Préaux, *Écon. Lag.*, Index, s. v. ἀναχώρησις and 'grève', esp. pp. 500 ff., and W. L. Westermann, *Am. Hist. Rev.* xliii (1938), pp. 276 ff. I cannot regard the 'anachoresis' as a right conceded to the natives by the government (Westermann). The 'walk-outs' and 'flights' were traditional in Egypt. The kings, faced with the stern fact of scarcity of labour and with the impossibility of replacing the 'folded hands', had only two means of combating the strikes: violence and negotiations. They used both of them, see C. Préaux, loc. cit. Nor can we say with Westermann that the 'anachoresis' was in the Ptolemaic period a group-action and in the Roman an individual one. Cases of individual flights are frequent, see in addition to *B.G.U.* 1797 (quoted by Westermann) the material collected by Mlle Préaux, loc. cit., cf. *Teb.* 895, 71, and 1008.

[180] F. von Woess, *Das Asylwesen Aegyptens* &c., 1923, cf. U. Wilcken, Introduction and notes to *U.P.Z.* 64, 119, 120, and 121, especially p. 571 (on the *asylia* granted to slaves); L. Wenger, *Phil.* lxxxvi (1931), pp. 427 ff.; C. Préaux, *Écon. Lag.*, p. 487 f., with a list of inscriptions (p. 487, n. 2). Cf. the important dedication and petition (95/94 B.C.) of Magdola, *O.G.I.* 740; *S.B.* 7259; *S.E.G.* viii. 466. In speaking of the *asylia* in my paper in *J.E.A.* vi (1920), p. 178, n. 10, I exaggerated its role in the life of Egypt in the second and first centuries B.C. I now return to my views on the subject set forth in my review of Otto's book (*G.G.A.* clxxi (1909), pp. 635 ff.) and in my *Kolonat*. I cannot share the view of Mlle Préaux that the rights of immunity, freedom from taxes (ἀτέλεια), and *asylia* granted to several temples in the first century B.C. were a kind of legally unnecessary supplement to the same rights already granted to all the temples, but not respected by the crown officials. I have explained above why I do not think that such a general grant was ever extended to the temples. The decrees of *asylia* confirm my point of view. Those who ask for the grant of *asylia* never mention that it is in fact a confirmation of rights already acquired. There is no doubt that by the decrees of *asylia* new rights were conferred on some temples.

Nor do I think that the immunity (exemption from liturgies) and *ateleia* conferred on the temples freed them from all the burdens imposed on them. The fact that the temples assure the rulers of their readiness to obey the laws shows that immunity and *ateleia* were partial, not general grants—freedom from *some* liturgies and taxes. I may mention that in the petition of 95/94 B.C. on behalf of the temple of Heron at Magdola, cited above, the two patrons of the temple complain not only of the general oppression of the temple by the officials of the crown (συκοφαντία καὶ σεισμός) but in particular of their endeavour (regarded by the patrons as unlawful) to collect from the χέρσος ἱερᾶς γῆς certain taxes (the ἔνατον and the ναύβιον). The officials certainly had reasons for doing so. Cf. G. A. Petropoulos, *Act. Ve Congr. Pap.* (1938), p. 338.

[181] F. von Woess, *Das Asylwesen*, p. 190; C. Préaux, *Chr. d'Ég.* x (19), 1935, pp. 114 ff.

[182] D. Schäfer, *Phil.* lxxxviii (1933), pp. 296 ff.; C. Préaux, *Chr. d'Ég.* x (19), 1935, pp. 109 ff., and *Écon. Lag.*, pp. 543 ff.; W. L. Westermann, *Am. Hist. Rev.* xliii (1938), p. 278. The earliest example of a πίστις is *Teb.* 741 (187/186 B.C.); cf. 895, ll. 37, 117, 124 (referring to the activity of Hippalus, above, Ch. V, n. 137). Mlle Préaux, loc. cit., p. 544, n. 2, gives a list of πίστεις of the Ptolemaic period.

[183] E. Seidl, *Der Eid im ptolemäischen Recht*, 1929, pp. 86 ff.; C. Préaux, *Chr. d'Ég.* x (20), 1935, p. 358 f., cf. H. Zilliacus, *Aeg.* xix (1939), pp. 70 ff. (esp. 73).

[184] C. Préaux, *Chr. d'Ég.* x (19), 1935, p. 114 f., and *Écon. Lag.*, p. 546.

[185] On collective responsibility, C. Préaux, *Écon. Lag.*, pp. 513 ff.

[186] On the 'Idios Logos' and its history see above, Ch. V, p. 707 ff., and notes 128 and 151, cf. *S.E.G.* viii. 468 (59 B.C.). On the ἀδέσποτα see the remarks of P. Collart and P. Jouguet, *Ét. Pap.* ii (1933), pp. 33 ff., based on G. Plaumann, 'Der Idios Logos', *Berl. Abh.*, phil.-hist. Kl. xvii (1918), p. 10, cf. C. Préaux, *Écon. Lag.*, p. 409. Some recent documents have supplied us with new evidence on this subject, esp. the inscription of Cyrene of 109/8 B.C. (?) quoted above, n. 157 (*S.E.G.* ix. 5, ll. 61 ff.): ἐάν τινες τῶν ἐπὶ χρείαις τεταγμένων | ἢ τῶν ἄλλων τῶν ὑπὸ τὴν βασιλείαν | τασσομένων ἀδέσποτα αἰτήσωνται | ἢ κατη⟨ι⟩τια-μένα, μὴ παρασφραγιζέσθωσαν | τὰ ὑπάρχοντα τῶν καταιτιωμένων μηδὲ | εἰς φυλακὴν παραδιδότωσαν μήτε αὐτοὺς | μήτε τοὺς οἰκέτας αὐτῶν ἄνευ τοῦ παρὰ | τῶν χρηματιστῶν κομίσαι χρηματισμούς. Cf. V. Arangio-Ruiz, *Riv. Fil.* lxv (15), 1937, p. 273 f. We may perhaps connect with the ownerless and confiscated property the 'unsold' property which appears occasionally in documents of the second and first centuries B.C., see *Teb.* 5, 9; 699, 6 (φιλάν-θρωπα of Euergetes II of 145/4 B.C. relating to the temples), and especially the amnesty decree of Euergetes II found in Cyprus, T. B. Mitford, *Arch. Pap.* xiii (1938), p. 32, ll. 8 ff.: καὶ κομ[ίζεσθαι τὰ ἔτι] | ἄπρατα ἀπὸ τῶν ἰδίων αὐτῶν τῶν διὰ ταῦτα [δημευθέντων (?)]. Cf. *Teb.* 716, 11 (158

B.C.). From the wording of the inscription of Cyprus we may infer that the ἄπρατα formed a special department of financial administration, which included confiscated private property not yet sold. The question of the management and real meaning of ἄπρατα must be studied in the light of the documents of Roman times dealing with ἄπρατα and γενηματογραφούμενα, see my *Kolonat*, pp. 133 ff., esp. 136 ff. and 150 ff. On the confiscated property in Cyprus and Cyrenaica see below, and on confiscated lands in Thera, assigned to soldiers of the Ptolemaic garrison, *I.G.* xii. 3. 327 (middle of third century B.C.).

[187] On the condition of Karanis, A. R. Boak, 'Irrigation and population in the Fayûm', *The Geographical Review*, xvi (1926), p. 361.

[188] On *B.G.U.* 1730 see W. Kunkel, *Arch. Pap.* viii (1928), pp. 212 ff., n. 15, cf. U. Wilcken, ibid. x (1932), p. 252, and W. Otto, *Hist. Zeitschr.*, clii (1935), p. 543. It is of interest to see that the government tries—before having recourse to its own grain stored in Alexandria—to ensure a supply of grain for Alexandria by pressure on the grain merchants. In normal times, therefore, Alexandria depended on private trade, on the surplus of grain produced in the χώρα. The king probably preferred to export his own grain and to sell it abroad for good silver. O. Krüger, 'Agricultural production in Hellenistic Egypt', *Bull. of the State Ac. of Mat. Civ.* cviii (1935), p. 102 f., (in Russian), suggests that the purpose of the order was not to secure grain for Alexandria but to keep grain in Middle Egypt, where there were bad crops in 50/49. I regard this interpretation as extremely improbable.

[189] F. Heichelheim, *Wirtsch. Schwank.*, pp. 33 ff. and 24, and for the prices, his lists, pp. 111 ff., cf. his *Wirtschaftsg.*, p. 456.

[190] W. W. Tarn, *C.A.H.* x, pp. 35 ff. There is a certain exaggeration in Tarn's panegyric of Cleopatra. The alleged fact that Egypt was quiet under her rule may be true (though based on negative evidence); but she was supported by Antony and his legions, and before that by Caesar. On the other hand, negative evidence in a period where the evidence is scanty is of very little use. The two famines of her time, though probably caused by a low Nile, were certainly aggravated by the bad condition of the dikes and canals and by the general depopulation of Egypt. This is obvious to every one who knows Egypt. Her popularity with the *laoi* is based on very slight evidence. Like the other Ptolemies, she was jealous of her treasury and was certainly very rich personally. This does not mean that the country was prosperous. Her granaries might have been full while there was scarcity of grain in the country. A good find of documents may shed much desired light on conditions in Egypt in her time. On Cleopatra's currency, Th. Reinach, *Rev. É.G.* xli (1928), pp. 182 ff., and F. Heichelheim, *Wirtsch. Schwank.*, p. 37. Note that the bronze coins of Cleopatra minted on a reduced standard (one-quarter of the weight of the bronze coins of Auletes) which were studied by Giesecke, *Das Ptolemäergeld*, pp. 71 ff., probably belong to the very beginning of her reign, see A. Baldwin Brett, 'A new Cleopatra tetradrachm of Ascalon',

A.J.A. xli (1937), pp. 452 ff., cf. Ph. Lederer, *Num. Chr.* lxxi (1938), pp. 65 ff. This shows that the economic situation in Egypt was no better in the early part of her reign than in the critical time before Actium. The only extant decree of Cleopatra, of 41 B.C. (*S.B.* 7337; Lefebvre, *Mél. Holleaux*, 1913, pp. 103 ff.; P. Collomp, *Rech. sur la Chancellerie et Diplomatique des Lagides*, 1926, p. 196), shows that the agents of the government were no better under her than before. Note how anxious Cleopatra, the Alexandrian queen, was to keep the Alexandrians in a good mood. Cf. *S.B.* 7457; E. Breccia, *Bull. de la Soc. Arch. d'Alex.* xxiv (1929), p. 66, n. 5.

[191] W. L. Westermann in his valuable and interesting paper, 'The Ptolemies and the welfare of their subjects', *Am. Hist. Rev.* xlvi (1938), pp. 271 ff., has briefly summarized the different views expressed by various scholars on the general policy of the Ptolemies and has stated his own. In combating the exaggerations of several modern scholars I am afraid that he himself exaggerates in his somewhat rosy picture of the Ptolemaic régime. In the main his views coincide to a certain extent with my own, as set forth above, and those of Mlle Préaux (see her *Économie royale des Lagides*). Mlle Préaux insists on the policy of the Ptolemies being 'royal', not racial. By 'royal' she probably means in accordance with the traditional policy of Oriental kings, who directed and organized the political, social, and economic life of their respective monarchies and protected the weak against the strong. While, however, the leading principles—the philosophy—of Oriental kingship remained one and the same for millennia, the application of them varied according to time, circumstances, and personalities. So it was with the Ptolemies. While at the outset their policy was in general the same as that of the other Hellenistic rulers, that is to say, personal and dynastic, it gradually became more and more connected with the land over which they ruled, i.e. more 'royal' in the Oriental sense than before. And yet under the pressure of circumstances it became ever more oppressive to the population at large, and unbearable to it. Cf. F. Heichelheim, *Wirtschaftsgeschichte des Altertums*, 1938.

[192] As regards Cyprus, see the papers of T. B. Mitford, quoted above, Ch. IV, n. 133. As regards Cyrene, G. Oliverio, *Documenti antichi dell'Africa italiana*, ii. 1 and 2; *S.E.G.* ix.

[193] The φιλάνθρωπα of Cyprus, T. B. Mitford, *Act. Vᵉ Congr. Pap.* (1938), pp. 291 ff., and *Arch. Pap.* xiii (1938), pp. 32 ff.; W. Otto and H. Bengtson, loc. cit., p. 26 f., and notes 4 and 5. The date 145/4 B.C. is certain. The inscription of Cyrene: *S.E.G.* ix. 5, cf. above, notes 157 and 186.

[194] Above, n. 157. I cannot repeat here the contents of the papers quoted in n. 157. I refer the reader to them for all the problems raised by the documents which are not treated in the text.

[195] See *Teb.* 61 a, ll. 20 ff., and 64 a, ll. 82 ff. (118/17 B.C.) and above, n. 186.

[196] Very interesting in this respect is a papyrus of the second century B.C., *Teb.* 886; cf. 728, 7. It is an account of an oil merchant. In it 'foreign oil'

(ξενικὸν ἔλαιον) bulks larger than the domestic (Αἰγύπτιον), though it is more expensive (80 dr. per *cotyla* as compared with 60 dr.). These two documents show that the restrictions on the importation of foreign oil into Egypt no longer existed in the second century and that foreign oil circulated freely on the Egyptian market. This may have been due to the fact that the domestic oil proved to be of inferior quality and was not produced in sufficient quantity. But additional reasons may be suggested. After Panium the excellent Syrian oil which supplemented the native olive oil was no more available on the same conditions as before, while the demand for olive oil of a better quality than the Egyptian remained heavy. This was an excellent opportunity for the Aegean and Syrian merchants to export one of their staple products to Egypt and for the kings of Egypt to attract Aegean and Syrian commerce to Alexandria, deriving at the same time a good profit from customs duties (this is the explanation of the difference in price—20 copper drachmas—between the foreign and the domestic oil: the customs duties would amount to one-quarter of the sale price). It is unfortunate that the document is not exactly dated and that we cannot therefore compare the price of foreign oil in Egypt with contemporary prices in the Aegean. The price of oil is too high for the ratio 1 : 60 of Philopator (8 silver obols). The copper drachma was certainly depreciated, but we cannot guess by how much.

[197] On the earliest wall decorations of the second style in Rome, G. E. Rizzo, *Monumenti della pittura ellenistico-romana*, iii, Roma, fasc. 1 : Le pitture della Casa dei Grifi, 1936, cf. H. G. Beyen, *Die pompeianische Wanddekoration vom zweiten bis zum vierten Stil*, i, 1938, pp. 46 ff., figs. 7, 8, 9. The date of the paintings of the House of the Griffins is probably the late second or early first century B.C. (early Sullan). Note especially the decoration of the lunettes of room 3, Rizzo, loc. cit., pls. B and IV; text-figures 16 and 17, which may point to Alexandria.

[198] One type of glass vessels may perhaps be recognized as a creation of Alexandria and Egypt in the first century B.C., viz. the glass vases covered with ornaments and figures painted on the surface in gold or in water-colours. We know this glass mainly from specimens found in Italy, South Russia, and Gaul, the earliest examples being dated in the first century A.D. The origin of this painted glass has been assigned with great probability to Egypt, Syria being the second best candidate. Now this glass is certainly a continuation of the gold glass of the Hellenistic period, which I have described above (Ch. IV, notes 165 and 166). The latest example of glass of this type is furnished by the fragments of a dish found in one of the monumental graves of the Galatian royal house of Deiotarus at Karalar (see above, n. 116) and thus belonging to the first century B.C., see Remzi Uguz, *Türk Tarih, Ark. ve etn. Derg.* ii (1934), pl. 13, facing p. 124 (Tumulus B). The sherd of the same type of glass in the Metropolitan Museum (pl. XLIII. 4), with gold and water-colour ornaments between two layers of glass, is certainly not Roman but late Hellenistic (*Bull. Metr. Mus.* xx (1925), p. 183). This may point to the first century B.C. as the time when the first specimens of painted glass

were produced in Egypt. Fine specimens of Augustan painted glass were on show in the Metropolitan Museum in its exhibition of Augustan art in 1939, see *Augustan Art*, 1939, p. 23, and figs. 51 and 52; cf. the painted bowls recently found at Locarno, D. Silvestrini, *Bull. d'Arte*, xvi (1938), pp. 430 ff., and F. Stähelin, *Anz. Schweiz. Altertumsk.* 1938, Heft 4 (my articles quoted above, Ch. IV, n. 165, were unknown to both writers). The most common type of painted glass (bowls with a peculiar rosette on the bottom, repeated on all the known specimens), were probably exported from one and the same place, the rosette being the trade-mark. Cf. Addendum to this note.

[199] I cannot enter here into a discussion of the late Hellenistic and early Roman or Augustan silver plate. It is, however, obvious that in the treasures of Hildesheim, Boscoreale, and the Casa di Menandro at Pompeii we have pieces which are purely Hellenistic in spirit ; some of them can be traced back to Alexandria. See the stimulating pamphlet of A. Ippel, 'Guss und Treibarbeit in Silber', *Winckelmanns Progr.* 97 (1937).

[200] My *Soc. and Ec. Hist. of the Rom. Emp.* (Italian edition), p. 111, cf. p. 82. It is certain that in Augustan times and later in the first century A.D. commercial relations between South Italy and Egypt were very lively. I am inclined to think that they were active long before, especially after the decay of Delos and the rapid growth of Puteoli. A splendid illustration of this fact is the recent find in Pompeii of a fine ivory statuette of the Indian goddess Lakšmi, of purest Indian style, which was almost certainly imported to Pompeii via Alexandria. Not being a specialist in Indian art, I cannot discuss the date of this statuette. My impression is that it belongs to the late Hellenistic period. On the export of ivory objects from India through Bactria, see my remarks on the find at Kapisa, above, p. 544 and n. 317 (cf. Addenda). On the statuette found in Pompeii, A. Maiuri, 'Statuetta eburnea di arte indiana a Pompei', *Le Arti*, i. 2 (1939), pp. 111 ff. Cf. Ch. VIII, n. 192.

[201] See my paper 'Foreign commerce of Ptolemaic Egypt', *Journ. of Ec. and Bus. Hist.* iv (1932), pp. 754 ff. On Lochus and the Delian inscription, see the comments of P. Roussel on *Inscr. de Délos*, 1526, and especially the discussion of his career and activity by W. Otto and H. Bengtson, *Zur Gesch. d. Niederg.*, &c., pp. 101 ff. I am not sure that Lochus was appointed *strategos* of the Thebaid in 127/6 B.C. after the capture of Alexandria. He may have held this office before and have participated in the capture as commander of the Thebaid part of the army. Nor have Otto and Bengtson produced any material to show that the Roman merchants helped Euergetes in the capture of Alexandria. It is not impossible that they did, but it is highly improbable. I see no reason why they should not have been on business in Alexandria and saved their life and property with the help of Lochus and Euergetes. If not, they might have had agents, goods, and ships in the harbour and the docks of Alexandria. On Stolus and on Simalus and his family, his wealth,

and his residence, see my remarks, *C.A.H.* viii, p. 649. On the Egyptian cults and on Alexandrians at Delos, P. Roussel, *Délos, col. ath.*, pp. 86 and 93, n. 4.

[202] U. Wilcken, 'Punt-Fahrten in der Ptolemäerzeit', *Zeitschr. f. Aeg. Spr.* lx (1925), pp. 86 ff., cf. E. Ziebarth, *Seeraub*, pp. 54 and 126, n. 24, and A. Wilhelm, *J.R.S.* xxvii (1937), pp. 148 ff. The date of the papyrus is not certain. The appearance of a Carthaginian among the sureties makes it probable, but does not necessarily mean, that Carthage was not yet destroyed. Carthaginian capitalists and merchants may have been residents in Alexandria before the catastrophe and may have remained there after it. On the role of Gnaeus see the interesting remarks of F. Heichelheim, *Aeg.* xiii (1933), pp. 187 ff., who compares the sea loans of Cato (Plut. *Cato Ma.* 21) and the role of his freedman Quintio, who sailed with the group of merchants to whom a loan had been granted by Cato. For the name of Gnaeus, cf. Gaius in Call. Διηγήσεις, v. 25 ff., and J. Stroux, *Phil.* lxxxix (1934), p. 305, n. 6; see also F. Altheim, *Weltherrschaft und Krise*, 1935, pp. 143 ff., and G. De Sanctis, *Riv. Fil.* xiii (63), 1935, pp. 289 ff. I may note in this connexion that Ptolemaic coins reached the Danube lands by way of Italy. A hoard of coins found at Mazin in Croatia (Noe², no. 666) and buried about 89 B.C. contained the savings of a family gradually accumulated or the copper deposit of a smith. In this hoard, besides *aes grave, aes signatum*, and *aes rude*, there were found large numbers of Sicilian, Carthaginian, Numidian, South Italian, and Ptolemaic (Ptolemy VIII and X) coins. The find shows the western orientation of Egyptian trade in the first century B.C.

[203] On the revival of the Oriental trade see M. Chwostow, *Studies in the history of commercial relations in the Hellenistic period and Roman Imperial times*. I. History of Eastern trade in Greco-Roman Egypt, Kazan, 1907 (in Russian); my paper, 'Zur Geschichte des Ost- und Südhandels im ptolemäisch-römischen Aegypten', *Arch. Pap.* iv (1907–8), pp. 304 ff.; H. Kortenbeutel, *Der ägyptische Süd- und Osthandel in der Politik der Ptolemäer und römischen Kaiser*, 1931, pp. 44 ff.; my paper quoted in n. 201; M. Cary and E. H. Warmington, *Les Explorateurs de l'Antiquité*, 1932, pp. 103 ff. For the relations with India, S. Levi, 'Alexandre et Alexandrie dans les documents indiens', *Mél. Maspero*, 1934, ii, pp. 154 ff. On the early relations with China (glass beads, perhaps imported from Alexandria), C. G. Seligman, 'The Roman Orient and the Far East', *Antiquity*, xi (1937), pp. 16 ff. For the ample literature of the subject see, besides the books and papers quoted above, the volumes of Kortenbeutel and Cary. In these books and in my paper in *Journ. of Ec. and Bus. Hist.* iv (1932), pp. 737 ff., and esp. 745 f., are discussed the various important controversies concerning some of the problems presented by the period we are considering.

On the traffic between Coptos and Berenice, and in general between the Nile valley and the shore of the Red Sea, in the time of Philopator, and on the hunting of elephants under Charimortus see L. Amundsen, *Ostr. Osl.* 1933, n. 2, pp. 8 ff., with the corrections of U. Wilcken, *Arch. Pap.* xi (1933), p. 139, n. 1, and A. S. Hunt, *J.E.A.* xx (1934), p. 125. On Egypt and the

Nabataeans in the time of Euergetes II, H. Kortenbeutel, loc. cit., p. 45; my paper in *Journ. of Ec. and Bus. Hist.* iv (1932), pp. 737 ff. Cf. W. Otto and H. Bengtson, loc. cit., pp. 214 ff.

[204] On Agatharchides of Cnidus, C. Müller in *G.G.M.* i, Prol., pp. liv ff., and fragments, pp. 111 ff., cf. F. Jacoby, *F. Gr. Hist.* 86. On his life and his work see the leading histories of ancient geography and literature, and especially F. Susemihl, *Gesch. gr. Lit. in d. Alexandrinerzeit*, i, pp. 685 ff.; M. Chwostow, loc. cit., p. 51 and 439 (both with bibliography); E. Schwartz, *P.W.* i. 739 f.; W. W. Tarn, *J.E.A.* xv (1929), p. 14; *Hell. Civ.*², pp. 209 ff.; H. Kortenbeutel, loc. cit., pp. 8 ff.; W. Otto and H. Bengtson, loc. cit., p. 195.

[205] On Eudoxus and on Hippalus see my paper in *Journ. of Ec. and Bus. Hist.* iv (1932), p. 745, and especially the masterly study of W. Otto and H. Bengtson, loc. cit., ch. iii, 'Die Aufnahme des direkten Seeverkehrs mit Indien in der Zeit des 2. Euergetes', pp. 194 ff. In the latter the reader will find all the evidence and a full bibliography. I may point out that in my paper quoted above (overlooked by Otto and Bengtson) I showed the connexion between Eudoxus and Hippalus. In the lines devoted to them in the text I accept most of the results of the study of Otto and Bengtson. Cf. J. H. Thiele, 'Eudoxus van Cyzicus', *Mededeel. Nederl. Ak. van Wettenschappen.* Nieuwe Recks, Deel 2, No. 8, 1939, pp. 187 ff.

[206] On the new office in the Ptolemaic administration see W. Otto und H. Bengtson, loc. cit., ch. i, 'Zu einer griechischen Weihinschrift aus Koptos von Jahre 110/9 v. Chr.', pp. 1 ff. and 215 ff.

[207] Strabo ii. 5. 12, p. 118; xv. 1. 4, p. 686; xvii. 1. 13, p. 798, and 45, p. 815. Strabo certainly thought that it was the Romans who were the first to organize maritime trade relations between India and Egypt on a large scale. On the statements of Strabo cf. W. Otto and H. Bengtson, loc. cit., p. 212. I cannot, however, accept their view of the gradual decay of the Egypto-Indian trade in the first century B.C. Our evidence does not support it. The trade could not, of course, be carried on to its full extent in this troubled time. But I see no reason to assume that the later Ptolemies would keep in existence the office of commander of the Red and Indian Seas if there was practically nothing to protect on these seas and no trade to watch and to organize.

CHAPTER VII

[1] For the history of the time of Mithridates and of the period of the civil wars, see the relative chapters of *C.A.H.* ix and x (with the appended bibliographies); cf. J. Carcopino, *Histoire romaine*, ii, 1936 (until 44 B.C.), and E. Kornemann, *Römische Geschichte*, i, 1938, pp. 411 ff. Surveys of the Hellenistic world and of Greece: Th. Reinach, *Mithridate Eupator* (I quote the German translation by A. Goetz, 1895); G. F. Hertzberg, *Histoire de la Grèce sous la domination des Romains*, I, 1887 (I use the French edition of this work, because it was revised by the author); G. Finlay, *Greece under the Romans*,

1844, i, pp. 28–36 (there are a German and a Russian translation of this book) ; J. A. O. Larsen, 'Roman Greece' in T. Frank, *Econ. Survey*, iv, 1937, pp. 422 ff. ; V. Chapot, *La Province romaine proconsulaire d'Asie*, 1904 ; T. R. S. Broughton, 'Roman Asia Minor', in T. Frank, *Econ. Survey*, iv, 1937, pp. 512 ff., cf. B. Haussoullier, *Études sur l'histoire de Milet et du Didymeion*, 1902 ; J. Dobiaš, *Dejiny Rimske Provincie Syrske* (Hist. de la province romaine de Syrie), i, 1924 (with French résumé). On the provincial administration of Rome, R. O. Jolliffe, *Phases of Corruption in Roman Administration*, &c., 1919 ; G. H. Stevenson, 'The provinces and their government', *C.A.H.* ix, pp. 437 ff. ; W. Kroll, *Die Kultur der ciceronischen Zeit*, 1933, pp. 99 ff., and J. M. Cobban, *Senate and Provinces 78–49 B.C.*, 1935 (superficial). All contain good bibliographies, which relieves me from quoting older treatments of the subject.

2 On the literary sources for the time between 133 and 44 B.C., *C.A.H.* ix, pp. 882 ff. (with bibliography). Masterly, though slightly antiquated, is the survey of sources in Th. Reinach's *Mithridate*, pp. 413 ff. On Strabo and his relations to the Bosporus, M. Rostovtzeff, 'Strabo as a source for the history of the Bosporus', *Volume in honour of Prof. Buzescul*, 1914, pp. 366 ff., cf. *Skythien und der Bosporus*, pp. 125 ff.

3 Besides the brilliant account by Th. Reinach, good surveys, all based on his work, will be found in *C.A.H.* ix, pp. 225 ff. (with bibliography, pp. 924 ff.), J. Carcopino, *Hist. rom.* ii, pp. 402 ff., and Geyer, *P.W.K.* xv. 2163 ff., s.v. Mithridates, no. 12. On the role of Athens in the first Mithridatic war, W. S. Ferguson, *H.A.*, pp. 440 ff., and S. Jebelev, *H.A.*, p. 226. Cf. the books quoted in n. 1.

4 On the identity of Athenion–Aristion, see on one side Th. Reinach (one and the same person, cf. Geyer, loc. cit. 2171), and on the other Niese, Wilcken, Jebelev, Ferguson and Wilamowitz (two successive leaders). Cf. U. von Wilamowitz-Moellendorf, *Kl. Schriften*, v. 1, 1937, pp. 204 ff., J. Carcopino, loc. cit., p. 389 (bibliographical note) and p. 417, note 106, and G. De Sanctis, 'Der Hellenismus und Rom', *Propyläen Weltgeschichte*, ii, p. 338.

5 The sources are quoted in the books named in note 1. For Sulla's levies in Greece, *S.I.G.*³ 744, honours bestowed by the *koinon* of the Aetolians on Ladameas of Calydon, who served in the army of Sulla and was honoured by him with military decorations. On the sack of Delphi by the Maedi and its date, G. Daux, *Delphes*, &c., pp. 392 ff. (85–84 B.C.), cf. for an earlier date (89/8 B.C.) A. Piganiol, *Rev. É.A.* xxxix (1937), pp. 108 ff.

6 Plut. *Sulla*, 12 ; App. *Mithr.* 30. The other sources are quoted by Hertzberg, loc. cit., p. 339, and Reinach, loc. cit., p. 151 (Reinach speaks of 100,000 pairs of mules : misprint ?).

7 Plut. *Sulla*, 19.12 ; App. *Mithr.* 54, and Paus. ix. 7. 5–6. The land was later restored to Thebes. On the temple of Amphiaraus, *S.I.G.*³ 747. Cf. G. Daux, *Delphes*, &c., p. 406. It is well known that Sulla and in his name his quaestor Lucullus issued in 87–84 B.C. both in Greece and in Asia Minor abundant

series of coins. These are partly Roman *aurei* and *denarii* of four types: with the name of Sulla only, with those of Sulla and his proquaestor L. Manlius (two types), and with the initial *Q(uaestor)* only. Besides these coins, however, abundant drachmas and tetradrachms of Greek type were minted in the Peloponnese and put into circulation by Lucullus in 87 B.C. They reproduce the Athenian coins of the time but omit the name of the city and add to the owl two trophies (to the r. and l. of the owl, see my pl. CV. 2.) The coinage of Lucullus issued in Sulla's name in Greece and Asia Minor is mentioned by Plut. *Luc.* 2. 2 and 4. 1. In the first passage: δι' ἐκείνου γὰρ ἐκόπη τὸ πλεῖστον ἐν Πελοποννήσῳ περὶ τὸν Μιθριδατικὸν πόλεμον, καὶ Λουκούλλειον ἀπ' ἐκείνου προσηγορεύθη καὶ διετέλεσεν ἐπὶ πλεῖστον, ὑπὸ τῶν στρατιωτικῶν χρειῶν ἐν τῷ πολέμῳ λαμβάνον ἀμοιβὴν ταχεῖαν. Plutarch in all probability refers to the Lucullan owls, as has been shown recently by G. Daux, *Rev. N.* xxxviii (1935), pp. 1 ff. These coins were known in Greece under the name of πλάτη, a nickname for the Sullan tetradrachms. They are mentioned in an unpublished manumission of Delphi of about 30–20 B.C.: ταῦτα ἐν ἑνὶ ἀπ[έδοντ]ο πλατέων Λευκολλε[ίων ἑ]κατὸν καὶ πέντε. In his article G. Daux gives a bibliography of the Sullan coinage in Greece and Asia Minor. Cf. Ch. Seltman, *Greek Coins*, p. 263, pl. lxiii. 12, *C.A.H.*, vol. of pls., iv, p. 10, n–p, E. J. P. Raven, *Num. Chr.* lxxi (1938), pp. 153 ff. On the Athenian coinage after the capture of the city by Sulla, M. L. Kambanis, *B.C.H.* lxii (1938), pp. 60 ff.

[8] Inscription of Sadalas, M. Holleaux, *Rev. É. G.* xxxii (1919), pp. 320 ff.; G. Daux, *Delphes*, &c., p. 401. Sadalas was a noble Thracian sent by King Amatocus to help Sulla. The inscription of Sadalas must be read in connexion with the famous story of Plutarch (*Cim.* 1 ff.) concerning Damon Peripoltas, a noble youth of Chaeronea and his tragic experiences, which cannot be retold here. Suffice it to say that the young man became the victim of the lust of a Roman officer stationed in the city. In sheer despair he organized a band, killed the officer and then the magistrates of the city, and finally took to brigandage. For his crimes his own city was made responsible and would have suffered severe punishment, had it not been for the intervention of Lucullus who, on his way back to Italy in 80 B.C., settled the affair and took the garrison of Chaeronea with him to Italy.

[9] Inscription of Daulis, *F.D.* iii. 4, no. 69; *S.E.G.* i. 175; G. Daux, *Delphes*, &c., p. 402.

[10] The inscription in honour of the man of Drymus, *F.D.* iii. 4, no. 54; in honour of Caphisias, ibid no. 55; *S.E.G.* i. 173; G. Daux, loc. cit., p. 400. On the interruption of the Pythia, see the inscription in *B.C.H.* liii (1929), pp. 34 ff., G. Daux, loc. cit., p. 405, a decree honouring a harpist Polygnoto of Thebes who was unable to take part in the celebration διὰ δὲ τὸν ἐνεστακότα [πόλεμον (or καιρὸν) οὐ συ]ντελεσμένου τοῦ ἀγῶνος.

[11] Capture and punishment of Delos: P. Roussel, *Délos, col. ath.*, pp. 317 ff.; F. Durrbach, *Choix*, p. 234 f. (comments on no. 146, cf. *Inscr. de Délos*

1742, with note) and p. 236, cf. pp. 239 ff., comments on nos. 150–1 (*Inscr. de Délos* 1710, 1854), based on archaeological evidence which shows the extent of the damage done by Archelaus' capture of the city to it and to the temple. The Athenians of Delos sided with the conservative party of Athens and offered resistance to the democratic leader in the hope of Roman help.

¹² The evidence about Asia Minor in the time of the first Mithridatic war has often been collected. There is no need to pile up references, which will be found in the books and articles quoted in note 1. In the following notes and in the text I refer either to certain basic texts or to texts and modern contributions that are not discussed in the principal historical accounts of Mithridates. In some of these notes I state my opinion on disputed questions.

¹³ On the treatment of Chios and the settlement of men from Pontus in the city, F. Koepp, *Rh. Mus.* xxxix (1884), p. 216; Geyer, *P.W.K.* xv. 2174–5. The policy of transplanting masses of new settlers from one place to another, some of them to recently founded cities—the traditional policy of Oriental monarchies—was adopted on a large scale in the period under review by Tigranes in Armenia, Mesopotamia, and Syria. Mithridates did the same in his Bosporan kingdom, drawing on his Pontic subjects (see my *Iranians and Greeks*, p. 149). An instance of the application of this policy may be found in the treatment of Olbia by Mithridates, if we accept as correct the ingenious restoration and interpretation of *I.O.S.P.E.* i.² 35, by A. Wilhelm, *Klio*, xxix (1936), pp. 50 ff. It seems that Mithridates transplanted to Olbia some time during his reign a colony (military?) of Armenians. To this colony an Amisene shipowner brought supplies from Amisus and, stopping on his way to Olbia at Sinope, took on board an Olbian embassy which had come to Sinope probably in order to see Mithridates as well as a reinforcement (βοήθεια) for the Armenian military settlers of Olbia, who practically formed a Pontic garrison there. For this service he was honoured by the city. Similar reinforcements were sent by Mithridates to other Pontic cities (during the second Mithridatic war?), as is attested in the case of Apollonia, Ch. M. Danoff, *Jahreshefte*, xxx (1936), Beiblatt, pp. 87 ff., and *Bull. Inst. Arch. Bulg.* xii (1939), pp. 235 ff. (in Bulgarian with German résumé), where the reinforcement may have been connected with the expedition of M. Terentius Varro Lucullus (F. Münzer, *P.W.K.* xiii. 414, esp. 417) in 72/1 B.C. against the cities of the NW. shore of the Pontus, cf. M. S. Lambrino, *C.R. Ac. Inscr.*, 1933, pp. 278 ff. (fragment of a *foedus* made at this time by Lucullus with the city of Callatis, cf. A. Passerini, *Athen.* xiii (1935), pp. 57 ff.).

¹⁴ *S.I.G.*³ 742, cf. J. H. Oliver, *Am. J. Phil.* lx (1939), pp. 468 ff. The decree or law of the *demos* of Ephesus is one of the most important documents relating to the economic life of Ephesus in the first century B.C.: see the comments on the inscription in *Inscr. Jur. Gr.* no. 4; Th. Reinach, *Mithr. Eup.*, p. 175; E. Ziebarth, *Seeraub und Seehandel*, p. 58, and T. R. S. Broughton, 'Roman Asia Minor,' pp. 518 and 559 (where part of the text is translated without comments or bibliography). It is to be regretted that the inscription

of Miletus, A. von Gerkan, *Milet, Erg. d. Ausgr.* ii. 3, *Die Stadtmauer*, 1935, pp. 129 ff., n. 400 (cf. i. 3, n. 172), assigned to the time of Mithridates, cannot be exactly dated. It mentions a certain Biares, who was in charge of the Didymeion, the city walls and towers, and the defence of the harbour (κλειστὸς λιμήν).

[15] A succinct summary of the acts of Mithridates is given by App. *Mithr.* 58, in the speech addressed to him by Sulla at their conference. Note that those who betrayed the conspirators to Mithridates were subsequently either executed by Sulla or committed suicide. Some fled to Pontus.

[16] On Sulla's punishment of some cities and grants of privileges to others, see the evidence collected in the books and articles quoted in note 1. Benevolent treatment of Cos by Sulla as a reward for its pro-Roman behaviour during the massacre (Tac. *Ann.* iv. 14) and after the evacuation of the city by Mithridates (App. *Mithr.* 23; Plut. *Luc.* 3) is suggested by the publication there, at Sulla's request, of his letter and the corresponding S.C. on behalf of the Dionysiac *technitai* (83–81 B.C.), M. Segre, *Riv. Fil.* LXVI (16) (1938), pp. 253 ff. On the contribution imposed by Sulla on Asia, see the following note.

[17] The basic texts relating to the burdens imposed by Sulla on the cities of Asia Minor are those which report the Ephesian speech of Sulla, which very probably reflects an official document, App. *Mithr.* 62, cf. 63, and Plut. *Sulla*, 25, and *Luc.* 4. 1, and 20. These texts and other notices of the same measures are discussed in the books and articles quoted in note 1, cf. C. Lanzani, *Riv. Fil.* xxxviii (1910), pp. 520 ff.; T. Frank, *Econ. Hist.*, 2nd ed., pp. 151 ff., and *Econ. Survey*, i, p. 342, and A. Momigliano, *Atti IV Congr. Naz. St. Rom.* i (1938), pp. 280ff. The subject of the five years' tribute and the indemnity imposed by Sulla is a controversial one, since the texts that deal with it are ambiguous and difficult to interpret. I am inclined to think that the sum of 20,000 talents mentioned by Plutarch means the amount of the war indemnity and does not include the five years' φόρος. The method of collecting the indemnity (and the φόρος) by means of special agents, appointed to special regions and accompanied by soldiers, was repeatedly used again by the successors of Sulla in the Near East and may not have been invented by him. The question of the survival of the regions is discussed by Chapot, *La Prov. rom. procons. d'Asie* 1904; cf. T. R. S. Broughton, *Quantulacumque*, 1937, p. 133 (without mention of Chapot).

Another controversial point is Sulla's elimination of the *publicani* from the collection of the *decuma*. The fundamental text relating to it (Cic. *ad Q. Fr.* i. 1. 33, quoted in full below, note 46) has been variously interpreted. In arguing about the *publicani* and the attitude of the Greeks towards them, Cicero says that the Greeks (i.e. the cities) have no right to take exception to the tax-contractors, since the system of tax contracts existed in Asia before the Romans, and moreover, when Sulla had distributed the *vectigal* equally among the cities, they were unable to collect it without the help of contractors. If we interpret *vectigal* as the five years' tribute and the indemnity, the text would mean only that the cities collected this εἰσφορά with the help of local *telonai* in order to hand it over to the special agents of Sulla. This, however, is not very probable. The usual meaning of *vectigal* is not an extra-ordinary contribution but a regular yearly tax such as the *decuma*. If the latter is meant, the conclusion is unavoidable that it was not the Roman *publicani* but the local *telonai* who collected the yearly *decuma* which Sulla distributed equally among the cities, making the cities themselves responsible for the payment. This looks like a return to the practice of the Seleucids and the Attalids, and vividly recalls the fiscal organization of Sicily, where the *scriptura* and the *portoria* were collected by Roman *publicani* and the *decuma* by local *decumani*. I interpreted the text in this sense in my *Staatspacht*, p. 29, and I am inclined to interpret it in the same way now. For a different interpretation, see T. R. S. Broughton, 'Rom. Asia Minor', p. 519.

Billeting of soldiers on cities and on private citizens was an ancient practice and lasted until the end of the ancient world. I have frequently spoken of it above. It is probable that the right of billeted soldiers to invite guests, who were fed at the expense of the host, was still the current practice in Dura in the third century A.D.: see the graffito published in *Dura Rep.* v, p. 39, cf. vi, pp. 176 ff. and 301 ff. It is interesting to note the abhorrence with which the people regarded the prospect of extraordinary contributions and the billeting of soldiers (and of other Romans also) on private houses. There is no doubt that every one tried in one way or another to escape this burden. The Dionysiac *technitai* of Asia who, like the other associations of *technitai*, enjoyed general immunity (granted or confirmed to them by the Pergamene kings) hastened to ask Sulla to confirm this immunity anew by a special letter and a corresponding S.C., which Sulla, a great friend of art and artists, graciously did. The relative documents were published in many cities and sanctuaries, among them Cos, where copies of a covering letter of Sulla, his letter to the *technitai*, and the S.C. have recently been found (M. Segre, *Riv. Fil.* lxvi (16) (1938), pp. 253 ff.). It will be of interest to repeat here the list of burdens from which the *technitai* were freed: λειτουργίαι and στρατεῖαι (compulsory personal service of whatever kind it might be and military service); εἰσφορά (extraordinary contribution) and δαπάναι (expense caused by some extraordinary measure, in the case of Sulla his reorganization of the province); ἐπισταθμία (billeting of soldiers or other foreigners), and παροχή or παρουσία (supply of foodstuffs, wood, and salt). All these extraordinary burdens were familiar to the Hellenistic world. They are known to us from many documents of the early Hellenistic period, as imposed by cities and kings (see Index s.vv.), and for the period of the Roman protectorate and domination, as demanded by the new masters: see, for example, the letter of a Roman magistrate to the artistes of Isthmus and Nemea (*I.G.* vii. 2413 f.; G. Klaffenbach, *Symb. ad hist. coll. art. Bacch.* 1914, pp. 26 ff.; R. Herzog, *Berl. S.B.* 1935, p. 974; G. Daux, *Delphes*, &c., p. 358; F. Poland, *P.W.K.* v. 2491; and above, Ch. VI, n. 17), and that of Antony to the *technitai* of Asia, below, note 117; cf. similar grants to private people, below, p. 971, n. 57.

[18] M. Gelzer, *P.W.K.* xiii. 380, who has collected the literary and epigraphical evidence bearing on the activity of Lucullus as quaestor and pro-quaestor (the Delian inscription, F. Durrbach, *Choix*, 154; *Inscr. de Délos*, 1620). Our tradition is unanimous in praising Lucullus' honesty and mildness in collecting the war indemnity, Plut. *Luc.* 4. 1; Cic. *Acad. pr.* 1. 1: 'ibi (i.e. in Asia) per multos annos admirabili quadam laude provinciae praefuit'.

[19] The *lex Gabinia–Calpurnia*: F. Durrbach, *Choix*, 163; *Inscr. de Délos*, 1511, and the comments of the editors (text much improved). Note that the name of Mithridates is mentioned in l. 28 of the fragmentary document. The tax (if a tax it be) for the *custodia publica* is puzzling. If we restore *frumenti* after *custodia publica*, we may think, with Cuq, of some tax connected with the grain-supply of the city. Σιτοφύλακες and σιτοφυλακία were institutions not unknown in Greek cities ·(Thalheim, *P.W.K.* iii A. 399 ff.: Athens, Tauromenium, Priene). The *frumentum publicum* of the cities was drawn upon by the governors of the provinces for the *frumentum in cellam* or *frumentum emptum* (e.g. Cic. *Pro Flacco*, 19. 45 'custos T. Aufidio praetore in frumento publico est positus'). Similar functions, i.e. selling public grain, are attested for the σιτοφύλακες of Tauromenium, *S.I.G.*³ 954 (second century B.C.). This, however, does not explain the Delian tax.

[20] *Lex Antonia de Termessensibus*, H. Dessau, *I.L.S.* 38; *C.I.L.* i.² 2, no. 589, cf. R. Heberdey, 'Termessische Studien', *Denkschr. Wien. Akad.*, phil.-hist. Kl. lxix, 3 (1929); id., *P.W.K.* v A. 732 ff., esp. 749 f. On the date, H. M. Last, *C.A.H.* ix, p. 896, who does not quote Heberdey's contributions. Encroachments on the customs duties of free cities were a common practice of Roman magistrates, though probably the act of Piso at Dyrrhachium was directed not against the city but against the *publicani*, Cic. *De prov. cons.* 3. 5.

[21] The evidence is collected by A. Wilhelm, *Jahreshefte*, xvii (1914), p. 101, cf. Hertzberg, *Hist.* i, p. 396, and the books and articles quoted in note 1.

[22] M. Segre, *Clara Rhodos*, viii (1936), pp. 240 ff. The inscription of the Coans comes not from Samothrace but from the temple of Zeus Urius: C. F. Lehmann-Haupt, *Klio*, xviii (1923), pp. 366 ff., cf. A. Maiuri, *N.S.*, n. 18, and F. Hiller von Gaertringen, *P.W.K.* xv. 1613, and Suppl. v. 802. There are several inscriptions in honour of Varro: at Delos (set up by the Italian and Greek *negotiatores*), F. Durrbach, *Choix*, 155; *Inscr. de Délos*, 1698; at Euromus, H. Dessau, *I.L.S.* 8773. Cf. *S.I.G.*³ 745; H. Dessau, *I.L.S.* 8772 (Rhodes). The epigraphical evidence quoted in this note is not mentioned by Broughton, loc. cit., p. 522.

[23] On the naval contributions, R. O. Jolliffe, *Phases of Corruption*, &c., pp. 33 ff. Jolliffe's collection of material is incomplete, cf. preceding note and notes 25 and 29. He bases his statements almost exclusively on the cases of Flaccus and Verres and mentions the other evidence only *en passant* (p. 47). Cicero (*De imp. Pomp.* 23. 67) caustically characterizes the methods of naval war used by the Romans before Pompey: 'videbat enim (Pompeius) praetores

locupletari quotannis pecunia publica praeter paucos, neque nos quicquam aliud adsequi classium nomine nisi ut detrimentis accipiendis maiore adfici turpitudine videremur.'

24 On the career and trial of Varro, F. Münzer, *P.W.K.* v A. 678 ff.

25 On P. Servilius Vatia Isauricus, F. Münzer, *P.W.K.* ii A. 1812 ff. On the date of the Athenian inscription, P. Foucart, *B.C.H.* vi (1882), p. 281 (expedition of Servilius); S. Jebelev, *H.A.*, p. 265 f. (expedition of Pompey). Chr. Blinkenberg, 'Triemiolia', *Det danske videnskabernes selskab*, arch.-kunsth. Medd. ii. 3 (1938), pp. 15 ff., dates the inscription in the second half of the second century B.C., and regards the commander of the squadron as a Rhodian despite the fact that the inscription is not written in the Dorian dialect. On the inscriptions of Aechmon, Kalinka in his notes to the inscriptions. He is inclined to assign the victories of Aechmon to a time earlier than Servilius' expedition. Cf. H. A. Ormerod, *C.A.H.* ix, pp. 354 ff.

26 On the raids of the Thracians, &c., A. Reinach, *B.C.H.* xxxiv (1910), pp. 322 ff.; Geyer, *P.W.K.* xiv. 762 ff. (art. 'Makedonia'). The northern neighbours of Macedonia never ceased their invasions between 85 (expedition of Sulla against them) and the third Mithridatic war.

27 On the war of M. Antonius Creticus, P. Foucart, *J. d. Sav.*, 1906, pp. 569 ff., and *Rev. É. G.* xxii (1909), pp. 405 ff.; A. Wilhelm, *Jahreshefte*, xiv (1917), p. 102; A. Passerini, 'La preparazione della guerra contro Creta nel 70 a. C.', *Athen.* xiv (1936), pp. 45 ff. On the Cloatii, J. Hatzfeld, *Les Trafiquants italiens* &c., 1919, pp. 80 ff., cf. A. Wilhelm, loc. cit., p. 63.

28 On the situation of Asia Minor and the measures of Lucullus, see the books quoted in note 1 and the full discussion of the evidence by M. Gelzer, *P.W.K.* xiii. 394. Most scholars who deal with the measures of Lucullus think that Plutarch and Appian are speaking of the same measures; they try therefore to combine the two reports. I regard their efforts as a failure (as do Th. Reinach, *Mithr. Eup.*, p. 348, and T. Frank, *Econ. Survey*, i, p. 343): the new tax of 25 per cent. on the harvest cannot be equivalent to the order of Lucullus to the creditors not to take more than $\frac{1}{4}$ of the income of the debtors. The second set of Lucullus' measures amounted practically to a restoration of the fiscal practice of the Seleucids and Attalids. The slave-tax and house-tax are of the same type as many of the so-called royal taxes of the Seleucids and Attalids, of which I have spoken above (pp. 469 ff., 643 f.). Nor is a land-tax of 25 per cent. of the harvest unknown to Hellenistic practice: there is evidence of such a tax or rent in Palestine (below, p. 1000). Like the taxes of Lucullus, some of the Hellenistic royal taxes were emergency taxes (e.g. the *Galatica*). The measures of Lucullus were afterwards repeated by Appius Claudius and Piso. The tax of 25 per cent. was probably collected in addition to the usual *decuma*, and without the help of the *publicani*. It is known that the *publicani* succeeded in the same year, 70 B.C., in getting from the restored censors the contract for the collection of the *decuma* for the next

lustrum. This implies that the *decuma* was not comprised in the new tax of 25 per cent. In 66 B.C. the *decuma* of Asia was certainly collected by the *publicani*; Cic. *De imp. Pomp.* 6. 15 ff. See V. Ivanov, *De soc. vect. publ.*, p. 102.

²⁹ Sack of Delos by the pirates. Five inscriptions in honour of C. Valerius Triarius at Delos: F. Durrbach, *Choix*, 159, 160; *Inscr. de Délos*, 1621, 1855–8. Three of them (*Inscr. de Délos*, 1855–7) were put up by the crews of ships manned, one by Milesians and another by Milesians and Smyrnaeans. Cf. B. Haussoullier, *Ét. sur l'hist. de Milet*, p. 248, and P. Roussel, *Syria*, xv (1934), p. 44. On the building activity of Triarius and his fortification of Delos, Phlegon of Tralles, *F.H.G.* iii, p. 606, cf. on the archaeological evidence Ch. Picard, *C.R. Ac. Inscr.*, 1911, pp. 872 ff.; Ch. Avezou et Ch. Picard, *Mél. Holleaux*, pp. 12 ff.; P. Roussel, *Délos, col. ath.*, p. 332, and *B.C.H.* xlix (1925), p. 446. The inscriptions cited above furnish a good illustration to Plut. *Luc.* 13. 4 (quoted above in the text) and show that the fleet of Lucullus consisted exclusively of ships supplied by the cities of the province. To the pirates on the sea corresponded brigands on the land, who made communications between Asia Minor and Syria and within Asia Minor very dangerous, see T. R. S. Broughton, 'Roman Asia Minor', pp. 524 ff. The measures taken by the Romans against these organized robbers were as spasmodic and as inefficient as those taken against the pirates. It was not till the time of Augustus that conditions improved.

³⁰ On the cities of Asia which were *liberae* and *immunes* after Sulla, see Th. Reinach, *Mithr. Eup.*, p. 204; a fuller list, A. H. M. Jones, *Cities*, &c., p. 62 f., and n. 51, cf. Broughton, loc. cit., p. 517. On Termessus, above, note 20. On Stratonicea, Tac. *Ann.* iii. 62; *O.G.I.* 441 (*S.C.* of 81 B.C.), and P. Viereck, *Sermo Gr.* no. xx, p. 41 (*S.C.* of 39 B.C.), cf. L. Robert, *Ét. Anat.*, pp. 416 ff. and pp. 461 ff. On Tabae, *O.G.I.* 442 and *M.A.M.A.* vi. 1939, no. 162. On Alabanda, E. Bikerman, *Rev. É. G.* l (1937), pp. 221 and 239 (additional note), cf. Jones, loc. cit. Other cities which became free and immune later are quoted by Jones, loc. cit. Add to his list Miletus, which in 62 B.C. recovered some important privileges of which it had been deprived since its defection from the Romans (unpublished inscription, B. Haussoullier, *Rev. Phil.* xlv (1921), p. 58, cf. L. Robert, *Ét. Anat.*, p. 428, n. 1). Cf. Addendum to this note.

³¹ L. Robert, *Ét. Anat.*, pp. 426 ff. He quotes also the establishment of the cult of Apollon Erathymios at Rhodes in 63 B.C. It is not improbable that to this gradual recovery of some of the cities of Asia we may ascribe with Robert the renewal in 58 B.C. of the minting of *cistophori* by Tralles, Pergamon, Laodicea, Apamea. I hesitate to postulate with T. R. S. Broughton, *A.J.A.* xli (1937), p. 248 f., a special law which reserved the silver of Asia Minor for Rome and forbade the minting of *cistophori*. The assumption of a shortage of silver and gold at Rome after the expedition of Pompey against the pirates is based on very slight evidence, and the measure as such has no parallel in Roman history and is improbable. On the other hand, the slow recovery of some of the cities of Asia after Lucullus and Pompey is a much better-

attested fact. Note that Aphrodisias does not seem to have begun to rise to importance until the first century B.C., L. Robert, *Villes d'Asie Mineure*, p. 64, and *Ét. Anat.*, p. 338.

[32] Strabo xiv. I. 42, pp. 648–9. On Pythodorus and Menodorus, members of rich Trallian families, above, pp. 819 ff., n. 98. On the fertility of the territory of Tralles and the prosperity of the city, O. Rayet, *Milet et le Golfe Latmique*, 1877, pp. 34 ff. and 71 ff., and the interesting remarks of L. Robert on the *ficeta* and *oliveta* of Tralles and of Caria in general in his *Ét. Anat.*, p. 416 and n. 7.

[33] An attempt to calculate the total amount of the revenue derived by the Roman government from its Anatolian provinces has been made several times. The results vary to a certain extent, but only in details. See V. Chapot, *La Province*, &c., pp. 324 ff.; K. Böttcher, *Die Einnahmen der römischen Republik im letzten Jahrhundert ihres Bestehens*, diss. Leipzig, 1915; Broughton, loc. cit., pp. 562 ff.; A. Momigliano, *Atti IV Congr. Naz. St. Rom.* i (1938), pp. 280 ff.

[34] On the *negotiatores*, see above, Ch. VI, p. 763 f., and note 29. A short but complete survey of the evidence about them, emphasizing the various aspects of their economic activity, which is based on Hatzfeld but contains some new contributions, will be found in Broughton, loc. cit., pp. 543 ff. There is no need to repeat here the well-known results reached by these two writers. In the following notes I shall merely quote some of the most important texts relating to the various aspects of the activity of the *negotiatores*.

[35] *Negotiatores* as landowners. A typical example is the famous Appuleius Decianus of Pergamon and later of Apollonis, a man of good Roman family, resident in Asia Minor for decades, who played such an important part in the lawsuit of L. Valerius Flaccus. Cicero in his oration for Flaccus gives a very instructive report of the way in which he became owner of an estate near Temnus which had belonged to Lysanias, a member of the Temnian aristocracy, and a still more vivid picture of how he came into possession of a large estate in the region of Apollonis which belonged to the mother-in-law of Amyntas, a prominent citizen of Apollonis (Cic. *Pro Flacco*, 51 and 70 ff.). Some other examples, which could be easily increased, may be found in Broughton, loc. cit., pp. 549 and 551 (on landowners who were not residents in Asia Minor).

[36] On the Delian families in the other islands and in Asia Minor, see the lists of Hatzfeld. An interesting enumeration of 'Romans' engaged in trade and money-lending in Asia Minor will be found in Broughton, loc. cit., pp. 549 ff.

[37] A collection of the evidence on the rates of interest in Asia Minor in the middle of the first century will be found in many books, the last being that of Broughton, loc. cit., p. 561 (without bibliography).

[38] On the *cistophori*, above, n. 31.

[39] See, for example, the sharp remarks of Cicero, a great philhellene, in his speech *Pro Flacco*, e.g., 4. 9 and 27. 64–6, and the notes of Du Mesnil to these passages.

[40] In his precepts to his brother Quintus (*Ad Q. Fr.* i. 1) Cicero eloquently formulates the high principles which guided the enlightened and 'humane' Romans in their government of the provinces, principles which probably go back to Panaetius and were similar to those which we find in the *mandata* of the Hellenistic kings to their subordinates (*Teb.* 703) and in the treatises περὶ βασιλείας addressed to the kings themselves by philosophers of various schools (below, Ch. VIII). See R. Harder, 'Nachträgliches zu humanitas', *Hermes*, lxix (1934), pp. 71 ff., cf. U. Knoche, 'Magnitudo animi', *Phil.* Suppl. xxvii. 3 (1935). I am convinced that Cicero was quite sincere in his advice to his brother and acted himself according to his own principles—so far as he could.

[41] Cic. *Ad Att.* v. 16. 2, cf. *Ad fam.* iii. 8. 5; xv. 4. 2; *Ad Att.* vi. 1. 3. For an interpretation of these passages, and especially the first of them, see my *Staatspacht*, p. 357 (29) f. The passages under consideration are misunderstood by R. Laurent-Vibert, *Mél. d'Arch. et d'Hist.* xxviii (1908), pp. 178 ff.; cf. H. Dessau, *Gesch. d. röm. Kaiserz.* i, 1924, p. 151, n. 2, and T. R. S. Broughton, *Am. J. Phil.* lvii (1936), p. 173, and 'Roman Asia Minor', pp. 567 ff., who give an exact interpretation of them, and T. Frank, *Econ. Survey*, i, p. 144. I do not think Broughton (loc. cit., p. 174) is right in explaining the *exactio capitum et ostiorum* as a new municipal tax introduced by the cities under the pressure of Appius. The two taxes, as well as an additional *tributum*, were levied by Appius (in imitation of Lucullus and of the Hellenistic kings, above, note 28) as new provincial emergency taxes, the cities being responsible for their payment; cf. below, note 93, on the same taxes levied in Asia Minor by Pompey, and note 68 on the *tributum* imposed by Ariobarzanes III of Cappadocia on his subjects *Appi instituto*.

[42] See note 23. I do not believe that Q. Cicero put an end to the practice and that it was not resumed before the civil war. The laws which regulated the practice were not abrogated.

[43] I cannot here collect all the evidence bearing on these exactions. Some instances have been quoted in the preceding paragraph of this chapter. For a fuller collection and more detailed discussion, see R. O. Jolliffe, *Phases of Corruption*, &c., pp. 7 ff. (quartering of troops), pp. 12 ff. (requisition of equipment and supplies), pp. 85 ff., esp. pp. 87 ff. (*hospitium*—παροχή, παρουσία —supplied to governors, their staff, and the *legati*, both official and *liberi*), and Broughton, loc. cit., pp. 571 ff., who never quotes Jolliffe's useful book.

[44] The naval contributions also may go back to the Hellenistic period. See my remarks on the τριηραρχία in the Ptolemaic Empire, above, Ch. IV, n. 84. The organization of the navies of the Seleucids, the Attalids, the Antigonids, and the other Hellenistic monarchies is very little known. But I have frequently mentioned above that the 'allied' cities were supposed to collaborate

with the kings in this sphere. On the Seleucid navy, see E. Bikerman, *Inst. Sél.*, pp. 98 ff. As regards the other extraordinary requirements of the State from its subjects and allies, see the Index to this book under εἰσφορά and ἐπίταγμα, ἀνεπισταθμία, ἐπισταθμία and σταθμός, ἀγγαρεῖαι, and παρουσία. In the East the Romans undoubtedly inherited the Hellenistic system and practice of requisitions. The problem of how far Hellenistic tradition influenced the establishment of the system of requisitions (as enumerated above) in Italy and in the western provinces cannot be discussed here.

45 I have dealt with this subject briefly in my *Geschichte der Staatspacht in der römischen Kaiserzeit bis Diokletian* (*Philologus*, Ergänzungsband ix), 1902 (in greater detail in the Russian edition of that book), where the reader will find quoted works prior to 1902 dealing with this subject, cf. my art. 'Frumentum', *P.W.K.* vii. 150 ff., esp. 154 (on Asia). Since the publication of my *Staatspacht* much has been written on the subject, most of it dealing with the system of taxation and tax-collection in Sicily as known from Cicero's *Verrines*. Of fundamental importance are J. Carcopino's contributions: 'Decumani', *Mél. d'Arch. et d'Hist.* xxv (1905), pp. 401 ff.; ibid., pp. 3 ff.; *La Loi de Hiéron et les Romains*, 1914–19; and his masterly presentation of the various problems connected with the *publicani* in *Hist. Rom.* ii, pp. 72 ff., 134 f.; cf. A. Schenk Graf von Stauffenberg, *König Hieron der zweite von Syrakus*, 1933, pp. 64 ff., and V. M. Scramuzza, 'Roman Sicily', in T. Frank, *Econ. Survey*, iii, 1937, pp. 237 ff. Excellent also is the short dissertation of V. Ivanov, *De societatibus vectigalium publicorum populi Romani*, 1910 (*Zapiski* of the Class. Section of the Imp. Russian Arch. Society, vi) which has remained unknown to most students of Roman history and law. Cf. T. Frank, *Econ. Survey*, i, pp. 255 ff., 342 ff.; Steinwenter, art. 'Manceps', *P.W.K.* xiv. 987 (with bibliography) and the articles 'Publicanus', 'Societas', 'Vectigal' in Dar. et Saglio, *D. d. A.*; cf. also the superficial survey of B. Jenny, *Der römische Ritterstand während der Republik*, 1936, pp. 8 ff., 68 ff.

46 The provincial taxes leased to the *publicani* are frequently enumerated by Cicero and other authors, see V. Ivanov, *De soc. vect. publ.*, pp. iii ff. All these taxes were inherited by the Romans from the past. Antony in his Ephesian speech ascribes the introduction of the *decuma* in Asia to the Romans. We have seen, however, that the *decuma* (δεκάτη) of the harvest was a very common tax in the pre-Hellenistic and Hellenistic period in Asia Minor (above, p. 441 and Index s.v.). It is very probable that a tax on cattle as a State tax existed in all the Hellenistic monarchies. The same, of course, is true of the *portoria*. There is also no doubt that most of the Hellenistic kings possessed more or less extensive crown estates (see my art. 'Frumentum', *P.W.K.* vii. 151 ff.). Besides State taxes city taxes were levied in all the cities of the Hellenistic kingdoms. I have dealt with these taxes and the mode of their collection above, Ch. V, n. 22. It is evident that they underwent no change during the period of the Roman protectorate and domination. Cicero repeatedly mentions municipal taxes and municipal *telonai* in Asia Minor. The most explicit mention of taxes and tax-collectors

in the time before the Roman domination is Cic. *Ad Q. Fr.* i. 1. 11. 33: 'ac primum Graecis id quod acerbissimum est, quod sunt vectigales, non ita acerbum videri debet, propterea quod sine imperio populi Romani suis institutis per se ipsi ita fuerunt. Nomen autem publicani aspernari non possunt, qui pendere ipsi vectigal sine publicano non potuerint quod iis aequaliter Sulla discripserat. Non esse autem leniores in exigendis vectigalibus Graecos quam nostros publicanos hinc intellegi potest, quod Caunii nuper omnesque ex insulis quae erant a Sulla Rhodiis attributae confugerunt ad senatum, nobis ut potius vectigal quam Rhodiis penderent.' This passage, no doubt, is ambiguous. We may understand the *vectigalia* which Greek cities paid *suis institutis* before the Roman domination to mean the royal taxes, not the city taxes. I think, however, that Cicero is speaking of Greek taxes and tax-collection in general without discriminating between royal and city taxes. City taxes levied in the cities of Cilicia are certainly meant in Cic. *Ad Att.* v. 16. 2 (above, note 41): 'audivimus nihil aliud nisi imperata ἐπικεφάλαια solvere non posse, ὠνὰς omnium venditas, civitatum gemitus, ploratus'. The ὠναί are municipal taxes leased to *telonai*, cf. Cic. *Pro Flacco*, 20. More difficult is the interpretation of Cic. *Pro Flacco*, 91. Here Falcidius buys the *fructus* of Tralles for 900,000 sesterces, and Flaccus was accused of interfering with the contract for a bribe. Various interpretations of this passage have been offered. Ivanov, loc. cit., p. 103, thinks that at that time (62 B.C.) the collection of the regular *decuma* was temporarily again in the hands of the cities. T. R. S. Broughton (*Am. J. Phil.* lvii (1936), p. 175) regards the *fructus* as municipal taxes. I would rather agree with Ivanov. Or it may be suggested that the *fructus* were a supplementary *tributum*, perhaps connected with the naval contributions exacted by Flaccus (above, note 23); cf. the remark of Cicero about the *tributum* imposed by Appius (*Ad Fam.* iii. 8. 5). The words of Cicero imply that legally the collection of the tax—whether it was the regular *decuma* or an additional *tributum* (similar to *alterae decumae* in Sicily)—was in the hands of the city itself. However, in the case of Tralles the government of the city, perhaps with the special permission of the governor, may have rented the collection of it to a 'Roman' *negotiator*, probably because the local *telonai* were not strong enough financially. The same apparently happened in Bithynia before its annexation, i.e. during the royal rule. For the payment of their φόρος to the king the cities had recourse to the good services of rich financiers of the province of Asia.

[47] The role of the Roman *societates publicanorum* was therefore approximately the same as that of the tax-contractors in Ptolemaic Egypt (above, pp. 273 and 328 ff.) and in Sicily in the time of Hiero II and later. Cicero defines it in precise language which cannot be misinterpreted (*Verr.* ii. 3. 11. 27): 'cum omnibus in aliis vectigalibus, Asiae, Macedoniae, Hispaniae, Galliae, Africae, Sardiniae, ipsius Italiae quae vectigalia sunt, cum in his, inquam, rebus omnibus publicanus petitor aut pignerator, non ereptor neque possessor soleat esse, tu de optimo, de iustissimo, de honestissimo genere hominum, hoc est de aratoribus, ea iura constituebas, quae omnibus aliis essent contraria?

Utrum est aequius, decumanum petere an aratorem repetere? iudicium integra re an perdita fieri? eum qui manu quaesierit, an eum qui digito sit licitus possidere?' This basic text has been discussed in all the books and articles quoted in note 46. See e.g. J. Carcopino, *La Loi de Hiéron*, p. 141 f. It is obvious that the *publicanus* as such had no administrative rights and was no more than a middleman between the State and the taxpayers.

[48] On the *lex censoria*, F. Kniep, *Societas publicanorum*, 1896, pp. 114 ff.; E. Weiss, *P.W.K.* xii. 2317, art. 'Lex'. On the provincial edict of the governor and the section on the *publicani* contained in it, Cic. *Ad Att.* vi. 1. 16.

[49] I cannot deal here with the topic of book-keeping and the archives of the Greek cities. I may refer to what I have said of it above, Ch. IV, n. 241, and to my *Seleucid Babylonia*, pp. 57 ff., esp. p. 61, n. 5 (on the archives of the cities of Asia Minor), cf. L. Robert, *Ét. Anat.*, pp. 453, 457 ff., 486 ff. The careful procedure which was followed when payments had to be effected by the city treasury is described for the period under consideration by Cicero, *Pro Flacco*, 19. 44.

[50] Our information on the *pactiones* in general (i.e. the agreements for all the provincial taxes) relates to Cilicia and is derived mainly from Cicero, especially from his letters of 51 B.C., when he was governor: *Ad Att.* v. 13. 1; v. 14. 1; vi. 1. 16; cf. for Asia *Ad Q. Fr.* i. 1. 12. 35, and for Syria *De prov. cons.* 5. 10 ff. For *scriptura*, *Ad fam.* xiii. 65. This evidence was collected and discussed by myself in *Staatspacht*, p. 357 (29); cf. F. Kniep, *Societas publicanorum*, p. 10, and Ivanov, *De soc. vect. publ.*, pp. 89 ff. On the *pactiones* in Sicily which were concluded between the contractors and the taxpayers with the participation of the cities, J. Carcopino, *La Loi de Hiéron*, pp. 12 ff., cf. my *Kolonat*, pp. 366 ff.; A. Schenk Graf von Stauffenberg, *König Hieron der zweite*, p. 66, and V. M. Scramuzza, 'Roman Sicily', T. Frank, *Econ. Survey*, iii, 1937, pp. 237 ff. On the *pactiones* in Egypt, my *Kolonat*, loc. cit., and *Large Estate*, pp. 75 ff. I regard the *pactiones* as annual agreements, while Broughton, loc. cit., p. 537, n. 18, thinks them to have been quinquennial. I cannot see how in a country like Asia the yield of the crops could be foreseen five years in advance. It is very probable that in reorganizing the collection of the *decuma* in Asia about 70 B.C., the Roman Senate followed, *mutatis mutandis*, the practice long established in Sicily.

[51] On the frequent inspections of crops by royal officers in Egypt, see *Teb.* 703, 40 ff., and the comments on this section of the document; cf. above, p. 279 f. On the large staff of the *publicani*, Cic. *De imp. Pomp.* 6. 16: 'quo tandem igitur animo esse existimatis aut eos qui vectigalia nobis pensitant, aut eos qui exercent atque exigunt, cum duo reges cum maximis copiis propter adsint, cum una excursio equitatus perbrevi tempore totius anni vectigal auferre possit, cum publicani familias maximas quas in salinis habent, quas in agris, quas in portubus atque custodiis, magno periculo se habere arbitrentur?' Cf. App. *B.C.* ii. 1. 13, and Ivanov, *De soc. vect. publ.*, pp. 74 ff.

[52] Cic. *De imp. Pomp.* 6. 15, cf. *Verr.* ii. 3. 11. 27; *De imp. Pomp.* 7. 17 ff.

[53] Such was the situation in 61 B.C. See the discussion of the texts relating to this affair by R. Laurent-Vibert, *Mél. d'Arch. et d'Hist.* xxviii (1908), pp. 176 ff., cf. T. Frank, *Econ. Survey*, i, p. 346. I do not believe that the success of the *publicani* was due, as Laurent-Vibert suggests, to a 'merger' of all the companies of *publicani* in the Anatolian provinces. See the discussion of the texts collected by Laurent-Vibert, and particularly of Cic. *Ad fam.* xiii. 9, by Ivanov, *De soc. vect. publ.*, pp. 19 ff., and esp. 24 ff. (cf. 26, n. 137, Th. Mommsen's opinion on this subject).

[54] See his letters *Ad Att.* v. 13. 1, 14. 1.

[55] On the affair of Salamis, see the remarks of and the bibliography compiled by M. Gelzer, *P.W.K.* x. 977, and W. Kroll, *Die Kultur der ciceronischen Zeit*, 1933, i, p. 93 f., cf. R. O. Jolliffe, *Phases*, &c., p. 104 f.

[56] On the problems mentioned in this paragraph, see T. R. S. Broughton, 'Roman Asia Minor,' pp. 540 ff., who quotes the meagre evidence referring to them. The alleged 10 per cent. commission secured by the *publicani* may faintly recall the 10 per cent. ὀψώνιον of the late Ptolemaic tax-contracts (*U.P.Z.* 112, v. 3–11, with Wilcken's comments) but its existence in Roman practice is a mere guess (based on Cic. *Pro Rab. Post.* 11. 30). The calculation of the net profit of the *publicani* founded on it is necessarily unconvincing.

[57] Some evidence on privileges granted by the rulers of the day during the first century B.C. to private people has been collected in my article 'Caesar and the South of Russia', *J.R.S.* vii (1917), pp. 27 ff., esp. 38. The privileges involved are enumerated in the inscriptions quoted in the text; cf. the letter of Sulla to the *technitai* of Asia Minor mentioned above, n. 16 f. On the inscription of Rhosus, P. Roussel, 'Un Syrien au service de Rome et d'Auguste', *Syria*, xv (1934), pp. 33 ff., esp. 51 ff.; M. A. Levi, *Riv. Fil.* lxvi (16) (1938), pp. 113 ff., and E. de Visscher, 'Les Conditions juridiques des nouveaux citoyens romains d'Orient', *C.R. Ac. Inscr.* 1938, pp. 24 ff., cf. 1939, 111 ff. Cf. Ch. Goodfellow, *Roman Citizenship*, 1935, esp. pp. 41 ff., 90 ff.

[58] The text of the passage of the inscription of Mytilene concerning the ἀτέλεια has been improved by L. Robert, *Rev. É.G.* xlii (1929), pp. 427 ff. The text of the edict of Cyrene, with bibliography, will be found in *S.E.G.* ix. 8, cf. my *Storia Ec. e Soc.*, p. 56, n. 6 a, and esp. 55, n. 5, where the reader will find some remarks on the privileged Roman citizens of Greek origin in the Greek communities of the first century B.C. It is evident to me that the persons who enjoyed immunity at Mytilene were not exclusively 'Roman' *negotiatores* (as Hatzfeld, *Trafiquants*, &c., p. 90 f., suggests) but both 'Roman' and local grandees favoured by the Roman administration. So it was at Chios (*I.G.R.* iv. 943), cf. Chapot, *Prov. Rom. d'Asie*, p. 125; Hatzfeld, loc. cit., pp. 95 ff. On the problem of immunity and citizenship in general, P. Roussel, loc. cit.; Goodfellow, loc. cit., esp. pp. 44 ff. (on the inscription of Rhosus); E. de Visscher, *C.R. Ac. Inscr.*, 1939, pp. 111 ff. (on the third edict of Cyrene).

[59] On Cilicia, see A. H. M. Jones, *Cities*, pp. 192 ff., and the books and articles quoted by him on p. 548, cf. J. Keil, *C.A.H.* xi, pp. 602 ff. (bibliography, p. 917). Cf. Addendum to this note.

[60] Sandon in late Hellenistic and Roman times, H. Goldman, *A.J.A.* xli (1937), p. 274. Linen industry: my *Storia Ec. e Soc.*, p. 211; A. H. M. Jones, *Cities*, &c., p. 207 f. and n. 28, cf. for Corycus J. Keil und A. Wilhelm, *M.A.M.A.* iii, pp. 131 ff., and Index s.v. λινοπώλης, λινυφαντάριος, ληνοπώλης, λινοξός, cf. T. R. S. Broughton, 'Roman Asia Minor,' p. 868 f. On the coinage of the Pamphylian cities, especially Aspendus and Side, above, pp. 655 ff.

[61] Cicero often speaks of these burdens of Cilicia and Cyprus, see esp. *Ad Att.* v. 21. 6–7.

[62] A. H. M. Jones, *Cities* &c., p. 203.

[63] *O.G.I.* 754; *I.G.R.* iii. 901; cf. *O.G.I.* 752 and 753, and the article by Stein, *P.W.K.* iv A. 2297.

[64] On these provinces, see the works quoted above, cf. J. Keil, *C.A.H.* xi, pp. 575 ff. (bibliography, pp. 915, 917), and Broughton, loc. cit., pp. 530 ff., cf. 525 ff. on the devastation of Bithynia and Pontus and on the war booty taken there by Lucullus and Pompey.

[65] On the *societas Bithynica*, Ivanov, *De soc. vect. publ.*, p. 107 f. Cic. *De l. agr.* ii. 15. 40: 'quid? quod disputari contra nullo pacto potest, quoniam statutum a nobis est et iudicatum, quam hereditatem iam crevimus, *regnum Bithyniae, quod certe publicum est populi Romani factum,* num quid causae est, quin *omnes agros, urbes, stagna, portus,* totam denique Bithyniam decemviri vendituri sint.' Cicero proceeds to compare with Bithynia the case of Mytilene whose *agri iucundi et fertiles* also became the property of the Roman people. A little later (section 50) he comes back to the territory which the *lex agraria* of Rullus intended to sell, and names territories of certain cities in Asia Minor which correspond to the territory of Mytilene in the previous passage, and then speaks of *ager publicus p. R.* in other former kingdoms, naming in the first place *agros Bithyniae regios, quibus nunc publicani fruuntur.* These two texts make it certain that the whole territory of Bithynia was regarded by the Romans as the property of the king and that it therefore became the property of Rome, *ager publicus p. R.* Of this territory Rullus proposed to sell the χώρα βασιλική, i.e. the land which did not form part of the territories of the Greek cities. The measures taken by the Romans in Bithynia may help us to a better understanding of the situation in Asia after the death of Attalus III, a crucial and hotly debated problem of which I have spoken above (p. 814 f.). It is evident that Bithynia was organized not after a new pattern but in the traditional fashion, that is to say, like Asia after its annexation. If Asia does not appear on the list of Rullus, this does not mean that Asia was originally organized on different lines from Bithynia, but simply that during the half-century of Roman rule in Asia the status of the χώρα βασιλική was definitely settled (above, Ch. VI, n. 88) and that Rullus (and behind him Caesar) did not venture 'quieta movere'. How it was settled we

do not know; but the analogy of Bithynia shows that originally after the annexation the whole territory of the Attalid kingdom became *publicum p. R.* and the *agri regii*, i.e. the χώρα βασιλική, which corresponded to territories not assigned to cities, became *ager publicus p. R.*

⁶⁶ *Bell. Alex.* 70, cf. 41. Strabo, xii. 3. 40, p. 562, describes the σανδαρακουργεῖον near Pompeiopolis in Pontus as exploited by *publicani.*

⁶⁷ On Paphlagonia, A. H. M. Jones, *Cities,* &c., p. 162 f.

⁶⁸ On Ariobarzanes, R. O. Jolliffe, *Phases,* &c., pp. 64 ff. As regards his situation, one of the letters of Cicero to Atticus (vi. 1. 3–4) of 50 B.C. is most instructive. It shows how deeply in debt he was, his chief creditor being Pompey, whose *sescenti procuratores* were active in Asia Minor. It may be noted that to pay the interest on Pompey's loan Ariobarzanes *Appi instituto tributa imperat.* This makes it certain that Appius' *tributa* (above, p. 962) was a provincial, not a municipal tax. Besides Ariobarzanes there were in Cappadocia two or three rich men, who were 'friends' of the king, while the rest of the people were apparently poverty-stricken. On the temple of Pessinus, its status, its vicissitudes, and its treatment by Clodius and Brogitarus, B. Niese, 'Straboniana, iv: Galatien und seine Tetrarchen', *Rh. Mus.* xxxviii (1883), pp. 588 ff. Cf. on Brogitarus, F. Stähelin, *Gesch. kleinas. Gal.,* 2nd ed. 1907, pp. 112 ff., cf. 88; R. O. Jolliffe, *Phases* &c., pp. 71 ff.; F. E. Adcock, *J.R.S.* xxvii (1937), pp. 12 ff.

⁶⁹ On Syria, see above, p. 869 f.; cf. A. H. M. Jones, *Cities* &c., pp. 227 ff., and bibliography pp. 549 ff.; J. Dobiaš, *Hist. de la province romaine de Syrie,* i. 1924 (in Czech with French résumé), and 'Les premiers rapports des Romains avec les Parthes', *Archiv Orient.* iii (1931), pp. 215 ff.; F. Cumont, *C.A.H.* xi, p. 613 (bibliography pp. 919 ff.); N. Debevoise, *A Political History of Parthia,* 1938, pp. 96 ff.

⁷⁰ On the Roman *negotiatores* in Syria in the middle of the first century B.C., Caes. *B.C.* iii. 102. 6 (Antioch); Strabo xvi. 4. 21, p. 779 (Petra), cf. J. Dobiaš, 'Les premiers rapports' &c., p. 253.

⁷¹ The most important evidence on Syria in the time of Gabinius is to be found in Cic. *De prov. cons.* 4. 9 and 5. 10 ff.; *In Pis.* 17. 41; 21. 48; *Ad Q. Fr.* ii. 11. 2; iii. 2. 2, cf. Cass. Dio, xxxix. 59, and Cic. *Pro Rab. Post.* 11. 30. All the texts relating to the *publicani* in Syria are collected in full and discussed by V. Ivanov, *De soc. vect. publ.,* p. 110 f. On Gabinius' activity in Syria, von der Mühll, *P.W.K.* vii. 427–8 s.v. 'Gabinius'; J. Dobiaš, 'Syrsky Prokonsulat M. Calpurnia Bibula', *Rozpr. Česke Akad. vet. a umeni,* phil.-hist. cl. lxv (1923), and *Hist.,* &c., pp. 97 ff., 553 ff. (with bibliography); and H. Box, *J.R.S.* xxii (1932), p. 183. Cf. the short remarks of E. Ciaceri in *Processi politici e relazioni internazionali,* 1918, p. 215 f., and *Cicerone e i suoi tempi,* ii, 1930, p. 136. On the restoration of many decayed cities by Pompey and Gabinius, A. H. M. Jones, *Cities,* &c., p. 259, and note 42.

⁷² The case of Tyre, Cic. *Ad Q. Fr.* ii. 11. 2; iii. 2. 2; Dobiaš, *Hist.* &c., p. 117,

and notes 119–21. Gabinius in fact legalized and perhaps extended the earlier privileges of the city. It is known that Tyre bought its autonomy from the Seleucids (above, Ch. VI, n. 126), and this grant was later confirmed by the Romans (probably not without a supplementary payment), Strabo xvi. 2. 23, p. 757. The confirmation of the Seleucid grant may have been in the first instance the act of Pompey or Scaurus, and may have been repeated by Gabinius. As regards the other cities and the rest of the country, Cic. *De prov. cons.* 5. 10: 'vectigalis multos ac stipendiarios liberavit'. Liberation of the cities from the *publicani* and the institution of direct contracts with the cities may be implied in the brief and rather vague statement of Cic. ibid. 5. 12: 'retinete igitur in provincia diutius eum, qui de sociis cum hostibus, de civibus cum sociis faciat pactiones'. The grant of these privileges to the cities may have had the effect of excluding the *publicani* and their agents from them. This may be the meaning of Cicero's rather obscure statement about Gabinius, ibid. 5. 10: 'quo in oppido ipse esset aut quo veniret, ibi publicanum aut publicani servum esse vetuit'. The cities which Cicero has in mind were probably excluded by Gabinius from the sphere of activity of the *publicani*. On the partial remissions, see the next note.

[73] Cic. *De prov. cons.* 4. 9: 'igitur in Syria imperatore illo nihil aliud ⟨neque gestum⟩ neque actum est nisi pactiones pecuniarum cum tyrannis, decisiones, direptiones, latrocinia, caedes' . . . . Since Cicero's main purpose is to describe the act of Gabinius directed against the *publicani*, we may interpret the '*pactiones* with the tyrants' as contracts about their φόρος made with them directly, which may have been connected with the recognition (of course for a certain fee) of their rule in the cities. The *decisiones* may mean contracts with the cities (which is the meaning of the term in the Verrines). In the Glossaries, however, this term is translated either by διάλυσις, i.e. *pactio*, *transactio*, or by ἀποκοπὴ χρέους, χρεοκοπία. See *Thesaur. l. L.*, s.v. Direct transactions with the native taxpayers—tyrants and dynasts—to the detriment of the *publicani* are also probably meant in *De prov. cons.* 5. 10: 'iam vero publicanos miseros . . . tradidit in servitutem Iudaeis et Syris, nationibus natis servituti'.

[74] Cic. *De prov. cons.* 5. 10: 'statuit ab initio et in eo perseveravit, ius publicano non dicere; pactiones sine ulla iniuria factas rescidit, custodias sustulit, vectigalis multos ac stipendiarios liberavit; quo in oppido ipse esset aut quo veniret, ibi publicanum aut publicani servum esse vetuit'. Cf. *In Pis.* 17. 41: 'nam ille . . . cum equites Romanos in provincia, cum publicanos nobiscum et voluntate et dignitate coniunctos omnis fortunis, multos fama vitaque privasset'.

[75] In *De prov. cons.* 5. 11, Cicero pleads for the Senate helping the *publicani* ruined by Gabinius. My remark in the text about the consequences of Gabinius' acts are directed against Dobiaš, *Hist.* &c., pp. 116 ff. (Fr. rés. 553 f.).

[76] Malalas, p. 225, 7–12, ed. Bonn., cf. Dobiaš, *Hist.* &c., p. 549, and G. Downey, 'Q. Marcius Rex at Antioch', *Cl. Phil.* xxxii (1937), pp. 144 ff.

77 Caes. *B.C.* iii. 31.

78 The facts will be found in Dobiaš, *Hist.* &c., pp. 1 ff.

79 Cass. Dio, xxxix. 56. 1 and 5; 59. 2, cf. Dobiaš, *Les premiers rapports*, &c., p. 250, on this and other evidence.

80 On the wars in the northern Balkan peninsula after Sulla, see A. Reinach, *B.C.H.* xxxiv (1910), pp. 322 ff.; A. Wilhelm, *Jahreshefte*, xvii (1914), p. 101 (Dolabella), cf. F. Münzer, *P.W.K.* iv. 1297, no. 134; C. Patsch, *Beiträge zur Völkerkunde von Südosteuropa*, v (*Wien. S.B.*, phil.-hist. Kl. 214. 1), 1932, pp. 34 ff. Cf. my review of this book in *Gnomon*, x (1934), p. 6; Geyer, art. 'Makedonia', *P.W.K.* xiv. 762 ff.; B. Lenk, art. 'Thrake', *P.W.K.* vi A. 441 ff. On M. Terentius Varro Lucullus, F. Münzer, *P.W.K.* xiii. 414 ff., esp. 417. Treaty with Callatis: M. S. Lambrino, *C.R. Ac. Inscr.*, 1933, pp. 278 ff.; A. Passerini, *Athen.* xiii (1935), pp. 57 ff.

81 On L. Calpurnius Piso Caesoninus, F. Münzer, *P.W.K.* iii. 1387 ff., no. 90. On his extraordinary power, Cic. *In Pis.* 16. 37; *De domo sua*, 23. 60; cf. the inscription of Delos (dedication of a temple by the Hermaists) dated by the proconsulate of Piso, F. Durrbach, *Choix*, 164; *Inscr. de Délos*, 1737, and the remarks of J. Hatzfeld, *B.C.H.* xxxiii (1909), pp. 522 ff., and of Durrbach, loc. cit. No critical survey of his administration in Greece and Macedonia, based on contemporary and related material, has ever been made in modern times. Hertzberg (*Hist.* &c., i, p. 400) and Drumann (Drumann–Groebe, *Gesch.* &c., ii, pp. 56 ff.) repeat without criticism the statements of Cicero. More recent students of Roman History devote to Piso's government short notices only (J. A. O. Larsen, 'Roman Greece,' p. 431, is not an exception). Cf., however, the short and interesting remarks of E. Ciaceri, *Cicerone e i suoi tempi*, ii, 1930, pp. 111 ff., and Ivanov, *De soc. vect. publ.*, p. 98. In the books by Jolliffe and Cobban, quoted above in note 1, Piso is, of course, mentioned several times under various headings.

82 On this dynasty and its role in the history of the time, B. Lenk, art. 'Thrake', *P.W.K.* vi A. 440 f. Cf. P. Collart, *Philippes, ville de Macédoine*, 1937, p. 245. The dynasty of Cotys and Sadalas ruled either over part of the Odrysi or over the Nesti.

83 On the military operations, see the bibliography quoted in notes 80 and 81. My reconstruction of them does not coincide with that given in the books and articles quoted in these notes.

84 Cic. *Pro Sestio* 43. 94: 'certam Achaeis in annos singulos pecuniam imperasse'; *De prov. cons.* 3. 5: 'cum interea quis vestrum hoc non audivit, quis ignorat, Achaeos ingentem pecuniam pendere L. Pisoni quotannis?' These payments were an ἐνιαύσιος εἰσφορά and can hardly be identified with the *aurum coronarium* exacted by Piso from the Achaeans, Cic. *In Pis.* 37. 90.

85 Cic. *In Pis.* 36. 87: 'quid? vectigalem provinciam, singulis rebus quaecumque venirent certo portorio imposito servis tuis a te factam esse meministi?' A tax on sales (ἐπώνιον) was a common feature of the royal

Hellenistic economy and of the financial organization of Greek cities (Index s.v. ἐπώνιον). Cf. what is said above on the extraordinary provincial taxes imposed by Lucullus and Appius Claudius, and below, p. 993 f. on the extraordinary taxes of Pompey.

86 Cic. *De prov. cons.* 3. 5: 'vectigal ac portorium Dyrrachinorum totum in huius unius quaestum esse conversum', cf. *Pro Sest.* 43. 94: 'cogere pecunias maximas a Dyrrachinis'.

87 Cic. *In Pis.* 35. 86 f.: 'qui modus tibi fuit frumenti aestimandi, qui honorarii? siquidem potest vi et metu extortum honorarium nominari. Quod cum peraeque omnes, tum acerbissime Bottiaei, Byzantii, Cherronesus, Thessalonica sensit. Unus tu dominus, unus aestimator, unus venditor tota in provincia per triennium frumenti omnis fuisti', cf. 37. 90: 'mitto rationem exacti imperatique frumenti'. On 'frumentum imperatum, aestimatum, honorarium', my art. 'Frumentum', *P.W.K.* vii. 165 f.; cf. the careful study of the problem by J. Carcopino, *La Loi de Hiéron*, pp. 172 ff.

88 Cic. *In Pis.* 36. 87: 'quid? illam armorum officinam ecquid recordaris, cum omni totius provinciae pecore compulso pellium nomine omnem quaestum illum domesticum paternumque renovasti? Videras enim grandis iam puer bello Italico repleri quaestu vestram domum cum pater armis faciendis tuus praefuisset'.

89 Cic. *In Pis.* 37. 90: 'mitto numerum navium'.

90 Cic. *In Pis.* 35. 86: 'nonne, hiberna cum legato praefectoque tuo tradidisses, evertisti miseras funditus civitates, quae non solum bonis sunt exhaustae, sed etiam nefarias libidinum contumelias turpitudinesque subierunt?' On Byzantium, Cic. *De prov. cons.* 3. 5–4. 7. Cf. *Pro Sest.* 43. 94, on the removal of statues, pictures, &c., from other Greek cities, which may be explained in the same way as the taking of pledges for the payment of the εἰσφορά.

91 Cic. *Pro Sest.* 43. 94: 'eundemque bona creditorum civium Romanorum cum debitoribus Graecis divisisse'; *De domo sua*, 23. 60; *In Pis.* 35. 86: 'nonne cum cc talenta tibi Apolloniatae Romae dedissent, ne pecunias creditas solverent, ultro Fufidium, equitem Romanum, hominem ornatissimum, creditorem debitoribus suis addixisti?' cf. 41. 98. See also *In Pis.* 34. 84 and *De prov. cons.* 6. 13, on Piso's encroachments on the rights of the *publicani*. On the Roman *negotiatores* in Macedonia in the time of Piso, J. Hatzfeld, *Les Trafiquants*, pp. 54 ff.

92 On the kingdom of Byrebista, C. Patsch, *Beitr. z. Völkerk. von Südosteuropa*, v (*Wien. S.B.*, phil.-hist. Kl. 214. 1), pp. 42 ff.; my remarks in *Gnomon*, x (1934), p. 6; B. Lenk, art. 'Thrake', *P.W.K.* vi A. 441; A. Alföldi, *C.A.H.* xi, p. 82 f.

93 The evidence on the mobilization of the East by Pompey has been frequently collected and interpreted. The best survey of the material will

be found in Hertzberg, *Hist.* &c., i, pp. 417 ff., and in T. Rice Holmes, *The Roman Republic,* iii, pp. 113 ff., p. 431 (on the Gabinians), and 432 (on Pompey's fleet; criticism of Kromayer's calculations in *Phil.* lvi (1897), pp. 433 ff.). Cf. F. E. Adcock, *C.A.H.* ix, p. 656 (bibliography, p. 955 f.), and J. Carcopino, *Hist. Rom.* ii, pp. 854 ff. On Caecilius Metellus in Syria, J. Dobiaš, *Hist.* &c., ch. 3 (Fr. rés., p. 556). On the size of the armies of Pompey and Caesar, see the works quoted above, and on the army of Caesar and Pompey in 49–48 B.C., A. von Domaszewski, 'Die Heere der Bürgerkriege in den Jahren 49 bis 42 vor Christus', *N. Heid. Jahrb.* iv (1894), pp. 157 ff., esp. 167 f. How general was Pompey's mobilization of the man-power of the East is shown, for example, by the famous story of the exemption of the Jews from military service by L. Cornelius Lentulus on behalf of Pompey. The official documents relating to this matter will be found in Fl. Josephus, *A.J.* xiv. 10. 13 (228 ff.). I cannot give here the voluminous bibliography of modern works dealing with these documents; see, for example, M. S. Ginsburg, *Rome et la Judée,* 1928, pp. 94 ff. On the passage of Caesar referred to in the text, Broughton, loc. cit., p. 579 f. I cannot agree with his translation of 'in capita singula servorum ac liberorum tributum imponebatur': 'a tribute was imposed on every head of slaves *and children*'. Such a special tax on children is never mentioned in our evidence. What Caesar means is a general poll-tax on *freemen* and slaves, the usual form of a poll-tax. Cf. Caesar, *B.C.* iii. 14. 3: 'qui de servis liberisque omnibus ad impuberes supplicium sumit' (I owe this quotation to Prof. G. L. Hendrickson). On Cicero's money at Ephesus 'lent' to Pompey or, as Cicero sometimes says, 'confiscated' by him, see Cic. *Ad fam.* v. 20. 9; *Ad Att.* xi. 1. 2; 2. 3; 13. 4, cf. 3. 3. I cannot enter into the discussion of this complicated case. Since legally the confiscation of the money was a loan, Cicero may have recovered part of this money in one way or another. Cf. O. E. Schmidt, *Ciceros Briefwechsel,* p. 186; J. Hatzfeld, *Les Trafiquants,* p. 200, n. 1 (with bibliography); W. Kroll, *Die Kultur der ciceronischen Zeit,* i, p. 115, and n. 116. Cicero's case must be viewed in the light of Caesar's description of the acts of Pompey in Asia.

⁹⁴ G. Daux, *Delphes,* &c., pp. 407 ff. On the pirates settled at Dyme in 67 B.C., Strabo viii. 7. 5, p. 388; xiv. 3. 3, p. 665; Plut. *Pomp.* 28; App. *Mithr.* 96. They left Dyme and returned to their old vocation during the civil war, Cic. *Ad Att.* xvi. 1. 3; Lucan, *Phars.* ii. 636.

⁹⁵ Gomphi: Caesar, *B.C.* iii. 80; App. *B.C.* ii. 64; Cass. Dio, xli. 51. 4; Florus, ii. 13, 41; Plut. *Caesar,* 41. 3. Athens and Megara: Cass. Dio, xlii. 14; Plut. *Brutus,* 8. 3–4.

⁹⁶ Cic. *Ad fam.* iv. 5. 4.

⁹⁷ Exactions from vassal kings in general (and among them Deiotarus): Cass. Dio, xli. 63. 1–3. On Deiotarus and his auctions, Cic. *Pro rege Deiot.* 14 and 25, cf. *B. Alex.* 34. On the kingdom of Deiotarus and his family graves, see above, Ch. VI, p. 836 f., n. 116.

⁹⁸ J. Carcopino, loc. cit., pp. 873 ff., esp. 884, cf. 919.

⁹⁹ The basic texts relating to the reform of Caesar are as follows: the Ephesian speech of Antony, App. *B.C.* v. 4; no mention is made here of any abolition of the *decuma*; Antony speaks of the elimination of the *publicani* and of the reduction of payments by one-third, and ends with the following words: ὑμῖν γὰρ τοὺς φόρους ἐπέτρεψεν ἀγείρειν παρὰ τῶν γεωργούντων, cf. App. *B.C.* ii. 92, and Plut. *Caes.* 48 (remission of one-third of the φόροι to the inhabitants of Asia). Cass. Dio, xlii. 6. 3 confirms the statements of Appian and Plutarch; he says: τοὺς γοῦν τελώνας πικρότατά σφισι χρωμένους ἀπαλλάξας, ἐς φόρου συντέλειαν τὸ συμβαῖνον ἐκ τῶν τελῶν κατεστήσατο. This means, of course, that the cities paid lump sums of money (the Hellenistic φόρος) which represented an *adaeratio* of the average yield of the δεκάτη, i.e. of the *decuma* or of all the provincial taxes (τέλη), just as they had done before, but which were not paid to the *publicani*. Of modern scholars who have dealt with the reform of Caesar I may quote first and foremost H. F. Pelham, *Transact. Oxf. Philol. Soc.*, 1881–2, pp. 1 ff., whose interpretation of the above-quoted texts I am inclined to accept, though it is rejected by V. Chapot, *Prov. rom. procons. d'Asie*, p. 329. Cf. T. Rice Holmes, *Rom. Rep.* iii, pp. 179, 482, and T. Frank's brief remarks, *Econ. Hist.*, 2nd ed., p. 195, n. 11, and p. 371, cf. his *Econ. Survey*, i, p. 337.

¹⁰⁰ M. Rostovtzeff, 'Caesar and the South of Russia', *J.R.S.* vii (1917), pp. 27 ff.; Ch. E. Goodfellow, *Roman Citizenship*, 1935, pp. 93 ff.; and notes 57 and 58 above.

¹⁰¹ See my article quoted in the preceding note, pp. 29 ff., 35 ff., and J. Carcopino, *Hist. Rom.* ii, p. 982. Cf. Broughton, loc. cit., p. 581. On Pergamon and the good services rendered by Mithridates of Pergamon, see above, Ch. VI, notes 86 and esp. 98. The fundamental text is the letter of Caesar to the Pergamenes regarding their privileges, which formed part of a long dossier dealing with the χώρα of the Pergamenes. The privileges granted to Pergamon were certainly of great importance; we cannot otherwise account for Mithridates of Pergamon, who was sent as ambassador to Caesar, being highly honoured at Pergamon and styled second *ktistes* of the city. See the text of the letter with comments in M. Segre's article, *Athen.* xvi (1938), pp. 119 ff.

¹⁰² On Caesar's colonization, J. Carcopino, *Hist. Rom.* ii, p. 986, and Broughton, loc. cit., p. 582. Note the string of cities which Caesar colonized, or on which he bestowed some benefactions, along the Straits, the Propontis, and the shores of the Black Sea: Lampsacus (and Parium?), Cyzicus, Apamea-Myrlea, Heraclea Pontica, Sinope, Amisus, Chersonesus—a set of important *points d'appui* during a presumably long and dangerous expedition in the East. Caesar's careful preparation for the expedition shows how seriously he took it and how far-reaching his plans were. Some of his colonies (Lampsacus and Heraclea) did not survive him.

¹⁰³ On the Seleucid system of taxation in Judaea, above, pp. 467 ff. On the taxes paid by Judaea in 152 B.C. and on the land-tax in particular, E. Bikerman, *Inst. Sél.*, pp. 131 f., 179 f. My suggestion in the text as regards the

interpretation of 1 Macc. xi. 34, and x. 30, is of course tentative. It accounts, however, for the reappearance of the land-tax in the time of Caesar.

[104] The passages of Josephus which refer to Caesar's reform of taxation in Judaea are as follows. Edict of 47 B.C.: *A.J.* xiv. 10. 6 (202–3): Γάϊος Καῖσαρ, αὐτοκράτωρ τὸ δεύτερον, ἔστησε κατ᾽ ἐνιαυτὸν ὅπως τελῶσιν ὑπὲρ τῆς Ἱεροσολυμιτῶν πόλεως, Ἰόπης ὑπεξαιρουμένης, χωρὶς τοῦ ἑβδόμου ἔτους . . . καὶ ἵν᾽ ἐν Σιδῶνι τῷ δευτέρῳ ἔτει [i.e. τῆς μισθώσεως, see below] τὸν φόρον ἀποδιδῶσι, τὸ τέταρτον τῶν σπειρομένων· πρὸς τούτοις ἔτι καὶ Ὑρκανῷ καὶ τοῖς τέκνοις αὐτοῦ τὰς δεκάτας τελῶσιν, ἃς ἐτέλουν καὶ τοῖς προγόνοις αὐτῶν. . . . There follow certain other privileges (ἀνεπισταθμία) and the prescriptions about the φόρος of the city of Joppa. Much shorter is Josephus' abstract of the edict of 44 B.C.: *A.J.* xiv. 10. 5 (200–1): ὅπως τε Ἰουδαίοις ἐν τῷ δευτέρῳ τῆς μισθώσεως ἔτει τῆς προσόδου κόρον ὑπεξέλωνται καὶ μήτ᾽ ἐργολαβῶσί τινες μήτε φόρους τοὺς αὐτοὺς τελῶσιν. These passages I interpreted in my *Staatspacht*, p. 148 (476) ff.(citing the modern works dealing with them in n. 313). My interpretation has not been taken into consideration by most recent students of the history of Judaea during the period under review, such as T. Rice Holmes, *Rom. Rep.* iii, pp. 210, 507 ff.; M. S. Ginsburg, *Rome et la Judée*, 1928, pp. 85 ff. and esp. 99 ff.; M. A. Levi, *Ottaviano capoparte*, 1933, i, pp. 169 ff. (with references to some modern works); E. R. Bevan, *C.A.H.* ix, p. 404 f.; J. Carcopino, *Hist. Rom.* ii, p. 980, and the interesting remarks of A. Momigliano, *Ann. d. R. Scuola Norm. di Pisa*, 1934, p. 34 f. (reference supplied by E. Bikerman). Ginsburg may be right in suggesting that the *stipendium* was generally paid in cash and only in the second year in kind. The delivery at Sidon is apparently the counterpart of the *deportatio ad aquam*, an obligation to transport the grain of Sicily to the harbours imposed on the *decumani* by the *lex Hieronica* (Cic. *Verr.* ii. 3. 14. 36, cf. J. Carcopino, *La Loi d'Hiéron*, p. 18). It is possible that the reduction of the tribute (from one-third to one-fourth) granted by Caesar was a compensation for delivery at such a distant place as Sidon. Caesar's edicts quoted by Josephus are without doubt genuine. They show striking similarities to those recorded in Mytilene, see my remarks, *J.R.S.* vii (1917), pp. 32 ff. On the activity of Caesar in Syria in general, see Ginsburg, loc. cit., and especially J. Dobiaš, *Hist.* &c., i, pp. 158 ff. (Fr. rés. p. 556 ff.). On the organization of Judaea by Pompey and Gabinius, my *Staatspacht*, pp. 146 (474) ff., cf. above, n. 71.

[105] The more detailed recent accounts of this period, with references to sources and modern works, are those of T. Rice Holmes, *The Architect of the Roman Empire*, 1928, and M. A. Levi, *Ottaviano capoparte*, i, ii, 1933, cf. *C.A.H.* x, chs. i (M. P. Charlesworth) and ii–iv (W. W. Tarn and M. P. Charlesworth). On the history of Syria, J. Dobiaš, *Hist.* &c., chs. 3 and 4 (Fr. rés. pp. 556 ff.). On Asia Minor, V. Chapot, *La Prov. rom. procons. d'Asie*, pp. 53 ff., Broughton, loc. cit., pp. 582 ff. On Greece, Hertzberg, *Hist.* &c., i, pp. 431 ff.; Larsen, loc. cit., pp. 432 ff.

[106] Laodicea: App. *B.C.* iv. 62; Cass. Dio, xlvii. 30. 7; Strabo, xvi. 2. 9,

p. 752. Tarsus: Cass. Dio, xlvii. 31. 3; App. *B.C.* iv. 64. Cf. T. Rice Holmes, *The Architect*, &c., p. 77. Note that both Dolabella and Cassius formed local fleets, Dolabella in Rhodes, Asia, and Egypt, Cassius in Phoenicia.

107 Fl. Jos. *A.J.* xiv. 12. 1 (297): συνεμάχει δ᾿ αὐτῷ [i.e. to Ptolemy, son of Mennaeus, the Ituraean dynast] καὶ Μαρίων, ὃν Τυρίων κατελελοίπει Κάσσιος τύραννον, τυραννίσι γὰρ διαλαβὼν τὴν Συρίαν οὗτος ἀνὴρ ἐφρούρησεν , cf. App. *B.C.* v. 10; U. Kahrstedt, 'Syrische Territorien' &c., *Gött. Abh.*, 1926, ii, p. 102, n. 1; L. Craven, 'Antony's Oriental Policy', *Un. of Missouri Stud.* iii. 2, 1920, p. 19.

108 On Dolabella's activity see the books and articles quoted in n. 105. Cf. R. Herzog, *H.Z.* cxxv (1921–2), pp. 190 ff. Dolabella's letter regarding the ἀστρατευσία of the Jews: Fl. Jos. *A.J.* xiv. 10. 11–12 (223–7). The system of hiring ships or crews from cities and occasionally of hiring squadrons of ships from pirates was commonly used by the Hellenistic monarchs (for the Ptolemies, *C.A.H.* vii, p. 118; for the Seleucids, E. Bikerman, *Inst. Sél.*, p. 100) but is not specifically attested in the case of any Roman governor of the East before Dolabella. The Roman magistrates in the East preferred the system, well known to the Hellenistic world, of compulsory levies of ships from the 'allies' and of special naval contributions (above, note 23). But our information alike for Hellenistic and for Roman times is very poor.

109 See the detailed accounts of Appian, *B.C.* iv. 73, and Plutarch, *Brutus*, 32, cf. Cass. Dio, xlvii. 33. 4.

110 Lycia, App. *B.C.* iv. 76–80 (Xanthus), 81 (Patara), 82 (the rest of Lycia); Plut. *Brutus*, 32; Cass. Dio, xlvii. 34, and the well-known correspondence of Brutus, cf. the full collection of texts, E. Kalinka, *T.A.M.* ii, pp. 98 ff., 146. On the correspondence of Brutus and the problem of its authenticity, Broughton, loc. cit., p. 584 (with tabulation of the data about the pillage of Asia Minor by Brutus). The correspondence, if genuine (and I see no decisive arguments against its authenticity), gives a vivid picture of life in Asia Minor at the time of the liberators' rule. However, Brutus in his dealings with the cities followed the example of his predecessors.

111 Ariobarzanes III and Cassius, App. *B.C.* iv. 63; Cass. Dio, xlvii. 33. cf. Plut. *Cato Minor*, 73.

112 App. *B.C.* iv. 74; v. 4–5, and Cass. Dio, xlvii. 32. 4, cf. App. *B.C.* v. 6: the Greeks described the burden of this contribution to Antony at the meeting at Ephesus; they said that they had handed over to Brutus and Cassius all their money and also their plate and jewels.

113 See this Chapter, p. 1003 and p. 1008.

114 App. *B.C.* iii. 79; iv. 75, 88; v. 75.

115 On the army of Brutus and Cassius and that of Antony and C. Caesar, T. Rice Holmes, *The Architect*, &c., pp. 80 ff.; M. P. Charlesworth, *C.A.H.* x, p. 23.

[116] A detailed account of the privileges granted to the cities will be found in App. *B.C.* v. 7.

[117] Letter of Antony (papyrus in the Br. Mus.): F. Kenyon, *Cl. Rev.* vii (1893), pp. 476 ff.; C. G. Brandis, *Hermes*, xxxii (1897), pp. 514 ff.; *S.B.* 4224, 1. A fragment of an inscribed plaque found at Tralles contained part of the same letter, J. Keil, *Jahreshefte*, xiv (1911), Beiblatt, p. 124; *Ann. ép.*, 1913, no. 58. Professional artists as friends of Antony, Plut., *Ant.* 24. 2–4. Franchise granted to soldiers and civilians: to soldiers, O. Cuntz, 'Legionare des Antonius und Augustus aus dem Orient', *Jahreshefte*, xxv (1929), pp. 70 ff.; Ch. E. Goodfellow, *Rom. Citizenship*, pp. 63 ff.; to civilians, ibid., p. 97 ff.

[118] Ephesian speech of Antony, App. *B.C.* v. 4 ff.; speech of Hybreas, Plut. *Ant.* 24. In general, Cass. Dio, xlviii. 24. 1. How radical were some of the changes which Antony made by setting up new kings in the existing vassal kingdoms and creating new kingdoms of the same type, is well known. These kings paid a regular tribute to Rome. Whether this was an innovation of Antony (Broughton, loc. cit., p. 585) or an established practice, we do not know. Cf. Addendum to this note.

[119] On the Antonii in Asia Minor, see my *Kolonat*, pp. 290 ff., cf. *Storia Ec. e Soc.*, p. 299, n. 1. Broughton, loc. cit., p. 587, cf. pp. 648 ff., rejects my explanation without suggesting a better one: the lavish bestowal of Roman franchise on obscure villages is not an explanation and does not account for the concentration of the Antonii in one region of Asia Minor. His arguments are based on negative, not positive evidence (the lack of evidence for *ager publicus* in Asia Minor in the Republican period and the scanty evidence for Augustan estates in the province of Asia). The state of our knowledge forbids me to regard such negative evidence as conclusive.

[120] In general, Cass. Dio, xlviii. 24. 1: after Philippi Antony came to Asia κἀνταῦθα τὰ μὲν αὐτὸς περιιών, ἐς δὲ τὰ ἄλλους πέμπων, τάς τε πόλεις ἠργυρολόγει καὶ τὰς δυναστείας ἐπίπρασκε. Boethus of Tarsus, Strabo, xiv. 5. 14, p. 674; Straton of Amisus, Strabo, xii. 3. 14, p. 547; Nicias of Cos, R. Herzog, 'Nikias und Xenophon von Kos', *H.Z.* cxxv (1921–2), pp. 190–216. Some other minor tyrants in Bithynia and Pontus (Adiatorix in Heraclea Pontica, Musa Orsobaris and Orodaltis, daughter of Lycomedes, in Cius) and in other parts of Asia Minor (the notorious Cleon, brigand-ruler of the Mysian Olympus, Aba at Olba) are listed by Broughton, loc. cit., p. 589. Cf. Addendum to this note.

[121] Antony in Syria, App. *B.C.* v. 7; 10. Palmyra, App. *B.C.* v. 9, cf. 10, and above, Ch. VI, n. 152; Aradus, Cass. Dio, xlviii. 24. 3; Hieron. year 1976 (Eus. ii. 139, ed. Schöne). In general, J. Dobiaš, *Hist.* &c., i, pp. 206 ff. (Fr. rés. p. 558); M. A. Levi, *Ottaviano capoparte*, ii, pp. 100 ff., and on the petty tyrannies in Syria generally, above, Ch. VI, notes 121 and 122.

[122] On the Parthian war of Labienus and Pacorus, T. Rice Holmes, *The Architect*, &c., pp. 121 ff.; J. Dobiaš, *Hist.* &c., pp. 210 ff. (Fr. rés. p. 559); M. A. Levi, *Ottaviano capoparte*, ii, pp. 113 ff.; W. W. Tarn, *C.A.H.* x, pp. 47 ff.;

N. C. Debevoise, *A Political History of Parthia*, 1938, pp. 108 ff. In these works will be found references to previous treatments of the subject.

[123] L. Robert, *Ét. Anat.*, pp. 324 ff. ; note the mention of ἀναγκαιότατοι καιροί twice in the short fragment in l. 6 f. and 10 ; the mention of ὁμόνοια in l. 3 points to internal disorders in the city.

[124] P. Roussel, *B.C.H.* lv (1931), pp. 91 ff. (Zeus of Panamara). Cf. Ch. Diehl et G. Cousin, *B.C.H.* xi (1887), p. 151, no. 56, and p. 161 f., no. 71—two inscriptions of the temple of Hecate: one speaks of the restoration by Augustus of the temple of the goddess ἀσεβηθείσης, in another are mentioned ἀ]σεβήσαντες in respect of the territory of the temple and some one who ἐπέβαλεν ἐλασσώματα.

[125] L. Robert, *Ét. Anat.*, pp. 312 ff.: fragmentary decree of the first century B.C. ; in addition to a bad famine (χαλεπωτάτη σιτοδεία) and a battle are mentioned ἀναγκαιότατοι καιροί (l. 2), πόλεμοι (l.5), and παντοδαποὶ κίνδυνοι (l. 7). The inscription is not exactly dated and may reflect the conditions of the Mithridatic war.

[126] P. Roussel, 'Un Syrien au service de Rome et d'Octave', *Syria*, xv (1934), pp. 33 ff. The grant of franchise and *immunitas* is not exactly dated. I regard 41 B.C. as more probable than 36 B.C., cf. Ch. E. Goodfellow, *Roman Citizenship*, pp. 44 ff., and above, note 57.

[127] App. *B.C.* v. 77 ; Cass. Dio, xlviii. 39. 1 ; 46. 1 ; Zon. x. 23 ; Hertzberg, *Hist.* &c., i, p. 445 ; A. Wilhelm, *Neue Beitr.* i, p. 37 ; M. Hadas, *Sextus Pompey*, 1930, p. 101 f., and n. 6 ; M. P. Charlesworth, *C.A.H.* x, p. 56 ; Larsen, 'Roman Greece', p. 434. Cf. Plut., *Ant.* 67. 3—execution by Antony of Lachares, father of the famous Eurycles ; the latter was one of the richest and most influential men in Greece in the time of Augustus. Lachares was executed for 'robbery', which illustrates the unsettled conditions in the Peloponnese. An additional motive for the execution may have been the wealth of Lachares. On Eurycles, his son, see the references in my *Storia Ec. e Soc.*, p. 65, n. 15, and p. 173, n. 13.

[128] On the army of Antony, W. W. Tarn, *Cl. Quart.* xxvi (1932), pp. 75 ff., cf. his paper, 'The Battle of Actium', *J.R.S.* xxi (1931), pp. 173 ff. On the mobilization of the East by Antony and on his army and fleet, W. W. Tarn, *C.A.H.* x, p. 100 ; on the army and fleet of C. Caesar, ibid., p. 102. In his paper on the battle of Actium, p. 179, Tarn has drawn attention to a note of Orosius (vi. 19. 5) in which he quotes a remark of Antony to the effect that there would be no lack of rowers as long as there was a man left in Greece. The same statement is made by Plut., *Ant.* 62. 1: Antony through his trierarchs was pressing into service in his ships 'from long-suffering Greece wayfarers, drivers, harvesters, ephebes'. This is a good illustration of Antony's methods.

[129] There is no need to adduce evidence for the gradual impoverishment of the Hellenistic world in the time of the civil wars. Even the richer

bourgeoisie, despite its privileged position, was declining in prosperity. I may quote a very instructive remark of Vitruvius (vi. 7. 4 [150, 7–13]). Speaking of Greek palatial houses—which the finest houses in Delos closely resembled and on which the larger houses in Asia Minor were probably modelled (see A. Rumpf, 'Zum hellenistischen Hause', *J.D.A.I.* 1 (1935), pp. 1 ff.)—Vitruvius describes the small apartments (*domunculae*) reserved for the guests, and proceeds: 'nam cum fuerunt Graeci delicatiores et *fortuna opulentiores*, hospitibus advenientibus instruebant triclinia, cubicula, cum penu cellas, primoque die ad cenam invitabant, postero mittebant pullos, ova, holera, poma reliquasque res agrestes. ideo pictores ea, quae mittebantur hospitibus, picturis imitantes xenia appellaverunt.'

¹³⁰ Above, Ch. VI, n. 146 (glass). On glazed pottery (supposedly lead glaze, not copper glaze as in Egypt) of late Hellenistic times imitating metal ware, R. Zahn, *J.D.A.I.* xxiii (1908), p. 74, and *Amtl. Ber. K. Kunstsamml. Berl. Museen*, 1914, July, p. 281; H. Kusel, *J.D.A.I.* xxxii (1917), Anz., p. 58; R. Zahn, Κτῶ Χρῶ, *Berl. Winckelmannspr.* lxxxi, 1923; A. Merlin, *Mon. et Mém. Piot*, xxx (1929), pp. 51 ff., and pl. v; G. M. A. Richter and Chr. Alexander, *Augustan Art*, 1939, p. 21. Cf. the *askoi* found in Alexandria, E. Breccia, *Le Mus. gr.-rom.* 1931–2, p. 19 and pl. vi, 23–4. The problems of date, origin, and relation to the other types of faience ware (Chinese, Mesopotamian and Syrian, and Egyptian) are under discussion. The whole material needs to be carefully studied afresh. Cf. my remarks in the description of pls. cvii and cviii. It may be noted in this connexion that even after the long period of anarchy in the time of Pompey and Caesar Antioch remained a great centre of art, as is shown by the beautiful marble portrait-head recently found there, F. Poulsen, *Syria*, xix (1938), pp. 357 ff.

¹³¹ Above, p. 927 f.

CHAPTER VIII

¹ I have dealt with Persia above in Chapter II. On the system of Persian roads much has been written. The subject has been treated from the technical point of view by C. Merckel, *Die Ingenieurtechnik im Altertum*, 1899, pp. 222 ff.; A. Neuburger, *The Technical Arts and Sciences of the Ancients*, 1930 (*passim*), and R. J. Forbes, *Notes on the History of Ancient Roads and their Construction* (Allard Pierson Stichting, Arch.-Hist. Bijdragen, iii), 1934, pp. 80 ff. (with a few bibliographical references), and from the commercial point of view by W. Götz, *Die Verkehrswege im Dienste des Welthandels*, 1888, pp. 161 ff., and F. M. Heichelheim, *Wirtschaftsg.*, pp. 362 ff., and n. 31, cf. my Chs. IV, n. 31, and V, n. 47 (ample bibliography on sea and land routes; no special section devoted to the Persian system of communications).

² It is unnecessary to enumerate here the modern contributions to the study of the development of ancient geography. It will be sufficient to mention the

leading and most reliable summaries: F. Gisinger, art. 'Geographie' in *P.W.K.* Suppl. iv. 521 ff. (Hellenistic period, 602 ff.) ; W. Kubitschek, art. 'Erdmessung', *P.W.K.* Suppl. vi. 31 ff.; R. E. Dickinson and O. J. R. Howarth, *The Making of Geography*, 1933; E. H. Warmington, *Greek Geography*, 1934 (with excellent translations of the basic texts) ; H. F. Tozer, *A History of Ancient Geography*, 2nd ed. 1935 (with notes of M. Cary) ; cf. M. Cary et E. Warmington, *Les Explorateurs de l'Antiquité*, 1932, and R. Henning, *Terrae incognitae*, i, 1936. On the maps, Kubitschek, art. 'Karten', *P.W.K.* x. 2022 ff., cf. W. A. Heidel, *The Frame of the Ancient Greek Maps*, 1937.

3 We know very little of the official itineraries of the Hellenistic period. On the *bematistae* of Alexander, H. Berve, *Das Alexanderreich*, &c., i, 1926, pp. 51 ff., cf. 44, and all later studies of the campaigns of Alexander (above, Ch. III). On the *bematistae* of Seleucus I, Pliny, *N.H.* vi. 63, and E. Bikerman, *Inst. Sél.*, p. 63. The postal service, well organized by the Persians (U. Wilcken, 'Alexander der Große und die hellenistische Wirtschaft', *Schmollers Jahrb.* xlv (1925), p. 357), improved by Alexander (Berve, loc. cit., p. 53 f.), and certainly maintained by the Hellenistic rulers, was probably based on these itineraries. On the σταθμοὶ Παρθικοί of Isidorus of Charax and on the date of Isidorus, my remarks, *C.A.H.* xi, p. 126, and W. W. Tarn, *The Greeks in Bactria and India*, pp. 53 ff. W. Kubitschek in *P.W.K.* ix. 2308 ff., art. 'Itineraria', does not mention the itinerary of Isidorus. The Dura map of σταθμοί: F. Cumont, *Fouilles de Doura-Europos*, p. 335. I cannot enumerate here the later discussions of this map.

4 All the statements in the text are of course hypothetical, based as they are on very slight evidence, see K. J. Beloch, *Gr. Gesch.* iv. 1, 2nd ed., pp. 280 ff. ; my remarks in *C.A.H.* vii, p. 175 ; F. M. Heichelheim, *Wirtschaftsg.*, p. 571. I may quote in support of my statements the ὁδὸς βασιλικὴ ἡ ἀρχαία in the Laodice inscription, *O.G.I.* 225, 41; Welles, *R.C.* 20, 10, and the information which we possess about the roads around Pergamon. In the Pergamene kingdom the upkeep of the roads in the territory of the city was, according to the well-known Astynomoi law of Pergamon (*O.G.I.* 483, 24 ff.), the duty of the owners of the land through which they passed ; the main roads had a prescribed minimum width of 20 πήχεις, the others of 8. The law, which is a royal law, and was still in force in Roman times, produces the impression that even the local roads in the Pergamene kingdom and ap-parently also in the Seleucid kingdom were a matter of much concern to the central government and were maintained in good condition. How much more assiduous must have been the care taken of the great military and commercial highways!

5 I cannot refer here to all the modern works dealing with the development of geography in the Hellenistic period and with the leading geographers of this period. A good summary of our actual knowledge on this subject will be found in the books and articles quoted in n. 2. Very useful is the list of

Hellenistic geographers in F. Susemihl, *Gesch. d. gr. Lit. in d. Alexandrinerzeit*, i, 1891, pp. 649 ff., and the articles on the individual geographers in *P.W.K.* On ps.-Scylax and his description of the Syrian and Palestinian coast, K. Galling, 'Die syrisch-palästinische Küste nach der Beschreibung bei Pseudo-Scylax', *Z. d. pal. Ver.* lxi (1938), pp. 66 ff.

[6] On the *periploi* see the recent article by F. Gisinger, *P.W.K.* xix. 841 ff., cf. A. Köster, *Das antike Seewesen*, 1923, pp. 187 ff. (on maps and *periploi*). The common use of *periploi* by travellers is excellently illustrated for the early Roman Imperial period by the epigram of Crinagoras, *Anth. Pal.* ix. 559, addressed to Menippus of Pergamon, probably the author of the well-known *periplus*: πλοῦς μοι ἐπ' Ἰταλίην ἐντύνεται · ἐς γὰρ ἑταίρους | στέλλομαι, ὧν ἤδη δηρὸν ἄπειμι χρόνον. | Διφέω δ' ἡγητῆρα περίπλοον ὅς μ' ἐπὶ νήσους | Κυκλάδας, ἀρχαίην τ' ἄξει ἐπὶ Σχερίην, κτλ. On the thorough revision of the *periploi* of the Black Sea by Diophantus and Demetrius of Callatis, my *Skythien und der Bosporus*, 1931, pp. 25 ff.

[7] On maritime traffic and maritime transport of goods and passengers in Hellenistic times, A. Köster, *Das antike Seewesen*, 1923, pp. 157 ff.; W. Kroll, art. 'Schiffahrt', *P.W.K.* ii A. 408 ff.; F. M. Heichelheim, *Wirtschaftsg.*, pp. 569 ff. and n. 33 (copious bibliography of works which mostly say very little or nothing of the Hellenistic period). On the forms of ships F. Miltner, art. 'Seewesen', *P.W.K.* Suppl. v. 917 ff. (on the merchant ships of Classical, Hellenistic, and Roman times). On the technical improvements in navigation: sextant (?) found at Anticythera (origin Hellenistic or Roman?), A. Köster, loc. cit., p. 196 f. The new technical devices attested by the discovery of the Nemi ships: A. Köster, 'Studien zur Geschichte des ant. Seewesens', *Klio*, Beih. xxxii (1934), p. 22; my *Storia Soc. ed Ec.*, p. 209, n. 40; G. Cultrera, 'Nemi', &c., *Not. d. Sc.*, 1932, pp. 279 ff.; A. W. Persson, 'Die hellenistische Schiffsbaukunst und die Nemischiffe', *Opusc. Archaeol.* iv (1935), pp. 10 ff., and *Mostra Augustea della Romanità*, Catalogo, 1937, i, pp. 256 ff., and ii (bibliography), p. 124. On the rudder, Comm. R. Lefebvre des Noettes, *De la marine antique à la marine moderne: La révolution du gouvernail*, 1935, cf. G. La Roëire, 'Les Transformations du gouvernail', *Ann. d'Hist. Ec. et Soc.* vii (1935), pp. 564 ff.; E. de Saint-Denis, 'Le Gouvernail antique. Technique et vocabulaire', *Rev. Ét. Lat.* xii (1934), pp. 390 ff., and the substantial review of Lefebvre's book by H. de Saussure, 'De la marine antique à la marine moderne', *Rev. Arch.*, 6 sér. x (1937), pp. 90 ff. (a general survey of Greek navigation in the light of climatic conditions in the Aegean Sea); see also L. Laurand, 'Note sur le gouvernail antique', *Rev. Phil.* xi (63) (1937), p. 131 f., and P. Nordmann, ibid. xii (64) (1938), pp. 330 ff. The giant ships of the Hellenistic period: the Syracosia–Alexandria of Hiero II of Syracuse (3,310 tons), A. Köster, *Das antike Seewesen*, pp. 158 ff., and the article by Persson quoted above; the pleasure-ship (*thalamegos*) of Philopator, A. Köster, 'Studien', &c., ch. iii, pp. 20 ff. The giant ships in the navy (competition of Hellenistic monarchs in building ever larger men-of-war): W. W. Tarn, *J.H.S.* xxx (1910), pp. 209 ff. (cf. his *Hellenistic Military*

and *Naval Developments*, 1930) ; cf. W. L. Rodgers, *Greek and Roman Naval Warfare*, 1937, pp. 254 ff. (on the flagship of Demetrius, with reconstruction). See also above, Ch. IV, n. 353 on the *octeres* of Heraclea.

[8] On the harbours, K. Lehmann–Hartleben, 'Die antiken Hafenanlagen des Mittelmeeres', *Klio*, Beih. xiv (1923), pp. 122 ff., cf. the descriptions of Pls. LXXV (and fig. 5), LXXVI, CXII. This is not the place to complete the bibliography for individual ports given by Lehmann–Hartleben. I may, however, make an exception in the case of the lighthouses by referring to my summary of the controversy concerning them, *St. Soc. ed Ec.*, p. 202, n. 34. Nor can I collect the scanty evidence which we possess on harbour regulations and harbour life in general. I may quote *exempli causa* the Thasian regulation concerning the beaching of ships and payment for it, M. Launey, *B.C.H.* lvii (1933), pp. 394 ff., cf. W. Peek, *Ath. Mitt.* lix (1934), pp. 35 ff.

[9] Here again the statement in the text is hypothetical and based on general probability. For instance, our information about the inns in the cities and the rest-houses on the great roads is meagre and scattered. The evidence on the inns has been collected by E. Ziebarth, 'Gasthäuser im alten Griechenland', *Εἰς Μνήμην Σ. Λαμπροῦ*, 1935, pp. 339 ff., and a little earlier by W. C. Firebaugh, *The Inns of Greece and Rome*, 1923 (not quoted by Ziebarth); it relates mostly to the great sanctuaries and the sea-ports of the Greek and Hellenistic world. I have spoken above of the *fonduqs*—religious and business centres of foreign merchants—at Delos, and I may quote the way in which Palmyra, in the first centuries A.D., equipped her caravan roads with wells and rest-houses (M. Rostovtzeff, 'Les inscriptions caravanières de Palmyre', *Mél. Glotz*, pp. 795 ff.). G. E. Kirk, 'Gymnasium or Khan? A Hellenistic building at Babylon', *Iraq*, ii (1935), pp. 223 ff., has endeavoured (not convincingly) to interpret the building connected with the Hellenistic theatre of Babylon, not as a *palaestra*, but as a khan. I wonder why a khan should be built as an annex of the theatre. In Kirk's paper the reader will find some material on the ancient inns and caravanserais (Firebaugh's book and Ziebarth's article are not quoted).

[10] On the organization of the police in Egypt, F. Oertel, *Die Liturgie*, 1917, pp. 50 ff., who quotes the previous works on this subject.

[11] On the παραφύλακες of the Hellenistic period, above, Ch. IV, n. 250. On the gendarmes of Palmyra see my paper in *Mél. Glotz* quoted in n. 9, and the evidence about the Palmyrene archers under the command of a *strategos* found in Dura but relating to Roman times only, see my *Dura-Europos and its Art*, 1938, p. 23.

[12] For transport by land only animal power was available in the ancient world. How efficiently this power was handled we do not exactly know. I have dealt with this question for the period of the Roman Empire in my *St. Ec. e Soc.*, p. 439, and have quoted the works of Lefebvre des Noettes, cf. A. Rehm, *Arch. f. Kulturg.* xxviii (1938), p. 160 f. For the Hellenistic

period the material is much less abundant (cf. W. L. Westermann, 'On inland transportation and communication in antiquity', *Pol. Sc. Quart.* xliii (1928), pp. 364 ff.). We do not know, for example, whether the horseshoe was ever used in Hellenistic times. Some prominent scholars (see the bibliography in F. M. Heichelheim, *Wirtschaftsg.*, p. 1096, and C. Blümlein, Bursian's *Jahresber.* cclxi (1938), pp. 53 ff.) are confident that it was commonly used as early as that period. I have my doubts about this. At Dura, in which large detachments of cavalry were stationed for about a century and which was a city frequently visited by caravans, not a single horseshoe (in the upper layers of the city modern horseshoes were found frequently) was found in circumstances that would guarantee its ancient origin. The same applies to the other ruins where horseshoes have been found. If they were used at all, it was only exceptionally, not as a common practice. Otherwise the ruins would have yielded scores of them, which is notoriously not the case.

[13] On the many and various recent studies devoted to the Κοινή see the report of A. Debrunner, 'Nachklassisches Griechisch 1930–1935', Bursian's *Jahresber.* cclxi (1938), pp. 140 ff.

[14] The statements in the text are based on the material adduced in the preceding chapters or in the various books and papers quoted in the notes to these chapters.

[15] I refer to the basic article on this subject by U. Wilcken, 'Antike Urkundenlehre', *Münch. Beitr.* xix (1934), pp. 42 ff., especially p. 55.

[16] I cannot cite all the modern books and papers which deal with the epigraphical evidence (our main source of information) relating to the Dionysiac *technitai*. I will only refer to the useful recent summary by F. Poland in *P.W.K.* v a. 2473 ff., cf. L. Robert, *B.C.H.* lix (1935), pp. 193 ff. It is to be regretted that we know so little of the role which the associations played in the business life of their members. Poland's remark concerning Antiochus IV and the *technitai* (loc. cit. 2490) is misleading.

[17] The theatre of Babylon: R. Koldewey, *Das wieder erstehende Babylon*, 1913, pp. 293 ff., cf. *Die Königsburgen von Babylon*, ii, 1932, p. 44. The inscription on an alabaster slab (not mentioned by B. Haussoullier, *Klio*, ix (1909), pp. 252 ff., nor by F. Cumont, *Fouilles de Doura-Europos*, pp. 452 ff., in their lists of the Greek inscriptions of the eastern parts of the Seleucid kingdom, nor reprinted in *S.E.G.* vii) speaks of the construction (or reconstruction?) of the theatre and the *skene*: Διοσκουρί[δης] | ὁ Φιλοδόξου | τὸ θέατρο[ν] | καὶ σκηνήν. It certainly belongs to late Hellenistic times (reign of Epiphanes or a little later?). My impression has been confirmed by a close examination of the lettering of the inscription by C. B. Welles, and the form of the *skene* supports this view: see my remarks, *C.A.H.* vii, p. 188; A. Frickenhaus, *Die altgriechische Bühne* (Schr. d. wissensch. Ges. in Straßburg, xxxi (1917)), p. 44, fig. 17; id., *P.W.K.* iii a. 444, art. Σκηνή; H. Bulle,

'Untersuchungen an gr. Theatern', *Bayr. Abh.* xxxiii (1928), p. 246, cf. 300;
C. Fensterbusch, Bursian's *Jahresber.* ccxxvii (1930), p. 42; on the *palaestra*
of this theatre, G. E. Kirk, *Iraq*, ii (1935), pp. 223 ff., cf. above, n. 9.

[18] Much has been written on the marriage contracts of Ptolemaic Egypt.
I am inclined to accept the view of F. Bozza, 'Il matrimonio nel diritto dei
papiri dell'epoca Tolemaica', *Aeg.* xiv (1934), pp. 205 ff.; R. Taubenschlag,
'Die Geschichte der Rezeption des griechischen Privatrechts in Ägypten',
Atti IV Congr. Pap., 1936, pp. 268 ff., and H. J. Wolff, 'Written and Un-
written Marriages in Hellenistic and Postclassical Roman Law', *Philol.
Monogr., Am. Philol. Assoc.* ix, 1939 (in these papers the reader will find a
complete bibliography). On intermarriage, O. Montevecchi, 'Ricerche di
sociologia', &c., *Aeg.* xvi (1936), p. 32, cf. C. Préaux, *Chr. d'Ég.* xii (1937),
p. 120. On the native concubines of Ptolemaic soldiers and foreign residents
in the Ptolemaic province of Syria and Phoenicia, see above, Ch. IV, pp. 343 ff.
and n. 135. I cannot mention all that has been written on the Dura law.
The text is to be found in F. Cumont, *Fouilles de Doura-Europos*, p. 309,
and an important correction by D. Pappulias in 'Συμβολὴ εἰς τὴν ἱστορίαν τῆς
ἐξ ἀδιαθέτου κληρονομικῆς διαθήκης ἐν τῷ Ἑλληνικῷ δικαίῳ', 'Ακαδημ. 'Αθην.
Συνεδρία, 28 Nov. 1929; cf. L. Wenger, *Arch. Pap.* x (1932), p. 130 f. (the
reading of Pappulias has been confirmed by C. B. Welles).

[19] On town-planning and the Hippodamian system in general, G. Cultrera,
'Architettura Ippodamea', *Mem. Acc. Lincei*, xvii (1924), pp. 357 ff.;
A. von Gerkan, *Griechische Städteanlagen*, 1924; K. A. Doxiadis, *Raumord-
nung im gr. Städtebau*, 1937. On Egypt, F. Luckhard, *Das Privathaus im
ptolemäischen und römischen Ägypten*, 1914 (diss. Bonn); H. Schmitz, *Die
hellenistisch-römischen Stadtanlagen in Ägypten*, 1921; P. Viereck, 'Philadelpheia', *Morgenland*, xvi (1928), and the bibliography *C.A.H.* vii, p. 894.
Cf. A. E. R. Boak and E. E. Peterson, *Karanis 1924–29*, 1931; *1929–31*, 1933;
A. E. R. Boak, *Soknopaiu Nesos*, 1935. On the rebuilding of ancient Egyptian
cities see the reports on the German excavations in Hermupolis by G. Roeder
and others, especially the last 'Bericht über die Ausgrabungen der deutschen
Hermopolis-Expedition', 1935, *Mitt. d. Inst. in Kairo*, vii (1937). I may remark that the Ptolemies never rebuilt the ancient Egyptian cities thoroughly.
This was reserved for the Romans. On Syria, the bibliography, *C.A.H.* vii,
p. 900 f. On Apamea, F. Mayence, *Ac. R. de Belgique, Bull. cl. d. Lettres*,
etc., xxv (1939), pp. 328 ff. On Dura-Europus, my 'Dura and the problem
of Parthian art', *Yale Cl. Stud.* x (1935), pp. 203 ff., and *Dura-Europos
and its Art*, 1938, pp. 33 ff. On Laodicea, J. Sauvaget in *Bulletin d'Études
orientales*, iv (1934), pp. 81 ff., cf. his note 'Le Plan de Laodicée sur mer',
ibid. vi (1936), p. 51 ff. On Damascus, J. Sauvaget, 'Esquisse d'une histoire
de Damas', *Rev. Ét. Islam.*, 1934, pp. 422 ff.

[20] A good study of the Ptolemaic private house will be found in A. R.
Schütz, *Der Typus des hellenistisch-ägyptischen Hauses*, &c., 1936 (diss.
Würzburg), with excellent bibliographical references; cf. the reports of the
Michigan expedition on the excavation of Karanis quoted in the preceding

note. On the private house in Dura-Europus see my two books cited in the same note. On the Greek house of the pre-Hellenistic and Hellenistic periods, D. M. Robinson, 'Prähistorische und griechische Häuser', *P.W.K.* Suppl. vii. 223 ff., cf D. M. Robinson and J. W. Graham, 'The Hellenistic House', *Excavations at Olynthus*, viii, 1938.

[21] I have given above in Ch. IV, n. 121 a bibliography of modern literature concerning the *status civitatis* of foreigners in Egypt. On the Seleucid kingdom, ibid. pp. 517, notes 292 ff. In this note I may quote the two references to laws and royal orders concerning the change of political status by the various groups of the population of Egypt which are discussed by Bikerman. In *B.G.U.* 1213 (list of laws and royal orders of the third century B.C.) we find in l. 3 the item: περὶ μετα[βολῆ]s πατρίδος καὶ ὀνομάτων. In *B.G.U.* 1250, 11 ff. (second century B.C.) in a complaint regarding unauthorized change of names we read: προστεταγμένον γὰρ | [πᾶσι τοῖς ἐπὶ τῶν πρ]αγμάτων μηθένα μετε|[νομάζειν μηδ' αὐτὸν] μηδὲ τὴν πατρίδα, εἰ δὲ [μή, τὸν ποιήσαντα θ]ανάτωι ζημιοῦσθαι (the form μετενομάζει is found again in l. 15). It is hard to believe that in such measures the kings were guided by purely administrative and fiscal motives.

[22] Bibliography, Ch. IV, n. 121.

[23] On the gymnasia see the modern works cited in Ch. IV, n. 121. Great importance attaches to the inscription recently found in Egypt and published by Kortenbeutel (*S.E.G.* viii. 641). It gives a good idea of the corporative life of a group of Greeks formed around the gymnasium (οἱ ἐκ τοῦ γυμνασίου). There was probably a fixed number of members and strict rules about admission of new members. The organization of the group is almost a copy of the city organization. It is a pity that we do not know whether the gymnasium of the inscription was that of Ptolemais (which is doubtful) or of a native town or village. Cf. *S.E.G.* viii. 694 (third/second century B.C. from Luxor). Close connexion between the gymnasia and the army: *P. Enteux.* 8 (221/0 B.C.); *S.B.* iii. 7245; P. Jouguet, *Raccolta Ramorino*, 1927, pp. 381 ff. (gymnasium built at Samareia by a well-to-do officer of the army settled there); *S.E.G.* viii. 531; P. Roussel, *Mél. Maspéro*, ii, 1934, pp. 37 ff., Aphroditopolis, 57/6 B.C. (Herodes, son of Demetrius ἱππάρχης ἐπ' ἀνδρῶν τῶν κατοίκων ἱππέων, a great benefactor of the gymnasium; he organized a grand reception for the στρατηγός and soldiers); *S.E.G.* viii. 357, third/second century B.C. (a group of officers of an unknown town or village honours their συστρατιώτης, the gymnasiarch). Οἱ ἐκ τοῦ γυμνασίου are frequently mentioned, for example, in inscriptions: *S.E.G.* viii. 504, 531, 641, 694. Gymnasial liturgy (λαμπαδαρχία ἀνδρῶν), connected with the *agones*: *B.G.U.* 1256 (first half of the second century B.C.); F. Zucker, *Aeg.* xi (1931), pp. 488, n. 4, and 493; the man who complains—curiously enough to the *komogrammateus*—about this burden imposed on him was a Macedonian ὀγδοηκοντάρουρος of Philadelphia. On the gymnasia and *agones* in the correspondence of Zenon, see my *Large Estate*, p. 174; E. Norman Gardiner, *Class. Rev.* xliv (1930), pp. 211 ff. Gymnasia owning land: *Teb.* 700 (124 B.C.).

24 The SCHOOLBOOKS found in Egypt have been carefully collected, edited, and studied by eminent scholars. The most important contributions are those of P. Bendel, *Qua ratione Graeci liberos docuerint*, &c. (diss. Greifswald) 1911; E. Ziebarth, 'Aus der antiken Schule', Lietzmann, *Kleine Texte*, 65, 2nd ed., 1913; H. J. M. Milne, *Greek Shorthand Manuals. Syllabary and Commentary*, with 9 pls., 1934 (Eg. Expl. Soc.); P. Collart, 'Les papyrus scolaires', *Mél. Desrousseaux*, 1937, pp. 69 ff. A spectacular discovery has been made recently: a fragmentary roll containing a school manual intended to give a Greek schoolboy in Egypt of the time of Philopator elementary notions of reading, spelling, mathematics, and literature, published and illustrated by P. Jouguet and O. Guéraud, *Un Livre d'écolier du IIIᵐᵉ s. av. J.-C.*, 1938 (Publ. de la Soc. R. Ég. de Papyrologie), cf. A. Körte, *Arch. Pap.* xiii (1938), pp. 104 ff., who shows how closely this manual resembles that of the late Roman Empire, *P. Bour.* 1.

On the FRAGMENTS OF BOOKS found in the *chora* of Egypt, some of which represent the remains of school libraries, see C. H. Oldfather, 'Greek literary texts from Greco-Roman Egypt', *Univ. of Wisc. Stud.* ix, 1923; F. G. Kenyon, *Books and Readers in Ancient Greece and Rome*, 1932, pp. 25 ff. (on the Hellenistic period). The remnants of books of the Ptolemaic period are of course less numerous than those of the first to third centuries A.D. It is interesting to note that remnants of books of the third century B.C. are more numerous than those of the second and first. This may be an accident, but perhaps it may be explained by the keener interest taken in books by the early settlers as compared with their more orientalized descendants.

The existence of LIBRARIES (well known for the Greek cities) is attested for the *chora* by many fragmentary lists of books found in Egypt, from the 'prophetic' papyrus of Petersburg from Memphis published by V. Jernstedt (U. Wilcken, *Chr.* 155) to that of Warsaw (G. von Manteuffel, *P. Vars.* 5), and to the highly interesting letter about 'useful' books recently published by A. Vogliano, *Dal Iᵒ volume dei Papiri d. R. Univ. di Milano*, 1935, no. 2 (cf. above, Ch. IV, n. 232). These lists belong to the imperial period, but there are two documents of the early Ptolemaic period which testify to the existence of libraries in early Ptolemaic times. One is *P. Col. Zen.* 60 (for my knowledge of this document, which will soon be published, I am indebted to Prof. W. L. Westermann), a fragmentary undated list of books (from the library of Zenon) which have been forwarded to his brother Epharmostus; the other (*P. Cairo Zen.* 59079), received by Zenon in 257 B.C. at Arsinoe Dionos, a place otherwise unknown, contains a list of pieces of furniture (among them κίσται) compiled by Dionysius, to whom the document probably gives the title of βιβλι[οφύλαξ], and may indicate the existence of a library or record office (or both ?) in the household of Apollonius the *dioecetes*. I may remind the reader that a list of books of Hellenistic times (a gymnasium library ?) has been found recently at Rhodes, above, Ch. IV, n. 83, and Ch. V, n. 113; cf. L. Robert, *B.C.H.* lix (1935), pp. 421 ff. (subscription list of Cos for the gymnasial library, of the second century B.C.) and the remarks of W. A. Oldfather, *Library Quarterly*, viii (1938), pp. 287 ff.

The architecture and equipment of ancient libraries has been studied more than once in the light of the new discoveries. The best-known ruins of a Hellenistic library are those of the library of Pergamon. On this library and the other known libraries of chiefly Roman times see B. Götze, 'Antike Bibliotheken', *J.D.A.I.* lii (1937), pp. 225 ff., and C. Wendel, 'Neues aus alten Bibliotheken', *Zentralbl. f. Bibliothekswesen*, liv (1937), pp. 585 ff., and lv (1938), pp. 641 ff. (with bibliography). The actual management of the ancient libraries is well illustrated by a short inscription recently found at Athens (*Hesp.* v (1936), p. 41), which appears to be an extract from the library regulations concerning the borrowing of books and the office-hours of the library. The inscription was probably put up somewhere in the library of Trajan at Athens, cf. W. A. Oldfather, *Library Quarterly*, vii (1937), p. 437. It is very probable that library regulations were first compiled in the great Library of Alexandria.

On SCHOOL LIFE in Egypt in Hellenistic and Roman times, C. Préaux, 'Lettres privées grecques d'Égypte relatives à l'éducation', *Rev. Belge de Phil. et d'Hist.* viii (1929), pp. 757 ff.; P. Collart, 'À l'école avec les petits Grecs d'Égypte', *Chr. d'Ég.* xi (1936), pp. 489 ff.; W. Peremans, *Vreemdelingen* &c., pp. 173 ff. The life of the schoolboys in the eastern Hellenistic monarchies was not different from that so picturesquely described by Teles περὶ τοῦ μὴ εἶναι τέλος ἡδονήν (ed. O. Hense, 1909, p. 50).

[25] I have cited the modern studies dealing with the guilds in Egypt, both native and Greek, in Ch. IV, nn. 105 and 121. The question of the origin of Ptolemaic private associations (we know several of them well enough, including the character of their statutes, from Demotic and Greek papyri) is controversial. M. San Nicolò and A. E. R. Boak, *Tr. Am. Phil. Ass.* lxviii (1937), pp. 212 ff., are inclined to regard it as highly probable that all the associations of Ptolemaic and Roman times had a Greek origin, while A. D. Nock in *Harv. Th. Rev.* xxix (1936), pp. 74 ff., points out many peculiarities in their statutes which cannot be regarded as Greek. My personal opinion is that in the late Ptolemaic period the two types influenced each other, while in pre-Ptolemaic and early Ptolemaic times they may have existed side by side. New evidence about a special type of religious and social associations, with a slight admixture of professional elements, will be found in the inscriptions of the γεοῦχοι from lower Egypt referred to above, Ch. V, n. 151. Associations of φιλοβασιλισταί and βασιλισταί, mostly military, have been recently discussed by U. Wilcken, *U.P.Z.* 161 (Hermias' lawsuit of 119 B.C.). To the list of professional associations compiled by M. San Nicolò (in the first volume of his *Vereinswesen*) many new items could be added, for example, the guilds of millers, picklers or fish-salters, and general dealers, *Teb.* 840, 841; cf. the beekeepers who have their own temple, *Teb.* 853. 26. I cannot deal here with the professional associations of the Ptolemaic period. I regard them as inherited from the past, and the πρεσβύτεροι of the γεωργοί of Ptolemaic times (similar to the πρεσβύτεροι of other professional guilds) as precursors of and models for the πρεσβύτεροι κώμης of Roman times; against

this view, which I first stated in my *Kolonat*, M. San Nicolò, *Vereinswesen*, ii, 1915, pp. 89 ff., cf. W. Peremans, *Vreemdelingen*, p. 88, and *P. Bad.* 170, A.D. 54 (a lease of 'public' land), which attests the existence of the πρεσβύτεροι γεωργῶν and of corporative organizations of δημόσιοι γεωργοί in early Roman times: see the useful introduction by G. A. Gerhard to this papyrus and the remarks of U. Wilcken, *Arch. Pap.* xiii (1939), pp. 239 ff. On the division of professional groups into δεκαταρχίαι, W. Hellebrand, *Festschrift Paul Ko-schaker*, 1939, pp. 247 ff. The right of property possessed by the βασιλικοί γεωργοί of individual villages (*Teb.* 53, 5 ff.) is not inconsistent with the character of their associations as stated in the text.

²⁶ The little we know of the professional associations in Syria and Meso-potamia belongs to the Roman imperial period, see F. M. Heichelheim, 'Roman Syria', T. Frank, *Econ. Surv.* iv, p. 208. The κοινὸν τῶν μαχαιροποιῶν (Clermont-Ganneau, *Rev. Arch.*, 3 sér. iii (17), 1891, pp. 107–8), may be, as Clermont-Ganneau suggests, a native Phoenician hellenized guild (the Phoeni-cian name was *gêv*). Much has been written on the *thiasoi* of Palmyra, and the question of their character is under discussion. There is no doubt, however, that associations of this kind go back to very early times (their Semitic name seems to be *marzah*), and that ritual banquets played a very important part in their life. See J. C. Février, *La Religion des Palmyréniens*, 1931, pp. 201 ff., cf. H. Ingholt, 'Un nouveau thiase à Palmyre', *Syria*, ii (1926), p. 135 f. and pl. xxxiv. On the ritual banquets for which special *triclinia* were built in the sanctuaries of Palmyra and its neighbourhood and of Dura, H. Seyrig, *Syria*, xiv (1933), p. 263, and D. Schlumberger, *J.D.A.I.* l (1935), Anz., pp. 595 ff., and esp. pp. 606 ff.; cf. the remarks of F. E. Brown in *Dura Rep.* vii–viii (1939), pp. 157 ff. On the clay *tesserae* connected certainly with these banquets, my papers in *J.R.S.* xxii (1932), pp. 107 ff., and *A.J.A.* xxxvii (1933), pp. 58 ff. A Corpus of the *tesserae* by H. Seyrig and H. Ingholt is in preparation. On the ἑταιρεία of Dura, C. Hopkins, *Dura Rep.* v (1934), pp. 112 ff., nos. 416 and 418.

²⁷ The evidence relating to the professional guilds in general and to those of Asia Minor has been frequently collected and discussed. Lists of extant inscriptions and other mentions of them will be found in J. P. Waltzing, *Étude hist. sur les corp. prof.*, &c., 1895; E. Ziebarth, *Das gr. Vereinswesen*, 1896, pp. 101 ff.; J. Oehler, *Eranos Vindobonensis*, 1893, pp. 277 ff.; F. Poland, *Gesch. d. gr. Vereinswesens*, 1909, pp. 116 ff., with the lists at the end of the book, cf. pp. 527 ff.; T. R. S. Broughton, 'Roman Asia Minor', T. Frank, *Econ. Surv.* iv, pp. 841 ff. (without quoting his predecessors). Based on the material thus collected are the summaries in E. Kornemann, art. Κοινόν, *P.W.K.* Suppl. iv. 915 ff.; Suppl. v. 453 ff.; Stöckle, 'Berufs-vereine', ibid. Suppl. iv. 155 ff.; Kahrstedt u. Poland, 'Synodos', ibid. iv A. 1415 ff. A Roman origin is the *communis opinio* of modern scholars, for example Waltzing, loc. cit.; H. Francotte, *L'industrie dans la Grèce ancienne*, ii, 1901, pp. 212 ff.; F. Poland, loc. cit.; R. T. S. Broughton, loc. cit., and several others. The possibility of local origin has been suggested by G. Radet,

La Lydie et le monde grec au temps des Mermnades, 1893, p. 226, n. 2; W. M.
Ramsay, *Cities and Bishoprics of Phrygia*, 1895, pp. 105 ff. and 440 f., and
accepted by E. Ziebarth, loc. cit.; J. Kaerst, *Gesch. d. Hell.* ii, 2nd ed.,
p. 161 f.; and myself, *Stor. Econ. e Soc.* pp., 210 ff. In combating the latter
opinion (which he speaks of as most generally accepted, while the contrary
is true) Broughton has not produced any new material nor added any new
arguments of value. None of the modern scholars has taken into consideration the striking fact that the notable development of professional organizations in the eastern Roman Empire was confined to Egypt and Asia Minor,
the two most prominent centres of industrial development in pre-Hellenistic
and Hellenistic times. It is unfortunate that evidence regarding Babylonia
and Phoenicia is so poor. As regards Phoenicia, however, see the preceding
note: Clermont-Ganneau makes it appear very probable that the κοινὸν τῶν
μαχαιροποιῶν of this city was a hellenized Phoenician *gêv*. Note that the name
of the dedicant (Heliodorus), president of the guild, is apparently a Greek
translation of a Semitic name, and that the anonymous 'holy god' to whom
the dedication is made is essentially Semitic (cf. Palmyra).

[28] On the legal development of Hellenistic Egypt see the modern works
quoted in Ch. IV, n. 121. The term πολιτικοὶ νόμοι is used, for example, by
one of the lawyers in the Hermias lawsuit, along with τὰ ψηφίσματα, in
opposition apparently to the Egyptian laws, as the basis of the jurisdiction
of the λαοκρίται, *U.P.Z.* 162, col. vii, ll. 8 ff. On the πολιτικοὶ νόμοι in
Ptolemaic times in general, R. Taubenschlag, *Atti IV Congr. Pap.*, 1936,
p. 259 f. On the terminology of Roman times, E. Bickermann, *Arch. Pap.* ix
(1930), p. 40 f. On the parchments and papyri of Dura and of Avroman, see
above, Ch. IV, n. 221 and Ch. VI, n. 139. In the papers of C. B. Welles quoted
in the former notes the reader will find mention of the contributions of other
scholars to the study of the Dura parchments and papyri. It is unnecessary
to remind the reader that it was L. Mitteis in his *Reichsrecht und Volksrecht
in den östlichen Provinzen des römischen Kaiserreiches*, 1891 (reprinted in
1935), who first postulated the existence of a Hellenistic system of law.
His work had a lasting influence (see L. Wenger, *Ludwig Mitteis und sein
Werk*, 1923, and 'Ludwig Mitteis und die hellenistische Rechtsgeschichte',
Archives d'Hist. du Droit oriental, i (1937), pp. 181 ff., cf. id. *Festschrift Paul
Koschaker*, 1939, p. 7 (of the reprint). Since work on the law of the papyri
is done mostly by Romanists, the main effort is directed not towards the
study of the growth, development, and various aspects of Hellenistic law but
towards that of the relations between the Roman and the little known
Hellenistic law in its different versions within the Roman Empire. On the
Jewish courts in early Roman Egypt, E. R. Goodenough, *The Jurisprudence
of the Jewish Courts in Egypt ... as described by Philo Judaeus*, 1929 (this
book gave rise to a lively controversy, which cannot be discussed here).

[29] I have dealt with the hellenization of natives and the orientalization of
Greeks in the previous chapters. The process is best seen in the sphere of
religious life. The hellenization of native cults was an outstanding pheno-

menon of the spiritual life of the period and has been frequently noticed and described by modern scholars. See, in general, in the first place the classical work of F. Cumont, *Les Religions orientales*[3], 1929, though his main attention is devoted to the period of the Roman Empire, and A. D. Nock, *Conversion*, 1933, but especially K. Latte, 'Religiöse Strömungen in der Frühzeit des Hellenismus', *Die Antike*, i (1925), pp. 146 ff.; W. Schubart, *Die religiöse Haltung des frühen Hellenismus* (Der alte Orient, xxxv. 2), 1937. In O. Kern, *Die Religion der Griechen*, iii (1938), very little is said on this subject. For Egypt in particular I may cite the useful summary of T. A. Brady, *The Reception of the Egyptian Cults by the Greeks* (330–30 B.C.), 1935, cf. E. Visser, *Götter und Kulte im ptolemäischen Alexandrien*, 1938, and F. W. von Bissing, *Ägyptische Kultbilder der Ptolemäer- und Römerzeit* (Der alte Orient, xxxiv. 1, 2), 1936, and for Syria the works of Bikerman and other scholars discussed and cited above in Ch. V, n. 125.

[30] A good bibliography will be found in F. M. Heichelheim, *Wirtschaftsg.*, p. 1113, n. 51. To this bibliography must be added the most important books dealing with Hellenistic literature and especially poetry, such as, for example, A. Rostagni, *Poeti alessandrini*, 1916; U. von Wilamowitz-Moellendorf, *Hellenistische Dichtung*, 1924; A. Körte, *Die hellenistische Dichtung*, 1925; W. W. Tarn, *Hell. Civ.*[2], pp. 235 ff.; and with Hellenistic philosophy as an exponent of Hellenistic mentality, for example, W. W. Tarn, *Antigonos Gonatas*, 1913; J. Kaerst, *Geschichte des Hellenismus*, ii, 2nd ed., 1926, ch. ii, 'Die philosophische Welt- und Lebensanschauung des Hellenismus', pp. 84 ff.; W. S. Ferguson, *C.A.H.* vii, pp. 1 ff. (with bibliography); W. W. Tarn, *Hell. Civ.*[2], pp. 290 ff., and several studies of the Stoics, Epicureans, and Cynics which cannot be listed here (the list would be a long one indeed). An excellent general picture will be found in A. D. Nock, *Conversion*, 1933, and the corresponding sections in the general histories of the Hellenistic Age quoted in Ch. I, n. 1. As regards the role of the metics or κατοικοῦντες in the settlement of the eastern Hellenistic monarchies, see F. M. Heichelheim, loc. cit., cf. A. Rehm, *Arch. f. Kulturg.* xxviii (1938), p. 154 f. (on the spirit of the metics and the part they played in the economic life of the Classical period of Greece).

[31] I cannot deal with this important and hotly debated problem of the constitutional life of the Hellenistic monarchies. I am inclined in general to agree with the view recently supported by E. Bikerman, *Inst. Sél.*, chs. i and ii (cf. above, Ch. I, n. 3), and by P. Jouguet in his substantial review of Bikerman's book, *Bull. Soc. Arch. Alex.* xxxiii (N.S. x. 2) (1939), p. 381 f.

[32] The letters of Zenon, other than those relating to his administrative and economic activity, should be collected and studied more closely than has hitherto been done. He certainly was very much devoted to his family, though it is characteristic of his mentality that his correspondence gives us a very vague picture of his own family life. We do not know for certain whether or not he was married and had children. On his literary interests see *P. Cairo Zen.* 59532–5, cf. G. A. Gerhard, *P. Bad.* 176, Introduction, and below, Addendum to n. 24.

[33] Some remarks on this point will be found in almost all the general works on Hellenistic history. The best presentation from the historical and philosophical points of view, dealing with both theory and practice in Greece in Classical and Hellenistic times, will be found in J. Kaerst, *Gesch. d. Hell.* ii, 2nd ed., ch. iii, 'Der rationalistisch-technische Charakter der hell. Kultur', pp. 146 ff. I do not intend to give here a summary of this chapter. My aim is to demonstrate by a few examples the importance of professionalism in the mentality and the social and economic life of the eastern Hellenistic world, collecting and illustrating material which has been dealt with by modern scholars from points of view different from mine. Cf. the somewhat confused and haphazard bibliography in F. M. Heichelheim, *Wirtschaftsg.*, p. 1100, n. 42.

[34] On the duties and training of the Hellenistic king see the books and articles on the various Hellenistic monarchies quoted in Ch. IV. On the queens cf. G. H. Macurdy, *Hellenistic Queens* (Johns Hopkins Univ. St. Arch. xiv), 1932, and on the later princesses her *Vassal Queens . . . in the Roman Empire* (ibid. xxii), 1937. On the treatises περὶ βασιλείας see above, Chs. III, nn. 15 and 24, and IV, nn. 83. I cannot here deal with these treatises at length. A careful collection of all the material is very much needed. Of the modern works dealing with this question, besides the general works on Hellenistic kingship quoted in my Chs. III and IV, I may cite at random the Marburg dissertation of G. Burner, *Comparantur inter se Graeci de regentium hominum virtutibus auctores*, 1889; W. W. Tarn, *Antigonos Gonatas*, pp. 254 ff.; J. Kaerst, *Gesch. d. Hell.* ii, 2nd ed., pp. 296 ff.; E. R. Goodenough, 'The political philosophy of Hellenistic Kingship', *Yale Class. Stud.* i, 1928, pp. 55 ff.; J. Bidez, *La Cité du monde* &c., pp. 26 ff. (267 ff.) (quoted in full, Ch. IV, n. 232); U. von Wilamowitz-Moellendorff, *Der Glaube der Hellenen*, ii, p. 284, n. 1. I may, however, point out that treatises περὶ βασιλείας are attested among the works of almost all the philosophical schools. In order to make this clear to the reader I may give some instances (fullness is not attempted). The subject was most popular with the early and late STOICS. I shall confine myself to the former: Persaeus, *S.V.F.* i, p. 96, no. 435; Cleanthes, ibid. i, p. 107, no. 481; Sphaerus, ibid. i, p. 139, no. 620; Chrysippus, ibid. iii, pp. 158 ff., nos. 617–22, cf. pp. 172 ff., nos. 685–9, 691 and 693. Stoics, natives of the Seleucid kingdom: see above, Ch. IV, n. 232. On Suidas' fragments, above, Ch. III, n. 24. For EPICURUS and his school, H. Usener, *Epicurea*, p. 94, cf. Philod. περὶ τοῦ καθ᾽ Ὅμηρον ἀγαθοῦ βασιλέως ed. Olivieri, 1909. The attitude of the CYNICS towards kingship may be inferred from some of their utterances. See, for example, the occasional remarks of Teles concerning the kings. The leading idea is that there is no essential difference between a king and an ordinary person, and that his power and wealth do not protect the king from need and distress. See Teles (ed. Hense): περὶ πενίας καὶ πλούτου p. 43, 9, cf. 37; περὶ φυγῆς p. 24, cf. 23; περὶ αὐταρκείας p. 5 f. On Teles, D. R. Dudley, *A History of Cynicism*, 1937, pp. 84 ff. PERIPATETICS: treatise ascribed to Aristotle, V. Rose, *Aristot. Fr.*, sect. lii, frs. 646–7; Theophrastus, Dion. Hal. v. 73; *P. Oxyr.* 1611, ll. 38 ff.

NEO-PYTHAGOREANS, E. R. Goodenough, loc. cit., cf. A. Delatte, *Essai sur la politique pythagoricienne*, 1922, p. 42 f. On the date of the various treatises, see above, Ch. III, n. 15. I may note that the justification of avarice on the part of a king by Diotogenes (Stob. iv. 7. 61 ff.) may indicate that this philosopher had Alexandrian connexions. I may quote as a curiosity the advice to the king (or to a king) to follow the economic policy of the Persian kings, *P. Ryl.* 20.

35 On Ptolemaic administration see all the general books which deal with the history and structure of Ptolemaic Egypt, especially Wilcken's *Grundzüge*, and Schubart's *Einführung*, and the works of Bouché-Leclercq, Mahaffy–Bevan, and Jouguet on the history of Ptolemaic Egypt. In addition to these there are several special books, papers, and articles. An interesting survey of the results of modern investigation will be found in V. Martin, 'Les Papyrus et l'histoire administrative de l'Égypte gréco-romaine', in 'Papyri und Altertumsw.', *Münch. Beitr.* xix, 1934, pp. 102 ff. A good up-to-date bibliography will be found in C. Préaux, *Écon. Lag.*, cf. *C.A.H.* vii, pp. 116 ff. and 893. On the professional training of aspirants to an administrative post see the remarks of U. Wilcken, *U.P.Z.*, p. 474. It is highly probable that the roll which contains the documents *U.P.Z.* 110, 144, and 145 was written by one of these aspirants, who copied some official documents which were regarded by his teachers as excellent examples of the official style. He added some other material (astrological), probably on his own account. Cf. Addendum to this note. On the moral principles which were supposed to underlie the conduct of Ptolemaic officials and were incorporated in the ἐντολαί (instructions) of a practical character issued by the king and higher officials of the crown to their subordinates, see above, Ch. IV, n. 83; cf. *Teb.* 703, Intr., p. 71, where I quoted a very interesting fragment of a comedy which reflects such treatises, A. Körte, *Arch. Pap.* vii (1927), p. 257. On the administrative structure of the Seleucid kingdom, E. Bikerman, *Inst. Sél.*, chs. ii and v, and above, Ch. IV, p. 440, n. 241. On the Pergamene kingdom, see the bibliography given in my sections on it, Chs. IV, V, and VI.

36 On the Ptolemaic army and navy, *C.A.H.* vii, pp. 116 ff., and bibliography, p. 893; cf. above, Ch. III, n. 7, and Ch. IV, n. 91. On the Seleucid army, E. Bikerman, *Inst. Sél.*, ch. iii. On the Pergamene army, *C.A.H.* viii, pp. 594 ff. and 788 f.; cf. above, Chs. IV and V.

37 On the treatises on tactics, J. Kromayer in J. Kromayer und G. Veith, 'Heerwesen und Kriegführung der Griechen und Römer', *Handb. d. Altertumsw.* iv. 3. 2, 1928, pp. 9 ff., especially pp. 12 ff. on Aeneas Tacticus (357/6 B.C.) and the later treatises. The only treatise of Hellenistic times is that of Asclepiodotus, a pupil of Posidonius, which was used by Aelian in the time of Trajan and through him by Arrian.

38 The question of the date of the known authors of poliorcetics and belopoiïcs is hotly debated. We know with certainty the dates of Ctesibius (time of Ptolemy II) and Biton (time of Attalus I) and of Philon of Byzantium

(about 250 B.C.). Opinions about the dates of Heron and Athenaeus are divided. But there is no doubt that all the extant treatises go back to the Hellenistic period and that the Romans did not add very much to the inventions of this time. See E. Schramm in Kromayer–Veith, loc. cit., pp. 209 ff.; Orinsky, art. *Μηχανή*, *P.W.K.* xv. 10 ff.; E. Pernice, 'Literarische Zeugnisse', in W. Otto, *Handb. d. Archäologie*, ii, 1937, pp. 260 ff. (with collaboration of A. Rehm); A. Rehm, *Phil.* xcii (1937–8), p. 319, n. 1, and *Arch. f. Kulturg.* xxviii (1938), p. 143. The excavation of the arsenals of Pergamon is very important: Ákos von Szalay und E. Boehringer, 'Die hellenistischen Arsenale', *Alt. v. Perg.* x, 1937, cf. my Pl. LXXI. It may be mentioned that hundreds of stone bullets exactly like those found in Pergamon have been excavated in Dura. They are remains of the last siege of Dura. Excellent analyses of extant fortifications of Hellenistic cities will be found in F. Krischen, 'Die Befestigungen von Herakleia am Latmos', *Milet: Erg. d. Ausgr.* iii. 2, 1922; A. von Gerkan, 'Die Stadtmauern', ibid. ii. 3, 1935, esp. pp. 124 ff., and his chapter in *Dura Rep.* vii-viii, 1939, ch. i, on the fortifications of Dura; cf. my *Dura-Europos and its Art*, p. 11 f. On naval warfare and the technical staff on the warships of the Rhodian navy, above, Ch. V, pp. 685 ff., nn. 100 and 101; cf. A. Köster in Kromayer–Veith, loc. cit., pp. 163 ff.

[39] Much has been written on the Museum of Alexandria. A good summary (with bibliography) will be found in the article *Μουσεῖον* by Müller–Graupa, *P.W.K.* xvi. 801 ff. The members of the museum enjoyed *ateleia* and received both board and lodging and a certain stipend. The expression *ἀτελεῖς σιτούμενοι ἐν τῶι Μουσείωι* is the official title of the members of the 'association of worshippers of the Muses' in Alexandria.

[40] On the Dionysiac *technitai*, above, n. 16. An interesting list of members and affiliated members will be found in the well-known inscription of Ptolemais, *O.G.I.* 51; cf. W. Peremans, *Vreemdelingen*, pp. 135 ff., and B. D. Meritt, *Hesp.* vii (1938), pp. 77 ff., no. 22. On Pergamon see above, Chs. IV and V, bibliography in n. 16, above, and on the Seleucids the full collection of our meagre information by E. Bikerman, *Inst. Sél.*, pp. 38 ff.

[41] I may refer to the recent treatment of this subject by M. Guarducci, 'Poeti vaganti e conferenzieri dell' età ellenistica', *Mem. Acc. Lincei*, Ser. VI, ii (1926–29), pp. 629 ff., cf. L. Robert, *Rev. Arch.* 5 sér. xxiv (1926), pp. 173 ff.; *B.C.H.* liii (1929), pp. 34 ff. Most of the inscriptions referring to poets come from Delphi and Delos. Inscriptions mentioning travelling musicians, historians, grammarians, philosophers, and even lecturing doctors are found all over the Hellenistic world.

[42] L. Robert, 'Pantomimen im griechischen Orient', *Hermes*, lxv (1930), pp. 106 ff., cf. his article in *R.E.G.* xlix (1936), pp. 235–54 (*ἀρχαιολόγοι, μειμολόγοι, βιολόγοι*).

[43] On acrobats and in general on 'Fahrendes Volk', H. Blümner, 'Fahrendes Volk im Altertum', *Bay. S.B.*, 1918, pp. 12 ff.; rope-dancers (*σκανδαλισταί*)

*S.I.G.*³ 847 ; A. Wilhelm, *Wien. Anz.*, 1922, ii–vii, pp. 17 ff. on the θαυματοποιοί in general, especially at Delphi, cf. L. Robert, *B.C.H.* lii (1928), pp. 422 ff. ; *R.E.G.* xlii (1929), pp. 433 ff., and W. Kroll, *P.W.K.* Suppl. vi. 1278 ff. Castanet-dancers are well attested for Egypt in Roman times, W. L. Westermann, 'The castanet dancers of Arsinoe', *J.E.A.* x (1924), pp. 134 ff., cf. ibid. xviii (1932), pp. 16 ff., and *P. Corn.* 9. Dwarfs, mimes, &c., as castanet-dancers and male and female dancers were favourite subjects of Hellenistic and later of Roman art. For the Hellenistic period I may refer to the famous dancing dwarfs of Mahdia (see my Pl. LXXXIV) ; cf. several similar bronze figurines of Galjûb (descr. of Pl. LXXXI), reproduced and described by A. Ippel, *Der Bronzefund von Galjûb*, 1922, pp. 45 ff., nos. 30–5, pl. iv. A set of other bronze figurines which represent the castanet dancers of Hellenistic and Roman times has been published and discussed in a masterly way by P. Perdrizet, *Bronzes grecs d'Égypte de la coll. Fouquet*, 1911, pp. 62 ff., nos. 101–3, and pls. xxix–xxxi ; cf. P. Ducati, *Jahreshefte* xiii (1911), pp. 167 ff., and I. Noshy, *The Arts in Ptolemaic Egypt*, 1937, p. 101, and in general pp. 97 ff. Copious material concerning the grotesque dancing figures used as decorative motifs on various products of minor or applied arts, has been collected by R. Zahn, *Amtl. Ber. Kön. Kunsts.* xxxv (1913–14), pp. 301 ff. and id. *Κτῶ χρῶ, Winckelmannspr.* lxxxi (1921).

⁴⁴ I shall not be expected to enumerate here even the leading works on Greek athletics and their history. The list would be endless. On the associations of professional atheletes, G. Glotz, 'Xystus' in Dar. et Saglio, *D.d.A.* v. 1027 ff. On the role of athletics in Greece in general, E. N. Gardiner, *Athletics of the Ancient World*, 1930.

⁴⁵ The comparatively abundant evidence on the medical profession in the Greek cities has been collected several times. See R. Pohl, *De graecorum medicis publicis*, Diss. Berl., 1905, esp. pp. 19 ff., a list of inscriptions which mention public doctors ; of twelve inscriptions of the pre-Roman period eleven belong to Hellenistic times ; on pp. 20 ff. are recorded the inscriptions relating to doctors who were honoured for their services by the cities ; many of them belong to Hellenistic times. Veterinaries: *I.G.* ix. 2. 69 ; *G.D.I.* 1447. Many additions to the lists of Pohl will be found in J. Oehler, 'Epigraphische Beiträge zur Geschichte des Ärztestandes', *Progr. Maximilians Gymnasium* in Vienna, 1907. An excellent summary of all the evidence, literary, epigraphical, and archaeological, on doctors, veterinaries, and druggists will be found in S. Reinach's art. 'Medicus' in Dar. et Saglio, *D.d.A.* iii. 1669 ff., and his art. 'Mulomedicina', ibid. 2011 ff. Cf. the interesting collection of some important texts of ancient medical writers (with translations) referring to the professional activity of the doctors by W. Müri, *Der Arzt im Altertum*, 1938. Since the time of Pohl, Oehler, and S. Reinach many new inscriptions and bas-reliefs referring to or representing doctors of the Hellenistic period have been found and some previously known inscriptions have been revised. I may quote some of them, without aiming at completeness.

Especially abundant is the series of inscriptions relating to COAN DOCTORS and found mostly at Cos. Some of them have not been published. They are mostly decrees of foreign cities in honour of Coan doctors: Cnossus (Crete)— R. Herzog, *J.D.A.I.* xviii (1903), Anz., p. 11; *S.I.G.*³ 528 (221–219 B.C.); *Inscr. Cret.* i. viii, no. 7* (for Hermias, a Coan doctor sent to Cnossus by the city of Cos); *Gortyn* (Crete)—L. Laurenzi, *Historia*, v (1931), p. 620 f. (for the same doctor, unpublished); *Aptera* (Crete), decree of second century B.C. for a Coan doctor, similar to the two preceding—R. Herzog, loc. cit., p. 198 (unpublished); *Iasus* (Caria), third century B.C.—R. Herzog, loc. cit. (unpublished); *Halicarnassus* (Caria)—Paton–Hicks, no. 13; L. Robert, *Rev. Phil.* xiii (65) (1939), p. 163 f.; *Delos—Historia*, v (1931), p. 620 (unpublished); *Delphi* (found at Delphi)—*B.C.H.* xxvi (1902), p. 269 f. (218/7 B.C.) In addition I may cite two decrees of Coan villages in honour of doctors— R. Herzog, loc. cit., p. 198 (unpublished). On the medical school of Cos and its activity outside Cos cf. R. Herzog, *J.D.A.I.* xlvii (1932), Anz., pp. 274 ff.; *Kos: Erg. d. Ausgr.* i, 1932, p. 72 f.; 'Die Asklepiosheiligtümer als Heilstätten und Gnadenorte', *Münch. Med. Wochenschr.*, Jubiläumsausgabe, 1933, pp. 1 ff.; cf. above, Ch. IV, n. 70.

Next to Cos comes DELPHI with a rich crop of inscriptions in honour of doctors. I may refer to a few of them: above under Cos, and L. Robert, *B.C.H.* lii (1928), pp. 172 ff., cf. the decree in honour of certain doctors of Pergamene origin but employed or educated in the Alexandrian Museum— A. Wilhelm, *Wien. Anz.*, 1922, pp. 20 ff.; *S.E.G.* ii. 332. In addition I may mention at random some typical decrees of other cities: ATHENS (for a Rhodian doctor, 304/3 B.C.), *S.I.G.*³ 335; GYTHIUM, above, Ch. VII, p. 952, n. 27; ELATEA (doctor as lecturer, second century B.C.), *I.G.* ix. 1. 104; A. Wilhelm, *Wien. Anz.*, lxi (1924), pp. 130 ff., no. 7; *S.E.G.* iii. 416; M. Guarducci, 'Poeti vaganti e conferenzieri dell'età ellenistica', *Mem. Acc. Lincei*, Ser. VI. ii (1926–29), pp. 629 ff.; SAMOS (decree of about 200 B.C. in honour of a public doctor of the city who was in its employment for several years and rendered splendid service during earthquakes), G. Klaffenbach, *Ath. Mitt.* li (1926), p. 28 f.; L. Robert, *B.C.H.* lii (1928), p. 178; A. Wilhelm, *Wien. S.B.* cclxiv (1932–3), pp. 48 ff.; L. Robert, *Rev. Phil.* xiii (65) (1939), p. 165 f.; TENOS and the Nesiotai (for a Milesian doctor, after 188 B.C.), *S.I.G.*³ 620; ANDROS, W. Peek, *Ath. Mitt.* lix (1934), pp. 67 ff., no. 23; ERESOS (Lesbos), *R.E.G.* li (1938), p. 448; PARIUM (benefactor paying for the services of a doctor during a fair, early second century B.C.), *S.I.G.*³ 596; COLOPHON (decree of the Asclepiasts of this city), *S.E.G.* iv. 566; L. Robert, *Rev. Phil.* viii (60) (1934), p. 272, no. XXXV; MESEMBRIA, A. Salač, *Rev. Arch.*, 6 sér., x (1937), pp. 14 ff.

The combination of scientific medicine and religious healing and the co-existence of the two in the same health resorts are best illustrated by the inscriptions of Epidaurus—R. Herzog, *Die Wunderheilungen von Epidauros*, &c., 1931 (a bibliography of the numerous works dealing with these inscriptions cannot be given here)—and by the history of the Asclepieum of Pergamon (the city was one of the great centres of medical research, especially in Roman times), for which see O. Deubner, *Das Asklepieion von Pergamon*,

1938; cf. R. Herzog, 'Ein Asklepios-Hymnus des Aristeides von Smyrna', *Berl. S.B.*, 1934, pp. 753 ff., and L. Robert, *Ét. Anat.*, pp. 384 ff. (on other Asclepieia). Cf. Addendum to this note.

⁴⁶ On the social standing of doctors in Greek cities, see preceding n. The best collection and illustration of surgical instruments will be found in J. S. Milne, *Surgical Instruments in Greek and Roman Times*, 1907; additions to his bibliography in H. Diels, *Antike Technik*, 3rd ed., 1924, p. 26 f., cf. also G. Lafaye, 'Note sur deux instruments antiques de chirurgie vétérinaire', *Bull. Soc. Ant. France*, 1927, pp. 194 ff. Medical analysis of some gynaeco-logical instruments: E. Buchheim, *Die geburtshilflichen Operationen und zugehörigen Instrumente des klassischen Altertums*, 1916, pp. 42 ff. (diss. Jena), and J. Kalthoff, *Die theoretischen und praktischen Grundlagen der operativen Geburtshilfe der Hippokratiker*, 1933, pp. 27 ff. (diss. München). I cannot quote here the many new finds of surgical instruments made since Diels's book was published. Very illuminating is the group found at Colophon, R. Caton, *J.H.S.* xxxiv (1914), pp. 116 ff., pls. x–xii. No new corpus of surgical instruments and no study of them from the historical point of view are known to me (cf. below, Add. to this note). On bandages see the excellent paper of J. Ilberg, 'Verbände in der griechischen und römischen Heilkunde', *Zeitschr. für Samariter- und Rettungswesen*, 1911, n. 24. Drugs and druggists: Theophrast. *Hist. pl.* ix. 16. 8, and 17; Teles περὶ φυγῆς (ed. Hense), p. 18: ὥσπερ εἰ τὸν ἄριστον ἰατρὸν ἀφέντες φαρμακοπώλην εἵλοντο καὶ τούτῳ τὸ δημόσιον ἔργον ἐνεχείρισαν. On drugs and pharmacies, S. Reinach, loc. cit., pp. 1679 ff.; A. Schmidt, *Drogen und Drogenhandel im Altertum*, 1924, pp. 75 ff., and 'Drogen', *P.W.K.* Suppl. v. 172 ff., cf. W. Morel, 'Pharmacopoles' *P.W.K.* xix. 1840 ff. and ibid. Suppl. vi. 1278, and H. Diller, *Wunderarzt und Aitiologe*, 1934. On pharmacological treatises, M. Wellmann, *Hermes*, lix (1924), pp. 129 ff., cf. ibid. lxviii (1933), pp. 93 ff.

⁴⁷ On the court physicians in the service of the Hellenistic kings, S. Reinach, loc. cit., pp. 1689 ff., cf. M. Wellmann, 'Beiträge zur Geschichte der Medizin im Altertum', *Hermes*, lxv (1930), pp. 322 ff., and on the Seleucids, E. Bikerman, *Inst. Sél.*, p. 36 f. 'Chief-doctor' of Antiochus IX Cyzicenus—*O.G.I.* 256; *Inscr. de Délos*, 1547. The office appears here as a court office. Craterus was first 'educator' of the king (τροφεύς), then 'chief-doctor', and finally chamberlain of the queen. And so was the chief-doctor of Mithridates VI, *Inscr. de Délos*, 1573. I cannot here deal with the history of medicine and the part played in its evolution by the schools of Alexandria, Pergamon, and Antioch, but I may refer to some recent works on its history: I. L. Heiberg, *Mathematics and Physical Science in Classical Antiquity*, 1922 (with short bibliography), and 'Gesch. der Mathematik und Naturwissen-schaften im Altertum', *Handb. der Altertumsw.* v. 1. 2, 1925; Ch. Singer, *Greek Biology and Greek Medicine*, 1922; G. Senn, *Die Entwicklung der biologischen Forschungsmethode in der Antike*, &c., 1933 (with copious biblio-graphy); A. Rehm und K. Vogel, 'Exacte Wissenschaften', in Gercke u. Norden, *Einleitung in d. Altertumsw.* ii. 2. 5, 4th ed., p. 58 f.; G. Sarton,

Introduction to the History of Science, i, 1927, esp. pp. 158 ff. and 175 ff. On the part taken by the Coan doctors in founding the medical schools in the great Hellenistic monarchies see the papers of R. Herzog quoted above in n. 45. Cf. Addendum to this note.

⁴⁸ On physicians as members of the Museum, Müller–Graupa, 'Μουσεῖον', *P.W.K.* xvi. 813; A. Wilhelm, *Wien. Anz.*, lix (1922), p. 20 f.; *S.E.G.* ii. 332; L. Robert, *B.C.H.* lii (1928), p. 178, cf. above, n. 45 (doctors of Pergamene origin trained in the Alexandrian Museum). On the organization of medical service in Egypt and on the ἰατρικόν, K. Sudhoff, *Ärztliches aus griechischen Papyrus-Urkunden*, 1909, esp. pp. 254 ff. and 266 ff.; U. Wilcken, *Ostraka*, i, 1899, pp. 375 ff.; C. Préaux, *Écon. Lag.*, pp. 45 and 132 f.; E. Breccia, *Bull. Soc. Arch. Alex.* xiv (1912), N.S. iii, p. 195. Note that in addition to the ἰατρικόν a special tax was paid by the cleruchs for the service of veterinaries (ἱππιατρικόν). No mention of the tax, since it was not levied in Roman Egypt, in Sh. L. Wallace, *Taxation in Egypt*, 1938.

⁴⁹ See art. Συνήγορος, *P.W.K.* iv A. pp. 1353 ff. (Athens in the fourth century B.C. by Latte, and Egypt by Seidl). Cf. the comments of U. Wilcken on *U.P.Z.* 161 and 162. No collection of material illustrating the activity of professional lawyers in Hellenistic times outside Egypt is known to me, though συνήγοροι are frequently mentioned in Hellenistic inscriptions as assisting the parties. See Addendum to this note.

⁵⁰ On the typical Greeks of Ptolemaic Egypt, above, Chs. IV, V, and VI. On the prevailing mood of the Greeks of the Eastern *diaspora* I may quote in addition to the works listed above, n. 30, my short Ingersoll Lecture: *The Mentality of the Hellenistic World and the After-life*, 1939.

⁵¹ I have dealt with slavery in Asia Minor in the sections of the preceding chapters devoted to that region and especially to the Pergamene kingdom (above, Chs. V and VI, cf. F. M. Heichelheim, *Wirtschaftsg.*, pp. 640 ff.). Holidays granted to slaves as to schoolboys are attested by many inscriptions collected and interpreted by L. Robert, *B.C.H.* lvii (1933), p. 521, esp. the decrees of Pergamon of 129 B.C., *S.I.G.*³ 694, l. 55, and of Magnesia *S.I.G.*³ 695, l. 25. Some texts which may be interpreted as referring to opportunities given to slaves of receiving a good education have been collected by E. Ziebarth, *Aus dem griechischen Schulwesen*, 2nd ed., 1914, p. 39, n. 1. I may quote in this connexion the formula 'schools for free boys' frequently used in deeds of donation. Does it mean that there existed schools where free boys sat on the same benches with slaves?

⁵² The best studies of the Greek cities in the Hellenistic period are those of W. W. Tarn quoted in Ch. IV, n. 2. Cf. the corresponding sections in my Chs. IV, V, VI, and VII.

⁵³ I know of no full collection of the few references in our literary and epigraphical sources to the salaries and wages of the *technitai* in Hellenistic times. The best known rates of remuneration are those of soldiers. I have

spoken of them above, Ch. III, n. 7. On the salaries of school-teachers, above, p. 1087 f. The highest recorded salary is that of a doctor (1000 drachmas a year), W. W. Tarn, *Hell. Civ.*², p. 100; cf. A. Wilhelm, *Neue Beitr.* iv, p. 56 f. From this scanty material we may draw one general conclusion. The average remuneration of technical service (with few exceptions) was about 1 dr. a day, sometimes less, sometimes a little more. The salary of a 'foreman' (for example a ἡγεμών in the military service) was no more than double the salary of a common *technites*. This shows how low was the standard of life of a *technites*: little more than a living wage, while the unskilled or half-skilled hired hands earned a little less than this living wage. Officers and soldiers had of course the prospect of living in enemy country at the expense of the population, of acquiring their own private booty, of receiving bonuses from their employers in case of victory. But we must not forget that their remuneration included not only the price of their skill but also that of their blood and life. Cf. H. Francotte, *L'Industrie dans la Grèce anc.* i (1900), pp. 309 ff.; F. M. Heichelheim, *Wirtschaftliche Schwankungen*, p. 125.

54 On the picture of Athenian life given by Menander and other contemporary writers and on the economic aspects of the life of the Athenian *bourgeoisie* of this period see above, Ch. III, pp. 161 ff. and n. 37; cf. A. Körte, 'Die Menschen Menanders', *Ber. Sächs. Akad.*, phil.-hist. Kl. lxxxix, 3 (1937), pp. 3 ff. (mentality of Menander's characters). On the *bourgeoisie* of Cos, above, Ch. IV, pp. 236 ff., and notes 70 ff. It is impossible to cite here all that has been written on Menander and the New Comedy in general and on Herondas and Theocritus. Many literary studies on these authors contain interesting remarks on the life and mentality of the men whose pictures are drawn by them. Cf. the references given above, n. 30.

55 I have never come across a study which endeavoured to present a full picture of the Greek *bourgeoisie* of Hellenistic times; cf. the bibliography given above in nn. 22 and 30.

56 The only statistical data about the numbers of the *bourgeoisie* at Athens are those reported by Diodorus (xviii. 18. 4–5) for 322 B.C. By order of Antipater the franchise was restricted to those who possessed more than 2,000 drachmas (reduced by Cassander to 1,000 at the time when Demetrius of Phalerum was appointed *epimeletes*, Diod. xviii. 74. 3). The number of these was 9,000, while those who were excluded numbered 12,000 (correction of 22,000), cf. Plut. *Phoc.* 28. 4. The total sum of citizens is the same as that of the census of Demetrius of Phalerum (the date is disputed: at the beginning of the rule of Demetrius, or 309 B.C.), which we know from Ctesicles (Stesicleides ?) of Athens (Athen. vi, p. 272 c; fr. 1, *F. Gr. Hist.* 245, cf. F. Jacoby's note ad loc.). The restriction of Antipater is explained by Diodorus as a political measure aimed at creating quiet conditions at Athens by the exclusion of all unruly elements from the roll of citizens. The nine thousand possessing more than 2,000 drachmas each were regarded by Antipater as quiet and reliable elements who would not desire *res novae*, the

well-to-do conservative *bourgeoisie* of Athens. On the census of Demetrius of Phalerum, see p. 1135 and n. 70.

[57] Much has been written on the various philosophical schools of the period. I cannot enumerate here all the histories of ancient philosophy and the monographs dealing with the Hellenistic schools of philosophy. I may, however, mention in addition to references in n. 30 some works in which the reader will find a detailed treatment of the attitude of the Stoics to political life. On Zenon's Πολιτεία, N. Festa, *I frammenti degli Stoici Antichi*, 1932, pp. 9 ff., and J. von Arnim, *S.V.F.* i, nos. 259–71. Cf. the most recent treatments of Stoic ethics in general: O. Rieth, *Grundbegriffe der stoischen Ethik*, 1933 (Problemata IX), cf. id., 'Ueber das Telos der Stoiker', *Hermes*, lxix (1934), pp. 13 ff.; E. Elorduy, 'Die Sozialphilosophie der Stoa', *Philol.*, Suppl. xxviii. 3 (1936) (with ample bibliography), and R. Philippson, 'Zur Psychologie der Stoa', *Rh. Mus.* lxvi (1937), pp. 140 ff. On the attitude of Panaetius and the Middle Stoa, W. Gemoll, *Der stoische Philosoph Hekaton*, 1934, and especially M. Pohlenz, 'Antikes Führertum: Cicero *de officiis* und das Lebensideal des Panaitios', *Neue Wege zur Antike*, ii. 3 (1934), and Lotte Labowsky, *Die Ethik des Panaitios*, 1934.

[58] The best collection of material illustrating the traditional religious life of the Greek cities in the Hellenistic period will be found in U. von Wilamowitz–Moellendorff, *Der Glaube der Hellenen*, ii, 1932, and O. Kern, *Die Religion der Griechen*, iii, 1938, pp. 152 ff. On the epiphanies of the gods in Hellenistic times, see above, Ch. VII. A complete and exhaustive treatment of the subject has, however, never been attempted.

[59] I have collected some material illustrating this activity of the city *bourgeoisie* in the preceding chapters, esp. Ch. V, pp. 618 ff. A fuller and better collection and study of the evidence may prove of great use to students of Hellenistic history. It has never been attempted. It must be based on a careful study of the life and ruins of the Hellenistic cities. A tabulation similar to that made by T. R. S. Broughton in his 'Roman Asia Minor' for the cities of Asia Minor in Roman times may yield very important results.

[60] My ideas on the tenacity, or rather the immortality (ἀθανασία, Isocr. *de pace*, p. 183 d), of the Greek city coincide to some extent with what J. Burckhardt had to say on the subject in his *Griechische Kulturgeschichte* (Gesamtausgabe, viii. i, 1930, p. 261). The new cities of the Oriental extension of the Greek world continued under the patronage of the kings, though in changed conditions and in their own way, the traditions of the ancient Greek city-state.

[61] On the sociological studies and ideas of Plato and Aristotle see A. Menzel, 'Griechische Soziologie', *Wien. S.B.*, phil.-hist. Kl. ccxvi. 1 (1936), who shows how keenly Plato and still more Aristotle considered the leading sociological questions and how in many respects they anticipated modern ideas on this subject. On the special problem of wealth and poverty as

viewed in the pre-Hellenistic period, see the Utrecht dissertation of J. Hemelrijk, *Πενία en Πλοῦτος*, 1925 (in Dutch with German résumé). The Hellenistic period (together with that of the Roman Empire) has been recently examined in another Utrecht dissertation: J. J. van Manen, *Πενία en Πλοῦτος in de periode na Alexander*, 1931 (in Dutch). I regret that my ignorance of the Dutch language has prevented me from making full use of this interesting paper. Cf. also some other studies quoted by F. M. Heichelheim, *Wirtschaftsg.*, p. 1114, n. 52. On the class struggle in Greece see my remarks in the sections dealing with that country in Chs. IV, V, and VI. I may refer again to the fine summary of F. Oertel, 'Die soziale Frage im Altertum', *N.J.f. Wiss. u. Jugendb.* iii (1927), pp. 1 ff.

[62] For Zenon cf. Diog. Laert. vii. 106; for Chrysippus *S.V.F.* iii, fr. 623, 689, and in general the Index to *S.V.F.*, s. vv. *Πλοῦτος* and *Πενία*.

[63] Epicurus and the Epicureans: frs. A, 25, 44*, 58, 67 (quoted in the text); D, 72 and 73 (Bailey), cf. Vita Epicuri 120ᵃ and 121ᵇ. On these and other fragments, C. Bailey, *The Greek Atomists and Epicurus*, 1928, p. 501; F. Castaldi, 'Il concetto della ricchezza in Epicuro', *Rend. Acc. Lincei*, Cl. di Sc. Mor., &c., Ser. 6, iv (1928), pp. 287 ff.

[64] R. von Pöhlmann, *Gesch. der Soz. Frage*, ii, 1925, pp. 274 ff.; J. Kaerst, *Gesch. d. Hell.* ii², 1926, pp. 149 ff., cf. 181 ff. and 373 ff.; W. W. Tarn, *Hell. Civ.²*, pp. 112 ff.; cf. above, Ch. VI.

[65] See E. Elorduy, 'Die Sozialphilosophie der Stoa', *Philol.*, Suppl. xxviii. 3 (1936), pp. 194 ff.; cf. above, n. 61.

[66] See F. Wilhelm, 'Die Oeconomica der Neupythagoreer Bryson, Kallikratidas, Periktione, Phintys', *Rh. Mus.* lxx (1915), pp. 161 ff., cf. A. Delatte, *Essai sur la politique pythagoricienne*, 1922 (Bibl. de la Fac. de Phil., &c., de l'Univ. de Liége, xxix), pp. 42 ff. (on *πενία* and *πλοῦτος* in the *Πυθαγορικαὶ ἀποφάσεις* of Aristoxenus) and p. 156 (similar doctrine of Hippodamus), cf. pp. 160 ff. (on Callicratidas). See also pseudo-Ocellus Lucanus, ed. R. Harder, 1926, paragrs. 52–7 and 46.

[67] On Menander see above, n. 54. On *πενία* and *πλοῦτος* as treated by Hellenistic poets, M. Pohlenz, 'Die hellenistische Poesie und die Philosophie', *Χάριτες* (Leos Festschrift), 1911, pp. 76 ff.

[68] Titles of the middle and new comedy referring to a profession occur occasionally, such as Menander's *Ἁλιεῖς, Γεωργός, Κιθαριστής, Κυβερνῆται, Ναύκληρος, Χαλκεῖα* and similar titles of comedies by other authors (see Kock's Index). But the extant fragments of the *Γεωργός* (Menander, *Reliquiae*, ed. A. Körte, i, 1937, pp. xlii ff. and 91 ff.) show that Menander's *γεωργός* was a well-to-do landowner, and those of *Κιθαριστής* (ibid., pp. xlvi ff. and 104 ff.) that the comedy was a regular *bourgeois* comedy, the *κιθαριστής* being a respectable Athenian citizen whose daughter was probably the heroine of the play; what role the father played in the comedy we do not know. We are

therefore unable even to guess whether or not in such comedies as the Αἰπόλοι of Alexis, Ἀμπελουργός of the same author, Ζωγράφος of several authors, Καπήλιδες of Theopompus, Κηπουρός of Antiphanes, Μυλωθρίς of Eubulus, Μυλωθρός of Alexis, Μυλών of Antiphanes, Σκυτεύς of Eubulus, Φαρμακοπώλης of Alexis and Mnesimachus, Χρυσοχόος of Anaxilas and Diphilus, the titles indicate that the life of men of these professions was represented on the stage. As regards the mimes, similar titles first appear among those of Laberius, but some 'Megarian' bowls suggest that the life of professionals and workmen formed the subject of earlier Hellenistic mimes. See my article in *A.J.A.* xli (1937), p. 99, and the description of Pl. xxv of this book.

CHAPTER VIII, PART II

[69] The standard work on the population of the ancient world is still the brilliant book by K. J. Beloch, *Die Bevölkerung der griechisch-römischen Welt*, 1886. The conclusions of this book are repeated, sometimes in slightly modified form, in the same author's *Griechische Geschichte*, and have been used extensively by other historians of the ancient world as a starting-point for their own calculations. Beloch's work ought to be carefully revised in the light of new evidence and reprinted. But even in a revised form it will retain its former character. The calculation of the population of the ancient world is based, in some cases, on the few (very few) figures which give the number of inhabitants of a certain part of it at a certain moment, the figures being mostly ambiguous and open to various interpretations. But in most cases the total population is derived by modern scholars from specific figures, casually mentioned in our texts, relating to the size of the armies and navies mobilized at a given moment, or to that of various political bodies, or to the quantity of corn consumed by the population, or to some other similar factor. Failing these, the population is estimated according to the size of the inhabited territory, whether that of some city or of a larger section of the inhabited area. It is obvious that conclusions drawn from such material are necessarily problematical and therefore controversial. Moreover they refer to certain moments only, and very seldom throw light upon the fluctuations of the population in one part or another of the ancient world.

[70] On the population of Athens and Attica in the fourth century B.C. see above, Ch. II, p. 95, and n. 30. On the census of Demetrius of Phaleron (Ctesicles or Stesicleides of Athens, fr. 1), *F. Gr. Hist.* 245, see W. S. Ferguson, *H.A.*, pp. 54 and 97, and the other modern contributions quoted in Ch. II, n. 30 (cf. F. Jacoby, note to fr. 1, *F. Gr. Hist.* 245, and P. Roussel in G. Glotz, *Hist. gr.* iv. 1, 1938, p. 327). According to Ferguson the total number of inhabitants was between 200,000 and 250,000 including the metics and slaves, a slight decrease as compared with the late fourth century. Later, even after the recovery of the early second century B.C., the population of Athens and Attica never reached the old level, though it did not decrease catastrophically. According to Ferguson (*H.A.*, p. 316 f.) the inhabitants of Attica, including metics and slaves, may, after the time of Perseus, have

numbered from 100,000 to 150,000, that is to say, 100 to 150 per square mile,
cf. K. J. Beloch, *Gr. Gesch.*² iv. 1, p. 279, n. 2. On the population of the
Peloponnese in the Hellenistic period, K. J. Beloch, *Bevölkerung*, pp. 155 ff.,
cf. p. 149. On the gradual depopulation of Greece in the late third and early
second century see above, Ch. V, pp. 623 ff. and notes 23–5, and on partial
recoveries in certain regions of Greece in the second century Ch. VI, pp. 750 ff.
For some hypothetical suggestions about the number and fluctuation of the
population of Greece in the Hellenistic period in general see K. J. Beloch,
Bevölkerung, p. 498; *Gr. Gesch.*² iv, p. 279; J. A. O. Larsen, 'Roman
Greece', p. 418 f. Some modern scholars are inclined to regard the tentative
suggestions of Beloch as ascertained facts. See for example A. Segré, *Bull.
Soc. Arch. Alex.* xxix (N.S. viii. 3) (1934), p. 292 (list of some Greek cities
with their population).

71 On the vicissitudes of Macedonia see the sections devoted to it in Chs.
IV, V, and VI. The general estimate of Macedonia's population in the Hellenistic period suggested by K. J. Beloch (*Gr. Gesch.*² iv, p. 331)—3 to 4
millions—is of course tentative, being based on the size of the armies mobilized in the times of Philip II and Alexander, and again during the second
and third Macedonian wars.

72 U. Wilcken, *Ostraka*, i, pp. 488 ff., cf. 239; K. J. Beloch, *Bevölkerung*,
pp. 254 ff.; C. Wachsmuth, *Klio* iii (1903), pp. 272 ff.; K. J. Beloch, *Gr. Gesch.*²
iv. 1, p. 330; A. Segré, *Bull. Soc. Arch. Alex.* xxix (N.S. viii. 3), pp. 256 ff.
The population of Egypt in pre-Ptolemaic times is estimated by E. Cavaignac,
Population et capital dans le monde méditerranéen antique, 1923, p. 2, at
5 to 6 millions against the explicit statement of Diodorus.

73 Diod. i. 31, 7: ἐπὶ μὲν γὰρ τῶν ἀρχαίων χρόνων ἔσχε κώμας ἀξιολόγους καὶ
πόλεις πλείους τῶν μυρίων καὶ ὀκτακισχιλίων ὡς μὲν ἐν ταῖς ἱεραῖς ἀναγραφαῖς
ὁρᾶν ἐστι κατακεχωρισμένων, ἐπὶ δὲ Πτολεμαίου τοῦ Λάγου πλείους τῶν τρισμυρίων
ἠριθμήθησαν, ὡς τὸ πλῆθος διαμεμένηκεν ἕως τῶν καθ᾽ ἡμᾶς χρόνων. τοῦ δὲ
σύμπαντος λαοῦ τὸ μὲν παλαιὸν φασι γεγονέναι περὶ ἑπτακοσίας μυριάδας καὶ καθ᾽
ἡμᾶς οὐκ ἐλάττους εἶναι [τριακοσίων] (the last word is emended to τούτων by
Wilcken). Wilcken's emendation has not been accepted by Beloch, *Gr. Gesch.*²
iv. 1, p. 330, and n. 2. He adheres to the text of the manuscript and interprets
the figure of 3 millions as including the male poll-tax-paying population only,
the total population being about 10 millions.

74 Diod. xvii. 52. 6: τὸ δὲ τῶν κατοικούντων αὐτὴν πλῆθος ὑπερβάλλει τοὺς ἐν
ταῖς ἄλλαις πόλεσιν οἰκήτορας. καθ᾽ ὃν γὰρ ἡμεῖς παρεβάλομεν χρόνον εἰς Αἴγυπτον
ἔφασαν οἱ τὰς ἀναγραφὰς ἔχοντες τῶν κατοικούντων εἶναι τοὺς ἐν αὐτῇ διατρίβοντας
ἐλευθέρους πλείους τῶν τριάκοντα μυριάδων. On this passage, K. J. Beloch,
Bevölkerung, pp. 259 and 279; U. Wilcken, *Ostr.* i, p. 487 f.; *Grundz.* p. 173;
K. J. Beloch, *Gr. Gesch.*² iv. 1, p. 287; A. von Premerstein (memoir quoted
in the next note), p. 48.

75 A. von Premerstein, 'Alexandrinische Geronten vor Kaiser Gaius' &c.

(P. Bibl. Univ. Giss. 46), *Mitt. Papyruss. d. Giess. Universitätsbibliothek,* v (1939), a posthumous paper by this much regretted historian of the ancient world. The document is preserved in fragments. Most of the text has been ingeniously restored by the editor. Fortunately the parts of the text concerning the gerusia and the 180,000 are almost intact and certain.

76 The gerusia-acts, col. i. 12 ff. (speech of the prosecutor): ἄκουσόν μου, Καῖ]σαρ. Ἀλεξανδρέων ὁ | [δῆμος ἐπιθυμεῖ, κύ]ριε αὐτοκράτωρ, πο|[λειτικῆς γερουσί]ας ἀπὸ ρ̄ γ̄ γερό[ντω]ν | [ἢ ἤδη ἐν συνόδῳ δ]έκα καὶ ὀκτὼ μυριάδα[ς] | [περιεχούσῃ ἐχειροτον]ήθη. Cf. col. ii. 2: ἔπλευσαν [οὖν οἱ] | [πρῶτοι τῶν] ρ̄ο̄γ̄ διὰ τοὺς ρ̄ο̄γ̄ καὶ Εὔλ[αλος] | [ὁμοῦ καὶ ἦλ]θον εἰς Ὠστίαν. [ἐκ]εῖθεν κέ[λευμα] | ἀ[νελάμβ]ανον τῶν μυρίων ῑη. The restorations, ingenious but rather hazardous, are by Premerstein.

77 On these data as studied by W. Schubart and A. Segré see Premerstein, loc. cit., pp. 49 ff., with bibliography.

78 On the number of Greeks in Egypt see my remarks about the calculations of A. Segré above, Ch. IV, p. 331 f., and n. 126. On the 6,475 'Hellenes' of the Fayûm see Premerstein, loc. cit., pp. 43 ff. (with bibliography).

79 See Premerstein, loc. cit., p. 55 (with bibliography) and above, Ch. IV, p. 498.

80 On the total population of Syria see the remarks of K. J. Beloch, *Bevölkerung,* pp. 242 ff., cf. *Gr. Gesch.*[2] iv. 1, p. 329 f.

81 On Miletus, the papers quoted by Hiller von Gaertringen, *P.W.K.* xv. 1610. For Asia Minor and its cities in general see the careful collection of material by K. J. Beloch, *Bevölkerung,* pp. 223 ff. As regards the city-less territories, we have some valuable figures for Galatia (ibid., pp. 238 ff.).

82 W. W. Tarn, *The Greeks in Bactria and India,* 1938, p. 6.

83 Cf. P. Roussel in G. Glotz, *Hist. gr.* iv. 1, 1938, p. 327. It may be noted that not all modern scholars accept the statement of Duris as exact.

84 Some remarks on men of great wealth in the Hellenistic world (without discrimination of time and place) will be found in K. J. Beloch, *Gr. Gesch.*[2] iv. 1, pp. 323 ff.; W. W. Tarn, *Hell. Civ.*[2], p. 102 f.; F. M. Heichelheim, *Wirtschaftsg.,* p. 566, with bibliography in n. 32, p. 1093. On the rich mine-owners of Athens of the middle fourth century, G. Glotz, *Hist. gr.* iii, 1936, p. 246 f., On Crates, D. R. Dudley, *A History of Cynicism,* 1937, pp. 42 ff. On the number of slaves owned by Aristotle and his successors, W. L. Westermann, *P.W.K.* Suppl. vi. 934.

85 On the inscriptions of Messene see above, Ch. VI, pp. 750 ff. and n. 21. What I have said in Ch. VI and here represents in a slightly modified form the results of Wilhelm's study. His interpretation of the data of the inscriptions especially as regards their bearing on the economic history of Greece, has

been recently challenged by E. Cavaignac, *Population et Capital*, 1923, pp. 128 ff., and F. Heichelheim, *Wirtschaftsg.*, p. 1093, n. 32. I cannot enter here into a discussion of their views. I must, however, observe that Cavaignac's method of calculation would yield exactly the same results for every period, good and bad. It is based on the total area of the cultivable territory, and takes for granted that it was all cultivated. He does not allow for the possibility that waste or half-waste land accumulated during wars and devastations, especially land on which vines and olives had been planted and which could not be reclaimed because of scarcity of labour and capital. The houses were there, but how many were in good repair and not depreciated? The slaves certainly existed, but how many were in the ownership of members of the *bourgeois* class? Mechanical calculations are worthless in history. On the causes of the impoverishment of the *bourgeoisie* see above, Ch. V, pp. 604 ff.

86 The fullest and best discussion of the figures dealt with in the text is that by U. Wilcken, *Ostraka*, i, pp. 412 ff., *Grundz.*⁸, cf. p. 172 f., and *Schmollers Jahrb.* xlv (1921), p. 392 f. (88 f.). The later discussions are all based on the material collected by Wilcken. I cannot here give a full bibliography. The last contributions are those of K. J. Beloch, *Gr. Gesch.*² iv. 1, p. 340; C. Préaux, *Écon. Lag.*, pp. 424 ff., and S. L. Wallace, *Taxation*, etc., ch. xviii. On the tribute of Egypt under Darius, E. Cavaignac, *Population et Capital*, 1923, pp. 1 ff., cf. E. Meyer, *Geschichte des Altertums*, iv. 1, ed. 3, 1939, pp. 78 ff. On the income of the Ptolemies in corn see A. Segré, *Bull. Soc. Arch. Alex.* xxix (N.S. viii. 3), pp. 277 ff. Segré's calculations, I need hardly say, must be regarded as very hypothetical, cf. C. Préaux, *Écon. Lag.*, pp. 136 and 148; S. L. Wallace, *Taxation*, pp. 336 ff. On the discrepancy between Cicero and Diodorus, C. Préaux, loc. cit., p. 424, and S. L. Wallace, loc. cit., p. 492, nn. 25 and 26. Their explanation (difference of currency in which the income is calculated) is more probable than that of Wilcken, who regards the sum named by Diodorus as representing the income from the land owned by the Alexandrians in the *chora*.

87 E. N. Adler, J. G. Tait, F. M. Heichelheim, F. Ll. Griffith, *The Adler Papyri*, 1939, cf. C. Préaux, *Chr. d'Ég.* xxviii (1939), pp. 393 ff.

88 Above, Ch. V, p. 732 f. (on the γεοῦχοι), and this chapter (on the clubs and associations). A very illuminating document illustrating club life (the most recent addition to our knowledge) is *Teb.* 894.

89 I need not insist upon this point. The importance of the *bourgeoisie* of Alexandria in its own eyes and in those of the Roman imperial government is well reflected in our texts relating to the struggle between it and the Jewish population of Alexandria (the bibliography of the 'acts of martyrs' of Alexandria will be found in the paper by Premerstein quoted above); cf. the famous letter of Claudius of 41 A.D., Hunt–Edgar, *Sel. Pap.* 212. I cannot refer here to all the modern contributions to the interpretation of this letter, see my *St. Ec. e Soc.*, p. 89, n. 2; cf. Fr. M.-J. Lagrange, 'La lettre de Claude aux Alexandrins', *Rev. Bibl.* xl (1931), pp. 270 ff., and A. Momigliano,

Claudius, 1934, p. 98, n. 25 (bibliography). I may add that the famous edict of Ti. Julius Alexander contains much material illustrating the role of Alexandrians in the life of Egypt, *O.G.I.* 669; cf. the recent revision of the text of the edict by H. G. Evelyn-White and J. H. Oliver in *The Temple of Hibis in El Khārgeh Oasis* (Metr. Mus. of Art, Egyptian Expedition Publications, xiv, 1939), part ii: 'Greek Inscriptions', nos. 3 and 4, pp. 23 ff.

[90] I have dealt with the *laoi* of Egypt above, in Chs. IV, V, and VI, and in this Chapter.

[91] See the general survey and very hypothetical calculations of E. Cavaignac, *Population et Capital*, 1923, pp. 107 ff.; cf. E. Bikerman, *Inst. Sél.*, pp. 106 ff., and above, Ch. IV, pp. 464 ff.

[92] H. Berve, *Das Alexanderreich*, i, 1926, p. 312 f.

[93] On Mnesimachus' estate and its revenues see Ch. IV, p. 465 f., and 495 f. and nn. 255 and 274. The text will be found in *Sardis*, vii, 1932, n. 1; cf. the corrections of the text by G. Klaffenbach, *Gnomon*, xii (1936), pp. 211 ff. An economic analysis of the Sardian estate of Mnesimachus, E. Cavaignac, *Population et Capital*, 1923, pp. 122 ff.

[94] Add to the references in Ch. II, J. R. Partington, *Origins and Development of Applied Chemistry*, 1935. The title of this book is somewhat misleading. The book is in fact a systematic survey of the sources of the wealth of the Ancient East from the earliest times down to Alexander (with occasional references to the later evidence) and of the technical methods adopted to utilize them. Especially important is the author's treatment of the various metals and their employment. For the Roman period see T. Frank, *Economic Survey of Ancient Rome*, ii (A. Ch. Johnson), 1936, pp. 1 ff. (Egypt); iv, 1938, pp. 127 ff. (Roman Syria by F. M. Heichelheim), and pp. 607 ff. (Roman Asia Minor by T. R. S. Broughton). For Thrace and the Danubian provinces some information will be found in the surveys of A. Alföldi and J. Keil in *C.A.H.* xi, 1936, pp. 540 ff. and 570 ff. For Thrace in the Classical and Hellenistic periods I may refer, in addition to the works quoted above, Chs. II, III, IV, V, and VI (sections which deal with the history of the Greek cities of the north-western coast of the Black Sea), to the valuable memoir of Chr. M. Danov, 'Zur antiken Wirtschaftsgeschichte der w. Pontusküste bis zur Niederlassung der Römer', *Bull. Inst. Arch. Bulg.* xii (1939), pp. 185 ff. (in Bulgarian with German résumé).

[95] On Crates of Olynthus or Chalcis, H. Berve, *Das Alexanderreich*, ii, 1926, p. 227, no. 448. Much has been written on the existing remains of the drainage work. The most recent contributions are: E. J. A. Kenny, 'The ancient drainage of the Copais', *Liv. Ann. of Arch.* xxii (1935), pp. 187 ff., esp. p. 204 (he ascribes most of the remains to prehistoric times, only one canal being the work of Crates), and U. Kahrstedt, *J.D.A.I.* lii (1937), Anz., pp. 1 ff. (he ascribes all the remains to the early Hellenistic period). On Larissa and Eretria, P. Guiraud, *La Propriété foncière en Grèce*, 1893, p. 461.

96 Strabo, xvi. 1. 10 (description of the canals of Babylonia) and 11, p. 740 f. (after Aristobulus, the work done by Alexander) ; Arrian, *Anab.* vii. 19. 3 ff., 21. Cf. U. Wilcken, *Alexander der Grosse*, 1931, p. 217 ; G. Glotz and R. Cohen in G. Glotz, *Hist. gr.* iv. 1, p. 180.

97 The classical books on this subject are still V. Hehn, *Kulturpflanzen und Hausthiere in ihrem Uebergang aus Asien nach Griechenland und Italien sowie in das übrige Europa*, ed. 8, 1911, and O. Keller, *Die antike Tierwelt*, i–ii, 1909–13, cf. Orth, art. 'Landwirtschaft', *P.W.K.* xii. 624 ff., and Olck, art. 'Gartenbau', ibid. vii. 768 ff., esp. 779 ff. Excellent are the remarks of H. Bretzl, *Botanische Forschungen des Alexanderzuges*, 1903, esp. pp. 234 ff. and 351 ff. See also the articles in *P.W.K.* on plants and animals ; a full list of them and some other bibliographical references will be found in F. M. Heichelheim *Wirtschaftsg.*, p. 1102 f., n. 46. For the history of Iranian plants in their migration to the east and south and to some extent to the west see the excellent book by B. Laufer, *Sino-Iranica*, Field Mus. of Nat. Hist. Publ. 201, Anthropol. Ser. xv. 3, 1919.

98 Lucerne: Orth, art. 'Klee', *P.W.K.* xi. 585 ; V. Hehn, loc. cit., pp. 410 ff. ; A. Jardé, *Les Céréales dans l'Antiquité grecque*, 1925, p. 89. Jardé's scepticism about the role played by lucerne in Greek agriculture in the fourth century and in the Hellenistic period is not entirely justified. Aristotle (*Hist. An.* iii. 21, p. 522 b, cf. viii. 8, p. 595 b) speaks of lucerne and cytisus as common green forage for domestic animals ; Theophrastus is well acquainted with it (*C.P.* ii. 15. 6 ; *H.P.* viii. 7. 7) ; and we hear that the famous Amphilochus of Athens wrote a special work Περὶ κυτίσου καὶ μηδικῆς (E. Oder in F. Susemihl, *G. d. gr. Lit. in Alex.* i, 1891, p. 836 f. ; M. Wellmann, *P.W.K.* i, 1940–1) in which he recommended its cultivation and gave advice on the subject. Pistachio: V. Hehn, loc. cit., pp. 421 ff. It must be noted, however, that while Theophrastus (*H.P.* iv. 4. 7) speaks of the tree on the basis of information which he had received from persons who had seen it in Bactria, Posidonius (*apud* Athen. xiv, p. 649 d ; fr. 3, *F. Gr. Hist.* 87) mentions the pistachio tree as producing excellent nuts in Syria, near Beroe–Aleppo. We may therefore suppose that it was in the time of the early Seleucids that the tree was first planted in Syria and thence introduced into Egypt. But we must take into consideration that Theophrastus' information about the flora of Seleucid Syria is rather poor. On the other hand, it is more than probable that the special Pontic variety of walnut tree was first planted in Greece in the Achaemenid period: walnuts were known in Greece and Egypt under the name κάρυα Περσικά or βασιλικά (Pliny, *N.H.* xv. 87 and 88) ; cf. M. Schnebel, *Landwirtschaft*, 1925, p. 314, and V. Hehn, loc. cit., pp. 393 ff.

99 Pyrrhus and his cattle-breeding in Epirus, cows and sheep called Πυρρικαί (βόες) or Πυρρικά (πρόβατα), Arist. *Hist. An.* iii. 21, p. 522^b23 ; after mentioning the peculiarly large animals and the rich pastures of Epirus the author adds: μέγιστοι δ' οἵ τε βόες εἰσὶ καὶ τὰ πρόβατα τὰ καλούμενα Πυρρικά, τὰ τὴν ἐπωνυμίαν ἔχοντα ταύτην ἀπὸ Πύρρου τοῦ βασιλέως and ibid. viii. 7, p. 595^b18:

διὸ οἱ ἐν τῇ Ἠπείρῳ τὰς καλουμένας Πυρρικὰς (πυρρίχας codd.) βοῦς ἐννέα ἔτη διατηροῦσιν ἀνοχεύτους ὅπως αὐξάνωνται· τούτων δὲ τὸ μὲν πλῆθος εἶναί φασι περὶ τετρακοσίους, ἰδίους τῶν βασιλέων, ζῆν δ' ἐν ἄλλῃ χώρᾳ οὐ δύνασθαι, καίτοι πεπει-ρᾶσθαί τινας. The last statement is repeated by Pliny, *N.H.* viii. 176, cf. Ael. *N. An.* iii. 34. The Pyrrhus mentioned in Aristotle's *Hist. An.* cannot be any other than the great Pyrrhus, who was born a few years after the death of Aristotle. The two passages are therefore interpolations, but certainly very early ones. One may suppose that they are due to Theophrastus or to the Peri-patetic philosopher who may have compiled the IXth book of the *Hist. An.* and may have used as his main source Theophrastus' περὶ ζῴων φρονήσεως καὶ ἔθους (see L. Dittmeyer in Teubner's edition of *Hist. An.* (preface, p. vii, and ad iii. 21)). On the herd of Neoptolemus, Plut. *Pyrrh.* 5: γυνὴ Σάμωνος τοῦ τὰ ποίμνια καὶ τὰ βουκόλια τῷ Νεοπτολέμῳ διοικοῦντος. Cf. B. Büchsen-schutz, *Besitz und Erwerb*, 1869, p. 222, cf. 219, n. 4; K. Zeissig, *Die Rinder-zucht im alten Griechenland*, 1934 (diss. Giessen), p. 28; O. Brendel, *Die Schafzucht im alten Griechenland*, 1934 (diss. Giessen), p. 47 (full of misquota-tions).

[100] I may add here to what I have said above, Ch. IV, pp. 302 and 355 ff. and notes 150–3, that sesame according to some modern scholars was first planted in Egypt shortly before the time of Theophrastus, Steier, art. 'Sesamon', *P.W.K.* ii A. 1849, cf. M. Schnebel, loc. cit., p. 197. Since, how-ever, sesame was extensively cultivated in Egypt in the reign of Philadelphus, it is perhaps more probable that it came to Egypt (from Babylonia) earlier, perhaps in Persian times.

[101] On vines planted in Babylonia and Assyria see the references in B. Meissner, *Babylonien und Assyrien*, i, 1920, p. 207 f. On Dura, above, Ch. IV, p. 489. I may remark that the methods of planting vines used by the Mace-donians in Babylonia are the same as Theophrastus, *C.P.* iii. 12. 1, pre-scribes for planting vines in humid soil. On the experiments of Harpalus, Theophr. *H.P.* iv. 4. 1; *C.P.* ii. 3, 3; Pliny, *N.H.* xvi. 144; Plut. *Symp.* iii. 2. 1; and H. Bretzl, loc. cit. (n. 97), pp. 234 ff.

[102] F. M. Heichelheim, 'Roman Syria', in T. Frank, *Econ. Surv.* iv, pp. 130 ff.

[103] Olck, *P.W.K.* ii. 270 f. (apricot); Steier, ibid. xix. 1022 ff. (peach); M. Schnebel, *Landwirtschaft*, pp. 312 ff. The μῆλα Ἀρμενιακά and μῆλα Περσικά, as the Greeks called apricots and peaches, are not mentioned in Egyptian papyri of Ptolemaic and early Roman times; the Περσικά first appear with the κίτρια in the late Roman period (Schnebel, loc. cit., p. 312). But Edgar has suggested that μῆλα ἐαρινά in the famous letter of Zenon about planting vines and fruit-trees (*P. Cairo Zen.* 59033) means not early apples but apri-cots. This is doubtful. But if it be so, we may agree with M. Wellmann in his contention that apricots, peaches, the pistachio tree, and the *citrus medica Risso* were known to Bolus Democritus of Mendes in Egypt (about 200 B.C.), a famous polyhistor with inclinations to mysticism and occult

science, who, among many other books, wrote one on agriculture (Γεωργικά).
I shall return to him in the following section. See M. Wellmann, 'Die
Georgika des Demokritos', *Berl. Abh.*, 1921, phil.-hist. Kl. no. 4, pp. 19
and 52, and frs. 51, 53, 54, 55, in which late Roman and Arabic writers on
agriculture, quoting Democritus, mention the trees named above. If these
trees were known to Bolus he certainly had observed them in Egypt. But
it is not certain that all the quotations from Democritus which occur in late
writers must necessarily refer to Bolus Democritus. It seems probable that
there circulated in late antiquity under the famous name of Democritus of
Abdera many writings falsely attributed to him, and that there existed
later editions of the *Georgica* of Bolus Democritus with additions. We
must await new papyrological discoveries for a clearer understanding of this
difficult question. Meanwhile it is safer to reserve judgement. The history
of the cherry-tree is peculiar. The wild cherry is a European tree. Sweet
cherries were well known in the Greek world; those of Mount Ida and those
cultivated near Miletus were famous. But we have no mention of cherries
in the papyri found in Egypt. To Italy the sweet-cherry tree was brought
not from Miletus or the Troad, but directly from Pontus by Lucullus, see
V. Hehn, loc. cit., pp. 404 ff.; Olck, art. 'Kirschbaum', *P.W.K.* xi. 509 ff.

104 On *Citrus medica*, V. Hehn, loc. cit., p. 456; H. Bretzl, loc. cit., p. 312,
and the preceding note. If *Citrus medica* was known and planted in Egypt
in Hellenistic times, the history of this tree in Italy appears puzzling. On
the pistachio tree, above, n. 98 to this chapter and Ch. IV, n. 152.

105 I cannot give references here to the modern works which deal with the
history of cotton. It will suffice to refer to the substantial treatment of the
history of cotton and of its cultivation in the Greco-Roman world by M.
Chwostow, *History of Oriental Trade of Greco-Roman Egypt*, 1907, pp. 130 ff.
(in Russian), and by E. H. Warmington, *The Commerce between the Roman
Empire and India*, 1928, pp. 210 ff. Cf. Wagler, art. 'Baumwolle', *P.W.K.*
iii. 167 ff., and on the cultivation of cotton in western Asia and Babylonia,
F. M. Heichelheim, 'Roman Syria', p. 131. On Egypt, F. Ll. Griffith and
Mrs. G. K. Crowfoot, 'On the early use of cotton in the Nile Valley', *J.E.A.*
xx (1934), pp. 5 ff.; A. Lucas, *Ancient Egyptian Materials and Industries*,
1934, pp. 143 ff.

106 V. Hehn, loc. cit., pp. 502 ff.; M. Chwostow, loc. cit., pp. 117 ff.;
E. H. Warmington, loc. cit., pp. 218 ff.; M. Schnebel, loc. cit., p. 100, and
F. M. Heichelheim, loc. cit., p. 129, n. 18.

107 On sugar, the notions which the Hellenistic and the Roman world
had about it, and its importation into the Roman Empire, M. Chwostow,
loc. cit., pp. 107, 124, 251; E. H. Warmington, loc. cit., pp. 208 ff.; Maur.
Schuster, art. 'Mel', *P.W.K.* xv. 372 ff.; cf. B. Laufer, loc. cit., p. 376 f.;
and for Egypt, A. Lucas, loc. cit., p. 24 f.

108 Mau, *P.W.K.* iii. 678; Blümner, art. 'Serica', *P.W.K.* ii A. 1724 ff.;

M. Chwostow, loc. cit., pp. 147 ff.; E. H. Warmington, loc. cit., pp. 174 ff. On the *amorgina* G. M. A. Richter, *A.J.A.* xxxiii (1929), pp. 27 ff. Silk in Egypt, A. Lucas, loc. cit., p. 144.

[109] Pistachio tree in Greece and Paxamus: E. Oder in F. Susemihl, *Gesch. d. gr. Lit. in Alex.* i, 1891, p. 842. On the pistachio tree acclimatized in Egypt, above, n. 104. Domestic ducks in Greece, Orth, *P.W.K.* vii. 903 ff., cf. Olck, art. 'Ente', v. 2639 ff. On the attempts to acclimatize foreign types of corn in the territory of Greek cities in the time of Theophrastus, and their (temporary?) ill success, A. Jardé, *Les Céréales dans l'Antiquité grecque*, 1925, p. 17 f.

[110] We may derive a good idea of the distribution of forests in the Hellenistic world by reading books iii–v of Theophrastus' *H.P.*; see esp. iv. 5. 5, a list of countries which produced the best timber for shipbuilding, and ix. 2, where the subject of resinous trees and the methods of collecting resin and pitch is dealt with (the statements of Pliny are derived from Theophrastus). It is evident from the material collected by Theophrastus that the countries richest in timber were Macedonia, some parts of Asia Minor mentioned in the text, and Syria. Whether by Syria Theophrastus meant the whole of it or the Lebanon only is not easy to decide. A sketchy enumeration of the regions rich in timber in Roman times will be found in T. Frank, *Econ. Surv.* iv, p. 134 f., for Syria, and pp. 616 ff., for Asia Minor. On Greece, P. Guiraud, *La Propriété foncière en Grèce*, 1893, p. 504 f., and A. Jardé, op. cit., pp. 99 ff.

[111] Exploitation of the forests of Cyprus, Theophr. *H.P.* v. 8. 1 (protection of the forests by the late Cyprian kings), cf. 7. 2 (on fir-trees and the Aleppo pines of Cyprus). Antigonus and Demetrius: Theophr. *H.P.* v. 8. 2; Pliny, *N.H.* xvi. 203, cf. Plut. *Dem.* 43. Gift of (Cyprian) timber to Athens in 306/5 B.C.: Diod. xx. 46, 4; Plut. *Dem.* 10; *S.I.G.*³ 334. Cf. n. 113.

[112] On Theophrastus and his botanical works, W. Christ–W. Schmid, *Gesch. d. gr. Lit.* ii. 1, 1920, p. 62 f. (with a short bibliography). Since 1920 many important studies have appeared on Theophrastus as a botanist and biologist: see especially the contributions of G. Senn enumerated in his *Die Entwicklung der biologischen Forschungsmethode in der Antike*, Veröff. d. schw. Ges. f. Gesch. d. Medizin u. d. Naturwissenschaften, viii (1933), p. 244 f. Especially important for the economic historian is the Vth book of Theophrastus' *H.P.*, a full and excellent survey of various kinds of timber, with extremely important technical remarks; a special section is devoted to firewood and to the preparation of charcoal, and another (ix. 2) to resin and pitch extracted from the resinous trees.

[113] The history of the forests of Cyprus may have been as follows: (1) early deforestation after Greek and Phoenician occupation of the island; (2) protection of trees and forests by the city-kings of the fourth century B.C.; (3) new period of intensive exploitation by Antigonus and Demetrius, and (4) management of the forests by the Ptolemies, perhaps on the lines adopted

by the Cyprian city-kings; we must not forget that the Ptolemies needed large quantities of wood from Cyprus, for their intensive mining work and shipbuilding in the island, and for exportation as building material to Alexandria and Egypt. On the re-afforestation of Egypt by the Ptolemies, above, Ch. IV, p. 298 f., n. 103. The most important evidence is *Teb.* 703, 191–211, cf. my remarks on this document. On the Roman management of the forests of the Lebanon, my *St. Ec. e Soc.*, p. 323, note 32. Protection of forests and of trees on plots of cultivated land was not unknown in Greece. We sometimes come upon passages referring to it in leases of land, see A. Jardé, op. cit., p. 100 f. Cf., on the leases of the phratry of the Clytidae of Chios (middle of the fourth century B.C.), the memoir by A. Wilhelm, 'Die Pachturkunden der Klytiden', *Jahreshefte*, xxviii (1933), pp. 197 ff., with a complete list of other contributions to the restoration of these important documents. See especially the collection of texts on p. 209 which testify to the protection of sacred groves. It is possible that the Clytidae required their tenants to carry out a partial re-afforestation of the grove by planting young trees (inscr. A, ii. 43 ff.).

114 Pliny's *N.H.* (xxxiii–xxxiv) contains a general survey of the methods of mining gold, silver, copper, iron, and lead. But this is naturally much more concerned with the West, which was much richer in minerals, than with the East. The relative passages have been reprinted, translated, and commented on by K. C. Bailey, *The Elder Pliny's Chapters on Chemical Subjects*, i, 1929 (Pliny, xxxiii, chs. 66–77 (gold), chs. 95–100 (silver)), and ii, 1932 (Pliny, xxxiv, chs. 2–4 (copper), ch. 142 (iron), ch. 156 (lead)).

115 On Gorgus, H. Berve, *Das Alexanderreich*, ii, 1926, p. 114 f.; U. Wilcken, *Alexander d. Grosse*, p. 181; G. Glotz–R. Cohen, *Hist. Gr.* iv. 1, pp. 159 and 247.

116 A careful exploration of Greece in respect of ancient mines has been recently carried out by O. Davies, *Roman Mines in Europe*, 1935, pp. 239 ff.

117 O. Davies, loc. cit., pp. 226 ff.

118 O. Davies, loc. cit., p. 17; A. Ch. Johnson, 'Roman Egypt', 1936, pp. 239 ff. I may quote in this connexion a fact mentioned by Pliny (xxxi. 78). One of the Ptolemies while building a camp near Pelusium discovered salt-mines. This discovery led to subsequent prospecting for salt-mines in the desert.

119 Above, Ch. IV, p. 381 ff., cf. J. R. Partington, *Origins and Development of Applied Chemistry*, 1935, pp. 32 ff.

120 Above, Ch. IV, pp. 297 f. and 339 f., cf. J. R. Partington, loc. cit., pp. 360 ff. I repeat that the yield of the silver-mines of Cyprus was probably very small.

121 On the mines of Asia Minor in Roman times, T. R. S. Broughton, 'Roman Asia Minor', pp. 620 ff.; for the earlier period, S. Przeworski,

'Die Metallindustrie Anatoliens in d. Zeit v. 1500–700 v. Chr.', *Intern. Arch. f. Ethn.* xxxvi (1939): on p. 91 there is an excellent map illustrating the distribution of copper and iron ores in Asia Minor.

[122] On the copper and iron ore of Edom (Idumaea), N. Glueck, *Bull. Am. School Or. Res.* lxiii (1936), pp. 4 ff. quoting the text of Ps.-Aristeas, and on Ezion–Geber, id., ibid. lxxi (1938), pp. 3 ff. On S. Arabia, A. Grohmann, 'Südarabien als Wirtschaftsgebiet', i, *Osten und Orient*, i. 4, 1922, pp. 164 ff.

[123] On the mines of Syria and Palestine, F. M. Heichelheim, 'Roman Syria', p. 156 f; J. R. Partington's survey is much fuller, loc. cit., p. 486 (silver), p. 488 (copper), p. 490 (iron). Cf. the instructive article by G. E. Wright, 'Iron: the date of its introduction into Palestine', *A.J.A.* xliii (1939), pp. 458 ff. The whole of the Lebanon and the Antilebanon belonged to the Ptolemies until the time of Antiochus III, K. J. Beloch, *Gr. Gesch.*, 2nd ed. iv. 2, 1927, pp. 323 ff.

[124] A useful survey of the mines of the Near East known from pre-Hellenistic, Hellenistic, and Roman sources will be found in the above-quoted book by J. R. Partington; cf., as regards the iron-mines, the articles by H. C. Richardson quoted in the next note and S. Przeworski's volume cited in n. 121. For references to the ancient sources and modern works I refer to these books and to the chapters on Roman Syria and Roman Asia Minor in T. Frank, *Econ. Surv.* iv.

[125] I cannot cite here all the books and articles in which the evidence about the Chalybes is discussed from various points of view, especially in connexion with the problem of the origin of iron. To the meagre and antiquated bibliography of J. R. Partington, loc. cit., p. 379 f., I may add the following: my remarks on a recently published fragment of Hellanicus, in *Skythien und der Bosporus*, 1931, p. 22 (with bibliographical references to works unknown to the authors of the most recent studies quoted below); A. W. Persson, 'Eisen und Eisenbereitung in ältester Zeit', *Bull. Soc. royale des Lettres de Lund*, vi (1933–4), pp. 111 ff.; H. C. Richardson, 'Iron, prehistoric and ancient', *A.J.A.* xxxviii (1934), pp. 555 ff., esp. 558; cf. Am. Hertz, ibid. xli (1937), pp. 441 ff.; H. C. Richardson, ibid., pp. 447 ff., and G. E. Wright, ibid. xliii (1939), pp. 458 ff. The fullest and best study of the early history of iron will be found in the book by S. Przeworski cited in n. 121.

[126] Much has been written in late years on bitumen and petroleum in antiquity. I shall quote here the most recent and fullest surveys only: R. J. Forbes, *Bitumen and Petroleum in Antiquity*, 1936 (with an excellent bibliography); id., *Mnemosyne*, Ser. 3, iv (1936), pp. 67 ff.; id. *Fifteen centuries of Bitumen*, 1937; A. Seguin, 'Recherches sur le pétrole dans l'antiquité', *Rev. Quest. hist.* lxvi (1936), pp. 1 ff.; id. *Nouvelles recherches sur le pétrole dans l'antiquité*, 1937, and 'Étude sur le pétrole', *Rev. Quest. Hist.* lxvi (1938), pp. 36 ff.; J. Toutain 'Histoire et Archéologie du pétrole', *Rev. Intern. d'Enseignement*, lxxxvi (1937), pp. 181 ff.; R. J. Forbes,

'Neues z. ältesten Gesch. d. Bitumens', *Bitumen* viii (1938), pp. 128 ff., and 161 ff.; id. 'Petroleum and Bitumen in Antiquity', *Ambix* ii (1938), pp. 68 ff. (which I have not seen). Coal was equally known to the ancients (Theophr. *Lap.* 16—lignite used in Elis by smiths) but never extensively used even in Roman times in provinces rich in coal-mines (O. Davies, *Roman Mines in Europe*, 1935, p. 153, n. 6).

127 On the quarries of the Hellenistic world in the Roman period, most of which were exploited in pre-Hellenistic and Hellenistic times, see T. Frank, *Econ. Surv.* ii, pp. 240 ff. (Egypt, A. Chr. Johnson); iv, pp. 156 ff. (Syria, F. M. Heichelheim); pp. 462 ff. (Greece and Macedonia, J. A. O. Larsen); pp. 624 ff. (Asia Minor, T. R. S. Broughton); cf. in general on mines and quarries of the Hellenistic period F. M. Heichelheim, *Wirtschaftsg.*, pp. 629 ff. and bibliography, n. 50.

128 On fishing and fisheries see the interesting set of essays on various aspects of Greek and Oriental fishing by W. Radcliffe, *Fishing from the Earliest Times*, 1921. There is no good study of Greek fishing from the economic point of view; some material has been collected by L. Bohlen, *Die Bedeutung der Fischerei im Altertum*, 1936 (diss. Hamburg). Cf. F. M. Heichelheim, *Wirtschaftsg.*, pp. 594 ff. and n. 45. The importance of fish even in the smaller cities of Greece is illustrated by the inscription of Acraephiae in Boeotia, which contains a list of sea and river fish with prices, above, Ch. IV, n. 35.

129 On the *Halieutica*, W. Susemihl, *Gesch. d. gr. Lit. in Alex.* i, p. 850 f., cf. 906. On Oppian and the development of zoology and the τέχναι of hunting, fishing, fowling, A. W. Mair, *Oppian, Colluthus, Tryphiodorus* (Loeb Library), 1928, Introduction. On the fish dishes, L. Lacroix, *La Faune marine dans la décoration des plats à poisson*, &c., 1937, cf. *Mél. Boisacq*, vi. 1938, pp. 49 ff. (on the names of fish in the Acraephiae inscription), and Ch. P., *Rev. Arch.* xiii (1939), pp. 290 ff. On the fish mosaics of Pompeii and their connexion with the South Italian pottery, E. Pernice, *Die hellenistische Kunst in Pompeii*, vi, 1938: 'Pavimente und figürliche Mosaiken', pp. 149 ff., and pls. 52 ff. Roman fish mosaics and their possible relations to illuminated treatises περὶ ἰχθύων, my *St. Ec. e Soc.*, p. 202, note. Fish mosaics are very frequent in the western provinces of the Roman Empire; those of Antioch (R. Stillwell and others, *Antioch-on-the-Orontes*, ii, 1938, pls. 38, 39, figs. 50, 51), and perhaps those of Italian Africa may go back to eastern Hellenistic originals. A charming mosaic from Leptis Magna representing various methods of fishing may be regarded as a copy of an Alexandrian original, see my paper in *Mélanges G. Radet* and my Pl. XL.

130 The two standard works on Greek land tenure and Greek agriculture are still P. Guiraud, *La Propriété foncière en Grèce jusqu'à la conquête romaine*, 1893, and A. Jardé, *Les Céréales dans l'Antiquité grecque*, i, La Production, 1925 (the second volume which was intended to describe the role of corn in the life of the Greek world never appeared). Cf. Olck, art. 'Ackerbau', in *P.W.K.* i. 264 ff.; Orth, art. 'Landwirtschaft', xii. 624 ff., and Olck, art.

'Gartenbau', vii. 768 ff. In these books and articles attention is chiefly paid to the archaic and classical periods of Greece. More bibliographical references concerning land tenure and agriculture in classical Greece will be found in F. M. Heichelheim, *Wirtschaftsg.*, pp. 386 ff., and n. 44. On the Hellenistic period, G. Glotz, *Le Travail dans la Grèce ancienne*, 1920, pp. 407 ff. (on Greece proper, pp. 413 ff.), and F. M. Heichelheim, loc. cit., pp. 596 ff., and notes 46–9. I regret not to have been able to read again for the purposes of this book the substantial study by B. L. Bogaevsky, *Outlines of the Agriculture of Athens*, i, ii, 1915 (in Russian). E. Savoy's *L'Agriculture à travers les âges*, ii, 1935, is of no importance to students of antiquity.

[131] On the estate of Phaenippus (*Prosop. Attica* 13978), P. Guiraud, loc. cit., p. 565; A. Jardé, loc. cit., pp. 157 ff.

[132] Above, Ch. VI, pp. 750 ff., and this chapter nn. 84 and 85.

[133] Early Greek writers on agriculture (after Hesiod) Ps.-Plato, *Minos*, 316 E (date is controversial); Arist. *Pol.* i. 11. 1258^b39 ff. (the whole paragraph on land economy is written from the point of view of the landowner, not of the peasant; the leading idea is how best to invest money and obtain a good return). Cf. E. Oder in F. Susemihl, *Gesch. gr. Lit. in d. Alex.* i, 1891, p. 832 f. On the literary sources of Theophrastus, S. A. Liaskovsky, 'Science of agriculture in connexion with the evolution of natural science in classical Greece before Theophrastus', *Bull. Ac. Hist. Mat. Civ.* cviii (1935), pp. 184 ff. (in Russian). Cf. the articles in *P.W.K.* referring to the individual authors quoted by Aristotle and Theophrastus.

[134] On Theophrastus, G. Senn, *Die Entwicklung der biologischen Forschungsmethode in der Antike und ihre grundzügliche Förderung durch Theophrast von Eresos* (Ver. schweiz. Ges. f. Gesch. d. Medizin u. Naturw. viii), 1933. The copious bibliography appended to this book relieves me from quoting here the standard works on Theophrastus.

[135] E. Oder in F. Susemihl, loc. cit.

[136] On Bolus Democritus and his handbook of agriculture, M. Wellmann, art. 'Bolus', *P.W.K.* iii. 676 f. and especially 'Die Georgika des Demokritos', *Berl. Abh.*, phil.-hist. Kl. 1921, no. 4. I shall return to Bolus in the next sub-section. The ingenious study by Wellmann shows how widely the *Georgica* of Bolus was used in later times. Cf. notes 103 and 176.

[137] M. Wellmann, *Berl. Abh.*, phil.-hist. Kl. 1921, no. 4, pp. 34 ff.

[138] See the list of these terms in F. M. Heichelheim, *Wirtschaftsg.*, pp. 1108 ff., n. 49. In the same note he gives a good bibliography of modern works dealing with the Roman *scriptores rei rusticae*. It is to be regretted that his list of terms is short and unsupported by argument and therefore not altogether convincing (especially the terms supposedly derived from new-Babylonian, Biblical Hebrew, and Phoenician). It is to be hoped that he will expand his note into a monograph on this interesting subject.

[139] A special study has been devoted to the Thessalian *penestai* by R. V. Schmidt, 'From the history of Thessaly', *Bull. Ac. Hist. Mat. Civ.* ci (1934), pp. 75 ff. (in Russian).

[140] There is no special study of the conditions of land tenure in Greece in the Hellenistic period; see above, n. 130. Some remarks on the evolution of land tenure in Thessaly will be found in the paper by R. V. Schmidt quoted in the preceding note, pp. 106 ff.; his conclusions about the decay of agriculture in Thessaly in Hellenistic times and the development of small holdings are not warranted by the evidence adduced by him. In Thessaly, as in the rest of Greece, land was gradually concentrated in the hands of corporative bodies and probably of private landowners also, while the prevailing mode of exploitation appears to have been by small tenants (including the *penestai*?). How many of the slaves in Thessaly (known from the frequent manumissions) were engaged in agricultural work it is impossible to say; cf. above, Ch. V, n. 30. A list of μισθώσεις or contracts of lease (among them leases of land) of the classical and Hellenistic periods for the Greek world in general (except Egypt) will be found in O. Schulthess, art. *Μίσθωσις*, *P.W.K.* xv. 2098 ff. I may add to his references some basic articles on the subject. *Attica*: A. Wilhelm, *Arch. Pap.* xi (1935), pp. 189 ff. *Boeotia*: the leases of land at Thespiae (third century B.C.), above, Ch. IV, n. 35. *Aetolia:* lease of land at Thestia (second century B.C.), G. Klaffenbach, *Berl. S.B.*, 1936, pp. 380 ff., cf. S. von Bolla, *Jahreshefte*, xxxi (1939), Beibl., pp. 170 ff. *Chios*: the leases of land of the Clytidae (fourth century B.C.), A. Wilhelm, *Jahreshefte*, xxviii (1933), pp. 179 ff. *Delos*: leases of temple estates, above, Ch. IV, p. 234, and n. 66, cf. J. A. O. Larsen, 'Roman Greece', pp. 402 ff.; and on the ἱερὰ συγγραφή A. Wilhelm, *Arch. Pap.* xi (1935), p. 215. *Olymus* and *Mylasa* in Caria: above, Ch. V, n. 82. In the articles by Wilhelm and Klaffenbach the reader will find quotations and discussions of many more leases of land only partially quoted by Schulthess. The only extant fragmentary contract of lease (of a house) between two private persons is that scratched on a sherd and published and discussed by E. Szanto, *Ausgewählte Abh.*, 1906, pp. 92 ff.

[141] On the plough, A. S. F. Gow, 'The ancient plough', *J.H.S.* xxxiv (1914), pp. 249 ff.; A. Jardé, loc. cit., p. 19 f.; A. G. Drachmann, art. 'Pflug', *P.W.K.* xix. 1461. No iron ploughshares found in Greece or Italy are registered by Drachmann (1466 ff.), while he discusses several found in the area of the western provinces of Rome (both prehistoric and Roman). On the wine- and olive-presses, above, Ch. IV, p. 364, and n. 158. Cf. Hörle, art. 'Torcular', *P.W.K.* vi A. 1727 ff.

[142] On the rotation of crops, A. Jardé, loc. cit. pp. 80 ff. Against his view, F. M. Heichelheim, *P.W.K.*, Suppl. vi. 834, quoting the lease of land at Sunium, *I.G.* ii.² 2493 (339/8 B.C.), which according to him attests the triennial rotation of crops. But this lease states explicitly ll. 7 ff.: ὁ δὲ μισθωσάμε[νος τὸ χωρίον] γεωργή|σει ἀρῶν τὴν γῆν ἐναλλ[άξ. τὰ μὲν ἡμίσε]α

πυροῖς καὶ κριθαῖς, τῆς δ' ἡμι[σέας τὴν μὲν ν]εὰν ὀσπρίοις, τὴν δὲ ἄλλην γῆν [χερρὸν οὐ σπερεῖ]. The restoration of this passage is doubtful, νεάν and χερρόν (*I.G.* ii.² 2492, l. 16, lease of the Aexoneis of 345/4 B.C.) meaning one and the same thing (fallow land). I do not know whether a more satisfactory restoration has been suggested. But the general sense is clear. The decisive word is ἐναλλάξ, which is the technical term for the biennial system, see the lease of Arcesine of the fourth century B.C., *S.I.G.*³ 963. 7, and cf. *I.G.* ii.² 1241 (lease of the phratry of the Dyaleis of 300/299 B.C.), l. 21: σπερεῖ δὲ τῆς γῆς σίτωι τὴν ἡμίσειαν, τῆς δ' ἀργοῦ ὀσπρεύσει ὁπόσην ἂν βούληται. Opposed to the system ἐναλλάξ ἀροῦν is that of sowing year after year, see lease of land at Delphi of the third or second century B.C., *S.E.G.* ii. 293, ll. 10 f.: τὰν δὲ γᾶν | [μὴ σπεί-ρε]ν ἀπ[αυστί, cf. the above-cited passage of the lease of Arcesine, *S.I.G.*³ 963, l. 7: τὴν δὲ γῆν ἀρόσει ἐναλλάξ καὶ οὐκ ἀμφιετεί.

143 On the points mentioned in the text, A. Jardé, loc. cit., pp. 19 ff. (Les techniques agricoles) and his summary, p. 29 f., cf. pp. 14 ff. (on seed corn). Jardé in my opinion takes an unduly unfavourable view of the attention paid to seed-corn. On διασπορεῖν, above, Ch. IV, p. 365, and n. 160.

144 On the writers about viticulture, E. Oder in F. Susemihl, loc. cit., p. 839 f. It is well known that Theophrastus pays special attention to vines (see the Indexes to Teubner's edition of Theophrastus and to the edition in the Loeb Library, s.v. ἄμπελος) and that large sections of the Roman works on agriculture and of the *Geoponica* are devoted to viticulture and the making of wine. On viticulture as it appears in the treatises of the Roman agronomists cf. R. Billiard, *La Vigne dans l'Antiquité*, 1913, esp. ch. v, pp. 156 ff., on the contracts of lease, and the excellent article 'Vinum' by A. Jardé, in Dar. et Saglio, *D.d.A.* v, pp. 912 ff., esp. 917 ff. (viticulture); cf. his article 'Vinitor', ibid. Jardé's treatment, however, is systematic, not historical.

145 On the treatises of Hellenistic times dealing with the cultivation of olive-trees and gardening, E. Oder in F. Susemihl, loc. cit., pp. 841, 845; cf. A. S. Pease, art. 'Oelbaum', *P.W.K.* xvii. 1998 ff. (systematic, not historical, treatment).

146 See my *Soc. and Ec. Hist. R.E.*, pl. x (Ital. ed., pl. xi). Cf. the remarks of F. M. Heichelheim, *Wirtschaftsg.*, p. 1104, n. 47, on the names of agricultural implements in general in Greece and Rome, which show that the implements used in Greece (including Hellenistic Egypt) and Italy were mostly identical. Only a few Latin names have no equivalents in Greek, while in general Greek terminology is richer; but it must be remembered that our evidence on the Latin names is much better than that on the Greek. It is to be hoped that Heichelheim will devote a special monograph to this subject and in doing so will make due use of the archaeological material. Many agricultural implements of Roman times (including those used for vine and olive plantations) have been found in Priene in Asia Minor and in Karanis in Egypt and other cities of the Fayûm (now in Michigan University,

the Toledo Museums, and the Museum of Toronto), and many more in the western provinces of the Roman Empire. See, for example, Priene, Wiegand und Schrader, *Priene*, p. 391, figs. 496–502; Gaul and the Rhine provinces, B. Champion, 'Outils en fer du Musée de Saint-Germain', *Rev. Arch.* iii (5me sér.) (1916), pp. 210 ff. (implements found in the villas near the forest of Compiègne); L. Lindenschmidt, *Altert. uns. heidn. Vorzeit*, v, 1906, pp. 255 ff., pl. 46; K. Schumacher, *Der Ackerbau* (Kulturg. Wegweiser durch das röm.-germ. Zentralmuseum), 1922, pp. 20 ff. Cf. in general R. V. Schmidt, *Problems of the History of Material Civilization*, 1933, nos. 5–6, on the agricultural instruments (in Russian). Wine and oil presses: above, n. 141. I may quote in this connexion a most interesting lease of a vineyard, an olive-grove, and perhaps a garden, of 228–221 B.C., in which various agricultural implements used especially in vineyards are enumerated, *Teb.* 815, fr. 6, col. iii. 69 f.; cf. 720, 5 (238 B.C.) concerning implements in the vineyard of Berenice, daughter of the king, and 878 (about 111 B.C.). In the first document, l. 69, I am tempted to read ἀ[ρπε]δόνας (cords).

¹⁴⁷ After Aristotle's books on zoology not very much was added to the stock of knowledge collected by him (cf. W. Kroll, 'Zur Geschichte der aristotelischen Zoologie', *Wien. S.B.* ccviii. 2, 1940). Special treatises on cattle-breeding are rarely mentioned. I may name the work of Alexander of Myndus, Περὶ κτηνῶν. In modern times ancient cattle-breeding has been studied chiefly by agronomists, see the set of Giessen dissertations by pupils of Prof. H. Kraemer: A. Hörnschemeyer, *Die Pferdezucht im kl. Altertum*, 1929; K. Winkelstern, *Die Schweinezucht im kl. Altertum*, 1933; K. Zeissig, *Die Rinderzucht im alten Griechenland*, 1934; O. Brendel, *Die Schafzucht im alten Griechenland*, 1934. Cf. the corresponding articles in *P.W.K.*: 'Schaf' (Orth), ii A. 373 ff.; 'Schwein' (Orth), ibid. 801 ff.; 'Pferd' (Steier), xix. 1430 ff. In these books and articles the reader will find good bibliographical references. On milk and cheese see the arts. 'Käse' (by Kroll) and 'Milch' (by G. Herzog-Hauser) in *P.W.K.* x. 1489 ff., and xv. 1569 ff.; cf. E. Hardi, *Die Herstellung und Verwendung des Käse im gr.-röm. Altertum*, 1917 (diss. Bern).

¹⁴⁸ Treatises on bee-keeping: E. Oder in F. Susemihl, loc. cit., pp. 838 ff., and on the treatment of this subject by Bolus Democritus, M. Wellmann, *Berl. Abh.*, phil.-hist. Kl., 1921, no. 4, pp. 23 ff. The fundamental modern study of ancient bee-keeping is that of J. Klek and L. Armbruster, 'Die Bienenkunde des Altertums', i. Aristoteles, ii. Varro und Vergil, iii. Columella und Plinius, iv. Die Biene in Aegypten, v. Die Spätzeit, *Archiv für Bienenkunde*, i (1919), ii (1920), iii (1921), viii (1926); cf. Olck, art. 'Biene', *P.W.K.* iii. 348 ff.; Klek, art. 'Bienenzucht', Suppl. iv. 211 ff., and Maur. Schuster, arts. 'Mel' and 'Met', xv. 364 ff. and 1298 ff. More popular and shorter is H. M. Fraser, *Beekeeping in Antiquity*, 1931 (with copious bibliography at the end). On bee-keeping in Egypt, above, p. 295 f. and n. 99, cf. P. E. Newberry, *Man*, xxxviii (1938), pp. 31 ff.

¹⁴⁹ See the sections devoted to Syria, Pergamon, and the other monarchies of Asia Minor in Chs. III, IV, V, and VI.

[150] On the plough used in Egypt in Ptolemaic and Roman times, M. Schnebel, *Landwirtschaft*, pp. 101 ff. To his material may be added that found at Karanis. I owe the information about the agricultural implements found at Karanis, of which I have made use in the text, to Prof. A. E. R. Boak of Michigan.

[151] A more detailed discussion of all the problems raised in the text will be found in my *Large Estate*. Nothing essential has been added to it by C. C. Edgar in his Introduction to *P. Mich. Zeno*. His brief discussions conclude generally in a confession of ignorance. This attitude I regard as too sceptical. F. M. Heichelheim, *Wirtschaftsg.*, pp. 616 ff., has analysed the sculptures of the grave of Petosiris from the economic point of view as if they were reflections of the life of a large οἶκος in early Hellenistic times. I am disposed to think that the subjects chosen are rather a traditional repetition of those represented in the graves of owners of large estates in the Early, Middle, and Late Kingdom of Egypt than reflections of actual life on the estate of Petosiris. The choice of subjects may have been suggested by real life, but it may not. 'Modernization' in the grave of Petosiris affected the style of the sculptures and the form of some of the objects represented, see above, Ch. II, p. 82 and n. 14, cf. A. Adriani, 'Rhyta', *Bull. Soc. Arch. Alex.* xxxiii (N.S. x. 2), pp. 350 ff. (on the date of the grave, p. 361). To the documents which deal with the cultivation of vines and the taxes paid by the owners of vine-growing estates (κτήματα) must be added a very instructive document of the Zenon correspondence in the Yale collection (soon to be published).

[152] On the state of industry in Hellenistic times see F. M. Heichelheim, *Wirtschaftsg.*, pp. 576 ff., with abundant bibliographical references in the notes. In this work the reader will find a discussion of the branches of industry which I have omitted in my sketch. The best surveys of ancient industrial technique based on independent research are the works of H. Blümner, *Technologie und Terminologie der Gewerbe und Künste bei Griechen und Römern*, vols. i–iv, 1875–87 (vol. i in 2nd edition, 1912), and, for the building and engineering craft, of C. Mercklin, *Die Ingenieurtechnik im Altertum*, 1899. The study of materials and industries in Egypt by A. Lucas, *Ancient Egyptian Materials and Industries*, 2nd ed., 1934, is likewise excellent and based on minute research. Very little is added to the data already collected by Blümner in A. Neuburger's *The Technical Arts and Sciences of the Ancients* (translation from German), 1930, and in F. M. Feldhaus's *Die Technik der Antike und des Mittelalters*, 1931 (the same author's earlier work *Die Technik der Vorzeit*, 1914, is more useful); cf. the short *compendia* of E. Stemplinger, *Antike Technik*, 3rd ed. (Tusculum Schr. iii) (arranged in historical order), and L. J. Peters, *Die Technik im Altertum*, 1925 (Kultur und Technik i). H. Diels, *Antike Technik*, 3rd ed., 1924, is a masterpiece of historical research, combining exact knowledge with ingenious interpretation of literary texts and archaeological material; cf. E. Kornemann, *Klio*, xvii (1921), pp. 287 ff. In the same spirit are written the valuable contributions

to the history of ancient technique by A. Rehm: see his short summary in Gercke und Norden, *Einleitung*, ii. 2. 5, 1933, pp. 55 ff. and 71 ff. (with up-to-date bibliography), and the general discussion of the role of technique in the Greek and Roman world in his paper 'Zur Rolle der Technik in der griechisch-römischen Antike', *Arch. f. Kulturg.* xxviii (1938), pp. 135 ff. Cf. various valuable articles in *P.W.K.*, for example Μηχανή, Μύλη, 'Schraube', &c.

[153] See the excellent study by H. A. Thompson of the pottery discovered at Athens in the American excavations of the Agora, 'Two centuries of Hellenistic pottery', *Hesp.* iii (1934), pp. 311 ff., on common pottery p. 464 f.; cf. above, Ch. III, n. 30. Of the other cities of the Hellenistic world, Priene and Pergamon have been best studied in this respect (see Chs. III, notes 35 and 44, IV, n. 311, and V, n. 66).

[154] On the spread of this pottery all over the early Hellenistic world see above, Ch. III, p. 159 f. and the corresponding notes.

[155] See on this pottery above, Ch. V, n. 66, and Excursus IV by F. O. Waagé at the end of this book.

[156] On the development of Hellenistic pottery in general see the recent handbook by C. W. Lunsingh Scheurleer, *Grieksche Ceramiek*, 1936, pp. 146 ff. (with bibliography).

[157] I cannot give here a complete bibliography of the books and papers which deal with Hellenistic painted pottery. I may refer to the excellent bibliographical references in the well-known books by E. Pfuhl, *Malerei und Zeichnung*, 1923, and M. H. Swindler, *Ancient Painting*, 1929, p. 460 f., in the articles by Thompson and Pease quoted in Ch. III, n. 30, and in the book by Scheurleer quoted in the preceding note. I may add some references which will not be found in those works. On the *lagynoi*, in addition to the studies by G. Leroux, *Lagynos*, 1913, and Ch. Picard, *Rev. Arch.* xxii (1913), pp. 161 ff., see H. A. Thompson, *Hesp.* iii (1934), p. 450 f. On the interesting Centuripae painted vases, precursors of Pompeian wall paintings, G. M. A. Richter, *Metr. Mus. Studies*, ii. 2 (1930), pp. 187 ff., and iv. 1 (1932), pp. 45 ff. Gnathia ware: C. W. Lunsingh Scheurleer, *J.D.A.I.* li (1936), Anz., pp. 285 ff.

[158] I have enumerated above, Ch. IV, n. 163, the leading works on Hellenistic relief pottery; cf. Ch. IV, n. 311, and Ch. V, n. 66, and Index, s.v. 'Pottery'. On the Pergamene ware with appliqué reliefs cf. O. Deubner, *J.D.A.I.* liv (1939), pp. 340 ff. (with bibliography; according to him the date of this pottery is 157–57 B.C.). On the relief vases with lead glaze, above, Ch. VII, n. 130. I must note here that the type of glaze used for this pottery is controversial pending a careful chemical analysis which is now being carried out in the Metropolitan Museum. On the technical devices used in Italy for the production of relief pottery, G. M. A. Richter, *Studi Etruschi*, x (1936), pp. 63 ff.

159 Above, Ch. IV, n. 163.

160 Above, Ch. IV, n. 311, and Ch. V, n. 120.

161 A. Lucas, *Ancient Egyptian Materials and Industries*, 1934, pp. 101 ff. On the Babylonian and Assyrian glaze, which is not different from that of the Mesopotamian faience, E. O. von Lippmann, *Entstehung und Ausbreitung der Alchemie*, ii, 1931, p. 95, and the article by A. Lucas in *J.E.A.* xxii (1936), pp. 141 ff. An exhaustive chemical study of the Mesopotamian glazed pottery will be printed in the appropriate section of the Final Report of the Dura Expedition (by N. P. Toll).

162 On Pliny and the books of his Natural History which dealt with metals see K. C. Bailey, *The Elder Pliny's Chapters on Chemical Subjects*, i, 1929, and ii, 1932 (the relative passages in Pliny with translation and comments).

163 On the passage in Apollonius Rhodius, J. W. Mackail, *Lectures on Greek Poetry*, 1910, p. 259 (he calls the Chalybian mining city an ancient Pittsburg or Middlesborough).

164 I have repeatedly referred (notes 116–25) to the books by S. Przeworski, J. R. Partington, and especially by O. Davies and to the articles by H. C. Richardson which deal with mining technique and the production of raw metals; cf. Orth, 'Bergbau' in *P.W.K.*, Suppl. iv. 108 ff. and R. V. Schmidt's useful though superficial summary of 'bourgeois' treatises (on which he heaps abuse), 'Studies in the history of mining and metallurgy in ancient Greece', *Bull. Ac. Hist. Mat. Civ.* cviii (1935), pp. 222 ff. (in Russian). Cf. U. Täckholm, *Studien über den Bergbau der römischen Kaiserzeit*, Diss. Uppsala, 1937.

165 F. Freise, *Geschichte der Bergbau- und Hüttentechnik*, i. Das Altertum, 1908, p. 63; Orth, *P.W.K.*, Suppl. iv. 125. On the *dioptra*, Hultsch, *P.W.K.* v. 1073 ff.

166 The two lamps I refer to are plastic lamps showing the figures of miners or smiths with the bellows before them. These lamps were first published by Licetus, *De lucernis antiquis*, 1652, pp. 739 ff., and after him by Bartoli, Montfaucon, and finally by E. Saglio to illustrate his article 'Follis' in Dar. et Saglio, *D.d.A.* ii. 1227, figs. 3133 and 3134. Doubts about their genuineness have been expressed by H. Blümner, *Technologie* ii, pp. 190 ff.; cf. Mau, *P.W.K.* vi. 2829. Prof. Zahn, whom I have consulted on the matter, is inclined to regard the two lamps as ancient and not as works of the Renaissance. In support of his belief he adduces the plain form of the lamps and a fragment of a clay lamp in the Saalburg Museum which was adorned with a plastic figure of a man warming his hands over the flame of the lamp. A metal-worker with a bellows of the usual form is represented on a Roman lamp from Tarsus, H. Goldman, *A.J.A.* xxxix (1935), p. 538, fig. 29.

167 I cannot give here a full bibliography of the works dealing with the technique of metal-working in the East and Greece. A few references to the

most recent contributions will suffice. JEWELLERY. *Egypt*: C. Ransom Williams, *Gold and Silver Jewelry*, New York Hist. Soc., 1924, and the chapter in A. Lucas's work quoted in the text. On Hellenistic jewellery in Egypt, above, Ch. IV, n. 168, and Pls. XLV and XLVII. *Greece*: The most recent work on Greek jewellery (with good bibliographical references) is B. Segall, *Katalog der Goldschmiedearbeiten*, Mus. Benaki, 1938, pp. 27 ff. (on the Hellenistic period) ; cf. on the new accessions to the rich Mus. Benaki at Athens *J.D.A.I.* liv (1939), Anz., p. 226, and figs. 3–7. On the methods of making gold wire and on filigree work, M. Rosenberg, *Geschichte der Goldschmiedekunst*: Granulation, 1918; H. Kuthmann–Kusel, *Ath. Mitt.* l (1925), pp. 183 ff.; R. Zahn, 'Zur hellenistischen Schmuckkunst', *K. Schumacher Festschrift*, 1930, pp. 202 ff. NIELLO (an ancient Egyptian technique very popular in Hellenistic and Roman times): M. Rosenberg, *Gesch. d. Goldschmiedekunst*: Niello, 1924. TOREUTICS. A good survey with an up-to-date bibliography will be found in G. Lippold, 'Toreutik', *P.W.K.* vi A. 1750 ff.; cf. on silver-gilding H. Nachod, *Röm. Mitt.* xxxiii (1918), pp. 103 ff. On the various schools, above, Ch. IV, notes 169 ff. (Egypt), 313 (Syria), and Ch. V, n. 65 (Pergamon). On the casts and moulds of Mit-Rahineh, above, Ch. IV, n. 169, and Pls. XLV and XLVIII, and on those of Athens, D. B. Thompson, 'Mater Caelaturae', *Hesp.* viii (1939), pp. 285 ff. BRONZE. Statuary: K. Kluge und K. Lehmann–Hartleben, *Die Antiken Grossbronzen*, i, 1927; statuettes: A. Ippel, *J.D.A.I.* liv (1939), Anz., pp. 350 ff.; cf. on the find of Galjub above, Ch. IV, n. 173. Vessels and implements: F. Winter und E. Pernice, *Die hellenistische Kunst in Pompeii*, iv. E. Pernice, 'Gefässe und Geräte aus Bronze', 1925. Instructive remarks on the early history of metal work will be found in S. Przeworski, *Die Metallindustrie Anatoliens in d. Zeit von 1500–700 v. Chr.*, 1939.

[168] Sir H. Carpenter and J. M. Robertson, *Nature*, cxxv (1930), pp. 859 ff.; A. Lucas, *Anc. Egyp. Mat. and Indust.*, pp. 198 ff.

[169] On the Damascene steel and its origin, N. Belaiew, 'Damascene Steel', *The Journ. of the Iron and Steel Institute*, xcvii (1918), pp. 417 ff.; H. C. Richardson, *A.J.A.* xxxviii (1934), pp. 580 ff.; cf. Sir Robert Hadfield, *History of Metallurgy of Iron and Steel*, 1915.

[170] H. C. Richardson, loc. cit., p. 581.

[171] Alexander: H. Berve, *Das Alexanderreich*, i, 1926, p. 193. Ptolemaic Egypt: J. Lesquier, *Les Instit. mil.*, 1911, p. 102. Seleucid kingdom: E. Bikerman, *Inst. Sél.*, p. 91 (no discussion of the question of supply). Apameans and Larissaeans, above, Ch. VI, n. 128. I may notice in this connexion that in the battle of Carrhae the Parthian king supplied his mounted archers with arrows transported on camelback. Arsenal of Pergamon, above, n. 38 to this chapter.

[172] M. Chwostow, *Outlines of the Organization of Industry and Commerce in Greco-Roman Egypt* (Papers of the Univ. of Kazan, 1912–14) and separately, 1914, pp. 1 ff. (in Russian).

173 On the finds of Noïn-Ula in Mongolia and the probably contemporary finds at Schibe and Pazuruk in the Altai see the works quoted in my *Skythien und der Bosporus*, pp. 544, note, and 579, note. Some textiles of Noïn-Ula have been analysed from the technical point of view in the *Bull. Ac. Hist. Mat. Civ.* xi. 7–9, 1932 (in Russian).

174 I cannot give here bibliographical references regarding the finds of textiles in general. I may, however, quote some books and articles which deal with the finds made in S. Russia, central Asia, and Mesopotamia. On the first two see the references in the preceding notes. On Mesopotamia and Syria: Palmyra—R. Pfister, *Textiles de Palmyre*, 1934; 'Études textiles', *Rev. d. Arts As.* viii (1934), pp. 84 ff. (Palmyra and Dura); *Nouveaux textiles de Palmyre*, 1937; *Textiles de Palmyre*, iii, 1940; cf. M. Th. Schmitter, 'Subsericae vestes', *Rev. Arch.*, 6e série, ix (1937), pp. 201 ff. Dura-Europus—F. Cumont, *Fouilles*, p. 251, and pls. xcii, xciii; *Dura Rep.* ii, pp. 178 ff. Halybieh—N. P. Toll, *Ann. Inst. Kond.* ix (1937), pp. 18 ff.

175 On the Egyptian loom, H. Kees, 'Aegypten', *Handb. d. Altertumsw.* iii, i 3, 1, p. 73; A. Lucas, *Anc. Eg. Mat. and Ind.*, p. 139 f. On the Greek loom, H. Blümner, *Techn. u. Term.* i, 2nd ed., pp. 135 ff. On the looms in Ptolemaic and Roman Egypt see *P. Fouad* 37 and the comments of J. Scherer on this papyrus. The papyrus is an apprentice contract. The boy will be taught τὴν λινυφικὴν τῶν καθημένων τέχνην (l. 2), which is the counterpart of ὀρθόϋφος (the standing weaver) *P. Grenf.* ii. 79, i, l. 3.

176 On Bolus Democritus and his Βαφικά and the two papyri containing recipes, M. Wellmann, 'Bolus', *P.W.K.* iii. 676 f.; H. Diels, *Ant. Techn.*[3], 1924, pp. 121 ff.; M. Wellmann, 'Die Φυσικά des Bolos Demokritos und der Magier Anaxilaos aus Larissa', i, *Berl. Abh.*, phil.-hist. Kl., 1928, no. 7; E. O. von Lippmann, *Entstehung und Ausbreitung der Alchemie*, i, 1919, pp. 1 ff. (on the papyri) and ii, 1931, pp. 58 ff. (on Bolus Democritus); W. Kroll, *Hermes*, lxix (1934), pp. 228 ff.; O. Lagercrantz, 'Das Wort Chemie', *K. Vetenskapssoc. Årsbok* (Uppsala), 1937, pp. 25 ff.; J. Bidez et F.Cumont, *Les Mages hellénisés*, i, 1938, pp. 117 ff., and passim. A fragment of a book which contained recipes for colouring various stuffs has been recently published by C. Gallavotti, *Riv. Fil.* lxvii (17) (1939), pp. 252 ff., cf. K. Reinking, *Die in den griechischen Handschriften aus dem Altertume erhaltenen Vorschriften für Wollfärberei*, 1938 (which I have not seen).

177 R. Pfister, 'Teinture et alchimie dans l'Orient hellénistique', *Sem. Kond.* vii (1935), pp. 1 ff., and *Nouveaux textiles de Palmyre*, 1937, pp. 10 ff.

178 I may mention in passing that the degradation of science into magic and occult practices may be observed in the history of the study of stones, especially precious stones, from Theophrastus and Sotacus to the Babylonian Sudines and his Babylonian offspring; see in general Hopfner, Λιθικά, *P.W.K.* xiii. 747 ff., cf. Kind, iii A. 1211 (Sotacus) and Kroll, iv A. 563 (Sudines). See also J. Bidez et F. Cumont, *Les Mages hellénisés*, i, 1938, pp. 191 ff.

179 There is a striking coincidence in plan and arrangement between the palatial house of Delos recently excavated, a house which apparently belonged to a rich Syrian merchant (J. Chamonard, *Expl. arch. Délos*, xiv (Les Mosaïques de la maison des Masques), 1933; cf. *B.C.H.* lvii (1933), pp. 98 ff.), and the above-mentioned description by Vitruvius of a Greek mansion in general. A minute comparative study of the two has recently been carried out by A. Rumpf, 'Zum hellenistischen Haus', *J.D.A.I.* l (1935), pp. 1 ff. The difference between these houses and the modest houses of Priene is very striking. Of the same palatial type is the early Hellenistic 'Rhodian' house, excavated by Pharmakovski in Olbia (B. Pharmakovski, *Bull. Comm. Arch.* xiii (1903), pp. 37 ff., and pls. xi, xii, cf. E. H. Minns, *Scythians and Greeks*, 1913, pp. 456 ff.). I may also cite the picture of a *nouveau riche* (Νεόπλουτος) drawn by Phoenix of Colophon (early third century B.C.), in which there is mention of his palatial house, worth many talents, with στοαὶ τετράστυλοι and floors of malachite (*Herodes, Cercidas*, &c., by A. D. Knox (Loeb Library), p. 248, vv. 7 ff.; cf. G. A. Gerhard, *Phoenix von Kolophon*, 1909, pp. 115 ff. T. Fyfe, *Hellenistic Architecture*, 1936, pp. 148 ff., is disappointing in this connexion (as well as in every other respect). The short remarks on Hellenistic architecture by A. Rumpf in Gercke und Norden, *Einleitung*, ii. 1. 3 (4th ed.), 1932, pp. 65 ff., are much more valuable; on pp. 66 f. and 68 he gives lists of Hellenistic temples and secular buildings of which the ruins are extant.

180 On Ctesibius, Philo, Archimedes, and their relation to ancient technique, see the works of H. Diels and A. Rehm quoted in n. 152. On their inventions, H. Diels, *Ant. Techn.*, 3rd ed., 1924; cf. on siphons and water-clocks A. G. Drachmann, 'Hero's and Pseudo-Hero's adjustable siphons', *J.H.S.* lii (1932), pp. 116 ff., and on Hero's screw-cutter id., ibid. lvi (1936), pp. 72 ff. On optical instruments, F. M. Feldhaus, 'Die ältesten optischen Hilfsmittel', *Sternfreund*, 1936, 1, pp. 41 ff. (this article I have not been able to consult). On the 'automobile' of Demetrius of Phalerum, A. Rehm, *Philol.* xcii (1937/8), pp. 317 ff. On siege engines and artillery, W. Sackur, *Vitruv und die Poliorketiker*, 1925, and above, n. 38. On the literary production of architects and engineers in general see the chapter of E. Pernice, 'Literarischen Zeugnisse' in W. Otto, *Handb. d. Arch.* i. 1, 1937; cf. above, n. 38 to this chapter (on the πολιορκητικά and βελοποιϊκά). On Vitruvius, A. Boethius, 'Vitruvius and the Roman architecture of his age', *Δράγμα M.P. Nilsson . . . dedicatum*, 1939, pp. 114 ff.

181 'Laterculi Alexandrini' is the modern name given by H. Diels to a text on papyrus (second century B.C.) found in Egypt, consisting of lists of names and facts which everybody was supposed to know. One of the lists, which contains seven names, has the title Μηχανικοί. See H. Diels, *Berl. Abh.*, 1904; *Ant. Techn.*, 3rd ed., p. 29 and pl. iv. I may add that several famous historians of the Hellenistic period described in their works some of the most spectacular constructions of their time. Athenaeus (v, 206 d–e, quoting Moschion) mentions among others the description by Diocleides of Abdera

of the *helepolis* of Demetrius Poliorcetes, that by Timaeus of the funeral pyre of Dionysius of Syracuse, and that by Hieronymus of the famous funeral carriage of Alexander, the design of which has been frequently reconstructed by modern scholars.

[182] On the high-pressure water-system of Pergamon, F. Gräber, *Alt. v. Perg.* i. 3, 1912–13, cf. *Berl. Abh.*, 1887. His description and illustrations are repeated by C. Mercklin, loc. cit., p. 504 f., and A. Neuburger, loc. cit., pp. 422 ff. Cf. A. von Gerkan, *Griechische Städteanlagen*, 1924, pp. 88 ff., who mentions aqueducts of Hellenistic times at Priene, Magnesia on the Maeander, and Ephesus.

[183] On the question of the slow development of technique in agriculture and industry see my *Soc. and Ec. Hist. R.E.*, pp. 302 ff. (Ital. ed., pp. 401 ff.) ; cf. A. Rehm, *Arch. f. Kulturg.* xxviii (1938), pp. 135 ff.

[184] Hellenistic trade has been discussed and the material referring to it often collected from different points of view and on different scales. As an element in the general economic development of the ancient world the subject has been carefully dealt with by F. M. Heichelheim, *Wirtschaftsg.*, pp. 458 ff. (the most detailed treatment of Hellenistic trade in existence, with copious bibliography). As part of the evolution of ancient trade in general, Hellenistic trade has been discussed by E. Speck, *Handelsgeschichte des Altertums*, i–iii, 1900–6, and H. Schaal, *Vom Tauschhandel zum Welthandel*, 1931. As forming one period in the history of Greco-Roman trade, it has been dealt with by Gummerus, art. 'Industrie und Handel', *P.W.K.* ix. 1381, esp. 1398 ff., and R. Cagnat and M. Besnier, art. 'Mercatura', Daremb. et Saglio, *D.d.A.* iii. 1754 ff. ; and as a section of Greek trade, by E. Ziebarth, *Beiträge zur Geschichte des Seeraubes und Seehandels im alten Griechenland*, 1929, cf. id. *Der griechische Kaufmann im Altertum*, 1934 (Tusculum Schriften, 18), and *Klio*, xxvi (1933), pp. 231 ff., and by F. Oertel in R. von Pöhlmann, *Gesch. d. soz. Frage*, &c., ii.² 1925, pp. 537 ff. ; see also my chapter 'Rhodes, Delos, and Hellenistic commerce', *C.A.H.* viii, 1930, pp. 651 ff. Several scholars have dealt with Hellenistic trade as a feature of the general evolution of the Hellenistic world. I have enumerated their works above, Ch. III, n. 1, and Ch. I, n. 1. On the evolution of Greek trade before the Hellenistic period see the bibliography in Ch. II, n. 25.

[185] Above, Chs. IV, pp. 386 ff., n. 185, and VI, pp. 923, ff., notes 203 ff. (for Egypt) ; Chs. IV, pp. 455 ff., n. 253, V, pp. 696 ff., and notes 116 ff., VI, pp. 861 ff., notes 147 ff. (for Syria) ; Ch. V, pp. 654 ff., notes 68 and 71 (for Pergamon). Cf. the copious but somewhat confused bibliography in F. M. Heichelheim, *Wirtschaftsg.*, p. 1084, n. 25.

[186] On the caravan routes in the Mesopotamian and Syrian deserts see above, Ch. VI, n. 152 ; cf. the preliminary remarks on the southern sections of those routes by Sir Aurel Stein, *C.R. Ac. Inscr.*, 1939, pp. 262 ff. On the inscriptions and sculptures of Palmyra and Dura which refer to the caravan

trade, my articles in *Mél. Glotz*, 1932, pp. 793 ff., and in *Berytus*, ii (1935), pp. 143 ff., and my *Dura-Europos and its Art*, 1938, pp. 18 ff., 66, 84; cf. H. Seyrig, *Syria*, xiii (1932), p. 266, and xiv (1933), pp. 152 ff., and D. Schlumberger, ibid. xviii (1937), pp. 295 ff. Cf. Addendum to Ch. VI, n. 152.

[187] See the bibliography to ch. i. of my *Caravan Cities*, 1932 (Ital. ed., 1934).

[188] A more detailed account, unfortunately biased by some preconceived ideas and made difficult to use by the absence of quotations from the ancient sources cited, will be found in F. M. Heichelheim's otherwise ingenious and useful survey of the various branches of international trade (*Wirtschaftsg.*, pp. 458 ff.).

[189] I may quote the fluctuation of corn prices at Delos in 282 B.C., which depended on the closing or opening by Lysimachus of the passage through the Thracian Bosporus, A. Jardé, *Les Céréales dans l'Antiquité grecque*, i, p. 168 f. Great interest attaches to the Athenian decree of 323/2 (at the end of the great famine) probably in honour of a resident on the Bosporus who helped 'those who were coming to the Bosporus' (ll. 8 ff.) and made a gift of corn: E. Schweigert, *Hesp*. viii (1939), pp. 27 ff., no. 7.

[190] Rhodes and the cities of the Black Sea, above, Ch. V, notes 87 and 93. Italy: T. Frank, *Econ. Survey*, i, p. 285 (second century), p. 355 (first century); H. Jefferson Loane, *Industry and Commerce in the City of Rome*, 1938, p. 16.

[191] I may here *exempli causa* mention one of the points on which I disagree with F. M. Heichelheim. In his *Wirtschaftsg.*, p. 469, he says: 'Zahlreiche Zeugnisse haben wir für die Zeit von Alexander bis Cäsar...für den Fernhandel mit Vieh. Er diente . . . auch der Fleischversorgung durch schlachtreife Massenware'. In n. 10 he quotes a set of texts none of which relates to anything like export and import of 'schlachtreife Massenware'. He might with more justification refer to *Teb.* 729 (time of Philopator), a fragmentary letter concerned apparently with mass seizure by the army of cattle belonging to a temple (?) εἰς τὰς σιταρχίας, which may prove that meat was a part of the soldiers' diet while on active service. But the document is obscure and this interpretation is doubtful. On the μάγειροι (butchers and dealers in meat and fat) in Egypt, above, Ch. IV, n. 106.

[192] I have cited above (Ch. VI, n. 200) the ivory statuette of Lakšmi found at Pompeii and the finds at Kapisa in Afghanistan (Indian ivories found with Roman glass) (Ch. IV, n. 317). On this statuette and some other fragmentary ivory statuettes perhaps also made in India (or at Seleuceia on the Tigris?) found at Pompeii, see A. Ippel, *J.D.A.I.* liv (1939), Anz. pp. 368 ff., figs. 16–18, cf. my Pl. LXI. 1.

[193] I have dealt with the problem of slave supply repeatedly in the previous chapters, especially in Ch. VI, in connexion with Delos and the growth of Cilician piracy (Ch. VI, pp. 778 ff., notes 46 ff.). I may remind

the reader that the institution of bondage and serfdom was deeply rooted in all the tribal States of the northern Balkan peninsula and South Russia.

194 On the role of Rhodes in the commerce of the late third and early second centuries and the distribution of Rhodian stamped jars see Ch. V, pp. 676 ff., and notes 93, 97 and 109; cf. F. M. Heichelheim, *Wirtschaftsg.* p. 1072, n. 12.

195 I cannot enter into a detailed discussion of the contents of the Rhodian jars and of the meaning of the stamps. I may refer again to the discussion of these problems by V. Grace, *Hesp.* iii (1934), pp. 197 ff.

196 On the different terms used to designate one or another type of merchants in the fifth and fourth centuries B.C. see the books and articles quoted in Ch. II, n. 25. A recent detailed discussion will be found in the paper by M. I. Finkelstein, *Cl. Phil.* xxx (1935), pp. 320 ff., who overstresses the confusion which, according to him, reigned in this terminology. For the Hellenistic period, F. M. Heichelheim, *Wirtschaftsg.*, pp. 493 ff. In Hellenistic Egypt ἔμπορος is a wholesaler, as a rule a Greek. Though this term occurs but rarely in the Ptolemaic papyri, when it is used it certainly means 'wholesale merchant' (*Rev. Laws*, 52. 25; 77. 7; 91. 5; 102. 2; *P. Cairo Zen.* 59573; *Teb.* 744 (245 B.C.), and especially the letter of Demetrius and *Teb.* 890 discussed in greater detail below). I may note that the ἔμποροι are not tabulated by Peremans in his *Vreemdelingen*, 1937. From the evidence available it appears that an ἔμπορος was not a specialist in a particular type of trade. Those who were such (ἐλαιέμποροι, λινέμποροι, ἐριέμποροι, &c.) were perhaps nearer to the retail traders styled ὀθονιοπῶλαι, ἱματιοπῶλαι, &c., and παντοπῶλαι than to the ἔμποροι, though of a higher standing (see the copious evidence in *Teb.* 890; below, n. 201; and for parallel material W. Peremans, loc. cit., pp. 135 ff.). The meaning of the term κάπηλος in Ptolemaic Egypt appears to be, not retail trader in general, but dealer in certain foodstuffs and caterer, keeper of an inn, of a tavern, or of a wineshop (καπηλεῖον). We know some of these who specialized in dealings in corn (σιτοκάπηλοι, Preisigke, *Wörterbuch*, s.v., cf. *Teb.* 890, 97, 180), oil (the κάπηλοι in *Rev. Laws*, coll. 47, 48 (differentiated from μετάβολοι) and ἐλαιοκάπηλοι, Peremans, loc. cit., p. 139), and wine (κάπηλος, *P. Enteux.* 34, cf. *Teb.* 724 (175 or 164 B.C.) and οἰνοκάπηλος, *P. Cairo Zen.* 59236, cf. 59748, 60 (?)). But in most of the texts κάπηλος means caterer, 'traiteur', innkeeper. Decisive evidence is supplied by the petitions *Teb.* 43 (118 B.C.), where people are having dinner in a καπηλεῖον, and 230 (end of the second century B.C.), where criminals spend a long time in the village inn before being arrested; cf. the unpublished *P. Col. Zen.* Inv. 272, 15 concerning a Greek, Antipater, who opens a καπηλεῖον in Hermupolis, and the tax καπηλικόν, C. Préaux, *Écon. Lag.*, p. 343. The same is probably true of *Teb.* 701, 156 (235 B.C.), 833, 44 (early second century B.C.) and of the many κάπηλοι mentioned in *Teb.* 890. I may suggest that the business of a κάπηλος was originally retail trade in corn (not to be confounded with the business of the ἀρτοκόποι, bakers), oil, and wine. It was natural to combine this business with that of an innkeeper. The ἐγδοχεῖς are mentioned

in the letter of Demetrius alongside of ἔμποροι, as in the Delian inscriptions. The ναύκληροι played in the life of Egypt a special role which I have discussed above, Ch. IV, p. 314 f. Some artisans were at the same time dealers in goods which they produced, see *Teb.* 890 and the lists in W. Peremans, loc. cit. The term μονοπώλης (as contrasted with παντοπώλης) appears in an inscription from Tavium in Galatia, G. Jacopi, *Dalla Paflagonia alla Commagene*, 1936, p. 14.

197 I have discussed the merchants' associations of Delos above, Ch. VI, pp. 788 ff., and notes 57 ff. On the associations in general see the books quoted in n. 27 to this chapter, and on the associations of merchants in particular E. Ziebarth, *Der griechische Kaufmann im Altertum*, 1934, pp. 26 ff. More up-to-date is F. M. Heichelheim, *Wirtschaftsg.*, pp. 572 ff.

198 On the foreign trade of the Ptolemies, above, Ch. IV, pp. 386 ff. with notes 185 ff., in which I have referred to my article on the foreign commerce of the Ptolemies in the *Journ. of Economic and Business History*, iv (1932), pp. 728 ff. On Apollonius as successor of Cleomenes and precursor of Cato, F. M. Heichelheim, *Wirtschaftsg.*, pp. 498 ff.

199 On foreign merchants in Panticapaeum at the time of Leucon, Polyaen. vi. 9. 2, cf. *C.A.H.* viii, p. 569.

200 I cannot adduce here all the evidence on the retail trade and the trade between Greek cities round the Aegean. A treatment of this question more detailed than mine will be found in F. M. Heichelheim, *Wirtschaftsg.*, pp. 531 ff. On the circulation of coins within a city see the bibliography quoted in my article in *Anat. St. pres. to W. H. Buckler*, 1939, pp. 277 ff., cf. below, Index, s.v. 'Coins'. Add to the references concerning Achaean coinage in the second century, Ch. V, n. 33 (cf. ibid., n. 29), M. Thompson, *Hesp.* viii (1939), pp. 116 ff. (hoard of about 146 B.C.).

201 No full list of retail traders exists. The tabulation of W. Peremans, *Vreemdelingen*, pp. 135 ff., is confined to early Ptolemaic times, contains several omissions, and must now be completed by the data supplied by *Teb.* III and other recent publications of early Ptolemaic texts. I have discussed the terminology above, n. 196.

202 This lends support to my contention (above, Ch. IV, n. 107) that in the field of textile industry there existed no strict monopoly, and that trade in linen and woollen stuffs and garments was considerable. The same remark applies to the goldsmiths and coppersmiths.

203 On banking in the ancient world in general see the relative sections of F. M. Heichelheim, *Wirtschaftsg.*, pp. 144 ff., 256 ff., 349 ff., 550 ff., and 722 ff. (with copious bibliographical notes). On banking in the Greek cities before and in the Hellenistic period, E. Ziebarth, 'Trapeza', *P.W.K.* vi A. 2194 ff., cf. Laum, art. 'Banken' and Kiessling, art. 'Giroverkehr', Suppl. iv. 68 ff. and 696 ff. On banking in Egypt the fundamental work is still F. Preisigke, *Girowesen im griechischen Aegypten*, 1910; the more recent works

are enumerated above, Ch. IV, n. 203; cf. for the Roman period my *Soc. and Ec. Hist. R.E.*, p. 541, n. 45 (some corrections in the Italian edition).

²⁰⁴ The best articles on the city banks of the Hellenistic period are those by E. Ziebarth quoted in the preceding note and above in Ch. IV, n. 203.

²⁰⁵ On the temple bank of Delos see the articles by E. Ziebarth quoted in the preceding notes (with bibliography).

²⁰⁶ On the Artemis temple at Ephesus and its banking operations see the collection of literary texts and inscriptions referring to them in *Forsch. in Ephesos*, i, 1906, pp. 261 f. (literary texts) and 279 (inscriptions); cf. Ch. Picard, *Éphèse et Claros*, 1922, pp. 81 ff. For Roman times, in addition to the literary texts, I may refer to the important role which the ἱερὸν μισθω-τήριον played in the life of the city and temple in that period. It is frequently mentioned in the inscriptions: *Forsch. in Ephesos*, iii, 1923, no. 50, p. 137; cf. the remarks of the editors on no. 65, pp. 147 ff., an inscription which attests the importance of private banking in Ephesus in the early first century A.D. (it mentions a special 'hall of bankers', τραπεζιτικὴ στοά, which can hardly have been a building of Roman times).

²⁰⁷ See bibliography in note 135. I know of no full collection of the texts of Hellenistic and Roman times which mention bankers and banks.

²⁰⁸ Cf. my *Soc. and Ec. Hist. R.E.*, p. 541, n. 45 (and the Italian edition).

²⁰⁹ More details will be found in C. Préaux, *Écon. Lag.*, p. 289 f.

²¹⁰ No doubt it is possible to assume that both parties were present in the bank when the payment was effected and that the money was handed over by the payer to the payee in specie and then deposited by the latter. But such a cumbersome procedure is highly improbable.

²¹¹ On the loans contracted between private persons C. Préaux, *Écon. Lag.*, pp. 280 ff., especially the list p. 281 f., n. 5. The existence in the reign of Philadelphus of a royal διάγραμμα, which was still valid in the first century B.C. (*B.G.U.* 1056, 9–10), dealing with private loans and probably prescribing a maximum rate of interest, is attested by the Columbia Zenon papyrus, *Inv.* 272, quoted in the text and by many other documents, and is certain. The other evidence which refers to it has been collected by Prof. W. L. Westermann and will be produced in his forthcoming publication of the Columbia papyrus; cf. C. Préaux, loc. cit. (*P. Cairo Zen.* 59341, 15, which she quotes, refers to the rate of interest valid at Calynda in Caria and probably prescribed not by a royal, but by a city, law). The various modifications and expansions of the term διὰ χειρός are recorded in F. Preisigke, *Wörterbuch*, s.v. χείρ.

²¹² See my *Soc. and Ec. Hist. R.E.*, p. 542, n. 48.

²¹³ A short bibliography will be found in Ch. III, n. 49. Cf. the much longer enumeration of books and papers in F. M. Heichelheim, *Wirtschaftsg.*,

p. 1061, n. 2 (with preponderance of books and papers dealing with Roman coinage); cf. his discussion of 'Geld und Kapital', ibid., pp. 420 ff. I have devoted to questions of coinage several sections of my Chs. II–VI. The reader will easily find them by consulting the Index, s.vv. 'Coins', 'Coinage'.

214 Cf. my general remarks on prices in Ch. IV, pp. 190 ff. and pp. 258 ff. and passim (see Index, s.vv. 'Price' and 'Inflation'); cf. the bibliographical references in F. M. Heichelheim, *Wirtschaftsg.*, p. 1065, n. 5, and p. 1064, n. 4 (rate of interest). On the growing importance of copper in money circulation, K. Regling, 'Münzkunde', in Gercke und Norden, *Einleitung*, II, 1, 2 (4th ed.), 1932, p. 21.

215 On Alexander's coinage, above, Ch. III, p. 134 f. and notes 6, 38, and 49. On the coinage of the time of the Successors, ibid., pp. 165 ff., 185 ff. On the coinage of independent cities, ibid., pp. 185 ff. and notes 50 and 51. On minting of Alexanders and Lysimachi in Greek cities before 197 and 189 B.C. ibid., n. 51. On the 'Ausgleichsmünzen', K. Regling, loc. cit., p. 21. Cf. my remarks on Pl. LXXIX. 12 (monetary alliance between Aradus and Ephesus in the second century B.C.).

216 On Seleucid coinage above, Ch. IV, pp. 446 ff., and Ch. V, p. 701 f.

217 The Attalids and their coinage, above, Ch. V, pp. 654 ff.

218 F. Hultsch, *Griechische und römische Metrologie*, 2nd ed., 1882; A. Segré, *Metrologia e circolazione monetaria degli Antichi*, 1928. On the conflicting methods of study in ancient metrology in general, C. F. Lehmann-Haupt, *Klio* xxix (1936), pp. 250 ff.

219 To the bibliography in Ch. VI, n. 9 add Ehrenberg, *P.W.K.* xv. 1485 (art. 'Metronomoi').

220 See above, Ch. IV, pp. 451 ff., n. 251, and Pls. LIV and LV; cf. the article by Ehrenberg quoted in the previous note.

221 A. Segré, loc. cit., pp. 95 ff.

222 For Ptolemaic Egypt, U. Wilcken, *Ostraka*, i. pp. 738 ff.; *Grundz.*, pp. lxviii ff.; cf. A. Segré, loc. cit., pp. 3 ff.

223 The writers on metrology: F. Hultsch, *Metrolog. script. reliquiae*, 1864–6; A. Segré, loc. cit., pp. 5, n. 4; 12, n. 1; 20. The term Πτολεμαϊκός connected with the names of various measures was never used in documents of the Ptolemaic period, although it has been restored recently in *Pap. Adler* G 19, l. 6.

224 The material is collected in the works quoted in n. 222; cf. A. Segré, loc. cit., pp. 497 ff.

225 A. Segré, loc. cit., pp. 69, 174.

226 The evidence and bibliography will be found above, pp. 314 ff.; cf. C. Préaux, *L'Écon. Lag.*, p. 146.

Excursus I

ATHENIAN COINS FOUND IN EGYPT

Extract from a letter by Dr. J. G. Milne.

'I have looked up some notes on Egyptian finds of Athenian coins, but cannot come on anything more certain than I told you—that Athenian coins of the style regarded as of the early part of the fourth century are commonly found, but there are not many which could be ascribed to the latter half of the century. The evidence of the finds from Naukratis seems to agree with this; Head has some useful material in his account of Petrie's work in his first campaign—*Num. Chron.* 1886, pp. 1 ff.; and some casual specimens from Hogarth's diggings and visits to the site which I catalogued are of the same date— probably not later than 350. As silver tetradrachms would not be likely to remain long in their original condition as coins in Egypt—the great Egyptian demand was for silver to be melted down, and the coins would not be regarded as currency by the natives—I think it seems most probable that anything now found was lost or hoarded soon after its importation, and, as the Athenians would not export old coins, but new, the pre- sumption is that there was little in the way of Athenian tetradrachms imported into Egypt after about 350. I should be inclined to put the cessation a little sooner, and connect it with Iachos and Chabrias: as I suggested in discussing the Beni Hassan hoard, it seems not unlikely that Chabrias brought some old Athenian dies with him, to strike 'owls' for paying the Greeks who served under him: the die published by Dattari in *J.I.A.N.* viii (1905), 103, looks like a rather worn genuine Athenian die which has been touched up; then local artists made more barbarous dies, to strike the inferior coins described by Dattari in the same article; and finally we get the coins with Aramaic legends described by Newell. Iachos and his fellows had realized that they could make coins that would pass muster with the mercenaries, and, as no coins came from Athens, they filled the gap.'

Excursus II

THE EGYPTIAN MINES ON THE SINAI PENINSULA

By Prof. R. P. Blake

Such personal observation of the ancient mines in the Sinai peninsula as the writer has made, namely at Serabiṭ-el-Khadem, in the Wadi' Maghārah and in the district adjacent to the Bir Naṣb, has left him with the definite impression that any mining operations of importance in these areas were carried out at an early period.[1] The Serabiṭ mines were the only ones carefully studied by the party; a merely cursory inspection was given to the two other centres. At the Bir Naṣb the substance sought after by early miners was copper.[2] This metal occurs frequently in the north-western part of the peninsula to the south of the plateau of eṭ-Ṭih and eastward in calcareous sandstone in the form of veins of copper carbonate. The green colour of this compound sharply differentiates it from the red, yellow, or white hues of the adjoining strata.[3] Smelting was certainly carried on at Bir Naṣb. The *siyyāl* trees, a species of mimosa or acacia, are even now abundant in the adjacent wadis, and their flinty wood makes excellent charcoal. The pebbles and lumps of silicious manganese oxide which abound in this region[4] were used by the early Egyptian workers as flux, and splashes of metallic copper are still found in the scoria heaps in the Bir Naṣb.[5] Sir W. M. Flinders Petrie's investigations have shown that at Maghārah certainly, and probably at Bir Naṣb, the workings date from the Old Empire.[6] The straight well-run galleries and cuts at the latter site show that ore veins of even thickness were being followed, which *a priori* implies a search for copper.[7] The sites selected were chosen for water as well as for ore supply.[8]

Under the Middle Empire[9] and probably earlier, active mining operations were carried on in search of a different substance. This was the turquoise, which occurs in the neighbourhood of the Bir Naṣb and eastward.[10] The operations at this epoch, while carried on sporadically at Maghārah, centred around the rocky ridge of Serabiṭ-el-Khadem, where the ancient nomad 'high place' (*bāmāh*) was transformed at this time into an Egyptian temple, highly unorthodox in plan, and the local goddess Ba'alat was equated with the Egyptian divinity Hathor.[11] She is termed in the inscriptions 'our lady of the *mfkt*' (conventionally vocalized *mefket*). This word unquestionably means turquoise, as it has now been shown definitely that turquoise and not copper was sought on the plateau. Many fragments of turquoise and of turquoise matrix have been recovered by recent Harvard expeditions from the tailings of the mine-workings which dot the plateau.[12] The mines are evidently excavations rather than galleries, where the workers were hunting for pockets of a substance connected by a 'tracer',[13] and were not following veins. Lastly, it is clear that copper was not being sought; a thick vein of copper carbonate was cut through in an open trench working above mine N, but was not followed.[14] Mining operations were difficult here, as there was no water within twelve miles, and the Egyptian inscriptions boast in some cases of the well-ordered transport of fluid which made their work possible. The Semitic inscriptions of the locality appear also to relate to mining operations.[15] No important work was carried on here after the Middle Empire.

We know that by this period Egypt was receiving large quantities of copper from the north—from Cyprus and Anatolia[16]—and the expensive operation of the Sinai deposits was no longer economically profitable. This was even more true in Hellenistic and Roman times, and no traces of work dating from this period were found in the areas we surveyed.

NOTES TO EXCURSUS II

[1] The chief book on this area is Sir W. M. Flinders Petrie, *Researches in Sinai*, London, 1906. The Egyptian inscriptions were published by Gardiner and Peete, 1917. The maps in Petrie's book, especially those of Serabiṭ-el-Khadem, leave much to be desired and should be checked with the work of A. Barrois (*Revue Biblique*, 1930, 601–21, and also the *Harvard Theological Review*, 1932, 101 f.: map after p. 209). Further investigations were carried on at this site in 1927 by the first Harvard expedition (*Harvard Theological Review*, 1928, 1 ff.), in 1931 (ibid. 1932, 95 ff.), and in 1935 (*Studies and Documents* edited by Kirsopp and Silva Lake, Fascicle vi: 'Excavations and Proto-Sinaitic Inscriptions at Serabiṭ El Khadem', by Richard F. S. Starr and Romain F. Butin, S.M., London, 1936).

[2] See Petrie, l.c., p. 51, 27.

[3] A geological study of this area was made by Prof. John Ball of Glasgow and is published in his book, *The Geography and Geology of West Central Sinai*, Cairo, 1916.

[4] The deposits are being worked by the Sinai Mining Company.

[5] Observations of the writer in 1931 (*Harvard Theological Review*, xxv. 97–8). Copper bars discovered there—Petrie, l.c., p. 27.

[6] Petrie, l.c., pp. 34 ff.

[7] The copper veins belong to the earlier geological period and simply form one of the multicolored sandstone layers.

[8] Water in this area is found in the main where granitic dykes have extruded themselves through antecedent strata of aqueous origin.

[9] See *Harvard Theological Review*, xxv. 133–5.

[10] Turquoise is collected and sold by the local Bedouin, as we ourselves were able to observe. The mines at Maghārah, according to Petrie, apparently produced turquoise. There is no copper there (l.c., p. 53), yet copper smelting was done there (l.c., pp. 51). There is some confusion here.

[11] Petrie, l.c., pp. 55 ff.

[12] See *Studies and Documents*, l.c., p. 22.

[13] This technical term means a hairline sedimentary trace which sometimes bulges out into pockets.

[14] Observation of writer. See Petrie, l.c., map 3 before p. 55.

[15] See R. Butin, *Harvard Theological Review*, xxv. 130 ff.

[16] See *Cambridge Medieval History*, vol. ii, p. 96.

Excursus III

THE COIN STANDARDS OF PTOLEMY I

By E. S. G. ROBINSON (*British Museum*)

When Alexander died in 323 B.C. the Attic standard was firmly established throughout the eastern Mediterranean as the one standard regulating the imperial coinage. It was a coinage of both gold and silver, and the metals stood to each other in a ratio of 10: 1, so that 20 silver drachmae (5 tetradrachms of 17·15 grammes) went to the gold stater or χρυσοῦς, a didrachm weighing 8·575 gm.[1] For ten years and more Ptolemy, as satrap of Egypt, continued the same system, issuing gold staters, and, with some modifications of type, silver tetradrachms, on the Attic standard, still bearing the name of Alexander.

Then, soon after 310, a period of change begins. In something less than twenty years the weights of both gold and silver coins fall by stages until they are stabilized in a combined issue of gold pentadrachms (τρίχρυσα) and silver tetradrachms, on the so-called Phoenician standard, which continues to regulate the coinage till the Roman conquest, though a further change of denomination is made under Ptolemy II. The issues of the various stages may be summarized as follows:

I. Gold staters and silver tetradrachms, both of Attic weight, but the latest accompanied by silver 'drachmae' weighing only 3·70–3·75 grammes and so bearing no obvious relation to the larger pieces (Svoronos, Νομίσματα . . . τῶν Πτολεμαίων, ii, nos. 34, 43, &c.).

II. After 310 the issue of gold staters was interrupted, and though the types and legend of the silver tetradrachm remained unchanged, its weight was lowered from 17·15 to 15·70 grammes. This weight is too heavy for the current description of 'Rhodian' (occasionally 'Phoenician') given to it.

III. After 306, while the silver is continued unchanged in weight, types, and legend (Ἀλεξάνδρου), the issue of gold is resumed with a change in all three respects. The staters (7·13 gm.) henceforward bear the portrait and name of Ptolemy as king, and weigh ⅚ths of the old Attic stater. This standard is conveniently, though erroneously, called Phoenician.

IV. After 300, but perhaps overlapping with the latest silver coins of III, comes the final stage. Gold (hemidrachms and pentadrachms 17·85 gm.) and silver (tetradrachms and occasional octadrachms) alike bear the portrait, type, and name of Ptolemy as king. All are now struck on the so-called Phoenician standard. These tetradrachms, however, appear in two slightly different weights, the earlier, usually with one monogram, is rather heavier (14·90 gm.),[2] the second (14·25 gm.) corresponds exactly with the gold issues.

These successive changes of standard, so far as their explanation has been attempted, are usually held to be due to the needs of commerce, either with Cyrenaica, or Phoenicia, or Rhodes and the Aegean basin. It is true that in Cyrenaica a parallel system of change may be observed, but there it is rather imposed by the suzerain than borrowed from the provincial dependency. Apart from the fact that the reduced weight of the fourth-century Phoenician coins gives a norm for the tetradrachm of about 13·30 grammes at Sidon, and of about 13·90 at Tyre, the Attic standard was firmly established in Phoenicia from Alexander's conquest down to the Egyptian occupation in 286. The fourth-century norm for Rhodian tetradrachms is 15·15 (at Ephesus 15·25), and for the radiate Rhodian tetradrachm of the third century 13·45 grammes. The discrepancy between these and any of the Ptolemaic weights is too great for commercial considerations to have played a leading part in determining the latter, though the approximations may have been found useful on occasion.

It has already been suggested[3] in connexion with the coinage of the Ptolemaic period in Cyrenaica (*B.M.C. Cyrenaica*, cclxx ff.) that the real reason for the change of standard is to be sought in the change in the ratio between the precious metals, and the suggestion may now be worked out in detail.

A steady appreciation of gold in relation to silver set in towards the end of the fourth century, which, as we know from the Zeno papyri,[4] by the middle of the third had produced in Egypt a ratio of something over 13:1. An intermediate stage, 12:1, is demonstrated among other things by the name τρίχρυσον applied to the pentadrachm of stage IV, which passed for 60 silver drachmae of the same weight. So thoroughly had the earlier χρυσοῦς, the Macedonian gold stater, fixed itself in popular speech as the gold equivalent of 20 silver drachmae, that even after the subsequent changes of standard a gold piece equivalent to 60 drachmae is automatically dubbed a τρίχρυσον.

Apart from the continuous changes in the coin-weights it will be noted that (1) the 'drachmae' of stage I bear no convenient relation in weight to their accompanying tetradrachms. (2) The weight of the silver tetradrachms of stages II and III is not found elsewhere except in the isolated issue of Cyrene. (3) The earlier and heavier form of silver tetradrachm in stage III is struck simultaneously with gold coin on the lighter scale. Without some general explanation of the kind suggested it seems impossible to cover all the facts. A similar explanation has already been proposed for similar and contemporary phenomena at Cyrene in the years immediately following its conquest by Ptolemy I (*B.M.C. Cyrenaica*, l.c.). There the process is easier to follow as it was the practice to strike a gold coin actually equivalent to the silver unit, and the falling weight of this little piece implies a rise in the ratio from 10 : 1 through 11 : 1 to 12 : 1.

If we apply this explanation in detail to the successive coinages of Ptolemy I enumerated above we find in

Stage I. (*a*) a ratio of 10 : 1, giving place, perhaps, towards the end, to (*b*) a ratio of $10\frac{1}{2}$: 1; for it may be suggested that the purpose of the 'drachma' of apparently irrational weight is to make up the necessary amount required over and above the five tetradrachms to exchange against a χρυσοῦς (*a*) 8·575 *N* ×10=85·75=17·15 Æ×5=85·75. (*b*) 8·575 *N* ×10·5=90·0375 =17·15 Æ×5+3·75 Æ=89·50.

II. The ratio next rises to 11 : 1 and the χρυσοῦς equals 6 tetradrachms of 15·70 grammes. 8·575 *N*×11=94·325= 15·70 Æ×6=94·20.

III. The new reckoning of six tetradrachms instead of five to the χρυσοῦς was not popular, so in III the weight of the χρυσοῦς itself is lowered to restore the old reckoning at the same ratio. 7·13 *N*×11=78·43=15·70 Æ×5=78·50.

IV. The next change, the last in the reign of Ptolemy I, shows a further fall in the ratio to round about 12 : 1; at first as the overweighted silver seems to imply, with a slight premium on the gold, later, at the strict ratio. 17·85 *N* ×12=214·20=14·25 Æ×15=213·75 Æ.

Finally under Ptolemy II a last attempt was made to stabilize the weights and exchange of the gold and silver on a ratio of $12\frac{1}{2}$: 1 by the issue of gold octadrachms, which were named μναεῖα because of their equivalence to a mina (100 drachmae) of silver. 8 *N*×$12\frac{1}{2}$=100 Æ.

We can see from the Zeno papyri referred to above that the attempt was unsuccessful, and that in the end variations in the exchange value of the two metals came to be met by an agio over and above the official rate.

NOTES TO EXCURSUS III

[1] None of the weights given have been arrived at by calculation from larger theoretical units such as the Euboic-Attic talent, &c. They are the normal weights of the various issues as determined from the coins themselves by the frequency table (*Num. Chr.* 1924, p. 76), and, as a rule, correct only to a twentieth of a gramme; hence the fractional discrepancies in the calculation of the equivalents in the last section, which, in view of these two facts, are surprisingly small.

[2] This unexpected and hitherto unnoticed fact emerges from a table based on the weights given by Svoronos (ibid., pp. 33–9) for tetradrachms with a single monogram and for two of his series with two monograms (nos. 240–4 and 266–8).

[3] T. Reinach, *Rev. É.G.* 1928, pp. 132 ff., has independently come to the same conclusion, but I cannot follow his detailed application of it.

[4] *P. Cair. Zen.* 59022, cf. Schubart–Regling, *Z. f. N.* xxxiii (1922), p. 73, and T. Reinach, l.c.

Excursus IV

'PERGAMENE' WARE

By Frederick O. Waagé

1. '*Pergamene*' ware.

In the past, the term 'Pergamene' ware has been used to denote a certain class of pale-bodied pottery dating roughly between the second century before and the second century after Christ. It is now evident, however, that this large class actually consists of two separate groups of pottery, rather similar in body and varnish, but totally different in shape and date. This complete difference in shape and date makes an entirely separate treatment of these two groups necessary; that is to say, it necessitates the division of the old 'Pergamene' ware into what, under the same terminology, would be called Hellenistic and Roman 'Pergamene' respectively. The fact must now be stressed that the term 'Pergamene' has no geographical significance whatsoever, since such evidence as has been reported from Pergamon is definitely against the supposition that non-micaceous, pale-bodied pottery originated in that city.

2. Hellenistic 'Pergamene'.

This can be readily distinguished from the later Roman 'Pergamene', even when the two are found mixed together, by the shapes, and it can be no less easily separated from contemporaneous Hellenistic wares by its red varnish and pale body as well as by its shapes (sketches of typical shapes, Fig. 12). At Athens it is first found in a deposit of the end of

FIG. 12. Hellenistic 'Pergamene'.

the second century B.C. and the beginning of the first (*Hesperia*, iii (1934), p. 422, nos. E151, 152). Reported occurrences of it in Palestine in the third and second centuries B.C. are disputed. It seems to have come to Antioch in the second half of the second century B.C., and during the first it is used almost exclusively, having driven the older Hellenistic shapes of local pottery off the market; the same appears to have been the case throughout the Hellenistic South-East (note the common occurrence of this ware at Alexandria, Samaria, Hama, Antioch, and Delos and its presence even at Dura), whereas the old-fashioned cities of the Greek mainland continued to use black-varnished wares, as did Athens, for instance. The rather sudden appearance of this particular red ware over a wide area, and the uniformity of its distinctive shapes, suggest that it originated in some one district; but the minor variations in colour and quality of body suggest also that branch factories were soon set up, or at least that it was successfully copied, elsewhere. The original source of the pottery is unknown, and there is no evidence to support the claim of any particular site where it is found. In view both of the necessity of having a specific name for this pottery and of the inappropriatenesss of the term 'Pergamene', even when limited by the adjective 'Hellenistic', one might venture the following terminology:

Hellenistic 'A': the usual black to brown or red pottery found throughout the Hellenistic world; it was of continental Greek and in large part of specifically Attic descent.

Hellenistic 'B': the distinctive red Hellenistic 'Pergamene' pottery.

3. Roman 'Pergamene'

It was probably during the first quarter of the first century A.D. that, at Antioch and other sites where Hellenistic 'Pergamene' was in wide use, its characteristic shapes were rapidly superseded by the typical early Roman ('sigillata') shapes copied from the popular Italian (Arretine, Puteolan) wares. Very likely some of the same factories which had been making Hellenistic 'Pergamene' shapes went on to make Roman

FIG. 13. Roman 'Pergamene'.

'Pergamene' shapes instead, but whether or not analyses prove body and varnish to be identical in some cases, the difference in date and shapes still requires a separate name and classification for each. This early Roman pottery (first to second centuries A.D.) with pale body is but one of several cognate and contemporaneous wares (all reproducing Italian shapes more or less closely), of which the Gaulish in the north and the Samian and Çandarli (Tschandarli) in the east are most readily recognizable as such. It is, however, much less distinctive than the Hellenistic 'Pergamene' or the Roman wares just mentioned, since its pale body often varies to darker and less characteristic shades of colour, and the minor differences in its shapes (as compared with those of other contemporaneous wares) have yet to be proved significant. Hence the need for a separate name is not so great here as in the case of Hellenistic 'Pergamene', and little is lost by describing it as 'Early Roman pale-bodied ware' or the like (for sketches of typical shapes see Fig. 13).

4. Classification of Red Wares.

It is evident that any classification which does not divide the old 'Pergamene' ware into a Hellenistic and a Roman group cannot be valid, since that division is an actual one. A case in point is 'Group II' of Mr. Iliffe's recent study, which in addition to both Hellenistic and Roman 'Pergamene' is also made to embrace Çandarli ware. Such a broad grouping as this 'Group II' is both archaeologically impossible and ceramically non-existent, since it contains (1) the Hellenistic 'Pergamene' of the second to first centuries B.C.; (2) the pale-bodied Roman 'Pergamene' of first–second centuries A.D.: (3) the distinct Çandarli ware, also of the first to second centuries A.D., but red-bodied and usually as distinguishable from Roman 'Pergamene' as are Arretine, Samian, or Gaulish. The sudden change of pottery shapes about the time of Augustus throughout the Hellenistic world must be made to mark the line between what is 'Hellenistic' and what is 'Roman' so far as the plain, wheel-made table-ware is concerned; the moulded and otherwise decorated fancy vases are things apart and are not under consideration here. Hellenistic 'Pergamene' must therefore be grouped as a distinct species under the same genus as other Hellenistic wares; Roman 'Pergamene' must be grouped as an only moderately distinct species under the same genus as other Early Roman wares. Other comments upon Mr. Iliffe's article, such as the presence of Samian potters' stamps at Antioch, will be found in my forthcoming review of it in the *American Journal of Archaeology*; but as this review was written several years ago, it does not bring out the necessity of recognizing the existence of two groups of pale-bodied pottery, which I have emphasized here.

ADDENDA AND CORRIGENDA

CHAPTER I

p. 51. It may be noted that the existence of a pact between Philip and Antiochus III is denied by D. Magie, *J.R.S.* xxix (1939), pp. 32 ff.

n. 12. Battle of Cos: add W. Peremans, *L'Antiquité Class.* viii (1939), pp. 401 ff.

n. 14. Add to the references: J. van A. Fine, 'The Background of the Social War of 220–217 B.C.', *Am. J. Ph.* lxi (1940), pp. 129 ff.

CHAPTER II

n. 4. In citing the chief works dealing with the economic life of the Persian Empire I have omitted to mention the short study of four Persian satrapies (Egypt, Babylonia, Syria, and Asia Minor) by E. Cavaignac, *Population et capital dans le monde méditerranéen antique*, 1923, pp. 1 ff. (chs. i–iv). Cavaignac studied the Persian tribute imposed on these four satrapies in the light of the contemporary evidence, but his study adds nothing essential to the general picture I have given in Ch. II. His calculations of the general produce of the four satrapies of the Persian Empire are highly hypothetical.

n. 9. Much has been written since 1937 on Ras Shamra (Ugarit). I may refer to the two recent summaries of his own work by C. F. A. Schaeffer: *Ugaritica. Études relatives aux découvertes de Ras Shamra*, Première série, 1939, and *The Cuneiform Texts of Ras Shamra-Ugarit* (The Schweich Lectures of the British Academy, 1936), 1939. On Alalkha or Alalakh, Sidney Smith, *Alalakh and Chronology*, 1940.

n. 11. A survey of Palestine (with good bibliography) will be found in F. M. Abel, *Géographie de la Palestine*, v. ii, 1938.

n. 48. A rich grave of the time of Philip II of Macedonia has been recently discovered near Gornjani in the region of Nevrokop: V. Mikov, *Bull. Inst. Arch. Bulg.* xi (1937), pp. 207 ff.

CHAPTER III

p. 126 and n. 1. The problems connected with the part played by the Greek cities in the development of the ancient world since the time of Alexander have been recently discussed by A. H. M. Jones, *The Greek City from Alexander to Justinian*, 1940. This book is a systematic supplement to his earlier volume, *The Cities of the Eastern Roman Provinces*, 1937, which I have often cited in the present work. It came to hand too late to be considered in my text and notes. In these short addenda I cannot discuss all the points on which I agree or disagree with the author.

p. 155 and n. 28. On the enlargement of Colophon, A. Wilhelm, *Anat. St. pres. to W. H. Buckler*, 1939, pp. 345 ff.; cf. L. Robert, *Rev. É.G.* lii (1939), p. 497 f.

p. 181 and n. 45. In dealing with the economic conditions in Greek cities during the late fourth century I was unable to consult the recent book by H. Michell, *The Economics of ancient Greece*, 1940. In enumerating the sources of income of Greek cities I have not mentioned the substantial income which they derived from fisheries. The rate at which they taxed the fisheries was very high: πέμπτη ἰχθύων is mentioned in inscriptions from Colophon and Calymna, a τετάρτη (probably also a tax on fisheries) in one from Cyzicus; see A. Wilhelm, *Anat. St. pres. to W. H. Buckler*, 1939, p. 361 f.; cf. for the later period Ch. IV, n. 71 and in general Ch. VIII.

CHAPTER IV

p. 257; cf. Ch. V, n. 151. F. Ll. Griffith, *The Adler Papyri*, 1939, p. 63, is inclined to regard all the papyri of a date earlier than 186–88 B.C. which are said to have been found at Gebelen as coming from other places. The Gebelen group deals exclusively with the affairs of the local Πέρσαι τῆς ἐπιγονῆς, and belongs to the second to first centuries B.C.

pp. 263, 320, 326, 411 ff., especially 414: cf. Ch. VIII. My view concerning the privileged position of the Greeks in Egypt in the third century B.C., a position bitterly resented by the natives and by other non-Greeks of high and low standing settled in Egypt, is supported by some recently discovered documents, unknown to me when I wrote these passages. One is *P. Yale Inv.* 1627–8 of the time of Euergetes I (unpublished). A priest of high standing in whose house a Greek cleruch was billeted says about his opponent in his *enteuxis*, l. 13: καταφρον]ήσας μοῦ ὅτι Αἰγύπτιός εἰμι. Another is one of the Zenon papyri now in Columbia University (*Inv.* 274), soon to be published in *P. Col.* iv. 66 by Prof. W. L. Westermann (to whom I owe my knowledge of it). An Arab in the service of Zenon in Philadelphia, put by the latter under the orders of Jason, complains about irregularities in the payment of his salary and says that he is so treated ὅτι εἰμὶ βάρβαρος (l. 19) and ὅτι οὐκ ἐπίσταμαι ἑλληνίζειν (l. 21). Cf. the excellent comments of Westermann. I may add in this connexion that in the list of qualities required in a Ptolemaic official (cited by me below in Ch. VIII, n. 35 and quoted in *Teb.* iii, no. 703, p. 71) there figures that of being φιλέλλην.

p. 316. The subheading should read: *Economic and Social Conditions in Egypt. The Greeks and the Natives*.

p. 339 f. A full and excellent survey of the history of ancient Cyprus will be found in Sir George Hill's *History of Cyprus*, i, 1940. The conditions prevailing in the period of Persian domination, touched upon in my Ch. II, are discussed in ch. vii, pp. 111 ff., those obtaining during the times of the Successors in ch. viii, pp. 156 ff., while ch. ix (pp. 173–211) deals with the period of Ptolemaic rule. For all the known facts concerning the political vicissitudes of this island, its administrative and military organization in the periods dealt with in my book, I refer the reader to these chapters of Hill's volume (which, I may note, have been revised by W. W. Tarn, while ch. ix was written in collaboration with T. B. Mitford).

pp. 392 ff. Commercial relations between Alexandria and the cities of the

north-western coast of the Euxine are attested for the Hellenistic period
by an inscription from Callatis recently published by Th. Sauciuc-Saveanu,
L'Archéologie en Roumanie, 1938, fig. 74: Θέων Ποτάμωνος | Ἀλεξανδρεύς.
This book and the inscription quoted are known to me from the mention
of them in R. Flacelière, J. Robert, L. Robert, *Rev. É.G.* lii (1939), p. 483,
no. 235, cf. 227.

n. 92, cf. Ch. V, n. 151. The documents of the archives of Horus found at
Gebelen and mentioned in these notes are now published by E. N. Adler,
J. G. Tait, F. M. Heichelheim, and F. Ll. Griffith, *The Adler Papyri*, 1939.

n. 131, cf. Ch. V, n. 75. A parallel text to the inscription of Samothrace
mentioned in this note has recently been found there. It was first published
by A. Bakalakis and R. L. Scranton, *Am. J. Ph.* lx (1939), pp. 452 ff.; new
readings and a different interpretation have been suggested by M. Rostovtzeff and C. B. Welles, ibid. lxi (1940), p. 207 f.; L. Robert, *Rev. É.G.* lii
(1939), p. 492 f.; cf. P. Roussel, *B.C.H.*, 1939. Unfortunately the new
inscription sheds no fresh light on the relations between Samothrace and
the Ptolemies.

nn. 156 and 159. Fragments of a waterwheel and some millstones have been
found recently at Venafrum (1st cent. A.D.); see L. Jacono, 'La ruota
idraulica di Venafro', *L'Ingegnere*, xii (1938), pp. 1 ff. (offprint).

n. 215, cf. 213. On Apollonius: R. Seider, 'Beiträge zur ptolemäischen Ver-
waltungsgeschichte', *Quellen u. Studien z. Gesch. u. Kultur d. Altert. u.
Mittelalt.* viii, 1938.

n. 216. A large production of wine on the former *dorea* of Apollonius in
Philadelphia is attested by *P. Yale Inv.* 1641 (unpublished) of the time of
Euergetes I (?). An order is given by Zenon (the former manager of
Apollonius' *dorea*?) to buy for him nine *keramia* παλαιοῦ Φιλαδελφείου οἴνου
(l. 20).

n. 223; cf. p. 481. A general idea of the economic and social aspects of life
in Hellenistic Antioch may be derived from the famous mosaic of Daphne
which depicts scenes from life in the fourth century A.D. along the road
leading from Antioch to Daphne. These scenes find striking parallels in
the modern life of Syria, which have not altered very much since Hellenistic
times; see J. Lassus, 'Dans les rues d'Antioche', *Bull. Ét. Or. de l'Inst. fr.
de Damas*, v (1935), pp. 121 ff. and pls. XII–XVII.

n. 227. On the lay-out of Seleuceia on the Tigris, C. Hopkins, *Antiquity*, xiii
(1939), pp. 440 ff.

n. 230. An Olympichus is mentioned in an inscription from Laodicea on the
Lycus, *M.A.M.A.* vi (1939), no. 4, cf. p. 14; but his identity with the
tyrant of the same name is questionable, see L. Robert, *Rev. É.G.* lii
(1939), p. 506.

n. 309. On prices in Babylon cf. E. Cavaignac, *Population et Capital*, 1923,
p. 111 f.

n. 311. The same sequence of brands of pottery as in Syria, Mesopotamia,
and Palestine has been revealed by the systematic excavations at Alishar
Hüyük in Phrygia, viz. black-glazed of Attic and of local make, West-slope

ware, Megarian bowls, which were all gradually replaced by the so-called Pergamene ware. See F. O. Waagé, 'Greek, Hellenistic and Roman Pottery from Alişar', in H. H. v. d. Osten, *The Alishar Hüyük, Seasons of 1930–32*, iii, 1937, pp. 74 ff.

n. 317. A full report on the first season's excavation at Kapisa will be found in J. Hackin, *Recherches archéologiques à Begram*, 1939. The exploration of the site has been carried on and has yielded among other things more specimens of painted Syrian glass and Indian ivories. On the finds of the first season cf. the remarks of A. Ippel, *J.D.A.I.* liv (1939), Anz. pp. 599 ff. New explorations in Afghanistan: E. Barger, *Ill. Lond. News* 1939, Apr. 22, p. 682 f.

n. 322. I should have mentioned in this note that Philetaerus apparently regularized the system of weights and measures in his *dynasteia*. The later *Scriptores Metrologici* knew of a special system of weights and measures styled the Philetaeric. See below, Ch. VIII.

n. 330. On the dates to be assigned to the gifts of Philetaerus to Cyzicus, M. Segre, *Athen.* viii (1930), pp. 488 ff. and xii (1934), p. 437. A special festival called Philetaerea was celebrated at Cyzicus, L. Robert, *Ét. Anat.* 1937, pp. 199 ff.

CHAPTER V

p. 617 and n. 18. In speaking of the material losses of Greece at the time of the Roman intervention I have omitted to mention the serious damage done to her by the loss of man-power: those killed in the wars and revolutions and those—freemen and slaves—who were exported as slaves from Greece to Italy were irretrievably lost to Greece. Though we have no statistics, we may safely assume that their numbers were very large.

n. 20. On the food supply of the Greek cities cf. K. Köster, *Die Lebensmittelversorgung der altgriechischen Polis*, 1939 (which I have not seen).

nn. 27 and 30, cf. Ch. VI, n. 49. New Delphian acts of manumission have been recently published by N. Valmin, *F.D.* iii. 6, 1939. Manumissions from Epirus: D. Evangelidis in Ἠπειρωτικὰ Χρονικά, i (1935), pp. 196 ff. (which I have not seen).

n. 33. Achaean coinage. A new hoard of Achaean federal silver has been published by M. Thompson, *Hesp.* viii (1939), pp. 116 ff.

n. 40. To what I have said about the situation of the 'free' cities of Asia Minor after Magnesia and Apamea I may add that, though legally independent, these cities were bound to be careful not to offend the Pergamene kings, since their prosperity depended to a large extent on their good relations with the rulers of a large part of Asia Minor. Rome, benevolent to them and ready to protect them in case of open encroachments on their liberty, seldom interfered in the affairs of Asia Minor. This situation changed somewhat after Pydna, but the main lines of Roman policy towards the Pergamene kings and the free cities remained the same. See the judicious remarks of D. Magie, *Anat. St. pres. to W. H. Buckler*, 1939, pp. 161 ff.

n. 44. On Antiochus III and the cities of Asia Minor, see the article by D. Magie cited in the preceding addendum.

n. 49. Add to the bibliography the article by D. Magie, l.c.

n. 55. A new restoration and a new interpretation of the decree for Cephisodorus have been recently suggested by L. Robert (*Rev. É.G.* lii (1939), p. 508 f.). According to him it was the city of Apamea (without the help of Cephisodorus) that supplied the Pergamene army with corn and rendered certain other services to Eumenes II during the war. After the war the king, in token of gratitude, bestowed on the city a gift of 3,000 drachmas. To this sum Cephisodorus added a substantial contribution of his own to be used for the needs of the Gymnasium.

n. 93. Add to the articles quoted in this note one by G. Cantacuzène, 'Considérations sur les timbres amphoriques découverts en Roumanie et sur les côtes du Pont Euxin', *Rev. hist. du sud-est européen*, xvi (1939), pp. 44 ff.; cf. the papers quoted in *Rev. É.G.* lii (1939), p. 482 f., nos. 228–31.

n. 99. On the Rhodian bas-reliefs and statues see L. Laurenzi, 'Rilievi e statue d'arte Rodia', *Röm. Mitt.* liv (1939), pp. 42 ff.

n. 132. On the date of the accession of Epiphanes, E. Bikerman, *Chr. d'Ég.* xxix (1940), pp. 124 ff.

n. 151. Σύνοδος γεωργῶν ἰδίων, discussed in this note, may be understood as landowners, residents in the given place as opposed probably to ξένοι, that is to say, to men whose ἰδία was somewhere else. Cf. *B.G.U.* 1589, and my Index, s.v. πράκτωρ ἰδιωτικῶν. The various meanings of the terms ἴδιος and ξένος in Ptolemaic and Roman Egypt need a careful special study.

CHAPTER VI

n. 10. Miss V. Grace has kindly allowed me to read her typewritten report to the Guggenheim Foundation on her recent study of stamped jar-handles found and stored in Egypt, Syria, Cyprus, and Greece. According to her observations, while the early Rhodian stamps are abundant in Athens, the late ones, found in large quantities at Alexandria and Carthage (until 145 B.C.), are very rare at Athens. She is inclined to connect this fact with the settlement of 166 B.C. I would suggest that the disappearance of Rhodian containers from Athens testifies to the gradual emancipation of Athens from the commercial hegemony of Rhodes, an emancipation which began earlier than 166 B.C. (see above, p. 629 f.) but was accentuated by the Roman settlement of the affairs of Greece after Pydna. I have noticed the same evolution at Pergamon (Ch. V, n. 68). It would be highly interesting to study from the same point of view the stamped jar-handles found at Delos and those of South Russia and the cities of the western coast of the Euxine.

n. 73. To the list of cities add Teos (?), *S.E.G.* ii. 580.

n. 80. D. Magie, *Anat. St. pres. to W. H. Buckler*, p. 181, n. 2, assigns the decree of Cyzicus, *I.G.R.* iv. 134, to an earlier date (135 B.C.). Phocaea as supporting Mithridates: Justin, xxxvii. 1. 1.

n. 152. Important new evidence on the Palmyrene trade in the Roman period has been recently discovered during the excavation of the Palmyrene *agora* by H. Seyrig. Several inscriptions give valuable information on the organization of the caravans, which was probably *mutatis mutandis* the same in Hellenistic times. See Seyrig's preliminary report in *C.R. Ac. Inscr.* 1940 (a typewritten copy of which was kindly sent me by the author).

n. 198. Large quantities of painted glass have been recently discovered at Begram in Afghanistan: see J. Hackin, *Recherches archéologiques à Begram*, 1939. To the published fragments many more have been added since the publication of Hackin's first report. The fragments from Begram must be carefully studied in the light of the other extant specimens. My impression is that the latter are in many respects different. While those found in Italy, South Russia, and Gaul were probably made in Egypt, those from Begram may be regarded as produced in Syria. On the finds at Begram see Add. to Ch. IV, n. 317.

n. 200. It is needless to remind the reader of the many features of life in Pompeii which reveal early connexions between that city and Alexandria. Suffice it to mention the temple of Isis, which was built in the late second century B.C. and rebuilt after the earthquake of A.D. 63. See R. C. Carrington, *Pompeii*, 1936, p. 126 f. (cf. 121 f.) and A. Sogliano, *Pompei nel suo sviluppo storico*, 1937, pp. 221 ff. See also the most recent Guides to Pompeii (Mau-Ippel, Warsher, Maiuri, &c.).

n. 203. The high customs duties levied at Leuce Come in Roman times (25 per cent. of the value of the goods) are paralleled on the one hand by the compensatory tariff on imported goods belonging to the reign of Philadelphus, and on the other by the τετάρτη levied in Roman times on the Parthian frontier, as attested by inscriptions recently found by H. Seyrig in the *agora* of Palmyra (see above, Add. to Ch. VI, n. 152). The latter may be interpreted as a protective tariff intended to divert Indian goods from the overland route which ran through Parthia to the sea-route which brought Indian merchandise to Egypt and Alexandria directly.

n. 205. On Eudoxus see the remarks (apropos of the suggestions of Otto and Bengtson) of W. W. Tarn, *J.H.S.* lix (1939), p. 324.

CHAPTER VII

p. 978 f. On the organization of Pontus by Pompey see W. G. Fletcher, 'The Pontic Cities of Pompey the Great', *T.A.P.A.* lxx (1939, published in 1940), pp. 17 ff. Mr. Fletcher is inclined to assume that Pompey did not attempt to colonize Pontus in the Hellenistic fashion, i.e. to create Greek or hellenized cities there, but that his division of Pontus into eleven cities (some of them created by him) was a measure of purely administrative and financial character, and was based on his experience in Spain and on Roman, not Hellenistic, traditions. There are no conclusive facts to support his contention. None of the Pontic cities have been excavated, and the archaeological and epigraphical material at our disposal is meagre. We know nothing of the plan, the architectural features, or the constitution of the Pontic cities in Hellenistic or Roman times. No conclusions can be based on such inadequate material. The parallel with Spain is far-fetched. In one feature at least, i.e. in giving to some of the new cities 'dynastic' names (Pompeiopolis, Magnopolis, Megalopolis), Pompey followed Hellenistic traditions. The further suggestion of Mr. Fletcher that the whole of the territory of Pontus was divided between the new administrative and financial centres cannot be proved. The data furnished by Strabo are not conclusive. Moreover, it is certain that a conspicuous part of Pontus—the estates of Mithridates—was not included in any city territory, and the same is true of the temple land of Comana and perhaps of some other temples. Another unproved assertion is that the new division into city territories put an end to serfdom in the country. I cite again the former estates of Mithridates and the temple land. Further, serfdom was not incompatible with the structure of a city-state, especially in Asia Minor. A more detailed discussion of Mr. Fletcher's paper is not possible here.

pp. 981 ff. On Gabinius' career and his personality see the substantial paper by Eva Matthews Sanford, 'The Career of Aulus Gabinius', *T.A.P.A.* lxx (1939, publ. in 1940), pp. 64 ff., esp. pp. 82 ff. on his administration of Syria.

n. 13. On the decree of Olbia, *I.O.S.P.E.* i.² 35, see L. Robert, *Istros*, ii (1936), pp. 5 ff.

n. 30. On the date of the grant of freedom to Tabae and Alabanda, D. Magie, *Anat. St. pres. to W. H. Buckler*, 1939, pp. 175 ff.

n. 59. On the history of the Roman province of Cilicia see the substantial article by R. Syme, 'Observations on the Province of Cilicia', *Anat. St. pres. to W. H. Buckler*, 1939, pp. 299 ff. On the relations between Appius Claudius Pulcher and Cicero, L. A. Constans, *Un correspondant de Cicéron Ap. Claudius Pulcher*, 1921.

n. 81. On L. Calpurnius Piso Caesoninus, R. Syme, *The Roman Revolution*, 1939, Index, s.v.

n. 105. To the works of T. Rice Holmes and M. A. Levi add R. Syme, *The Roman Revolution*, a detailed account of the history of the period from the death of Caesar to that of Augustus, with a few words on Pompey and Caesar.

n. 118. On the policy of Antony in respect of the vassal States cf. L. Craven, 'Antony's Oriental Policy until the Defeat of the Parthian Expedition', *Univ. of Missouri Stud.* iii. 2, 1920, and R. Syme, *Roman Revolution*, 1939, pp. 259 ff., who does not cite Craven's paper.

nn. 118–20. Some remarks on Antony's activity in the East in collecting money will be found in E. Groag's article in *Klio*, xiv (1914), p. 49 f.

n. 120. On the petty tyrants of Asia Minor in the first century B.C., especially on Antipater of Derbe and Laranda, R. Syme, *Anat. St. pres. to W. H. Buckler*, 1939, pp. 309 ff.

CHAPTER VIII

p. 1061. The fragments of Herodotus and Appian (*Bell. Mithr.* 101) found at Dura are discussed and reproduced by C. B. Welles, *T.A.P.A.* lxx (1939) publ. in 1940), pp. 203 ff.

n. 7. On the forms of merchantmen in Greece and Rome, Fr. Moll, *Das Schiff in der bildenden Kunst*, 1929, Section B iv. His book is a useful, but not complete, repertory of monuments of art and artistic industry on which ships are represented. The text to the copious reproductions contains some valuable technical remarks. In the section dealing with Greece no discrimination is attempted between the Classical and the Hellenistic periods. Cf. the same author's article, 'Der Schiffbauer in der bildenden Kunst', *Deutsches Museum, Abh. u. Ber.* ii (1930), pp. 153 ff., and E. Pfuhl, 'Sepulcrale Bilder von Segelschiffen', *'Eφ.' Aρχ.* 1937, pp. 92 ff.

n. 24; cf. nn. 32 and 35. To the private library of Zenon of Philadelphia may have belonged the literary works of which fragments were found in his house. One of these works (perhaps one of the tragedies of Agathon) has musical annotations (*P. Cairo Zen.* 59533; cf. C. C. Edgar, *P. Mich. Zen.*, Intr. p. 49, and H. I. Marrou, *Rev. Phil.* xiii (65), 1939, pp. 308 ff.).

n. 35. Very interesting in this respect is the Columbia papyrus quoted in n. 24 (*P. Col.* iv, 'Zenon and other Ptolemaic Papyri', no. 60). In this fragmentary letter Zenon is informed about some books (βιβλία), probably belonging to his library, which had been sent (ἃ κατηνέχθη) to Epharmostus his brother. The two books mentioned in the fragment are συναγωγαί of the Peripatetic school (one by Callisthenes), that is to say, 'collections of materials which were so characteristic of the activities of the Peripatetics' (Westermann, *P.W.K.* x, 1685). It is natural to suggest that a study of such books, if not required from Ptolemaic officials, was regarded by them as a useful background for their administrative and diplomatic activity in the service of the king, and the ability to quote them in conversations with their superiors as a help in their career. On the συναγωγαί cf. Westermann's introduction to the papyrus cited above.

nn. 42 and 43. Add to the references L. Robert, *Ét. ép. et phil.*, 1938, pp. 7 ff.

n. 45. An interesting instance of the combination of scientific and religious healing may be seen in a votive bas-relief found in the Amphiareum, which represents Amphiaraus acting as a doctor, that is to say, performing a surgical operation, V. Leonardos, *'Eφ. 'Aρχ.* 1916, p. 120.

n. 46. Add to the references for surgical instruments P. Capparoni, 'L'armamentario chirurgico greco e greco-romano', *Atti e Mem. Acc. Stor. Arte Sanitaria*, 2 ser. iv (1938), pp. 169 ff., and N. Scalinci, 'Sui alcuni strumenti di chirurgia oculare', ibid., pp. 225 ff.; cf. J. Orient, 'Röm. chirurg. Instrumente aus dem Randgebiet Pannoniens', *Arch. f. Gesch. d. Medizin*, xxxii (1939), p. 136 (which I have not seen).

n. 47. In addition to the references given in this note I may mention that Diog. L. vii. 186 speaks of a doctor of one of the Ptolemies, named Chrysippus, 'who on a false charge was dragged about and castigated with the lash', which shows that the life of a court physician was not one of continuous enjoyment. The popularity of medical science in the Hellenistic world is illustrated by a terracotta statuette found in Pompeii, but made probably in Egypt, representing a doctor feeling his own pulse. It has been suggested that the statuette represents the famous Herophilus, the discoverer of the pulse. See A. Ippel, *J.D.A.I.* liv (1939), p. 367 and fig. 15 (with bibliography).

n. 49. Add to the documents in which lawyers appear as assistants of the parties the inscription of Calymna published by M. Segre, *Epigraphica* (presented to the First Congress of Epigraphy), 1938, pp. 9 ff. (which I have not seen); cf. L. Robert, *Rev. É.G.* lii (1939), p. 488, no. 270: a decree of the city (end of the fourth or beginning of the third century B.C.) in honour of a Milesian lawyer (συνάγορος) Hecatonymus, son of Prytanis. Like the doctors, the lawyers were not bound to one place.

MINOR ERRATA

Page 35, line 8 from foot, *for* Chalcedon *read* Calchedon
   79,   21 from foot, delete Emesa
   151,   6, *for* Mitylene *read* Mytilene
   232,   6 from foot, *for* Chalcedon *read* Calchedon
   298,   3, *for* νῖτρον *read* νίτρον
   363,   17, *for* κηλώνια *read* κηλώνεια
   493,   9 from foot, *for* Pitana *read* Pitane
   507,   8, *for* Hierapolis *read* Hieropolis
   510,   8, delete Hemesa
   609,   10, *for* Lacaedemonian *read* Lacedaemonian
   660, pl. LXXIV, 3. The artist's signature does not belong to the
        mosaic reproduced in the Plate.

LIST OF ABBREVIATIONS USED IN CITING TITLES OF PERIODICALS, &c.

Abbreviations used in citing editions of ancient authors and collections of inscriptions and papyri will be found in Index II.

Abh. Bayer (*or* Munich) Akad. *or* **Bay. Abh.** = *Abhandlungen der bayerischen Akademie der Wissenschaften.*

Abh. Sächs. Ges. (*or* Leipz. Akad.) = *Abhandlungen der k. sächsischen Gesellschaft der Wissenschaften.*

Ac. Roum., Bull. de la Sect. Hist. = *Bulletin de la Section historique de l'Académie Roumaine.*

Acta Arch. Mus. Nat. Hung. = *Acta archaeologica Musei nationalis hungarici* (= *Arch. Hungarica*).

Aeg. = *Aegyptus: Rivista italiana di egittologia e di papirologia.*

A.E.M. aus Oest. = *Archaeologisch-epigraphische Mittheilungen aus Oesterreich.*

A. (*or* Am.) J. A. = *American Journal of Archaeology.*

A. J. Num. = *American Journal of Numismatics.*

A. (*or* Am.) J. Ph. = *American Journal of Philology.*

A.v.P. *or* **Alt v. Perg.** = *Altertümer von Pergamon.*

Am. Hist. Rev. = *American Historical Review.*

Amtl. Ber. K. Kunstsamml. (*or* Ber. Kgl. Kunsts.) = Berliner Museen: *Amtliche Berichte aus den königlichen Kunstsammlungen.*

Ann. Br. Sch. Athens = *Annual of the British School at Athens.*

Ann. d'Hist. éc. et soc. = *Annales d'histoire économique et sociale.*

Ann. ép. = 'L'Année épigraphique', in *Revue archéologique* and separately.

Ann. Inst. d. Phil. et Hist. Orient. = *Annuaire de l'Institut de Philologie et d'Histoire orientales de l'Université libre de Bruxelles.*

Ann. Inst. Kond(akov) = *Annales de l'Institut Kondakov.*

Ann. Mus. Gr. Rom. = Municipalité d'Alexandrie: *Annuaire du Musée Gréco-Romain.*

Ann. Sc. Ital. = *Annuario della R. Scuola archeologica di Atene.*

Ant. Class. = *L'Antiquité Classique.*

Ant. Denk. = *Antike Denkmäler.*

Antiquaries Journ. = *Antiquaries Journal.*

Anz. Schweiz. Altertumsk. = *Anzeiger für Schweizerische Altertumskunde.*

Arch. d'Hist. du Droit orient. = *Archives d'histoire du droit oriental.*

Ἀρχ. Δελτ. = *Ἀρχαιολογικὸν Δελτίον τῆς δημοσίας ἐκπαιδεύσεως.*

Arch. Eph. (*or* Ἐφ. Ἀρχ.) = *Ἀρχαιολογικὴ Ἐφημερίς.*

Arch. f. Kulturg. = *Archiv für Kulturgeschichte.*

Arch. Hungarica = Magyar nemzeti múzeum: *Archaeologia hungarica* (= *Acta Arch. Mus. Nat. Hung.*)

Arch. Journ. = *Archaeological Journal.*

Arch. Orient. = *Archiv orientální.*

Arch. Pap. = *Archiv für Papyrusforschung.*

Athen. = *Athenaeum: Studii periodici di letteratura e storia dell'antichità.*

Ath. Mitt. = *Mitteilungen des deutschen arch. Inst., Athenische Abteilung.*

Atti Acc. Tor. = *Atti della R. Accademia delle scienze di Torino.*

Ausgr. d. d. Or. Ges. in Babylon = *Ausgrabungen der deutschen Orient-Gesellschaft in Babylon.*

Avhandl. Ak. Oslo *or* Avh. utgitt av det Norske Videnskaps-Akad. = *Avhandlinger utgitt av det Norske Videnskaps-Akademi i Oslo.*

Babelon–Blanchet, *Cat. d. Br. de la Bibl. nat.* = E. Babelon et A. Blanchet, *Catalogue des bronzes antiques de la Bibliothèque nationale,* 1895.

Bayer. S.B. = *Sitzungsberichte der bayerischen Akademie der Wissenschaften.*

B.C.H. = *Bulletin de Correspondance hellénique.*

Berl. Abh. *or* Abh. Berl. Akad. = *Abhandlungen der preussischen Akademie der Wissenschaften.*

Ber. aus den Preuss. Kunstsamml. = Berliner Museen: *Berichte aus den preussischen Kunstsammlungen.*

Berl. S.B. *or* Sitzb. Berlin Ak. = *Sitzungsberichte d. preuss. Akad. d. Wissenschaften.*

Ber. Sächs. Ges. = *Berichte der sächsischen Gesellschaft.*

Bibl. de l'Inst. Fr. d'Arch. Or. = *Bibliothèque de l'Institut français d'Archéologie orientale.*

Bibl. Éc. H.-Ét. = *École pratique des hautes études. Bibliothèque. Sciences philologiques et historiques.*

Bikerman, *Inst. Sél.* = E. Bikerman, *Institutions des Séleucides,* 1938.

B.M.C. = *British Museum Catalogue.*

B.M.Q. = *British Museum Quarterly.*

Boll. d'Arte = *Bolletino d'Arte.*

Bull. Ac. Hist. Mat. Civ. (of U.R.S.S.) = *Bulletin of the State Academy of the History of Material Civilization (of U.R.S.S.).* (in Russian).

Bull. d. l'Ac. d. Sc. de l'U.R.S.S. = *Bulletin de l'Académie des Sciences de l'U.R.S.S.* (in Russian).

Bull. de l'Ac. Royale de Belgique = *Bulletin de la classe des Lettres de l'Académie Royale de Belgique.*

Bull. Am. Sch. Or. Res. = *Bulletin of the American Schools of Oriental Research in Jerusalem and Bagdad.*

Bull. Comm. = *Bulletino della Commissione archeologica communale di Roma.*

Bull. Comm. Imp. Arch. = *Bulletin de la Commission impériale archéologique de Russie* (in Russian).

Bull. Hist. Soc. Sofia = *Bulletin of the Historical Society of Sofia* (in Bulgarian)

Bull. Inst. Arch. Bulg. = *Bulletin de l'Institut archéologique Bulgare* (in Bulgarian).

Bull. Inst. d'Égypte = *Bulletin de l'Institut d'Égypte.*

Bull. Inst. Fr. Arch. Or. = *Bulletin de l'Institut français d'Archéologie orientale.*

Bull. Inst. Hist. of Medicine = *Bulletin of the Institute of the History of Medicine, Johns Hopkins University.*

Bull. Metr. Mus. = *Bulletin of the Metropolitan Museum of Art, New York.*

Bull. Soc. Ant. Fr. *or* **Bull. Soc. Nat. Ant.** = *Bulletin de la Société nationale des Antiquaires de France.*

Bull. Soc. Arch. Alex. = *Bulletin de la Société archéologique d'Alexandrie.*

Burl. Mag. = *Burlington Magazine.*

Bursian = Bursian's *Jahresberichte über die Fortschritte der klassischen Altertumswissenschaft.*

C.A.H. = *The Cambridge Ancient History,* 1923–39.

Cat. Sculpt. Mus. Ott. = G. Mendel, *Catalogue des sculptures grecques, romaines et byzantines.* Musées impériaux ottomans. Constantinople, 1912–14.

Chr. d'Eg. = *Chronique d'Égypte.*

Class. Journ. = *Classical Journal.*

Cl. Phil. *or* **C.P.** = *Classical Philology.*

Cl. Quart. = *Classical Quarterly.*

Cl. Rev. = *Classical Review.*

Cl. Weekly = *Classical Weekly.*

C.R. Ac. Inscr. = *Comptes rendus de l'Académie des Inscriptions et Belles-Lettres.*

C.R. de la Comm. Arch. = *Compte rendu de la Commission Impériale Archéologique* (in Russian).

Dar. (*or* **Daremberg**) **et Saglio, D. d. A.** = *Dictionnaire des antiquités grecques et romaines,* 1877–1919.

Denkschr. Wien. Akad. = *Denkschriften der österreichischen Akademie der Wissenschaften.*

Diss. Pont. Acc. = *Dissertazioni della Pontificia Accademia romana di archeologia.*

D. Literaturz. = *Deutsche Literaturzeitung.*

Enc. Ital. = *Enciclopedia Italiana.*

Ἐφ. Ἀρχ. *or* **Eph. Arch.** = *Ἐφημερὶς Ἀρχαιολογική* (since 1910 *Ἀρχαιολ. Ἐφημ.*)

Eph. Ep. = *Ephemeris Epigraphica.*

Ét. de Pap. = *Études de papyrologie.*

Eur. Sept. Ant. = *Eurasia Septentrionalis Antiqua.*

Expl. Arch. de Délos *or* **Expl. de Délos** = *Exploration archéologique de Délos,* 1909–.

Ferguson, H. A. = W. S. Ferguson, *Hellenistic Athens,* 1911.

Forsch. u. Fortschr. = *Forschungen und Fortschritte.*

Frank, Econ. Surv. = T. Frank, *An Economic Survey of Ancient Rome,* 1933–40.

Gaz. Arch. = *Gazette Archéologique.*

Geogr. Journ. = *The Geographical Journal.*

Gercke u. Norden, Einl. = A. Gercke u. E. Norden, *Einleitung in die Altertumswissenschaft.*

G.G.A. = *Göttingische Gelehrte Anzeigen.*

Gött. Abh. *or* **Abh. Gött. Ges.** = *Abhandlungen der Gesellschaft der Wissenschaften zu Göttingen.*

Gött. Nach. = *Nachrichten von der k. Gesellschaft der Wissenschaften zu Göttingen.*

Greifsw. Beitr. z. Lit. und Stilfr. = *Greifswalder Beiträge zur Literatur- und Stilforschung.*

Harv. St. Cl. Phil. = *Harvard Studies in Classical Philology.*

Harv. Theol. Rev. = *Harvard Theological Review.*

Head, *H. N.*² = B. V. Head, *Historia Numorum*, 2nd ed., 1912.

F. M. Heichelheim, *Wirtschaftsg.* = F. M. Heichelheim, *Wirtschaftsgeschichte des Altertums*, 1938.

Hesp. = *Hesperia.*

Hist. = *Historia.*

H.Z. = *Historische Zeitschrift.*

Jahreshefte = *Jahreshefte des österreichischen archäologischen Institutes* (cf. Oest. Jahresh.)

J. Am. Or. Soc. *or* **J.A.O.S.** = *Journal of the American Oriental Society.*

J.D.A.I. = *Jahrbuch des deutschen archäologischen Instituts.*

J. d. Sav. = *Journal des Savants.*

J.E.A. = *Journal of Egyptian Archaeology.*

Jebelev, *H.A.* = S. Jebelev, *History of Athens from 229 to 31 B.C.* (in Russian), 1898.

J.H.S. = *Journal of Hellenic Studies.*

Jones, *Cities &c.* = A. H. M. Jones, *The Cities of the Eastern Roman Provinces*, 1937.

Journ. Ec. and Bus. Hist. = *Journal of Economic and Business History.*

Journ. internat. Arch. num. *or* **J.I.A.N.** = *Journal international d'Archéologie numismatique.*

Journ. Palest. Or. Soc. = *Journal of the Palestine Oriental Society.*

J.R.A.S. = *Journal of the Royal Asiatic Society.*

J.R.S. = *Journal of Roman Studies.*

Kaerst, *Stud. z. Entw.* = J. Kaerst, *Studien zur Entwickelung und theoretischen Begründung der Monarchie im Altertum*, 1898.

Krit. Vierteljahresschr. = *Kritische Vierteljahresschrift für Gesetzgebung u. Rechtswissenschaft* (München).

Liverp. Ann. of Arch. (and Anthr.) *or* **Ann. of Arch. and Anthrop.** = *University of Liverpool, Annals of Archaeology and Anthropology.*

Mat. for the arch. of S. Russia = *Materials for the Archaeology of South Russia* (in Russian).

Mél. d'Arch. et d'Hist. = *Mélanges d'archéologie et d'histoire de l'École Française de Rome.*

Mél. Univ. St. Joseph = *Mélanges de l'Université Saint-Joseph.*

Mem. Acc. Lincei = *Memorie della classe di scienze morali, storiche e filologiche dell'Accademia dei Lincei.*

Mem. Amer. Acad. in Rome = *Memoirs of the American Academy in Rome.*

Mém. de l'Ac. d. Inscr. = *Mémoires de l'Académie des Inscriptions et Belles-Lettres.*

Mém. de. l'Ac. r. d. S. et d. Lett. de Dan. = *Mémoires de l'Académie royale des sciences et des lettres de Danemark.*

Mém. Délég. Perse = *Délégation en Perse* (later *Mission archéologique de Perse*): *Mémoires,* 1900–.

Mem. FERT = *Memorie pubblicate a cura dell'Istituto Storico-Archeologico FERT e della R. Deputazione di Storia patria di Rodi.*

Mém. Inst. Fr. Arch. Or. (du Caire) = *Mémoires de l'Institut français d'Archéologie orientale du Caire.*

Mem. pubbl. a cura dell' Ist. Storico-Archeol. di Rodi *or* **Mem. d. Ist. St. Arch. di Rodi** = *Memorie pubblicate a cura dell'Istituto Storico-Archeologico di Rodi.* Cf. *Mem. FERT.*

Mém. Soc. Ant. Fr. *or* **Mém. de la Soc. d. Ant.** = *Mémoires de la Société nationale des Antiquaires de France.*

Metr. Mus. St. = *Metropolitan Museum Studies.*

Mitt. Altor. Ges. = *Mitteilungen der altorientalischen Gesellschaft.*

Mitt. d. schles. Ges. f. Volkskunde = *Mitteilungen der schlesischen Gesellschaft für Volkskunde.*

Mitt. Vorderas. Ges. = *Mitteilungen der vorderasiatisch-aegyptischen Gesellschaft.*

M.M.A. = *Metropolitan Museum of Art.*

Mnem. = *Mnemosyne.*

Mon. Ant. = *Monumenti antichi pubblicati per cura della R. Accademia dei Lincei.*

Monatsschr. f. Gesch. d. Judent. = *Monatsschrift für Geschichte und Wissenschaft des Judentums.*

Mon. et Mém. Piot = *Monuments et Mémoires E. Piot.*

Müller–Otto, *Handbuch Alt.-Wiss.* = *Müller–Otto, Handbuch der Altertumswissenschaft,* 1886–.

Münch. Beitr. (Pap.) = *Münchener Beiträge zur Papyrusforschung und antiken Rechtsgeschichte.*

Münch. Mediz. Wochenschrift = *Münchener medizinische Wochenschrift.*

Mus. Belge = *Musée Belge.*

N. Heid. Jahrb. = *Neue Heidelberger Jahrbücher.*

Neue Phil. Unters. = *Neue philologische Untersuchungen.*

N. J. f. Wiss. (und Jugend.) = *Neue Jahrbücher für Wissenschaft und Jugendbildung.*

N. J. Kl. Alt. = *Neue Jahrbücher für das klassische Altertum.*

Not. d. Sc. = *Notizie degli Scavi.*

Notiz. Arch. d. Min. delle Colonie = *Notiziario Archeologico d. Ministero delle Colonie.*

Num. Chr. = *Numismatic Chronicle and Journal of the Numismatic Society.*

Num. Notes and Mon. *or* **N.N. and M.** = *Numismatic Notes and Monographs* (American Numismatic Society).

Num. St. = *Numismatic Studies* (American Numismatic Society).

Num. Z. = *Numismatische Zeitschrift.*

Oest. Jahresh. *or* **Jahreshefte** = *Jahreshefte des österreichischen archäologischen Institutes.*

Phil. *or* **Philol.** = *Philologus.*

Phil. Stud. (Kath. Univ. te Leuven) = *Philologische Studien* (Kath. Univ. te Leuven).

Ph. W. *or* **Phil. Woch.** = *Philologische Wochenschrift.*

Pol. Sc. Quart. = *Political Science Quarterly.*

Préaux, *L'Écon. Lag.* = C. Préaux, *L'Économie royale des Lagides*, 1939.

Proc. Brit. Acad. = *Proceedings of the British Academy.*

Publ. Pal. Sect. Mus. Pennsylv. = *Publications of the Palestine Section of the University Museum, U. of Pennsylvania.*

P.W.K. = Pauly–Wissowa–Kroll, *Realencyclopädie der classischen Altertumswissenschaft*, 1894–.

Quart. Dep. Ant. Pal. = *Quarterly of the Department of Antiquities in Palestine.*

R.É.A. *or* **Rev. É. A.** = *Revue des études anciennes.*

R.É.G. *or* **Rev. É. G.** = *Revue des études grecques.*

S. Reinach, *Rép. d. peint.* = *Répertoire de peintures grecques et romaines,* 1922.

Rend. Ist. Lomb. = *Rendiconti dell'Istituto Lombardo di scienze e lettere.*

Rend. Linc. = *Rendiconti della R. Accademia dei Lincei.*

Rend. Pontif. Acc. Rom. Arch. = *Rendiconti della Pontificia Accademia romana di Archeologia.*

Rev. Arch. = *Revue archéologique.*

Rev. Art ancien et mod. = *Revue de l'Art ancien et moderne.*

Rev. Assyr. = *Revue d'Assyriologie.*

Rev. Belge = *Revue Belge de philologie et d'histoire.*

Rev. Bibl. = *Revue Biblique internationale.*

Rev. de l'Ég. Anc. = *Revue de l'Égypte ancienne.*

Rev. des Arts Asiat. = *Revue des Arts asiatiques.*

Rev. Ét. Islam. = *Revue des Études islamiques.*

Rev. Ét. Juives = *Revue des Études juives.*

Rev. Ét. Lat. = *Revue des Études latines.*

Rev. Hist. *or* **Rev. H.** = *Revue historique.*

Rev. hist. de Dr. fr. et étr. = *Revue historique de droit français et étranger.*

Rev. Hist. Rel. = *Revue de l'histoire des Religions.*

Rev. Internat. des Études Balkaniques = *Revue Internationale des études balkaniques.*

Rev. Num. *or* **Rev. N.** = *Revue Numismatique.*

Rev. Phil. *or* **Rev. d. Phil.** = *Revue de philologie, d'histoire et de littérature anciennes.*

Rev. Quest. hist. = *Revue des Questions historiques.*

Rh. Mus. = *Rheinisches Museum für Philologie.*

Riv. d. Stor. Ant. = *Rivista di storia antica.*

Riv. Fil. = *Rivista di Filologia e d'Istruzione classica.*

Riv. R. Ist. Arch. e St. dell'Arte = *Rivista del Regio Istituto d'Archeologia e Storia dell'Arte.*

Röm. Mitt. = *Mitteilungen d. deutschen archæologischen Instituts, Römische Abteilung.*

S.B. (or Sitzb.) Heid. Akad. = *Sitzungsberichte der Heidelberger Akademie der Wissenschaften.*

Schmollers Jahrb. = *Schmollers Jahrbuch für Gesetzgebung, Verwaltung und Volkswirtschaft im deutschen Reich.*

Schr. d. Königsb. Gelehrten Ges. = *Schriften der Königsberger Gelehrten Gesellschaft.*

Sem. Kond. = *Seminarium Kondakovianum.*

Soc. R. d'Arch. d'Alexandrie = *Société Royale d'Archéologie d'Alexandrie.*

St. d. Sc. Pap. = *R. Accademia Scientifico-Letteraria in Milano: Studi della Scuola Papirologica.*

St. It. Fil. = *Studi Italiani di filologia classica.*

S.V.F. = *H. v. Arnim, Stoicorum veterum fragmenta, 1903–24.*

Tr. Am. Phil. Ass. *or* **T.A.P.A.** = *Transactions and Proceedings of the American Philological Association.*

Tübing. Beitr. = *Tübinger Beiträge zur Altertumswissenschaft.*

Un. of Missouri St. = *University of Missouri Studies.*

Wien. Anz. = *Anzeiger der Akademie der Wissenschaften in Wien.*

Wien. Blätter f. Freunde d. Antike = *Wiener Blätter für Freunde der Antike.*

Wien. S.B. = *Sitzungsberichte der Akademie der Wissenschaften in Wien.*

Wien. St. = *Wiener Studien.*

(Berl.) Winckelmannspr. = *Archäologische Gesellschaft, Berlin, Winckelmannsprogramme.*

Wiss. Ver. d. d. Or.-Ges. = *Wissenschaftliche Veröffentlichungen der deutschen Orient-Gesellschaft.*

Woch. f. kl. Phil. = *Wochenschrift für klassische Philologie.*

Yale Class. St. = *Yale Classical Studies.*

Z. D. Pal. Ver. = *Zeitschrift des deutschen Palästina-Vereins.*

Zeitschr. d. Morg. Ges. = *Zeitschrift der deutschen Morgenländischen Gesellschaft.*

Zeitschr. f. Ass. = *Zeitschrift für Assyriologie.*

Zeitschr. f. ges. Staatsw. = *Zeitschrift für die gesamte Staatswissenschaft.*

Zeitschr. f. Semitistik = *Zeitschrift für Semitistik u. verwandte Gebiete.*

Z. f. Aeg. Spr. = *Zeitschrift für ägyptische Sprache und Altertumskunde.*

Z. f. neutest. Wiss. = *Zeitschrift für neutestamentliche Wissenschaft.*

Z.N. = *Zeitschrift für Numismatik.*

Z. Sav.-Stift. = *Zeitschrift der Savigny-Stiftung für Rechtsgeschichte (Romanistische Abteilung).*

INDEXES

I. NAMES AND SUBJECTS

It has been no easy task to compile a useful index of names and subjects for a book of such length and such varied contents. The Index is arranged in alphabetical order according to the Latin alphabet. For the Greek words no special index has been made: they are incorporated in the general index. The recalcitrant letters θ, χ, and ψ are to be found under their Latin phonetic equivalents, *th*, *ch*, and *ps*, while υ and φ are classed with the Latin *u* and *f* respectively. The Greek words given in the text, either in transliteration or in their Greek form, appear in English or Greek characters, according to the frequency of their occurrence. No translations of Greek terms are given. I regret my inability to include in the Index the names of modern scholars whose printed works I have cited and sometimes quoted. Exception has been made in the case of those scholars who have contributed some *inedita*—remarks, references to sources, or archaeological material.

Vol. I contains pp. 1–602; Vol. II pp. 603–1314; Vol. III pp. 1315 ff. A reminder is printed in the inner margins of the headlines of these indexes.

Aba, tyrant, 1580.
Abae, 1471.
Abandoned property (*res derelictae*), 907.
Abbaitis, 556.
Abbukome, 561.
Abdemoun, 226–8.
Abdera, 111, 759, 762, 764, 766–8, 1501.
Abderite coinage, 1510.
Abduction of freemen and slaves, 203, 207, 608, 1258, 1360, 1364, 1514; *see* Captives.
Abgarus, 842.
Abolition, of debts (χρεῶν ἀποκοπή, χρεοκοπία), 42, 141, 208–10, 612, 757, 943, 944, 1128, 1367, 1460, 1509; of contracts (ἀσυναλλαξία), 722, 757, 1509.
Abonuteichus, 978.
Abrettene, 556.
Absentee landlords, 524, 1521, 1565.
Abusir, 258, 1229.
Abydus, 232, 556, 560, 585, 586, 712, 1453, 1496; coinage, 1356.
Abyssinia, 381, 382.
Acanthus, grove of, 299.
Acarnania, 90, 212, 606, 1190, 1501.
Acarnanian League, coinage of, 1291.
Acarnanians, 220.
Acarno-Aetolian treaty, 1316, 1317.
Accadian tablets, 1436.
Acclimatization of animals, 358, 1162–4, 1167, 1609; of plants, 353, 357, 1162–7, 1609–12.

Accounting, 266, 269, 273, 405, 1079, 1283, 1310, 1380.
Accounts, 257, 358, 359, 362, 403, 404, 419, 967, 1144, 1150, 1276, 1284, 1285, 1393, 1494, 1496, 1500; of the *hieropoioi*, see *Hieropoioi*; of the temple of Delos, *see* Delos; of temples, *see* Temples.
Achaea, 41, 56, 197, 612, 741; relations with Rome, 48, 739, 763, 815, 986, 993, 1013.
Achaean, cities, 212, 987; invasion of Attica, 217; League, 24, 31, 32, 38, 42, 56, 204, 206, 209, 1109, 1317, 1467; coinage of, 604, 628, 751, 755, 1291, 1356, 1469, 1504, 1629, 1646, relations with Rome, 58, 1502, role of, 36, 39, 41; War, 739, 741, 745, 748–50, 755, 800, 1127, 1460, 1501, 1502, 1507.
Achaeans, 193, 194, 605, 607, 612, 772, 1365, 1467.
Achaemenids, 434, 849, 850, 1163.
Achaemenid art, 1446.
Achaeus, governor of Asia Minor, 43, 49 1142.
Acmonia, 1515.
Acornion, 675, 1511.
Acraiphia, 1341, 1363, 1369, 1615.
Acrobats, 1596.
Actium, battle of, 53, 69, 910, 929–31, 1012, 1013, 1102, 1581.
Actors, 1085, 1086, 1096, 1124; *see* Dionysiac *technitai*.

Romani, 814–17, 966, 978, 982, 1007, 1477, 1525, 1571, 1572; *regius*, 468, 815; *stipendiarius*, 345, 468, 814–16, 1526; *vectigalis*, 748, 815; see *Agri*.

ἀγγαρεῖαι, 315, 964, 1305.

Agis IV of Sparta, 24, 41, 205, 208, 209, 1146, 1318, 1367.

Aglibol, 438.

Agonothetes, 952, 971.

Agorai, 1271.

ἀγοραῖα τέλη, 444, 445.

Agoranomia, 621.

Agoranomoi (ἀγορανόμοι), 451, 453, 454, 486, 952, 1124, 1431.

ἀγοραστός (σῖτος or πυρός), 316.

Agri, 640; *excepti*, 748; *Attalici*, 338; *Bithyniae*, 571, 978, 1571; *Mithridatis*, 978, 979; of Pergamon, 1525, 1572; *Ptolemaei Telmessii*, 647, 1399.

Agrianes, 1444.

Agricultural, cities, 157, 178, 179, 212; implements, 260, 362, 363, 1186, 1197, 1618–20; labour, 96, 97, 287, 327, 343, 754, 1099, 1116, 1149, 1182, 1184, 1196, 1260. *See* Slave labour.

Agriculture, 446, 615, 1116, 1143, 1160, 1166, 1180, 1182, 1194–6, 1204, 1237, 1415; methods of, 158, 1180, 1182, 1184–7, 1237, 1303; technique of, 1302, 1626; treatises on, *see* Treatises; use of metals in, 362, 363, 386, 587; writers on, *see* Greek writers; in Asia Minor, 81, 98, 287, 366, 563, 618, 671, 672, 957–9, 1021, 1185, 1195, 1196; in Babylonia, 78, 79, 364, 1161, 1164–6, 1610, 1611; in Bactria, 545, 1166, 1609; in Bithynia, 917, 1251; in Bosporan Kingdom, 596, 917, 1249, 1331; of Celts, 581; in Cos, 240; in Cyprus, 339; in Egypt, 81, 274, 287, 331, 359, 411, 421, 719, 1168, 1380, 1381, 1389; control of government over, 275, 279, 280, 290, 291, 299, 303, 313, 366, 1197; decline of, 711, 717, 726, 893, 904, 918; increase of production, 287, 290, 360, 365; labour, 287, 327, 343, 1099, needs of, 362, 363, 386, 396, organization of, 275, 290, 291, 317, 353, 360, 366, 381, 1161, 1196, 1197, 1199, 1200, 1382; technical progress, 362, 364, 365; Greece, 94, 96–8, 100, 101, 109, 210–12, 287, 365, 754, 764, 1116, 1160, 1181–7, 1190, 1352, 1507, 1615, 1616, trade in products of, 90, 93, 104, 110, 750; Macedonia, 633, 759, 1471; Media, 77; Mesopotamia, 536, 697, 1164; Palestine, 81, 348; Pergamon, 556, 563–5, 650, 654, 777, 803, 804, 1451; Persia, 78; Persis, 77; Phoenicia, 618, 697; Pontus, 572, 917; Priene, 178, 179, 1196, 1618, 1619;

Rhodes, 221, 236; Rome, 1259; Seleucid Empire, 157, 363, 365, 462, 488–90, 510, 523, 536, 541, 618, 697, 859, 860, 864, 1161, 1195, 1196, 1253; Thrace, 1161.

Agroi in Pergamon, 561.

Ahenobarbus, Cn. Domitius, 972.

Ahura-Mazda, 434, 438, 576.

αἰχμάλωτοι, 148, 199, 203, 206, 342, 634, 1360, 1364–6, 1459, 1514, 1516, 1519; see Prisoners of war.

Aigiale, 1364.

αἰλουροβοσκοί, 1383.

Aiorix, 1452.

αἱρέσεις, 1059.

Aisymnetai, list of, 533.

Akabah Gulf, see Aelanitic.

Ake, see Ptolemais Ake.

'Ακεσᾶς, weaver of Cyprus, 1412.

ἀκληρονόμητος, 840.

Akrasos, 645.

ἀκροφύλακες, ἀκροφυλακῖται, 348, 490.

Alabanda, 1009, 1363, 1472, 1480, 1564, 1649.

Alabaster, 112, 417, 1176.

Alalcomenae in Boeotia, 942.

Alalkha or Alalakh, 1323, 1643.

ἀλαζονεία, 624.

Albania, 1335.

Albinus, Sp. Postumius, 1460.

Alcetas, 6, 7, 128.

Alchemistic treatises, 1225.

Alchemy, 1225.

ἀλειτουργία or ἀλειτουργησία, 1006, 1394.

Aleppo, 485, 1163, 1274, 1353, 1612.

Alexander the Great, 3, 50, 52, 127, 473, 547, 1098; army of, *see* Armies; coinage, 161, 186, 253, 442, 446–8, 1338, 1510, posthumous issues, 448–50; coins of, 131, 135, 136, 161, 164, 448, 1324, 1353, 1357, 1431, 1502, hoards of, 186, 1352, 1353, 1356, imitations of, 583, 659, 743, 1289, 1489, 1510, posthumous, 10, 449, 450, 656, 1292, 1293, 1417, minted by cities, 655, 657, 659, 694, 743, 1356, 1480; colonization, *see* Colonization; consequences of conquest, 127, 129, 130, 132, 151, 160, 161, 168, 252, 615, 617, 1019, 1026, 1031, 1032, 1035, 1053, 1054, 1136, 1145, 1161, 1180, 1338; cult of, 145, 268, 1047; currency, *see* Currency; descent of Hellenistic rulers from, 267, 431, 434, 849; economic policy, 132, 138, 139, 152, 443, 444, 455, 472, 1155, 1337, 1338, 1340; Empire of, 5, 7, 23, 127, 129, 183, 185, 187, 248, 1056, organization of, 134, 135, 151, 183, 249, 439, 522, 579, 1034, 1038, 1046, 1160, 1172, 1351, 1471, 1609; mints of, 1355; monetary policy, 134, 135,

of Alexander the Great, 3, 128-31, 143, 144, 147, 151, 252, 263, 284, 498, 1136, 1172, 1220, 1314, 1346, 1623; of Antigonus the One-eyed, 144, 148, 1342, 1346; of Bithynia, 571; of Egypt, 144, 267, 283, 324-7, 334, 414, 914, 1345, 1346, 1453, 1497, 1498, 1595, 1627; gifts to, 327, 878, 1396, organization of, 262-4, 284-7, 708, 709, 714, 727-9, 887, 1220, 1221, 1339, 1397, 1400, 1623, relations to king, 69, 325, 722, 898, 915, revolts, 871, 873, strength of, 332, supply of animals, 292, 293, 384, 432; of the Epigoni, 143; Greek, 767; Macedonian, 149, 152, 500, 632, 633, 1074, 1136, 1314, 1319, 1342, 1346, 1459, 1470, 1472, role of, 3, 6, 8, 9, 19, 20, 23, 26, 144, 145, cavalry, 128, 150, 497, 500, infantry, 497, phalanx, 3, 497, 500, 708, military equipment, 373, 391, 408, 424, 638; of Mithridates VI, 935, 942; Pergamene, 809, 810, 1449, 1524, 1595; of Persia, 262, 1232; Persian in Egypt, 1150, 1151, 1155; of Rhodes, 680, 687, 1221, 1487; of Roman leaders, 821, 822, 937, 939-41, 945-7, 953, 988, 991, 993-5, 1005, 1007, 1013, 1557, 1576, 1579, 1581; of the Seleucid Empire, 144, 284, 430, 431, 438, 487, 491, 497, 499-501, 517, 518, 860, 1221, 1232, 1435, 1439, 1440, 1538, 1595, 1623; of Successors, 144-9, 262, 284, 1074, 1136, 1342-5, economic role of, 129-31, 137, 143, 145-8, 151, 152; *see* Garrisons, Mercenaries, Soldiers.

Armour, 93, 100, 106, 107, 112, 113, 123, 124, 260, 1212.

Arms, supply of, 152, 677, 1623; *see* Weapons.

ἀρώματα, 307, 313, 926.

Aromatic shrubs, 572.

ἀρωματική, 392.

Aroura (Ἄρουρα), 352, 410.

Arrears, 708, 724, 751, 752, 884, 901, 946, 947, 953, 1507; liquidation of, 954, 962, 967-9; remission of, 713, 714.

Arretine pottery, 171, 176, 654, 919, 1024, 1303.

Arrhidaeus, *see* Philip III; satrap of Hellespontine Phrygia, 588, 590, 1453.

Arrian, 2, 566, 567, 570, 1595.

Arsaces, king of Parthia, 430; coin of, 802.

Arsacid era, 855.

Arsacids, 50, 430, 468, 550, 855, 859; coinage of, 855.

Arsenals, 639, 661, 1220, 1221, 1481, 1596.

Arsinoe, name of queens, 370; wife of Philadelphus, 22, 40, 270, 336, 368, 388, 417, 439, 1078, 1399, 1407, 1419, coins of, 18, 184, 188, 401, cult of, 283, 796, 902.

Arsinoe-Crocodilopolis, 361, 405, 722, 1495;

-Dionos, 1589; in Palestine, 347; in the Peloponnese, 1398.

Arsinoite nome, 309, 353, 356, 360-2, 715.

Art products, commerce in, 380, 399, 744-6, 760, 761, 778, 1212, 1505, 1506, 1519.

ἀρταβιεία, 286, 714.

Artaxerxes I, 1353; III Ochus, 83, 105, 262, 266, 281, 1330.

Artemidorus of Ephesus, geographer, 458, 1039, 1040; a friend of Antony, 1006; of Perge, 1346, 1489.

Artemis, temple of, at Ephesus, *see* Ephesus; temple of Lusoi, 201, 1364, temple of, at Sardis, *see* Sardis, Kindyas, 1523; Leukophryene, 667, 820, 1122; Munichia, 1514; Nanaia, 1428.

Artemision, cape in Euboea, 1505; of Magnesia on the Maeander, 820, 824, 1528.

Arthaśāstra, 550, 551, 1448.

Artillery, 1083, 1232, 1625.

Artisans, 445, 1204, 1211, 1220, 1222, 1227-9, 1257, 1260; of Asia Minor, 937, 1066; of Babylonia, 78; of Bosporan cities, 596, 601; of Egypt, 82, 301, 322, 323, 331, 420, 1063, 1099, 1154, 1205, 1277, 1285, 1388, relations to government, 298, 300, 301, 316, 1101; of Galatia, 584; of Greece, 100, 210, 300, 753, 783, 1117, 1272-4, 1276, 1629; of Italy, 123; of Pergamene kingdom, 564, 565; of Priene, 178; of S. Russia, 110; of Seleucid Empire, 471, 506, 519, 1157.

Artistic industry, 744-6, 760, 799, 1212; *see* Art.

Artists in industry, 123, 159, 298, 380, 420, 438, 539, 596, 601, 650, 652, 684, 702, 742, 746, 760, 793, 798, 799, 820, 1332, 1410, 1446, 1447, 1451, 1490, 1491, 1506, 1519; of the theatre, 234, 519, 1085, 1113, 1117, 1561, 1580, *see* Dionysiac artistes.

ἀρτοκόποι, 1628.

Arybbas, 488.

Asander, king of Bosporus, 998, 999, 1340.

Ascalon (Ashdod), 702, 847, 1402, 1517, 1551; mint of, 936, 1324.

Asclepiades, S. C. concerning, 1506.

Asclepiades of Aradus, 793.

Asclepiasts, 1598.

Asclepieum, of Cos, 221, 237, 240, 243, 569, 804, 1122, 1373; of Pergamon, 564, 1448, 1481, 1525, 1598.

Asclepiodotus, 1595.

Asclepius, 1088; priesthood of, 1475; temple of, at Buttos, 1466, 1515.

ἄσημος (ἄργυρος and χρυσός), 1277.

ἀσφάλεια, 775, 1506.

Asia, policy of Demetrius Poliorcetes, 17,

516, 519; industry, 78, 84, 698, 1201 : metal, 863, papyrus, 541, 1447, pottery, 1350, 1442, 1622, terracottas, 1442, 1461; textiles, 698, 1222, 1226, 1227, toreutics, 376, woollens, 540; land, *see* Land; political conditions, 12, 13, 860, 861; Parthian domination, 451, 457, 697, 841, 864, Persian domination, 78, 537, 1033, 1322, 1427, 1643, Seleucid domination, 9, 12, 429, 480, 512, 515, 516, 519; priests, 78, 513, 515; religious life, 282, 435–7, 439, 512; routes, *see* Routes; slaves, *see* Slaves; taxation, 468, 470, 471, 514–16; temples, *see* Temples; trade, 78, 90, 450, 458, 572, 863, 866, 1246, 1257, 1278, 1486; urbanization, 1436; weights, 451, 1298, 1431.

Babylonian, art, 84; chronicle, 2, 13, 24, 1318; cities, 1051, 1438; culture, 77, 78; cuneiform tablets, 259, 423, 425, 450, 451, 513, 1321, 1322, 1439; law, 79, 512, 513, 515, 1067; learning, 513; names, 436, 523, 1442; seals, *see* Seals; semi-Babylonian States, economic life of, 80.

Babylonians, 473.

Bacchon, 140.

Bactra, 461, 543–5.

Bactria, agriculture, *see* Agriculture; archaeological evidence, 427, 1424; art, 548, 1457; coinage, 446, 447, 547; coins, 46, 427, 544, 936, circulation of, 584, 1539; colonization, 131, 477; economic structure, 78, 543–5, 547, 549, 550, 1288, 1447; Greek cities in, 547, 1053; Greeks in, *see* Greeks; Hellenism in, 248, 936, 1098; industry, metal, 433, 540, 546; political conditions, 31, 43, 50, 65, 67, 248, 429, 447, 459, 542, 543, 549–51, 705, 1318, 1338, 1425, 1493; routes, 457, 461, 546; trade, 461, 544–7, 676, 702, 795, 1248, 1484, 1539, 1554.

Bactrian cavalry, 545, 549.

Bactro-Siberian art, 850.

Baetocaece, 494, 510, 1434, 1440.

βαφεῖς, 1225.

βαφικά, 1225, 1624.

Bag-bellows, 177; *see* Bellows.

Bagous, satrap of Egypt, coins, 1324.

Bahrein Islands, 1166, 1174.

Bakers, 1628.

Balance of power, idea of, 23, 24.

βαλανεῖα, 312.

Balbura, 150.

Balbus, T. Ampius, 972.

Balkan peninsula 1316, 1511 1515; coin circulation, 768, 1504, 1510; colonization, 156, 157; currency, *see* Currency; economic development, 161; invasion by

Celts, 25, 360, 581, 955; political conditions, 70, 118, 161, 248, 566, 768, 770, 955, 1016, 1054, 1574; serfs, 1184, 1185, 1515, 1628; trade, 93, 120, 121, 161, 447, 743, 1337, 1510, 1518.

Balkan Thracians in Asia Minor, 758.

Balsam, 386.

Baltic Sea, trade of, 80.

Bambyce (Hieropolis), *see* Hieropolis.

Banana trees, 1166.

Bankers, 78, 804, 946, 947, 1110, 1278–81, 1518, 1519; of caravan trade, 1247; in Delos, 190, 798, 959, 1268, 1281; in Egypt, 405, 406, 1071, 1287, 1418; in Greece, 952, 1046, 1112, 1116, 1133; Italian, 785, 787, 795, 798, 922; of Rhodes, 172, 232, 393, 688, 1267, 1280, 1281, 1485, 1486.

Banking, 1278–81, 1287, 1288, 1303, 1629; in Asia Minor, 672; in Athens, *see* Athens; in Babylonia, 78; of Bithynian kings, 828; in Cyzicus, 586, 587; in Delos, 190, 231, 233, 795, 798, 959, 1268, 1281, 1372, 1373; in Egypt, 302, 404–6, 411, 903, 1282–8, 1629; in Ephesus, 1630; in Greece, 99, 101, 212, 405, 1278, 1279, 1287, 1352, 1629; of Italians, 749, 763, 764, 959, 970; in Rhodes, 236, 677, 680, 691, 777, 787; in Seleucid Empire, 1281, 1282; of temples, 231, 406, 495, 648, 672, 995, 1278–80, 1282, 1371, 1418, 1483, 1630.

Banks, 187; private, 1278–81; State control of, 1288; in Alexandria, *see* Alexandria; in Athens, 405; in Egypt, 326, 1286, 1287, 1418; accounts, 1494, 1496, 1500; central State, in Alexandria, 1283, 1284, corn, State, 328, 406, 1276, 1283, 1287, 1419, country, royal, 1276, 1277, private, 326, 402, 406, 1283, royal, 328, 402, 404–6, 1283, 1284, 1286, 1418; in Greece, city-banks, 670, 1279, 1281, 1283, 1287, 1288, 1482; in Rhodes, 173; in Roman Empire, 1288.

Banqueting tent of Philadelphus, 380.

Bargates, M. Perennius, 176.

Bargylia, 527, 809, 1523.

Baris (castle), 508, 1441.

Barley, 240, 300, 308, 489, 1181, 1187, 1450.

Barter trade, 119, 121, 263, 403, 450, 1247, 1288, 1418.

Basalt, 1176.

βασιλεία, 1345–7.

βασιλικὰ χρήματα, 1392.

βασιλικὰ προστάγματα, 527.

βασιλικαὶ παιδίσκαι, 565.

βασιλικὴ οὐσία, 488.

βασιλικὴ (οἰκονομία), 74, 75, 440, 442, 443.

βασιλικὴ πλινθίς, 109.

tiochus IV, 625, 703; Greek, *see* Greek; of Prolemy I, 149, 482; of Seleucids, 157, 158, 457, 472, 476–80, 490–3, 496, 499, 501, 502, 516, 525, 538, 625, 1075, 1103, 1141, 1142, 1162, 1436, 1438; of Seleucus I, 157, 427, 472, 477–80, 482, 487, 516, 704, 1103; of the Successors, 156–8, 472, 1349.

Colophon, 93, 137, 151, 155, 567, 641, 943, 1346, 1349, 1463, 1598, 1599, 1643; coinage, 1480, tax, 1644.

Colophon Nova, 1474.

Columella, 1183, 1189, 1192, 1194.

Columnaria, tax, 994.

Comana, temple of, 576, 839, 978, 1649.

Comanus, 715, 731, 1494.

Commagene, 434, 784, 851, 1231, 1524, 1533; coinage, 849; economic and social structure, 849, 976, 979, 1440, 1535; hellenization, 849; political conditions, 842, 977, 980, 993; temple-state of, 505, 506, 1440.

Commerce, *see* Trade.

Competaliasts, 1517.

Compulsion, 622, 714, 721, 724–6, 889, 909, 990; against temples, 695.

Compulsory, contributions in Egypt, 725, to the Successors, 1345; gifts in Greek cities, 155; levies in Greece, 192; levies by Rome (ἀνδροληψίαι), 809, 810, 937, 940, 947, 951, 1003, exemption from, 952, of ships, 1579; loans in Greek cities, 155, 621, 1399, to Pompey, 994, 995; measures of Athenian Empire, 183, 186, reminting of money, 1417; sacrifices at Cos, 241, 242; sale of grain in Egypt, 316, 327; service in Chaeronea, 1013, in Egypt, 271, 411, 882, 890, 901, 912, 1392, immunity from 1561, in Teos, 182, *see* Liturgies; supply of slaves to Romans, 1502, of transport, 964, 1242, 1305; use of local coinage, 1292, of royal currency, 1293; work in Egypt, 271, 299, 317, 320, 411, 912, 1102, 1380, 1543: in cultivation of land, 717, 720, 721, 726, 908, 1495, 1498, of draught animals, 182, 275, in irrigation, 275, in manufacture of woollen stuffs, 308, in reclamation of land, 361, in transport, 315, 317, freedom from, 275, 286, 322, 325, in Euboea in mines, 221, in Greek cities, 1124, in Seleucid Empire, 1104; *see* Criminals.

Concessionaires, in Egypt, 296, 305, 308, 313, 314, 406, 1071, 1274, 1277, 1389; in Seleucid Empire, municipal mints, 448.

Concubines, of Greeks, 343, 344, 1435.

Conductores, 758.

Condylus, hyparch of Maussolus, 1433; a fisherman, 722.

Confiscated property, in Egypt, 907, 1398, 1550, 1551.

Confiscations, in Egypt, 290, 326, 328, 708, 714, 724, 894, 906; in Greece, 141, 208, 610, 611, 614, 626; by Mithridates VI in Asia Minor, 942, 943; in Pergamon, 648; by Romans in Greece and the East, 739, 748, 940, 947, 948, 995, 1003, 1004, 1007, 1576.

Conflicts in Egypt, between population and administration, 411–14; between civil and public law, 904, 905.

Conon of Dura, 488, 862; of the Sarapeum, 735.

Constitution of Greek cities, *see* City.

Contractors, at Cos, 241, 243; at Delos, 1370, 1371; in Egypt, 290, 298, 299, 326, 331, 361, 411, 421, 898, 906, 1188, 1390, 1401, 1402: in government monopolies, 882, of oil production, 303–5, of revenues, 309, 328–30, 336, 888, 889, 904, 907, 1386; in Judaea, 349; in Roman provinces, 758, 966; in Spain, 1212; *see* *Publicani, telonai*.

Contracts, cancellation of, 722, 757, 810, 1509; in Babylonia, 436; in Delos, 234, 1371; in Egypt, 257, 317, 328, 722, 889, 905, 906, 922, 1101, 1276, 1285, 1382, 1546; farming of, 302, for collection of revenues, 328–30, 338, 411, for cultivation of land, 278, 280, 328, 345, 1382, for fishing, 297, of makers of linen, 306, of stone-cutters, 298, for transportation, 315; in Greece, 1161, 1185, 1188, 1189, 1368, 1404, 1617, 1618; in Roman provinces, 817, 967, 1483, 1573; in Seleucid Empire, 487, 490, 1438, 1445.

Contrascriptor (ἀντιγραφεύς), 269.

Contributions, to Hellenistic kings, 1475, 1476; to Ptolemies of ships by Island League, 222, by dominions, 352, extraordinary, 708, of temples, 884; to Romans, 751, 752, 810, 937, 942, 947–9, 951–5, 983, 984, 987, 988, 990, 991, 993, 994, 996, 1002–6, 1008, 1501, 1502, 1579; extraordinary, 956, 979, 1561, of ships, *see* Ships; to Seleucids, of Greek cities, 529, 531, of temples, 506, 695, 696, 940; to Successors, of Greek cities, 138–40, 142, 156, 223, 231.

Control, of economic activity, in Babylonia, 78; in Egypt, 273, 291, 313, 729, 731, 733, 913, 1242, 1389: over agriculture, *see* Agriculture, over domestic animals, 292, over flax-production, 306, over industry, 312, 367, 377, 1205, 1274, over mines and quarries, 298, over oil-production, 303–5, over prices, 314, 1274, 1275, over temples, 282, over trade, 313, 314, 331, 402, 928, 1274, over vine growing, 1404, over weights and

915; forests, 1168–70, 1255, 1256, 1612, 1613; hellenization, *see* Hellenization; industry: pottery, 1209, 1446, textiles, 1222; metals, *see* Metals; mint of, 399; pirates, 202, 774, 1364; political conditions, 14, 17, 336, 965, 975, 976, 1326: dominion of Ptolemies, 13, 16, 332, 334, 338, 339, 351, 873, 875, 876, 1375, 1400, relations with Phoenicia, 80, 339; trade, 88, 93, 169, 339, 368, 381, 630, 1613, in grain, *see* Grain.

Cyrenaica, amnesty decrees, 907; economic and social conditions, 333, 916, 917, 1398; grain of, *see* Grain; horses of, *see* Horses; industry, terracottas, 212, 616; orientalization, 71; political conditions, 332, 333, 336, 774, 875, 876, 993, 1150; royal land, 815; trade, 368.

Cyrene, 168, 332, 333, 973, 1110, 1354, 1398, 1552; coinage of, 399; inscriptions, 915–17, 1313, 1329, 1542, 1550, 1570.

Cyrrhestica, 479, 843.

Cyrrhus, 479, 1439.

Cyrus, king of Persia, 77.

Cyrus (Kura), river, 456.

Cythnos, 949, 1191.

Cytisus, 1609.

'Cyzicenes', 587, 1453.

Cyzicus, 809, 926, 1221, 1453, 1454, 1647; clearing-house for Euxine trade, 586, 587, 1264; coinage, 76, 587, 830, 1356, 1454; coins, 114, 117, 136; economic conditions, 589, 673, 830, 977, 1144, 1273, 1454; industry, metal, 650; navy, 772; political conditions, 27, 35, 185, 588, 589, 674, 827, 829, 830, 953, 1348, 1355, 1453, 1454, 1523, 1530; relations with Bithynia, 567, 588, 589, 772, with Byzantium, 590, with Pergamon, 554, 556, 588, 589, 641, 1444, 1448, 1450, 1453, 1646, with Rome, 944, 977, 998, 999, 1577; tax on fisheries, 1644; trade, 117, 175, 228, 232, 245, 585, 587, 589, 830, 1454.

Daimachus, embassy to India, 459, 1217.

Dairies, on royal estates, 1190.

Dakke, 382.

Dalmatian coast, 1511, 1512.

Damas, of Pergamon, 565.

Damascene, steel, 1218, 1623.

Damascus, 351, 510, 511, 848, 867, 1231, 1441, 1536, 1538; economic structure, 79; plan of, 485, 1051, 1587; routes to, 462, 841, 865; 865; trade, 697; vine-planting, 1163; weights of, 454.

Damiadas, 952, 953, 1112.

Damion, 753.

Damon Peripoltas, 1558.

δαμοσία χώρα, 1375.

Dancers, 747, 1085–7, 1597; castanet dancers, 747, 1087, 1597.

δάνεια ἐμπορικά, 670.

Daniel, Book of, 47.

Danube, 118, 120, 985, 986, 989; Celts on, 25, 581, 1351; fisheries, 1177; Scythians on, 596.

Danubian, Celts, coinage of, 161; regions, coin hoards, 1504; trade, 93, 103, 118–20, 161, 768, 769, 1253, 1264, 1355, 1518, 1555.

δαπάναι, 1561.

Daphne, 67, 497, 518, 699, 703, 1350, 1645.

δαψίλεια, 1359.

Dardanelles, 12, 572, 586, 1315.

Dardanians, 39, 758, 759, 985–7; slaves, 1262, 1515.

Dardanos, 560.

Darius I, the Great, 77, 82, 281, 1150, 1163, 1607; III, 128, 262, 281, coin, 76; son of Pharnaces, 979.

Dascylium, 128, 561, 590.

Dates, 319; prices of, 537; taxes on, 467.

Daulis, 941, 1558.

Dea Syria, 438, 506.

Dead Sea, 1176.

Debasing of silver coinage, 712, 1494; *see* Coinage.

Debtors, selling into slavery of, 894.

Debts, abolition of, *see* Abolition; of cities, 953, 954, 973, 1371, 1464, 1467; collection of, by Delos, 139, 140; to the State in Egypt, 317, 1547, 1548; private, 317; of vassal kings to Rome, 980.

Decisiones, 1573.

Declaration, of domestic animals, 295; of property, 1499; of slaves, 342, 343.

Decuma, 467, 812–18, 946, 955, 965–7, 982, 997, 1526, 1560, 1561, 1563, 1564, 1567–9, 1577; immunity, 818; *see* δεκάτη.

Decumani, 1561, 1578.

Dedications, to temples, 165, 219, 220, 230, 1372, 1411.

Deditio, 529.

Deforestation, 91, 1021, 1168–70.

Deigma, of Rhodes, 681.

Deinocrates, 1235.

Deiotarus, Galatian tetrarch, 821, 837, 996, 1194, 1532, 1576.

δεκαταρχίαι, division into, 1591.

δεκάτη, tax, 337, 444, 445, 464, 466, 467, 470, 562, 1434, 1440, 1450, 1526, 1567, 1577; remission, 1434; see *Decuma*.

δεκατῶναι, 387.

Delicacies, trade in, 745.

Delos, 779, 1355, 1369, 1370, 1468, 1488, 1513, 1519, 1596, 1598; archaeological evidence, 221, 1371; associations, *see* Associations; Athenian cleruchy, 231, 233, 738, 741, 778, 788, 1502; banking, *see* Banking; clearing-house for trade, *see* Clearing-houses; collection of loans, 139, 140; cults, 792, 794, 922, 1491, 1518, 1555; currencies of, 742, 743, 1502, 1503; economic conditions, 127, 139, 190, 191, 221, 233, 235–7, 585, 736, 778, 798, 1145, 1371, 1505; foreigners in, 190, 225, 233, 236, 741, 742, 790, 791, 798, 922, 1271, 1370, 1505, 1517, 1531, 1555, 1585: Italians *see* Italian merchants *and* Italians; Orientals, 793, 864, 870, 1247, 1491, 1492; free port, 738, 741, 742, 771, 777, 778, 788, 1242, 1267; gift of grain to, 232, 1486; industry, 798: art products, 1519, bronze ware, 100, 796, metallurgy, 376, mosaics, 379, 702, 793, 1519, 1540, pottery, 616, 651, 742, 797, 1407, 1461, 1502, trade, 653, 797; pirates, 198, 202, 223, 954, 955, 1362, 1564; political conditions, 231, 236, 827, 838, 864, 947, 998, 1024, 1448, 1469, 1502, 1518, 1532, 1554: relations to Athens, *see* Athens, to Macedonia, 39, 232, 1375, to the kings of Pontus, 833, 834, 941, 1558, 1559, to Ptolemies, 38, 226, 231, 232, 692, 794, 1280, 1488, 1518, to Rhodes, *see* Rhodes, to Rome, 787, to Seleucids, 692, 693, 702, 1489, role in the Aegean, *see* Aegean; prices, *see* Prices; revenues of the city, 234; slaves, revolt of, 756, 798, 807; social structure, 790, 799, 1186, 1359; supply of foodstuffs, 1273, 1488; taxes, 233–5, 242; a temple city, 190, 221; temple of Apollo, 190, 230, 231, 310, 790, 1122, 1144, 1484: accounts of, 190, 191, 231, 233–5, 258, 259, 311, 796, 798, 1255, 1373, 1374, 1490, banking activity, 231, 1279, 1280, 1371, economy of, 230, 233–6, 1373, 1617, inventories, 165, 463, 796, 1333, 1371, 1409, 1422, 1446, 1490, 1492, votive offerings, 371, 463, *see* Gifts; trade, 190, 221, 233, 235, 654, 788, 790, 799, 869, 959, 1169, 1268, 1372, 1373, 1518: competition with Athens, 216–18, in caravan goods, 778, 795, in grain, *see* Grain, international, 702, 741, 744, in slaves, *see* Slaves, transit, 190, 744, 786, 788, in wine, 790, 1488, in the Aegean, 139, 190, 230–3, 741, with Alexandria, 235, 397, 761, 791, 920–3, 1555, with Asia Minor, *see* Asia Minor, with Bithynia, 791, with the Bosporus, 598, with Chios, 245, with Egypt, 216, 231, 392, 794, 795, 797, 922–4, 927, 1488, 1518, with Greece, 742, 743, 794,

797, 1518, with Italy, *see* Italy, with Lampsacus, 589, with Macedonia, 218, 232, 253, 1255, Oriental, 179, 180, 702, 787, 1491, 1492, with Pergamon, 654, 797, with Phoenicia, *see* Phoenicia, with Pontus, 834, with Rhodes, 231, 235, 744, 797, 1488, with Rome, 1267, with S. Russia, *see* Russia, with Seleucid Empire, *see* Seleucid Empire, with Sinope, 831; weights, 1431.

Delphi, 220, 221, 565, 740, 756, 1218, 1320, 1371, 1506, 1507, 1596–8; *asylia*, 197, 200, 609, 1363; economic conditions, 218, 614, 1618; foreign judges, 613, 614; foreigners in, 609, 614; gifts to, *see* Gifts; manumissions, 207, 626, 1262, 1466–8, 1501, 1515, 1646; political conditions, 39, 197, 216, 219, 220, 613–15, 940, 995, 1484, 1517, 1534, 1557: Celtic invasion, 26, 200, 218–20, 1123; relations with Aetolians, *see* Aetolians, with Bithynian kings, 783, 827, with Pergamon, 803, 827, 1448, 1451, 1473, 1520; slaves in, 627, 783, 1466, 1468; a temple-city, 190, 212; temple of, 165, 200, 219, 614, 675, 748, 756, 763, 783, 940, 1122, 1144, 1363; *theoroi*, 216, 608, 609, 676, 1460; trade, 618, 675, 676.

Delphinion, in Miletus, 665.

Delta, 162, 318, 361, 711, 733, 1198; irrigation of land, 363, 364; reclamation of, 362, 1161.

Demaratids, 151.

Demas, 1093.

Demeter, temple of, in Pergamon, 554, 661, 1449.

Demetrian war, 39, 41, 199, 217, 222, 1361, 1364, 1365, 1368, 1369.

Demetrias, 21, 137, 157, 251, 613, 626, 632, 1264, 1265, 1467, 1471.

Demetrius I Poliorcetes of Macedonia, 2, 15, 18, 1315, 1354, 1434, 1612, 1626; coinage, 185; coins of, 184, 1357; cult of, 1315; currency, 1356; expedition to Babylonia, 12–14, 476; financing of military operations, 138–40; fleet of, *see* Fleet; foundation of cities, 251; relations to army, 19–21, 144, 148, 1345, to Greece, 14–17, 19, 20, 141, 142, 193, 215, 216, 1255, 1341, to Greek cities of Asia Minor, 153, 154, 173, 1348, 1362, 1363, of Macedonia, 250; to Greek islands, 15, 16, 29, 231, 237; with pirates, 147, 185, 196, 1361; ruler of the Aegean, 19, 22, 31; struggle for empire, 11, 12, 14–17, 19–21, 23, 158, 1315, 1316, 1340, 1365; struggle with Rhodes, 15, 16, 146–8, 225, 463, 677, 1149, 1233, 1236, 1340.

Demetrius II of Macedonia, 31, 39, 216–18, 232, 250, 253, 255, 1317, 1372.

Diophanes of Bithynia, 1183, 1194.
Diophantus, 1512, 1584.
Dioptra of Heron, 1214, 1622.
Diorite, 1176.
Dioscuri-Cabiri, 833.
Dioscurias, 586.
Dioscurides, *dioecetes*, 725; of Samos, artist, 1506.
Dioskome, 504.
Diotimus, banker, 947; son of Dionysius, 341.
Diotogenes, the Pythagorean, 1347, 1595.
Diphilus, of Athens, 1146; of Siphnos, physician, 357, 1090; of Sinope, writer of comedies, 1604.
Disintegration of Hellenistic world, 69, 71.
διαπορεῖν, 365, 1187, 1405, 1406, 1618.
Disturbances in Greek cities (ταραχαί, ἔχθρα, διαφορά), 140, 209, 224, 225, 1527.
Divine descent of Hellenistic rulers, 431, 1426.
Dnieper, river, 106, 108, 596, 599, 1177, 1263.
Dniester, river, 106, 1177, 1263.
Dobrudja, 599.
Docimium in Phrygia, 1176, 1425.
Docimus, 1425.
Doctors (ἰατροί), 519, 883, 1117, 1133, 1374, 1598, 1600, 1650; in the armies, 146; chief, 1091, 1093, 1599; court, 1093, 1094, 1544, 1599; lecturers, 1596, 1598; public, 1091, 1597, 1598; salaries, 1601; ship's, 686; *see* Medical and Physicians.
Dodona, temple of, 201, 212, 1364.
Dogs, 359, 1162, 1164.
δοκιμασταί, 1419.
Dolabella, C. Cornelius, 948, 985, 1002, 1003, 1574, 1579.
Doliche, temple, 510.
δόμα, 1339.
Domains, of Hellenistic kings, 1195; of Attalids, 338; of Macedonian kings, 250–3, 758; of Persian nobles, 81; of Ptolemies, 717, 906, 1196, 1198; of Successors, 156; *see* Estates.
Domestic animals, in Egypt, 203, 292–5, 315; acclimatization of, 1162, 1164; improvement of breeds, 359; registration, 294, 295; trade, 1276.
Dominium in solo provinciali, 1525.
Domitian, emperor, 932.
Don, river, 106, 118, 769, 1177.
Donations, in Greek cities, 1463, 1464; to cities and temples, 1278, 1279, 1474; *see* Gifts.
Donkeys, 292, 293, 315, 359, 536, 1190, 1386; taxes on, 314.
Dora, 843.

Doreai (δωρεαί), 1195, 1307, 1339, 1340, 1421; given by Alexander the Great, 1314, 1340; in Asia Minor, 278, 640, 1155; in Egypt, 277, 278, 289, 291, 297, 353, 411, 414, 415, 420, 422, 718, 903, 906, 1071, 1153, 1180, 1197, 1378, 1396; commercial activity of owners of, 1270, 1275; industry on, 1229; in form of revenue from taxes, 896, 1421, 1498, 1499, 1548; system of granting of, 731, 732; in Pergamon, 561, 563, 1450; in the Seleucid Empire, 493, 1103, 1104, 1155; of the Successors, 137; of Apollonius the *dioecetes*, 289, 420–2, 718, 731, 1197–9, 1396, 1420–2: acclimatization of plants, &c., 1164, 1165, agriculture, 364, 365, 1198, 1199, bee-keeping, 1386, cattle, 293, 294, 358, 359, 1386, commercial dealings, 1275, documents concerning, 256, 1422, Greeks in, 331, 420, 421, 1074, 1199, industry, 308, 381, 1389, 1390, 1412, irrigation, 360, labour, 322, 1420, 1644, planting of trees, 299, 354–7, 420, 1199, 1404, of vines, 353, 354, 420, 1199, 1403, production of olive oil, 355, 356, reclamation of land, 361, ships, part of, 314, use of iron, 362, 363, 1197, 1405; *see* Zenon; of Ptolemy, son of Lysimachus, 336, 647, 1477.
δορίκτητος χώρα, 267, 482.
Dorimachus, 611.
Dorion, 1420.
Dorylaus, 833.
Dowries, in Athens, 163; in Delphi, 614.
Drainage, 360, 728, 1160, 1161, 1214, 1232, 1608.
Drangiana, 461; mines, 1175.
δραπέται, 754.
Draught animals, 319, 1190; compulsory service of, 182, 275; private, in Egypt, 292, 314, 421; registration of, 292; requisition of, 192, 315, 894, 1013; royal, in Egypt, 292; shortage of, 292, 720; taxes on, 242, 314; cattle, distribution of, in Egypt, 293.
Drave, river, 120.
Dresses, 164, 1257, 1352.
Drivers, 315, 317, 940, 1451.
Druggists, 1089, 1597, 1599: drugs, 1599.
Drymus, 941, 1558.
Dualism in Egyptian organization, 267, 400, 405.
Ducks, 1167, 1193, 1612.
Dues, harbour, *see* Harbours; for hunting in Egypt, 296; from private land in Seleucid Empire, 496; in kind from peasants in Egyptian dominions, 1401; right of collecting in Egypt, 415; of serfs in Seleucid Empire, 495.

Dumatha, 458, 867, 1541.
δυνάμεις, 1344.
Dura-Europus, 489, 523, 536, 541, 1141, 1437.
1537, 1561; archaeological evidence, 862,
1038, 1100, 1223, 1583, 1624, 1649; architecture, 1052, 1053, 1588, 1596; associations
in, 1062, 1065, 1591; *bourgeoisie* of, 1156;
coinage, 489; coin circulation, 448, 451,
1430, 1431, 1539; colony of, 427, 461, 488,
491; constitution of, 482, 485–7, 840, 857,
1438; documentary evidence, 423, 425,
1047, 1313, 1423; excavations of, 427,
1051, 1424; foundation of, 476, 483, 491,
1436; gods of, 424, 438; Greeks in, 519,
1061, 1075; industry: pottery, local, 1350,
imported, 160, 651, 700, 1351, 1446, 1491;
irrigation, 1162; laws, 1050, 1587; Macedonian settlers, 487–9, 497, 498, 501;
military settlement, 484, 491, 501; mint,
489; orientalization, 522, 523, 1443;
Parthian domination, 427, 483, 486, 856,
857, 861; plan of, 485, 1051, 1587; relations
with Palmyra, 424, 522, 791, 1517, 1585;
royal judges, 508, 1429; slaves, 1435;
social and economic conditions, 856–9,
1438; territory of, 488, 489, 511, 697, 857,
1162; trade, 463, 489, 540, 1486: caravan,
1246, 1626, local, 1271, 1272; vine-planting,
1165.
Duris, 1361, 1606.
Duties, on export and import, 633; on
maritime commerce, 229; on frontiers of
satrapies, 44; *see* Customs duties.
Dyaleis, phratry of, 1618.
Dyed stuffs of Phoenicia, 1222.
Dyeing, 564, 1225, 1226, 1624; materials,
1245.
Dyes, 386, 1226.
Dyme in Achaea, 142, 722, 757, 995, 1346,
1472, 1576.
Dynasteiai (δυναστεῖαι), in Asia Minor, 248,
336, 589, 592, 646, 979; in Cyprus, 336; in
Cyrenaica, 336; in Pergamon, *see* Pergamon; in Seleucid Empire, 336, 507, 848.
Dynastic, coins, 656, 659, 840; cults, 145, 439,
486, 661, 704, 857, 1047–9, 1438, 1499;
names of cities, 479, 482, 570, 703, 1438,
1649; troubles in Hellenistic States, 43, 68,
71, 72, 430, 530, 597, 696, 719, 720, 781, 783,
784, 841, 843, 871, 874–8, 921, 1075, 1516,
1542, 1554.
Dynasts (δυνάσται), 502, 743, 839, 843, 849,
860, 865, 982, 991, 1001, 1005, 1347, 1399,
1440, 1533; coinage of, 659, 853.
Dyrrhachium (Epidamnus), 48, 120, 769,
988, 1562; coinage, 769, 1292, 1512.

Ebony, 107, 366, 409.
Ecbatana, 435, 461, 480, 1427.
Ecclesiastes, 351, 1403.
Economic, initiative in Egypt, 273, 274, in
Greece, 273; isolation of Hellenistic kingdoms, end of, 249; organization, types of,
75, 440–2, in the Persian Empire, 77; ruin
of the Hellenistic world, 71; sanctions,
737, 738; self-sufficiency, *see* Self-
sufficiency; unity of Hellenistic world,
654, 737, 1019.
'Economics' (book II) ascribed to Aristotle, 74, 75, 440–6.
Ecphantus, 1343.
Ecron, 494.
Edessa-Orrhoe-Antioch, 476, 477, 479, 491,
510, 842, 866, 1533, 1540; coin of, 694.
Edom, mines of, 853, 1614.
ἐγχώρια νόμιμα, 1069.
ἐγχώριος νόμος, 1069.
ἐγδοχεῖς (or ἐκδοχεῖς), 228, 692, 742, 1268,
1275, 1518, 1628.
ἔγγυοι, 273, 328, 1498.
ἐγκάτοχοι, 735, 1497.
ἐγκλήματα, 446.
ἔγκτησις γῆς καὶ οἰκίας, 204, 205, 446.
ἐγκύκλιον, 316, 445, 1392.
Egnatia, via, 987.
Egypt, 248, 261, 262, 318, 350, 421, 637, 1405,
1417; agriculture, *see* Agriculture; aristocracy, *see* Aristocracy; army, *see*
Armies; art, 82, 86; *bourgeoisie*, see
Bourgeoisie; χώρα, *see* χώρα; city-like
settlements, 361, 420, 476; communications, improvement of, 132, 134; cults,
438, 439, 1063, 1429, 1593, *see* Royal and
Dynastic; currency, *see* Currency; dualism in organization, 267, 400, 405; economic conditions, 77, 81, 82, 158, 403, 407,
409, 410, 414, 586, 734–6, 891, 1021, 1250,
1296, 1551, 1552: corn economy, 1286, dis-
organization of, 712–18, 724, 734, 878, 906–
10, 1029, 1241, 1286, 1551, distribution of
wealth, 1153, 1154, self-sufficiency, 263,
271, 352, 366, 367, 381, 401, 707, 1241, 1295;
foreigners, *see* Foreigners; Greek aspect
of, 264, 265; Greek cities in, *see* Greek
cities; Greeks, *see* Greeks; hellenization,
351, 367, 882, 883, 886, 889, 912, 1063, 1071,
1072, 1099, 1139, 1168, 1544, 1593; industry,
81, 207, 300–2, 331, 366, 378, 918, 1422, 1620:
conflicts in, 411, foreigners in, 326, 331,
hellenization of, 367, 1227, labour in, 322,
343, methods of, 352, needs of, 386, 396,
organization by Ptolemies, 301–8, 311, 313,
356, 366, 367, 381, taxes on, 337; faience,

military colonies, 645, 647, 648; monetary policy, 633, 655, 1293; political activity, 58, 59, 61, 610, 634–7, 659; relations to Greek cities, 528, 529, 640–3, 803, 1473, 1474; with Rome, 71, 738, 799, 800, 826, 1340, 1472, with temples, 648, 1443; wars, 636, 665, 673, 767, 801, 1320, 1476, 1512, with Galatians, 800, 836, 1519.

Eumenes, brother of Philetaerus of Pergamon, 554.

Eumenes, dynast of Amastris, 578.

εὔνοια, 526, 1343, 1344, 1347, 1358, 1495.

εὐνομία, 209; of the Rhodians, 684.

Eupatoria (Magnopolis), 978.

Eupatoristai, 1022.

Euphrates, 363, 478, 479, 490, 865, 866, 1174, 1177, 1239, 1540; routes of, 79, 173, 461, 484, 697, 831, 865, 866.

Eupolemus, tyrant of Iasos, 136, 149, 152, 429, 1425.

Euromus, 671, 775, 1483, 1513, 1562.

Εὐρωπός, ἐν Παραποταμία, 1437; πρὸς Ἀραβίᾳ, 1437; see Dura.

Europus, name of cities, 479; -Dura, see Dura; in Macedonia, 483, 759, 1509; in Media (Rhagae), 480.

Eurycles, 1581.

Euryclides, 199, 218, 1360.

Eurydice, wife of Ptolemy I, 22, 338; wife of Philip Arrhidaeus, 6, 8, 9, 149.

Eusebeia, 838, 839.

Euthycrates, 1146.

Euthydemus, king of Bactria, 67, 542, 543, 549, coins of, 1492; of Mylasa, 822, 823, 1528; writer, 1336.

Eutychidas, 424.

Eutychus, 1373.

Euxine, 252, 566, 567, 591, 595, 665, 832, 835, 985, 986; fisheries of, 1177; Greek cities of, see Greek cities; mining, 1175; *periploi*, 1036, 1037; trade, 245, 572, 578, 585–7, 827, 829–31, 1025, 1144, 1264, 1512; currency of, 587, 588, in fish, see Fish, with Greece, see Greece, with Egypt, 107, 386, 392, 393, 593, 594, 598, 676, 1025, 1455, 1484, 1644, 1645.

ἐξ ἀξίας, 718, 726, 1498.

Exactio capitum et ostiorum, 962, 1566.

Exactions, by Mithridates VI, 942; by officials in Egypt, 894, 897; by Romans, 606, 983, 984, 993, 994, 996, 1002, 1003, 1008, 1012, 1013, 1018, 1566, 1576; by Successors, 1347.

Exactores, for collection of contributions, 994.

ἐξαίρημα, 496.

Exchange business, in Egypt, 402, 405, in Greece, 1287, 1292; exchange of goods in

the Aegean world, 585, in the empire of Alexander, 183.

Exclusion of foreign currencies, 1242.

Execution against the person, 317, 343, 344.

Exegetes of Alexandria, 1091.

Exemption, from compulsory work, 275, 286, 322, 325, 1381, 1561; from customs duties, 463; from demands of *publicani*, 749; from furnishing quarters, 971, 976, 1001, 1006, 1561, 1578; of individuals from imposts, 971, 997; from military service, 97, 200, 952, 1001, 1003, 1397, 1576; from pillage, 194; from rent, 726; from requisitions, 952, 956; from royal exactions and jurisdiction, 845; from taxes, 309, 956, 966; from tribute, 1001.

Exhaustion, of mines, 1021; of soil, 1021.

ἔξω πόλεις, 1397.

Exomides (ἐξωμίδες), 100.

Exotic trees brought to Egypt, 409.

Exploration, of the Red Sea, 925; of sea route to India, 927–9; work of, 1037.

Export, of goods in royal economy, 443; duties, 384; licences, 385; taxes, 316.

Exposure of children, 96, 623, 892, 1127, 1261, 1465, 1547.

Extraordinary, burdens, 323, 1561; financial measures in Athens, 217; imposts, 529, 530, 750; service from cleruchs, 286.

Ezida, temple of, 435, 437, 1427.

Ezion-Geber, 1174, 1614.

Factories, 616, 1010, 1220; Arretine, 176; in Egypt, 303, 306, 307, 311, 312, 317, 892, 899: in *dorea* of Apollonius, 421, royal, see Royal, temple, 322, workmen in, 317; in Greece, 100, 113; in Pergamon, 564, 565.

Factory-like establishments, 1210, 1211.

Faience, 1208, 1209, in China, 1208, 1209, 1433, 1446; in Egypt, 366, 368, 370, 372, 375, 1011, 1208, 1209, 1407, 1408, export, 107, 169, 369, 676, 1257, 1446, 1484; in Italy, 1010; Mesopotamian, 699–701, 1011, 1208, 1209, 1446, 1491, 1622; in S. Russia, 1010; Syro-Anatolian, 1010, 1011.

Fairs (πανηγύρεις), 444, at Cyzicus, 589, 1454.

φάλαγξ, 1397.

Falcidius, 1568.

Familia publicanorum, 967, 977.

Famines, 1250; in Asia Minor, 1012, 1520, 1581; in Egypt, 1551; in Greece, 95, 168, 619, 622; in Greek cities, 593, 674, 765, 951, 1110, 1248, 1273, 1329, 1627; in Samos, 224, 1445. See Food (shortage).

φαρμακοπῶλαι (druggists), 1089.

Farmers general of revenues, 345.

Farming, law of Mylasa, 466; of contracts, 302; of monopolies, 330; of revenues, *see* Revenues; of *stipendium* in Judaea, 1000; of taxes, *see* Taxes.

Fayûm, 266, 295, 724, 881, 899, 902, 1366, 1404, 1544, 1550; agriculture, 1200; copper mines, 297; documentary evidence, 256–8, 260, 388, 1313, 1410, 1618; fisheries, 1177, 1180; Greeks in, 1051, 1140, 1606; land in, 276, 282, 1496: drainage of, 1161, irrigation, 360, 1381, reclamation, 203, 256, 361; oil, 305, 355, 356; sheep-breeding, 358.

Federal, constitution of Greek Leagues, 72; State, 36, 41.

Federation of Greek cities, 154.

Feeding of Government agents while travelling, 964.

Ferry service, 1482.

Feudal, aristocracy of Bactria, 549, of Persia, 77, 81, 507, 549, of Pontus, 576; lords of Asia Minor, 81, 782, 783, 849, 1515, of Macedonia, 1314, of Persia, 1103; origin of δωρεαί, 1339, 1340; structure of Commagene, 849, 1515, 1536, of Persia, 77, of Pontus, 979; tendencies in Egypt, 82, in Oriental monarchies, 272.

Figs, 229, 247, 357, 1189, 1254.

φιλάνθρωπα, in Egypt, 879, 885, 887, 898, 902, 905, 1399, 1543; of Ptolemy Auletes, 879, 1543; of Ptolemy Epiphanes, 713, 714, 718, 723, 878, 879, 885; of Ptolemy Euergetes II, 339, 873, 874, 878–82, 884, 885, 887, 888, 890, 891, 893, 894, 897, 899, 907, 914, 916, 1541, 1543, 1546, 1550–2; of Ptolemy Philometor, 723, 879; of Ptolemy Philopator, 710, 713, 714, 878, 879, 899, 1494; of Ptolemy Soter II, 915, 916, 1542; in Pergamon, 1522, of the Seleucids, 467, 469, 509.

φιλανθρωπία, 1358, 1359.

φιλία, 526.

φιλοβασιλισταί, 1590.

φιλοχρημοσύνη, 624.

φίλοι, of Antiochus II, 224, 1445.

φίλος πρῶτος, 1476.

φιλοτεχνῖται, 1085.

φιλόξενοι, 569.

Fimbria, C. Flavius, 830, 944, 945.

Finance, theory of, 440.

Financial, agents of the crown, 1044; crises, 74, 217, 440; difficulties of Greek cities, *see* Greek cities; managers of temples, 648; officials, 130, 343, 515, 516; organization (οἰκονομίαι), forms of, 74; system of cities, 643.

Fines, in Egypt, 340, 342; imposed by Romans, 945, 962, 963, 991, 1003, 1004, 1016.

Fir trees, 357, 1612.

Firewood, 1168, 1169, 1612.

Fish, 618, 1177–80, 1193; dishes (pottery), 1615; in Greece, 93, 106, 210, 394, 621, 1615; mosaics, 1615; pickled, 394; prices of, 1369, 1615; salted, 1336, concessionaires for sale of, 314; salters, guild of, 1590; sauces, 394, 1254; tax on catch of, 297; trade, 297, 1177, 1179, 1254, 1271, 1273, 1336, 1387; of Azov Sea, 1263, of Euxine, 106, 586, 587, 589, 595, 831, of Thrace, 111.

Fisheries, 1177, 1178, 1180, 1615; in Asia, Roman, 966; of Byzantium, 591; of Cos, 241, 242, 1374; of Egypt, 1150, 1177, taxes on, 337, 1644; of Ephesus, 648; of Greek cities, 1644; of Lesbos, 247; of Pergamon, 556, 1157; of Persian kings, 1151; of Seleucid Empire, 472; of Sinope, 593; of Thracian Bosporus, 586.

Fishermen, of Cos, 243; Egypt, 296, 297, 317, 1387.

Fishing, 92, 211, 235, 599, 1177–9, 1615; in Egypt, 296, 297, 299, 317, 1387, control over, 313, taxes, 297.

Flaccus, L. Valerius, 821, 822, 949, 961, 963, 970, 987, 1562, 1565, 1568.

Flamininus, 44, 53, 56, 605, 606, 617.

Flax, 1257; in Cilicia, 975; in Egypt, 280, 300, 377, 421, 1383, 1416, control over, 306, dealers in, 1277; Euxine, trade in, 586; in Greece, 91.

Fleets, of Alexandria, 334, 397; of Athens, 7; of Demetrius Poliorcetes, 14–16, 22, 146, 147, 1169, 1345, 1585; of Ephesus, 807; of the Island League, 333; Rhodian merchant, 687; of Roman military leaders, 948, 949, 953, 954, 963, 991, 993, 1005, 1012, 1013, 1564, 1576, 1579, 1581; of Successors, 146, 147; transport, of Apollonius, 314; *see* Navies.

Flour mills, 176.

Flowers, 247, 572.

Fodder, 334, 1163.

Fonduqs, 80, 702, 791, 1024, 1517, 1585.

Food, requisitions, 991, 993; shortage, 1250: in Egypt, 1254, in Greece, 94–9, 168, 211, 393, 619, 765, 952, 1187, 1248, 1251, 1369, on Greek islands, 223, *see* Famines; supply of armies of Successors, 137, 1470, in Egypt, 297, 334, in Greek cities, 31, 91, 106, 168, 393, 618–22, 951, 1124, 1248–51, 1269, 1271–3, 1354, 1464, 1562, 1646, of Greek islands, 182, 235, of Roman armies, 953, 995.

Foodstuffs, 98, 99, 147, 618, 1241, 1248, 1254; Babylonia, prices of, 537; Bosporan

649, 782, 836, 837, 977, 980, 993; population of, 1141, 1606; serfs in, 1515.

Galatian, chiefs, 581, 584; mercenaries, 571, 584, 836, 1005, 1082, 1397, 1452, 1453; military equipment, 638; royal graves, 1553; slaves, 691, 836, 1532; State, 32, 248.

Galatians, 30, 503, 582–4, 592; invasions of, 25, 27, 33, 37, 61, 529–32, 581, 583, 667, 669, 1009, 1028, 1455, 1519; pacification of, 527; relations with Bithynia, 568, 578, 584; settlement in Asia Minor, 429, 552, 568, 578–80, 1453; social and economic structure, 578–81, 584, 837, 1452; wars, 635, 636, 803, 829, 836, 1142, 1444, 1450: with Pergamon, 33, 35, 43, 59, 553–5, 557, 559, 635, 643, 800, 801, 836, 1519, with Pontus, 578, 831, 943, with Seleucids, 32, 429, 432; expedition of Vulso, 584, 635.

Galatica (Γαλατικά), 1563.

Galilee, 349, 351; land taxes, 467; Sea of, 347.

Galjub near Cairo, 375, 730, 1222, 1597.

Gallic terror, 531, 800.

Gallius, C., 952.

Gamala, 843.

Gambreon, 563.

Game, in Egypt, 296.

Gandhara, 78, 863.

Gardening, 77, 221, 750, 859, 958, 1618; treatises on, 1164, 1189.

Gardens, 182, 286, 289, 290, 496, 523, 536, 545, 556, 887, 888, 1199, 1619; taxes on, 290.

Gargara, 560, 1356.

Garlic, 357.

Garments, *see* Clothing.

Garrisons, of Alexander the Great, 144; in Greek cities, 8, 140, 198, 215, 642, 644, 951; Macedonian, *see* Macedonian; of Ptolemies, 265, 334, 695, 1151, 1220, 1339, 1397, 1551; of Seleucids, 518, 527, 530.

Gate-toll, 335–7.

Gaul, 91, 93, 581, 865, 922, 1553, 1619, 1648.

Gauls, in Delphi, 26, 200, 1123; in Greece, 26, 38, 41; in Macedonia, 25; in Asia Minor, *see* Galatians; statue of dying Gaul, 558.

Gaza, 12, 130, 132, 228, 347, 351, 387, 841, 843, 1339, 1419; battle of, 148, 149; coins of, 1324, 1325; mint of, 399.

Gaziura, 576.

γαζοφύλαξ, 440.

γῆ ἀνιερωμένη, 277, 281, 727, 1545, 1546.

γῆ ἀρχαία, 1381.

γῆ βασιλική, 913; in Egypt, 276, 277, 281, 283, 1382; Lycia, 336; Macedonia, 251; Priene, 179.

γῆ δημοσία, Pidasa, 671.

γῆ ἐν ἀφέσει, 276, 277, 280, 913, 1381; ἐν δωρεᾷ, 277, 731, 732, 1381; ἐν συντάξει, 277, 289, 1381.

γῆ ἰδιόκτητος, in Egypt, 277, 289, 290, 327, 732, 1450; Pergamon, 562.

γῆ ἰδιωτική, 1382.

γῆ ἱερά, in Egypt, 277, 280–4, 322, 714, 727, 884, 1200, 1375, 1384, 1495, 1496, 1500, 1545, 1546; Pidasa, 671.

γῆ κληρουχική, 277, 289, 727, 916, 1384, 1385.

γῆ πολιτική, 276, 1381, 1382, 1385.

Gebelen, documents of, 257, 1376, 1644, 1645.

Gedrosia, 457.

Geese, 292, 294, 1193, 1385, 1386; gooseherds, 294.

Gelon, 1249, 1256.

Gems, 107, 108, 1258.

Gendarmerie, of Miletus, 669.

Gendarmes, of Palmyra, 1585.

γενηματοφύλακες, 280, 890.

γενηματοφυλακία, 1496.

γενηματογραφούμενα, 1551.

Genusus, river, 48.

Geodetic instruments, 1214.

Geographers, 1583, 1584.

Geographical works (γεωγραφίαι), 1035–40.

Geography, development of, 1582, 1583.

γεωμετρία (measurement of land), 275.

Geoponica, 1183, 1188, 1192, 1618.

γεωργεῦντες, 690.

γεωργοί, Cyrene, 333; Egypt, 1199, 1421, 1590.

γεοῦχοι, 732, 733, 1154, 1200, 1499, 1590.

γέρα, 513, 1384.

Gerasa, 776, 867, 1424.

Gergitha, 560.

Gerillanus, Maraeus, 798.

Gerkan, A. von, 664.

Germans, raids on Macedonia, 985.

Gerontes, of Alexandria, 1138.

Gerrha, 457, 458, 841, 1247, 1433.

Gerrhaeans, 457–9, 696, 702, 1244, 1246.

Gerusia acts, 1138, 1139, 1606.

γῆς ἀναδασμός, *see* Redistribution of land.

γῆς περίοδοι, 1036.

Gessia, P. l. Fausta, 992.

Gessius, P., P. l. Primus, 992; P. f. Rom(ilia), 992.

Getae, 118.

Gêv, 1065, 1591, 1592.

Gezer, 85, 651, 1324, 1325, 1349, 1445; coins, 402; weights, 454.

Gift estates, see *Doreai.*

Gifts, of cattle, 493, 494, 1450, 1451; of cities to kings, 640, 641, 644, 1474; of grain, 232, 381, 463, 492, 565, 593, 629, 777, 803, 806, 941, 1141, 1248, 1249, 1354, 1455, 1467, 1476, 1486, 1520, 1627; of land, 250, 251, 435, 493–5, 529, 562, 649, 884, see *Doreai*; of metal, 1256; of olive oil, 529, 1124; of slaves, 227, 565, 783; of timber, 1255, 1612; to army, 821, 878; to Athens, 216, 629, 630, 803, 805, 997, 1255, 1340, 1520, 1612, 1627; to Delos, 232, 1486; to Greek cities, 137, 143, 153, 155, 174, 531, 621, 622, 641, 703, 806, 819, 822, 828, 941, 1110, 1149, 1305, 1340, 1375, 1399, 1455, 1520, 1521, of Pergamene rulers, 559, 777, 803–5, 1450, 1451, 1467, 1473, 1474, 1520, 1646, 1647; to Miletus, 174, 338, 494, 641, 667, 669, 803, 804, 1141; to officers, 137, 327, 410, 1339; to Rhodes, 230, 463, 631, 663, 777, 803, 805, 1110, 1249, 1255, 1256, 1265, 1433; to temples, 435, 439, 564, 938, 1122, 1427, 1450, 1451: of Delos, 231, 234, 236, 371, 463, 554, 1373, 1422, 1433, 1434, 1490, 1502, of Delphi, 219, 220, 565, 783, 803, 1520, of Didyma, 174, 459, 666, 676, 824, 825, 1344, 1447, 1451, of Egypt, 710, 714, 878, 884, 885, 1384, 1411, 1494, 1545, of Jerusalem, 376, to Pan-hellenic sanctuaries, 554, 569, of Thespiae, 554, 1368, 1448; *see* Grants.

Giro, 1279.

Glabrio, M. Acilius, 614, 1461.

Glass, 539, 918, 919, 1021–3, 1211, 1212; in Egypt: industry, 366, 370–4, 539, 698, 1024, 1211, 1408, 1409, 1446, 1553, 1554, trade, 107, 112, 169, 370–4, 396, 676, 918, 1257, 1409, 1484, 1553, 1648; Italy, 371, 1409; Phoe-nicia, 539, 698, 861, 1211, 1446, 1538, trade, 861; Syria, 539, 698, 1024, 1446, 1538, 1539, trade, 546, 795, 1646, 1648.

Glaucias, 723.

Gnaeus, 922, 1555.

γναφεῖς, 309, 1277.

Gnathia, pottery, 162, 396, 538, 1207, 1209, 1408, 1415, 1621.

Goats, 203, 292, 294, 421, 563, 1162, 1190.

Gobelin type of textiles, 1224.

Gold, 123, 230, 386, 388, 402, 409, 414, 530, 981, 1170–5, 1277, 1353; articles: Egypt, 375, 376, 1411, Greece, 108, 113, 596, S. Russia, 110, 596, 600, 1332, Siberia, 535, 548, Syria, 540, 699, as capital, 1171, 1282; confiscation of, 940, 1003, 1004; dust, 409; gifts of, 137, 327, 410, 1339; industry, 1215, 1216; mines: Altai, 447, Chalcidice, 1173, Egypt, 297, 298, 381, 382, 1150, 1173, 1413, India, 1172, Macedonia, 252, 758, Nubia, 297, 298, 381–3, 1173, 1213, 1219, Pergamon, 556, Persia, 83, Thasos, 221; mining, 1613;

plate, 92, 106, 108, 165, 174, 234, 374, 376, 1212, 1257, 1411, 1490, as capital, 1171, 1204; prices of, 165, 399; smiths, 375, 378, 699, 730, 1216, 1277, 1629; supply: Bactria, 546, 1430, Egypt, 381–4, 386, 711, Near East, 447, Rome, 1290, Seleucid Empire, 447, 1490.

Gomphi, 995, 1576.

Gongylids, 151.

Gonnoi, 613, 764, 1470, 1471.

Gordium, 579, 580.

Gorgus, of Iasus, 151, 1346; engineer, 1172, 1613.

Gortyn, 199, 1374, 1598; coin of, 972.

Gotarzes, coins of, 1490.

Gourds, 1165.

Gracchus, C., 812, 813; Tiberius, 1131.

Grace, Miss V., 1647.

Graeculi, 1097, 1125.

Grain, as currency, 279, 300; gifts of, *see* Gifts; payments to Romans in, 1001, 1578; prices, 1046, 1250, 1354; for prisoners, 1365; production, 1190, 1249–52, 1462; supply, 618, 1462; trade, 98, 168, 360, 587, 630, 676, 1248–52, 1354, 1462; Aegean, prices, 236, trade, 172, 393, 630, 632, 692, 918, 1252, 1265, 1372; Africa, trade, 619, 765, 1243; Asia Minor, production, 98, 366, 671, 1251, 1252, subscriptions for, 810, trade, 587, 1354; Athens, fund, 629, prices, 1353, trade, 89, 111, 168, 169, 217, 218, 629–32, 676, 692, 795, 1329, 1462, supply, 89, 106, 168, 1329; Babylon, prices, 537, 1445; Bosporan king-dom, trade, 111, 232, 595, 598, 1249, 1251, 1252, 1372; Byzantium, trade, 591; Carth-age, production, 1250, trade, 619, 675, 765, 1251, 1462; Cos, trade, 244; Cyprus, pro-duction, 98, 360, trade, 89, 111, 172, 384, 1354; Cyrenaica, production, 333, 360, 384, trade, 384; Delos, accounts of buyers, 235, gifts to, 232, 1486, prices, 235, 393, 692, 1372, 1414, 1627, supply, 1462, 1562, trade, 217, 218, 232, 235, 393, 591, 632, 676, 692, 795, 1373, 1462, 1486; Egypt, 300, abstrac-tion of, 892, compulsory sale of, 327, gifts of, 381, 593, import from dominions, 360, 384, 385, improvement of, 365, land, private property, 289, prices, 236, 259, 316, 1414, 1469, production, 280, 331, 360, 365, 421, 720, 1198, 1199, 1249–51, 1381, supply of Alexandria, 909, 1551, trade, *see* Egypt, transport, 280, 314, 315, 1151, 1300, 1382, 1391, 1543, 1545, used for payments, 279, 300, 1382; Ephesus, trade, 169, 1354; Greece, prices, 619, 628, 1187, production, 91, 1187, 1188, requisition, 988, 1013, ships,

98, 1372, trade, 93, 98, 101, 105, 106, 111, 122, 156, 359, 360, 619, 777, 1252; Heraclea Pontica, trade, 578, 592, 630; Italy, trade, 98, 111, 122, 359, 1250; Judaea, payments to Rome, 1000, 1001, 1578; Macedonia, production, 1249, 1251, trade, 253, 633; Numidia, trade, 619, 1252, 1462; Pergamon, gifts of, 565, production, 630, 1251, 1450, for soldiers, 1476, trade, 565; Phoenicia, production, 98, 360, trade, 111, 172, 360; Pontic cities, production, 674, trade, 111, 586, 587, 674, 675, 831, 1265; Rhodes, loan to, 1340, trade, 169, 172, 225, 393, 632, 676, 680, 692, 777, 795, 1251, 1252, 1462, 1485; S. Russia, production, 98, 360, 1250, trade, 111, 359, 360, 366, 630, 1462; Samos, regulations, 673; Seleucid Empire, gifts, 463, 492, production, 536, 1249, 1251, trade, 587, 1354; Syria, trade, 89, 172; Thrace, production, 98, 359, 360, 366, 1249, 1462, trade, 98, 359, 360, 1249, 1462; *see* Agriculture, Corn, Famines, Food (shortage).

γραμματεύς, 339, 348.

γραμματοφυλακία, 1429.

Granaries, 280, 589, 1001, 1151, 1287.

Granite, 297, 1176.

Grants, in Egypt: of revenues, 731, 1494, of royal land, 286, 338, 420, 422, 494, 727, 1153, to temples, 281, 283, 1546; Greece, of citizenship and *proxenia*, 1109; Pergamon, to Greek cities, 529; in Seleucid Empire, of land, 495, 1103, 1427; see *Doreai* and Gifts.

Grapes, 536, 572; taxes on, 467.

Grass, 274, 280, 286, 421, 1382.

Grazing, 77, 81, 299, 545, 581, 750, 859, 958, 1259, 1507.

Greco-Anatolian Empire of Mithridates VI, 835; -Egyptian cults, 791, families, 883, 889, silver ware, 1411; -Iranian art, 110, 390, 546; -Italian industry, 183; -Macedonian cities, 477, 478, 842, 1438, stratum in Seleucid Empire, 517; -Oriental religion, 64, world, unity of, 135; -Phoenician cities, hellenization of, 130; -Phrygian civilization, 837; -Scythian settlements, 108; -Semites in Seleucid Empire, 703; -Syrian industry, 534, 535; -Thracian State, 26, silver, 114.

Greece, 919, 933, 934, 1556, 1578; agriculture, *see* Agriculture; banking, *see* Banking; *bourgeoisie*, see *Bourgeoisie*; coin circulation, 76, 99, 186, 449, 1338, 1480, 1502–4; coinage of Roman leaders, 972, 1504, 1557, 1558; currency, 187, 449, 604, 655, 1529; economic conditions, 72, 77, 90–6, 126,

208, 211, 613, 624–7, 750–5, 869, 1250, 1251, 1327, 1328, 1358, 1460, 1461: balance of production and demand, 99, crises, 94, 99, 101, 125, 127, 1127, decline, 243, 617, 618, 628, 632, 736, 917, 939, 1021, 1250, depopulation of, 623–5, 1127, 1136, 1464, 1465, disequilibrium of demand and supply, 168, 169, distribution of wealth, 1143–8, 1617, effects of the conquest of Alexander, 129, 130, 132, 151, emancipation of the East from, 1028, emigration from, 332, 519, 624, 625, 770, exploitation of natural resources, 210, 1143, 1168, 1169, 1171, 1172, 1175, 1180, 1613, food shortage, *see* Food shortage, impoverishment, 203–7, 210, 615, 617, 623, 626, 1026, 1028, 1241, 1366, 1494, influence of wars, 98, 189, 191–5, 210, 1026, insecurity of life, 200, 202–4, 330, 612, 615, 625, 1109, monetary anarchy, 655, overpopulation, 92, 1026, periods of prosperity, 158, 161, 163–5, 183, 187, 617, 628, 750–5, 1028, 1328, poverty of soil, 204, 624, scarcity of raw materials, 204; industry, 91, 94, 99–101, 104, 123, 159, 163, 176, 177, 210, 212, 300, 1026, 1143, 1490: capitalistic development of, 100, emancipation of the East from, 207, 208, 615, labour in, 96, 97, 100, trade in products of, 90, 92–4, 104, 107, 110, 119, 538, 768: artistic products, trade, 745, 746, 760, 761, 1505; jewellery, 183, 1215, 1623, metal, 100, 539, 540, 1215, 1222, trade, 92, 93, 103, 106, 108, 112–14, 117–19, 122, 183, 596, 1271, 1325, 1447; pottery, 100, 370, 615, 616, 651, 1209, 1335, 1354, 1406, trade, 85, 93, 106, 108, 117, 122, 183, 538, 596, 598, 1325, 1326, 1335, 1337, 1354, terracottas, 170, 212, 593, trade, 106, 122, textiles, 1223, 1224; intermarriage, 204, 205, 523; Italians in, *see* Italians; labour, *see* Labour; life in, 170, 171, 565, 627, 1086, 1113, 1329, 1468; piracy, *see* Piracy; political conditions, 17, 23, 36, 56, 72, 74, 135, 185, 189, 204, 209, 210, 219, 222, 571, 603, 624, 625, 628, 1108, 1508: attempts to unify, 36, 41, 42; policy of Caesar, 998, 999; relations with Macedonia, *see* Macedonia and individual kings; with Mithridates VI, 757, 834, 935, 937, 939, 941, 942; with Pergamon, 554, 1450; with Ptolemies, 39, 217, 334, 407, 1416, 1420; with Rome, 47–9, 52, 53, 55, 56, 58, 59; role of Aetolians, *see* Aetolians; Roman domination: economic conditions, 606, 607, 616, 617, 738, 741, 952, 953, 1012, 1013, 1015, 1145, 1311, 1312, 1462, 1501, 1646, political conditions, 62, 606, 608, 610, 616, 739, 741, 745, 748, 750,

1606, relations to temples, 503, 504, 506, 507, 824, 825, slavery in, 1106, status of, 525, 528, 640–4, 815, 1343, taxes, 466, 467, 531, 644, 1577, trade, 80, 81, 84, 107, 169, 245, 407, 532, 653, 701, 1272, 1526, *see* individual cities; of Bactria, 547, 1053; of Bithynia, 33, 567, 568, 570, 571, 663, 1481; of the Bosporan kingdom, 594, 769, 770, 1330, of the Crimea, 586, 665, 768, 833; of the Dalmatian coast, 1511; of Egypt, 156, 264, 265, 276, 324, 401, 415, 846, 1052, 1069, 1381; of the Euxine, 573, 585–7, 1126: economic conditions, 91, 183, 674, 675, 764, 768, 1143, 1147, 1148, 1159, 1462, 1484, industry, 107, navies, 772, political conditions, 29, 35, 573, 590, 591, 665, 766, 767, 832–4, 985, 986, 989, 1455, 1456, 1511, 1532, 1559, slaves, 675, 1484, trade, 106, 107, 111, 216, 587, 674, 676, 768, 831, 1253, 1263, 1485, 1645, in grain, 111, 586, 587, 674, 675, 765, 831, 1265, *see* individual cities; of Gaul, 91; of Greece, 181, 1369: coinage, 186, 253, economic conditions, 90–2, 183, 211, 212, 585, 619, 1110, 1142, 1467, education, 1059, life, 1107, 1108, political conditions, 8, 13, 17, 27, 36, 42, 56, 192–7, relations with Attalids, *see* Attalids, to Rome, 749, 750, 951, 1013, social revolutions, 8, 94–6, 209, 210, *see* Greek cities and individual cities; of the Hellespont, 229, 528, 529, 556, 585; of Illyria, 48; of the Islands, 181, 1143: coinage, 229, 655, 656, 1469, 1480, economic conditions, 140, 183, 221, 223–5, 531, 585, 619, political conditions, 11, 16, 27, 30, 156, 641, trade, 93, 225, *see* Greek islands and individual cities and islands; of Italy and Sicily, 47, 91, 122, 124, 1144, 1301; of Macedonia, 91, 250, 251, 253, 1470; of Mysia, 554; of Parthian kingdom, 840, 856–9, 861, 976; of Pergamene kingdom, 529, 554, 556, 557, 559–62, 648–50, 807, 808, 817, 818, 1157, 1158, 1294, 1450, 1481, *see* Pergamon; of Phoenicia, *see* Phoenician cities; Pontic, *see* of the Euxine; of Pontus, 33, 570, 573, 576, 577, 653, 768, 978; of the Propontis, 183, 229, 585, 673, 674, 1230; of the Ptolemaic dominions, 333–5, 337–9, 352, 1417; of S. Russia, 106, 108–10, 183, 586, 600, 676, 1331; of the Seleucid Empire, 464, 477, 478, 480–2, 485, 491, 501, 507, 512, 514, 515, 518, 519, 703, 847, 1051, 1061, 1075, 1141, 1443: coinage, 447, 448, 1293, cults, 424, of ruling king, 431, freedom of, *see* Autonomy and Freedom, foundation of, 703, 704, 1436, 1438, 1587, land of, 465, 469, 493, 495, 496, 509, orientalization, 71, relations with

kings, *see* Seleucids, with native cities, 510, 512, social and economic structure, 643, 856, 861, 1104, 1310, taxes, 528–30, 642, *see* Greek cities of Asia Minor and individual cities; of semi-Hellenistic monarchies, 859; of Spain, 91, of Thrace, 91, 111, 112, 116, 585, 586, 594, 766, 1334.

Greek city-states, 133, 249, 1029, 1031, 1097, 1119–21, 1358, 1379; arms supply, 1221, 1222; economic conditions, 74, 75, 90–2, 97, 101, 104, 154–6, 185, 1027, 1288; in Italy, 1301; political conditions, 4, 72, 135, 204, 619, 1108, 1109, 1026, 1304.

Greek islands, 221, 245: agriculture, 240, 1160, cities, *see* Greek cities, class war, 209, currency, 229, 744, economic conditions, 91, 191, 221–5, 247, 519, 1143, 1251, 1358, piracy, *see* Piracy, political conditions, 15, 16, 29, 35, 36, 39, 142, 146, 148, 189, 231, 237, 332, 333, 337, 463, 531, 607, 942, 963, 991, 1485, 1508, population, 1135, trade, 109, 225, 407, 651, 691, 1518.

Greek, accounting system, 266, 273, 1079, 1283; architecture, 1052; art, 213, 1010, 1143, 1487, influence of, 86, 110, 116, 872, 1456; artists, 123, 438, 793, 820, 1446, 1447; aspect of Hellenistic world, 1035, 1040; bureaucratic machinery, 1079; business life, 101, 133; capitals of Hellenistic monarchies, 149, 264, 568; civilization, 68, 71, 179, 249, 473, 551, 681, 848, 851, 912, 961, 1020, 1040, 1057, 1097, 1106, 1125, 1542, unity of, *see* Unity; classics in Egypt, 422, 1060; coins, 84, 88, 104, 119, 124, 125, 135, 164, 1324, 1334, 1351; colonies, 481, 552, 567, 573, 1143, 1281, local industry of, 118, 159, trade, 92, 93, 100, 105, 110, 111, 120, 159, 679; colonization, 92, 111, 502, 552, 572; economic system, 135, 273, 1031, 1127, 1507; education, 882, 1047, 1058–61, 1071, 1099; emigrants, 249, 1027, 1054–6, 1072–4; façade of Egypt, 264; front of Bithynia, 568, 570, 663, of Pontus, 665; harbours on Persian Gulf, 1245; houses, 1052, 1053, 1230, 1231, 1625; identity of Hellenistic monarchies, 1097; international usage, 141; kings of Bactria, 50, 549, 550; of India, 550; kingdoms of India, 551; language, 130, 266, 418, 519, 522, 882, 1045, 1060, 1061, 1065, 1079, 1545; law, 324, 522, 614, 1050, 1067–70, 1114, 1240; life, 106, 159, 366, 409, 421, 422, 622, 703, 704, 1050, 1071, 1098, 1304; mentality, 268, 421, 422; merchants, 82, 130, 388, 569, 1024, 1452; military technique, 262; names of cities, 361, 478, 479, 510, 511, of gods, 522, 523,

Hagesandrus, 682.
Hagne of Cyzicus, 828.
Halab (Aleppo), 79, 491, 510, 511.
Haliartus, Boeotian city, 741, 1501.
Halicarnassus, 151, 179, 240, 334, 335, 339, 432, 949, 956, 973, 1231, 1313, 1399, 1400, 1598; bank in, 1418; coinage, 1417; war of Aristonicus, 809, 1523.
Halieutica, 1177, 1178, 1615.
Hallstatt, 113, 1333.
Halmyros, Thessaly, 1503.
Halys, river, 571, 572, 578.
Hamath (Hama), 79, 491, 510, 511, 700, 866.
Hana, kingdom of, 491.
Hangings, 379, 918, 1257.
Hannibal, 48, 52, 383, 663.
Hanse, Northern, 568, 587, 977; Pontic, 591, 1265, 1268.
Harbours, 132, 173, 183, 1025, 1043, 1230, 1263–5, 1585; of Alexandria, 417, 418, 1042, 1404; of Cnidus, 1266; of Cos, 244, 245; of Delos, 780; of Heraclea Pontica, 1454; of Lindus, 678; of the Red Sea, 924, 1245; of Seleucids, 478, 1043, 1245; dues, 227, 316, 389, 444, 742, 749, 771, 1486.
Harmon, A. M., 826.
Harpalus, 1162, 1165, 1610.
Harvest, guarding of, 217; transportation, 315.
Hasmonaeans, 68, 852, 853, 859, 1536; coins of, 853, 1536; taxes, 1000.
Hatchepsut, 1166.
Hauran, 425, 512.
Hay, delivery of, 1386.
Head-tax (*exactio capitum*), 962; for medical service, 1092.
Heads of villages (κωμάρχαι), 275, 279, 320, 344, 896.
Healing, religious, 1598.
Health, resorts, 221, 1598; service, 182, 242, 244, 1124; see Medical service.
Hecades in Dura, 488.
Hecataeus of Abdera, 1092, 1132, 1137, 1389.
Hecatomnus of Caria, 151; coins of, 1324.
Hecatonymus, 1651.
Hedonists, 1329.
Hegemony, 249, 381, 403, 603, 707, 1028, 1029, 1031; Aegean, see Aegean; commercial, of Athens, 169, 1264; of Rhodes, 1647; Panhellenic, of the Aetolians, 48, 55; of Rome over the East, 70, 71.
Hegesias, 1329.
Heichelheim, F. M., 1186, 1202, 1270, 1434, 1499.
Hekate, temple of, 824, 1528, 1581.
Helianax, 833, 834, 1531.

Heliasts, oath of, 1368.
Heliocles, king of Bactria, coin of, 936.
Heliodorus, regent of Syria 63; president of a guild, 1592.
Heliopolis, capital of Ituraeans, 842; of Iambulus, 808.
Heliopolitai, 808.
Helios, temple of, 681.
Hellas of the East, 1112.
Hellenes, 1109, 1110; of the East, 1020, 1073; in Egypt, 729, 913, 1394, 1606; in Hellenistic monarchies, 1057, 1071, 1073, 1075, 1087; in Seleucid Empire, 499, 515, 542, 848, 1401, 1535; see Greeks.
Hellenic League, 15–17, 48, 1315; war, see Lamian.
Hellenization, 1071–3, 1079, 1097, 1106, 1227, 1593; in Anatolian monarchies, 663, 837–9, 848, 849, 856, 1532; in Arabia, 478, 853, 855; in Asia Minor, 85, 523, 532, 1043, 1053, 1098; in the Crimea, 770; in Cyprus, 85, 127, 1071; of the East by Alexander, 131, 473, by the Successors, 156, 249; in Egypt, see Egypt; in India, 551, 936, 1098; in Italy, 1415; of Latin world, 1301; in Macedonia, 1056; in Palestine, 127, 351, 519, 848, 853, 1043, 1061, 1536; in Phoenicia, 85, 127, 130, 341, 519, 1043, 1071, 1325, 1401, 1443, 1536; in the Seleucid Empire, 476, 478–80, 499, 502, 515–17, 519, 522, 523, 703–5, 848, 853, 1053, 1065, 1071, 1072, 1075, 1156, 1165, 1403, 1443, 1593.
Hellespont, 640, 772, 1364, 1512, 1520; cities of, 229, 528, 529, 556, 585.
Hellespontine Phrygia, 590, 635, 642.
Helots, 203, 247, 611, 1360.
Hemesa (Homs), 79, 510, 842, 849, 851, 852, 866, 1491, 1533.
Hemicleria, 285.
Hemp, 91, 300, 305, 421, 586, 1257, 1277.
Hendrickson, G. L., 1576.
Henotheism, solar, 704, 808.
Hephaistion of the Sarapeum, 735, 736.
Her, priest, 886.
Hera, temple of, at 201, Argos, 1364; in Pergamon, 661.
Heraclea, under Latmus, 426, 666, 667, 670, 672, 775, 1455, 1483, coins of, 1481; -Lyncestis, 1461; -Pontica, 2, 47, 592, 933, 1454: coinage, 1356, economic and social conditions, 591, 673, 829, 977, 1103, 1273; industry, pottery, 1334, navy, 1455, 1585, political conditions, 26, 35, 185, 566, 567, 590, 591, 665, 674, 826, 829, 836, 953, 1455, 1580, relations with Bithynia, 568, 662, 663, with Rome, 954, 977, 999, 1577, trade,

Hopkins, C., 535.

Hor, priest, 886.

Horace, 53.

Horrea, 661, 798.

Horses, of Antigonus the One-eyed, 13; in Bactria, 545; in Bosporan kingdom, 595; in Cyrenaica, 293, 333, 381, 385, 396; in Egypt, 1386, 1404, breeding, 293, 359, import, 293, 352, 381, 384, 385, 396, royal, 293, 315, studs, 292, 385, taxes, 293; in Greece, 1190; in Media, 77, 480; in Pergamon, 556, 563, 565, 1450; in Pontus, 572; in S. Russia, 601; in Seleucid Empire, 461, 480.

Horse-trappings, 108, 116, 117, 119, 378, 676, 1334.

Hortensius, L., 767.

Horticulture, 489, 536, 563.

Horus, son of Nechontes, 1153, 1499, 1500, 1544, 1645.

Hostages, system of, 1512.

Household (οἶκος), *see* οἶκος; production, *see* Home production.

Houses, 181, 1052, 1053, 1231, 1587, 1588, 1625; prices of, 190, 259, 537; taxes, 316, 954, 962, 1563; in Delos, 231, 234, 741, 742, 1052, 1231, 1232, 1625; in Egypt, 289, 327, 417, 420, 888, 889, 1422.

Housing of Government agents, 964.

Humanitas, idea of, 1358.

Hungary, 118, 375, 1335, 1504.

Hunters, 296, 317.

Hunting, 296, 299, 313, 317, 383, 384, 1062, 1387, 1398, 1615.

Hurgonaphor, king of Nubia, 1496.

Hyarotis, 1172.

Hybreas of Mylasa, 822, 823, 1006, 1007, 1528, 1580.

Hybrida, C. Antonius, 948, 985–7.

Hybristas, 609, 1460.

Hyderabad, ore of, 1218.

Hydraletes, 365.

Hydraulic engineers, 1160; works, 1160, 1161.

Hyllarima, 1512.

Hymettian marble, 417.

Hypaepa, 943.

Hypanis, *see* Bug.

Hyparchies, 341, 640, 1400.

Hyparchoi, 440, 1433.

Hypata in Thessaly, 1503.

Hyphasis, 1172.

Hypsicrates of Amisus, 934.

Hyrcanus, John, 853, 859.

Hyrcanus II, 1001, 1002.

Hyspaosines, dynast of Mesene, 1492; of Bactria, 1492.

Iamblichi, dynasty of, 842.

Iambulus, 808, 1132, 1523.

Iasus, 429, 641, 671, 945, 1464, 1472, 1473, 1475, 1598.

ἰατρικόν, 242, 286, 1092, 1600.

ἰατροκλύστης, 883, 1093.

Iberia, 1515.

Iberian civilization, 1020.

Iberians, 93.

Ibn Al-Saj, 1422.

ἰχθυϊκή ὠνή, 297.

Ichthyology, 1177, 1178.

Ida, Mount, 556, 560, 1168, 1375, 1611.

Identity of king and country, 271, 272.

ἰδία (place of residence), 277, 278, 725, 879, 1382, 1522, 1647; ἴδια (private possessions), 444, 1499, 1647.

ἰδιοκτήμονες, 891, 1547.

ἴδιος λόγος, 444, 708, 908, 1493, 1550.

ἰδιῶται, 1382.

ἰδιωτικὰ φορτία, 311.

ἰδιωτική (οἰκονομία), 74, 75, 440, 442, 445, 446.

Idumaea, 347, 351, 520, 1173.

Idumaean mercenaries, 1542; mines, 1174.

Idumaeans, 347, 853.

ἱερά, 844–6, 1109, 1534; καὶ ἄσυλος, 844, 1534.

ἱερὰ πρόσοδος, 277, 280, 281.

ἱερὰ συγγραφή, 234, 1373, 1617.

ἱεραὶ ἀναγραφαί, 1137.

ἱεροδουλία, 321, 1383.

ἱερόδουλοι, 280, 322, 343, 506, 1383, 1396, 1435.

ἱερὸν μισθωτήριον, 1630.

ἱεροσυλία, 201, 605, 1362.

ἱερόσυλοι, 200, 1364.

ἱκέται, 735, 901; *see* Refugees.

Ilian League, 154.

Ilium, 426, 431, 556, 944, 945, 998, 1344, 1349, 1451, 1526; coinage, 1356.

Illyria, 32, 48, 53, 119, 250, 763, 767, 955, 1335, 1515; trade, 93, 119, 120, 759, 1238, 1262.

Illyrian civilization, 1020; pirates, 47, 48, 120, 196, 203, 985, 1365; State, 47, 74, 248.

Illyrians in armies of Brutus, 1005; of Successors, 146.

ἱματιοπῶλαι, 1277, 1628.

ἱματισμός, 1339.

Imbros, 221, 631, 741, 1459, 1512, 1514.

Immunes, cities, 641, 642, 947, 1564; individuals, 1018; territories, 818.

Immunity (ἀτέλεια), 647, 812, 813, 1005, 1006; to cities, 463, 466, 528, 529, 530, 947, 948, 976, 981, 982, 1450; to individuals, 492, 952, 971, 1012, 1545, 1546, 1570, 1581; to members of the Museum, 1084, 1596; to *technitai*, 200, 1056, 1561; to temples, 816, 899, 1477, 1549, 1550.

Olympene, 556.
Olympia, 54, 200, 563, 569, 1313; coin hoards, 164, 1352, 1416; temple of, 190, 212, 748, 940, 1122, 1144.
Olympians (gods), 1122.
Olympias, 8, 9.
Olympichus of Caria, 1426, 1645.
Olympus, Mount, 566, 1169, 1481.
Olymus, 672, 1483.
Olynthus, 1052, 1144, 1412.
Olyra, 365.
Oman, copper mines, 1174.
Omboi, 883, 889, 1545.
ὁμόνοια, 209, 1124.
ὠναί, 302, 303, 309, 327–9, 962, 1390, 1568; ἁλική, 470; χαρτηρά, 311; ἰχθυική, 297; πορφυρική, 336; τραπεζιτική, 406.
ὀνηλάται, 314, 315, 1392.
ὤνια, 314.
Onias, 348.
Ophelas, 1344.
Opifices, 1526.
Opis, 479.
ὁπλοφύλαξ of Alexander, 151.
Oppian of Anazarbus, 1178, 1615.
Oppida non libera, 640.
ὀψώνια, 327, 329, 710, 759, 1339, 1387, 1570, 1601.
Opus, silversmith, 1277.
Oranges, 1166.
Orchards, 617, 1199; taxes on, 336, 337.
Orchomenus, 141, 142, 944, 972.
Oreus, 606.
ὄργανον, 363.
Oricus, 48.
Oriental monarchies, economic organization, 75; States, basic principles of, 272.
Orientalization in Hellenistic monarchies, 71, 1070, 1072, 1096–8; of Euxine regions, 835; in Seleucid Empire, 63, 64, 71, 502, 522, 523, 703, 835, 850, 858, 862, 1098, 1105, 1426, 1442, 1443.
Ormuz, Gulf of, 457.
Ornithones, 1193.
Orodaltis, daughter of Lycomedes, 1580.
ὀροφύλακες, 669.
Orontes, satrap of Mysia, 76, 554, 1449.
Orontes, river, 85, 363, 697.
Orophernes Nikephoros, ruler of Cappadocia, 653, 670, 806, 819, 820, 824, 1468, 1478, 1483, 1520, 1527.
Oropus, 211, 212, 676, 748, 940, 1456, 1470.
Ortiagon, 636, 836, 1473, 1519.
Osrhoenes, 866.
Osrhoenian Arabs, 842; dynasty, 849.
Ossa, 1169.

Ostia, 1201.
Ostiaria, 994.
Ostrich eggs, 383; feathers, 383.
ὀθόνια, 1389.
ὀθονιηρά, 302, 305, 1411.
ὀθονιοπῶλαι, 1276, 1277, 1628.
Othrys, mines, 1173.
Otranto Straits, 48.
Ouadd (god), 1492.
οὐσίαι, 269, 488, 1499, *see* Domains, Estates.
Ovens, portable, 181, 370, 616, 742, 797, 1371, 1407, 1461, 1502.
Over-population of Greece, 92, 95, 96, 132; of islands, 225.
Ownerless property, *see* ἀδέσποτα.
Ownership of the State by king, 267–9, 271, 272, 277, 402, 403, 444, 482, 706, 1309, 1380.
Oxen, 292, 293, 1164, 1190, 1197, 1277, 1386.
Oxus, river, 78; treasure, 390.
Oxyrhyncha, 902, 908.
Oxyrhynchite nome, taxes in, 328.
Oxyrhynchus, 1547.
Ozolian Locrians, 90.

Pacorus, 822, 984, 1009, 1580.
Pactiones, 967–70, 982, 997, 1000, 1569, 1573.
Paeonia, 216, 250.
Paeonians, 1444.
Paerisades I, ruler of Bosporus, 595–7; II, 232, 392, 393, 597, 598, 602; IV, 667, 676, 1484; the last, 769, 1512; coin of one of the Paerisades (III–VI), 694.
Pagasae, 251.
Pahlav kings, 428.
Pahlavi, 490, 544.
παιδάριον, 1393.
παιδίσκη, 1393.
Painters, 1096, 1117, 1232.
Paints, import to Greece, 92.
Pais, 1390.
παῖς, 1393.
Palacus, Scythian king, 769, 776.
Palaemagnesia, 149.
Palaescepsis, 563.
Palestine, archaeological evidence, 423, 425, 427, 853, 1313, 1424; coinage, 84, 105, 659, 1325, 1338; coins, circulation of, 84, 401, 451, 1417, 1430, 1535, hoards, 1324; colonization, 157; currency, 402, 658; economic conditions, 81, 536, 1156; emigration from, 1054; Greeks in, *see* Greeks; hellenization, *see* Hellenization; industry: glass, 439, pottery, 1445, 1446; mines, 1174, 1614; political conditions, 12, 50, 65, 68, 71, 1105: Persian domination, 1033, 1323–5,

1442; coinage, 446, 802; coins, circulation, 698, 1430, 1489, 1490, 1539; Greek cities in, *see* Greek cities; Greeks in, 486, 550, 859, 1075; Hellenism in, 1098; industry, pottery, 699, 1208, 1350, steel, 1218; mints, 547; political conditions, 42, 248, 543, 547, 841–3, 864, 1425, 1437, 1541: growth, 50, 71, 72, 543, independence, 64, 430, 459, 542; relations with Rome, 53, 62, 870, 962, 984, 1002, 1008, 1016: expeditions of Roman leaders against, 866, 984, 998, 999, 1001, 1005, 1008, 1012, 1580, invasions of Roman provinces by, 822, 955, 984, 985, 990, 1009, 1010, 1142; relations with Seleucid Empire, 60, 67, 430, 459, 480, 551, 699, 703, 705, 841, 860, 864, 1105, 1538; routes through, 1243, 1244, 1648; structure of, 770, 855; taxation, 1435; trade, 697, 698, 854, 858, 863, 865, 867, 1238, 1248, 1267, 1433, 1490, 1539; use of money, 1288.

Parthian, archers, 1010; Babylonia, 451, 457, 697, 841, 864, documents, 425; domination in Dura, 427, 483, 486, 856, 857, 861, in Seleucia on the Eulaeus, 858, 859, 861; elements in Nabataean kingdom, 853; style in sculpture, 863; temple at Orchoi, 1424.

Parthians, advance of, 65, 67, 68, 447, 841, 864; in army of Brutus, 1005.

Particularism in Greece, 36, 42, 204, 205, 1109, 1114, 1291–4.

Partners, of contractors of revenue (μέτοχοι), 328, 330; of *publicani*, 970.

Pasparus, Diodorus, of Pergamon, 563, 805, 810, 813, 1521–4, 1528.

Pasturage, 210, 536, 566, 650, 1021, 1451; taxes on, 337, 445, 1386.

Pastures, 221, 291, 292, 295, 336, 445, 649, 1386, 1609; taxes on, 295, 302, 346, 817.

Patara, 1004, 1579.

Παθυμίας, weaver in Egypt, 1412.

Pathyris, 1385, 1499.

Pathyrites nome, 1542, 1544.

πάτριος πολιτεία and νόμοι, 635.

Patrocles, explorer, 456, 1432.

Patronage (σκέπη), 325, 901, 903–5, 1396, 1495.

Patrons of temples, 899, 901.

Paulus, jurist, 688.

Pausanias, 2, 44, 629.

Pausistratus, Rhodian commander, 608.

Pax Romana, 930.

Paxamus, 1167, 1612.

Payments in kind, *see* Kind.

Peace proclamations or amnesty decrees, *see* φιλάνθρωπα.

Peach trees, 1166.

Peaches, 1610.

Pearls, 386, 1245.

Peasant, economy, 1184, 1185, 1190, 1196; landowners, 1149, 1181, 1182.

πηχισμὸς περιστερεώνων, 294.

Pecunia vectigalis, 949.

Pedieis, 179.

Pedii, Italian *negotiatores*, 921.

πεισιθάνατος, 1329.

πηλαμυδεῖα, 1179.

πελάται, 1515.

Pelion, 1169.

Pella, in Macedonia, 251; coinage of, 76, 633, 1472, 1480; in Seleucid Empire, 479; in Transjordan, 347.

Pellana in Achaea, 197.

Peloponnese, 1135, 1143, 1507, 1605; civil strife in, 141, 209, 210; coinage of cities, 655, 1469, of Lucullus, 1558; coins, hoards of, 1352; economic conditions, 205, 206, 212, 222, 750, 752, 1469; political conditions, 9, 15, 19, 38, 39, 41, 42, 56, 332, 608, 1416; during Roman rule, 947, 951, 993, 1581; trade, 394.

Peloponnesian war, 94, 95, 200, 1144.

πελτασταί, 1397.

Pelusium, 228, 385, 1613.

πέμπτη, on crops, 279; ἰχθύων, on fisheries, 1644.

Pemsais, 722.

Penestai, 1617.

πενία, 1129, 1133; *see* πλοῦτος.

πεντηκοστή, 233.

Pepper, 387.

Peraea (Rhodian), 687, 690, 1487.

Percote, 563.

Perdiccas, 2–6, 23, 144, 158, 1340, 1348; colonization, 157, 1349.

Perfumes, 84, 92, 107, 389, 699, 920, 1245, 1257, 1258, 1391.

Pergamene *basileia*, 553, 555; *dynasteia*, 553–7, 559–63, 637, 1449, 1474; Empire, 555.

Pergamon, 552, 553, 638, 809, 1313, 1448, 1449; agriculture, *see* Agriculture; army, *see* Army; art, 593, 650, 796; artists, 1451; *bourgeoisie*, see *Bourgeoisie*; currency, 187, 1293; economic conditions, 659, 662, 736, 803–5, 813, 1157, 1158, 1175, 1251, 1252, 1310, 1521; Greek cities of, *see* Greek cities; industry, 563, 564, 650, 1451: metal, 376, 650, 651, 1451, trade, 651, 676, 1478, mosaics, 660, 1227, 1481, parchment, 564, 565, pottery, 368, 533, 616, 651, 653, 654, 1206, 1207, 1351, 1444, 1446, 1479, 1621, trade, 598, 651, 653, 654, 797, 1479, 1646, terracottas, 616, textiles, 563–5, 918, 1226, 1526, toreutics, 650, 652, 1478; land, *see* Land; large estates, 561–3, 649; medical schools, 1090, 1598, service, 1093; mercenaries, 625; navy, *see* Navy; political conditions, 43, 49–51, 62, 151, 603, 610, 636, 801, 804, 827, 868, 1472, 1508: independence, 33, 37, 43, 248, 429, 530, 552, 555, role in Asia Minor, 58, 59, 61; population of, 561, 1142; slaves, 243, 564, 565, 1106, 1158, 1159, 1261, 1521, 1600; subdivisions of, 561, 562, 1473, 1474; temples, *see* Temples; trade, 310, 556, 565, 651, 654, 676, 777, 797, 804, 805, 1157, 1257, 1265, 1268, 1479: with Egypt, 392, with Greece, 565, 630, with Rhodes, 775, 777, 1479, with S. Russia, *see* Russia, with Seleucid Empire, 654, 659, 701, 805, 868, 1479; villages, 561, 654, 1106; weights and measures, 1299, 1646.

Pergamon, city of, 554, 556, 560, 649, 659, 661, 804, 1468, 1481, 1521, 1522, 1573; buildings of, 557–9, 561, 638, 639, 1084, 1205, 1221, 1232, 1236, 1449, 1590, 1596, 1626; χώρα πολιτική of, 811; coinage, 1564; constitution, 559, 811, 813; economic conditions, 641, 807, 810; excavations, 426, 553, 919, 1478; fortress of Lysimachus, 553, 554; political conditions, 800, 813, 817, 1473, 1526.

περὶ βασιλείας (treatises), 441, 1078, 1081, 1346, 1347, 1379, 1566, 1594, 1595.

περὶ ἰχθύων, 1615.

περὶ κτηνῶν, 1619.

περὶ λίθων of Theophrastus, 1212.

περὶ μηχανημάτων, 1236.

περὶ μεταλλικῶν μηχανημάτων of Straton, 1212.

περὶ μετάλλων of Theophrastus, 1212.

περὶ ταρίχων, 1336.

Perictione, 1133.

περιηγήσεις, 828, 1035, 1036.

Perinthus, 479, 762, 1356, 1509.

περίοδοι, 1035, 1041.

Perioeci, 203, 247, 1360, 1375.

Peripatetics, 268, 440, 1192, 1359, 1594, 1650.

Peripatos, 1146.

περίπλους, 927, 1035–7, 1039–41, 1584.

περιπόλια, 1460.

Perithebas, *strategos* of, 722.

Perperna, M., 809.

Perpetuus mercenarius (hireling for life), 1126.

Persaeus of Citium, 1426, 1594.

Πέρσαι τῆς ἐπιγονῆς, 1385, 1644.

Persea tree, 299, 1167, 1404.

Persephone, festival of, 926.

Persepolis, 428, 516, 1425, mint of, 461.

Perseus, 437.

Perseus, king of Macedonia, 55, 57, 59, 1461; army, 633, 1472; coinage, 604, 1294, 1472; economic policy, 632–4, 1172, 1470, 1471; use of pirates, 1522; wars, 739, 1136, with Rome (Persean War), 53, 65, 610, 633, 634, 737–9, 741, 750, 766, 787, 1501, 1509, 1514.

Persia, 428, 1033, 1034, 1163, 1321: administration, 1033, 1299; army, 262, 1232; coinage, 76, 83, 89, 446, 1278, 1325, 1338, monopoly of, 442; coins, circulation of, 84, 85, 186, 1324, hoards of, 1539; currency, *see* Currency; economic organization, 75, 77–9, 83, 84, 132, 441, 1163; feudal aristocracy, 77, 81, 507, 549; financial organization, 74, 442, 472, 1429; industry, 84: glass, 539, jewels, 1354, steel, 1218, textiles, 1222, 1226, toreutics, 539, 540, 1447; land, *see* Land; mercenaries in, 1033; policy of kings, 82, 83, 99, 129, 151, 153, 473; political conditions, 94, 105, 128–30, 430, 567, 573, 579, 1032, 1033, 1098, 1346: domination in Babylonia, *see* Babylonia; in Cyprus, 1326, in Egypt, 81, 82, 89, 261, 262, 265, 388, 1033, 1062, 1321, 1323, 1330, 1643: agricultural work, 359, income of kings, 1150, 1151, private land, 289, 1380, relations with temples, 281, 412; in Palestine, 1033, 1323–5, 1643; in Phoenicia, 81, 83, 84, 1033, 1321; in Syria, *see* Syria; postal service, 1583; roads, *see* Roads; royal property, 179, 444, 495; satrapies, *see* Satrapies; satraps, *see* Satraps; seaports, 85; sea routes, 83, 134; social structure, 1103; taxation, 83, 139, 443, 464: land, 444, royal, 469, salt, 470; trade, 78–82, 84, 85, 173, 443, 532, 540, 1257, 1258, with Greece, 84, 85, 89, 90, 93, 98, 104, 105, 127, 1033; use of money, 1288; weights and measures, 1298–1300.

Persian 'archers' (coins), 186; archives, 1034; art, 84, 110, 548; cuneiform script, 425; inheritance in Seleucid Empire, 434, 439, 440; itineraries, 1038; kings, ancestors of Hellenistic rulers, 434, 832, 850.

Persian Gulf, 133, 134, 457–9, 546, 841, 1174, 1177, 1239, 1243, 1245, 1246.

Persicus, Paullus Fabius, 1375.

Persis, 77, 429, 457, 480, 516, 1425.

Pessinus, 579–81, 649, 801, 803, 837, 980, 1452, 1520, 1529, 1572.

Petearoeris, 722, 723.

Petenephotes, 1548.

Petetum, lawsuit of, 716.

Proxeny, 205, 220, 763, 1109, 1366.
Prusa, 663, 1481.
Prusias-on-the-Hypios, 663; -on-the-Sea, 663.
Prusias I of Bithynia, 59, 578, 826, 827; gifts to Greek cities, 230, 667, 1255; policy of, 58, 570, 591, 662, 663, 1481; wars, 636, 673, 679, 1473.
Prusias II, 766, 772, 773, 800, 826, 827, 830, 1267, 1513, 1522.
Prytanis of Carystus, 629, 1317, 1469.
ψηφίσματα, 1060, 1069, 1592.
Psenamosis, 732, 1499.
Psenemphaia, 732, 1499.
Psephisma of Pergamon, 821, 822.
Psichis, 723.
ψιλαὶ Περσικαί, 1412.
ψιλὴ γῆ, 1471.
ψιλοὶ τόποι, 537, 909.
Psinteo, 731.
Ptôion, 214, 1144.
Ptolemaeus, of the Heracleopolite nome, 1285.
Ptolemaeus, nome of, 732.
Ptolemaic, court, 419; dynasty, 27, 255, 333; Egypt, 318; end of, 69, histories of, 1313, terminology of law of, 276; Empire, 399, 401, 418, 637, 912, 914; mints, *see* Mints; queens, 270, 872; sculpture, 872, 886; standard of coins, 395, 399, 401, 719, 853, 868, 1294, 1535, of weights, 1299; pre-Ptolemaic Egypt, 82, 301, 324, 347, 365, 403, 1053, 1079, 1101, 1137, 1201, 1389, 1394.
Ptolemais-Ake, 244, 347, 399, 847; coin hoard, 1356; coinage of, 1535.
Ptolemais in Egypt, 149, 156, 157, 265, 276, 324, 717, 1048, 1051, 1055, 1140, 1313, 1381, 1382, 1395, 1596.
Ptolemies, 265, 267, 414, 415, 431, 872, 1037, 1085, 1205, 1231, 1587; acclimatization of plants and animals, 353, 357, 358, 1164–6; administration of, 263, 264, 297, 440, 560, 561, 707, 708, 882, 885, 928, 1137, 1196, 1556, 1595, corruption of, 881, 893–5, 902, 912, 914, 917; animal husbandry, 292–4, 357–9, 377, 1191, 1385; bureaucracy, 1079–81, 1097, 1644; coinage, 184, 185, 386, 398–401, 446–9, 604, 1416, 1417, 1494; coins, 10, 18, 66, 260, 409, 584, circulation of, 263, 264, 395, 451, 658, 719, 1242, 1248, 1294–6, 1415–17, 1430, 1500, 1555, hoards of, 449; commercial policy, 30, 381, 385, 411, 658, 795, 923, 924, 928, 1042, 1044, 1243–5, 1269, 1270, 1415; construction of Alexandria, 557, 559; cult of, 268, 283, 368, 1379; dominions of, 216, 332, 368, 369, 426, 462, 519, 520, 693,

695, 848, 914–17, 1397–9, 1401, 1402, 1534: administration of, 337–40, 343–9, 351, 914, 1165, 1398, 1429, building of cities, 346, 347, 511, currency of, 401, 402, 449, 1417, economic conditions, 536, fiscal organization, 334–7, 340, 341, 344, 345, 348, 349, 351, gifts from, 227, grain supply from 360, 384, 385; λαοί in, 341–5, 508, 511, loss of, 603, 696, 713, 1256, policy in, 438, 519, 634, 1403, revenues from, *see* Revenues, royal land in, 336, 338, 345, 385, 494, 815, taxes in, 334, 335, 337, 338, 345, 349, 351, 418, 469, 470, trade with, *see* Egypt, *see also* Palestine, Phoenicia, Syria; dynastic troubles of, 68, 875, 876, 878; economic organization, 271–4, 289, 316, 328, 411–14, 1101, 1340, 1378, 1388; planned economy of, *see* Planned economy; exploitation of natural resources, 82, 264, 272, 273, 291, 298, 352, 1170, 1173, 1174, 1613; finances, 297, 300, 328, 329, 404, 472, 707, 708, 964, 1063, 1080, 1283, 1286, 1287, 1299, 1345, 1551; foreign policy, 31, 381, 403, 561, 637, 707, 711; hegemony in the Aegean, *see* Aegean; industry, organization of, *see* Egypt; juridical system of, 1067; land policy, 290, 718, 728; military colonies of, 348, 499, 500; monetary policy, *see* Monetary policy; monopolies, *see* Monopolies; organization of Egypt by, 371, 372, 707, 708, 1027, 1137, 1285, 1309, 1546, of production, 272, 313, 316, 352, of supply of elephants, 296, 383, 384, 388; ownership of the State, 267–9, 271, 272, 277, 402, 403, 444, 706, 1309, 1387, 1396; policy in Egypt, 29, 289–91, 326, 421, 475, 476, 724, 733, 872, 911, 1072, 1073, 1102, 1396, 1552: towards Greeks, 269, 331, 352, 496, 706, 887, 1027–9, 1139, 1541, natives, *see* Natives, slavery, 342–4, 1260, 1262, 1263; political activity, 12, 14, 50, 51, 69, 217, 253, 254, 478, 561: struggle with Seleucids, *see* Seleucids, relations with the Aegean islands, 39, 240, 332, 333, 337, Aetolia, 41, Asia Minor, 29, 30, 35, 50, 216, 240, 429, 531, 532, 551, 666, 713, 1173, 1174, 1416, Bithynia, 392, 393, 568, 569, Bosporan kingdom, 597, Carthage, 395–7, 404, Delos, *see* Delos, Greece, *see* Greece, Island League, 29, 154, 222, 333, Nabataeans, 387, 388, 455, 458, Nubia, 382, 383, 719, pirates, 196, 619, 774, 784, 1259, 1360, 1361, Rhodes, 172, 226, 230, 463, 692, 1249, 1255, 1256, 1265, Rome, 57, 62, 63, 69, 72, 395, 396, 871, 876, 910, 912, 913, 931, 993, 1013, 1320, Sicily, 395, 396, with temples, *see* Temples and Priests; religious policy, 438, 439, 887,

1012, 1570, 1580, 1581; intervention in the affairs of the Hellenistic world, 55, 63, 70, 71, 73, 603, 737, 1029, 1311, 1312, theory of, 1014; *laoi* in provinces of, 815, 816; monetary policy, 655; organization of provinces, 640, 758, 811–18, 931, 955, 961, 970, 971, 974–81, 999, 1001, 1017, 1474, 1571, 1578, 1648, 1649, *see* Asia, Lucullus, Pompey, Syria; policy in the East, 43, 47, 52, 55, 56, 63, 65, 68, 70–2, 999, 1015, 1319, 1320, 1458, 1460: in the Aegean, 59, 62, 781, 963; towards Antiochus IV, 67, 737, 738, 871; in Asia Minor, 636, 662, 803, 912; towards Bithynia, 826–8; in Cappadocia, 838; towards Carthage, 787, 788; in Cyrenaica, 876; towards Galatians, 836; in Illyria, 48; of liberation, 629, 654, 655, 1291; towards Mithridates VI, 831, 832, 834, 835; towards pirates, 774, 784, 785, *see* Piracy; in Pontic cities, 529, 767, 768, 829, 830, 977, 978, 985, 986, 988, 998, 999, 1577; towards *publicani*, 758, 782, 818, 968, 969, *see* Caesar, Cicero, Gabinius, Piso, Sulla; towards temples, 506, 816, 978; relations to cities in provinces, 807, 808, 824, 966, 969, 1514, 1522, 1523, *see* Confiscations, Contributions, Exactions, Fines, Indemnities; to classes of population, 612, 749, 755–7, 816, 819, 821–3, 1106, 1306, 1308, 1125, 1128; with Delos, 738, 740, 787, 788; with Delphi, 609, 614, 740, 756, 1363; with Paphlagonia, 979; *see* Achaea, Aetolians, Asia Minor, Athens, Attalids, Attalus III, Bithynia, Cappadocia, Corinth, Cyzicus, Ephesus, Eumenes II, Greece, Greek cities, Greek cities of Asia Minor, Lycia, Macedonia, Miletus, Parthia, Peloponnese, Pontus, Ptolemies, Rhodes, Seleucid Empire, Seleucids; revenues, *see* Revenues; roads, 869, 1039; rule of, resentment against, 937, 956, 965, 1530; taxation, 466, 471, 812–14, 817, 945, 946, 954, 957, 962, 965–71, 978, 982, 983, 987, 988, 994, 997, 999–1001, 1005, 1017, 1288, 1450, 1560, 1561, 1563, 1567–9, 1577, 1578, *see* Arrears, εἰσφοραί, φόρος, *publicani*, *Stipendium*, Tribute, *Vectigalia*, and separate taxes; trade dislocation by political measures of, 1242; tyrannies in provinces, *see* Tyrannies; unity, establishment of, 1025; urbanization, *see* Urbanization; vassal kings, *see* Vassal kings; war booty, *see* Booty; wars: with Dardanians, 986, 987, *see* Achaean War, Antiochus III, Aristonicus, Macedonia, Mithridatic wars, Perseus, Philip V, Punic wars, Seleucids; *see also* individual Roman leaders.

Ropes, production of, 300.

Roses, plantations of, 357.

Rosetta stone, 706, 713–15, 729, 884, 885, 893, 1493, 1545.

Rotation of crops, 98, 280, 292, 1186, 1197, 1617, 1618.

Round-gourd oil, 302.

Roussel, P., 788.

Routes, caravan, *see* Caravan; sea, *see* Sea routes; trade, 16, 29, 30, 134, 249, 785, 804, 864, 1024, 1243–5, 1263, 1648; of Anatolia, *see* Asia Minor; of the Balkans, 120, 1264; of the Black Sea, *see* Black Sea; from Central Asia, 456, 1024, 1263; Chinese silk, 456, 696, 697, 864, 1024, 1243, 1539; to Egypt, *see* Egypt; of the Euphrates, *see* Euphrates; from India, *see* India; of Mesopotamia, 134, 462, 484, 1038, 1246, 1626; of the Nile, *see* Nile; from Pontus, 572; of the Seleucid Empire, 456, 457, 459, 461, 462, 579, 659, 841, 865–7, 1243, 1244, 1433, 1540, 1585; of the Tigris, *see* Tigris. *See* Roads.

Rowers, 315, 317, 754, 991, 994.

Roxane, 3, 4, 9, 11.

Royal, banks, *see* Banks; coinage of Successors, 186; couriers, 1045; cult, *see* Cult; dairies, 1191; domains, *see* Domains; domestic animals, 280, 292–4, 315, 1451; economy, 74, 75, 440, 442, 443, in Egypt, 281, 300, 1062; estates, *see* Estates; factories in Egypt, 300, 312, 317, 389, 1229, in Pergamon, 564, 565; herds, 203, 1164; horses, 556, 563, 565; house, *see* οἶκος; industry: in Bosporan kingdom, 109, in Egypt, 300; judges, 440, 486, 508, 522, 562, 857, 1067, 1429, 1438, 1476, 1544; jurisdiction, 1067, 1068; land (γῆ βασιλική), 1194: in Bithynia, 571; in Egypt, 276–81, 283, 285, 291, 345, 726, 888, 906, 907, 913, 1071, 1197, 1198, 1382, 1496, cultivation of, 275–7, 279, 280, 292, 1421, in dominions, 336, 338, 345, 385, 494, 815; in Macedonia, 251, 1471; in Pergamon, 562–4, 649, 1106, 1157, 1450; in Persia, 179, 495, 1103; in Priene, 179, 529; in Seleucid Empire, 338, 435, 465, 468, 492–6, 503, 507, 509, 529, 589, 1103, 1104, 1195, 1427; see *Agri*; laws, 515, 1067, 1069, 1101, 1438, 1475; management of commerce, 313, 1269, 1270; money, management of, 405, 406, 1071; *oenochoai*, 270, 368; officials in Egypt, 266, 287, 320, 885, 893–7, 901, 902, 906, 1079–81, 1102, 1547, Parthian, 857, in Seleucid Empire, 465, 486, 518; orders to Greek cities, 527, 528; peasants in Egypt (γεωργοί or λαοί

Sarapion, *hypodioecetes*, 1496.

Sarapis, 1497; statue of, 593, 1456; -Zeus, 434, 704.

Sardis, 81, 426, 477, 1066, 1472, 1476, 1521; coinage, 972, 1480; coins, hoards of, 657; cultivation, 1196; industry: metal, 650, textiles, 563, 564, 1412; land tenure, 495; *laoi*, 465; political conditions, 555, 800, 943, 1434, 1519, 1527; temple of Artemis, 439, 495, 504, 648, 672, 1443, banking of, 1280, 1282.

Sarmatian, graves, 601, 1457; kettles, 584; monarchies in S. Russia, 248.

Sarmatians (or Sarmatae), 360, 596, 599, 601, 769, 770, 1238, 1433; art of, 116, 546, 1448; slaves, 675, 691, 1262, 1484, 1515.

Sasanids, 516; taxation, 468, 1435.

Šašanu, slaves in Babylon, 1435.

Satarchaeans, 675, 767.

σατραπικὴ οἰκονομία (satrap economy), 74, 75, 440, 442–5, 464.

Satrapies, of Alexander the Great, 130, 161, 271, 444, 464; of Antigonus the One-eyed, 13, 158; Iranian, *see* Iranian; of Parthia, 248; of Persian Empire, 77–9, 81, 83, 89, 248, 464, 552, 554, 1032–4, 1151, 1155, 1298, 1321, 1322, 1324, 1643; redistribution after Alexander's death, 4, 6; of the Seleucids, 27, 31, 43, 64, 427, 448, 457, 464, 465, 481, 516, 517, 695, 1065, 1318, 1436.

Satraps, of Alexander the Great, 5, 7, 9, 11, 161, 249; pre-Alexandrian, coins of, 76, 89; Parthian, 859; of Persian Empire, 74, 440, 445; of Seleucids, 50, 843, 1533.

Satyra, harpist, 419.

Satyrus I, ruler of Bosporus, 595.

Saumacus, revolt of, 757, 769–71, 807, 1508, 1512.

Savaria, 120.

Save, river, 120.

Scaevola, Q. Mucius, 819, 1527.

Scaurus, M. Aemilius, 984, 1573.

Scented oils, 699.

Scents, 313, 389.

Scepsis in the Troad, 138, 155, 156, 1314.

Scholars, emigrant, 519, 1096.

School books and libraries, 1589.

Science, development of, 362, 363, 365, 1180, 1237, 1302.

Scientific, discoveries, 1302; expeditions, 382; investigation, 362; medicine, 1088.

Scientists, 1083, 1084, 1234, 1235.

Scilurus, king of Scythians, 675, 767–9, 776.

Sciri, 985.

Scopas of Aetolia, 611.

Scordisci, 758, 985.

Screw, of Archimedes, 363, 1224, 1235; -presses, 364.

Scribes, 266, 275, 419, 513, 1382; village, 275, 279, 320, 345, 896, 1588.

Scriptores metrologici, 1299, 1646; *rei rusticae*, 1182, 1183, 1616.

Scriptura (tax on cattle), 295, 471, 812, 814, 817, 946, 957, 965, 1561, 1569.

Sculptors, 799, 1096, 1117, 1232.

Scylax, Ps.-, 1033, 1036, 1040, 1584.

Scymnus, Ps.-, 828, 1530.

Scyros, 631, 741, 1162.

Scythia, 360; economic emancipation of, 108–10, 125.

Scythian Empire, 595, 596, 599, 1457; graves, 108, 110, 183, 596, 599, 601, 1218, 1331, 1333, 1335, 1457; influence in Thracian production, 118; kettles, 584; monarchy in S. Russia, 248.

Scythians, 32, 108, 118, 161, 596, 767, 1351; in the Crimea, 596, 597, 599, 767–70, 1508, 1512; industry, 119, 1333; iron, production of, 1217; nomadic economy, 75; trade of, 119, 595, 675, 768, 776, 1238, in slaves, 675, 691, 1262, 1484, with Greece, 93, 106, 108, 112, 586, with Thrace, 113, 116, 118.

Scytho-Persian lake, the Black Sea, 571; -Sarmatian steppes, 676; -Thracian style, 117, 1334.

Sea routes, 83, 134, 387, 388, 457–9, 546, 659, 781, 867, 869, 924, 927–9, 985, 1243, 1245, 1264, 1433, 1582, 1648.

Seals, Babylonian, 425, 470, 471, 513, 514, 521, 1441.

Sebennytus, 731.

Secession, 291, 413, 725, 879, 898, 899, 908, 914, 1102; *see* ἀναχώρησις and ἀνακεχωρη-κότες.

Security, for contracts, 330; for loans, 223.

Seed-corn, 279, 286, 303, 905, 1187, 1197, 1618.

Seistan, 543.

Seleuceia, dynastic name of cities, 479.

Seleuceia on the Calycadnus, 477, 505.

Seleuceia on the Erythraean Sea, 457.

Seleuceia on the Eulaeus (Susa), 86, 423, 428, 436, 448, 480, 482, 491, 538, 697, 1061, 1075, 1161, 1429, 1442, 1537; coin hoards, 701, 1491; constitution, 486, 487, 489, 490, 840, 858; manumissions, 1435, 1445; mint, 461, 1417, 1428; temples, 435, 696, 1427, 1428; trade, 680, 701, 1486; Parthian domination, 858, 859, 861; *see* Susa.

Seleuceia in Pieria, 85, 157, 423, 437, 479, 1075, 1313, 1320, 1350, 1437, 1534; coinage, 694, 846, 864, 1534, 1535; constitution, 482,

458; Greeks, *see* Greeks; Iranians, 434, 473, 475, 516; Jews, 349, 467, 469; *laoi*, 1104; lower classes, 1105; natives, 519, 1027; serfs, 509; temples, *see* Temples; political activity, 30, 31, 65, 67, 68, 71, 429, 430, 783, 841, 923: relations with Asia Minor, *see* Asia Minor and Greek cities of, with Delos, 692, 693, 702, 791, 794, 1489, 1491, 1518, with Parthians, *see* Parthians, with pirates, 774, 784, with Ptolemies, 30, 31, 65, 455, 478, 875, with Rome, 53, 59 62–4, 68, 69, 70, 72, 695, 703, 737, 869, 912; wars: with Ptolemies, 24, 37–9, 43, 49, 67–9, 196, 336, 407, 414, 429, 530, 533, 536, 709, 719, 847, 870, 1028, 1318, 1320, 1343, 1421, 1445, with Rome, 52, 55, 57, 608, 610, 611, 626, 628, 629, 632, 762, 1029, 1480; private estates of, 465, 495, 503, 589, 1195; religious policy, 434–9, 1426; revenues, *see* Revenues; royal territory of, 488, 503, 509; rule, character of, 430, 431, 434, 437, 1426; urbanization, *see* Urbanization; wealth of, 703, 860, 861.

Seleucus I Nicator, 2, 205, 422, 424, 434, 473, 634, 1316, 1426; army organization, 144, 284; coinage, 185, 434, 435, 449, 1428; coins, 18, 184, 432, 450, 535, 1357; colonization, *see* Colonization; commercial policy, 174, 455, 456; cult of, 431, 486; elephants, supply of, 383, 459; foreign relations, 459. 463, 553, 554, 588, 590; gifts to cities and temples, 174, 459, 463, 1344, 1433, 1434, 1447, 1490; harbours, creation of, 131, 174, 478, 1043; hellenization of Babylonia, 480; policy in the Empire, 430, 475, 478, 507, 527, 1161, 1165, 1433, 1436; political activity, 7, 9, 12–17, 19, 21–5, 33, 173, 429, 475, 484; portraits of, 18, 28; religious policy, 437–9; urbanization, *see* Urbanization.

Seleucus II Callinicus, 240, 463, 494, 542, 1344, 1363; dynastic wars, 43, 430; financial policy, 466; gifts to Rhodes, 230, 1249, 1255, 1433; relations to cities, 526, 528, 846, 1440; to temples, 507; religious policy, 435; wars, 39, 429, 1343.

Seleucus III, 43, 463.

Seleucus IV, 59, 63, 64, 703, 841, 846, 1320, 1489, 1493, 1534; portrait, 604; relations to temples, 695, 696, 1282.

Seleucus, navarch of Rhosus, 971; *strategos*, 904.

Σελευκίς (Seleucid Syria), satrapy, 478, 479, 1437, 1538.

Σελεύκειον (weight), 453.

Self-administration in Bactria, 549; -en-

slavement, 342, 1383; -governing bodies in Syria, 464; -government of cities, 324, 334, 527; -sufficiency, 249, 615, 1241, 1242, 1293, of Egypt, *see* Egypt, of Greece, 91, 154, 185, 750, 1291, 1292; of Persia, 83.

Selge in Pisidia, 643, 691, 801, 1481, 1519, 1520; coinage, 1356.

Sellasia, battle of, 24, 42, 194, 195.

Semites, 146, 862, 1247, 1271; hellenized, 264, 703, 1426.

Semitic, conception of life, 1426; gods, 862, 1592; names, 523, 862, 1545; parts of Persian Empire, 78; of Seleucid Empire, 503; religious associations, 1064, 1065, 1591; towns, 518, hellenization of, 704.

Senpoeris, 897.

'Separate income' (κεχωρισμένη πρόσοδος), 732.

Serbia, 1504.

Seres, 1218.

Serf economy, 1184, 1185.

Serfdom, 251, 1435, 1512, 1515, 1628, 1649.

Serfs, 495, 496, 509, 511, 512, 524, 562, 577, 589, 591, 595, 783, 808, 1184, 1185, 1237, 1307, 1435, 1515, 1617, 1628.

Seriphos, 1531.

Sertorius, 45.

Sesame, 1164, 1610; oil, 302, 303, 537; price of, 1445; tax on, 337.

Sesmaios, 520.

Sestus, 585, 586, 809, 811, 1520, 1523, 1524.

Settlements, of Hellenistic monarchies, 1038, 1051, 1593; Macedonian, *see* Macedonian; of Pergamon, 556; of Seleucids, 429, 472, 476, 479, 491, 499, 519; of Successors, 157; of soldiers, 149, 251, 284, 285, 361, 422, 465, 487, 561, *see* Military.

Settlers, in Hellenistic monarchies, 1030, 1196, 1241; in Egypt, 266, 324, 348, 355, 420, 421; in Pergamon, 642; in Seleucid Empire, 63, 475, 477, 487, 488, 497, 498, 500, 514, 517; soldiers in Egypt, 420, 421, 718, 720, 726, 727, 887, 890–2, 906, 1199, 1397, 1453, 1497, medical service for, 1092; in Seleucid Empire, tax paid by, 467; remission of, 1434; *see* Military.

Seuthes, 1332, 1351.

Seyrig, H., 438, 452, 453, 1432, 1648.

Shami in Khuzistan, 66, 858, 859, 863, 1428, 1490.

Shapur, Sasanian king, 427.

Shareholders of the *societates publicanorum*, 970.

Sheep, 182, 536, 572, 601, 1162, 1190, 1191; in Egypt, 203, 292, 294, 358, 377, 411, 421, 1164, 1257, 1386; in Epirus, 1163, 1164,

σιτηρέσιον, 1339.

σιτοφύλακες, 1562.

σιτοφυλακία, 1562.

σιτοκάπηλοι, 1276, 1277, 1628.

σιτολόγοι, 280, 896, 1283, 1287.

σιτῶν, of Cyrenaica, 1398.

σιτῶναι, 232, 235, 253, 486, 1124, 1269, 1486.

Sitonia, 620, 1469.

σιτωνικόν, 235, 1373.

σιτώνιον, 1339.

σῖτος, 1339; βασιλικός, 1392.

Situlae, 113, 1334.

σκανδαλισταί, 1087, 1596.

Skenai, 866, 867, 1540.

σκηνῖται (Arabs), 866.

σκέπη, *see* Patronage.

Skerdilaidas, raids of, 203, 1365.

σκοπαί, 242, 243, 1179.

σκυτεύς, 1277.

Slavery, 1030, 1132, 1258, 1260, 1357, 1375, 1465, 1468; in Asia Minor, 1106, 1261; in Bithynia, 782; in Egypt, 321, 322, 343, 1393, 1394, 1547; policy of Ptolemies, *see* Ptolemies; in Greece, 321, 343, 1365, 1394; Orientzl, 1401; in Pergamene kingdom, 1106; in Seleucid Empire, 1261, 1435; sale into: for debts, 894, 953, 1003, 1547, of free citizens, 625, 626, 781, 942, by pirates, *see* Pirates, by robbers, 203; of population of cities, 203, 606, 752, 766, 1002, 1259, 1458, of prisoners of war, 147, 148, 204, 1365; transformation of bondage into, 342, 782, 783, 1515; *see* Enslavement.

Slaves, 781, 1111, 1112, 1119, 1465, 1600; abduction of, 203, 1360; in the army, 767, 942, 1435, 1502, 1507; in Asia Minor, 670, 672, 1259, 1435, 1521, 1522; associations of, 691, 1062, 1111; *asylia* for, 754, 1549; in Babylonia, 471, 537, 538, 1261, 1435; in Cos, 242–5, declaration of, 342, 343; in Egypt, 203, 321, 322, 536, 1099, 1138, 1154, 1393; gifts of, 227, 565, 783; in Greece, 96, 97, 207, 225, 623, 625, 1126, 1133, 1136, 1149, 1258, 1259, 1515; hiring out of, 163, 182, 1116; home-bred (οἰκογενεῖς, παράτροφοι), 538, 691, 1261, 1367, 1465, 1468, 1502; labour of, 96, 97, 163, 179, 207, 208, 225, 322, 421, 565, 670, 754, 756, 778, 798, 1127, 1199, 1237, 1260, 1261, 1521: in agriculture, 97, 178, 243, 489, 524, 781, 784, 806, 1106, 1116, 1158, 1159, 1182, 1184, 1196, 1260, 1261, 1302, domestic, 670, 1127, 1205, 1227, 1483, in industry, 100, 243, 322, 564, 1106, 1116, 1157, 1159, 1222, 1228, 1260, 1261, 1273, in mines, 806, 1116, 1219, 1220, 1260, in trade, 322, 1416; λαοί as slaves, *see* λαοί; libera-

tion of, 208, 942–4, 948; in Macedonia, 251; manumissions, *see* Manumissions; numbers of, 97, 203, 627, 1127, 1146, 1258–60, 1366, 1367, 1393, 1465, 1466, 1606; pedagogues, 1087; price of, 190, 537, 627; protection of, from piracy, 197; in Pergamon, *see* Pergamon; public (δημόσιοι), 239, 670, 691, 1111, 1117, 1260; ransom, 199, 202, 204; registration of, 346, 1402; requisition of, 1013; revolts of, 140, 756, 757, 798, 807, 808, 938, 1106, 1502, 1504, 1508; in Rhodes, 675, 690, 691, 1149; Roman, 751, 783, 784, 975, 1259; royal, 564, 565, 1435; sacred, 280, 282, 321, 322, 343, 469, 506, 515, 537, 576, 783, 1062, 1103, 1104, 1157, 1260, 1282, 1307, 1383, 1396, 1435, in Seleucid Empire, 487, 496, 517, 522, 1435; supply of, 97, 781–4, 806, 1258–62, 1465, 1466; taxes on, 242, 316, 322, 346, 471, 954, 994, 1260, 1261, 1563, 1576; tax-collectors of Piso, 987; *technitai*, 1117; trade, 627, 691, 777, 778, 781–4, 786, 787, 806, 826, 959, 1258–60, 1262, 1445, 1515, 1516, 1532; in Asia Minor, 782, 783, 828, 1262, 1515, in Delos, 756, 778, 788, 794, 795, 798, 1262, 1515, in Egypt, 351, 383, 385, 536, 1276, 1393, 1394, 1401, 1402 (regulations concerning, 1242, 1260, taxes on, 322), of the Euxine, 586, 675, 831, 1484, of Greece, 92, 836, 1515, 1532, of Italy, 756, 781, 836, 1259, 1262, 1267, 1540, 1646, of pirates, *see* Piracy, of *publicani*, 782, 828, 1515; wealth of, 205, 1146.

Smelting of metals, 1173, 1213, 1215, 1220.

Smugglers, 897.

Smuggling, 305, 411.

Smyrna, 149, 813, 1158, 1230, 1274, 1346, 1449, 1514; *asylia*, 1363, 1440; city army, 1472; coinage, 972, 1356, 1480; economic conditions, 532, 1273; freedom granted, 526; immunity, 466, 528; industry, terracottas, 616; political conditions, 35, 137, 462, 530, 938, 943, 993, 1343, 1344, 1349, 1472; trade, 525, 672, 1264, 1265.

Soap, 309.

Sobk (or Sobek), club of the god, 1499; temple of, 1383.

Social, problems in Greece, 612; revolutions, 605, 610–13, 615, 617, 722, 739, 751, 755, 757, 933, 943, 944, 948, 1028, 1125, 1128, 1134, 1365; *see* Civil wars.

Socialism, 1367, 1368.

Societas Bithynica, 979, 1571.

Societates vectigalium publicorum p. R. (or *societates publicanorum*), 748, 749, 812, 965, 966, 968, 970, 977, 1568.

Societies of tax farmers in Egypt, 273.

Socii of Rome, 526, 963, 1014, 1016, 1017.

Socrates, son of Nicomedes III, 828.

Soda, 309, 310.

Sogdiana, 78, 131, 477, 542, 543, 545, 547, 549.

Sogenes, 799.

Soil, exhaustion of, in Greece, 98; poverty of, in Greece, 91, 204.

Soknopaios, temple of, 886.

Soknopaiou Nesos, 722, 886.

Soldiers, owners of slaves, 321, 1260, 1438; pay of, 890, 1339; supply of, to the Romans, 751, 991, 994, *see* Levies of; of Egypt, 321, 326, 327, 403, 880, 881, 890; of Pergamon, 649, 1450, 1522; *see* Cleruchs, Military colonies, Settlements, Settlers.

Soli, coinage of, 1356.

Solon, son of Attalus, 1476.

Somaliland, 381, 384, 386, 711, 713, 918, 922, 923, 927, 1246, 1247, 1269, 1271, 1462.

σώματα, 205, 783, 1365, 1393, 1515; λαϊκά, 341–3; λαϊκὰ ἐλεύθερα, 340, 342; ὄντα οἰκετικά, 343.

Sopeithes, 1172.

Sophilus, 254, 1360, 1412.

Sornatius, 1515.

Sosander, 1520.

Sosibius, minister of Philopator, 707, 709, 731, 1220.

Sosiphon, 354.

Sostratus, 398, 1235.

Sosus, 1416.

Sotacus, 1624.

Sotades, 86.

Soteria, 41, 197, 219, 1317.

Σωτήριχος Βιθυνός, 288.

Spain, 80, 91, 93, 228, 396, 580, 581, 865, 1353; mines of, 1212, 1214, 1219, 1290.

σπάνις σίτου, 952.

σπανοσιτία, 1372.

Sparta, 24, 608; coinage, 186, 446, 628, 1429; coin hoard, 1416; economic conditions, 41, 95, 96, 205–9, 212, 247, 618, 1128, 1146, 1366; industry, pottery, 616, 1461; political conditions, 19, 26, 31, 32, 36, 37, 42, 56, 195, 208, 608, 611, 947; serfs, 1185.

Spartacus, 1508.

Spartocids, 595–9, 770, 1162, 1270.

Spartocus II. ruler of Bosporus, 595.

Spartocus III, 216, 597.

Speculation, 168, 172.

Sphaerus, 1131, 1367, 1594.

Spices, 84, 92, 107, 174, 366, 387, 392, 409, 546, 1165, 1245, 1391.

Sponges, 210, 211.

σταδιασμοί, 1036.

Stadiasmus Maris Magni, 1036.

στάμνοι, 1502.

Stamps, on jars, *see* Jars; on pottery, 1479; on tiles, 109.

Standard of coinage, 185, 229, 399, 442. 461, 712, 1278, 1292, 1294, 1295, 1494; *see* Attic, Phoenician, Ptolemaic, Rhodian; of weights, 451, 454, 455, 1297, 1299, 1300.

στασιασταί, 412.

στάσις, 877.

στατάριον, 1515.

State, control, 272, 273, 291, 729, 731, 1029, 1242, 1288, 1309, 1310; economy of the East, 1031; ownership by the king of, *see* Ownership; property, revenues from, 444; theory of, 271–3.

σταθμοί, 285, 334, 518, 893, 1385, 1547, *see* Quarters.

σταθμοί (itineraries, geographical works), 1033, 1035, 1038; Παρθικοί, 1583.

σταθμὸς βασιλικός, 1433.

Statues, 106, 122, 123, 394, 799, 1178.

Steel, production of, 1217–19.

στεφανιτικός φόρος, 469.

στέφανοι, *see* Crowns.

Stein, Sir Aurel, 66, 859, 1246, 1428.

Stephanephoria, 667.

Stephanus Byzantius, 842.

Stewards, 1146; of the king of Egypt (οἰκονόμοι), see *oeconomi*; of the *dioecetes* Apollonius, 419.

στιβεῖς, 309.

Stipendium, 982, 1000, 1001, 1578.

Stoa (philosophy), 1121, 1602.

Stoic philosophy, 1071, 1426.

Stoicism, 1347, 1426, 1523.

Stoics, 192, 268, 1110, 1123, 1130–2, 1359, 1426, 1593, 1594, 1602.

στολάρχης, 1275.

στολισταί, 1092.

Stolus, 922, 1554.

Stone, 297, 298, 300; bullets, 639; cutters, guild of, 298; precious, *see* Precious; quarrying of, 1176; *see* Quarries.

Storehouses, 228, 355, 397, 588, 639, 661, 742, 780, 830, 1116, 1267, 1342, 1370, 1398, 1416, 1481; royal, in Egypt, 280, 302, 314, 328, 389, 406, 1151; *see* θησαυροί.

Strabo, 45, 47, 120, 333, 506, 536, 573, 576, 577, 588, 589, 673, 681, 684, 685, 783, 784, 794, 807, 821, 822, 830, 838, 839, 843, 847, 860, 861, 864–6, 929, 933, 956, 1004, 1006, 1007, 1039, 1040, 1138, 1171, 1557, 1649.

Straits, cities of, 29, 35, 392, 673, 1145, 1159, 1230, 1577; control over, 31, 591, 609, 663, 773, 827, 935, 998, 1250, 1512, 1513; fisheries of, 1177.

Taska, 468.

Tatas, 1093, 1544.

Tathemis, 735.

Taurians, 586, 769; pirates, 608, 609, 676, 767.

Tauromenium, 1562.

Taurus, 21, 81, 625, 1175.

Tavium, 837, 1629.

Tax, collectors, 320, 328, 329, 351, 518, 748, 882, 888, 889, 905, 946, 966, 978, 987, 1310, 1390, 1396, 1567, 1568: δεκατῶναι, 337, λογευταί, 328, πράκτορες, 277, 889, 1382, 1547, τελῶναι, 273, 296, 297, 328, 349, 405, 725, 966, 970, 1402, 1403, 1463, 1561, 1567, 1568; contracts, 328–30, 338, 411, 817, 967, 1560, 1563, 1570, 1573, see *Pactiones*; de-faulters, 907; farmers, 159, 233, 234, 241–4, 273, 328–33, 337, 338, 345, 349, 354, 518, 669, 708, 725, 782, 785, 888, 889, 904, 962, 966, 970, 1017, 1071, 1115, 1283, 1310, 1386, 1401–3, 1498, 1560, see *Publicani* and *Societates publicanorum*; laws: of Hieron II (*Lex Hieronica*), 337, 395, 968, 1578; of Ptolemy Philadelphus, *see* Ptolemy Phila-delphus, *see also* νόμοι τελωνικοί; lists, 182, 241–3, 245; payers, 317, 328, 329, 725, 751, 752, 906, 962, 968, 983, 1374, 1507; receipts, 257, 1392.

Taxation, 443–5, 1046, 1079, 1475, 1567; of Alexander the Great, 443, 444; in Asia Minor, 139, 337, 464–7, 471, in cities of, 138, 139, 182, 242, 337, 338, 466, 467, 531, 644, 667, 669, 672, 1355, 1374, 1434, 1644, *see* Roman (below); of Attalids, 466, 562, 804, 813, 814, 957, 1157, 1440, 1450, 1526, 1561, 1503; in Babylonia, 468, 470, 471, 514–16; in Byzantium, 673, 679; in Cos, 241–3, 693, 1374, 1489; in Delos, 233–5, 242; in Egypt, 227, 256, 257, 273, 279, 283, 285–7, 290, 293–7, 302, 303, 305, 309, 310, 312–14, 316, 322, 323, 325–31, 354, 385, 404, 470, 471, 648, 707, 710, 890–2, 906, 912, 1071, 1152, 1283, 1286, 1296, 1347, 1392, 1499, in Egyptian dominions, 334–8, 340, 344–6, 348, 349, 351, 418, 469–71, 1402; in Greece, 206, 471, 1392; Greek cities, 241–3, 619, 620, 669, 753, 1047, 1374; Greek islands, 140, 680; in Judaea, 467–9, 472, 999–1001, 1577, 1578; in Macedonia, 252, 471, 633, 1172; in Palestine, 346, 349, 445, 467–70, 1402, 1563; in Persian Empire, 83, 139, 443–5, 464, 469, 470, 1151; at Rhodes, 679, 1512; Roman, 466, 471, 812–14, 817, 937, 945, 946, 954, 957, 962, 965–71, 974, 978, 982, 983, 987–91, 994, 997, 999–1001, 1005, 1017, 1288, 1450, 1560, 1561, 1563, 1567–9, 1572, 1575,

1577, 1578; in Seleucid Empire, 346, 349, 443, 445, 464–72, 514, 516, 517, 522, 528–30, 541, 562, 642, 648, 845, 860, 1104, 1402, 1434, 1435, 1477, 1526, 1561; of Successors, 138–40, 152.

Taxes, *adaeratio*, 466, 1577; arrears of, 708, 724, 751, 884, 893, 901, 967–9; assessment of, 329, 340, 443, 466–8, 518, 812, 968, 1450; auction of, 316, 338, 418; collection of: in Egypt, 283, 327–30, 337, 338, 340, 345, 349, 351, 354, 415, 708, 724, 901, 906, 967, 968, 1094, 1300, 1310, 1499, 1500, by Romans, 466, 817, 945, 946, 954, 955, 962, 965–8, 970, 982, 983, 987–9, 997, 1000, 1005, 1288, 1310, 1560, 1561, 1567–9, 1573, 1578, in Seleucid Empire, 466, 468, 469, 1561; exemption from, 153, 309, 349, 528, 529, 609, 643, 669, 714, 749, 956, 966, 971, 997, 1170, 1450; farming of, 243, 256, 327–30, 335, 966, 970, 1396, 1397; immunity from, *see* Immun-ity; payments of in kind, *see* Kind, in money, *see* Money, *pars quanta* and *quota*, see *Pars*; reduction of, *see* Reduction; remission of, 337, 466, 467, 642, 713, 714, 812, 880, 938, 945, 997, 1434, 1546, partial, 643, 982, 997, 1476; responsibility for, 328, 329, 345, 354, 708, 725, 907, 1305, 1310, 1399, 1550; συγγραφαί, 337, 967; supervision of, 326, 328, 329; underwriter of, 326.

Taxes, ἀνιππία, 293; on apiaries, 296; paid by artisans, 316, 445, 471; *aurum coro-narium*, 987, 988; on baths, 312, 313; on beans, 337; on beer, 308, 904; on business transactions, 316, 444, 445, 1392; on cattle, 242, 295, 337, 340, 344, 346, 444, 445, 471, see *Scriptura*; city, 334, 337, 445, 464, 528–30, 642–4; on commerce, 229, 233, 316, 337, 385, 445; on *cleroi*, 1526; paid by cleruchs, 285–7, 290, 293, 327, 562, 1404, 1600; on corn, 335, 337, 1287; on crops, 279, 303, 467, 957; crowns, *see* Crowns; on dates, 467; *decuma*, see *Decuma*; δεκάτη, *see* δεκάτη; διάλαυρα, 1115; on domestic animals, 295; on donkeys, 314; on draught animals, 242, 314; for embankments, 286; emergency, 471, 531, 750, 751, 1566; ἔνατον, 1550; on fish, 297; on fisheries, 337, 1644; on foodstuffs, 242; on foreigners, 323; on forest products, 337; on frankincense, 242; on fruits, 467; *Galatica*, 1563; on gardens, 290; gate-toll, 335–7; on grapes, 467; for guard service, 286, 1386; head, 962, 1092, 1566; on horses, 293; on house rents 242; on houses, 316, 954, 962, 994, 1563, 1566; on industry, 242, 337; on inheritance, 316; on inns, 1628; καταγραφή, 316; on kitchen

War, booty, *see* Booty; casualties, 195; chariots, 1232; economic effects of, 191–5, 625, 1242, 1243, 1250: supply of slaves, 627, 1258, 1262; indemnities, *see* Indemnities; industry, 1232, 1233; laws in Greece, 192–4; material, 639, 677, 993, 1255; methods, Greek, 142, 143, 192–5, 201, 603, 605–7, 1110, 1359, 1360, 1364, 1365, 1458, Roman, 605, 606, 739, 1458, 1462, 1473, 1501, 1562; prisoners, *see* Prisoners; profiteers, 152; profits, 326, 327.

Warehouses, 87, 88, 183; owners of (ἐγδοχεῖς), 397, 788, 1268, 1270, 1275, associations of, 791; *see* ἐγδοχεῖς.

Warships, 991, 1277, 1318, 1388, 1596; *see* Men of war, Ships.

Water, mills, 364, 365, 1405; supply in Egypt, 274, 275; in Priene, 181; system in Pergamon, 1626; -wheel, 363, 1214, 1645.

Wax, 586, 1191.

Wealth (πλοῦτος), 193, 409; accumulated, 1143–7, 1149, 1150, 1154, 1156, 1157; concentration of, 96, 206–8, 618, 753, 755, 1026, 1129, 1135, 1148, 1158, 1271, 1606; distribution of, 141, 1129, 1130, 1131, 1133, 1143–8, 1153–7, 1367, 1368, 1617; standard of, 1147, 1148, 1204.

Weapons, 1175, 1212, 1218, 1220, 1221, 1232; Egypt, 260, 378; Greece, 91, 92, 100, export of, 93, 106, 112, 119, 1325; Italy, 123, 124; Pontic, 107; Thrace, import of to, 112, 113.

Weavers (ὑφάνται or λίνυφοι), 306, 307, 377, 380, 1222, 1228, 1277, 1412.

Weaving, 300, 305, 1390.

Weights and measures, 1296–1300; at Al Mina, 88; Athens, 1297, 1431, 1432, 1503, 1506; Attic, *see* Attic; at Delos, 1431; in Egypt, 888, 1300; Pergamon, 1299, 1646; Roman, 1506; of Seleucid Empire, 451–5, 517, 1298, 1300, 1301, 1431, 1432.

Welles, C. B., 446, 495, 508, 620, 658, 718, 1049, 1435, 1440, 1477, 1586.

Westermann, W. L., 1286, 1589, 1644.

Wheat, 240, 335, 359, 366, 1164, 1168, 1187, 1406, 1416, 1450.

Wholesale dealers, 596, 1268, 1270, 1271, 1275, 1277, 1628.

Wine, 1177, 1187, 1253, 1618; presses, 364, 1190, 1224, 1405, 1617; trade, 1187, 1252–4, 1268, 1271, 1273; in Asia Minor, production and trade, 109, 671; Babylonia, 1189; Cos, 240, 1488, tax on, 242; Cyzicus, trade, 589; Delos, trade, 790, 1488; Egypt, customs duties on, 355, 1252, 1300, 1404, production, 297, 300, 353, 354, 362, 1645, shops, 1628, taxes, 302, 327, 336, 354, 884, trade, 313,

335, 384, 1253, 1403, 1416, 1538, 1628; Greece, price of, 628, production, 101, 109, 1181, trade, 88, 90, 93, 94, 101, 107–11, 120, 123, 156, 394, 596, 601, 745, 768, 1252, 1253; of Greek islands, production and trade, 93, 109, 120, 221, 229, 240, 247, 332, 1488; of Italy, 1253, trade, 795, 1254; Macedonia, trade, 764; Persia, 83; Rhodes, 236, 240, trade, 229, 236, 677, 1253; S. Russia, production and trade, 109, 110, 1331; Syria, 536, 1253, trade, 227, 384, 1538; Thrace, 111.

Winter quarters of armies, 144, 147, 810, 964, 976, 988, 994, *see* Quarters.

Wood, 299, 300, 940, 1318, 1613; rare, 387, 1258; tax on, 242.

Wooden, furniture, 107, 108, 1325; implements, 363.

Woodwork, 100.

Wool, 1257, 1277; Arabia, 358; Calymna, tax on, 242; Cos, 243, tax on, 242; Egypt, 292, 294, 300, 357, 358, 377, 1257, trade, 307, 308, 394; Greece, 100, 358; Italy, 124; Milesian, 182; Phrygian, 822.

Woollen, clothes, 124, 182, 307, 308, 357, 1257; industry, 307, 367, 377, 540, 563, 1229, 1390, 1411; stuffs, 302, 305, 307, 308, 380, 540, 563, 918, 1222, 1390, 1411, trade in, 122, 1223, 1257, 1412, 1629.

Woolley, Sir Leonard, 85, 131.

Workers, 1221, 1228, 1232, 1233; associations of, 1066, 1389.

Working classes, 1072, 1073, 1103, 1104, 1119, 1134, 1204, 1205, 1240, 1357; in Asia Minor, 806; in Egypt, 320, 880, 881, 892–5, 908, 913, 917, 1099, 1101, 1102, 1154, 1237, 1296, 1393; in Greece, 143, 168, 610, 1126, 1149; in Pergamon, 807, 1158; in Seleucid Empire, 522, 1156.

Workmen, in Bosporan kingdom, 770; in Delos, 191, 798; in Egypt, 298, 303, 304, 306, 317, 322, 331, 342, 361, 403, 735, 906, 1396; in Rhodes, 688.

Workshops, 301, 374, 380, 386, 389, 421, 1116, 1127, 1216, 1227, 1228, 1272, 1273, 1412; see *Ergasteria*.

Wuswas, 1427.

Xanthus, 949, 1004, 1005, 1579.

ξεναγός, 1393

ξένια, 227, 315, 1403.

ξενικὸν ἔλαιον, 385, 1417.

Xenocrates, 164.

ξένοι (foreigners), 277, 561, 690; (non-residents), 884, 908, 1647; οἱ εἰσπλέοντες, 1275; *see* Aliens, Foreigners.

Xenon, sculptor, 799.
Xenophon, 566, 569, 570, 697, 1034, 1181, 1182, 1332, 1358; see Πόροι.
Xerxes, 82, 1324.
ξυλική, 336.
ξυλίνων καρπῶν, 337.

Yarn, 306.
Ye-chi, 547, 549.
Yehud, 1325.

Zahn, R., 534, 535, 574, 850, 1208, 1447, 1456, 1622.
Zamaspes, 859.
Zela, 577, 978.
Zeleia, 589, 1103, 1453, 1454.
Zenodotus, son of Glaucus, 388.
Zenon, admiral of Soter, 140; brother of Abdemoun, 226, 228; philosopher, 1071, 1132, 1145, 1329, 1353, 1517, 1602, 1603; of Laodicea, 822, 1528.
Zenon, steward of the *dioecetes* Apollonius, 339, 909, 1096, 1275; accounts of, 358, 359, 362, 419, 1393; archives of, 256, 310, 402, 403, 421, 1073; business activity in Palestine, Phoenicia, and Syria, 227, 340, 343, 351, 389, 1400–2, 1413; management of *dorea*, 293, 354, 355, 358, 359, 362–4, 420, 421, 1164, 1199, 1387, 1390, 1610, 1644; private affairs of, 285, 325, 329, 359, 1074, 1387, 1416, 1419, 1589, 1593, 1650; wealth of, 411, 1153; see *Doreai*.

Zenon's correspondence, 226, 245, 260, 277, 287, 295, 296, 299, 308, 311, 326, 331, 340, 346, 347, 351, 364, 384, 385, 388, 397, 411, 420, 519, 524, 909, 1076, 1096, 1192, 1198, 1232, 1253, 1262, 1270, 1275, 1276, 1284, 1376, 1386, 1413, 1422, 1588.
Zephyrium, 976.
Zeugma-Apamea, 865.
Zeus, 486, 704, altar of, 800, temple of, 557; of Aezani, 493, 1478; Ammon, 1497; Atabyrios, 681; Baetocaecenus, 494; Bronton, 1523; Casius, 437; Ceraunius, 437; Chrysaoreus, 505, 507; Megistos, 485; Olbius, 439, 505, 1454; Olympius, 424, 434, 485, 486, 523, 704, 1443, 1492; of Panamara, 1009, 1581; Sosipolis, 193; Soter, 1359; Stratios, 576; Urius, 948, 1518, 1531, 1562.
Zeuxis, 492, 1439.
Ziaëlas, king of Bithynia, 240, 567, 569, 826, 1452.
Zibelmius, Thracian king, 766.
Zion, Mount, 704, 1492.
Zipoites, king of Bithynia, 27, 567, 568.
Zipoition, 568.
Zois, papyri of, 1385, 1498.
Zonaras, 44.
Zonarii, 1526.
'Zoo', of Alexandria, 417, 1422.
Zoological treatises, 318, 1615, 1619.
Zopyrion, 161, 1351.
ζυτηρά, 302.
ζυτοποιοί, 308.

II. INDEX OF SOURCES

I. CLASSICAL AUTHORS [VOL. I, pp. 1–602]

Strabo *cont.*

3. 10, p. 421 .	. .	1415
5. 16, p. 437 .	. .	1177
x. 5. 4, p. 486 .	. .	744
5. 6, p. 486 .	. .	224
xii. 1. 4 ff., p. 537 .	.	838
2. 9, p. 539 .	829,	1515
3. 11. p. 545 .	. .	1179
3. 11, p. 545 f.	. .	1456
3. 14, p. 547 .	. .	1580
3. 19, p. 549 .	. .	1175
3. 30, p. 556 .	. .	365
3. 31, p. 557 .	. .	506
3. 40, p. 562 .	1213,	1572
5. 3, p. 567 .	. .	1529
8. 11, p. 575 .	. .	830
8. 11, p. 575 f.	. .	588
8. 11, p. 576 .	. .	590
8. 14, p. 577 .	491, 506,	1177
8. 16, p. 578 .	. .	1528
xiii. 1. 14, p. 588 .	. .	560
1. 18, p. 589 .	. .	589
1. 28, p. 595 .	. .	560
1. 58, p. 611 .	. .	560
1. 70, p. 616 .	. .	560
2. 5, p. 618 .	. .	1415
4. 17, p. 631 .	1142,	1173
xiv. 1. 23, p. 641 .	. .	1478
1. 24, p. 641 .	. .	1520
1. 26, p. 642 .	1478,	1526
1. 38, p. 646 .	. .	1521
1. 41, p. 648 .	. .	1006
1. 42, pp. 648–9 .	.	1565
1. 42, p. 649 .	. .	821
1. 46, p. 650 .	. .	493
2. 5, p. 652 .	169,	678
2. 5, p. 653 .	622,	685
2. 5 ff., pp. 652 ff.	681,	684
2. 24, p. 660 .	. .	1528
2. 24–5, pp. 659–60 .	.	1528
2. 25, p. 660 .	. .	507
3. 2, p. 664 .	783,	785
3. 3, p. 665 .	. .	1576
5. 2, p. 668 .	. .	794
5. 2, pp. 668 ff.	.	783
5. 2, p. 669 .	773,	1516
5. 14, p. 674 .	. .	1580
6. 5, p. 684 .	. .	1170
xv. 1. 4, p. 686 .	. .	1556
1. 18, p. 692 .	. .	1166
1. 20, pp. 693–4 .	.	1167
1. 30, p. 700 .	. .	1172
1. 69, p. 718 .	. .	1419
2. 10, p. 724 .	. .	1175
2. 14, p. 726 .	. .	1174
3. 11, p. 731 .	. .	1164

Strabo *cont.*

xvi. 1. 7, p. 739 .	. .	1227
1. 10 and 11, p. 740 f.	.	1609
1. 27, p. 748 .	. .	1540
2. 4, p. 749 .	. .	1538
2. 5, p. 750 .	. .	1140
2. 7, p. 751 .	. .	1533
2. 8, p. 751 .	. .	1535
2. 9, p. 751 f.	. .	1538
2. 9, p. 752 .	. .	1578
2. 10, p. 752 .	. .	1538
2. 10, p. 753 .	. .	1533
2. 11, p. 753 .	. .	1437
2. 12, p. 753 .	. .	1535
2. 14, p. 754 .	1516,	1534
2. 16, p. 755 .	. .	1538
2. 18 and 20, p. 755 .		1535
2. 19, p. 756 .	. .	1539
2. 20, p. 756 .	. .	1538
2. 23, p. 757 .	1534,	1573
2. 23 and 24 f., p. 757 .		1538
3. 3, p. 766 .	. .	458
4. 2, p. 768 .	. .	1406
4. 18–19, p. 776–8 .	.	458
4. 21, p. 779 .	. .	1572
4. 26, p. 784 .	. .	1174
xvii. 1. 13, p. 798 .	1153,	1556
1. 35, p. 809 .	. .	356
1. 40, p. 812 .	. .	319
1. 45, p. 815 .	. .	1556
3. 6, p. 827 .	. .	1415

Suidas, s.v. Leschides . . 1090

S.V.F. (H. v. Arnim, *Stoicorum veterum Fragmenta*, i–iv, 1903–24).

i. nos. 259–71 .	. .	1602
p. 96, no. 435 .	. .	1594
p. 107, no. 481 .	. .	1594
p. 139, no. 620 .	. .	1594
iii. p. 27, no. 115 .	.	1358–9
p. 33, no. 138 .	.	1130
pp. 158 ff., nos. 617–22 .		1594
no. 623 .	. .	1603
nos. 685–6 .	. .	1131
pp. 172 ff., nos. 685–9 .		1594
no. 689 .	. .	1603
no. 691 .	. .	1594
no. 693 .	. .	1594

Tacitus, *Ann.* iii. 62 . . 1564

iv. 14 .	. .	1560
xii. 13 .	. .	1490
62 .	. .	1523
63 .	. .	591

Teles (ed. Hense)

περὶ αὐταρκείας, p. 5 f.	.	1594
ii .	. .	1353
περὶ πλούτου καὶ πενίας, p. 29. 6 .		409

2. INSCRIPTIONS

3. PAPYRI

PRINTED IN
GREAT BRITAIN
AT THE
UNIVERSITY PRESS
OXFORD
BY
JOHN JOHNSON
PRINTER
TO THE
UNIVERSITY